Private Faces *and* Public Places

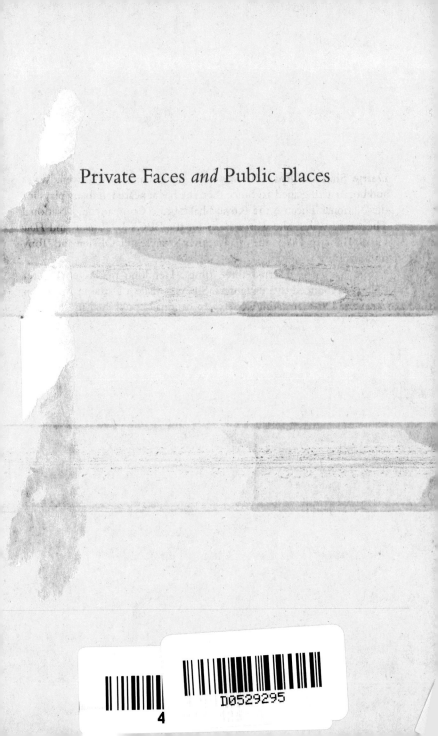

Dame Siân Phillips CBE was born in Gwaun-Cae-Gurwen, Wales and began acting aged 11. Since then she has appeared in many plays for the National Theatre, the Royal Shakespeare Company and National Theatre of Wales. She won a Bafta for the BBC's *I, Claudius* and *How Green Was My Valley* and many other awards and Olivier and Tony nominations.

She has been married three times. Her long marriage to Peter O'Toole produced two daughters. She was made a Dame in 2016. Her two volumes of autobiography were originally published in 1999 and 2001.

Private Faces
and
Public Places

SIÂN PHILLIPS

SCEPTRE

First published in Great Britain in 1999 and 2001 by Hodder & Stoughton
An Hachette UK company

First published in paperback in 2000 and 2002 by Sceptre
An imprint of Hodder & Stoughton
This paperback edition published in 2021

1

A CIP catalogue record for this title is available from the British Library

Paperback ISBN 978 1 529 37363 9
eBook ISBN 978 1 529 37364 6

Typeset in Bembo MT by Hewer Text UK Ltd, Edinburgh
Printed and bound in Great Britain by Clays Ltd, Elcograf S.p.A.

Hodder & Stoughton policy is to use papers that are natural, renewable
and recyclable products and made from wood grown in sustainable
forests. The logging and manufacturing processes are expected to
conform to the environmental regulations of the country of origin.

Sceptre
Hodder & Stoughton Ltd
Carmelite House
50 Victoria Embankment
London EC4Y 0DZ

www.sceptrebooks.co.uk

Contents

Foreword   vii

Private Faces   I
Public Places   227

Foreword

After filming ends, actors may be summoned to view their scenes, and then re-voice their work where the sound is deemed inadequate. It used to be called post-syncing or dubbing. No one likes doing it (well, imagine – your face looking silly . . .).

One day O'Toole came home bruised after a day of this and, as he lowered himself into his favourite armchair, remarked, 'I've realised something: hell isn't other people, it isn't paddling in boiling oil, it isn't even being dined on by rats; it would be having to post-sync your entire *life*.' Imagine that . . .

As I read my autobiographies for the first time in twenty years I realised, not for the first time, that he had a point. Reading what you write of your life is a bruising process. And some of it defies belief. Most of the time you find yourself questioning (you'll see I'm sneakily including you, the reader, here). As you share my story you will, I swear, be saying 'Why did she do *that*?' 'Why did she not *explain*?' 'Why did *they* do that?' '*How* could she have said such a thing?' You ignore the good bits: 'Yes, yes, very nice, very nice, turn page, turn page. Aha! Here we are; another piece of folly and madness . . .'

There were moments when I hardly recognised this girl. There were moments when I foolishly wondered if 'she' would live to tell the tale. A great deal of the story exasperated me beyond belief as I watched her make the same mistake again. And again. But quite often I admired her optimism (largely unfounded), her cheeriness (also unfounded). I really admired her ability to gain solace in the natural world, and, in the end, I liked the small shoots of what might become a capacity for friendship.

There were more questions when I looked at my notebook and diary accounts of the next twenty years. Why call her '*her*'? She's '*you*'. Have you learned anything during the years after *Public Places*, that has endured? Do you wish you could go back? Obviously, I learned something important, because I stopped making some of my more lurid mistakes, and that made for – hello! – Happiness. *There's* a word. And no, I would have to be dragged back.

Life changed. I acquired friends. I learned to cook. I acquired exceptionally good acquaintances. I became a really good gardener. I spent a great deal of my time looking after and entertaining my Burmese cats, and along the way I rather lost interest in myself except to feel a new sense of entitlement; a sense that I was in 'my' place.

All this happened somewhat unnoticed, but one unexpected thing occurred and it couldn't be ignored: I began to get younger! At the same time, I hasten to add, I aged in appearance in a perfectly normal manner . . . but there was no doubt about it: I was not getting older.

I've read of people experiencing a huge surge of energy and it wasn't like that. Rather, I looked about me, I became curious. This manifested itself in the kind of work I did and also in how I lived, or rather where I lived. I embarked on a kind of tour of London that continues to this day. I have always had a mild urge to move house, but was never able to indulge it to the full. Guyon House was home for twenty years, but then I set about moving. I made a garden everywhere and moved only because I wanted to experience a new neighbourhood and a different way of living. I love packing and buying and selling and building and digging and planting.

The only person I have met who shares this particular and peculiar hobby is Lesley Manville. We were sharing a dressing room at a gala at the Festival Hall and wondering aloud how it was that we had never met before, and I happened to mention an address in Spitalfields, 'Oh,' she said, 'I nearly bought that.' 'So did I!' I exclaimed. 'But then I move a lot.' 'So do I!' she said. And then, in the middle of the excitement of finding a kindred spirit, we had to go and do what we were being paid to do and never did finish the conversation. But I have never met anyone else who enjoyed the inconvenience so. I went on to live briefly in W1, and then Mayfair, and Islington for the first time, and Barnsbury and Kensington and Islington again at the Angel – then Spitalfields, and now the lockdown has found me and my unpacked boxes in the City itself, somewhere I had always wanted to live.

None of this interfered with work. Due to my job, I travel enough not to need or want holidays, so I don't see a space in the diary until the first lockdown, when everything almost stopped, until I realised that my voice could now step up and do its bit, so I built a (tiny) studio in my (small) study, and my PA, Jane, extended her (formidable) battery of skills to include that of engineering (I just crossed my fingers and hoped for the best). In my tiny box – with room only for me, a violin stand for scripts, a little table for water, a minute lamp – I sweltered through the first lockdown. The studio frame was festooned with duvets. (Kindly LA voice to Jane: 'You can't overdo the duvets, Jane.') I became a Voice for Hire, which was very exciting.

Work – any work – always is exciting. It just is. And part of becoming 'younger' affected the kind of work I found myself doing. I remembered my childhood wish that work should be the main part of my life. And remembered the years when this had been impossible. I had been made to feel guilty, made to think that what I wanted was wrong. I tried really hard to live a different kind of life to please other people, or maybe out of fear. They may even have been well meaning. Then, liberated, I worked. Life became easier, sweeter. I remembered my mother, my conventional mother, in a rare moment of candour, warning me against living a conventional domesticated life. I was by then of an age to feel scared by the future she saw for me (and by what it said of her existence). And we never spoke of it again when we shared the difficulties and rewards of the life I chose to embark on. She was horrified when I remarried, and I know she would have been relieved and pleased when I came to my senses some years later, not long after she died. One change was that I became a great deal more interested in other people. And what people they were! Far too many to mention them all here, but every year was full of surprises and adventure.

Playing the hugely demanding singing role of Marlene Dietrich in Pam Gems' *Marlene* in the early noughties was scary. Going to Dublin to perform in the Beckett festival in 2006 and driving in from the airport to see Sam Beckett's beautiful, haunted face hanging from every single lamppost was – thrilling. The joy of rehearsing Alan Bennett at the National – the joy of playing Alan Bennett's *People* for the National in Leeds in 2013 was exhilarating and lasting. I can still feel the excitement in the air as the audience rose to the play by their favourite son. The whole week was unforgettable (and I fell backwards down the cement stairs leading to the stage door and was saved by my mother's Bonnie Cashin leather coat, so I may have been concussed as well. I just didn't care).

I noticed how theatre was changing. The directors and the methods of working were, literally, dying off. Of course I continued to be offered parts that would always come my way (I loved playing Lady Bracknell, Mrs Patrick Campbell, Miss Havisham and so on), but I began to branch out in sometimes alarming ways. Kind friends looked askance when I jumped at the chance of playing a seventy-five-year-old Juliet in *Juliet and her Romeo* at the Bristol Old Vic in 2010, and a big test to my comfort zone came in the form of Physical Theatre. Quizzing Steven Hoggett and Scott Graham of Frantic Assembly on what I might be expected to do as part of their production, I was raised aloft mid-sentence and thrown good-heartedly from one to the other. It was lovely. I joined.

In *Les Blancs* at the National in 2016, I was, for the first time in my life, part of the ethnic minority and without a thought I shaved my head in 2015 to play a prisoner in Auschwitz alongside a company of young women in a production of Arthur Miller's *Playing for Time* in Sheffield. I was probably following the advice of my good friend and director Frith Banbury, who, on being questioned on how he remained so 'um . . . er . . . lively' at ninety-one, instantly responded: 'Cultivate young friends, my dear.'

In 2019 I made a film, a love story, *Time & Again*, where I played a lesbian partner to my great friend Brigit Forsyth and became a 'Dykon' in the LGBTQ film world, according to the director. Who would have thought?

So when you meet 'her' in *Public Places*, don't lose heart. She finally saw some of the light.

Much of what passed for Life as opposed to Working Life would have been utterly different were it not for a chance encounter I had some twenty-seven years ago. In short, I received the greatest, most undeserved, unlooked-for present of my life. I may have stopped doing some of the foolish things that characterised my life in *Public Places*, but I had done nothing to earn the wonderful, enduring friendship that came my way and that endures to this day. I was living alone for the first time and loving it. I looked about for a cat sitter so that I could go abroad to work. Thierry (a friend from the National) said, 'Oh, I'm sure my boyfriend could do that. He's got exams coming up and could do with the peace and quiet.' I left for New York. On my return I had another travelling job and asked the young man (one Fabi Waisbort) if he could stay on. He could. On my return, we were both busy and rarely bumped into each other. Many things happened in his young life; he graduated, he became well known. He became very well known. He and Thierry parted. Mark came into our lives. Fabi and I looked at each other with bemusement one day and realised that we had lived together for seventeen years. Seventeen happy years during which our roles had been upended and reversed many times, unnoticed. I could never have wished for this. I could never have bargained for it. It just growed like Topsy. I officiated at his marriage to Mark and now some twenty-seven years later we no longer live together, but Fabi and Mark and Jane and her family and I are neighbours. I don't do a great deal that isn't noted by them. It is the best thing that ever happened to me.

As I write it is spring again and we are still in lockdown, but everything seems so different. Now the quiet is over. Traffic is heavy. I do television. And soon I shall go back to theatre; to the National to play in *Under Milk Wood*, which I love (and I can walk to work!). I love to work. It is what I have done since childhood and it makes me happy, but it is also the reason why my life has a faint undercurrent of that untranslatable Welsh word '*Hiraeth*' ('Longing'? No. 'Wishing for times past'? Maybe). I knew, when I was old enough to understand that everything has consequences, that my decision to be an actress meant I would have to leave 'home' as soon as I could. So I prepared myself, and that coloured my (happy) childhood with sadness. Even so, I was ill-prepared when the moment came for me to move to Cardiff to begin my university life. Having to live in a city broke my heart. The paths and fields and mountains of my childhood really were the 'happy highways where I went and cannot come again'. I assumed that the move to London to train at the Royal Academy would be worse. It wasn't. I fell in love with London, but I had learned that I could never again form such a huge emotional attachment to a landscape, a place. Now, in a life of travel, I have learned how to settle down anywhere. I am happy with the turns my life has taken. I don't take anything for granted. Maybe I would be derailed if I suffered some dreadful reversal. I hope not.

When I was given the wonderful book *The Smith of Smiths* by Hesketh Pearson at the age of fourteen, it made me laugh a lot. Over the years it has kept me laughing and it has taught me a great deal. This is a tiny part of his letter to his great friend Lady Holland, after he found himself not quite where he might have wished to be in his career:

'If it be my lot to crawl, I will crawl contentedly, if to fly I will fly with alacrity, but as long as I can possibly avoid it, I will never be unhappy.' And so say I.

Siân Phillips, London, April 2021

Private Faces

For Sally and Dai, my mother and father

Acknowledgements

My thanks to my agent Mark Lucas, without whom I wouldn't have started, and my editor Rowena Webb, without whom I wouldn't have finished this book.

I thank Gethin Lewis and Meriel Lewis for help with family history and Patricia Myers (registrar at RADA) for reminding me of the geography of RADA past.

Huge thanks to Nina Humm for dealing with my terrible handwriting and for being so patient and resourceful throughout.

Most especially my thanks to William Corlett for understanding the problems of a novice and for his constant guidance. To him and Bryn Ellis, my thanks for refuge and light entertainment.

'Thank you' seems an inadequate expression of what is due to Thierry Harcourt and Fabi Waisbort for their daily, unfailing love and support.

Private faces in public places
are wiser and nicer
than public faces in private places

Orators, by W.H. Auden

Private Faces

I was born on a farm on a windy mountain in south-west Wales. Mountain? Some would call the Betws a hill. It is modest where it stands opposite the Black Mountain range. In the valley between the big mountains and the little one lies Gwaun-Cae-Gurwen (G.C.G. to even the most ardent Welsh speaker) – a street or two of small granite houses, a few pubs, a chapel, a Miners' Welfare Hall doubling as a cinema, and a coalmine. They say this place is wetter than Borneo and certainly the life into which I was born and which I thought would stay the same for ever is as curious and remote now as the lives of strange people, in an unknown country, far away.

Chapter One

I was almost out of the back door of Tŷ mawr, my grandparents' farm where I was staying, when my grandmother, emerging from her cold, slate larder carrying a basin of milk, called 'Oi' in the firm but neutral tone she would use to address an errant beast. Jerking her head, she indicated the almost cold basin of washing water. I hated that tepid water with its pale blue soapy scum even more than I hated the face-flannel, cut from the tail of one of my grandfather's flannel shirts, striped and slimy with soap. Holding my breath, I dabbed at my nose and chin and, eyes tightly shut, reached for the towel. Brisk, capable hands lifted my face and scrubbed at my head and neck. I could feel water trickling down inside my jumper, but knew better than to complain. She towelled me dry and reached for a comb, deftly undoing my plaits with one hand. Useless to say, 'Mammy lets me do my tangles first.' My hair was brushed, combed and plaited with the same calm speed with which cows were milked, dough kneaded and family discussions chaired around the large, black-leaded range with its gleaming brass fender.

I knew she wouldn't pause to look at me again when she was done, and as she returned to her milk and flour and butter I stood on tiptoe to catch a quick glimpse of myself in the only looking-glass in the house, which hung in the darkest corner of the kitchen. At six I could just glimpse my hair and my eyes. The little mirror was there for the men when they shaved, but I sneaked regular looks so as not to miss the day when, as promised if I ate bread crusts, my hair would become thick and blonde and curly. Nothing doing today. Nondescript straight wisps. I looked back into the darkness of the big kitchen with its small window set deep in the far wall, the big settle and the little settle framing two sides of the scrubbed table, my grandfather's chair with its back to me, the grandfather clock in the corner, and the fireplace with its overmantel serving as a filing cabinet; the yellow *Farmers Weekly* and advertisements for cattle feed jammed behind the brass candlesticks. A larger window illuminated the long table where I had just been washed, at the far end of which my grandmother was now working. It was a thick slab of wood, scrubbed white, and on special days two men would turn it over to reveal a side polished like a conker.

I was thin and white and on the frail side, and this exempted me from helping, and I had never known my grandmother to delegate to anyone, but, taking no chances, I gently backed away down the length of the table, past the larder, then – whirling round – I was out of the back door, across the clean scrubbed flagstones of the little yard, past the dairy, then across the big, dirty yard skipping over the drying cow-pats and on down to the seclusion of the cowsheds, cool and dim and at this hour of the morning empty and smelling more of disinfectant than cows and cow-dung. I loved the cows and knew them by name, but I found their personal habits hard to bear.

For a country child I was squeamish and ashamed of that and went to great pains to conceal it, having no wish to add to my list of oddities that my auntie Meriel, my mother's sister who lived at home on the farm, put down to my being a bit S-P-O-I-L-E-D. She mouthed this over my head by way of explaining why I read unsuitable books and why I politely but firmly rejected fresh eggs, milk warm from the cow, salty home-made butter and home-cured ham in favour of water, margarine and Spam. Her explanation of my behaviour as spoiled was just that – an explanation, uncritical and even tinged with humour. Behind an impassive face I wondered how she could imagine I couldn't hear her semi-spoken mouthing and how she could think I was unable to spell such a simple English word as 'spoiled' when I was already known as a GREAT READER. 'Go on – spell "epiglottis".'

Now, hauling myself into one of the enormous vats of dry cow-cake in the corner of the cowshed, I wriggled into a comfortable position out of sight – just in case – and contemplated the limitless possibilities of the day. The only checks and hindrances would be meals. Adults were, without exception, obsessed with food; collecting it, slaughtering it, cooking it and never-endingly sitting down to eat it. How many times a day did my grandmother climb up on to the hedge near the spring calling people in to eat? Too many times, it seemed to me. Strangers passing through Tŷmawr land were corralled into the kitchen and urged to 'Eat! Eat!' My grandmother brought out one of her three English sentences in the service of food. Addressing English itinerant labourers, she would call, 'Man, come to dinner!' – open vowels and a rolled 'r' at the end. John Dineen, the Irish itinerant who came to work on the farm each summer, was considered to be almost Welsh, was spoken to in Welsh and had to make the best of it. I shared his fondness for potatoes and ate such phenomenal amounts that I was referred to sarcastically (though never in John's presence) as 'the Irishman'.

Potatoes aside, I picked at food and my grandmother worried about my lack of appetite. She needn't have. I ate my way through the day and tasted everything I came across, knowing enough to avoid poisonous leaves and berries. Sitting unseen in the kitchen garden, I despatched spring onions, carrots and radishes straight out of the earth (a quick rub on my knicker leg got rid of most of the dirt). There was always something new to eat; peas in the pod, gooseberries, cooking apples, sorrel, dandelion leaves, nuts, even hawthorn berries weren't too bad, and now, luxuriating in the huge feed bin, I nibbled a cow-cake: the size of a fingertip, brown and earthy tasting. Filling too. No one had ever said, 'Don't eat cow food', but I kept it to myself all the same.

Restored after the irritations of getting up, I lowered myself out of the feed bin and set off past the stables, making for the hen-house. Most of the hens were scratching about outside, but I knew that some of them would be perched inside. I longed to see a hen lay an egg and spent part of every day sitting on my heels in the hen-house, watching and waiting, scarcely breathing, but the hens never forgot I was there. Heads tilted to one side, then the other, they made comfortable noises that might have been the prelude to the laying of an egg but never was. After a bit, resigned, I straightened my stiff legs and left them to it. (This part of my day I never talked about.) How could animals be so patient? I would lie for hours in the field behind my parents' house in nearby Alltwen watching the skylark high in the sky, waiting for her to forget I was there and come down to her nest. She never, ever did and I always gave up first.

I was now working my way up the Betws Mountain through a small wood at the back of the farmhouse. This was where we collected hazelnuts. Part of the wood was dark and sinister; the earth on the steep slope had leached away from the roots of the trees and they reached down in contorted rope-like shapes around the mouths of small hiding places, hardly big enough to be called caves. This place was always the setting I described when recounting the nastier parts of The Story – a rambling, ongoing tale of adventure and death that I made up to tell my friends at infant school in Rhos, near Alltwen. It was along the lines of a 'Famous

Five' adventure as told by Edgar Allen Poe. I loved *Tales of Mystery and Horror from Poe to Arlen* and borrowed plots to add to my own. There were few of my stories that didn't feature a ceiling or the roof of a cave that descended slowly and inexorably on a couple of trussed-up children dressed in blazers and wearing belts with snake buckles. Snakes! Speckled bands (deadly snakes) circled the heads of plucky girls with fresh complexions and naturally curly hair as they sat, not daring to move, until they were rescued by a boy in a blazer.

My young audience believed me only too completely, and when one, then two, then three children were found crying with fright in their beds, there was a delegation of mothers to our house and a good deal of eye-rolling and head-shaking and whispering. My mother was unaccustomedly nonplussed by this unusual crime. She was all for originality: 'Go on, write a story! Use your imagination!' was an often-heard refrain in our house. Never before at a loss for words, she was now reduced to a rather feeble, 'RIGHT! Upstairs, and no coming down 'til I tell you.' The following day I was forbidden to tell any more stories until the fuss had died down and even then not to tell any that didn't have happy endings. 'Invent HAPPY things,' Mother said, at the end of her tether. Struggling through the dark, sinister undergrowth, I thought I wouldn't bother.

I reached the top of the Betws Mountain and sat down, out of breath, and looked about. Down below was the farm with the lean-to washhouse and the long slope of the blue slate roof. Smoke rose steadily from the chimney. A long way below was the string of granite houses that made up the village of Gwaun-Cae-Gurwen. Carmel Chapel was very big. The coalmine was so discreetly placed as to be scarcely visible. Reaching away to the horizon were the slopes of the Black Mountain, smooth like the flanks of an elephant and dun-coloured with the darker shadows of the few clouds, moving slowly today. One of these peaks I had selected as my Test. The Bible was very familiar to me – my grandmother seemed to know the whole of the Old Testament and few arguments at home were settled without a triumphant, apt quotation from it. My mother was more keen on the New Testament and I was already learning and reciting long pieces from that. Faith moving mountains had made a deep impression on me and I strained every nerve to move my chosen peak. I knew it would take a while and I wasn't even going to try today. It was something I did when I felt particularly 'holy' and ready to do battle with nature. Now I leaned back and did nothing.

Below and to the left, smoke rises from Llwyncelyn, which is a yellow house. My grandmother's house stands granite-dark and symmetrical, and its outhouses are whitewashed. Llwyncelyn is smaller, more picturesque, maybe even prettier, but white seems more correct for a farmhouse than yellow. There is one farm I know that is outlandishly pink, and some years, when the mix goes wrong, it becomes a vivid raspberry, and when it rains, which is most of the time, it looks too bright by far. My grandmother's way in this, as in most things, is best. I sense that even my mother thinks this, but at home in Alltwen we do things her way, which is slightly, ever so slightly, different. I sit up and go on looking around, doing nothing. I spend a great deal of time here, in Tŷmawr. I hear people say I'm not 'the strongest'. I may not be the strongest, but I feel fine and this life suits me fine. This is the countryside I know best and I like spending most of my time just looking at things. My mother comes over from Alltwen and nods approvingly at me, but she looks anxious. She doesn't need to be. On his day off my father comes as well and works on the farm. I love going home on the bus with them, but sometimes they leave me here and we're all sad when we say goodbye, although once they're out of sight I cheer up right away. I don't know why they call me 'delicate'.

When I can tell from the feel of the day that soon it will be time for the midday meal, I still have time to take the long, easier way down, entering the farmyard from below and stopping at the spring where we draw our water for the house. Very quietly I lift a few of the big mossy stones. The toad isn't there. There isn't anything there. The spring rises above a field of fairy rings and it seems to me reasonable that fairies would spend time around this very convenient, pleasant spot. Auntie Meriel made a face when I told her this, but my mother didn't because she was in the house when I *saw* a fairy, years ago when I was really small – maybe three or four years old. It wasn't a dragonfly and it wasn't a butterfly, so what could it have been but a fairy? All the same, I'm beginning to think that I'm never going to see another one. It's like the hens' eggs and the skylark.

My grandmother's metal-tipped boots are making a ringing sound on the flags as she moves quickly between the range and the work-table and the table where we eat. I slide into the little settle where I left my book last night. Life outside a village means life without electricity. My uncle Davy, the third of my grandparents' children, is a teacher and a councillor. He lives in a lovely white modern house called 'Pen-y-bryn', which he's built on a meadow below the farm, and he is working hard on something called 'rural electrification' ('Go on, spell what Uncle Davy's doing'). He hasn't managed it yet and at night everything has to take place around the Tilley lamp in the kitchen, and since Uncle Davy, when he was a student home from the university, set fire to himself, reading in bed, and my grandmother saved him and the house by throwing the burning mattress into the yard, there's been a strict rule against reading in bed by candlelight.

I read a bit now until all the places around the table are taken. It's cawl – Welsh stew – so that's all right. My grandmother ladles it into basins; lamb, carrots, swedes, potatoes, chopped leeks and great handfuls of parsley. The top is shiny with stars of fat. I pray there aren't too many bits of fat at the bottom of my basin. Tomorrow we'll eat the cawl again and it will taste even better. On day two it's called 'cawl aildwym' – second-time-warm cawl. I hate Sunday food because there's always beef, which has a lot of fat, and the worst trial of all hangs above my head: a huge side of bacon that is nearly all fat with thin stripes of pink meat. I don't really like the Welsh cakes or the pancakes that are made on the bake-stone over the fire, nor do I care for my grandmother's famous pastry. What I like best is *siencyn*, which the men eat after the first few hours of work, early in the morning. It's a basin of bread and butter, with sweet milky tea poured to the top of the basin and old cheese grated over it all. It's lovely.

The only members of the family not here are my mother, who is in her house in Alltwen with my father, and her brother, Davy (the bed-burner), who is at school, teaching.

Daniel, my grandfather ('*Tadcu*' in Welsh), sits at the head of the table and is served first. He's a shadowy figure to me and I don't really like his moustache or his clothes, which seem to have moulded themselves to his shape, but I do like his moleskin trousers – washed and washed until they are white – which make a 'whip, whip' sound as he walks. He is the son of Sali from Wernwgan farm – a 'hedge school teacher' who taught anywhere that was dry and convenient (did those teachers ever teach actually sitting in a hedge?), and the Welsh Bible was their only textbook. He looks fairer and much bigger than his mother, Sali, in the photograph of her in the parlour that shows a small, shrunken, beetle-like little woman, holding her Bible firmly between her and the world.

When he was younger, Daniel's passion was not farming but horses, and his dream was to breed a good racehorse. Needless to say he never succeeded in this and the failures were seconded to farm work, for which they were completely unsuited. My mother, when she was a girl, lived in daily dread of entering the stable to put one of these high-spirited, nervous monsters between the shafts of a hay-wain or a milk float. Their eyes rolled and they backed away from her, rearing up and lashing out with their hooves. 'Don't hurt that horse,' my grandfather would say as he passed the stable where my mother was trying to avoid serious injury to herself. Once the job was done and the float was backed out on to the yard, she had to fling herself aboard as the horse took off with a determination and speed never displayed in its earlier, racing life. They thundered down the stony dirt track to Gwaun-Cae-Gurwen, milk churns sliding perilously around her legs, only slowing to an exhausted, sulky trot as they took the sharp turn over the little river and began the steep climb up to the village.

Daniel's brother was a coal-miner and *his* dream was to find the big seam of anthracite that he was sure existed just outside the village. The little foothills of the Betws were pitted with small openings and shafts where he'd probed for his Big One. When he'd saved enough money, he would stop working for the Mining Company and start his own dig again. The big strike was as elusive as his brother's champion horse, but his dream was no impossible fantasy and after his death the big seam was found a few yards beyond one of his little shafts that had been discontinued for lack of funds. He enjoyed prospecting as much as my grandfather enjoyed playing with horseflesh; they weren't bitter in their disappointment and their wives were only mildly (and silently) exasperated.

My grandmother, Elizabeth ('*Mamgu*'), was born in the room in Tŷ mawr where my uncle and aunt and my mother and now I had been born. Medium tall, medium slim, she was unremarkable save for her swift, athletic walk and the deftness and certainty of her gestures. Married to Daniel, who loved to talk and linger down in the village, she was, above all, a skilful worker. Plain living and high thinking, was it a secret vanity that drove her, even after cold water had been piped through to the farm, to walk through the two farmyards to draw water from the spring to wash her face? Her feet, shod in laced-up boots, were as white and unblemished as a girl's. Her hands, gnarled as an old man's, didn't seem to belong to the unlined face and smooth feet. Her hair was scraped back under a faded cotton cap, elasticated behind and turned up at the front, giving her a deceptively girlish air. She wore dark dresses and, over them, sleeveless overalls, small prints on black cotton. Indoors, over these she wore large, clean, light-coloured starched aprons and outdoors these were replaced by aprons made of clean sacking. There were 'day' clothes; then there were 'end of the day' clothes ('best' clothes past their best), which she would wear on week-days to visit neighbours or receive visitors. 'Clothes of respect' were best clothes worn only to chapel and to weddings and funerals. All these were made by a relation, Syrviah, who, along with her treadle sewing machine, would be met in the village and brought up to the farm on the horse-drawn milk float. She would stay for a week or two, making shirts and suits for the men and a sparse wardrobe of dresses and aprons and coats for the women and children.

My grandmother read the Bible daily and it was said that if all the Bibles in the village were burned, Mrs Thomas, Tŷ mawr, would prob-ably be able to write out the whole of the Old Testament. *All* of it? I wondered some years later. Not allowed to read the *Sunday Despatch* while it was running excerpts from *Forever Amber*, I spent many Sundays reading 'improving' books and, in an excess of zeal and virtue, decided to read the whole of the Old Testament. I struggled to keep my face impassive as, delighted and astonished, I plunged ever deeper into the scarcely credible accounts of sex and violence among the tribes of Israel. Occasionally my mother would look up from her knitting and I could feel her mild surprise at my good behaviour. (There was always some-thing grudging in her approval of me, as though she sensed I was less biddable than appearances would suggest, and even when I *was* up to no good I resented her sceptical look and tone of voice.)

Now, making rapid strides in my sex education, I wondered if this kind of carrying on was limited to times past and life in a different climate? It seemed improbable that there could be quite so much smit-ing, cleaving unto, lying with and begatting by the wrong people in the non-conformist villages of the Swansea Valley. Was it possible that my grandmother had memorised *these* bits? Was it possible that she'd even *read* them? These pages were never opened in Sunday school where we laboured over such subjects as 'Everyday Life in the Time of Jesus, with Special Reference to Cooking and Hygiene' and yet, there they were. Such was my regard for my grandmother's lofty cast of mind and my awe of the gloomy parlour where the family Bible lay on a table in the window that it seemed to me quite possible that by some Methodist alchemy these pages became temporarily invisible when Elizabeth

Thomas, née George, opened the great cover and turned past the pages of our less exuberant, rather puny begats. For one thing, what could she have made of Onan? I had to go and look it up in the dictionary and she didn't even *have* a dictionary. Her poise and serenity were legendary and I wondered if a calm conviction such as hers could only be achieved and maintained by not reading all the pages of anything – ever.

My mother told me that even she, *quite* calm and serene, would go to any lengths not to be present on the day the slaughterer came to the farm. Only my grandmother kept her composure. After a strenuous bout of killing, the slaughterer would emerge, blood-stained, and call my grandmother and any others in the vicinity to view his work, then, taking his knife, he would cut a thin slice of raw meat and, holding it up to the light, say, 'Sweet as a nut, Mrs Thomas, sweet as a nut.' 'And then,' said my mother, lowering her voice a tone, 'he *ate* the meat.' She left a pause so that I could fully dwell on the horror and then, almost in a whisper, continued, 'And then, asking to be excused, he would climb on to the pile of warm, bloody skins and, drawing a hide over himself, *go to sleep.*'

Severely shaken, everyone beat a retreat. My mother – no cissy – went for a wash and a lie-down. My grandmother merely inclined her head to acknowledge the compliment to the quality of her beasts, said that supper would be ready in an hour, also hot water for his toilette, and that he would be welcome in the house, after which she walked sedately back to her kitchen, pausing only to shake her head in mild reproof at two farm-hands engaged in a violent pantomime of stabbing and eating and throwing up. One shake of the head from her was enough to stop what she called 'nonsens' (much crisper sounding than the English 'nonsense'), by which she meant exaggeration and excess of any sort. Much as I admired her for her stamina and her complexion, her frugal eating habits and her slim figure (her children were all inclined to run to fat), I thought that I'd like to have more fun than she did.

I never know precisely what my grandmother thinks about anything. I know that her views of right and wrong are identical with God's and that, if anything, she admits fewer shades of grey than He does so it isn't necessary for her to go into detail; the white and black are simple and plain for all to see. I am always surprised by her silent tenderness with small animals and by my earliest recollection of her; I must have been a baby when she held my outstretched hands and I sat facing her, sitting astride her raised ankle, bouncing into the air as she chanted 'Pedoli,

pedoli, peDINK!' and made as if to drop me. 'Cheboli, cheboli, CHUBUT!' (What did it mean?) Now, at the age of six, regarding her across the dark kitchen from my corner near the clock, I could hardly credit that she had ever been so playful.

John, the living-in help, looks lovely as he eats silently. I have never seen a film, but I imagine that film stars look like him. And only the other day he spent ages trying to catch me a mole as it rose in its little molehill. And he did it! (That's another one of the Impossibles, like eggs and skylarks and fairies.) I think Meriel likes him a lot. Auntie Meriel has fun. More than most grown-ups. Her face is large and shiny and bright pink. It might sometimes look irritated, but I can't imagine it looking frightened. She spends most of the day working out of doors and she drives the milk float down the hill and through the village in her khaki milk-delivering coat and wellingtons, looking like a warrior queen standing on the springy back step where I am not allowed to stand. She calls 'Milk–o' in a special tune and measures out the milk, collecting all the village news, then 'Gee-up!', expertly negotiating the level-crossing and the sharp turn over the little bridge and back up the rough, stony path to Tŷ mawr. Riding with Meriel is my favourite thing.

At last I'm allowed to get down from the table and now I'm told that my mother is coming for me tomorrow and I'm well enough to go home and maybe go to school. I quite like the school. I go there so seldom I feel like a visitor. But now I shall have to rush around, visiting the animals and saying goodbye and checking up on things. I have so much to do every day on the farm.

Why do grown-ups have to do everything so suddenly?

Chapter Two

This time, when I got home from Tŷ mawr I began to feel really unwell. The doctor was called and he arrived, in a hurry as usual, swearing under his breath, banging down his bag and demanding what I had been up to now. He was the only person who addressed me familiarly in the second person singular, as '*ti*'. It was customary for parents to call their children '*ti*', but for some reason mine used the more formal '*chi*' and I was never wholly comfortable with this implied closeness between the doctor and myself. I felt he was no friend of mine.

When he left, instead of being put to bed with a fire in the bedroom grate and all my treasures ranged around me (I knew and appreciated the advantages of being slightly ill), I was wrapped, still dressed, in a shawl and my father carried me from room to room, glancing out of the front windows each time he passed them. Then, horror of horrors, the ambulance drew up outside our house.

Now, tuberculosis, 'the lung', was rife in the neighbourhood. People were taken away for long periods and sometimes they didn't return. Miners sufficiently ill with silicosis ('the dust') were taken away, and when they came back, *if* they came back, they never got better. The ambulance was a chariot of doom and death, and when it passed by we would stop, look away, hold our collars and chant, 'Never swallow, touch your collar, never catch a fever.' Now it had come for me. I couldn't believe it. What was worse, it was taking me away – on my own. In an instant, a panic-stricken instant, my universe lost its foundation, its wall against the world, its sheltering roof. This was as bad as my dog dying. My bones turned to water. It was as though I had nothing inside me except my pounding heart. My mother half-extended her arms towards me, but what could she do? Other arms were taking me and laying me on a bunk. The ambulance door closed on my father's handsome, anguished face and I felt that the Worst Thing had happened to me.

It was dark when we arrived at a big house surrounded on three sides by black, dripping trees with open country stretching away on the fourth side. I was undressed and put into bed in a large, dimly lit, high-ceilinged room. Where was I? No one had told me anything; I suppose they'd thought that I was too ill to hear or understand. I did feel terrible. I lay there, afraid to move. There were the shadowy outlines of other beds and there was silence except for the sound of rain and something that tapped the window behind my head. When dawn broke I recognised the room; I had seen it with its high, dirty, damp-spotted ceiling in almost every drawing by Phiz in my mother's set of books by Charles Dickens. I hadn't thought such a room could exist in real life and now I was in one. Later I learned that the house was an isolation hospital. I spelt 'isolation' in my head.

There were thirteen of us in the room, boys and girls together; some much bigger than me. We all had scarlet fever. Humiliation was heaped on misery. I had to pee in a chamber pot in full view of everyone. Worse was to follow. As I grew more and more ill and couldn't get out of bed, the bedpan appeared and the boys on either side of me made my life hideous with their jokes about it. My squeamishness was against me and in a single day I was defeated and at their mercy. Even my imagination was against me. Peter Rice and Peter Boiling, the boys on either side, convinced me that unspeakable horrors lay under my bed, waiting for me to go to sleep before they heaved themselves up, and slithered towards my face . . .

I believed them. I believed everything they said. I would never be allowed home. I might die. I grew thinner and paler, grubbier, more anxious. But I didn't die. 'Oh, she's turned the corner,' someone said.

One day they told me to stand on my bed and look out, and there in the distance were my parents. They were holding up my colouring pencils and a doll and some books. I hadn't expected ever to see them again and for a moment I felt a rage as all-consuming as the misery I had felt at losing them. I had been gone six long weeks and I knew now that everything I possessed in the isolation hospital would be burned when I left. Didn't *they* know this? They were dismayed to be confronted with a pinched little creature with unkempt hair and a dirty nightgown, gesticulating wildly and crying tears of anger and frustration. My precious things were delivered to me. No one had understood my sign language or my distress. I looked at the pile on my bed and couldn't bring myself to touch anything. My beautiful long pencils had been snapped in half so that I should have something to draw with when I went home. They were ruined. 'She's an only child. A bit spoiled,' said one of the nurses. I glowered at them, hating them all. They weren't like the nurses in any of the books I'd read and I thought they were hopeless.

'Now you're getting better you can have a bath,' one of them said brightly, and on Friday night a large zinc bath was pulled into the room and thirteen of us were bathed in it, one after the other. I came after one of the Peters and didn't need him to tell me as he climbed, grinning, into his bed that he had peed in the bath. 'Thank God I don't have brothers and sisters,' I thought as I stepped into the dirty water.

Now I have something called eczema. There's a nasty crack outside each ear where my ear lobe joins my face. They say they'll cure it before I go home and they're painting my ears purple with 'permanganate of potash' – which I can spell. I've got over my anger and I'm happy. The Peters have gone home and I shall go soon; I don't care if I look strange.

Going home was an anti-climax. I've grown taller and none of my clothes fit. My possessions are sadly depleted and that makes me cross all over again. No school for a while. My mother is making a big effort to do something about my eczema, which is much worse now. The hospital didn't make it better. We visit doctors and specialists and hospitals and herbalists. All the 'cures' are time-consuming and useless. There are long walks to the nearest bus stop, long journeys, then more waiting in ante-rooms. I'm learning a lot of poetry by heart. Chunks of the New Testament as well. Some of the cures make me look peculiar. For a while I'm covered in grease and wrapped in bandages with holes for my eyes, nose and mouth. When that doesn't work I'm unwrapped and a sharpened matchstick, dipped in white liquid, is drawn through the cracks in my skin. It turns brown and it burns me. The eczema has spread everywhere. Permanganate of potash is tried again at intervals so I have weeks when I'm purple all over. I'm not really bothered. I'm reciting a lot in chapel and Sunday school and my eczema goes away from my face just before I make a public appearance. At home my hands are bandaged so that I don't scratch myself, but I manage perfectly with my grubby, bound paws and I've learned to sleep flat on my back. Soon I'm returned to Tŷ mawr, to Mamgu.

I might be here for a long time and I don't mind that. School is very nice, but not being at school is also very nice. I like my friends, but I don't mind not seeing them for a while – there are plenty of animals to play with and it doesn't really matter if I don't do lessons either. I like learning songs and listening to stories and writing compositions, but I have plenty of books to read and I can write my own stories. I couldn't understand the sums or the clock and I don't think I ever will, but I don't really need to; I don't have any money so I don't need to add and subtract, and I always know when it's time to get up or stop playing and go home.

I go down to Uncle Davy's house and walk along the white front behind the pillars and pretend it's mine. He has thousands of books and lets me read them. Sometimes he and Auntie Maya, his wife, make me spell words and I write things for them. Maybe they don't know it but every teacher I ever met has asked me to write 'A day in the life of a penny' and 'Callers at my door'. It doesn't take me a minute to write a composition. I learn English grammar from one of Auntie Maya's old books and I like that, but when they get out the paper, ruled into little squares, I know what's coming and I say I'm not feeling very well and run up the Betws to the farm where no one makes me do arithmetic. My mother gives me poems to learn from *Palgrave's Golden Treasury*, but mostly I just wander about and have a really lovely time.

My eczema is a bit of a nuisance and sometimes visitors stare at me if the cracks are bleeding. My mother and father have explained that only rude or inconsiderate people will stare at me and I am not to feel upset or shy. I should feel sorry for the people who can't help gawping. And that's what I do.

Chapter Three

Alltwen, Gwaun-Cae-Gurwen, Cwmllynfell, Bryn Amman. The ring of villages gave me a different perspective on the same familiar landscape of mountains and valleys where my grandparents and *their* grandparents had worked, farmed, ridden and walked over. My grandmother had travelled weekly from Tŷ mawr in G.C.G., over the mountains through Alltwen to Neath to sell her butter, carried in panniers on either side of her pony. One of my great-grandmothers had ridden from her farm near Carreg Cennen Castle, over the Brecon Beacons to be married, carrying her dowry of gold coins in her apron. My grandmother's mother, Elizabeth George, had climbed the Betws Mountain from Cwmamman with her husband to build the first little farm in what was now the orchard of Tŷ mawr.

I was aware of being at home everywhere. And I was especially aware of the line of women stretching back behind me. Men were deferred to, made much of, 'tended' to, even referred to sometimes as 'The Boss', but I was aware that I lived in a matriarchy. Women balanced the books, paid the bills, made the decisions and, when necessary, ran their own small farms and businesses alone. My parents came into focus for me as people now as I continued to spend time at home instead of going to school. I adored my father but realised that the force I had to reckon with was my mother, Sally Fâch Tŷ mawr, Little Sally Tŷ mawr.

My mother lived austerely so that the few pieces of frippery that remained from her past life, a life I knew little about, were so strange and so uncharacteristic that they assumed for me the quality of magical relics, and when I was allowed, I lifted them carefully from the drawer in the bedroom, handling them, smelling them and laying them out, before returning them carefully. I don't think they were ever looked at or touched except by me. There was a box of unused pink powder labelled 'Coty', dotted all over with drawings of swansdown powder puffs with ebony handles on an orange background. It made no sense to me; the unbroken seal, the colour called 'Rachelle' (what kind of colour was 'Rachelle'?). Then there was a little mirror with a coloured silk tassel attached that pulled it out of its black grosgrain silk case. I thought it was the prettiest thing I'd ever seen. (My mother never looked at herself in a mirror.) The silk handkerchief had a black paisley pattern on white and was only used for chapel-going. There was a bottle – an empty bottle – of 'Evening in Paris' scent, dark blue with a silver moon and the Eiffel Tower on the label, and an almost empty bottle of 'Californian Poppy'. (My mother never smelled of anything but soap.) As for powder, what sort of person wore powder? But oh, the smell of that box of Coty!

When I was seven and old enough to respect books and papers, as a special treat I was allowed to look at my mother's photograph album. Slowly I lifted the interleaves of tissue-paper, never tearing or creasing them. She was barely recognisable and I found it hard to credit the reality of her life before my advent, but there she was – the schoolteacher, dark and slim and intense, wearing the fashionably flat-chested dresses of the day, waists low on the hips, bodices cut in a low 'vee' and filled in with silk 'modesty vests' decorated with drawn threadwork and French knots. Her legs, crossed neatly at the ankles, were shiny in pale stockings, her feet encased in immaculate, fine leather louis-heeled shoes. She described each outfit in the photographs and eventually I knew them all by heart; even the price of the 'fur' tippet (10s 6d), the bottle-green coat (two guineas) – 'Very daring to wear that colour to school; green was safer if it was moss or leaf.' What colours there were: blue could be marina, saxe, misty, French navy or powder; pink was at its most ladylike (and therefore desirable) when it was 'dusty'. I was too young to appreciate the subtleties of grey; dove, pearl, charcoal and clerical. Hard to imagine a black so much blacker than everyday black that it became 'jet' black. Light brown was called fawn or donkey and didn't show the dirt.

My mother was at her most vivid and tender when she spoke of her time at Cwmamman School in the Amman Valley, which led west from G.C.G. She and her brother, Davy the bed-burner, both taught in this valley, but it had only been possible for Davy to go to the university. My mother's pupil-teacher salary paid for his digs and every Friday she would post a parcel of fresh food to him so that their mother could rest easy in the knowledge that he ate properly once a week at least. My mother shrugged aside my suggestion that it seemed unfair that she hadn't been allowed to go to university. 'That's how it was. Boys came first.' Then, meaningfully to me, 'But I wouldn't like to think it could happen today.' When they were both teaching, they rose early – in summer John Dineen, the Irish labourer, would take a pitchfork and tap on Davy's window at 4.15 a.m., Davy would wake his sister and they would work in the fields or with the animals until it was time to breakfast and wash and change into teaching clothes; then, still wearing boots, their shoes tied around their necks, they ran over the fields (never time to take the dirt track), the mile or so down the hillside and, leaving their boots at a neighbour's house, they boarded the little bus for school, decently shod, breathing hard but ready for the classes of some seventy pupils that awaited them.

Before my mother married, while she still lived in Tŷ mawr, her week was long and hard because at night and at the weekend there was household work awaiting her after the day's teaching. Once a week, with her younger sister, Meriel, who was still a schoolgirl, she emptied and black-leaded the big range and polished the brass fender and fire-irons and the brass door knobs and handles and the twenty candlesticks that stood on the big oak dresser. The dresser was, she said, like an altar, and she knelt before it cleaning the willow-patterned plates and the fifty lustre jugs. She wasn't put upon; everyone worked long hard days. 'Hard work harms no one,' she would say at this point, looking at me over her glasses for extra emphasis. Nothing, however, dampened her enthusiasm for her 'real' work at school. Married women were not allowed to continue teaching, so she'd been obliged to retire before I was born, but she still kept all her notebooks and teaching schemes for the year; beautiful, copperplate labelling; pressed flowers and leaves, ways of coaxing 'slow' children to read. She especially loved the not-so-bright and explained how she kept them in a special, unthreatening corner of the big classroom until they knew enough to join another group.

'Were there any children who couldn't learn?' I asked, thinking of my hopelessness at arithmetic and hoping that there had been many like me, as bad, maybe worse. 'Not one,' she said firmly. This was the moment to ask about Billy. 'Tell me about Billy.' 'Oh well,' she would say as though I'd surprised her with the request, '*Billy* . . . well now . . . Billy *was* – *slow* – no use denying that, well the whole *family* was slow, so what do you expect? Lovely people, mind – children beautifully clean and tidy. Billy learned to read and write and count a bit in the end – and he got a nice little job when he left school, though he could hardly talk – cleft palate – poor dab.

'One year, on April the first, we all did April Fools in the morning. The headmaster didn't join in, of course, but he turned a blind eye. Billy couldn't do an April Fool. We explained it to him but it was no good. He laughed and nodded his head, but he didn't understand. And the term went by and one afternoon before the summer holidays the classrooms were nice and quiet, everyone working, and suddenly there was all this shouting in the yard. I told the children to sit still and went to see what was wrong.

'The headmaster had come out of his study and was standing in the yard looking at Billy, who was pointing at the roof and saying something that sounded like ball – "all-all", he cried. He was so distressed that Mr Williams went for a ladder and climbed on to the roof – it was quite low over the entrance, but when he couldn't find anything he called down, "I'm sorry, Billy. Are you sure it's up here?" Billy's face opened into a huge smile and he doubled over clutching himself in an ecstasy of laughing. "Bill-foo!" he gasped. "Bill-foo!" April Fool, of course! It had taken him from April to June to work it out, but he'd *done* it. Mr Williams came down and picked him up and hugged him and said, "Well done, Billy bach." Well, all the teachers had tears in their eyes. Oh yes, *everybody* can learn if you give them time.' We both looked at the album and she had a sad look on her face. I wondered gloomily if Billy had mastered long division.

It was a former colleague of hers who told me what a wonderful teacher she was. 'You're a very lucky young lady, especially since your school attendance is so poor. Not that that's your fault, I suppose. Your mother can teach *anyone anything*.' I didn't reveal that for some reason I wasn't being taught at all at home. My mother had said I could read anything I wanted, so I did, but I still couldn't add, subtract or multiply, and as for decimals . . . Grateful to be left alone, I kept out of the way. 'You might very well never have been born,' continued the same teacher. 'Your mother was spreading her wings. She had her passage booked and a teaching post waiting for her in Edmonton, in Canada. Then something happened and she couldn't go. Tragic waste. Coaching is all very well, but it's not the same.' Canada! I could see that any impediment to such an adventure, myself included, could be classed as 'Tragic waste'.

My mother looked startled when I asked her about it. 'Oh, old history,' she said briskly, not even looking at me and she wouldn't be drawn. Her brother told me that something happened on the farm and his salary and my mother's were both needed to ride out the crisis. Meriel had to leave school to come home and work with their mother. I never found out what it was that happened or what my mother felt about it, but I guessed that since she wouldn't talk about it, it was something important to her. There were so many things that remained secret. I was insatiably curious and I watched the grown-ups and listened as still and quiet as a little animal, but they were too clever for me as a rule. There were secrets I never learned.

When I was seven and eight, I rarely had to be up early to go to school, so I was allowed to stay up later than my friends. Together, my mother and I would begin an evening by listening to *Children's Hour*, which was at once so foreign and so much a part of my life. We spoke Welsh at all times, but I could say 'Goodbye, children, goodbye' just like Uncle Mac with his lovely English voice. We were alone; the fire glowed in the clean fireplace, supper had been prepared, so my mother was free to sit and knit, her glasses perched on the end of her nose. There would be no more radio for ages (programmes were chosen ahead of time and we all sat down to listen properly). As a special treat, if my mother was in a good mood I was allowed to play hairdressers and 'do' her hair. Her own style was exasperatingly plain; hair drawn back and clamped in a kind of doubled-over pipe-cleaner, then rolled up and secured at the nape of her neck in what was practically a bun. I gave her rolls piled high on either side of a side parting and I reversed the pipe-cleaner and bun part into a page-boy. Without the drama of lipstick, the effect was never quite what I hoped for, but it made her look different and less like a mother. She looked at herself in the mirror and considered before shaking her head at our foolishness and telling me to put it all back as it was before.

She was beginning to put on weight and I couldn't understand why, since food was rationed and she'd given up sugar during the war and often went without so that my father and I should have more (we accepted this without comment as something that mothers did). She was clever with food and clever with money and clever with books and poetry and maths, but there her energy and inventiveness seemed to give out. Gone was the elegant schoolteacher of not so long ago, and her thickening figure was dressed in the same four-square, dun-coloured

costume and brown riding hat year in, year out. At home she wore a
shapeless brown skirt and hand-knitted jumpers under a cotton overall.
Undoubtedly she used her clothing coupons for my school uniforms
and concert dresses and my father's immaculate three-piece 'best' suit. I
didn't think to ask and disloyally wished she wore prettier clothes and
lost weight.

She spent most of our time together 'improving' my mind and
making sure I knew the difference between Right and Wrong, never
missing a chance to point up a moral. Stories of children who Went to
the Bad were recounted with gruesome relish.

Our conversations were hardly ever exchanges. I was kept in my
place. I answered questions, I was lectured to, I listened. Sometimes I
absorbed, sometimes my mind wandered. Now, as I asked a question,
for once, my mother looked surprised, almost taken aback. Then she
looked shy and there was silence as she considered this new departure
in our relationship. Maybe she was nervous of advancing me to a position of equality as a confidante. If so, the temptation to speak was too
strong and there in the warm, bright living room she told me the story
of her other daughter, my sister whom I had never known, someone I
had only heard mentioned on the edges of conversations that faded as I
approached.

The Perfect Baby was called Gwenith Mai (born, like me, in May, I
supposed). My mother described her clothes, who gave them to her
and which ones my mother knitted for her and in what colour. Her
complexion, her hair, her sleeping and eating habits were described.
Nothing, no detail however small, was forgotten or considered too
trivial to be laid out between us now; laid out and considered and added
to. 'And then, one day when she was nine months old, I fed her and
changed her and put her in her new nightie, the flannelette with the
pin-tucks above the waist and small appliqué daisies round the hem, and
I wrapped her in the shawl that Mary-Annie had crocheted for her, and
she was beautiful and clean and going to sleep – and she went still. Too
still. I put her on my shoulder and patted her, and I looked at her again,
but now she was stiff, and I called out, loud, and Mrs Fred Phillips next
door came running in and she took her from me and rocked her. Then
she lowered her head as though she was listening, and then she looked
up at me and shook her head.' My mother's hand lifted from her lap in
a small gesture. 'She was gone.' There was old surprise in her face. She
shook her head, tears gathered in her eyes and rolled down her face. She

didn't make a sound. The fire crackled and the clock ticked and the silence thickened in the bright room shiny with polished wood and old brass and new chromium. It smelled good and ordinary and safe, but as we sat, each in our own little circle, I could see that nothing was safe at all. I walked over to her and put my arm around her shoulders. She didn't move and I don't know how long it was before she raised and dropped her hands again in the same small gesture of not understanding and, wiping her eyes on the corner of her overall, she rose and walked into the kitchen.

There was the clattering sound of pots and dishes. I thought maybe I would like to cry but decided to save it until later, in bed. I laid the table without being asked and my mother and I were very nice to each other for the rest of the evening. Until I went to the grammar school I was called by my third name, Ailwên. It was a made-up name and meant 'second smile', and now I knew why I'd been given it.

Soon after the end of my mother's dream of emigrating, she was standing in Prince's shop (it was called that because Mr Jenkins who ran it used to be the landlord of the Prince Albert pub, down the valley). Prince's sold *everything*; groceries on one side, hardware on the other, and little metal boxes with bills and change whizzed about overhead between the counters and the cashier's raised boxed-in desk. Across the busy room, she told me, she saw a stranger in police uniform towering over everyone in the shop. Times were hard for everyone in the Twenties; most of the local lads were out of work and depressed (and Welshmen on the whole are on the short side). The newcomer, wonderfully good-looking, looked very different from everyone around. 'Who is that?' she whispered to Mrs Jenkins. 'Well now,' beamed Mrs Jenkins, sensing a likely match, 'that's young Phillips from Llanelli. Just arrived and I'll introduce you.' He had a beautiful voice. He sang. He played the piano. He played cricket. He was a useful all-round athlete. So much my mother told me – once. This was not one of the told and retold stories, and I think she felt that for me to be told about the courtship and the marriage would have been completely inappropriate. She married this handsome, sweet-natured man whose grave smile could not have given her a clue to the sadness he carried inside him. Or maybe it did. She was no one's fool.

Chapter Four

He was the handsomest man I knew and he could do everything. He didn't like too much talk, so from infancy I followed him around, keeping a still tongue in my head and hoping to be given little jobs. I held hammers and measuring tapes, shone torches, dug the garden. As I grew up I filled his fountain-pen, changed the blotter and tidied the pigeon-holes of his desk, turned the pages of his music scores, learned bass-baritone solos with him, and, to my mother's despair, clad in wellingtons and gloves on the hottest day, helped him dispose of the night soil when we lived in a house that had an outside privy – squeamish right through, I didn't flinch when I worked alongside my father. When I was small I could see that I slowed him down, but when we walked together he never lost patience with me. Not once.

Even I could see that he was in the wrong job and as I grew older, at eight or nine years, I could see that he had somehow withdrawn himself from a major part of his existence. The Welsh word for police force is '*Heddlu*', peace-force. So, in a way, I thought, he did his job very well because in our village peace reigned. When, on the pay-day, there was a brawl outside one of the two pubs at closing time, my father would contrive to be strolling past, looking the other way and, in appreciation of the policy of non-interference, there would be a jumble of 'All right now, boss', 'No trouble now, boys', 'Good man, boss.' My father's expression remained fixed and inscrutable and maybe his reticence was misinterpreted as a grand aloofness or possibly even menace. He and the postmistress and the chapel minister were great friends, and held the secrets of the village and served as marriage-guidance counsellors, therapists and occasionally judge and jury. It was understood that nothing heard between the walls of the police station was ever to be revealed to anyone outside.

I would sit at the top of the darkened staircase at night while people poured out their hearts to my father, who would have paid good money, if he'd had any, to be spared the intimate confidences. I, on the other hand, was delighted. Grave and shy and beautiful, he sat and listened, seldom speaking, and one night, one of his 'regulars' – a miserable wife who gave her husband as good as she got (even I knew that) – sensing that she wasn't arousing enough feeling in my father cried, 'And another thing! Do you know what he called you? Do you?' No response, of course. 'I'll tell you then! "Bloody waster!" You!' Dramatic pause, then in a crescendo: 'You! A man who carries *the weight of British justice on his shoulders.*' 'Mmm,' said my father while, upstairs, my toes curled with delight. 'Mmm. Look, I'll have a little word with him.' Realising that she would have to content herself with this, she allowed herself to be ushered out, and as he closed the door he dropped his head for a moment, shutting his eyes, shoulders shaking slightly with laughter. Looking up he caught sight of me on the stairs. Taken aback, he shook his head and turned into the middle room. I understood that it was all right to enjoy the joke, but not all right to acknowledge it. I scurried back to bed, still laughing.

After an illegal pig-slaughtering during rationing, he required everyone to be extra discreet when contraband sausages and faggots and brawn were handed round the village. Baskets had to have a decent layer of blameless apples or cakes on top. To my mother's unspoken but evident displeasure, he refused our share of the feast. When Jones the Post, who was a talented poet writing in the old metre, turned to drink while wrestling with an ode and collapsed, surrounded by undelivered mail in a place where it was impossible not to notice him, my father expected to be notified as soon as possible so that he could get him out of sight and finish the mail round himself.

There were darker events. Once a little girl was found dead on the mountainside and my father sat all night next to her body until the doctor could come in the morning. He didn't speak for almost a week after that. Every so often there would be an outbreak of poison-pen letters in the village. They were handed to my father, who was only too aware of the author's identity. I knew where to look for the things I was not supposed to see and was enthralled by the letters, the blackmail threats and the blurry 'Peeping Tom' photographs of adulterous couplings. There was nothing there to upset or surprise me at the age of eight, nothing I hadn't read about in the Old Testament or my mother's French novels. 'A little word' was delivered and the letters would stop for a while. And people seemed plagued by what they referred to as 'nerves'. Occasionally I would be moved to the couch downstairs and my room given over to someone 'suffering from the nerves' who needed looking after for a while. I understood that I was never to reveal anything I saw or heard. I learned discretion and duplicity became second nature.

My father was accountable to his superiors in the nearest small town, Pontardawe. They were a rough lot, I privately thought. One of them with a passable singing voice was about to be received into my father's choir and as I passed him a cup of tea he remarked, '*The Messiah* – great! I don't think that I know it, though. How does it go? Could you hum it?' I was transfixed by such ignorance. I gathered that my father's position was uneasy and made even more precarious by the way he did his job and by the way we lived our life. His interpretation of his work was to keep everything ticking over as quietly as possible and to 'have a quiet word' rather than to make an arrest. Quite rightly, the lack of arrests was viewed with disapproval as it was considered unlikely that our village should be peopled only by the innocent. I dimly understood that our way of life was disapproved of as unsuitable. My mother directed children's plays and coached me as I began to make a name for myself locally and then nationally. My father accompanied singers, sang himself, trained a choir and organised 'Celebrity Concerts', raising money for charity. In the police force this was considered to be inappropriate behaviour leading to undesirable familiarity, and from time to time I sensed that warnings were issued from above. An uneasy compromise would follow. My father made sure that his paperwork was impeccable, he took course after course, stepped up his night-school activities, passed exam after exam up to Inspectorate level and, having become over-qualified, proceeded to run the tiny fiefdom in his unorthodox and to official eyes, hopeless, manner. Selfishly, I was grateful that my activities were never curtailed. We were very much at the centre of village life, yet slightly apart, keeping other people's secrets, never taking sides.

Once, during the war my father went away on a course and returned as a Bomb Disposal Officer for the neighbourhood. While Swansea, nine miles away, was pounded by bombs for three days and my mother carried me, wrapped in a blanket, into the garden and told me to remember that she was reading the paper at night by the light of Swansea burning, we experienced only one bomb that fell silently into a bog and disappeared. The yellow poisonous gas detector rusted on the lawn

– was it green or red for danger? We forgot. I sat, enthralled, hidden among the piled-up gas masks while the Home Guard met in the parlour for tea and Welsh cakes. The meekest, most God-fearing chapel deacon was all for sharpening the pitchforks against the marauding Germans.

My father went on another course and returned with a rifle and a gun licence. When an envelope arrived addressed to the Home Guard, 'To be opened in the event of an invasion', a meeting was held where it was naturally decided to open the envelope there and then since the day of invasion might be a very busy and confusing one with no opportunity to be reading letters. The letter read, in effect, 'If you see one or two Germans, shoot them. If there are more, bury the rifle.' There was an unheroic rumble of approval at this piece of good sense. The more excitable members of the Special Police and Home Guard were convinced that there were spy rings to be uncovered in every chapel and one of the most dramatic events that occurred during the war was Mr Evans' wild midnight ride. He thought he'd seen a parachute and, mounted on a white shire-horse, he galloped from village to village armed with a wooden klaxon, crying in Welsh, 'Arise, arise! Invasion! Invasion!' After a cursory peep through the window at the empty countryside, the village turned over and went to sleep. There were sharp words in the big police station in Pontardawe. My father shrugged.

Meanwhile, music was my father's 'real' life in the same way that teaching was my mother's. I could see that both of them were obliged to live once removed from the things that mattered to them. However happy she was with my father and however pleased she was to have a child, marriage and motherhood had spoiled my mother's life. My father's joy in life had been destroyed by circumstance. As a child, the oldest of a miner's five children, his facility at the piano had brought him to the attention of a local music teacher who gave him free lessons once a week. At the end of the hour, he would run home and immediately pass the lesson on to his brother, Ronald (like all families, however poor, they had a piano). Together they played and sang and learned to play the violin and the flute as well (and Ronald went on to be the organist at the Baptist Chapel in Bynea).

My father never spoke of these days and it was his brother who told me that when they formed a small glee club and began to give concerts, my father was one of the boys 'spotted' by a London talent scout who scoured the industrial valleys of Wales looking for good voices. He was given free voice training as a tenor (and then, interestingly, another coach thought a mistake had been made and he was retrained as a bass-baritone). Several of his friends left for London, most of them to the chorus of the Carl Rosa Opera Company, but at this moment his father's health failed, he was silicotic and unable to work, and my father became the breadwinner of the family. The events of these years – the aborted musical career, the job in the steelworks and then, thanks to his height and his talent for cricket, his seeming 'escape' to the comparative security of the Glamorgan Police Force at a time when unemployment was at its worst – were taboo subjects.

He never complained, but I knew that he was 'making do'. When he organised concerts and artists from London came down, some of them friends of his, I wondered how he could bear to be reminded of how much better his life could have been. But he didn't display any regret or envy; he was simply happier than he was at any other time. Tom Williams, Dafen, a friend of his who had become a soloist in London, would stay with us and they would sing duets into the small hours. I loved seeing him in his element. And I loved running around, fetching and carrying for Eva Turner, Heddle Nash, Edith Coates, Vanessa Leigh, Olive Gilbert, Webster Booth and Anne Ziegler (her crinoline couldn't pass through our front door and she dressed in the backyard next to the coal-house). The clothes, the jewels, the 'nerves', the rows, were pure pleasure.

It never occurred to me to doubt that I was adored by my father. His undemonstrative manner, his formal, rather distant polite way of relating to me, did nothing to shake my conviction that I occupied a central place in his world. Although I never felt poor, I assumed that like everyone else we had little money. One of my chief concerns was to make sure that my father was never saddened by his inability to give me something that I must have wanted. So I pretended that I didn't want anything because I didn't know what anything cost and if I did, I didn't know if that was expensive. My parents found this very difficult when it came to buying Christmas and birthday presents. I managed to cancel birthdays altogether, but Christmas was another matter and my parents made inspired guesses and bought me things I secretly longed for. I don't know how he came by it, but when my father gave me a beautiful old microscope, I thought I would die of love and pleasure.

Some of the presents were a bit odd. One Christmas when I was eleven, we had a Christmas tree for the first and only time, and it snowed. I was going through an intensely religious phase and Christmas Eve was mysterious and romantic, and my father gave me a very expensive book with a foreword by Julian Huxley that impressed me no end. It was called *Living Things and Their Evolution* and it suggested that maybe God *didn't* create the world, which was a notion I had never heard mentioned. 'Well,' he said, 'it's something for you to think about.' A year later he gave me the complete works of Oscar Wilde with no comment at all. That certainly gave me something to think about. I read: 'One's real life is often the life one does not lead.'

Nothing could change my idea that something went badly wrong for my father around this time. He gave away all his Caruso and Gigli records and stopped playing the gramophone. He stopped buying the Gollancz yellow-covered left-wing books. Doors closed with quiet finality. He began to read 'escape' literature, Zane Grey Westerns, one after the other. He played Beethoven hour after hour and every day I would see him reading a book in a plain, brown, loose cover. I couldn't see where he kept it until one day I saw him reach up and drop it behind a set of Galsworthy novels. Hating myself, but needing to know, I climbed on to the arm of a chair, fished out the book and saw that it was a well-thumbed New Testament.

There were times when he seemed to occupy a barely defined position in a family No Man's Land.

One day when I was little – about seven – I'd been sent by my mother up to my room and told to stay there until further notice. I was in real trouble and I was going to be taught a Big Lesson. I had finished crying. I couldn't cry any more and I sat on my single bed with its huge mattress filled with down from Tŷ mawr geese, my legs dangling, not reaching the linoleum-covered floor. I was looking through the window of my small, lovely bedroom with its painted furniture. Below, the sun shone on the meadows of the nearby farm in Alltwen; the lane leading to it was out of sight behind high hedges and so was the field where I had intended to play, near, but not too near, the witch's house (she had once tried to put buttermilk on my sunburned shoulders and ungratefully I'd roared with fright as she approached, bent almost double, toothless, wearing long, dark, cotton skirts). Out of sight I and my friends lit fires (which was strictly forbidden) and 'cooked' potatoes and ate them almost raw, and we made 'lemonade' from dandelion flowers or daffodils; anything that would turn water yellow. It was probably a forbidden drink. We were lawless in a quiet way. Nothing but the bedroom for me today and probably tomorrow as well.

It had all started because of my habit of investing ordinary things with almost supernatural powers – I 'acquired' as talismans and charms things that to other eyes seemed commonplace. When, as a four-year-old, I first saw scillas in the garden next door, I couldn't rest until I had cut them all and 'planted' them in our garden. I *had* to have them by me. There had been a huge row and I had finally understood that other people's things must be left alone, but now, three years later, it had happened again, only this time the property wasn't another *person's* and I hadn't seen the harm until it was too late.

I was in one of my periods of not being ill and I'd been to Rhos School, which I loved, and I'd learned a bit of sewing. The class had been set the task of sewing little 'worms' of coloured cotton, stuffed with cotton threads. There were dozens of these little coloured tubes, designed to be part of some great plan, unknown to me. I didn't know why it was, but I desperately wanted to keep mine. They were lovely. They were magical – and I decided to take them home. No one would notice that three were missing. At the end of the day the teacher said, 'There are three of these missing. Where are they, please?' Horrified, I froze. My moment to own up passed. 'All right,' she said, 'all desks open.' Inspired, I, the 'good' girl, the invalid what's more, raised a hand and asked to be excused. I had a brilliant idea. Racing down the yard, past the lavatories, I stood on tiptoe and hurled the treasures over the tile-capped wall. All right, I could never get them back from that nettle-filled ditch, but at least I would never be found out.

The teacher who had watched all this from the classroom window was waiting when I returned. She was 'disappointed' (she was probably confused as well; the magic of these inanimate objects was not easily apparent to grown-ups). I knew what 'disappointed' meant. It meant coming to the house and telling all to her friend, my mother. It meant making trouble for me. Sure enough, she arrived for tea and a long chat where I couldn't eavesdrop. After she'd gone, there was a long silence, then my mother, calling me in, sat down and just looked at me. Finally she spoke. 'I'm going to give you a dressing-down you'll never forget,' she said, 'and then we'll decide whether or not you'll have to be sent away to Reform School.'

Reform School? Reform School? I'd heard of them. They were for hopeless cases; really bad, bad children. That was like going to prison. I took in the point of the lecture that followed. Public property was like *private* property. Property was sacred even when there were no visible owners. Yes, yes, yes, I could observe the laws of property if they were that serious, but now I was feverishly reviewing my behaviour over the past few months and trying to work out my chances of survival. There had been a lot of Badness, I knew that far better than she did. Maybe this was the end of the road. My mind raced ahead. I'd read enough Victorian stories to know that, often, Badness led to Death and that deathbed scenes with confessions and forgiveness before the darkness fell on the criminal were the best ending for everyone concerned. I could see myself lying there, surrounded by *disappointed* people, being forgiven before I drifted off to a dubious afterlife. I howled and howled. My mother shook her head sorrowfully, reprised the lecture and asked me over and over again what I wanted the sewing *for*. Sodden with tears, I was beyond speech, but I couldn't have explained anyhow.

And there was the incident of the poem to consider. That had happened only last week. Mrs Rogers-up-the-road had come to the house (looking *very* disappointed) bearing a poem, a love poem I'd written to her son, my friend, Geoff, with whom I walked to school. I was very taken with him because I could tell he liked me as I was the one whose skirts he lifted up in the lane beside the school when the boys chased us, flicking up our skirts and running away crying '*Ach-y-fi* – disgusting' before collapsing with laughter and regrouping. We girls pretended to be scandalised and offended, but it was a game we liked a lot for the few weeks we played it before tops or hoops took its place. My poem, inspired by this proof of affection, had rhymes and looked just like a poem should, but my mother was furious and I had cried and promised never to do it again, though I cried only because I'd been found out and I couldn't really see why Mrs Rogers and my mother were so very upset. That, I now thought gloomily, probably made me even more bad. It was a small mercy that she didn't know we had shown the boys our knickers. Anyway, I had, it seemed, 'done it' now and I resigned myself to my fate. My mother had gone out. Would I know what was to become of me when she returned? When would that be? I waited.

My bedroom door opened and my father looked in. Then, without saying anything he went downstairs. Why had he opened my door? Tentatively I crept out on to the landing and, having loitered awhile in the bathroom where I used to write my poetry on the marble wash-stand, I slowly descended the stairs and sat at the bottom. My father had been playing the piano as he did every day, repeating the tricky bits over and over again, but now he began to play 'my' pieces, pieces he played for me to dance to. And now it was 'In a Monastery Garden' by Mr Ketelby. This was music for one of my sad, wafty dances.

I entered the middle room and made a few moody movements round the table. Next he played 'In a Persian Market' by the same composer. This music was for foreign, sultry dancing and now, gaining confidence, I twirled round the entire room. There was so much furniture that 'dancing' was mostly a matter of keeping to the beat while not bumping into things or jumping over them. My father sat with his back to me and played and played, mazurkas and waltzes and polkas and Souza marches and folk tunes about leaving home that made me cry each time I heard them and today, especially, provoked a storm of grief.

Then my father stopped playing and gave a small final-sounding cough. I was glad he didn't say anything because I couldn't decide what was right to say. My father had done me a kindness and I was grateful, but I knew and he must know that my mother was right to be punishing me. I didn't think that he would want to be disloyal to my mother either. It was confusing and sad and it was all my fault. I packed myself off upstairs and settled down again to wait, with an empty fearful place under my ribs. The shadows were lengthening along the hedges. I didn't want to be sent away – if it was decided that I had to go, might my father be able to save me? I stifled that thought at birth. I worshipped my father but I didn't want to test him.

Life was difficult for my father, but I couldn't decide if something went wrong or whether he simply ran out of steam. He loved me and feared for me and didn't involve me in his problems, but I thought about them all the time until selfishly, in the way of teenagers, I stopped thinking about my parents as interesting, separate beings. Something of my preoccupation with their story remained, however, like an infection in the blood, a residual unease, a fear of being crushed by circumstance. The overturning of a way of life. An expulsion from Eden.

My mother forgave me and I wasn't sent away.

Chapter Five

My first appearances on a stage had not left a deep mark on me. When I was four my mother washed and dressed me for my first recitation in chapel and left me to wait for her in the back garden. I fancy I remember the sunshine there and the colour of my dress – yellow – and the warmth of the sun on my bare arms. I think I remember being lifted up on to the Big Seat in chapel, where the sunlight beamed in through the large, plain windows and the varnished pews shone the colour of dark honey but smelled strongly of chapel: mints, bleach and polish. What I recited I don't remember, only that I felt happy and at home, as though I'd done this lots of times before. I have no recollection of taking off my knickers in the backyard and hiding them in a privet hedge as I was told I'd done, but I do remember that in chapel, when my mother lifted me down from the seat beside her and felt my bottom bare, she gripped me by my shoulders and hissed urgently, '*Don't bend over.*' That was the first piece of direction that I received. Mine must have been a rain-soaked childhood, but my memories are delightfully Mediterranean.

My first acting part in the same year was remarkable only for the fact that at the end of it I needed stitches in my face. The auntie of the famous writer and journalist, John Ormond-Thomas, taught us village children to dance (for years after, I treasured my tiny bit of 'tap' as one of my chief skills) and I was the smallest fairy – in what play I haven't the faintest idea. But those fairy *wings*! Wings with bunches of silver trim smelling of rusty tin cans and utterly beautiful in my eyes. The dress was adequate and the socks were a disaster, but my silver shoes and my wings filled me with pride. I thought, if only my feet could stay the same size I would always have these silver shoes. It didn't occur to me that I could ever have another pair. Little threads became unpicked from the strange material from which they'd been made and they also smelled curiously of metal.

The performance passed off unremarkably until the exit of the fairies, when, as the smallest dancer, I led off and was seized by a sudden notion that I could add lustre to my performance by showing the audience what beautiful manners I possessed. I would graciously *give way* to the bigger girl coming along behind. I made an elegant side-step, improvising a few arm movements, and then another little hop – on to the masking 'blacks' down-stage right, and disappeared, chin first, into the front row of the stalls. Mercifully the wings, being at the back of my costume where wings belong, were safe from the blood pouring from my nose and chin. I don't know if the show went on. I went to the surgery and as they clamped my chin I managed to convey through gritted teeth what was uppermost in my mind. '*Mind my wings*,' I growled. And they did. Everything worked out quite well. I was told never to do anything on stage that hadn't been *practised*, but almost in the same breath people were heard to say, 'Lovely manners she's got though.' Fifty per cent success and my wings survived intact.

Like most Welsh children I was expected to sing in public. My father taught me my first solo, 'You in your small corner and I in mine', learned phonetically in English, which no one spoke, and I sang it in the same chapel where I gave my first recitation when I was four. As usual, I was lifted on to the deacon's bench so that I could be seen. My father was to accompany me on the piano that had been brought in for the occasion, the pipe organ being considered too intimidating. My mother was completely unmusical and anxious I shouldn't make a fool of myself; neither was my father too sure that I could acquit myself well. They kept asking me, was I nervous? I was not. Not at all. My moment finally came and I waited for the usual buzz of conversation to die down, then turned slightly in my father's direction. He, waiting to give me an encouraging smile and a signal that he was going to start playing the introduction, was mortified to receive from me an imperceptible nod that he should begin playing *now*, please. As the years went by, my talent did not keep pace with my composure, and in that intensely musical environment I was relegated to being a chorister.

During my scarlet fever convalescence, when I was six and she was in her mid-seventies, my grandmother and I made a momentous journey from G.C.G. to Swansea. Together, we made our first visit to a theatre and my life changed for ever. I decided to become an actress and never forgot that afterwards, not for a single day.

Except for visits to chapel in the village, my grandmother never went anywhere, so her appearance on a *bus* – to *Swansea* – underlined for me the gravity of the excursion as we set off for the Swansea Empire. Swansea was large and dirty and dangerous. A 'Swansea wash' was a lick and a spit. Swansea people ate shop cake and tinned meat and they stole children who didn't stay close to their parents. This was a big journey. My mother and her sister, Meriel, had fretted over the wisdom of taking my grandmother to a theatre – a place where *her* mother had believed the devil lurked high up in the dark corners – and they were apprehensive as we sat down. I felt like a queen in my velvet seat, waiting for the pantomime to begin. What was a pantomime? What kind of place *was* this?

Suddenly there was loud music – where was it coming from? The lights dimmed and the huge red-and-gold curtain rose slowly. My lips parted in wonderment and my jaw dropped slightly. Occasionally I closed my mouth and swallowed, then my mouth would open again in silent wonder. I didn't understand the story but I was transported. When everything stopped I shook my head, silently refusing to leave my seat or eat a sweet. This was magic. I had never known anything so absorbing and I didn't want to speak or move in case I broke the spell. I wondered how it was that a place could be at the same time so dark, hugely dark, and so brilliantly alight. There was more light here than I could have imagined possible.

I wasn't rendered stupid, however. There was a principal boy, but she was a woman and her legs were too fat and I hated the way she boomed and scooped with her voice as she sang, 'I don't want to set the world on fi-ire but I do-o want to set a fla-ame in your heart'. No, it was the whole thing that captured me. That and the chorus girls! When they linked arms and kicked up their legs, I smiled the serene smile of perfect certainty. I knew what I wanted to be: I would spend my whole life in the theatre and I would be a chorus girl.

When the curtain descended again and the pantomime was over, I was speechless and remained so, hugging my moment of revelation to myself. My grandmother's reaction was nervously awaited. Solemnly she shook her head. Like me she had been entranced by the chorus girls and they were exempted from the disdain that would have been heaped on anyone else's unclothed lower limbs. Finally she spoke. 'Skin,' she said, 'perfect skin. Never, anywhere, have I seen such perfect skin.' Faces, innocent of so much as a dab of powder on the nose, beamed at one another in happiness at an afternoon well spent.

After the pantomime my mother took me home to Alltwen. When I got home I took out one of my most treasured possessions: a large Boots diary, two years out of date. I opened it and wrote in English, 'I am now resolved to be an actress.' My mother, passing behind me, looked over my shoulder and tossed her head good-naturedly, giving a small 'what next' laugh. I was affronted and hardened my heart a little against her. What was there to laugh at?

Brim-full of lofty purpose, I decided to start preparing for my vocation. The chorus girls had linked arms and – so it seemed to me – had kicked both legs in the air at once. Down in the backyard I stood on the stone flags, my back to the granite wall of the house, and tried to pluck up courage to do the same. One, two, three . . . No! Too scary – one foot would descend to save me. For days, whenever my parents weren't looking, I stood out in the yard, fists clenched, willing the courage to come from somewhere. Finally it did. Up went *both* legs! And I don't remember a great deal more. My bottom landed on the flags and my head hit the granite wall and as I crawled into the house, feeling sick, I reflected that there must be a secret method. I would be taught it later, when I was a student chorine.

As soon as I could move about more easily, I thought I would see how well I could manage the Fairy Queen's pose when she stood on tiptoe on one leg and, leaning forward with her wand, held the other leg out behind her, waist high. I thought I'd got it right but I couldn't be sure, so I climbed on to the chair in front of my mother's dressing-table with its triple-mirror, which began low down, near the floor. This was great, I would be able to see everything. Up on to the back of the chair, arms outstretched, leg up and crash! – down into the mirror – which didn't break. I was so grateful it remained in one piece that I ignored the pain in my ankle. My stripy socks gave me away; the sprained ankle swelled and swelled and the navy stripes became thinner as the sock stretched. 'What's that?' said my mother, accusingly. 'I don't know,' I said, looking at my foot as though I'd never seen it before. 'This ankle is sprained,' said my mother as she cut off the hand-knitted sock. 'You must know how you did it.' Wild horses wouldn't have dragged the truth from me. There is more to this pantomime business than meets the eye, I thought sadly.

After the revelation of my future that had occurred at the pantomime, I did not find a great deal to nourish my resolve to be an actress (preferably an actress in fishnet tights and six-inch heels). My own appearances in chapels and town halls up and down the valleys surrounding Alltwen were immensely interesting and enjoyable, but only so-so in my grand scheme. Wales was populated by amateur actors, and my mother took me to plays, mainly 'kitchen' comedies or melodramas about the demon drink. I remained hatchet-faced and unappreciative. She bought hardback editions of the 'best' West End plays of the year for herself and these I read over and over again. They included a few photographs and I became fascinated by an actress with a very ordinary, Welsh name. Edith Evans' face became as familiar to me as my own as I drew her over and over again in my big sketch-book. Even at eight I was good at drawing likenesses. Nothing going on around me could equal those plays, which I had never seen.

Later at grammar school I played in one-act plays by Miles Malleson with the other Good Actor, John Lloyd, and then a full-length play by James Bridie, *Tobias and the Angel*, with Dafydd Rowlands. I loved *that* play, and playing the Angel Raphael was almost as marvellous as singing and dancing in fishnet tights. I read my first 'rave' notices and felt pretty smug until I looked at the photograph in the paper and thought, 'Oh no!' I had thought I looked better than that. The picture showed a schoolgirl with lank hair, dressed up in what looked like (and were) old curtains, whereas I'd *felt* like a Towering Angel with a flowing mane of hair, shimmering in my gold brocade tunic. Nothing was quite measuring up to my private notion of what I wanted to be and what I thought I should look like. Except . . . There was an evening that swept me off my feet and reminded me.

My father took me to the cinema: the Lyric in Pontardawe. This was a most unusual event. Everything about it was novel; the long walk in the dark down the steep hill to the little town, everything looking different at night, everyone's curtains tightly shut, the streets empty. The Lyric itself, wedged between two shops, seemed huge to me – what age could I have been? Probably eight years old. It was a double-feature programme with a news report as well. I liked the frantic music that accompanied the Pathé gazette news and the over-excited voice of the man, but the news held no interest for me and I looked about in the darkness wondering, as usual, how grown up I appeared, sitting in my rather scratchy, balding seat. I hoped it would seem as though I was there alone. I leaned away from my father, surreptitiously licking the index finger of my left hand in order to make a little kink in the hair that hung straight over my left ear. The hair on the right side of my face was firmly secured by a large, much detested, silk bow, but I felt that the sophisticated twist on the left side negated the childish ribbon and gave me a touch of glamour. I licked my lips and sucked in my cheeks to make interesting hollows and hoped I was being *seen*.

The first film began. I was so overwhelmed that I didn't understand a word of it. Apart from the panto, it was the first entertainment I'd seen in English and for all I know this film may have been American. It didn't matter; it was the funniest thing I had ever watched. Men climbed in and out of outsized machinery and sat on things I couldn't identify. It seemed to be called *Helsappopin*, but I wasn't sure of that. The cinema was not full. People chuckled a bit and so did I, then they laughed aloud a bit. I laughed aloud a lot, then more – and more. I rolled in my seat, I patted my chest, trying to catch my breath. It was no good, I was transported by side-splitting, choking, ungovernable roars of laughter.

My easily embarrassed father was probably aghast by this unexpected turn – I was a quiet child. He gave me a nudge. There was a man standing over him in the dark. 'I'm very sorry,' he hissed, 'but she'll have to be taken out if she can't keep quiet.' I wasn't abashed, I thought the man was mad, but I didn't want to be taken out, oh gosh, I didn't. I smothered my laughter as best I could, exploding into the occasional whoop, never prolonged enough to justify my eviction.

The film ended and I leaned back, damp and exhausted and beaming with satisfaction. 'Do you want to go? Out?' said my father tentatively. I supposed he meant, did I want to go to the lavatory? Not likely. I was in an enchanted place and I wasn't about to waste a minute of the evening in a lavatory. I shook my head and waited impatiently for the lights to go down again. I didn't understand much more of this second film's dialogue either, but it was sad. *Very* sad. By the time the hero was sitting with his little boy in a kind of – workhouse? soup kitchen? – penniless certainly, hungry as well, and the unseen orchestra was playing something that I thought was 'Danny Boy', I was in paroxysms of grief. Tears poured unchecked down my face; my hankie was a sodden little ball, my nose ran and my frame was shaken by violent sobs that grew in volume. The man was there again. 'I'm very sorry but if she doesn't stop crying she'll really *have* to go out.'

My father half stood up to go. Mulishly I sank down in my seat, moaning as quietly as I could. My father sat down again and handed me his big handkerchief and I wiped my entire face with it as though it was a face-flannel. 'Why,' I thought, 'did they show such films if they wanted people to be quiet, for heaven's sake?'

Somehow I got through to the end of the evening. My hair was damp, the curl hung straight, the ribbon had wilted; I was exhausted and purged and I felt wonderful. My father and I didn't speak at all as we climbed the hill back to Alltwen. I was hardly aware of getting home, and when my mother opened the door to us, I scuttled off to bed silently, washing and cleaning my teeth and brushing my hair without being prompted, anxious to preserve this wonderful feeling and take it, intact, to my bed.

Between the ages of eight and twelve or thirteen, my very best friend was Mair Rees. We lived near enough to each other to be playmates when I was too ill to go to school, and after the scholarship exam we both went to Pontardawe Grammar School. She had curly blonde hair so I felt her to be by nature superior to me. We both took lessons from the same piano teacher and played duets together in chapel concerts until, by virtue of regular practice and attention to correct fingering, she became my superior in technical skill as well as hair and continued as a solo pianist while I went on strike and at ten stopped taking those awful music exams and those interminable lessons where my lack of practice was exposed as I threw myself at the North Face of a chromatic scale, only to end up time and time again in a mangled heap of wrong notes. After Mrs Williams Music had departed clutching her tiny fee, my mother would appear holding the implements of whatever cooking task she had interrupted and stand there, shaking her head. My father couldn't begin to understand what sort of person would not *want* to practise, so he didn't know what to say to me. He still played scales for at least half an hour every day. 'You've got a nice touch,' he once said encouragingly, but we both knew that I didn't 'have it'.

The private lessons were discontinued. I studied music at school and took cello lessons there because I liked the Augustus John portrait of Suggia. I was not a musical asset to the school orchestra, but I looked very convincing. Mair and I were both in the school choir and the times spent learning Miss Caryl Williams's ambitious programmes of Purcell and Pergolesi were among the happiest of my school-days. When I became house-captain I had my own, smaller house choir and I thought I'd died and gone to heaven the first time I conducted it.

I was a stranger to self-doubt at this time and thought that it would be a really good move to write just one 'pop' song and try a bit of what the wireless called 'Variety'. 'Can't be hard,' I thought, and found a venue where my forays into light entertainment could be tried out. Mair was a reluctant, long-suffering partner in this venture. She loathed performing and it took a lot of bullying on my part to get her singing and dancing (I had somehow acquired a dim perception of something called a jitterbug) and playing bad supporting roles in my comic sketches. She was necessary because she was my acknowledged 'official' best friend and our mothers allowed us to spend all our spare time together, so we had ample rehearsal opportunities. She was also the daughter of Phil Rees, the Oil, who had a little shop alongside his house, and the upper part of the shop was a garage with double doors that opened on to a small back road, where theirs was the last house before the road narrowed to a track past the cemetery. With the double doors opened wide and a sheet hung inside the empty garage, hiding the supplies of paraffin at the back, this was a perfect little theatre with considerable passing trade among people going to tend graves or taking a short cut to the chapel vestry.

We could only perform when Mr Rees was out on his rounds in the van and when Mrs Rees was also out for the afternoon. We charged a halfpenny, not for admission exactly because the auditorium was the road and the audience stood leaning on the hedge across the way or sat at our feet, which pleased us more because then no one could pass through to the cemetery and had to politely dawdle awhile, holding their buckets and trowels and other grave-tending equipment until we came to a stop. My big finish was a dance number set to a song I'd heard on the radio. It was really up to the minute, I felt, and a nice contrast to my affecting rendition of 'Christopher Robin saying his prayers' that preceded it. I'd copied down the words; they didn't make much sense but never mind. 'Maisie Dotes and Dozey Dotes and little Amsie Tivey, a Kiddlee Tivy too, wouldn't you?' we bellowed, and I was really pleased to see that it sent people on their way smiling. Some gave us more than a halfpenny.

Later, refining the jitterbug, I persuaded Mair to let me throw her over my shoulder, but it didn't work out at all as I'd hoped. I heaved her over my head, singing all the while, and instead of landing on her feet and doing something interesting, she fell on to the stone floor and just lay there. When her mother arrived home, she was still sitting on the floor holding her head and bawling. I was furious and scared in equal parts. Surely, at eight, she should know better than to just *fall* in the middle of a dance and she was making a terrible noise. But what if I'd hurt her really badly?

As Mrs Rees began to try to make sense of the state of the garage and the money on the table and the possibility that Mair was concussed, I sidled towards the door saying, 'I think my mother wants me home now.' Neither mother quite got to the bottom of things, but the Oil-Shop Theatre was closed and I gave up trying to be a songwriter and concert party producer. I never did manage to write more than four lines of a 'pop' song, so I decided to stick to performing for a while.

I never saw a variety show but I did see an amazing entertainment at Pontardawe. Next to the steelworks and the polluted, evil-smelling river, there was a ratty bit of open ground. It wasn't a place where you'd care to walk, except for the one and only time that the circus came to town. It must have been after the war and I must have been ten, a bit old to have been so ignorant. 'A what?' 'A circus and we're going tonight.' 'What is it?' 'Oh, I can't describe it, you'll have to wait.' I forgot about it. I didn't know what I was waiting for.

As we walked in the dusk down towards Pontardawe there was an unaccustomed smell in the air above the bad smell of the steelworks and there were lights where there had never before been lights, not even when all the lights went on after the war ended. There was a glow in the air and, as we drew nearer, I saw that the glow came from ropes of small coloured lights strung between the biggest tent imaginable and little – what were they? They looked like small, brilliantly lit, open-fronted shops and there was a merry-go-round and bumper cars and music everywhere, different tunes, clashing with each other, yielding one to the next as we walked on. The smell was overpowering; the damp downtrodden scrub underfoot mixed with the smell of cooking onions and animal droppings and some kind of scent.

Inside the big tent there were trapezes and a high wire, which didn't seem very high, and clowns who didn't seem very funny, and everywhere girls in fishnet tights. They didn't seem to do much and I wished I was one of them until they jumped up on to the ponies and did things I knew I could never manage, not even on long-suffering Tŷ mawr Daisy, tired out after her milk round. But I *could* wear a top hat and, whip in hand, point at the entrance as the drum rolled. I wanted to do *something*. The performance wasn't very long but by the end I was drunk on the atmosphere and the noise and the smell.

We walked about among the carousels and the little booths, and my father, who was a good shot, won me a pink toy that broke and a fish that died. Strolling in that unusual light was like being on stage and I stood up straighter and longed to belong to this strange, exotic and mysterious world. Curiously, I noticed that although the circus was all to do with fun and diversions and happiness, the people left a lot to be desired. Their eyes were distant and bored and they scarcely bothered to look pleasant, let alone smile. They were strangely bad at entertaining and I thought I could do much better. I had plenty to think about as we climbed home; I simply had to get into a world where I could feed my addiction to lights and music and noise, living and belonging on the other side of ordinary life.

On my way to school in the morning I made a detour down to the field. It was squalid and dirty, litter underfoot, a cold, grey Welsh light all around; no music, the people were shabby as they walked around with buckets and brushes, doing the housekeeping. But looking at it, I remembered what it was like disguised by lights, the people clothed in silk and spangles, and I wanted to belong to a world like this one and I was jealous of its inhabitants, even in their shabby morning selves.

Chapter Six

After my first brush with death at the age of six, I had scarlet fever again, chickenpox twice, measles and yellow jaundice once, a broken wrist, a sprained ankle, fainting fits, tonsillitis several times and chronic eczema, but my life as an invalid was packed with pleasure. My father did something called 'beating the bounds', which, I suppose, meant walking around the whole area he looked after: a couple of villages, a hamlet, a few mountains and lots of smallish farms. From the age of seven to ten, unless the weather was very bad, I would be allowed to accompany him. He didn't like idle chatter so we walked in companionable silence and I lengthened my stride more nearly to match his, only occasionally having to break into a little trot. From time to time he would motion me to stop and lift me up on to a five-barred gate to watch rabbits playing in a field and, once, hares boxing; we would stand still and watch a buzzard idling until it dived down to its prey, then resume our steady pace.

For much of this time I lived in anguish at the savagery that lay beneath the scents and winds and changing colours through which I moved, half submerged and half asleep. I realised as I rolled like a colt in the grass that I was destroying dozens, probably hundreds of small living things and that as I collected stones and fallen branches for my own amusement, I was obliterating domestic arrangements too small and too complex for me to understand. There were times, when I must have been eight years old, when I would tear out of the house in the early morning and then stand stock still, thinking how I could move without creating havoc, and on our long walks I would sometimes step in my father's tracks and pay attention to where I placed my feet in scuffed Clarks sandals, in case I stepped on and killed some small insect. I just couldn't understand why God had organised things in such an impossibly difficult way. Time after time I abandoned the conundrum and, faced with a long, inviting slope of soft grass, I broke into a murderous, unheeding gallop.

It was during these years that I took it into my head to try to look at everything as though I would never see it again. 'Look thy last on all things lovely' lodged, misunderstood, in my mind, and I was like a tourist in an exotic country, and would jink home at dusk, eyes aching, having failed yet again, half aware that I was setting myself impossible tasks and more than ready for a deserved Ovaltine and a re-read of something soothing – *What Katy Did* or a book by Enid Blyton – to reduce the pressure. I was only too good at letting myself off the hooks I manufactured for myself, and when my friends weren't at school we all rampaged together, interfering with nature without a qualm; we dammed streams, flooded meadows, climbed trees, lit fires, stole windfalls and one year collected scores of ladybirds day after day, keeping them cooped up in matchboxes for hours and hours.

I do not know what my father thought as we walked and walked, but for much of the time I didn't think of anything at all, fully absorbed in the constantly changing surroundings, tasting unfamiliar leaves and berries, sucking minute traces of honey from flowers and touching – touching everything. I knew I had as much right to be in the landscape as the oldest oak tree. I felt as small as an ant and as fierce as a lion.

Once out of the village, the countryside was bare of people. The farms were isolated and built in such a way as to be invisible until you were almost upon them. Some were small enough to be worked by two people and more often than not we would be greeted by silence as we entered the farmyard. Repeated hullo-ing from a bit of high ground eventually brought a faint reply and we would settle down to wait. The kitchen door was invariably open, but it would have been unthinkable to enter even if the weather was bad. The bachelor farmers employed housekeepers, and my mother, when she asked for news of our day, always overstressed their respectability. (Had it not been for this it wouldn't have occurred to me to think that they might *not* be respectable.) Then I noticed that they also overstated their propriety in many ways, assuming a massive severity of dress and manner, and when they offered food and drink as befitted a woman of the house (men were not expected to be able to make tea or lay a table), the feeling was nicely conveyed that the Welsh cakes they had baked were not actually *theirs* to offer, nor were the chairs they invited us to sit on. Nor did the farmer behave proprietorially. Each party deferred to the other and their behaviour was underpinned with formality. A chapel-going housekeeper would know that I was a Reciter and I would be invited to 'do' a piece and, that done, I could escape the horrible strong tea and cake and skip off to have a good nose around in their outhouses, highly critical of anything organised in a way that differed from my grandmother's.

Far more interesting to me than these good and ordinary people was the lady tramp whom we encountered once every six weeks as she walked in a great circle through the countryside. She was tall and strong and she strode out vigorously. My mother threatened the usual dire but unspecified consequences if we failed to treat her with respect, and suggested it would be even better to ignore her, which is what she would like best. My mother said that the woman was from a 'good' family and had *decided* to live as a Traveller, and who was to say that that was wrong? (I could imagine my mother's face if I told her that I had decided to take up Travelling . . .) My father was the only person who knew where she was on a given day or where she went, and I wasn't to be nosey, but I occasionally followed her at a discreet distance and never saw her sit down or slacken her speed and always had to turn home before I saw her do anything that might tell me something about her.

Sometimes we would visit a tramp who had built himself a home deep in a wood on the land around the Big House belonging to the squire, Mr Lloyd. As we approached through the undergrowth my father would clear his throat a few times and stamp about a bit so as not to take the old man by surprise. Maybe he wasn't old at all; he was heavily bearded and his long reddish-brown hair protruded under his jaunty, greasy pork-pie hat, and I may have mistaken his shabbiness for age. He wore a muffler and a shiny raincoat tied around the middle with twine. His shoes were past repair and he wore a sock *over* one shoe. Since I never saw him move from his house, I supposed he didn't really need shoes.

His cabin was a makeshift affair, not much better than the kind of ramshackle 'houses' I would build with my friends, but unlike any man I knew he could cook and I was so intrigued by his domestic arrangements – this was 'playing house' in a big way – that I would make an exception and accept the hateful, inevitable tea. Sipping it, I wondered if my mother would be pleased at my good manners or furious that I should be drinking from a tin can. I knew enough to make myself scarce when it was time for my father to have private conversations with these people and knew better than to ask tactless questions, so their stories remained a mystery. I was given *The Wind in the Willows* for Christmas when I was eight and it occurred to me that the animals in the book behaved rather as I was expected to; in some circumstances certain things went unasked, many things were better left unsaid, in the same way that the Wild Wood wasn't talked about, though who devised this subtle code of behaviour and how I learned it was another mystery.

Old people fascinated me. Not just old to me, but truly old; over eighty years old. One of the deacons in Alltwen Chapel was over ninety and he was my favourite of them all. On Sunday I would walk slowly behind him as he climbed the steep hill home. He was spotlessly clean (I had no fondness for grubby old people) with round pink cheeks and snow-white, fluffy hair, just as I imagined Mr Pickwick to be, but older. I only ever saw him formally dressed in a warm flannel shirt with a small, stiffened, round white collar and a thin tie, a watch and chain hung across his waistcoat under a heavy tweed jacket. I longed to be his friend and occasionally crept up beside him and walked slowly along-side until he turned in at his gate before Bwlch y Gwynt in Alltwen. Concentrating on his climb, he never spoke to me, but this did nothing to lessen my devotion and I plagued my mother to ask his family if they wouldn't like to hand him over to us so that I could fetch and carry for him and take him for walks and read to him. 'You are eight years of age and old enough to know that old people are a lot of work. They are not *pets*.' Since I never lifted a finger at home, I knew no such thing and finally I took matters into my own hands and called on his family to explain how, because I was hardly ever at school, I could give their aged relative far more care and attention than they could.

The youngish woman I talked to was non-committal and I thought the talk had gone rather well, so was genuinely surprised and disap-pointed to see her avoid my eye as she left our house later in the day when I came home for tea. My mother called me in and, wearing her only too familiar sorrowful face, sighed heavily as she began: 'I don't know where to start.' She knew where to start all right. And how to go on – and on and on. I couldn't understand why she was so angry or why they were so upset. I was given orders to keep my distance so I admired him from afar and thought, 'What a shame, what a waste.'

Most old people welcomed my attention. The old lady who lived alone next door (she was an exception, most of my old friends were gentlemen) let me play in her back garden out of sight of our back garden. Together we soaped an old plank of wood and leaned it up against the garden wall (strictly forbidden by my mother) and I climbed the high wall and slid down to my heart's content until a huge splinter embedded itself in my bottom and the two of us silently struggled to get it out, fleeing indoors so I could sob without being overheard as we dabbed on the iodine. All illicit injuries were kept from my mother until they could no longer be hidden and then the scolding was far worse than a festering wound or sprain.

When the old lady died I loitered about in the backyard until one of the mourners asked if I would like to view the body. Would I just! I shot through to the parlour and there, in the room where I used to pretend to play the piano on the polished table while she played gramophone records for me to mime to, was the open coffin. I gazed with interest at my first dead person, feeling that I ought to be a great deal sadder. I tried to muster a little tender feeling and a few appropriate tears, but it was no use. I knew what it was to feel grief and as I looked at my old friend's body I remembered the agony I felt the previous year when I saw my dog being run over. My stomach tightened at the recollection of the nights I had spent crying myself to sleep under the bedclothes. I didn't want to feel as bad as that again if I could help it and no, this was nothing like as bad, though I felt it ought to be. I accepted a Welsh cake and left.

My passion for old people, my fondness for wearing a hat at all times except at night in bed, my pastime of delivering long impassioned sermons from the top of the pigsty wall generated no more than a mild and amused shake of the head; the place was stiff with real eccentrics and there was a sprinkling of mad people who were referred to as 'simple' or 'innocent'. These *real* lunatics interested me, but I couldn't achieve the sophistication of those who looked after them. Their families liked them, and found them amusing as well as occasionally infuriating.

The little old lady I saw most frequently was cherished at home by her family and also offered rather proudly as home entertainment. Her 'madness' took the form of behaving like a little girl, and visitors were invited to marvel at her as she scampered about, saying mildly rude words and giggling behind her hands. I was astonished that someone so old could be so agile; she really did look as though she had become a little girl again. When she ran into the road and lifted her long skirts to show her bloomers to the headmaster as he drove past, I was scandalised, but her daughter could hardly keep a straight face as she lifted her finger saying, 'Naughty girl. Naughty, naughty girl. What have I told you?' The old lady laughed while hanging her head and sucking her thumb. I didn't care for any of that. I was not so old that I couldn't remember behaving a bit like that and I didn't like to think that such behaviour and such scoldings couldn't be left behind and finished with for good after a certain age. I didn't care for her little head, with its clean cotton cap, the sly toothless face and demure dress and apron, and those skipping feet. I couldn't manage the robust easy-going attitude that I admired and envied. But I had reason to be grateful for it.

During these years it seemed there was nothing one could do that was so awful that people wouldn't find it amusing. Except for my mother, that is. I tried her patience sorely with my pretensions. My affected attempts at grandeur must have been very embarrassing to her. I have a recollection of sitting in a rather smart front room when I was very small and being thought to know no English at all, so it must have been round about my fairy wings time when I would have been four. I had invited myself into the house of a newcomer to the village – an English woman, the first I'd been near, and I couldn't wait to get closer. My mother arrived in pursuit, apologetic and flustered, to be told that my visit had been most entertaining. It seems I'd accepted the offer of tea in the front room and had asked if I might go upstairs to the bathroom. When I came down I settled in the parlour – *much* posher than anything I'd ever seen – and the conversation – my very first in English, which I'd only heard spoken on the radio – went something like this.

Me: 'Well, I *love* your lav.'
'Oh, thank you.'
'Yes, I love it because it's got a chain' [pronounced the Welsh way to rhyme with 'mine'].
'Ah, yes.'
'Mind you, I think ours is *cleaner*.'
'Oh, yes?'
'That's because my mother has just *gwyngalched* it' [Welsh for 'whitewashing'].
'Yes?'
'Yes, we *gwyngalch* all the time because we've got *môch-y-cod*' ['woodlice'].
'I see.'

On the way home my mother shook me as we hurried along and said in Welsh, 'Did you *have* to tell her that our lavatory is outside and that we're plagued with woodlice?'

Shortly after this I was a bridesmaid, dressed in blue, chiffon velvet with a white collar. My hair had been put in rags to curl it and when I looked in the mirror I thought I was the most beautiful, sophisticated sight I'd ever seen. As we drove along in convoy to the church in Pontarddulais, my mother, in the car behind mine, couldn't understand why the road was lined with laughing, pointing people. After the service, an embarrassed relative of the bride sought out my mother and said, 'Could you stop your little girl from doing that on the way to the reception?' 'Doing what?' 'She's making strange faces and she's lifting her arm up and down just like the Duchess of York in the pictures.' Well, I felt so *grand* in my blue frock and curls, it seemed appropriate to wave at the dear common folk.

'Look straight ahead and don't you *move* or you go straight home and this'll be the last wedding for *you*, my girl.'

Chapter Seven

Only a generation away from a time of large families, I had just four relatives close to my age – my first cousins, Auntie Meriel's children, born, like me, in the front bedroom in Tŷ mawr farm. Huw was the first child, born in 1940. I looked and didn't touch and more or less ignored him until, in what seemed a remarkably short time, he made his presence felt as a capable, gifted farmer even before he was packed off to boarding school at the age of ten. I was impressed – from afar.

Babies held no interest for me, so I scarcely noticed the next child, Gethin (born a year after Huw) until, at five or six, he was old enough to reveal a congenial aptitude for idling away the day while the rest of the family toiled. We would sit on a five-barred gate concealed by high hedges, companionably taking in the view across to the Black Mountains. We swung our legs and didn't even bother to exchange glances as, from time to time, we heard our names called in tones varying between mild exasperation and this-is-the-last-time-I'm-calling shrillness. Bonded by our uselessness, we were fond of each other and once I was even moved, in a brief moment of cousinly tenderness, to put on his shoes for him before we set off for the village. 'Oh, come ON! Faster! Run! – Run!' I cried, and it must have been a sign of his fondness for me that he did his best to keep up, hampered though he was by shoes firmly laced on to the wrong feet. It was evident that he would never make a farmer, but as he grew up he made an effort to help while I resolutely maintained my 'totally *hopeless*' status.

Elizabeth, born six years later, was pretty and clever and – I could tell – capable. It seemed as if Gwyn, the last baby, born when I was in my teens, would never grow up to look like the rest of the family; white and sickly, he spent his time, summer and winter, wrapped in a shawl on my grandmother's knee as she coaxed him to eat a little egg yolk or a spoonful of creamy rice pudding.

So, there we were – five of us; four and a half, given Gwyn's fragile hold on life. My grandfather had five brothers and sisters and my grandmother was one of eight children. She was Elizabeth George, the daughter of Evan George, a shepherd from Rhiwe Farm in Llanddeusant and Elizabeth Colman, who ran a dairy in Garnant. My grandmother Elizabeth George was their youngest daughter and it was her skill and good management that made the Tŷ mawr thrive. She was a true, intelligent farmer like her mother-in-law, Sali. This generation produced enlightened women who realised that education was the only hope towards a freedom from the harshness of much of their life. That is not to say that there weren't softnesses in their life.

The communities were warm and self-sufficient. We had relations in Gorslidarn Farm to the right (where Auntie Kate dressed like a man and tended the sheep up on the hills while her husband, Uncle Dafydd, looked after their daughters at home) and Llwyncelyn Farm to the left of Tŷ mawr. There was a local herbalist who took care of everyone and who would 'order' the harvesting of special leaves and roots. His skill as a healer was streets ahead of his talent as a soothsayer. *All* his predictions were wrong and the women shook their heads at such ungodly carryings-on while the credulous men could hardly wait for the next revelation. In time something was bound to come true, they said optimistically.

Farming skills were partly passed down and were partly the result of observation. There was a strong awareness that men were in partnership with nature. Even as a little girl I was aware that the margin between survival and catastrophic ruin was frighteningly small. Farmers seemed to harbour feelings of love and respect and fear and resentment in equal quantities towards the land, much as sailors must feel for the ocean, I thought. The softnesses and the grace of life were offset by harshness that still obtained when I was a child (for one thing, it isn't easy to farm land where there is not a single level field), but I gathered that this was nothing compared with the grimness of life a generation or two earlier. There was a strong sense of having lived through and survived not-to-be-forgotten hard times, which might very well return.

The background to life was poverty and insecurity; the rural economy had gone through a long period of weakness with the price of dairy produce at rock bottom (three of my grandmother's brothers had left for America during one of the exceptionally bad periods). I came to see that nothing was forgotten. My parents were Liberals and when

I heard them speak of the iniquitous Tory feudal system under which tenant farmers voting Liberal were evicted, I assumed that these awful events had probably occurred while I was in hospital having my appendix removed the previous year. It was some time before I realised that they were speaking with passion and resentment about something that had happened in 1859. My mother profoundly disapproved of anyone who did not respect the hard-won secret ballot.

The pace of life was determined by horse power and horses were a source of pride – not the crazed, failed racehorses favoured by my grandfather but the clever, enduring shire horses that pulled the plough and the small cobs who worked at harrowing and drilling. The horses would walk twenty miles in an eight-hour day and some man-and-horse teams were experts at the 'turns', where the chains could tangle in a second of inattention. There was no sense of rush. There was no point in hurrying work. It took a week to plough and harrow a three-acre field and that was that.

There was, however, unspoken tension in the air at haymaking time. Six fine days were needed to cut, turn, rake and carry the hay home. Friends and neighbours in the village would stop work and arrive, unasked, to help once the hay was cut. The first sound in the morning was the chink-chink of knives being sharpened and the clop-clop as the big home-made rakes with their wooden teeth were knocked and tapped to check that they were in good repair. Women and children raked in the gleanings, but I did next to nothing and contrived to ride to and fro on the 'gambo' (the hay-wain). Two men would pitchfork the hay up and a third would build up the load. I sat higher and higher until the load was completed, then rocked precariously back to the barn thinking this must be exactly like riding an elephant.

Rabbits, mice and voles ran for cover, buzzards hovered overhead. Meriel and my grandmother and mother brought out tea and food, but there was very little talk. Even I appreciated it was desperately important to get the hay in before the capricious Welsh weather broke.

And meanwhile Meriel and my grandmother went on with the relentless business of milking. Meriel had married the glamorous John, and he, very advanced, had started making silage. I loathed the unbelievably horrible smell of the silo pit where the cut grass was packed and squeezed in with molasses added to it until the whole airless horrible mess fermented. The cows *adored* it, thrived and gave good, plentiful milk. They were all named and had distinctive characters, the natural leaders doing most of the herding on the way home from the fields. '*De – re, de – re, de – re*' (Come, come, come) was the human cry that encouraged them on their way, the dogs darted about on the periphery, but it was the clever ones among the cows that nudged the convoy into the cowshed where each cow made for her own stall and filled the air with soft, fragrant, grassy belches.

Occasionally I would help in the dairy. The milk parlour was as up to the minute as funds would allow, but it was hard work straining and cooling the milk, and everything had to be washed and washed and washed in cold water until one's hands and feet had no feeling even on the hottest day. And as for the butter churn . . . it seemed to take hours of churning before the slap-slap of milk turned into the clurp-clurp of butter almost ready. I didn't have what it took and I couldn't wait to get back to my books.

Before the Second World War, about six thousand women farmed alone in Wales and there must have been more by 1945. I dare say many of them shared my lack of enthusiasm for the work, but, unlike me, they had to persevere.

Chapter Eight

Many of my recollections of childhood are probably not recollections at all but stories I was told about myself or which I heard told as I sat under a table or chair, half asleep in one of those small, clean, brightly lit, over-heated village kitchens while my mother and three or four neighbours sat around the fire in the range knitting, sewing or crocheting and talking, talking, talking. 'I'm just going out for a little "*clec*",' my mother would say in Welsh as she put on her shapeless brown hat to go and visit a neighbour. I can't translate '*clec*'. What was it? More intense than mere chatting, not as high-flown as discussing, certainly not gossiping (although a great deal of gossip was exchanged, thinly disguised as cautionary tales: 'Let that be a lesson to us all, eh?').

Too young to be left at home alone, I used to have to accompany my mother, and I dreaded those evenings, with the notable exception of the ones spent at my 'Auntie' Hilda's house after she took delivery of a washing machine! With a porthole in the door! The village divided itself into fours and sat, night after night, contentedly '*cleccan*', not in front of the fire but around the Bendix as the clothes whirled around inside. It was wonderfully entertaining. Normally, nothing so interesting took place and I would read my book, wishing we were at home, only occasionally moved to prick up my ears. I didn't bother trying to make sense of the conversation when the voices were lowered and long silences were punctured by gusty sighs (I had no interest in death and obstetrics). When the tone remained low but the pace returned to normal and they talked of 'her' and what 'she' had done, the chances were that I was the topic of conversation. The variety of illnesses I presented meant I was a problem that exerted considerable fascination, not least of all to me.

They all knew a great deal about each other (and in my privileged position as my father's daughter, I knew that there was a great deal they *didn't* know about each other) and because a part of every day was spent exchanging information and discussing what had befallen people or conjecturing what might have happened, which was even more pleasurable, each person acquired a known history, a story that was added to at intervals, each addition modifying and enhancing the overall portrait. Highlights from people's stories were aired at regular intervals and, familiar though they were, I do not recall anyone being crass enough to interrupt the patterns of the storytelling. Never did anyone say, 'Yes, yes, we know all that, get to the *point*.' The long process of telling shaped the point, when it eventually arrived.

When my mother talked of *her* childhood I always waited for the bit where she described how, not much older than I was now, maybe nine, and entrusted with cleaning the big fender, she split her finger in two, such was the zeal of her polishing, and as she fainted her father caught her and ran her down the mountainside to the herbalist, who saved her finger, 'who knows how'.

When my father, as a young lad of fourteen, fainted in front of the big furnace in the Llanelli steelworks ('and he shouldn't have been there in the first place at that age. It's criminal'), his grandmother, who also worked there, came and dragged him out and revived him and took him home, forbidding his mother to send him back, and *she* took his place in her clogs and long skirt, with a man's flat hat on her head. I would nod to myself at the chorus of 'Terrible times, they were.' This was always followed by a cheerful account of how my father saved a life in the Llwchwr estuary 'and would you believe, they only found out by accident. Didn't tell a soul. Typical.'

Mrs Rogers, a youngish widow who kept house for her brothers who took care of her and her son, would describe how she knew her husband's time had come when he 'turned his face to the wall and wouldn't look back into the room'. This made me cry quietly, no matter how often I heard it. Turning one's face to the wall . . . it seemed the saddest thing imaginable.

The brilliance of people 'who came up from nothing' was a deep well, visited often. My favourite was the story of the young son of a neighbouring farm to Tŷ mawr on the Betws who, during my mother's youth, 'discovered and *proved* the existence of a star' ('pages and *pages* of workings out!'). As he passed through our farmyard at the start of his long, long journey to the Royal Society in London, they concealed their dismay when they saw that he was wearing someone else's suit, which his mother had altered for him and she'd made one leg shorter than the other. 'Imagine! One leg shorter than the other. To lecture! In London!' Another story told how Mrs Hopkins-the-Farm reached up for a loaf that was hanging in a basket and it fell on her head and the crumbs got into the cut and she was dead 'in a week!'. Dying 'in a week' was somehow worse than dying on the spot or after a decent illness.

There was very little in the way of gentry: just one small family, the Lloyds, who made no impression on the surrounding villages and took no part in Welsh life. When the squire left his wife and daughter in the big house, never to return, it was un-Welsh enough and sufficiently typical of something alien to be worth a mention. My mother would fall silent. She knew and I knew that the squire wrote to my father regularly, arranging to meet him in secret in the dingle. My father kept an eye on the estate and would tell him how things stood. The squire would write to my father telling him that he wanted to visit and my father would meet him and they would walk through the wood and then into the dingle and sit silently, looking at the house and stables in the distance.

After about an hour, the squire would get up and shake my father's hand and leave as silently as he'd arrived. And his beautiful daughter would ride her horse recklessly through our tiny gate, up the narrow steps round the lawn to the front door, dismount, and fall into the house, and I would be sent out to play and later told never to tell what I'd seen. I longed to grow up to be like her even if she was 'three sheets to the wind', whatever that meant. 'Her mouth was a red gash and she was a fearless horsewoman,' I described her to myself. Agony for my mother not to be able to share these stories. None of these things were ever to be revealed outside the house.

The mythology of the village reinforced its reality, but as I grew older I could hardly relate to the 'child' of four and five, and the stories they told of me seemed more remote and less meaningful than those they told of the childhood of my mother and her friends. Could I ever have been so small and stupid? Where I was concerned my mother was fairly loyal, but although she would have given me the food from her plate (this, it seemed, was a standard requirement among good mothers), her allegiance at the first sign of conflict was with authority: the teachers, or nurses or doctors.

'Odd' was an adjective that recurred in describing me and, in all fairness, had to be allowed. I wasn't prepared to mend my ways, but I could see that it *was* a bit odd to wear a hat indoors and out for over a year ('and the *same* one – oh, it looked terrible!'). It was 'odd' to assemble all the dolls in the house (except Teddy), line them up on the stone slab outside where the washing was pounded on Mondays and then, having rehearsed and conducted them in the Hallelujah Chorus from *The Messiah* for two whole weeks ('Oh we were fed up with Handel'), take them up the steps to the garden where my father was planting runner beans and bury the lot with three doleful hymns and a funeral oration. I didn't remember burying dolls, but I had not long given up delivering long, emotional sermons, full of '*Hwyl*' from the high wall of the old pigsty and there hadn't been any dolls in the house for years, so I supposed my mother was not exaggerating. In any case, I wasn't embarrassed; nothing I did would raise many eyebrows.

I half-remembered the Moonlight Sonata-on-the-Swansea-Bus story and that happened before I was five. Vivid in my mind was the longing I had to seem alone and independent, and I always sat apart from my parents on public transport. One sunny afternoon on an excursion to Swansea I sat alone in the front seat of an almost empty bus and, as usual, began to sing – quietly at first. My repertoire of Welsh folk songs and Edwardian bass-baritone drawing-room ballads was extensive, but on this day I began humming the music my father had been practising on the piano for weeks and, getting into the swing of things, la-la-ed my way through the whole of the Moonlight Sonata. My mother said, 'People were laughing. It seemed to go on for ever and I had to let her go on. It would draw more attention to us if we had walked down the bus to stop her.'

When I finally came to an end a gentleman sitting alone rose and sat next to my parents and asked if I belonged to them. He handed my father his card saying that I had given him a most unusual experience and he hoped that they would provide me with the formal musical education I surely deserved and they could call on him for advice on the matter. My father's jaw dropped when he read the name Sir Walford Davies, Composer. 'Imagine,' said my mother. 'She's got no voice worth speaking of and her piano playing will never be more than fair. She's got a good memory, that's all. The talent for music has completely passed her by. All the same – Sir Walford Davies! Can you believe it?' I didn't mind that they thought little of my musical ability. 'What use was music to an actress?' I thought when they told me the story.

My oddness was disconcerting but my piety, when it took hold a few years later, must have been even harder to bear. Everyone said a short grace before one meal a day, but now, in our house, grace spoken by me became longer and more detailed and had to be said before anything was eaten or drunk at any time. The minister, trying to down a quick cup of tea on his way through the parish, was startled to hear an admonishing cough and, looking over the cup, saw my upraised finger and reproachful look before I bowed my head and offered lengthy thanks on his behalf. Useless for my mother to try to widen the concept of godliness to include good manners and tolerance. I was smugly impregnable on the moral high ground.

Searching around for my most precious possession to give away, I lighted on my new (my only) overcoat and took it along the road to a house where there were six children, always shabby. 'Are you sure this is all right?' asked the startled mother. I grandly assured her that it was *more* than all right and went home bathed in a golden glow of virtue. 'But the Bible says—' I began when my mother found out what I had done. 'That's it! Enough! Go down there and fetch it back!' 'Fetch it back? I can't do that.' 'Do you want a good shaking? Go!' It was agony. I went, I fetched it back, my humiliation great. 'Don't ask me what Jesus meant,' snapped my mother, hanging up the coat. 'He *didn't* mean that you could give away your coat, your HARRIS TWEED coat that I've been saving and saving for.' My mother was not one of those who kept their young in line with the – very often truthful – refrain, 'I've given you the food from my plate . . .' In fact she never even talked about money, so for her to mention saving money meant I'd done something seriously wrong in her eyes and I was silenced.

When I remembered to, I did One Good Deed a Day and did Good by Stealth, but I longed to advertise my holiness. Only once again did I try to apply the lessons of Sunday school to real life. Realising now that we were all fairly equally situated and that there weren't any Poor to give things to, nor did I have anything to give as a rule, I hit on the next best thing, which was to give to the Undeserving. They had no thought for the morrow and so, on the eve of an examination week, I gave my carefully compiled revision notes to a friend who hadn't done any preparation at all. If the incident of the coat had exasperated my mother it was as nothing to her reaction when she realised what I'd done with my schoolwork. 'I want those books back on your desk NOW!' 'But I've done most of my revision and Jesus says—' 'Stop, before I shake you!' 'Her need is greater than mine.' 'Right, that's it! Do you seriously think that Jesus Christ wants to see you working behind the counter of Woolworth's? Because that's what it'll come to if you're not in the top three in your class. GET THOSE BOOKS.'

Not longer after that I gave up wanting to be a nun, which involved practising mortifying the flesh by standing on the cold lino in front of an open window in my nightdress. (I knew my mother would kill me if she found out about that.) I became a Freethinker instead and gave my parents a whole new range of embarrassments.

By the time I was nine I was almost well after my long catalogue of illnesses and my years of running wild were coming to an end. I had a secure place in my world. By now every detail of my territory was familiar to me because I had covered it slowly on foot, in all weathers. I could see, with my eyes closed, the pale *café-au-lait* dust of the lane with living rock protruding in wonderful shapes, smooth and safe for the passage of horse-drawn carts, the hay-wain and the milk float. The little trickle of water in the gully that quickly became a torrent when it rained was familiar and always astonishing. I knew where the birds nested year after year (never tell the boys; they took the eggs and 'blew' them). There was just one five-barred gate where lizards basked on hot days. I knew the best place for frogspawn and where to go for the one half-hour in the summer when you could see the sky full of flying ants. I collected the first mushrooms at five o'clock in the morning, I knew the secret damp patches where the biggest clumps of celandine grew and how to hop, skip and jump across the treacherous boggy field, where it was safe to ford the stream, when to see baby spiders hatching out and tiny black toads flinging themselves out of the water. I could smell rain hours away, but it never drove me indoors. There were areas of my life where I felt unsafe and times when I was wretchedly unhappy, but my worst feeling could be transformed in an instant into radiant happiness by a change in the weather.

Everything was familiar and everything was marvellous. My feeling of security went hand in hand with a feeling of insignificance. The mountaintops were exhilarating and awe-inspiring with their great windy views of the valleys below and sometimes there was nothing to see but the big sky and more mountains beyond. Not a house in sight, no roads, no trees, and a huge silence. More than once that silence had driven me, frightened, running down the mountainside, filled with relief to see the first disused cart track or broken, drystone wall; signs of human life. I knew exactly what Wordsworth meant when he wrote of 'low breathings' coming after him.

However dimly perceived, it was all these things that I fought for as a little girl of five when I flatly refused to stay at the primary school in which I had been placed; the nearest one to my home in Alltwen. It was a tall, ugly building, positioned under a frightening rock-face in the little town of Pontardawe, which looked to me like a vision of hell, with its steelworks and polluted river and evil-smelling smoke and trees black with greasy dust. Not a natural rebel, I don't know where at that age I found the strength to overcome the strict well-meaning, implacable adults who were ranged against me, but after what seemed like an eternity of silent, dry-eyed misery when I stood day after day with my face pressed against the playground railings, neither speaking nor eating, nor moving, *willing* something or someone to save me, I was allowed, one morning, to go home and to make the long walk in the other direction, deeper into the countryside, to a beautiful little white, one-storey school, set in fields on the edge of the village of Rhos. I hadn't known of its existence, but I wasn't surprised when we came to it. I recognised it as the place where I wanted to be.

As things turned out, my illnesses began almost at once and I didn't very often attend school, but when I did I loved it. Because I was left undisturbed for years during my illnesses, when the time came for primary schooling to end, it wasn't at all clear how much I knew. It was assumed that my knowledge of arithmetic must be patchy, but who knew what all that reading had done for me? My parents had decided on a policy of non-interference where my reading was concerned. They had never suggested that anything might be too difficult or unsuitable. Consequently, I read Shakespeare and Enid Blyton and Louisa M. Alcott and the *Dandy* and the *Beano* alongside Zane Grey and Mrs Humphrey Ward and old *Magnets* and Dickens and A.A. Milne and Trollope and *Sunny Stories* and the *News Chronicle*. My mother's nerve did fail a few times. She absolutely forbade me to read *Forever Amber* (so I read it in secret) and there were bits of *Antony and Cleopatra* that she wished she hadn't let me read. I wondered why she'd forgotten what a racy read the Old Testament was. The only publication against which my face was set was Arthur Mee's *Children's Newspaper*, which my parents had delivered for me and which I rightly suspected to be Good for me.

I was over-sensitive in some regards and given to storms of grief over sad endings – fictional – or the death of pets – only too real and frequent – but (rightly, as it turned out) my parents thought I had a steely streak and was not given to undue 'nerves', so it was decided that, at the age of nine, I should be allowed to have an early 'go' at the scholarship examination, which determined one's future at the age of ten and eleven. This was just for practice, they said, and at least it would reveal what I needed to be taught. If there was pressure, I was blithely unaware of it and had a delightful day out, back at school.

I read the Arithmetic paper with mild interest; baths of water empty-ing faster than they could be filled, trains travelling at X miles per hour, arriving after trains travelling at Y miles per hour, men working all day, failing to accomplish what three men working half a day could – or was it the other way round? These riddles contained very little to interest me, so I spent my time with my chin in my hand watching the clouds in the sky outside. This was not considered to be a good sign, but there was always the English paper. Horror of horrors, halfway through the allotted time I laid down my pen and, chin in hand, resumed my study of the sky.

My teacher reported back to my mother that things didn't look too good. No one wanted to worry me, so they left me alone except to ask, casually, how it went. 'Oh, fine, fine.' 'Arithmetic all right?' I laughed, shaking my head, and tried to remember some of the sillier questions about taps and trains. 'How about the English?' 'Oh, easy-peasy.'

My mother hid her disappointment and resolved to start coaching me as soon as summer ended. She was bewildered and unbelieving when my name was posted alongside the older children who had made it over the all-important hurdle. Confusion deepened when someone called round to explain that, alone among the pupils of South Wales, I had been given nought in the Arithmetic paper but that for the first time in the history of the examination they had been moved to award me 100 per cent for my English paper.

'What did you do?' my mother asked. I tried to remember. 'Well, Grammar – easy.' 'What about the Composition?' 'Oh yes, Shakespeare.' 'What do you mean, "Shakespeare"?' '*The Merchant of Venice*.' 'What about *The Merchant of Venice*?' 'Usury.' 'Usury?' 'Yes. Can I go out now?'

My mother nodded slowly. The post-mortem on the hopeless Arithmetic paper was postponed.

I took a great deal more interest in the scholarship when I realised there was a Uniform involved and Houses and Hockey and a Debating Society just like the schools in my mother's Angela Brazil books. I began to shape up for a new life.

Chapter Nine

The new life, when it came, was wonderful and frightening and a bit beyond me. I was still only nine and a year or so younger than the other new pupils, but in my naiveté I was five years behind them. But that uniform! My mother had sent for samples of tussore silk from somewhere called Devon. Blouse lengths were ordered, and navy gabardine from Swansea. Auntie Syrviah, the Tŷ mawr dressmaker, was alerted and I went back to G.C.G. time and again to fit my tunic with its deep box pleats and 'secret' pocket for a handkerchief and a fountain-pen pocket and hems and turnings so generous that the same tunic lasted the whole of my seven years at Pontardawe Grammar School. However many times it was let out, it always had to be the regulation two inches above the knee (hated by the big girls, who wanted long skirts like their mothers). The dressmaker also made my pale green, Greek-style P.T. clothes and my silk blouses with deep cuffs and big collars with rows and rows of stitching (not strictly allowed but very smart).

My blazer had to be bought; cheap, navy-blue 'utility' material, made magnificent by the badge. I breathed over my mother as she sewed it on to the breast pocket, willing her (no seamstress) to get it straight. The motto read, '*Bid Ben Bid Bont*' – 'Who would be a leader let him be a bridge for others'. Would I ever be able to live up to this? 'Yes!' I thought. 'I want to be *good*. I want to be the sort of person worthy of this magnificence.' There was a blue-and-maroon tie and even more than the tie I loved the satchel and my pencil box and rubber and fountain-pen and mysterious geometry set and my big ruler, but I *hated* my navy raincoat.

My mother's determination to make everything last had run riot in the rainwear department. The coat was *huge* and came down to my ankles with a turned-up hem a foot deep. It submerged the glory of the blazer and tunic and I looked as though I was wearing someone else's coat. My navy hat had also suffered under my mother's prudent hand

and sported a wide, childish elastic band stretched under my chin. I wanted to cry when I looked at myself, fully dressed. The Mallory Towers/Angela Brazil look, racy, confident, needing only a hockey stick under the arm to complete the picture, was gone and I looked puny and worried – a pinched, white face half hidden by the hat above and huge collar below and then a mass of navy blue bulking down to my socks and small, protruding lace-ups. The disappointment was crushing and I silently raged against my mother, who stood back admiring her handiwork. When he was brought in to inspect me, my father nodded his approval, which was no consolation to me. Daddy would always think I looked perfect.

Every day when I started out for school, as soon as I was out of my mother's sight, off came the hated coat and I slung it over my shoulder, shivering in the cold and getting wet in the rain but feeling ever so smart. The walk to school was exciting, away from the beauty of Alltwen, from Llygad yr Haul – the eye of the sun – round Bwlch y Gwynt – the windy gap – where the wind *did* always blow, down to Pontardawe, across the little town with its grimy buildings, then up another hill to the beautiful, big white school that rose in terraces towards the fields and trees above.

It was a place of enchantment to me. I loved the confusion, the complications; you may walk here, seniors only on the bridge, prefects only beyond this point, no talking to the boys, walk in twos here, single file only here. I was in a perpetual state of pleasurable excitement. I loved the life but I couldn't live it. The playing fields, the cloakroom, the changing rooms, the miles of road leading from school to my home were littered with my books, pens, gym shoes, textbooks, hockey stick, gym tunic, all picked up and returned to my mother, who didn't know what to do with me. I *was* very young. It would have taken a lady's maid to get me through the day and there were worried conferences about my chaotic behaviour.

Blissfully unaware of this, I became more and more enthusiastic about every aspect of school life. There were 'traditions', some of which were being invented as we went along, and I embraced each one avidly and formed passionate attachments to the staff and the big girls, and I adored my form mistress, Miss Inkin, who also taught Greek History and was in charge of physical training and games and reigned over the gymnasium, which was the strangest, most wonderful building I had ever seen. I would have done anything to please Miss Inkin and I quickly became a good, fearless gymnast (this was my one area of competence). It was this devotion that brought about my last childhood brush with death and at the same time gave me a breathing space to catch up with myself.

I had read enough boarding-school story books to know that 'decent types', 'bricks', 'good sorts' didn't 'cry off' from games and gym when they didn't feel well. They kept a stiff (English) upper lip and soldiered on. So when, during one of our beautifully organised, almost balletic gymnastic lessons, quietly shinning up ropes, threading through square ladders, vaulting over the horse and the buck, balancing on the high bars and making perfect 'landings', I began to feel slightly, then extremely ill, it did not occur to me to ask if I could be excused. By the end of the double period that finished the day I could hardly move for pain. I must have showered and dressed and set off for home carrying my satchel with its six textbooks and six exercise books, and I must have got myself across Pontardawe, but I don't remember. Nor do I remember beginning the long steep climb to Alltwen. I *do* remember climbing slowly and more slowly towards Bwlch y Gwynt and thinking, 'I'll just lie down here for a while.'

And it was there, lying on the pavement, that the baker found me and took me home in his van, laid out among the crumbs. I was dimly aware of the ambulance and 'apperitonitis and pendicitis' or was it 'peritonitis and appendicitis' and nothing more until I woke up in Swansea Hospital with a huge plaster on my stomach, feeling not bad at all. Hospitals – even this big one – no longer held any terrors for me and – wonder of wonders! – I wasn't homesick. This time I *understood* about temperatures and bedpans and screens and the importance of keeping the bed tidy and the supreme importance of seeming to stand to attention while lying down, cheerful and silent as Matron passed by. She was much grander than the consultants to whom she displayed a wonderful condescension even as she deferred to them. She never smiled and I watched her with keen admiration as she progressed regally around the ward holding her huge, starched headdress high. It was grand not to be confused and afraid. I spared a pitying half-contemptuous thought for my six-year-old self in the fever hospital and settled down to enjoy myself.

They kept me there for quite a long time and then, instead of sending me home, despatched me to a convalescent home in Cwmdonkin Park, where a little speck of coal dust drifted through the window and, landing on a stitch, gave me a blue mark, like a miner's scar on my stomach. I wasn't allowed home for weeks. Maybe I'd been more ill than I had thought. I read voraciously, as usual, but now I found myself sleeping with a similar hunger. I could feel something happening to me as I lay there. I was growing, although it was impossible to tell for sure because I wasn't allowed to get out of bed. And I was becoming stronger by the day. Each morning when I woke, I lay still, assessing the new, different me. And it wasn't just that my body was changing; I was pretty sure that henceforward I would have an extra skin, be less prone to melancholia, find that I was more *able* for the world. I watched myself lying there, gathering strength, looking forward to something wonderful.

I didn't burst out of my chrysalis like a butterfly and the outside world had to wait for what seemed like a long time before I re-joined it, but when I took my first, wobbly steps I realised that I'd guessed right; I was becoming tall, in fact I was altogether bigger and I was bubbling with suppressed energy. Once home and 'downstairs' I organised and reorganised my desk, my father's desk. I catalogued all the books and, looking through the school work I'd done before I became ill, I realised that my head was now clear of muddle. The days of being swept along like a twig in a stream were over. I longed to return to school and still I was held in the doldrums of convalescence. Then, practising with my hockey stick on the sloping field behind the garden, I ran into a rabbit hole and broke my ankle.

I could scarcely credit my bad luck and my mother was furious ('No one's going to test you in hockey, you know'). At least I could lie on the couch downstairs, reading and looking out at March Hywel mountain. One day, I realised that I was seeing that precious landscape with different eyes. It had lost something for me. I couldn't explain it even to myself, but I knew that I had lost the key to some kind of magic that had been mine for ten years. It made me sad, but not very sad, to realise that I was ready to move on. And that I was going to be able to leave this place I loved when I needed to go away to become an actress. Not once since I was six had I wavered in my determination to go into the theatre, but I had wondered how I could live without the loveliness I was accustomed to. The relief at the realisation that I was going to be able to do so far outweighed my sense of loss and I lay on my couch reading and waiting and learning patience.

Chapter Ten

When I was a girl in the Forties, during and after the war, life was still chapel-driven. It was becoming fashionable in 'advanced' circles to sneer at non-conformism, with the inevitable hypocrisies that attended it. The University of Wales, 'our' university as it was thought of proudly even by people who would never see it, was described by George Bernard Shaw of all people as a 'non-conformist hole in Wales', but without religion it is quite conceivable that by the time I was a child, Wales would have become a cultural annexe of England. In the second half of the nineteenth century, the 1870 Education Act decreed that Wales should be anglicised. Westminster observed: 'The Welsh language is a vast drawback to Wales and a manifold barrier to the moral progress and commercial prosperity of the people.' Where I grew up, people were still smarting over this insult. My mother, when she was little and was caught talking Welsh at school, had to stand out in the yard as a punishment with a board saying 'Welsh Not' hung around her neck.

It was chapel that kept the language alive and it remained the language of home, of literature and of entertainment. Hundreds of chapels were built in the nineteenth century; even when I was little there were three Sunday services and several meetings during the week. The chapel choir rehearsed all winter. Meriel remembers giving five spring performances of *The Creation* and *The Messiah* and I remember my father's never-ending rehearsals of *Judas Maccabeus*. All children learned Bible verses and, like it or not, built up a good working acquaintance with the Old and New Testaments. When I made up and delivered my own sermons from the high wall behind the apple tree, even at the age of eight or nine, I was well able to keep going for a generous half-hour, thundering against sin and lawlessness with threats of hell and damnation, making deadly eye contact guaranteed to chill the unfortunate singled-out gooseberry bushes, before exhorting the entire congregation of runner beans, broad beans, peas, potatoes, lettuces, radishes, fruit bushes and solitary apple tree to rise up, joined in the glory of redemption. My mother and Meriel once or twice paused near the pulpit and nodded sagely. 'Well – Rosina,' they said. Grown-ups were given to gnomic utterances usually not worth pursuing, so it was some time before I bothered to ask my mother, 'Why "Well, Rosina"?' 'She would be your great-aunt and she was a bit – oh, I don't know, ask your Uncle Davy.' 'She was a bit what?' I asked him on my next visit to his house in the meadow below Tŷ mawr.

'Oh *jiw, jiw,*' he replied. 'She was a bit of a case, really. Anyway, you met her when you were – let's see, you'd have been five when she came to stay in Tŷ mawr when she last preached here in Carmel. You stared at her all afternoon.' 'Preached?' 'Oh yes, she was a *famous* evangelist. You'd have to turn up very early to get a seat when she was preaching, and in fine weather they'd open all the windows and people would fill the graveyard, standing to listen to her. Sang too. People loved it. But we never knew where to look, we were so embarrassed. Horrible voice like a hooter and it was *peculiar* to see a woman in the pulpit, say what you like. There's a book about her in the front room. And there's all that business about our land too.' 'What business?' I asked, scenting drama. 'I can't go into it and you'd better leave it alone too. She was – I don't know – very *extreme.*'

Davy was a busy councillor as well as an overworked headmaster, and I'd used up the time he could spare me in a day that began at 5.30 a.m. and rarely finished before midnight. I took myself off to look for the book about Rosina and stayed overnight in the spare room, reading about my unlikely ancestor who brought the first whiff of exoticism into my known background of strong, down-to-earth, deadly earnest realists. An exotic evangelist? That's what it seemed like and as I read the rather pedestrian book, little more than a detailed chronicle of her extraordinary day-to-day engagements, a picture emerged of a woman half in love with her own glamour and half determined to suppress it. When she was staying at a house in Lleyn, someone wrote of her, 'as she entered I thought Ellen Terry had walked into the room'. In one of her photographs the pose was similar to that of the actress on one of her postcards, so Rosina ordered that all of hers should be destroyed. She was twenty at that time and leaving Wales to preach in London where she stayed at the Grange in Highbury with one of her many patrons, Mrs Jones (of Jones Brothers department store in the Holloway Road).

At Mrs Jones's house she sang, accompanying herself on the piano and wasn't averse to recording that a professor from the Royal Academy enthused over her 'contralto with pathos' and a retired diva, hearing her, said, 'The Lord Jesus Christ will lose her; Opera will snatch her up at once, the world will want her.' 'You will make a fortune as a tragedienne,' declared another after she had preached one of her hour-and-a-half sermons ('sixty-four converts' she recorded). 'Oh no, that will never be,' she replied. 'There is nothing tragic in my nature and I know nothing of the stage. I have been saved from the love of earthly things. He gave me a voice to sing the Gospel . . . I am only a girl, the love song of the cross wins their hearts.'

Well. 'Did she really have a terrible voice?' I asked Davy. 'Oh *jiw*, don't talk. It was awful. But she could hypnotise people – not the family, of course, but people really thought she was Madam Patti. She could preach though, fair do's.'

I returned to my reading. These women! As soon as I thought my days were full and well accounted for, all my aims and duties and ambitions neatly lined up and dealt with, I would come across another extraordinary woman whose energy and application made my efforts look feeble. Rosina, I read with a mixture of admiration and dismay, had begun preaching for the Salvation Army at the age of ten and, against her parents' wishes, began to tour as 'The little Welsh Girl' evangelist and singer. When I read that she left home saying, 'I must be about my Father's business', I wondered whether I would have liked her – evidently she wasn't bothered by self-doubt. Still, when she was seventeen she sang and preached *every day* for ten months. She read the Bible and she read Shakespeare, then 'I communed with God and went straight into the pulpit and the Lord filled my mouth'.

I wasn't interested in her godliness; it was her workload that fascinated me. The endless travelling. She loved America – preached to the Welsh surrounded by Indians in Mankato on the Prairies, on to Minneapolis, Cambria (Wisconsin), Columbus, Milwaukee, Racine, Chicago, then California and Los Angeles, which she thought 'quaint and delightful'. She must have added to the quaintness when she gave a concert, singing in Welsh costume before going to watch a film being made. In Los Angeles she suffered one of her bouts of total exhaustion and even, in true West Wales fashion, 'turned her face to the wall'. This meant that she lingered in California and, having made the acquaintance of a Dr Hubble, became a mature student at Los Angeles University.

'God bless the land of the free', she wrote in Beverly Hills, before tearing herself away to Coal Creek and Salt Lake City where she preached to 25,000 people, then on to Denver, Colorado. My eyes travelled down the list of 'engagements'. I didn't know where these places were – Williamsburg, Minneapolis, Gomer (Ohio), a North Welsh settlement, Lima, Cincinnati, Toronto, Palmyra, Pittsburgh, Ebensburg, West Bangor, Utica, New York – of course. She was 'well guarded by the Ninety-First psalm'. And I was intrigued to read that she preached to all denominations and refused a salary. Money just came. 'A miracle,' she explained.

'Oh, she made *plenty* of money,' said Uncle Davy. 'Enough to try and reclaim our land – the huge Garreg Amman estate. She took the case right up to the House of Lords and then even she had to give up.' Land. Wrongfully appropriated estates. It was all like something in a book. It *was* something in a book. There was no getting around it, I was jealous. How could I possibly have a career like Rosina's when I had to go to school? I worked it out that Rosina was living by faith, travelling and working non-stop, saving souls by the dozen every night and accompanying herself on the organ when she was thirteen, and that would have been in the late 1870s when it must have been a *lot* harder for a girl to strike out in the world. I could picture my mother's face if I left the house to go on the stage saying, 'I must be about . . .' Well, no, I couldn't say anything like that because going on the stage wasn't anything like saving souls. All the same, the singing and preaching didn't seem very different from acting.

I went home on the bus from Uncle Davy's to Cwmllynfell feeling more than usually restless. I thought I remembered the tall woman in black with jet jewellery and a precious Gladstone bag, precious because her writing was in it and it had to be put in the parlour. I *thought* I remembered her in the pulpit in Carmel, but I couldn't be too sure about that.

I was so busy thinking about Rosina and admiring my blurred reflection in the bus window that only gradually did I become aware that the man sitting next to me was fingering my leg just below the knee. We were in the third row, for heaven's sake. The conductor was standing a few feet away, facing us with his back to the driver. I couldn't think what to do. The man, whom I couldn't bring myself to look at, was fumbling away in a completely hopeless sort of way. I couldn't make a fuss and the fingering went on, so I sat very still for ten minutes until the bus drew into my village. I shot out of the bus, not a bit nervous once I was on the road. Even if he got out, I was sure I could outrun him. He didn't get out so I stood and took a quick look at him sitting now in my window seat. Nobody I knew. An ordinary, small, middle-aged man. Shabby. It hadn't been very nice and I felt I should have reacted differently. Maybe pinched his hand. Or given him a Look. Well, I'd been too embarrassed for both of us to do anything.

I thought it best not to tell my mother and father and I took myself off to bed, washing extra thoroughly, brushing my hair a hundred times and scrupulously crabbing my way up and down my bedroom, doing the exercises Miss Inkin had recommended to strengthen the arches of my feet. Finished, I looked around. My bedroom looked lovely in the diffused light I'd arranged by draping the old runner from the piano top over my bedside lamp. Everything was in perfect order and I knew that the contents of each drawer and cupboard were in immaculate order. My books were arranged by subject and size. I got into bed, sinking into the feather mattress. What could I *do* to speed up the beginning of my REAL life in the Theatre? How would Rosina have dealt with my mother and the staff of Pontardawe Grammar School?

Chapter Eleven

It seemed to me unlikely that school-days really would be my happiest days. It stood to reason that, vividly imagined, grown-up life was bound to be more fascinating, more thrilling. Meanwhile, school was just fine; so fine that I scarcely bothered looking beyond the present. So, at ten, I said a cheerful goodbye to the only school I 'knew', the one in my imagining, with its tuck-boxes and 'dorms' and 'caves' and midnight feasts where I was a freckle-nosed, curly-haired captain of games in the books of my mother's school-days; a 'good egg' and just about the pluckiest girl at Status-quo Towers. Why did all that upper-class bric-à-brac utterly beguile so many girls raised just this side of republicanism, exhorted to know their place and bend the knee to no man at one and the same moment? (I don't think boys were visited by a similar malaise.) Suddenly and overwhelmingly, reality in the shape of Pontardawe Grammar School loomed again, larger than fiction, fresher, brighter, absorbing and totally demanding.

My false start was over and done with and I was now back with pupils of my own age, though still the youngest in the class, a position I rather enjoyed. 'Now listen,' said my mother for the umpteenth time, 'this is your big chance. You've got to give it everything you've got. You've got to give MORE than you've got.' Well of course I had to. Without that last rider it wouldn't have been a true Sally Tŷ mawr-ism. For once, she needn't have worried – I felt as if I'd been given the run of a huge adventure-playground-cum-sweetshop and I was going to explore and devour every bit of it. I wanted it all. It seemed that every small, bright kitchen rang with the same words: 'Education is your Passport, don't forget, and it's the only thing they can't take away from you.' We compared notes ruefully but with the minimum of disloyal complaint. We knew it was the truth. Surprisingly, it did nothing to dampen our spirits; the grim facts of life were acknowledged, understood and forgotten in the enjoyment of the newness of everything;

new languages that we'd be speaking in no time, English emerging from between the covers of books; and brown, fretwork-fronted radios as the language of new manners, new feelings even. Welsh assumed a new stature, something rather grander than my everyday, Swansea-Valley Welsh, the language of play; it was the language of poetry like Shakespeare's. I longed to take my hair out of plaits and speak French NOW. There was even a *dead* language. That was surely worth a full-page visa in the Passport to Life.

Pontardawe – the bridge on the River Tawe, 'Ponty' out of earshot of the staff – was a small school, though it seemed enormous to me. We were about three hundred and fifty pupils; equal numbers of boys and girls, looked after, chivvied, spied on, bullied, manipulated and cherished by a staff of twenty who did the work of forty. Schools were talked of in military terms; some were perceived as being better than others, super-charged launching pads of human missiles, and in a way this lessened some of the usual pressures of school life. Very occasionally there would be the whispered taunt of 'Swot!' if someone did spectacularly well at something, but it was a half-hearted, feeble jibe. Brains were admired. Coming top was desirable. Our pin-ups were the barristers and scholars 'who'd come up from NOTHING, mind'. I don't think that the girls felt they were under pressure to prove themselves; it was assumed that we were equal with the boys and it was rather fun to put in a bit of extra effort and get ahead of them. The staff and Mr Rees, the headmaster, introduced a new element to add to the Passport concept of getting on in life: education, they conveyed to us, wasn't *for* anything; it was there, intrinsically good and ours for the taking. A posh job would be desirable, but that wasn't the point. At home, this was thought about for a moment, then heartily embraced. Ethically sound personal advancement – what could more thoroughly fire up the Welsh parental heart?

The staff worked long hours for us. Every night, after school, they stayed on to supervise society meetings or take choir practice or dancing classes. I joined everything I could and found out in Mr Lines's art club that I could draw, and then, because I desperately wanted to please Miss Agnes Thomas-Biology-Botany (who ran the Welsh Youth Movement at school and taught us traditional dancing and 'action songs', which were all the rage), I applied myself to botanical drawing and, showing promise, delivered myself, not for the last time, into my mother's hands. She embraced any enthusiasm I displayed that gave her the chance to divert my attention away from the theatre and all that 'nonsens'. Now, she supplied me with beautiful cartridge paper and Indian ink and mapping pens and I drew sections of all the vegetation I could lay my hands on, doing rather well it was thought, until I found myself making the long journey to Cardiff for a meeting with Dr Iorwerth Peate at the National Museum. Here my drawings were looked at and I felt a complete fraud to be treated with such encouragement and kindness and told to bring in more work if I was still serious about it in a few years' time. As for my mother, I felt sorry for her as she gradually realised that yet another of her stratagems was a failure.

It was an awkward situation for me. Provided that I did very well at school, I could go on performing. I actually enjoyed doing well at school and found no difficulty in combining the hours of homework each night with the long walks from Alltwen to Pontardawe and my involvement with the house choir, the gymnastic display group, the Debating Society, the Welsh Society, the Dramatic Society, the French Society, the Youth Movement dance troupe. I had boundless energy and felt like a round peg in a round hole. Apart from my terror of arithmetic, which become so acute that mathematics days were preceded by secret bouts of crying in bed, there was nothing but contentment in my life for the time being. I could, however, see that my problems would multiply. Then something happened that took me a significant step nearer what I wanted.

My mother spent long hours practising for the Eisteddfodau – literally 'Sitting places' – where people gathered each week in different villages and towns to sing, compose music, write poetry and recite, and to listen to long, detailed adjudications. They took place on Saturdays in chapels. The 'champion' Saturday reciters were as famous as the preachers who occupied the same spotlight in the pulpit on Sunday. The fashionable reciting style of the day was declamatory and dramatic, owing much to the fervent oratory and 'hwyl' of the pulpit. My mother adopted a different approach for me; simpler, more colloquial. I was much too young to be competing at this level and she deployed the only weapons at her disposal: surprise and stillness and quiet. Initial reactions varied from amused tolerance to hostility, but in a remarkably short space of time I began to be successful and in demand for concert work, and it was because of my mother's strategy that at the age of eleven I became a broadcaster. Greatly daring (and adding a year to our ages) she entered Mair Rees, my best friend, and myself in the big, annual National Eisteddfod in the category 'Dramatic Recitation for two, 12–16 years'. (This was after the closure of the Oil-Shed Theatre.) The 'National' was a very different proposition from the weekly Saturday Eisteddfodau I was used to. It attracted audiences of more than fifteen thousand people a day and lasted for an entire week. Unique in the whole of Europe as an Arts Festival, they said. I was impressed.

The set piece was difficult and unsuitable: a 'conversation' in strict metre between a disconsolate man and his more cheerful self. The task my mother set herself was formidable. Not only did she teach us the meaning of words unused for hundreds of years; she made sure we faultlessly observed the internal and external rhyme schemes and the intricate vowel and consonant patterns (the rules for the twenty-four-beat metre used in Cynghanedd verse were laid down in 1450) and, having achieved that, she said, 'Now, I want it to sound like Mr Jones next door and Mr Morgan down the road having a bit of a chat.'

We practised all through the spring and on a summer morning made the long journey to Llandybie, then walked from the station looking for the hall where the eliminating contest was to be held. That found, we settled down to wait and Mammy found a place for us to have a nice damp tomato sandwich from the pile she made early that morning. We had a last practice in a field before going into the hall. I began to realise that this was a new experience for all three of us: these people were in deadly earnest, a lot of them knew each other, they were all older than we were and the hall was packed. No one gave us a second glance. An hour went by and we listened to the same piece over and over again. It sounded 'dramatic' all right. Loud too. My mother looked thoughtful and said nothing.

At last it was our turn. My mother's only nod in the direction of 'dramatic' had been to 'stage' the recitation. I was to ask for a table and a chair. 'Ask politely and wait without fidgeting until you get them. Look pleasant. Don't look worried.' When the furniture was brought, Mair (the disheartened man) sat slumped in the chair (this was easy as she was by now very nervous) and I perched on the table looking perky as the more cheerful self (this was also easy; I was now very, very excited).

It was over quickly and I knew we'd remembered everything, but my mother said nothing. Mair said she felt sick and my mother said it was her imagination. Then we walked round the town until we found the place where the results would be posted. When the man came with the paper that bore the names of the four finalists, my mother walked up to the board quite slowly, then turned to us and nodded without smiling. We're through!

It was now the afternoon and time for more tomato sandwiches and a drink from the thermos flask. We had to find a lavatory and a tap so that we could be cleaned up. Then we walked towards the roar of the thousands of people on the Eisteddfod field where we could just make out the top of the huge marquee with the amplifiers relaying the contests and the adjudications to the people outside and red dragons flying everywhere. Mair said she really was going to be sick and she wasn't going to go on. I was so horrified that I had no words of sympathy for her. I could tell that my mother was furious and I prayed that she would find a way of getting Mair on stage. I walked away from them and thought about the piece. Our names were called and I looked round. My mother was smiling. Mair looked terrible but she was on her feet and heading in the right direction, up the steps and on to the enormous stage. There was a smell of damp, trodden-down grass and wood shavings and the murmur of more people than I had ever seen. 'Ask politely for a table and chair. Don't look worried', and a new note, 'Wait, wait, *wait* until they are all quiet.'

The performance seemed to last longer this time and these people understood old Welsh because they laughed at the jokes that had until now felt embarrassing and less and less funny as the weeks of rehearsal went by. We were a riot! And we won! Hands down! My mother said, 'Well, there you are, you see.' Mair said she still felt sick. We were photographed by the press and went to the BBC mobile studio to repeat our triumph. We fell asleep on the train and then on the bus and I don't remember walking the last steep mile home to Alltwen.

None of this was meant to lead to showbusiness; my mother still maintained that it was 'educational', 'to improve the memory'. 'And don't go thinking you're anything special just because you've got your picture in the paper,' she said, but I knew shortly after, when I started to work for the BBC on a regular basis, that I had made a significant step forward on my chosen path. Fortunately for me the BBC was, to my mother, as respectable as chapel.

I was now extra careful to do well at school. The better I did the stronger was my mother's determination that I should go to university and take up a solid profession. My resolution to be an actress kept pace with my mother's determination, but I had learned not to argue.

Then there was another obstacle to overcome. There must have been discussions about my future that included the possibility of my becoming an actress. After all, I was by now being written about in the press and offered more work than I could deal with, and I began to hear a new objection. 'She's got talent but she doesn't have the *steel*.' 'She's too sensitive.' 'She'll never be able to take the *knocks*.' 'She's the wrong *type*, altogether.' It was bad enough that they talked about me as though I wasn't there; how *dare* they presume to know what I was able for? And what did *they* know about the theatre? Or me? I was *sure* I knew what it would be like. And I was *sure* I could do it.

When I was younger, maybe eight or nine, after hearing my mother unsubtly holding forth about the rigours of the acting profession, I myself had wondered about my ability to survive the 'dreadful hardships', whatever they might be, and embarked on a toughening-up programme, getting out of bed after my parents were safely asleep and making my bed on a blanket on the cold, linoleum floor. It was a bit like training to be a nun, I thought. I had practised eating less than I would have liked and had finally decided that I *could* live a perfectly miserable life of privation if I had to. Now, three years on, I realised that I was going to have to learn something a great deal more difficult than patience and discretion if I was going to move forward. I was going to have to show my hand and force the issue. But how? Fortunately for me I acquired a few allies.

Chapter Twelve

When Eic Davies came to Pontardawe as Welsh master, my life took an upturn. I had been obliged to choose between Welsh and French as a matriculation subject and had chosen French, partly because I wanted to be able to speak French and partly because Miss Vivienne Williams-French wore wonderfully tailored suits by Deréta and blouses with silk bows at the neck and suede shoes and came to work from Clydach, which was almost Swansea, and it was rumoured with some awe that she'd been seen 'out' with a handsome American officer. I had hitherto thought that teachers stayed in all the time, marking homework after school, and I wanted to hang about near this dashing, daring woman, so I tackled my irregular verbs with the extra energy due to such a sophisticate. I wasn't a student of Eic's but, fortunately for me, he became a friend of the family and volunteered to coach me in Welsh at weekends and after school.

By this time I was thirteen and we had moved from Alltwen to Cwmllynfell, a small village forty-five minutes by bus up the valley at the foot of the Black Mountain; Eic and his family settled in the village below our farm in G.C.G. Corpulent, with a noble head, a country-man's red complexion and a huge mane of hair, he wore Welsh tweeds and knitted ties and walked the school corridors as though he was walking the deck of a ship, an evil-smelling pipe clamped between his teeth. He was the Welshest person I'd ever met; not just Welsh by accident of birth but passionately Welsh; Welsh Nationalist Welsh; cultured, educated Welsh. *He* told *me* about my great-grandmother, 'Sali Wernwgan' and he knew about my great-aunt, Rosina Davies, the evangelist. I began to consider Wales and the Welsh afresh and thought that were it not for the fact that I needed to get into the theatre, I would be very happy to remain at home.

Our Swansea-Valley Welsh was peppered with English words for which there were no Welsh equivalents. Eic now challenged us to invent new words to keep up with modern life and to speak pure Welsh with no Englishisms. He himself earned a place in Welsh history at this time by translating rugby terms into Welsh – inventing a whole rugby vocabulary – so that he could broadcast Welsh radio commentaries. Under Eic, Welsh grammar became a game and, thanks to him, I knew enough, in time, to sit and pass my university entrance in Welsh. He also renamed me. At school I was called by my first Christian name, 'Jane'. Out went the name along with 'sitting room', 'centre-forward', 'telly'. In came 'Siân', '*blaenwr*', '*lolfa*', '*tele-wele*'.

Siân, which was Welsh for Jane, hadn't been used for generations and it puzzled people even in Wales. When, a few years later, I got into an Arts Council production of a new Welsh play and, full of myself, took a bus to Aberdare to see my first grown-up billing in a play, I stood across the road from the theatre and, mortified, read very near the bottom 'with STAN PHILLIPS'. Stan . . . it was worse than all the other names I'd become used to: Sean (a boy's name), Sy-an, Shane, Cheyenne. I was too unimportant for anyone to bother correcting the poster, so I remained Stan wherever we played. Eic laughed it off. 'Don't worry,' he said, eyes twinkling through the smoke from his pipe, 'give it a year or two and they'll know who you are, all right.' My heart skipped a beat. What did he mean? Did he mean that he agreed I could be an actress? Had he talked about it with my mother? I was too afraid to ask in case he only meant that my name, like all the other familiar Welsh words, would in time catch on.

I knew that he thought I was good. He wrote successful comedies for children and translated French and Spanish plays into Welsh, which we performed in school under his direction. He'd listened to my first broadcasts and, very tactfully, urged me towards better microphone technique ('more thinking, less acting'). He introduced me to his friends at the BBC, and so I widened my circle of possible employers. For some reason, my mother never questioned the wisdom of my spending time at the BBC. Mr Rees, my headmaster, and she and my father all said, 'So long as she keeps up her school work.' I knew that one bad report would bring my career to a sudden end. My fellow pupils didn't find my unorthodox school life very remarkable. They were used to the fact that I led a public life. I wasn't secretive about my work, but I kept it separate from my life at school. My pay cheques were modest and the money was put aside for books. Like everyone else, I received no pocket money.

I loved this budding career at the BBC, but the early years were nerve-racking for all sorts of reasons. At thirteen, fourteen, fifteen, I was growing fast and outgrowing clothes faster than they could be replaced, but the school tunic had limitless turnings and the gabardine was standing up to the countless spongings and pressings, so there were periods when my school uniform was the smartest thing I could wear to work. I didn't mind this, but it did emphasise my slightly awkward position, very much a junior and very much a beginner on the fringe of the resident repertory actors and the very experienced part-time actors who made up the large company that was needed for the big weekly output of plays, stories, drama documentaries ('features', as they were called), poetry programmes, schools' programmes and *Children's Hour*.

I had to struggle not to appear as gauche and panic-stricken as I felt while I gradually picked up the actors' and directors' shorthand. 'Wait for the flick then take a beat after the spot effect before you do a medium approach on page four.' Wha-at? Why didn't I ask? I was shy and everyone was always in a mad rush and simply forgot that I had no way of knowing the things that they took for granted.

The fact that everything was live intensified the pressure. It was *imperative* that no mistakes were made. This was before television had resumed properly after the war and Wales had very little professional theatre, so everyone listened to the radio and hung on each word, reacting sharply to faults. Many of the plays were fed into the network and my first *Saturday Night Theatre* (in which I played a large number of public-school *boys*) was like going over Niagara in a barrel. Eic told me to imagine that I was playing to *one* family sitting together in one room, and that did make the whole thing a little less intimidating. A little. It was bad enough, acting in Welsh, but English . . . I agonised over every syllable. And regional accents . . . I wasn't to know that accents were never to come easily to me and I cursed myself for being so slow.

The actors in the company were wonderful. I never tired of watching them as they rehearsed, making it all seem so natural and easy. However, some of them were decidedly eccentric. When I had to give a full account of my experiences at home ('No, no, start from the beginning. You got off the bus . . .'), I censored out some of the racier conversations. I didn't think my parents would approve of anything 'bohemian'.

There were two actors who stood apart from the others: Norman Wynne and Ennis Tennusché. They were marked by an un-Welsh air.

Norman drank, I thought, although here in the city it wasn't the crime it would have been in our almost teetotal circle. Still, it was better left out of my description of Norman. He looked grumpy and artistically dishevelled and not entirely happy with his lot. And he cooked! I had never met a man who could cook (not counting the tramp), but Norman would amble late into the studio, just in time to avert hysteria and disaster, and invariably carried a string bag bulging with groceries, some of them *very* strange; things that could *only be bought in Cardiff.*

One day as I stood at the microphone during transmission, wondering what would happen if, for once, Norman didn't make it, the door opened gently and in he sidled. He crept up to the microphone and extracted from the string bag a rather grubby script that had been rolled around a bright red lobster. I had only ever read about lobsters. How wonderful, I thought, to be so insouciant and so sophisticated in one's eating habits – and so good at acting. He *was* good or his insubordination would have cost him his job. It did not escape me that the director, Elwyn Evans, who seemed to be seven feet tall, appeared even more inscrutable and frightening when, eyes narrowed, he looked through the glass window of the control cubicle at four actors stepping over Norman's lobster as they wove their way around the microphone.

Ennis Tennusché was beautiful. She looked like a model. As I stood beside her, I felt over-athletic, over-fed, over-healthy. She was thrillingly thin, her skin pale as ivory, her hair silvery blonde, pulled back into an immaculate chignon. It seemed to me that she only ever wore silvery colours; grey suits with long pencil-slim skirts, a little slit cut at the back so that she could walk in her incredibly high-heeled shoes. In the street she wore little jackets, nipped in at the waist, and carried a long, furled, black umbrella. Under her arm she held a large, flat, rectangular handbag and on her head she wore a small, flat, pancake of a hat. The only colour was the dark red of her lips, which I never saw unpainted. She was the only person I'd ever seen who looked like an actress. It goes without saying that she had a lovely voice, and when she chatted during breaks I found it an effort to keep my countenance neutral, partly because of the beauty of the sound and partly because I was truly shocked by the way she spoke of private things in public. Once she referred to her 'ex-lover' and the things he did that infuriated her. I blinked a few times and focused on the ceiling. 'Ex-lover'? What kind of talk was that? Boyfriends, husbands and fiancés, fathers and brothers were the total of possible roles for the men in one's life – outside books, that is. Ennis's conversation *was* like something in a book.

The other ladies, mindful of my age, looked faintly disapproving. They were *very* Welsh. Rachel Howell-Thomas had been senior to my mother at Ystalyfera Grammar School. Untrained, she was a remarkable, experienced actress, married to a doctor, quiet, discreet, successful, plain, her large Slavonic face (a bit like my mother's) completely bare of make-up, hair scraped back into plaits wound round into unbecoming, flat 'ear-phones'. She had thick ankles and wore sensible shoes and suits. She looked nothing like an actress, but she made movies and Paul Robeson had said she was one of the best actresses he'd ever worked with. She was always cordial, but when she looked at me I felt my mother's eyes on me, filled with faint suspicion. As the years went by, I gave her no reason to revise her doubts about me as, increasingly restless and longing to be up and away, I looked for mischief and found it.

Rachel played good women. Dilys Davies, her contemporary, played shrews, gossips, nags and viragos, and she was first-rate. She had a voice like a corncrake that could be heard three blocks away. Also married to a doctor, she was rich and, if not exactly pretty, striking; slim and bold with an inexhaustible wardrobe of bright, new clothes. She took me under her wing in a kindly, impersonal way and was always ready with advice, usually preceded by, 'The doctor says'. I never did find out her husband's name; he was always referred to as 'the doctor' and I was given to understand that he was infallible. 'The doctor says never wear bedroom slippers in the home. It's slack' and 'Always have a wash and put some make-up on before transmission. And always put a drop of scent on. It makes all the difference.'

The fourth established actress was Olive Michael. She was a widow; young and pretty and *tiny*. If I felt hearty alongside Ennis, when I stood next to Olive I felt like a giant. She looked like a little French juvenile, but she carried with her a faint air of tragedy, strangely at odds with her cheerful manner and her facility for playing children; little boys and girls, lots of them, all in the same play, all totally different.

My only contemporary was Gwenyth Petty: blonde, as sunny as she was beautiful, immaculate with flawless skin and beautiful clothes. We worked together for years and I looked up to her, though I sensed that our ambitions would take us in very different directions.

Prysor Williams and Moses Jones ('Moss') were the character actors and, unlike Norman, *very* Welsh. Ex coal-miners, they were short, slightly stooped, blue scarred and 'chesty from the dust'. Prysor was sharp and quick and foxy. Moses had a softness and a simplicity that would break the heart. I watched them carefully and realised that I was learning more from them than I was from the actresses.

The leading man was *such* a leading man ... John Darren was absurdly handsome with, of course, a heavenly voice and a great deal of what I had just learned to identify as sprezzatura. He was so poised, so cool, so unruffled, so effortless in all he did.

Everyone, no matter how experienced, suffered from nerves in the days of live broadcasting. As the seconds ticked away and the warning red light came on, the silence grew palpable, and as the voice of the continuity announcer up on the first floor identified the station and began to introduce the programme, we waited like greyhounds for the green light to signal the cue to begin. In those seconds, everyone prayed that they wouldn't be the one to stumble, make an unpardonable 'fluff', or turn over two pages by mistake, or fail to squeeze into the correct place on a crowded mic. The studio floor would be littered with discarded pages cut at the last moment and my special prayer was always: 'Please God, don't let me have thrown away the wrong pages.' Studio managers stood by with their strange assortment of tin cans, old nuts and bolts, maybe a washboard, which were to be pressed into service for 'spot-effects', and one had to be very careful not to get in their way.

There were a thousand things that could go wrong, and we all twitched and frowned and waved our arms about looking thoroughly unappealing – except for John, who, if he was anxious, never betrayed it as he negotiated his way through the chaos like a man strolling in his own garden. Except that – and again maybe it was hell for him, but he gave no outward indication of discomfort – he walked with the most attractive Byronic limp; the legacy of a cricketing accident at Oxford. Sunshine, green grass, dreaming spires, a lock of hair on the forehead, tie knotted at the waist, the song of willow on leather, gilded youth, sudden calamity, English voices ... it was too romantic and the girls mooned over him. I, from very far off. When he casually complimented me on some little piece of acting, I was struck quite dumb and could only nod gracelessly. He made the boys at school seem very – boyish, and he made the 'old' men in their forties who bought me meals and paid me compliments seem very – well – old and heavy-handed. As the years went by and I got to know him a great deal better, I never quite forgot that most delicious of states, the schoolgirl crush.

I think John was glad when a new actor of his own age was chosen to complete the company. Michael Aspel was the latest heartthrob and the two dashing young men played all the dashing young parts and seemed to be having a lovely time. They were so capable and remarkably nice – for God-like creatures.

The company was augmented by people like me who came and went. Well, hardly like me – Donald Houston and Clifford Evans and Hugh Griffith occasionally descended. And Richard Burton, whose adoptive father, Philip Burton, had been a BBC director. Richard was a really lovely 'boyo' of a man with a huge capacity for beer and singing; a typical South Walian, good humoured and quick to make friends. A real man's man, I thought approvingly, and I was still in my teens when I was moved to revise that judgement. What did I know about men? Then there were character actors who had 'proper' jobs as well. (An awful lot of Welsh solicitors had equity cards.) One of them would drive me home to the west, saving me an overnight stay and a series of bus journeys. I adored speed and he drove way over the legal limit and, on very late nights when the road was clear, he would let me take the wheel. It was bliss and my mother would have killed me, but I thoroughly enjoyed being as bad as I knew how.

By the age of fifteen I had achieved my full height of five foot seven and three-quarter inches, and if Eic was in the show and I wasn't in my school uniform, he would slip me into the BBC club or the upstairs bar of the Park Hotel, which was an unofficial annexe of the BBC in Park Place. There, I would sit quietly in a corner, nursing my orangeade until it was time for me to be taken back to West Wales by Eic, who wouldn't have dreamt of letting me drive but who rightly thought it worthwhile taking the chance of getting both of us into an awful lot of trouble in order to let me sit in the bar and listen to some of the remarkable characters who inhabited the BBC at that time as they relaxed after work.

My very first under-age escapade was wonderful and I forgot my apprehension as Dylan Thomas *and* Gwyn Thomas filled the room with the kind of conversation I could never have imagined possible. It wasn't like any exchange I'd ever heard. Neither inhibited the other and the words cascaded between them, flashing like water. Not for the first time I thought that only second-rate talkers resented other people's cleverness and couldn't wait to push in and claim the attention. The two Thomases were lordly and careless, profligate with their brilliance.

I thought I would suffocate as I laughed and laughed, trying to be inconspicuous. I was taken home before too much drink was taken, so my impression of Dylan Thomas on a night out was of a witty, brilliant gentleman.

We broadcast together a few times, reading poetry. There would be four or five readers and it was quite usual for people, as they finished their pieces, to tiptoe out of the studio. Once, I was on last – petrified, as usual – and not at all sure if I felt better or worse for having the great poet sitting with me in the big Studio 2, waiting politely for me to bring the programme to a close.

On the whole I was remarkably well looked after in this adult environment, which was my other life, running parallel with my school life. Naturally, as time went by, less care was taken to censor the conversation that went on around me, and from time to time my view of the world was given a severe jolt and I would mentally reshuffle the opinions I'd been fed at school and at home by my mother, who had an exaggerated respect for authority, insisting that *all* figures of power and influence were people of irreproachable moral standards. In her book, clever men and women merited respect by virtue of their cleverness. Whether she really believed all this I didn't know, but she handed down the belief as if it were written on a stone tablet from on high and I went along with it without too much thought. When I did think about it, I assumed that human nature in Wales was just different from human nature anywhere else, past or present. Only gradually did it dawn on me that a large proportion of the people my mother looked up to were just like the people in books – sometimes liars, adulterers, drunks and philanderers – but they were terribly nice and, more importantly, terribly nice to me. The heavy fog of non-conformism hid a multitude of sins from general view, and I would not have dreamt of revealing my fragments of insight to anyone in my other life at home.

The only people I came to dislike were aggressively puritanical – very establishment Welsh – chapel-going, narrow and disapproving of anything outside their own culture. I found it hard to conceal my dislike and there were a few directors I didn't work for at all, once we got the measure of each other.

There were fascinating people at the BBC whom I never got to know well; they appeared briefly and were gone again. John Heath-Stubbs, the poet, was one of these. He had very poor eyesight so I took him to and from the canteen and picked up his things as he dropped them. I doubt that he registered my presence and I was more than content to watch him and listen to him.

Richard Hughes was the first important novelist I met and worked with. He took me under his wing and escorted me to a café in a desolate, bombed-out area of Swansea, near the BBC in the Uplands. The desolate café had the desolate food of the time. He undertook to improve my education and said, 'Now, remember this.' I perked up, thinking I'd have something special to write in my diary. 'Remember,' he said, slowly, 'everything tastes better if you smother it in Worcester Sauce.' I'd never heard of Worcester Sauce – such a thing never featured on the shelves of our village shop – but for years after that, when eating out, and very pleased to know how to pronounce it, I requested Worcester Sauce and poured it over most things, heedless of the raised eyebrows, confident that I was doing the right thing on the very best recommendation.

I was young when I sat my matriculation (university entrance) examination – fourteen – and such was my fear of being made to give up work (acting was already work and school was a delightful sideline) that I prepared ten subjects and passed them all well, with distinctions in three. I was pleased because I felt very much in charge of my life for a brief while. The examination fortnight – sunny and peaceful in the big, airy gymnasium, with no sound but that of paper rustling faintly, the click of pens put down, picked up, tapped gently, dropped, the occasional gusty sigh and the soft tread of the invigilator – was restful after the frenzy of revision. When I found myself challenged to write about something that I hadn't revised, it was rather exciting – a bit like the nervous excitement before a performance. My eleventh subject was Arithmetic and, of course, I failed it. My maths teacher was delighted that I'd somehow managed to master geometry and trigonometry and we tacitly agreed to ignore arithmetic. When I turned up for the exam he said, 'Look, it's a nice day, why don't you just write your name, then go and read in the field.' I could have hugged him. Why had I been so frightened of him for so many years?

That summer the excitement of passing exams wore off and now I was truly becalmed and more and more frustrated as the weeks went by and I drifted towards the sixth form to prepare my chosen three subjects, which, in two years' time, I would begin reading at a second-year level at a university. This was not without charm – in fact it was immensely attractive – but in my heart I felt that it wasn't what I ought to be doing. My acting was getting no better. If anything, I felt that it was getting worse. I'd outgrown my mother, I'd won the National Eisteddfod four times and had stopped competing. I didn't want to recite any more, I wanted to act, but I'd outgrown school plays. The occasional Arts Council stage play never lasted long enough for me to be able to try out some of the acting methods I read about in books and in actors' autobiographies, and, in any case, I felt I was no longer able to help myself. The people who could and did help me were all at the BBC, but I was desperate to work in theatre.

I walked and walked on the Black Mountains and on the Gwrhyd Mountain as though I could somehow walk away my problems. I went round in circles, my mind went round in circles. How was I going to achieve a life where acting – on stage – every night, night after night, week after week, was my proper occupation, not something I was grudgingly allowed to squeeze in between other 'legitimate' activities? I was fifteen and no one understood my wretchedness. Well, Eic did, but he was no longer talking about it. A few people at the BBC were 'interested' to see if I would find a solution and they were 'sure' I would.

Despite myself, I was consoled by books, by the loveliness of my surroundings and by my own physical well-being. That summer I read a huge amount of Wordsworth and happiness kept breaking through in spite of everything. I felt a traitor to my sense of purpose as I relished the swing in my stride and smiled at the sun transforming the wet mountains when the sky grew huge and clear all around me. I laughed aloud as I raced home, trying to outstrip the thunderstorm I could smell in the air. During the long evenings at home, I brooded in my room and wrote sad poems about hopelessness and indifference. Unknown to me, my headmaster, S.G. Rees, was not only thinking about me, he was taking steps to help me.

Chapter Thirteen

'Report to the Head's study at the end of the morning.' The prefect looked around the door of the lower-sixth-form common room. 'Uh-huh,' said Audrey Watkins, my best friend at grammar school, but I wasn't apprehensive. I may have been seen talking to a boy (still not allowed) on the bridge to the refectory, the favoured place for assignations and the passing of notes. I may have been spotted walking with a boy outside the school gates and, much worse, been seen not wearing my hat in the street, but I doubted it. Deception was a large part of my life and I was good at it and rarely brought to book.

Before he became headmaster at Pontardawe, S.G. Rees had been a gifted English master and he still amused himself – and us – by taking the occasional class. He flattered us in the sixth form by telling us mildly risqué jokes, making us feel very grown up and sophisticated. His old school, Gowerton Boys' Grammar School, was about to present Shaw's *St Joan*, and when the leading 'lady' fell ill, Mr Rees came to their rescue by lending me out to play Joan. 'Learn it this weekend,' he said casually. I jumped at the chance and, not entertaining the possibility of failure, spent a very enjoyable weekend getting to know the play. By Monday I knew my part. It was really *my* part by Tuesday; I was sure I was going to play it better than it had ever been played. On Wednesday the young man recovered and I was told to stand down. I was disappointed but looked on the bright side and went on thinking about 'my' part against the day when I would, *surely*, play it.

Mr Rees may have felt slightly in my debt, because he'd decided that I should forgo tennis lessons in order to work on a programme of drama study that he would oversee. Life was full of these conflicts, I thought miserably. I was still a fanatically keen and good gymnast, a useful all-round athlete and an enthusiastic, if not at all good, hockey player and, of course, I adored Miss Inkin, the PE and Games mistress who had by now become a friend of the family and had taken me to my first ballet and my first opera and had, without offending my mother, given me the length of navy-blue silk to make what she (and I) regarded as an appropriate concert dress.

Under her guidance I'd forsaken my longing for waves and curls. 'All that prettiness looks common on you,' she'd said ('common' was a term of opprobrium widely used in those days) and, surveying the results of her handiwork in the big mirror in my parents' bedroom, I had to admit that, got up like a modern Jane Eyre, I certainly looked different and quite fetching in an odd way. I longed now to be in her tennis class and become a brilliant player, but it was plain to me that learning about plays was more to the point, so I made my excuses and hoped I wouldn't lose her regard. She didn't say anything, but a week later she gave me a history of drama by Allardyce Nicoll and I breathed a sigh of relief and settled down to my private classes with Mr Rees. He was a wonderful teacher and loved theatre, so the lessons were laced with accounts of productions and performances he had seen and admired – or not admired; he could be caustic.

Now, he looked quizzically over his glasses as I entered his study. 'I assume you're familiar with *Twelfth Night*?' I was. 'You know Viola's meeting with Olivia, leading up to the willow cabin speech?' I did. 'Here's my cut of the scene; learn it by the end of the week. I'm going to have you assessed. Maybe you should move on. Hugh Griffith is coming to look you over.' Hugh Griffith! I was speechless. Emlyn Williams excepted, Hugh Griffith was our greatest actor. He'd played in America. *And* in the West End. *And* in movies. He'd played King Lear, in Welsh as well as in English. He rarely played in Wales and it was unbelievable that he was coming here – to Pontardawe – to see *me*! My lungs were overfull of air. I needed to take a breath and I couldn't. I must have changed colour in the silence and Mr Rees said briskly, 'All right, all right! That's all. Off you go.'

Off I went. Out into the dark corridor with its wood-block floor and smell of polish. There was no one to tell. This was the most important thing that had ever happened to me and I had to keep it to myself. I had good friends at school, but my life was increasingly different from theirs and I was reluctant to talk about anything that pointed up the difference. My priorities were crystal clear and my mother – confusingly – had always made sure that they never went out of focus. 'You can't do your school work *and* act *and* . . .' go dancing, go to the swimming baths, go to the youth club, join the Brownies. All that was acceptable. Well, it had to be acceptable. The only thing I wasn't prepared to forgo was boys and somehow, in spite of my almost total lack of spare time, I managed to maintain a series of somewhat ritualistic 'courtships'. My mother sniffed dismissively but wisely left well alone. But where did the acting fit into her plans for me? We hadn't had an argument about it for years, but that was because I never brought up the subject. Now what was going to happen? If Hugh Griffith said I was no good, I'd persevere anyway. If he said I *was* good, what would that mean for me? Would my parents feel obliged to treat me seriously? Would he suggest that I left school? If he did, what would I do? My mind raced ahead. The thought of London terrified me. I couldn't imagine how I would live in a city, speaking English all day. Would I be capable of it?

At home that night I merely said that Hugh Griffith was coming to school and I was going to play a scene for him. I didn't say that he was coming specially to see me. I could tell that my mother wasn't sure how she should react. 'Oh, yes?' she said, evenly. In my room I began working on the scene, going over it again and again and again. In the morning I got up early and went through it over and over again before breakfast. On the bus I ran it silently in my head. After three days Mr Rees called me into his room and asked: did I know it? Know it? I felt as though I'd *written* it. Friday came and I went to school as though it was just another day and not the day when my life might change utterly. During assembly and morning prayers I rehearsed in my head. In the corridor I passed Eic. 'Okay?' he mouthed. I nodded. So he knew. No one else seemed to. Or maybe they didn't care. Somehow, I got through the morning, then rushed to the lavatory to go over the scene a few more times. When would he arrive? What if he didn't come?

At last, after lunch, I was sent for and told to go to the assembly hall and, heart pounding, I entered and shook hands with a real actor. Now that the longed-for moment had arrived, I was barely conscious. Everything I did seemed unreal, as though it was happening to someone else. Climbing the steps to the stage, walking to the centre, looking down at Mr Rees and Eic and at Hugh Griffith who sat apart from them, I was losing all sense of myself. I suppose I was saved by the amount of work I'd done, because I got to the end of the scene and no, I *hadn't* fainted and he hadn't stopped me and now he was asking Mr Rees and Eic if they would leave us alone.

As he began to talk about the scene, my mind cleared for the first time and my perceptions returned, sharp and clear. He was *directing me!* This was what I'd been longing for. I was astonished and delighted that there was so much more work to be done on the scene. Hugh altered everything; I played it twice as fast, then faster again. How could I have been so slow? Now I was too fast. 'No, no *'merch I.* Throw it away, girl, but don't lose it.' Oh God. How? Try again. Hugh's faced loomed larger and larger as he joined me on stage; all eyebrows and nose and sardonic mouth and the brightest, most piercing eyes. I don't know how long we worked, but suddenly he was saying, 'All right, my girl, once more – last time.'

After all the work I'd done and all the work we'd done combined, I felt like a new person; lighter, more agile than I'd ever imagined being. I finished and turned to him, absolutely sure that I'd done what he'd asked for, and laughed with pure pleasure. I'd never had such a good time. He smiled his inscrutable smile and said, 'There you are. Who'd have thought it, eh?' 'Well done' would have been nice to hear. He said nothing and my newfound confidence began to drain away. I didn't know what to say. 'I'm just going to have a word with Eic,' he said, speaking Welsh for the first time except for saying '*merch*' for 'girl'.

After he'd gone, I waited uncertainly on the stage. The hall looked like the ordinary, familiar hall of everyday life. The magic had evaporated as Hugh left. I descended the steps and, opening the door, looked out into the corridor. Hugh and Eic were standing outside Mr Rees's study, deep in conversation. They didn't look in my direction and I began walking away from them and turned into the empty common room to look at my timetable. My heart was pounding now. My tongue felt strange. I didn't know how long I'd been in the hall. There was nothing to do but to slip back into the afternoon's classes. 'Excuse me please, I've been with the headmaster.' I felt ill now and had to force myself to concentrate.

Before school ended I was sent for again. Mr Rees was alone in his study. Hugh had gone and Eic was teaching. Mr Rees said calmly, 'It seems you're on your way. Mr Griffith thinks you might well win a scholarship to the Royal Academy and he thinks you should try for one next year when you're sixteen. What do you think of that?' I couldn't tell him what I thought. I wasn't thinking. I was feeling relief so profound that I longed to drop to the floor and burst into tears. I didn't think that Mr Rees's study was the place for that, so I managed a polite 'That would be wonderful. Thank you very much, sir.' I'd been right, all along, ever since I was six years old. I *was* meant to be an actress. I was going to *be* an actress. How could I have doubted that, today, everything would start going my way?

Chapter Fourteen

What followed was the happiest and then the most desolate part of my life. It seemed as though my dearest wish was about to come true. Now that Hugh had made it clear that he was impressed, someone would be bound to do something and my parents would be obliged to cave in. Hugh wrote to them; I knew the letter was on its way and I was beside myself with excitement. I don't think my mother even replied to the letter. The rejection was total. There was no discussion, or if there was one, I was not included in it. The decision was final and my mother was implacable. Provided of course that I passed my exams, there was no question of my not going to university.

There was a part of me that hated my mother that year as I resumed the routine of school life; more and more homework, long bus journeys to and from the BBC in Cardiff and in Swansea. The resentment never quite left me. And yet, I could see why she behaved as she did. And I could see that everything she said made perfect sense. But not to me. What I most fretted over was my feeling that she had no faith in my ability. She had seen everything I'd ever done, except my rehearsal with Hugh Griffith, and it must be that she found me wanting. I got on with my preparation for university, determined to get through everything in record time and determined to prove my mother wrong.

Had I possessed a greater dislike of my life, or had my resentment of my mother not been tempered by some understanding of her thought-process, then I suppose I would have rebelled more vigorously at this stage. Only once did I openly oppose my mother. When she forbade me to do something or other on a fine Saturday afternoon, saying, yet again, 'You can't expect to be allowed to act if you don't give up your spare time to catching up on your school work,' I heard myself protesting that I felt 'exploited', that I wasn't living a 'normal life' and that it 'just wasn't *fair*', and as I spoke, I felt deeply embarrassed to be saying anything so crass, uttering such clichés. Had my father been present I wouldn't have been so rude. My mother looked disdainful and said nothing. I muttered an apology and was safely inside my bedroom before I began to cry from confusion and shame. 'Take what you want and pay for it' I had written in my notebook. I knew what I wanted and, most of the time, I was happy to pay the price, but there were moments when the dull, mundane payments – no heroic gestures required – alas, seemed to stretch ahead without end. I would be so *old* before I could be a proper actress. Maybe too old.

Meanwhile it was luxurious to have only three subjects to work on instead of ten. I read voraciously and now that I had evolved a rough form of rapid reading, my appetite was increasing to match my capacity. I made sure that my eye made a diagonal from the end of one line to the beginning of the next (rather than running back horizontally before dropping down). I tried, as well, to 'drink in' the whole page before I began reading and, of course, I practised 'skipping'. There was probably more to it, but this makeshift method helped me considerably. Set books formed only a small proportion of my reading, as my parents and Miss Inkin began to buy me modern novels. One by one my parents gave me Aldous Huxley's novels in a pretty Chatto & Windus edition, and when the set was complete and sitting on my dressing-table, between two rather nasty bookends in the shape of galleons, I enjoyed looking at them before I went to sleep as much as I had enjoyed reading them.

What I really wanted at this time was to understand Cyril Connolly's column in the *Observer* and to know what he was writing about in his review column on the Sunday; even more, I wanted to be able to walk into a room and *talk* to Cyril Connolly! (*The Unquiet Grave* was my favourite book.) The retired schoolmistress next door gave me her old Conrads and her brand-new volumes of Osbert Sitwell's *Left Hand: Right Hand*. I couldn't believe people could live such a life. I thought, 'How wonderful to *be* a Sitwell', stepped up my output of inferior poetry and made myself a turban out of the pretend silk runner on the piano. Miss Inkin gave me French novels in a lovely edition. *Mademoiselle de Maupin* was what I thought of as a *real* French novel and I thought how lovely to behave so badly in such wonderful clothes. She also gave me big books about Russian and British ballet, full of photographs of dancers, who became intimates as I drew them over and over again. There was very little I didn't know about the physiques of Anton Dolin, Sally Gilmour, John Gilpin and Galina Ulanova after I'd sat night after night at the kitchen table with my back to the anthracite fire, copying their photographs in mid-leap and listening to the Third Programme of the BBC issuing from the wooden face of the Ferranti wireless on the windowsill.

Miss Williams-French, still perfectly coiffed and suited, was not only dragging us inexorably through the thickets of the subjunctive and requiring us to learn by heart long pieces of sad, romantic poetry and particularly gloomy bits of Victor Hugo (which rather suited my mood); she was also telling us about French *movies* – not that there was any chance of us seeing any – and bringing us photographs of actors and actresses, so completely un-English and giving us a whole new look to aspire to – not that there was the smallest chance of my achieving that, either. As I became confident enough to begin bandying about the names of Gide, Malraux, Claudel and Jean-Paul Sartre – Miss Williams's extra gift, nothing to do with our set work – I *felt* sophisticated and gorgeous, as though I too possessed an eighteen-inch waist, bound in a huge black patent belt, and wore a fringe over huge black eyes, with lots of dark, dark lipstick on my small mouth like those French ingénues in the photographs. I lived a life of fantasy much of the time, tried on new personas for size and had to admit to myself that in spite of everything I was, on the whole, happy. I got on well with my schoolfriends and the staff and always had a romance on the go to liven up the day.

I was distracted by an increasing and greatly frowned-upon pre-occupation with boys at school, young men outside school and, even more interesting to me, secret flirtations with totally unsuitable older men, which would have completely 'cooked my goose' had they ever come to light. My mother looked askance when I went to the Miners' Welfare Hall to see a movie on Saturday night (and this could only happen when I wasn't working – I would never have dreamt of refusing work in order to keep a 'date'). She didn't actually say anything, but I thought it wise to be very discreet about my 'steady' boyfriends from school.

One day Rhydwen Williams said something that really upset me. He was one of Wales's most brilliant preachers, with the dark poetic good looks that matched his fame as a crowned poet. He was in huge demand as a guest preacher and some years before, when we lived in Alltwen, he had pressed me into service to help out during long exhausting Sundays when he would preach two major sermons. I would recite from the Gospel of St Luke – my mother's favourite – and he would take a little breather. He introduced me to the plays of Emlyn Williams and, back at the house after the evening service, performed his favourite scene from *The Corn is Green* (I had to give my twelve-year-old reading of Miss Moffat). Now he came back into our lives as a friend of Eic's in Cwmllynfell.

I think they were enjoying a kind of pub-crawl with a very august personage from the BBC in London. They must have run out of things to do one night because my mother woke me up and said that there was a car waiting to take me to the Boblen – a tiny, inaccessible pub on the Gwrhyd Mountain above the village, presided over by a mountainous, good-humoured woman called Bessie'r Rock, who was a stranger to licensing hours and sleep alike. I scrambled into my clothes and into the cold Austin Seven, which bumped up the dark mountain road and turned left into the yard in front of the tiny pub. Inside there was a coal-fire burning and it was stiflingly hot after the chill outside. There was a brilliant, central, overhead light. Bessie made a place for me while the ten or so men told stories, extemporised verse and drank steadily.

At last, they cleared a place for me to stand and I recited for them for about half an hour. Eic had said only that it was *quite* important for me to do my best as there were one or two people who wanted to see for themselves whether I was as good as I'd been cracked up to be. Not knowing my audience but enjoying the challenge, I showed off, beginning with the St Luke version of the Prodigal Son in Welsh, then moving on to the Nightmare Song in English, then continuing with my edited version of the trial scene from *St Joan*, and then a little Baudelaire in French. What they made of this indigestible programme, heaven knows, and I certainly didn't know because, as usual, I was packed off home as soon as I'd finished and was asleep the second I climbed into bed.

Rhydwen called on my parents the following day. 'You know she *is* going to be an actress,' he said in Welsh. They seemed gratified to hear me praised by someone they regarded so highly, and when he sat down and wrote an ode to me there and then, they were impressed. He took me for a turn around our garden. It was cold in the east wind that blew through the village, from Cefn-Bryn-Brain. 'Don't worry too much,' he said in Welsh, using the familiar '*ti*' form of the verb, something my parents never did. It gave me a jolt. 'It *is* going to happen, but there's no hurry. You're not going to come into your own until you're forty.' Forty? What could he be talking about? All my pleasure evaporated and

I felt deeply exasperated and actively disliked him as he stood in the winter-untidy vegetable patch, looking at me with an amused expression on his handsome face. What he'd said was completely absurd, but how on earth was I going to be able to prove him wrong, imprisoned as I was in school? 'Lulled in the doldrums of immaturity' I'd copied into a notebook. 'That's me,' I thought, miserably.

'I'll show you,' I thought to myself. After he'd gone I looked at his poem to me written in small, neat handwriting. It was very flattering and I especially liked the bit where he wrote that the curtain call was the one moment when *I* would bow. At all other times I would shine like Orion and *they* would bow before me. Well! My mother reached over my shoulder. 'I'll take this,' she said, and it disappeared along with my prizes and newspaper cuttings and silver cups, and I never saw it again. Rhydwen's words had no practical effect on my mother and father.

For the rest of my time at school there was nothing but disappointment and frustration. Jill Craigie came to our village to make *The Blue Scar*, a film about coal-miners. Everyone auditioned for it in the Miners' Welfare Hall. Everyone except me. It was summer and I longed to join the queue. 'Revise,' said my mother tersely, and I sat in the garden reading and thinking that nothing would ever go my way.

At school Eic began to direct *Blodeuwedd*, a play by Saunders Lewis in which I played the enormous, wonderful, title role of Blodeuwedd, the girl created from flowers. It was the best part I'd ever worked on and Saunders was the most controversial, glamorous figure on the literary and political scene. He sent me a signed copy of the play and then, halfway through rehearsals, the play was abandoned. We were censored and banned. I was stunned. The play *was* very un-Welsh, full of illicit, joyful sex and violent death. There was an outcry in the press against faint-hearted bigotry, but the school governors held firm. I was beside myself. It was so unfair! The play was no more unsuitable than a great deal of Shakespeare, but no, what was acceptable in English iambic pentameters from the seventeenth century was beyond the pale in modern Welsh. The disappointment made me ill and, to my surprise, my mother was sympathetic. She was busy directing operettas in the Miners' Welfare Hall, but she made sure that there was a supply of delicious titbits to get me through the evenings when I was at home writing essays instead of playing Blodeuwedd. Was nothing *ever* to go right?

The kitchen was a no-go area for me. My mother was a wonderful cook, but she taught me nothing. I made a few half-hearted attempts to learn something from her. 'How much flour, then?' 'Oh, just a handful.' 'How long do you stir it?' 'Till it's done.' I knew a great deal about cleaning, however, having learned 'Housewifery' in the junior school where we were taught to make soap, if you please, and learned how to whiten stone steps with bricks of something called 'Monkey Brand'. Modern methods were frowned upon. I loved cleaning and had a great sense of order, so my room was always spotless and as neat as something in a magazine. I arranged and rearranged the furniture, banished the overhead lamp and rigged up the only indirect light in the house, in all probability the only indirect light for miles around. At night, having completed my exercises to improve and strengthen the arches of my feet (Miss Inkin's suggestion, turned into an iron rule by me), I would lie in bed, reading and admiring the perfect order all around me. I exercised control where I could.

It had seemed as though my two years in the sixth form would never come to an end. I liked school, I had once loved it, but now at sixteen I longed for examination time and an end to it all. Mr Rees entered me for an exhibition to London University and made arrangements for me to sit the exam in his study. Eic thought I should go to Bristol, which was the only university offering a drama course, under Professor Tommy Taigh. I didn't really care where I went. As usual, I rather enjoyed the exams and I got through everything with no trouble at all. It was expected that I should do well in English and French, but I had done so little work in History that failure was almost a certainty. When I saw the paper I realised that it was one of those question papers that cause short-lived academic scandals; completely 'off' the subject. I dredged around in my mind and came up with enough material from historical novels and plays to keep me writing busily, vaguely but entertainingly. When his better students failed or did badly and I passed, my history master made no secret of his displeasure. The knack of passing exams, he implied, was something *girls* had and it was a bit cheap and quite without merit.

I was unrepentant and glad to be finished with his subject, but I wasn't as pleased with myself as I had been when I matriculated. It was good to have cleared another hurdle, but now I had another three or four years to get through before my real life could begin and I didn't know if I would be able to manage it. My attention had moved dangerously far away from the academic and it might be difficult for me to keep my two worlds from cancelling each other out.

While I was brooding over my general problem, a specific difficulty arose that woke me up and threw me into a frenzy. London University could not take students under the age of eighteen years. I was just seventeen. Mr Rees said that an extra year at school was not really such a long time to wait. I couldn't even consider it and only now realised how very desperate I was to get out. Representations were made to Bristol and I was accepted there instead. Carter Paterson, the carriers – the Pickfords of university trunks – picked up and took away my baggage containing all the required clothes for undergraduate life. In fact it contained everything I possessed. Then it was discovered that Bristol also had an age limit. My parents made frantic phone calls. My uncle did the same and the University of Wales agreed to squash me in at the last minute. They had no objection to an undergraduate aged seventeen.

Thoroughly unsettled, I took the bus to Cardiff, to Aberdare Hall, where first-year female students were obliged to live. My trunk was careering around the West Country and no one could find it. I had no clothes except the ones I stood up in. I looked around the college; endless queues everywhere, dim lights, confusion, the hateful city outside. However bad things had been, I realised that they were about to get a lot worse.

Chapter Fifteen

From the Mond Nickel Works onwards down the valley, Swansea had always presented to me a vision of hell. Acrid smells penetrated the red, single-decker Western Welsh bus. The black and grey smoke was shot through with sulphurous yellow, occasionally with a sinister little snake of green in the dark sky above some copper workings. The town itself in its blitzed, ruined state was warm and friendly and very Welsh, and I always knew that at the end of the day I would be in another low, red bus climbing steadily past the dirt and stench of the Tawe Valley through the narrow Twrch (boar) Valley with space for nothing but a narrow road and a turbulent little river on the valley floor, until suddenly, as the bus pulled slowly up the steepest part of the road, Cwmllynfell presented itself in its full, top-of-the-world, Hollywood-orchestrated glory. Violin music swelled in my head as the bus swung round towards the chapel. The landscape was limitless. That moment was like leaving a river for the ocean and it never failed to fill the air with exhilaration and grandeur. Every day I travelled up and away into a freedom that was as psychological as it was physical. It hadn't occurred to me that I was addicted to big landscapes and large skies.

Now I had to contend with Cardiff. Until now it had been a place that housed the BBC in Park Place; somewhere to leave as soon as work was done. I had been dimly aware of the civic centre – very white – and I remembered the museum from my school-days. I knew the route from the bus station to Broadcasting House and I knew the little tobacconist where, greatly fearing, I had slid half-a-crown across the counter for ten Du Maurier cigarettes. No bomb damage here. No slums as far as I could see. It was an eminently nice, clean, safe city and I hated it.

My father had left the police force and was now running a further education centre in the Vale of Glamorgan, outside Cardiff. My parents had arrived in the middle of a staffing crisis and my mother, who had never cooked for more than a small family, had stepped into the breach and was completely preoccupied running a large kitchen staff and cooking for hundreds of people. 'It's only arithmetic – multiplication,' she said breezily, composing menus and making dinky posies for the dining tables. They were meeting old friends from all over Wales and staying up late, entertaining in their flat. My mother had been bequeathed an ancient, fierce parrot that adored her, and my father was furiously painting landscapes in a small outhouse he'd turned into a studio. He was watched by an adoring dog who used to be mine and I was slightly put out to realise that I had moved far away from the centre of their attention; even the dog was perfunctory in his greeting. Of course, I had longed to be left alone and now suddenly I *was* – quite free and quite discomfited. It was as though, after all the years of fuss and struggle, they'd got me more or less where they thought I ought to be (not at all where *I* wanted to be) and, having done that, they'd rather run out of puff as far as I was concerned and discovered an interesting life of their own.

And my trunk was in Bristol! I pitched up in Corbett Road in Cardiff at an annexe of Aberdare Hall. The warden didn't really understand why I was late arriving or why I had no luggage, but made it plain that I was a bit of a nuisance, and I for my part struggled not to betray my dismay at my surroundings. For the first time I felt the impact of post-war austerity. Everything was brown and fawn. The furniture was cheap 'Utility' and seen at its worst in the common room, which was arranged like a doctor's waiting room. The single, dim overhead light in its beige parchment shade with pretend leather stitching illuminated the upright chairs arranged around the room, the few bare 'occasional' tables and the grudging, unlined cotton curtains barely covering the frame of the bay-window that looked out on to the darkening topmost edges of the fabled civic centre.

We climbed to the top floor and I was shown into what had once been a box-room; little brown wooden-framed bed, regulation desk, small wardrobe, chest of drawers, 'easy' chair, bare walls. 'Your bed must be made perfectly and everything that you have put away in the wardrobe or inside the drawers before my inspection at 7.45 a.m. or you will remake your bed and miss breakfast in the Main Hall. As an Arts student you ought to be rooming with someone from a Science faculty, but what can I do?' She shrugged. I couldn't really take her in. In fact, my mind wasn't really taking in anything much. I could hear her explaining the rules governing the kitchen (use of) and the penalties for staying out after 10 p.m. (dire but unspecified). Ten p.m.?! There was something about lights out and after that I decided not to listen at all. What had I let myself in for? I dumped a small bag with soap, towel and toothbrush and a hair brush – 'Not on the bed, I think.' 'Oh, so sorry' – and followed her down the stairs, bidding her the briefest 'Good afternoon and thank you' as she made for her own study.

There was no one about and I walked into the fading autumn day. It was damp and it was to stay damp for months. I walked down Park Place towards the Students' Union. Beyond was the BBC; familiar, warm, brilliantly lit, with real carpets and 1930-ish light fittings and furniture. I stood there feeling completely cut off from everything I cared for. Now that my parents had moved, I had no way of going 'home' to the west. I was going to have to learn to abide by myriad childish rules and deal with people like the warden. Who was she, the warden? I didn't care.

I walked round to the front entrance of the university building and nervously inched my way into the crowded, none too brightly lit interior. Why was it so *dark* everywhere? My heart sank as I realised that I was going to have to spend hours queuing in order to register for my first year's studies. Now was my chance, however, to alter my programme slightly. Naturally, I would join the English and French Schools at a second-year level, but I would drop History – I knew that although I'd done quite well in the exam I was way under the required standard. My matriculation result enabled me to read Welsh instead. Good old Eic. He'd given me another option. Obviously I was going to have to tackle all this in the morning.

What of the fourth subject that I was obliged to read and that would be started at a first-year level? Education seemed to be the favoured 'filler'. The queue was enormous. Well, I was *never* going to teach and the subject held no appeal for me. I drifted from notice board to notice board and came to rest in a deserted corner of the building. For the first time that day my interest awakened and it was with considerable if inexplicable excitement that I made my way to a desk with no queue at all. The man seated behind it looked discouraging. He seemed content not to be doing business. We went through the formalities and he said, 'Why do you want to join this school?' I replied that, honestly, I had no idea but I was quite sure that I *did* want to. So the first thing I did at the university was to enrol myself as an intermediate student of a subject that I was to pursue with love and passion for the next three years and beyond. It was the only smart thing I did that term. Philosophy became my chief interest and my hobby. And quite unexpectedly, along with Latin and Physical Training, it turned out to be the only really useful subject I ever studied. English was a pleasure and I was always grateful for the yards of poetry that I'd been made to learn parrot-fashion and that floated to the front of my mind, digested and comprehended in their own good time, but Philosophy—! It was philosophy and logic that held me together as I stumbled from one confusion to the next. It also provided me with amusement – something that was sadly lacking in the life I was to lead in this alien, un-Welsh city.

Back at the Aberdare Hall annexe (I hated it even more on second viewing) I heard the click-click of higher heels than would have been considered 'proper' by our mothers, and nearly cried with relief as I saw the huge dark eyes, bright red lipstick, upswept rolls of hair, pussy-cat bow and tailored shoulders of my best friend at school. By all that was wonderful I'd wound up on the same floor as Audrey Watkins. 'Where are you?' 'Next room.' 'Soon change that.' 'We're not allowed, we're both Arts and we know each other.' 'Rubbish. Leave it to me. Done your registering?' 'No.' 'Do it tomorrow. Where's your housecoat?' (Required packing. Not a dressing gown. A *housecoat*.) 'In my trunk. In Bristol.' 'Soon get it back. Banked your grant?' 'No.' 'Never mind. Do it tomorrow.' Sure. Thank you, God. Thank you, Audrey. Everything would get done tomorrow. And maybe, just maybe, life in the Ladies' Seminary mightn't be too bad, after all. My mother would be furious. She thought Audrey and I were bad for each other. Could be. I could feel a big smile coming on.

Chapter Sixteen

I moved in with Audrey and the fearsome warden looked confused but let it pass. My father drove into town in his new car, took me for a spin round the block and helped me open a bank account at Lloyds in St Mary's Street. Sitting there, depositing the first part of my grant, I could scarcely credit my transformation at seventeen into a woman of substance, with responsibilities; bills to pay, books and food and clothes to buy. Hitherto it had never occurred to me to carry money other than the sums my mother doled out to me for my books, bus fares and meals. I knew that a hardback book cost 7s 6d, that lunch could be bought for 3s and that by eating a bit less I could buy cigarettes and no one would be any the wiser. My interest stopped there. Now all that would have to change.

From time to time I made an ineffectual dab at locating my trunk, but Carter Paterson was a law unto itself and my trunk circled the south-west of England for weeks, returning to me in Wales just before the end of term. It didn't occur to me to buy more clothes, so I was the girl in the brown-checked costume and made as if it was a deliberate fashion statement. Audrey got me registered and showed me around, and I addressed my complete unpreparedness for normal, day-to-day living. I'd never made tea or boiled an egg or mended a seam or set an alarm clock or washed a pair of stockings. It seemed I'd done nothing with my life but read, learn lines, perform, do my homework, write poetry, draw, flirt with boys, and moon about. Especially moon about. I was too embarrassed to admit to my ignorance and pretended to take everything in my stride. I was exhausted and homesick for a house that no longer existed. Everyone had a home. So where was mine? Was Cardiff home now? No, not by a long chalk. I never became reconciled to the décor at Corbett Road and in fact everything all over the city seemed to be brown, damp and dim. The rain seemed wetter here, or maybe getting wet mattered more than it had in the country. I wore gloves and wrapped my college scarf round my head, but I was cold, and whereas at home a bit of a run warmed me up in no time, here city pavements and too many people and city shoes slowed me down to a sedate, brisk walk.

Audrey and I made friends with the other girls at Corbett Road and we settled down to some sort of routine, the principal part of which consisted of wasting time, sitting in the only place that would allow us to make one cup of coffee last the entire morning. This was the foyer café of the Capital Cinema in Queen Street at the bottom of Park Place. I don't know what we talked about. Mostly, I just looked at people and listened. Looking at the Park Hotel across the way I could scarcely believe that I had had another, different life; one in which I actually sat composedly inside the building that was now far too grand and expensive a place for me to enter in my present life. Was I going backwards? I couldn't tell. There was one other café on Queen Street, a Kardomah where they served a more 'real' kind of coffee and where I was taken once or twice by older students (much, *much* older – those young men who had come to the university after doing their National Service) and where coffee was drunk at a more reasonable speed. There were two hotels, the Angel, opposite the Castle, and the BBC 'extension', the Park. The only restaurant I was aware of was The Louis in St Mary's Street. Long and narrow and staffed by waitresses, it offered dull food; most things were arranged to be consumed on toast, tea was offered with food, coffee was thin and bitter, the china thick, and good behaviour, while not specified, seemed to be expected. When my parents took me there for high tea we spoke very quietly and chewed long and decorously with a lot of napkin work.

There just wasn't much fun and I couldn't get accustomed to that. City life was constrained and muted and I didn't care for it. Now, more than ever, I worried about my future life in London, which must be a hundred times more of a city than Cardiff and would be a hundred times more difficult for me to live in. In my mother's absence I imagined what she would say. It would be something along the lines of 'You're not *in* London, yet and you're not in Cardiff to have fun.'

Months had gone by since I'd been offered a job at the BBC and this was the longest I'd ever gone without acting. Maybe no one would ask me to act again, I thought miserably, and since we were already halfway through the Michaelmas Term I decided that I'd better take a serious look at the academic work I might reasonably be expected to get through. Also, with a faint sense that it was a mistaken move, I joined the University Dramatic Society.

English lectures were heavily subscribed and took place in the largest room in the building: Room 102. The Reverend Moelwyn Merchant swept on to the stage looking deceptively mild; bald head shining above a cherubic, rosy-cheeked face, black robed, grey suit underneath. Rather cheery, I thought. My pen was poised above my notepad and it stayed there, my jaw dropping slightly as Moelwyn, like a high-octane performer, got a few laughs, touched on the affairs of the day, gossiped aloud about people I'd barely heard of and then 'Gave his All' for ten to fifteen minutes. Hang on, I thought, desperately trying to keep up. If we were, as I'd supposed, looking at the Romantics, why was he talking about gardening? Anyway what was picturesque? Or was it The Picturesque? And what was that joke about his friend, John Piper and the Swan on Lake Windermere? I was still trying to get up to speed when, with a pleasant 'Good day', he was gone! I sat there for a moment, bruised but exhilarated, and realised that I was going to have to make a huge mental stretch if I was going to keep pace, let alone get into the Honours School at the end of the year. The room might be brown and cold, but Moelwyn was technicoloured and hot to boiling point.

At the other extreme there was *Beowulf* to contend with. Sweet's *Anglo-Saxon Reader* seemed manageable. The Norse sagas had a just-discernible appeal. But *Beowulf*! I held the big book in my hand and it felt like a ton weight. The possibility of my ever knowing what it meant seemed remote. I didn't think I had it in me to take on that kind of steady drudgery, but I was going to have to try. Even literature students *had* to know their Anglo-Saxon.

A friend of my father's from Llwynhendy near Llanelli was Professor of French so I tried to bring my written French up to scratch, but every time I delivered an essay I was confronted by my wretched carelessness. At my last oral I'd been given an unusual 100 per cent. *Talking* was fine, it was like giving a performance and now it cut no ice at all. I wasn't quite ready to accept the awful fact that for the first time in my life I was going to have to try really hard. My life of ease was over. Even Welsh had its equivalent of *Beowulf*, with a twist to the torture in that whereas I *knew* I didn't understand any Anglo-Saxon I felt that I half understood or at least could make a good guess at understanding old Welsh. No so. More real work stretched ahead.

Had it not been for Philosophy my spirits would have been lowered to a point of no return. There were very few of us in the school and Professor de Selincourt was my chief source of entertainment as he provoked his fluffy white hair into agitated spirals when threatened with insuperable problems concerning the day of the week (what could it be? – and in which term?) and where his car might be parked or whether he should go home in a bus (but whence might it depart?). Crouching under the desk out of sight, 'Am I here?' he intoned. Then, leaping up with surprising agility, 'Or am I only here when you can see me?' Fun had returned to my working life. I'd read Plato's *Republic* at home so I half knew what the year's work was about. A little unexplored corner of my mind clicked into action when we began the Logic course. It was heaven not having to struggle to understand. I had a bit of a knack for it. Doctor Evans had the shiniest, clearest mind I'd ever encountered and I finished each of his logic lectures wide-eyed, feeling as though I was stepping off an ice-rink. Not that Cymllynfell boasted an ice-rink, and if it had, would Sally Tŷ mawr ever have let me go to it? But I had a sound imagination and following Doc through an argument was just like executing a 'triple Lutz', I thought.

Occasionally, I allowed a worry to rise to the surface. There was probably a good reason why universities had an age limit for admission and was I too young for all this? I was old enough to see my limitations and to see that this place was rather above 'getting through'. I stifled the thought. I was committed to getting through as fast as possible and to getting *out* and *on* to London. It wasn't ideal, but it was what I had to do. I don't know why, but it never occurred to me to drop out.

Chapter Seventeen

I got down to work and it paid off. I still didn't much *like* having to make such an effort, but it was the way it had to be. I did get into the English Honours School and loved collecting the books for the two years that lay ahead. After a year of living at Aberdare Hall I was allowed to take lodgings in the town and perversely lead a less raffish life than I had when I wasn't allowed to. I had become adept at climbing silently through a bathroom window at the rear of the annexe long after the prescribed curfew. My school romances, in spite of our protestations of fidelity, had withered on the vine and I'd acquired a succession of young men, all students, but all much older than myself, old in the way that people senior to one in any institution seem and remote as well. 'What could it *feel* like to have graduated and to be writing a thesis?' I wondered to myself, as we queued for the 1s 9d seats at the cinema or stepped out, dressed in unaccustomed finery, to a student ball.

My affections were never much engaged. I realised that I was a bit of a sucker for brains and status. We were all, I suppose, preoccupied with sex in the formalised way of the Fifties, which didn't seem to have developed much beyond the formalised way of the Forties. Fear was at the root of our behaviour. I remember when I was a little girl, all the children in the congregation at Alltwen Chapel had been sent out into the front courtyard after the morning service and, only half interested, hung about playing and waiting for our parents to emerge. When the big doors opened, out ran a friend's big sister, crying as she rushed past us. We were completely riveted. She had been expelled from 'the body of the Chapel'. I could tell that my mother was torn between seizing the moment to preach a huge lesson and wishing to protect my young ears. When we compared notes afterwards, we realised that all the mothers had encountered the same problem and we had all been warned of the dreadful consequences of 'Getting into Trouble'; being driven out of the congregation was the least of them. Getting into

Trouble meant the end of everything that made life worthwhile. Gradually, we divined that Trouble was something to do with having babies. I noticed as well that when we walked home late at night after a concert in Pontardawe on the little dirt track leading to The Graig there were lights and noise in the houses where the Bad Women lived and that was something to do with Babies (and with Drink) and *those* women were never to *get on* in the world either.

By the time we'd got it all worked out, we knew quite clearly that getting pregnant was the worst thing that could befall us. The girls were threatened with a lifetime behind the counter at Woolworth's and the young men knew that their contribution towards such a fate ensured that they would become providers, working at the most boring jobs imaginable while remaining chained in a dutiful and probably loveless marriage. Nothing much occurred to change this precautionary approach to life. Condoms were not a hundred per cent reliable, 'proper' contraception was available only to the legally married, so the Act was something that belonged only within marriage. In the horrible phrase of the day, 'anticipating marriage' was at best foolish and usually disastrous. Divorce was unheard of, so a marriage too hastily entered into for the sake of respectable regular sex could lead to a lifetime of duty and resentment unless there was a case of true love. What did we know of true love at our age, we were asked, with no pause for an answer.

So as undergraduates we all drove each other half-mad and a great deal of that was hugely enjoyable. Looks were analysed, the touch of a hand pondered over. Was that accidental or deliberate? Inflections and cadences of speech were examined. Advice was sought from the sisterhood. Excitements were curiously dated, almost like the thrilling glimpse of an ankle. When avowed lust had overtaken these protracted, complex manoeuvrings, foreplay was elevated to an exquisitely tortured art form. There was always great anguish – mostly feigned – and 'if only' figured largely in the late night, usually cold collisions in dark, discreet corners of the city. I seemed to spend an inordinate amount of time bruising my lips while freezing in the outdoor tennis courts in winter.

Morals didn't enter into it; I wanted to be as bad as possible, but my conditioning held me in thrall; as with all my friends and contemporaries, Getting into Trouble was unthinkable, unwanted pregnancy not an option. 'He married her to get rid of her' was the Irish saying I knew and recognised. Now I was beginning to get engaged in rather the same spirit. In the absence of a driving commitment on my part, young men grew testy and impatient. For me, given my ambitions, marriage, in any foreseeable future, was out of the question and the next best thing was an engagement. I correctly assumed that even in her preoccupied, frantically busy state, my mother would raise the roof if I pitched up for the weekend, betrothed, so these short-lived liaisons were a closely guarded secret, not even shared with Audrey and the rest of the girls. Since they were so secret, I couldn't quite see what purpose they served anyone, save to take the heat off me by putting a temporary stop to discussions about the future.

The future. I knew what I wanted it to be and that did not include being engaged, far less married, but faced with a general refusal on the part of my young men to take my plans seriously or, even worse, their confident belief that I would never make good my escape, I did what I'd been doing all my life: I stopped talking about things that mattered most to me. I could see that this effectively put paid to real friendships, let alone love affairs, but I felt that my hold on my own life was too flimsy for me to be in a position to sacrifice one ounce of the resolve I had first formulated so long ago. Frustration was making me more implacable. But I liked being pursued and I liked having dancing partners. Fuelled by irritation and anger at not being understood, I thought it a fine thing to be a Belle Dame. I could even see that this wasn't attractive behaviour, but I was too unhappy to be kind.

Around about this time I realised something that should have given me greater pause. I was acting again. People had obviously been right when they'd said that I lacked 'push'. It hadn't occurred to me to go to the BBC to tell them where I was and ask for a job; I'd rather supposed *they* would find *me*. Indeed, I ran into a director on the street one day and he sent me a script, and from that point on I was in constant employment, my anxieties for the time being quietened. Since *I* thought that actors and actresses were the most interesting, admirable people imaginable, I assumed when I was acting and generally drawing attention to myself that this would make my admirers admire me even more. And I was genuinely surprised to realise that, on the contrary, the admiration of the many diminished the regard and goodwill of those who were, or ought to be, closest to me. Faced with reactions of hostility or displays of possessiveness and what I saw to be unreasonable demands, I thought merely 'how odd' and backed off. Love affairs foundered and engagements were broken, and foolishly I never took the time to consider what had emerged as a pattern of behaviour.

Work – at this stage always for the BBC – took over all my time. My brief spell with the University Dramatic Society had not been a success. I played Desdemona for David Jones, a post-graduate student who went on to teach drama in America, and my Othello was a mature student who was reading Philosophy with me after training at RADA and renouncing the theatre. Peter Gyngell was good but he was a mystery to me. How could anyone give up the theatre and go into – what was it? – something I'd never heard of (Computers, did he say?). Lyndon Harris, the President of the Students' Union – a very important and dashing figure – played Iago, very well, I thought. *They* were fine but I was ill at ease and tormented because I couldn't make anything work for me. My hair (dyed blonde – quite exciting) was wrong, my dress was wrong, rehearsals felt wrong, *I* felt wrong and didn't know enough to make myself right.

It was absurd but I had still not seen any theatre that I truly admired. When as a schoolgirl I won the National Eisteddfod in Colwyn Bay I had made my mother take me to a performance at the small seaside theatre. I *saw* the leading man and leading lady in the street, looking actorish – I envied the remnants of stage make-up still visible on their faces. His camel coat, casually draped over his shoulders, may have been a bit of a cliché even then, but I loved the look. I tried to love the performance, but I couldn't. The scenery was awful, the actors were far too actorish. I was embarrassed.

Worse, there had been a charabanc trip to Stratford-on-Avon to see *Hamlet* with a famous dancer in the leading part. I was beside myself with excitement, but in the event sat there, pressing back into my seat, embarrassed again and unable to admire anything, especially not the famous dancer (this time the scenery seemed almost *too* good). The dancer leapt about a lot. Now, in Othello, I was embarrassing *myself* with my own inadequacy. I had a Platonic idea of 'Theatre' and so far hadn't seen or taken part in anything approaching it.

It was a puzzle and I was intent on solving it, but obviously I needed help. I needed RADA, I thought longingly. Meanwhile, at the BBC, I was receiving lots of help from everyone. Well, almost everyone. I was slowly learning a little diplomacy and how to adapt to different directors, but I was also learning that I had an uncontrollable resistance to being directed in what I considered the 'wrong' direction. A quiet, biddable girl, the last thing I wanted was to make trouble and I was only too aware that I was in no position to antagonise my employers. Also, my own lack of experience was perfectly clear to me, so I was horrified by what occurred when I had a second opportunity to play in *Blodeuwedd* for one of the radio directors, who was mounting it in a theatre for a summer festival.

When I was offered the part, I had an immense feeling of everything coming out right after all. Like all good things, it was meant. I *should* have played it for Eic when I was fifteen, but maybe that had been too young and now, surely, I was the right age at eighteen; I'd had time to think about the part and Eic was pleased and Saunders Lewis himself sent me a message and planned to come and see me. The press was interested because of the scandal of the censorship when I was younger. This was important and I knew how to play the part. I was *sure* that although this hadn't been written for me, I was a natural Saunders Lewis heroine.

The director and I locked horns almost at once. I hated his ideas for the play and especially for Blodeuwedd herself. I tried to compromise and failed. I could scarcely believe it was happening when I took the script, walked over to my director, put it in his hands, told him quietly to find someone else with whom to do the play, and quit. I think he was pleased to lose me, and I was on the bus to my parents' place outside Cardiff before the tears came and kept coming after I'd descended from the bus and walked a mile down the deserted country road on the most beautiful sun-drenched afternoon. In the dining room I went to the huge armchair, curled up, and wept and wept until I fell asleep.

I never explained what had happened to anyone, least of all the press. I was heartbroken, disappointed, but also a little unnerved by my own intransigence. This could have serious consequences for me in and outside the BBC, but I consoled myself with the knowledge that I couldn't have done differently. '*Reculer pour mieux sauter*,' I repeated to myself. I had a genuine contempt for the director's ability and I resolved to ride out the débâcle and trust that the doors of the BBC wouldn't be closed against me. They weren't. I never worked for him again, but when I joined the repertory company soon afterwards and anxiously scanned the board every Monday, I saw that enough people had engaged me for their shows to ensure my continuing place in the Company. All the same, it had been an unsettling, worrying summer – and I still hadn't met the great Saunders Lewis, 'the Garbo of Wales' as the *Western Mail* rather inappropriately called him.

It should have worried me more, this lack of enthusiasm I felt for most of the acting I saw, but it didn't overly concern me. Somewhere,

I felt sure, there were people doing what I would think of as wonderful things. (I wasn't at all supercilious in the manner of undergraduates.) I really wanted to like, to admire, and it surprised me when, for example, I couldn't warm to D.W. Griffith's *Intolerance*, hailed as a masterpiece at the University Film Society, and I was relieved beyond measure to encounter and love Ingmar Bergman in our one foreign movie house in Roath. The Hollywood of the Fifties dampened my spirits also and it was wonderful to discover that there was another world inhabited by foreign movie actors who looked just like people, only more so.

Smart West End actors (a specific genus in those days) passed through Cardiff on their way to London and I wasn't lucky enough to see anything inspiring until, one afternoon, an actor playing in Cardiff came to visit us at the university. The biggest lecture hall was crammed to bursting and it wasn't full of people who had come to cheer. The received wisdom of the day was that Donald Wolfit was a 'ham' actor. Stories abounded about his self-centred productions in which he hogged the centre of the stage while the rest of the company languished in the gloom on the sidelines. He was old-fashioned, said the Dramatic Society luminaries, his style of acting was *passé*. I didn't know what to expect as I sat there, waiting.

The door on to the bare dais opened and in walked a florid-complex-ioned gentleman in a pin-striped business suit, followed by a brisk little lady with a somewhat fixed jolly smile on a face surmounted by a perky hat. She must be Rosalind Iden, his wife. They looked nothing *like* actors, I thought disappointedly. Then he began to speak; beautiful voice – easy to hear right at the back where I was perched. He talked about *Tamburlaine* briefly. The overhead light didn't do much to augment the fading winter light outside the big windows. I couldn't get over his ordinary appearance.

Then without any warning, he was acting Tamburlaine. Those who had come to mock began to pay attention. The silence was profound as he began to recite, 'Ah, fair Zenocrate, divine Zenocrate! Fair is too foul an epithet for thee', stocky in his business suit, Miss Iden standing by. Making no effort to charm, he took us all by the hand and gave us an unforgettable experience. 'Old-fashioned', 'ham', 'modern', 'contemporary' were meaningless adjectives to apply to something that clearly was the Real Thing. At the end of the performance, he acknowl-edged the tumultuous reception and was gone, striding out rapidly and nimbly, leaving his still-smiling wife to scurry after him as best she could. The artist wasn't much of a gent, I thought, even as I savoured the wonder of the afternoon. It was good to see the abashed faces in the auditorium that he had conquered.

A few months later I was made despondent by a conversation I over-heard among those same bright, young men of the Dramatic Society who had been cowed and abashed that day by the quality of Wolfit's acting. 'Ah well,' said one, 'it's an old-fashioned style, of course.' Brutes, I thought, realising the fearful tyranny of fashion.

That was the best acting I saw while I was an undergraduate and for the rest of the time I had to content myself with reading about actors whom I imagined to be wonderful. Edith Evans, whom I'd never seen, was still my favourite, and I read and re-read her autobiography and her notices and the parts she played until I imagined I could hear her voice.

Chapter Eighteen

My workload at the BBC increased and it became apparent that some kind of plan had to be formulated. Moelwyn Merchant had been my first tutor when I entered the Honours School. He became an ally. He shared my opinion of myself in *Othello*. 'Oh, you poor dear,' he exclaimed the morning after the first performance. 'That hair! That pink dress! You looked like a meringue.' Pleased and maybe surprised that I took this in good part and agreed with him, he threw me a crumb. 'On the whole *not* good, but that is exactly the way to play the willow scene.' He knew that I was wearing a track between the back door of the university and the front door of the BBC. He also knew and approved of my intention of going into the theatre and understood that I really did need to graduate for my parents' sake. He drew up a plan for me and said, 'Now, this is the work you *must* do; these are the essays you *must* write and this is the minimum attendance below which you *cannot* fall. Let's see how you get on.'

Well, I got on. Just. There were some awful moments. By now I was working as a 'relief' announcer as well as acting, and this meant that I opened the station very early in the morning and closed it late at night after the Epilogue and, in between, did a lot of the jobs that no one else wanted. I was never paid much for what was a prodigious amount of work. Iris Evans, who wrote the cheques at the BBC, used to say, 'Having your name in the *Radio Times* is worth £1,000 per year. No dear, I can't pay you more money.' It never bothered me. I always seemed to have enough money, but I was never aware of having lots more than my fellow students. Some of my friends were rather wealthy. I bought books, as usual, and began to buy a few smart clothes as well.

I loved presentation work. When I began I was a well-covered ten stone three, which was about right for my five foot, seven and three-quarter inches. Within months I was eight stone, the result of living in a permanent state of high anxiety (which I loved). I had always been dreamy – never wore a watch, never knew what day it was – and now I had to alter completely because from the moment I sat at my console in the tiny continuity suite, I was in control of everything that went out over the air, from my studio, and from all the other studios all over Wales and England. The least adept person imaginable, I had three turntables to operate; one on either side of my central control 'pot' (microphone control) and one large one on which I played daily 'soaps' or programmes lasting twenty minutes. Minutes and seconds had to be calculated precisely. I had to learn to write announcements that would last exactly the required number of seconds before I faded myself out and brought up another studio. It was a nightmare.

Morfydd Mason-Lewis, a wonderful broadcaster and a senior announcer, the best-known voice in Wales, was teaching me the ropes one day and I was thinking that this was a terrible venture, best forgotten, when she said, 'All right, I'm off. Take the next shift,' and left the room. My thumping heart moved high into my chest and stayed there. My damp hands slipped on the controls as I frantically added and subtracted and scribbled. Occasionally, through the glass panel on my right, I saw my engineer, grinning broadly. I had no sense that anyone was listening to me, but my mother had heard my voice and stopped in her tracks, horrified. 'Oh, it was terrible,' she said. 'I kept expecting everything to go wrong.'

I would wake up at night convinced that I'd announced the wrong programme or allowed everything to overrun and had been late joining the *Nine O'clock News* – the worst crime imaginable. Becoming a radio actress had been a breeze compared with the rigours of being engaged as an announcer. It was assumed that one was fluently bilingual, decent at one other European language and canny with foreign words in general. Every broadcast sound passed through the little continuity studio, so announcers were expected to be deft with the turntables and their controlling knobs, familiar with the pronunciation sheets that came in from London each day, careful at noting timing of programmes or the length of recordings, and tactful with one's own announcements or one's filling in of unexpected gaps so that one programme seamlessly fed into the next. Technical mistakes were unacceptable. 'Kerfuffles', as the Head of Continuity called them – one's own, or hitches occurring in studios – were carefully logged and explanations and excuses noted. The Kerfuffle Column was amazingly empty considering that we were all on the air live most of the time.

The BBC was proud of its technical near-perfection and the rest of us were expected to keep up. Overrunning was a cardinal sin. Having to fade out a programme in order to re-join the schedule on time or link up with London or Scotland was embarrassing in the extreme and somehow became a continuity error. It was expected that we should exert a tight grip on everyone's activities. The tension was killing. I had to strain every nerve to exert more care than ever before in my slapdash life.

And that was just the beginning; there was Attitude to cope with. One had to speak with authority tempered with a neutral friendliness – not *too* distant, be human; not too chummy, you're *not* anyone's friend, you're entering someone's home and you are expected to be one hundred per cent reliable, but remember always that you don't know what is *happening* in the home; don't impose a mood on them. You are speaking to millions and you are speaking to one or two people. Be natural. Being 'natural' wiped me out and I ached all over at the end of a shift.

Advancing to the status of newsreader was even worse and my first time out – twenty-five minutes of terror in English and Welsh – half prepared and half unseen, was listened to everywhere in the building. The ordeal was made worse by the sympathy and good wishes that came my way as I left Tom Richards, the editor, in the newsroom and raced back to my studio, clutching what there was of the news bulletin (extra bits arrived when we were on the air). Everyone knew that it was a major hurdle to get over. I was just eighteen and I had added two years to my age in order to be considered for the job. As I switched myself on to the air, identified the station and, taking a deep breath, forced a smile on to my face and said 'Here is the six o'clock news,' I'd wished I'd never been born. Twenty-four minutes and ten seconds later I was reading the last story – one I'd never seen – with one eye on the second hand and, coming into harbour at twenty-four minutes and fifty seconds, I reached for my previously written announcement for the next programme, timed and checked before the News began. Then I switched through to another studio, waited for the programme to begin, and laid my head on the desk among the mountain of discarded bits of paper. Looking up, I saw the engineer next door raise his fists in a victory salute. I felt as though I had climbed a mountain.

There had been no mistakes, but that was taken for granted; there was more Attitude to absorb. Light-hearted news stories were not to be presented as 'jokes', they were to be presented to the listener 'clean'. People weren't supposed to be *made* to laugh. Serious or tragic items were not to be dramatised or sentimentalised or sensationalised; the 'appropriate' tone had to be found. One had to get a move on without ever seeming to hurry, nor should it ever be apparent that one was stretching an item to fill in time. The list of dos and don'ts was endless. At the post-mortem of my maiden voyage, it was Attitude that took up most of the time. It was a bit like an acting job – trying to be the sort of person that people wanted in their homes. The chief note to me was 'No acting' and I thought it better not to reveal that I would have to act 'no acting' if I was going to make a go of this complicated job, which I grew to love. I was very well taught by Morfydd Mason-Lewis and her deputy Harvard Gregory, and I didn't ever make a mistake or 'fluff' during a news bulletin. My parents thought I'd had a personality change and for the first time I think my grandmother was impressed.

Of course I made some awful mistakes along the way, some so bad that they got me suspended. One of my nastiest moments in the studio occurred when, after having started the Epilogue disc in a tired state one night, I then had to lean over it to read the duration time. As I revolved my head gently in time to the slow circling of the turntable, my chiffon scarf caught in the special rod that held the playing-arm steady. With one hand I flapped wildly at the window to the engineer's cubicle as my face was slowly and relentlessly drawn down towards the turntable. As I tried to hold steady, keeping disaster at bay until the last possible moment, I feverishly attempted to compose in my head an announcement that would explain the horrible noise and the untimely end of the Epilogue that was about to occur at any moment. 'We must apologise to listeners but the Epilogue just ate my scarf.' Hardly. The engineer happened to look up and, seeing my unnaturally still head and an agitated arm, stampeded out of his little studio, through my ante-room, crashing into the studio just in time to cut me free and gently unpick the chiffon from the machine. 'Now, believe it or not, Siân,' he said, 'that's never happened before!' The engineers were my friends and saviours, which was just as well.

I had by now joined an Arts Council Theatre Company, dedicated to establishing a Welsh-speaking National Theatre. Raymond Edwards, who was later to become the first principal of the Welsh College of Music and Drama, was our young director of *Uncle Vanya* in which I played Elena. There weren't enough 'real' theatres in Wales, so we toured for a year, all over the country, playing in buildings that were more or less the right size and more or less suitable.

Waking one morning in my flat in Roath Park, very tired after a one-night stand of *Uncle Vanya*, goodness knows where (I very rarely knew exactly *where* we were playing), I reached out an arm and turned on the radio in time to hear a London voice saying, '. . . and now we hand you over to Siân Phillips in Cardiff'. Nothing happened for a moment, then with one bound, collecting my mac and shoes on the way, I was in the street running towards the main road in my pyjamas. It was early and the roads were deserted; a solitary car happened along and the driver, seeing my desperate face, stopped and rushed me to the BBC, rather enjoying the drama (which I was not).

Fortunately, Cardiff is a compact city and, with no traffic on the road, I was in my chair within twelve minutes and switching off Bow Bells, which had been playing over and over again since the London handover. The Bow Bells record was used as a filler, but *never* for more than twenty seconds. That was a Rule. The outbreak of World War Three might just justify ten minutes of bells – might, but probably not. I switched on my microphone and announced, 'We must apologise to listeners for . . . [thinks] . . . a technical fault at the transmitter,' I lied. I maligned the engineering department. I was an outcast. The phone didn't stop for hours. By ten o'clock I was on the carpet in the Alun Oldfield-Davies Suite where I had never before set foot and never would again. I think the august Reithian figure of the Head of Welsh Programmes may have wanted to see what sort of creature could commit such a crime. My suspension didn't last long and I was soon back in the bosom of a forgiving bunch of engineers.

I loved those days. The hours were long and the work was very demanding. I began to travel with the BBC Orchestra on outside broadcasts, writing their scripts and timing the programmes, and meeting the artists from London and taking care of them. Our orchestra did broadcasts of *Concert Hour* and *Music of the Masters* from halls and chapels all over the valleys near Cardiff, and artists were sometimes a little taken aback by the primitive conditions. I remember wondering whether one artist would be able to do the show as she lay on the floor of the shabby vestry in a none too glamorous concert frock while her worried husband poured warm oil into her ear (it seemed she was a martyr to pains in her cranial passages). When she struggled to her feet and began to sing, I was stupefied. I was no expert but this was surely a *major* voice.

Why wasn't she a star? I looked up her name again in order to give her a terrific back-announcement. 'You have been listening to . . .' – Joan Sutherland – surely she deserved better than a village chapel in the back of beyond.

Rae Jenkins, the conductor, was lovely and always impatient. 'Where's that bloody girl?' ringing around the corridors was my cue to appear with my clipboard and with everything he might need to know at my fingertips. Only once did I let him down. The visiting soprano was about to reach for an inadvisable high note, and Rae leaned forward over the podium, but I – miles away in a reverie – was too slow to switch off the mic as Rae hissed at the first violins urgently, and '*Drown 'er, boys!*' went out over the air. He didn't speak to me for a week.

I was engrossed in this world and was finding enough time on the tour of *Uncle Vanya* to be able to put some of my notions about acting into practice. Sometimes I was, I thought, almost getting there. Mostly, not. In spite of this, I was coming in for a great deal of flattering attention.

I wrote my English essays in the continuity suite and it showed. My new tutor was S.L. Bethel. 'Pretty lousy,' he said, smiling sweetly as he returned to me the first of my 'BBC' essays for him. Oh help. My worst mark ever. What to do? Briefed by Moelwyn, he also became a friend. He and his wife invited me to tea and outlined a strategy for me. I was terminally tired and, to further complicate things, I had become 'properly', publicly, engaged. 'You're far too young,' said everyone. My fiancé, Don, was a post-graduate student whom I'd known off and on since I came up. I had also been on holiday with him. My mother had been thoroughly against my proposed trip to Sweden with two young men from the university, Don and his friend, Ray. I was nineteen and they were older. I'd first seen Don playing Troilus in *Troilus and Cressida* at College. He was a good actor, handsome, neat, incredibly well-organised, mad about cricket. I found him so capable that I thought of him as belonging to an older generation altogether. He seemed to know what he was doing and for a brief while I enjoyed believing him when he said he knew what I should be doing. Ahead of him lay two years of National Service and another couple of years in Paris completing his doctorate. 'You must be *amazingly* clever,' I thought, looking at him sideways as we walked along Queen Street.

My parents were guarded in their response when we returned from Sweden somewhat closer than we'd been when we departed. They liked and respected Don, but they had Doubts. So did Don's parents. This was why they'd been reluctant to let us go off for a summer in Scandinavia. Although I'd asked permission, I'd been determined to go. I could fund the journey myself and the young men were respectable and so were my prospective hosts, friends of Ray's. Their estate was beautiful and – well, there was nothing she could put her finger on, but my mother felt it was Wrong and would lead to Trouble. She couldn't, though, think of a way of forbidding the trip without saying something coarse and I enjoyed her discomfiture.

For the first time I was going to do something that had no obvious advantageous outcome. My mother was better off than she had ever been, but holidays still didn't enter into her scheme of things. Of course, they didn't enter into mine either. When I said, 'I'm going to Sweden for the summer', I felt as though it was someone else talking and, unreasonably, I pretended to my mother that I thought taking the summer off was a perfectly natural thing for me to do. I blamed her for the fact that I was secretly appalled by the waste of working time and by the daring company I'd chosen. She brooded silently, spoke little, and glowered at me when our eyes met. I made as if I didn't notice and enjoyed infuriating her.

It was difficult for my parents. They had moved away from their families. Life near the big city was very different from life at 'Home'. There was no telephone on the farm. (Her brother's telephone was never used for chatting.) They were isolated; there were no neighbours. There was no village with its terms of reference and clear guidelines for behaviour. My parents didn't quite know what kind of life I was leading. They were adrift without a map and so was I to a certain extent, but I wanted to make a new map for myself. Defiantly, I drew a line from Wales to Sweden.

Sweden was beautiful beyond my imagining and on one of the long summer nights I became engaged. Together with Ray, Don and I spent the idyllic summer walking and idling and dozing through the days, eating delicious food. We were there for the crayfish season and went to Kräftor parties that went on late into the night – huge trestle tables piled high with red crayfish set up under the trees, and we were fed a sip of schnapps between each bite of crayfish. It never got really dark at night and we scarcely slept. The schnapps and the party atmosphere and the long lilac nights were a heady combination. Don and I grew closer and closer, and what could be more delightful than to arrive at an understanding in such a romantic situation? He was not only attractive and charming; he took care of me when the idyll ended and I became ill on the long journey home. We were in love by the time we returned to Wales, and had it not been for my ambition – conveniently forgotten during the romantic holiday – there was no reason why our proposed marriage shouldn't have turned out well. He was everything a normal woman could want in a husband.

After I returned I tried not to spoil our happiness with thoughts of how this marriage could accommodate my plans for myself, plans that hadn't changed at all but that appeared unrealistic to everyone except me. I hid my head in the sand. I hadn't told my mother anything much on my return, but now that, a few months later, I was about to become publicly, officially engaged, with a ring – and presents – my parents had to be told about it. I didn't want to tell them and was filled with apprehension.

Their reaction was everything I feared. They were taken aback. There was silence. Why, I thought, couldn't they just say 'How wonderful! Congratulations'? The fact that I myself was filled with anxiety was utterly beside the point. My fiancé-to-be was everything they could have wished – clever, brilliant, handsome, sober, reliable – and they didn't want it to happen. I could tell. I was furious. I knew from the way my mother's remarks were heading that she was trying to raise the question of my possible pregnancy. Did I *have* to get married was the question she couldn't bring herself to say and I wanted to smash crockery, I was so enraged. How dare she pry into my private life and how could she think I could be so *stupid*? Even as I sat looking at the floor or paced about looking everywhere except at them, I understood that they were trying to articulate the fears that were running riot in me.

Understanding how unreasonably I was behaving did not prevent me from becoming even more contrary. I had tapped into a vein of resentment against my mother that threatened to engulf me. Engagements logically lead to weddings. Where did a wedding fit into my plans? It didn't. It couldn't. The moment my mother pointed out this problem, the engagement was determinedly *on*. The future might never arrive. My fiancé went to Paris to write his doctorate and I missed him and moped and worked and tried not to think of the problems I was laying up for myself.

After graduating I would need a miracle to get me out of Wales and headed for the Theatre, and I didn't know anyone who had managed it.

It hadn't come to my ears that a girl from Aberystwyth University had already done the seemingly impossible and was *in* the theatre in England. Rachel Roberts from Swansea was bold; she was a free spirit; she took all her clothes off in public – in *Aberystwyth*, such a stiflingly respectable non-conformist heap in those days that the odd swear-word would have been enough to damn her as a loose woman. The enormity of Rachel's behaviour seemed to have paralysed the authorities. She wasn't sent down, but she was talked about in hushed tones for years after in the Principality. But just when I needed her most, her fame had not spread south to Cardiff, and when it did, it merely depressed me.

If that was *it*, if that was what it took, then I was *never* going to be able to behave like an actress. I couldn't even *look* like one. The leading lights of the University Dramatic Society were outstandingly good-looking and very *noticeable*. They were English-speaking with voices that carried effortlessly across the Union dining room. They always seemed to be at the centre of a merry throng, they tossed their heads and laughed, and they were clever with clothes. My wardrobe was still full of mistakes that I had to live with. All the things I needed and wanted were hideously expensive and most of them were unavailable in Cardiff.

I tried not to think of Christian Dior and concentrated on my real problems, which were multiplying as the weeks went by. I was approaching the end of my time at the university; one year to go and Moelwyn called me in for one of his infrequent but uncomfortably worrying chats. We sat in a garden, I on a swing, and I knew I wasn't going to enjoy the ensuing half-hour. 'Your life,' he began. 'I don't think you've given enough thought to your engagement and what it is that will quite reasonably be required of you.' He was going to be the Reverend. He doubted whether I was going to be able to do the Right Thing. Had I considered my vocation? Better to stop now than create havoc later. Did I realise what a fine, sensitive person I'd become involved with?

I was accustomed to feeling like a victim and now he was making me feel like the Witch of Endor, and I didn't like that at all. I couldn't tell him that I was feeble-minded enough to dread upsetting the apple cart almost more than I dreaded messing up two lives. And why me? Why wasn't he having this conversation with my fiancé? I looked glum and said nothing much.

'Please consider carefully,' he said pleasantly enough. 'Now – work,' he said, to my relief. 'I am assuming that you are not prepared to give up your position in the Arts Council Company. Nor, I take it, would you want to stop working at the BBC. Nor,' he went on as I made to speak, 'do I think you should.' That surprised me; I'd been expecting a sophisticated version of the Sally Tŷ mawr lecture that I'd been hearing since I was ten. 'You now have to make a choice,' he went on. 'Having considered your work for me, I think there is a chance that, were you to concentrate on your work for the whole of next year, to the exclusion of everything else, you could – just could – do well enough to get a First. If you continue with your outside work then you will not. This is the moment to choose what you want.' It was horribly grown-up; actions to choose, consequences to accept.

Then he closed that conversation and we talked of other things, and he shocked me into laughter as he spoke of a recent Shakespeare performance on film, almost universally praised, which he had found particularly brainless and appalling. We said goodbye and I went to visit my parents feeling more ill at ease than usual. Whatever my choice I doubted that it would please my mother; good work at the university and marriage. No marriage, possibly a bad result and a career. Career? That was completely unknown territory – every chance of total failure. As usual I dithered and confided in no one.

Chapter Nineteen

So I embarked on what were to be my last few years in Wales and the most difficult to account for. The sequence of events had no logic, no shape, no meaning for me. Maybe I had dug myself into a hole so deep that I stopped reviewing my scanty escape routes, and more than possibly, as I floundered mindlessly from one month to the next, I became increasingly reluctant to confront my behaviour except in isolated, appalled moments, quickly shaken off and put aside. At nineteen I looked back at the child and the young girl who had lain in bed and reviewed the contents of the day just past, assessing and judging or approving and tidying up before composedly going to sleep. I had cleaned my house each day and now I was depressed to see how far I had fallen from grace – grace gone for good, it seemed, as I flung myself into an exhausted, comatose state or read until the book fell from my fingers and woke in the bright lights of morning and my bedside lamp.

It was as though, after years of focused behaviour, of keeping true to my private resolves, of making sacrifices where necessary and living a life the nature of which was dictated by discipline and feeling the constant pleasure of moving forward in the right direction – knowing I was doing the right thing and *approving* of myself – now I became childish and thoughtless and foolish and I *dis*approved of myself and was miserable. So I slipped and floundered and stumbled and kept my head above water – just. I didn't know and I didn't dare discover why I was so angry with my mother, for example, but it was clear that relations between us took an ugly, inexplicably violent turn.

By this time, I had taken lodgings in Richmond Road with a Mrs Lewis. My home was a large front room in her house where she lived as a widow with her two grown-up sons who lived upstairs while she and I occupied the ground floor and shared her bathroom. She fed me in the cosy back living room next to the kitchen and I can't imagine that she profited at all during my two years with her because she overhauled my slapdash eating habits (mostly cigarettes with tiny amounts of food in between packets) and saw to it that I ate two huge 'proper' meals daily during the week and three meals a day at weekends, charging me £2.25 for board and lodging. She was white-haired and pink-and-white complexioned, inclined to stoutness and in manner the softest spoken, most gentle person I had ever been close to and we *were* close; she was happy to have a daughter-figure in whom to confide and to fuss over, and I was delighted to find in myself a simple, uncomplicated, affectionate daughter.

We lived in perfect harmony in spite of the fact that she was a fervent spiritualist trying, and never succeeding, in her efforts to persuade me along to a 'meeting'. That is until, on a sunny, spring day in Cardiff, every garden overstuffed with daffodils, I found myself in a little parlour where a cheerful little medium described in detail the layout and contents of the announcer's suite in the BBC in Cardiff. Then she seemed to be describing a much bigger broadcasting house, which was strange to me because at that time I had never worked at Bush House in London. I wish that I had known then that the doorway she described, flanked by two stone figures, was 62 Gower Street in London, the home of the Royal Academy of Dramatic Art. As it was, I wondered, after a moment's surprised pause, how she knew about the continuity suite, a place seldom visited even by the staff of the BBC, and then dismissed her sympathetic warnings of a 'Bad Time' to come before the 'Good Time', when I would enter the building with the big stone figures at the door. 'Well, what did you think to her?' asked Mrs Lewis as we walked to the bus stop. 'Miss-us Lewis,' I said, giving her an affectionate squeeze. We each shook our heads, smiling at the other's limited sensibilities.

On other matters we agreed, and I, who had never confided anything in anyone, enjoyed our chats – heavily censored on my part – about Boys and Food and Frocks and she told me about her wonderfully happy marriage. 'He was such a good man – never . . .' – whispering now – '*bothered* me too much. You know . . .' I was so enjoying my dear daughter role that I, who couldn't imagine anything better than to be constantly bothered, nodded enthusiastically. She made it easy for me to be thoroughly 'nice', and I hoped that she would never know what a fiend I could be.

The academic year drew to a close and I stopped working in order to prepare for the Honours exam. Don came home for a holiday and there were rumblings of discontent on his part over my acting plans for the summer. These deepened into arguments about the future – our future; more specifically my future as a wife. Well, of course, I *had* no future as a wife on a campus – in Cardiff or anywhere. I began to inch the conversations around to this, making tentative noises about the possibility that a mistake had been made and that maybe we should call the whole thing off. (I had found that this was the usual progression of events and although it always made me sad for a while, well, it wasn't the end of the world.) But events did not follow this course and I began to see that I was not going to be allowed off the hook with just a few tears of regret. He was angry and hurt and terribly, terribly upset, and intent on holding me to my side of the bargain.

I was alarmed. The situation had escalated in no time at all from a difficult one, fraught with future problems, into a compelling, very present crisis with no apparent solution. Exams were looming. Even mild-spoken Mrs Lewis (who had seen her own schoolteacher son through his exams) said, 'I hope you're not going to be seeing each other during the next few weeks.' My mother, with a flash of her old, confident conviction said, 'You stay at home, alone, and SWOT for the next few weeks.' A 'few' weeks were negotiated down to two weeks and, feeling hard done by, I grimly settled down to a fortnight of cramming against the two weeks of exams that followed. Normally this would be something to be enjoyed, but now, thoroughly unnerved by the turn of events, I was rattled. However, I managed to pull myself together and my temperament came to the rescue; at my best in a tight spot, I kept my head and organised myself back on track. Exams began well and I got into the swing of things and even coped nicely with the dreaded *Beowulf* and the other language papers. My best paper was metaphysical poetry, and the night before the exam I heaved a sigh of relief as I flicked through the texts with which I was truly familiar. Tomorrow was going to be a good day, my best, my easiest day. And we were almost at the end.

There was a tap at my window. It was Don. He'd not been able to keep to our arrangement that I should be left alone for the two weeks of exams. But he wouldn't stay long, he said. There were just a few things bothering him. Before we knew it we were in the thick of a huge, emotional discussion about my intentions, my future, our future. Hours went by. Mrs Lewis tapped at the door. Normal bedtime had arrived. Then her son looked in to the room and retreated. It seemed that nothing could halt this awful circular argument. There was a big bag of cherries at my side, which I mistook for an ashtray. I chain-smoked and ate dirty cherries covered in damp ash and cried and lost my temper, and finally, in the early hours of the morning, we parted and I spent the few remaining hours throwing up in the bathroom.

In the morning I managed to make it to the examination hall in time, but, fighting waves of nausea, did very little writing. I kept thinking I would have to leave and be sick, but that would mean I couldn't return and somehow I remained in the room hoping I would, miraculously, feel better. I didn't and I left the building hardly able to believe my ill fortune. And as I began to recover, misery and disappointment were replaced by outrage that he could have treated me so badly in a situation that he of all people should have understood.

The sense of outrage never went away, but we never spoke of this awful night and its consequences for me. He must have felt guilty. It cost me dear, though; in the event, it was one of those years that happen from time to time when the marking was so strict that people dropped a class below the one expected and there were a few Thirds and even Unclassifieds. There was a bit of a rumpus and complaints were made, and then, as usual, the fuss died down. Moelwyn mourned my Lower Second (my mother couldn't bring herself to speak about it). I didn't tell him or my mother that I'd fatally missed out an entire paper.

It was the first time in my life that I'd not met or exceeded the expectations of those closest to me, and while I did not enjoy the sensation of failure it was so much a part of the malaise within me that I experienced not a sharp regret at a moment of opportunity missed, but a resigned dull disappointment each time I thought about it. And every time I thought of my engagement, I *did* think about it and of my weakness that night during exams. *Why* had I not been able to put my foot down and refuse to get drawn into a row? It should have been a simple matter to postpone the argument and let Mrs Lewis show him the door. I would have been within my rights at that moment, during the most testing week of any student's career. This was *my* time. *My* future.

What had happened was that for the first time I was being called to account. This relationship was not going to fade away gently and, regretfully, it was clear that I was going to have to answer for my behaviour. I had summoned up feelings I couldn't control in a person who was not inclined to be fobbed off by some vague expression of regret. And I felt guilty. It was my own lax behaviour, my sentimentality, my lack of responsibility that had led to a situation where I stood bereft of any sense of what was due to me; I felt as though through my bad behaviour I'd forfeited my own rights and everywhere I looked a door seemed to close. I was trapped and full of regret; mutinous and resentful at the same time.

Confiding in no one, I went back to work at the BBC and was actually happy while I was there. I couldn't accept the possibility that maybe this was the only way I could be happy – at work. It seemed so unwomanly to say outright that work was so much more significant than my emotional life. My mother seemed to be on the brink of saying something of the sort whenever the conversation came round to marriage, the position of women or my future. I headed her off. I didn't want that said aloud. What was it about me that made all those who cared most for me, who wanted to help me, shake their heads, smile ruefully and say, 'Sorry but it's not for you'? Childishly, I wanted everything. 'I want. I want. I want. Why *not* me?' And to what end was I supposed to be renouncing my private life? I was marooned with no prospects of getting away, getting on.

In the middle of this confusion I decided to see through a project I'd undertaken earlier. Philosophy had become my favourite subject and I'd managed to get into the Honours School. There were only three of us and Professor de Selincourt really resisted taking on a woman, but I'd worn him down and now I wanted to complete a Philosophy degree. It seemed ludicrous to take on what was really another diversion, but in fact it was the only sensible thing I did during this period and it afforded me endless solace and enjoyment. The patterns of logic were so beautifully inevitable and so *manageable*. While I tried to follow complex arguments, time stopped and life – horrible, messy life – was excluded for a while. In a year I was to marry – all discussion on this subject had been exhausted. My life seemed fixed, but I didn't really believe it.

Chapter Twenty

If I'd worked hard before, it was as nothing compared to the regime I now set myself. *Uncle Vanya* was still touring. We travelled the Welsh countryside by special bus and it was evident that the Welsh appetite for drama was unquenchable. We were paid very little, were often cold and damp, but Nesta Harris of the Welsh Arts Council did her level best to look after us and I felt very lucky to be experiencing a kind of theatre that I suspected had long died out elsewhere. Some weeks, we were literally barn-storming, arriving in a village in the late afternoon, unpacking our costumes, fitting up our, by now, ramshackle scenery and unloading furniture, the actors and stage manager running round the shops, the post office and the pub (men only here, of course) to remind people that we had arrived.

I loved being an Actress in Town. It felt great to be striding down the deserted main street of a village, knowing that in a few hours' time everyone would be crowding into the little hall to watch the play. Two muffled, capped, old men leaned on the windowsill of the village store smoking their pipes and one of them removed his pipe to say to his friend in Welsh as Maggie John and I passed by in the deserted street, 'Duw – there's a pair of high-steppers for you!' I glowed. It was true! In my yellow jersey and my red shoes, blue skirt swinging, I felt like a thoroughbred pony.

At 7.30 p.m. miraculously, as if from nowhere, there was an audience that was augmented during Act I with people from outlying farms arriving after milking was done. Playing in the country was very different from playing in town. It was pretty certain that Chekhov had never been performed in some of the halls and chapel vestries where we were touring, and the play, which had previously been respectfully received and well liked, now provoked gales of laughter and loud comments that startled me at first, but that I quickly became used to and indeed grew to like. I hadn't known that Chekhov was supposed to be so funny, but this felt all right. The response was artless and uninhibited, never coarse or mindless. We were, of course, acting in Welsh, and that Chekhov world that all actors love to inhabit for the few hours allotted to them each night had never seemed so seductive, so convincing as it was then, played in my own language.

I was Elena, and some nights I was good, I could tell I was good, but I didn't know why and I couldn't reproduce my better performances. Some nights I was painfully aware that I was bad and I couldn't put things right. The harder I tried, the worse I became. These were awful nights and afterwards I lay awake feeling as if the whole point of my existence was disappearing. I did all the wrong things to try to remedy matters; I tried and tried and strained and struggled and read Stanislavski and tried to implement his exercises and got everything wrong. I read books about actors long dead. I filled exercise books with notes, took advice from anyone, anywhere, kept a journal that mostly charted and analysed my failures. Praise was no help at all; I simply didn't believe it. I *knew* I was all over the place. I prayed for help to turn the corner into some kind of competence. I longed to be efficient. I longed to be *professional*. It was a sacred word. Once I was a professional most of my problems would solve themselves, I thought. Infrequently, but often enough to save me from going mad, I did what I knew to be a bit of good acting. On these occasions the relief was so great that afterwards I could not imagine feeling happier.

Towards the end of *Uncle Vanya* I became ill and played through what was later diagnosed as pleurisy. I still didn't know how ill you were supposed to be before you stopped working. I had read that *real* actors worked no matter how ill they were, and after the tour finished, as I lay alone in my room in the flat I was now sharing with friends in Cardiff, I took my medicine and drifted in and out of a sick sleep, and for the first time in ages I was pleased with myself.

I recovered and in no time was back at work, mainly at the BBC, taking care to keep well up to date with Philosophy, which wasn't difficult. The BBC was claiming more and more of my time and attention. I was deeply fond of the institution where I had, more or less, grown up. I loved the studios and the storerooms and the library and the staff, some of whom had been there since the early days of broadcasting. The commissionaire had 'seen *everyone* come and go, Siân'. He told me that once, during a live drama performance many, many years ago, he'd brought a cart horse in through the big front door, turned left past the front desk, then right down a pair of steps to the wide corridor outside Studio 2, and, at the appropriate moment in the play, the studio manager had flung open the door and he'd walked the horse up and down on the hard floor while the actors played a rustic scene involving a cart horse on a microphone positioned inside the door, as another assistant stage manager stood guard at the front door to make sure that no one came through making inappropriate noises. 'They were a bit short of effects disks in the beginning. Naturally, we took the phone off the hook at the front desk for the duration of the scene.'

I leaned on his desk at night when the staff had gone home and we were almost the last people in the building, and he talked on and I listened and I didn't bother to wonder if he was being strictly truthful. I wanted to be part of the fable of my favourite place. I never turned into the walkway between two converted houses in Park Place without feeling a kick of excitement in my middle. The continuity suite office was a former box-room on the first floor of one of the houses, not much wider than its window that overlooked the front entrance. Sitting there, writing scripts or making up the skeleton shape of pages for *Radio Times* with little descriptions of the programmes, I could keep an eye on everyone entering or leaving the building, and since I was there very early I was able to observe who came to work early and eagerly, and who came in late – hungover, blinking against the light as they hurried up the short drive.

One famous lady director always came late, making a star entrance, svelte in black, fur stole slung on one shoulder, an Osbert Lancaster figure in a big hat, accompanied by her small, less imposing husband (he was an engineer with a trembling hand – a bad combination). Once ensconced in her office she took off the trappings she showed the world as she retrieved her considerable mind from the fog induced by the excesses of the night before and vigorously laid about her. Running for cover, her secretary would come and sit in my office for brief respites from the mayhem upstairs. 'Oh Miss Phillips, can I sit for a minute? She's *in*. Her feet are on the table and her teeth are in the in-tray. It's terrible this morning. We've got a day ahead of us.'

When I joined as a child, until I left at twenty-one, it was still very much an 'us' organisation. Live radio was exciting and in a crisis all hands went to the pump; cleaners and canteen staff chipped in unasked with praise and blame. Everyone in the building scrutinised everyone and everything.

The directors were almost without exception buccaneering types with a touch of the Red Queen about them. Working for drama director John Griffiths involved delicious terror. During transmission he would shake his fist at us from his directorial chair if he felt the performance was slipping a bit. We were on the air live, so there wasn't much else he could do, but if goaded beyond endurance, he would leave the control cubicle and there would be muffled thuds as he made his way through a series of soundproofed doors and into the studio. He was the only person I knew who could stamp on tiptoe. He would interpose his furious face between one's script and the microphone, and semaphore violent instructions. And he did a lot of on-the-air editing (which is really living dangerously) and would dash around the studio tearing pages out of our scripts and throwing them on the floor. (This was in the days when the BBC could afford lovely thick paper that didn't rustle, though oddly enough the loo paper has always been hopeless – little leaves, stiff and shiny and quite horrible.) John turned out first-class programmes, but he was a law unto himself.

So was Lorraine Davies, a dark, gypsy beauty and one of the most brilliant directors at the BBC, with the temper and temperament of a Cecil B. DeMille. The control console table in the director's cubicle could only just withstand the pounding of her fists as she lashed the company on to greater efforts. I think the directors were so on the edge and so volatile because radio is a maximum-effort medium. It demands huge amounts of physical energy. Lorraine gave me one of my first big star parts; it was to play a male cat called Ginger Tom in a *Children's Hour* serial and that was more draining than Saint Joan or Medea ever proved to be. Shortly after I began to present programmes on television, I was told that TV is a cool medium and demands a much more relaxed approach. Less, on camera, is invariably better than more. That may be. Radio is hot. *That* I know.

I was so beguiled by the BBC that, immensely flattered to be approached, I seriously considered an offer to join the staff and train as an 'anchor' on current affairs programmes, eventually to replace a famous woman broadcaster in London who was planning to retire. I'd begun interviewing and had even done a small outside-broadcast commentary. All this was still frightening me to death, but I did love it and my mother would have been *so* pleased with me. In her eyes, working for the BBC was as good as becoming a teacher. (And I was right – my grandmother *was* impressed.) At the last moment I drew back, remembering what I wanted to be. Politely it was pointed out to me that I had very little chance of success in the theatre, so why not pursue the attainable. I felt that maybe I was making a ludicrous mistake. After all, I was as far away as ever from my dream of being a *real* actress.

All this while my personal life, patchy as it was, became more unruly than ever before. I smoked ferociously, and didn't drink to excess only because I was so naturally high the whole time that alcohol would have pitched me completely off kilter. Ignoring my engaged status, I scarcely slept and took up with a string of fascinating and unsuitable men, most of them middle-aged and well-off, with big cars and, in one instance, a trusty chauffeur-cum-valet who became my devoted slave and I doted on him rather more than I did on his master. I made up for those frightened, unhappy, chilled years in Cardiff by turning it into my nocturnal playground. A street where I'd once stood, looking west, pining for home, was transformed into the street where I'd watch the dawn come up sitting under a cashmere rug in the back of a Rolls-Royce. I drank champagne where I'd been fearful. I redrew the map of the city where I'd been so frustrated and so cold. It couldn't ever again look the same; in the small hours I made it mine, and in the daytime I faced it down and found that it had lost its power to intimidate me. I was much heartened by this piece of magic I'd wrought on my surroundings, only now that it was over, admitting to myself how deeply wretched a time I'd had, torn from my roots for what seemed an insufficient reason. Homesickness had completely overpowered me for three entire years and had been all the more severe a malady because I knew that there was no reclaiming my land of lost content. I was sure that it was gone for good. I knew it.

I began to write a novel. It was about loss and exile and loveliness, and I wept gently as I wrote. There was a café I'd found, upstairs on Churchill Way on the corner of Queen Street, and I installed myself there when I wasn't at the BBC, and drank coffee, and wrote and wrote for hours on end. I was a stranger to the writer's block. I think I was trying to write a solution to my life. One day, I thought, I would look down at the page and there it would be: the answer! Eureka! The end. Or rather the end of the beginning. The heroine was a musician, but she looked remarkably like me. I tried to extricate her from the impossible chains of duty and obligation and liberate her into a world of happiness and music. But I couldn't. She became more and more enslaved. Dreadful things happened to her. I couldn't stop the torrent of misfortune and I wept. The pages were blotched with coffee and salt water.

At night, when I slept, I dreamt that I had done something so bad that it could never be forgiven. What was it that I'd done? On waking I half thought that I'd killed someone and lay there, heart racing, feeling a bit sick. It was amazing to me how life – ordinary, rather cheerful life – could continue above such a layer of confusion and darkness. There was never any question that I couldn't get on with my work, and though I had a sense that something bad was going to happen to me I also had a tiny, inexplicable feeling that something wonderful was just around the corner.

My relationships, all illicit since I was an engaged woman, were rather charming and I couldn't feel bad about them. They were desultory, which I liked, they were undemanding, which I loved, and they were at all times pleasant and pleasurable and civil. Maybe I took a little more than I gave, but good manners prevailed throughout. I think I liked my diplomat best. He had low taste in food and we gorged ourselves on Kraft cheese slices on toast, served by a butler on the best Spode. We both had reason to be discreet and on the whole we were circumspect, but as I scandalously ran into my future father-in-law as I emerged from the Angel Hotel after an afternoon's dalliance, I realised that I truly wanted to be found out. As is the way of these things, I wasn't.

My marriage approached. I tidied up my personal life. That is, I said a fond farewell to my gentlemen. I passed my last exams. Now, if ever, was the time to get on with my life as I wished it to be. But how? There were rows and tears and scenes, endless scenes. No one seemed to notice. It was like living in a waking dream. I was making my fiancé so unhappy already. Part of me could remember why it was that we had fallen in love in the first place and I was so sorry that it had come to this; part of me, however, just wanted to survive, and that part had teeth and claws and was cruel. In the end, the coward's part prevailed. I couldn't bear to be the cause of any more unhappiness and I chose a funereal wedding dress – grey. Grey shoes, grey gloves, NO flowers.

As I put on my silly pink hat in the bedroom, my father rocked me to my foundations by saying quietly, 'You don't *have* to do this, you know.' He *knew*? I looked at him in silence. I had been feeling numb, but now I experienced a surge of conflicting feelings and the chief one I recognised was anger. Anger at my beloved father standing before me, still the handsomest man I knew, not speaking and I knew he would say no more. I loved him at that moment and was also sorry for him, but fair or unfair, reasonable or not, I was also full of animosity towards him. Why hadn't he spoken before? Why wouldn't he say more now? What pointless questions, I thought. Spiky and resentful and ungiving, I looked away and shook my head. 'I'll be all right,' I said briskly and walked out of the room.

The rest of the day was spent concealing what I could only identify as irritation; hardly a grand emotion, but I was not in a grand story. My store of anguish was all used up and when I set up home in a rented flat I did so in a calm and methodical manner, feeling that my part in the affair was all over; I'd done as much as I could and now everything could unravel naturally in its own time. My husband deserved better than this, better than me, but I also deserved better. My husband was doing his National Service. I was a faithful wife – no more wild nights. I lived alone in Cardiff and waited for what was to happen next. Soon, I thought.

Chapter Twenty-one

When Herbert Davies walked into the room I nearly laughed aloud in recognition of the arrival of a kindred spirit. He was the rescuing cavalry in the form of a well-dressed, bohemian figure spreading chaos as he moved across the space between us, scattering papers, displacing furniture, his reporter's eyes darting everywhere, not dwelling on anything but, nonetheless, hoovering up every detail. I felt as though he'd seen everything he needed to know about me in the first minute. We shook hands and he moved away at once, restlessly picking up chairs, putting them down, sitting down, standing again, looking at the view through the window, darting the occasional quizzical glance in my direction. I stood still, hardly breathing, wanting to make sure that I absorbed and remembered everything that was happening. He was talking to me about plays, about acting, and I listened with half my attention; I could afford to catch up later. For the moment the important thing was to allow this meeting to unfold uninterrupted. My fairy godmother had given me the talent of being aware of happiness as it occurred and I was happy now, more than completely, overflowingly happy. Something wonderful was happening.

I knew that Herbert was a director and a journalist on the *Western Mail*. He was soon to become the Head of the Central Office of Information in Wales and then a full-time director at the BBC in Wales before moving to Australia. At this moment he was offering me a part in a new play; maybe I was being asked to read for a part. It didn't matter. I was, I knew, going to perform as Iris in Saunders Lewis's new play – his first modern one. Herbert told me the plot and described the character. There'd be a bit of money. I wasn't interested in money. The Arts Council would produce. Saunders would emerge from his eyrie and attend rehearsals! I couldn't believe he would do that; he never went anywhere.

I left the large house in Llandaff with *Gymerwch chi Sigaret?* clutched in my arms and went home to my neat, cheerless flat and read the play twice. After the second reading I was beginning to know my lines. They really were *my* lines; this part could have been written for me. I couldn't go to bed and I read it again. Now I *did* know a good deal of it. In bed I lay and thought about the play. Had I been offered it? I hadn't been listening. I woke early, still thinking about the play, and went to work for the repertory company, finding it hard to concentrate on the schools' programme I'd been assigned to. If I played *Gymerwch chi Sigaret?* my days of doing programmes like this would be numbered I realised, pleased. I'd paid my dues, meeting visiting artists from trains, fetching their cups of tea, smoothing their way, and now *my* turn had come.

Herbert was in touch with me merely to tell me the time and date of the first rehearsal. So I *was* Iris. It was just as well. I would have died if I hadn't been given the part. The first reading was terrifying. Saunders was there and I found it very difficult not to stare at him the whole time. He was tiny *and* big, his slight, energetic figure supporting a large, noble head with a high forehead and fly-away hair and, most notice-able, huge, beautiful eyes and a sweet mouth. His voice was high and remote, and his accent, unexpectedly, northern Welsh. He was formi-dable and there was nothing he could have done to put me at my ease. I was keenly aware of being in the presence of our greatest living Welsh writer, one of our Great Thinkers, a Hero. I knew and loved yards of his verse; there was no possibility of my feeling at ease. But I did think that I understood the heroine he had written and my fears dropped away as we began to read the play.

Rehearsals were wonderful and went on for long hours – as long as they needed to. When the rehearsal rooms were closed for the night, we went to Herbert's house and his wife fed us and gave us coffee and we went on working. The most thrilling part of rehearsing was showing work to Saunders and having him correct it or approve of it or decide that he needed to rewrite. Working with Saunders as he worked on a play was the most exciting thing that had ever happened to me. And I was being helped. Herbert was able to teach me as we went along, and I began to feel like the 'real' actress I was desperate to be as Herbert met my demands and gave me more time and attention than I had any right to expect. We lived, breathed, ate and slept the play and the opening night was like a dream unfolding.

Rehearsals had been dark; the winter nights had been dark, the rehearsal rooms had been dimly lit, so had Herbert's front room. Now there was colour everywhere; *real* light, *real* colour, the kind that I'd seen in the pantomime in Swansea. I waited alone on stage in my bright red skirt (my great-grandmother's long red Welsh flannel underskirt, her *pais*, cut down to something approaching a New Look, 'foreign' sort of skirt). There were lights on me as I stood there on tiptoe, but as the curtain rose and I began to dance the opening scene to the music of *Rosenkavalier*, I was dazzled as more and more light flooded on to the stage, and it was the best I'd ever felt.

Herbert had rehearsed me to the point where I had no worries, no fears, no self-consciousness; the play, worked on now by the audience, entered a different dimension and altered, and I altered with it, half guiding it, half swept along by it and not knowing which state was which or where the new path was leading, but never in danger of missing my footing; the familiar and the unfamiliar existed side by side in the same moment.

Expectations had been high for a new play by Saunders Lewis; the audience was glittering, we were being covered by the English press (what could *they* make of it?), the response at the end was overwhelming. 'Remember tonight,' someone said afterwards. Saunders actually appeared and caused a sensation. Herbert looked as though he was relishing a private joke. He didn't say much, but he had to be pleased. We were a hit, a huge hit.

The entire tour was as exciting to me as the opening night had been. Once again, we played what seemed, on the surface, improbable, unlikely places. It didn't make any difference; performing the play was like riding the big dipper; farm-hands, sophisticates, townies, academics, all responded in the same way – rapturously – and I never wanted the ride to end.

Before it ended, Herbert and Saunders summoned me to a meeting. They made an odd pair; Saunders was so small, so wispy, so unbendingly tough and Herbert so large, so physically present, so flexible and enquiring. Now he deferred to Saunders – the poet as the strategist. To my amazement, Saunders, the Welsh Nationalist, opened the conversation by saying that it was time for me to leave Wales. 'You must train,' he said, 'and you must train in the best place, surrounded by the best theatre. So you must go to London as soon as possible.'

I looked at Herbert, who remained expressionless. My heart was pounding and I couldn't respond. Did he know that I had just married? This was non-conformist Wales and at that moment I was all non-conformist girl. Didn't being married effectively preclude any chance I might have had of getting away? I didn't voice my question. I could feel Herbert regarding me quizzically. How much did he know? How much had he told Saunders about my situation? There wasn't much he could have said. No one except myself knew anything about the circumstances of my marriage, only that it had abruptly occurred. If I appeared to be uncertain, they might both turn away from me.

Saunders was waiting for me to speak and the silence was lengthening. Making some huge omissions I said, speaking the literal truth, 'That is what I most want.' 'Very well,' said Saunders briskly. 'Understand that this is not going to be an easy road to travel. Examine your motives very carefully and be prepared for considerable hardship.'

I nodded and Herbert took over, saying that he would send for the application forms to the Academy and coach me for my audition. 'However,' he went on, 'in my opinion you won't get anywhere much until you are forty, so I suggest that we make it clear that unless you're good enough for a scholarship you are not going to go to RADA at all.'

I was appalled. Forty? Again I remembered Rhydwen's words years ago. At twenty I couldn't even imagine being as old as forty. It was a lifetime of waiting. What did he mean? It wasn't the moment to start an argument and I stifled my protests. I did, however, question the wisdom of holding out for a scholarship. I had no idea how good I was, so surely getting into RADA would be difficult enough. It seemed insane to limit my chances by making clear this rather grand condition. Herbert was implacable. If no scholarship, then no training, no 'proper' career, no England.

'You'll have to get accustomed to being poor,' Saunders concluded, 'so I suggest that you make an appointment to see the Director of Education in the City Hall and ask him for a grant. I'll give you a letter of recommendation.' That seemed to be all, so I left them and walked down to the Capitol Café for a cup of coffee, a packet of cigarettes to chain-smoke and to think.

Chapter Twenty-two

In my mind, RADA was a fabulous place peopled by gods and goddesses. My dream at fifteen years of age, of a place where nothing mattered except acting, where I would belong and be content and live the life I wished to live, had persisted into my grown-up twentieth year. I had never thought of the reality of it. Unattainable and wonderful, it had remained fixed and unchangeable like a fairy tale. 'Once upon a time and far away, there was a wonderful place . . .' And I had also grown accustomed to not being allowed to go to the ball. Now, almost casually, RADA was being talked about as something reachable and possible in a knowable dimension, but the years of vainly waiting had left me a legacy of inertia and I drew back from the ordinariness of writing a letter to the Academy and licking a stamp and walking to the postbox. Surely it couldn't be as simple as that? I couldn't allow that the business of making a dream into reality could be so easy.

Where *was* RADA? 'Oh, I've done all that,' said Herbert. 'We should get the prospectus any day.' And still we didn't talk of my changed circumstances, and the fact that I wasn't free to go anywhere. Just once Herbert said, 'So why *did* you get married? When I heard about it, I assumed that you were pregnant and had to marry and that you'd subsequently lost the child.' 'No,' I replied, rather shocked by his matter-of-fact tone, 'it wasn't that at all,' but I couldn't bring myself to confide in him. Also, I didn't have a reasonable explanation. He did not seem very interested and the subject was dropped, but it had become my ceaseless internal monologue. What to do? And then, how to do it? I didn't know anyone who had ended a marriage, nor, I was sure, did anyone in my family; divorce was not an option in our lives. Confused, I went about my work and talked to no one. When I wrote to my husband, I told him nothing of this.

The prospectus arrived! It lay on the table between us. Herbert and Joyce, his wife, were interested and pleased. I drew it towards myself and as I began to read, my confusion vanished. The words before me were almost familiar, as though I'd read them before. Guilt and remorse might well remain, but I knew what I was going to do, no matter what it cost. If it was within my power, I was going to go to this place that I was recognising as though I'd been there in a dream. It seemed like home beckoning me. I would rather have died than voiced any of this, and when Herbert began to consider audition pieces I shed my fancies and joined him in a practical and none too serious consideration of ways of displaying any strengths I possessed while concealing my weaknesses – 'And there are plenty of those,' said Herbert.

There were set audition pieces, including a piece of scripture – rather dull. 'We'll do that,' said Herbert. 'No,' I protested. It was completely undramatic and it was short – over in a flash – no chance to shine. 'Leave it to me,' said Herbert and he suggested I should offer as my own choice the Willow Song from *Othello*. A song? I was aghast. 'Trust me,' he said. The scholarship pieces were not, it seemed, so crucial. The important thing was to walk into the room on the first day and make an immediate, unassailable impact.

· Yes, I could see that, but I'd never done an audition. I'd never even had to do an interview and most of my energies in everyday life were bent towards being as self-effacing as possible. 'And keep your voice down; people don't like *loud* girls.'

'All right then,' Herbert was saying. 'Rehearse the pieces on Wednesday and Friday next week?' 'Yes, I'll know them by then.'

I don't know what I was expecting him to do. I was accustomed to working things out for myself and having someone apply a little polish. Herbert was asking me to do things that sounded completely mad. The piece from the Bible was being taken very slowly with big pauses and impossible upward inflections. 'What did I sound like?' I wondered, listening to my own alien delivery. A bit like Dylan Thomas maybe. A bit like a revivalist preacher, possibly. My accent was standard English but the effect was strangely Welsh. Was that good? He said I *had* to do it his way and I obeyed.

He re-directed the Willow scene, which he'd seen me play. 'Not good enough,' he said to my chagrin; I'd been rather pleased with that bit. We edited the scene with Emilia so that I could play it alone and I became acquainted with it as though for the first time. It was more interesting, more affecting, more frightening than I had appreciated. I went through a downcast period when I realised how much more work there was to do than I had hitherto appreciated. Then my high spirits revived as we rehearsed again and again, week after week, and I could tell that I was improving and sounding less odd as the audition grew nearer. But still I had no idea if I was really bad or really good. Herbert said nothing. It was time to negotiate some leave from my jobs at the BBC and find somewhere to stay in London in the neighbourhood where all Welsh people stayed, in Paddington near the Great Western Railway terminus, where as a nation we got off the train and, seemingly too apprehensive or too tired to go further, set up as suppliers of milk or mistresses of respectable boarding houses with Welsh-language chapel timetables in the hall.

It was also time to tell my parents what I was about to do. Full of apprehension, I boarded a small red Western Welsh bus and made yet another miserable excursion to the Vale of Glamorgan. Very rarely had I been the bearer of good news recently, I reflected sadly. The journey passed far too quickly and I tried to make the mile-long walk to the house last longer than it should. I was hoping for inspiration as I walked along, but when I found my parents doing accounts in the office of the big house and went with them to their apartment for tea, my mind was still a muddle of discarded opening gambits.

No matter how I dressed it up or justified it I was going to have to tell them that I was going to run away and that, if I could help it, I wasn't coming back. I couldn't begin to calculate the strength of their reaction. How many levels of trouble was I dealing them? There was the scandal to contend with. Shame, loss of face, the collapse of appearances were powerful and important elements that I had inherited and was trying to dispense with. How much more potent they must be to my parents who, with *their* parents' example, before them, had in a seemingly unchangeable society not only been given a framework of rules and values, but had inflexibly lived by them. It was the fashion to deride the inevitable hypocrisies of the narrow code of conduct by which we lived in Welsh Wales, but, although I was about to break new ground in bad behaviour, I believed that there was something heroic in the self-denial, the self-control, the strength required to live through days and weeks and years of duty rather than inclination. I looked at the two faces before me in the big airy sitting room, very un-Welsh with a formal English garden outside, and I saw the same serious, level expressions that looked out from those damp-spotted family portraits at 'home'. Home was far away and sorrow for my disenfranchised parents overtook my fears and nervousness for myself. It should have been so easy for me to make my parents happy and proud. It seemed so unfair to be bringing home more trouble.

And there was the less lofty question of security; mine and, in a way, theirs. Although I had chosen an unorthodox route, I had, surprisingly, arrived at a position that might be even more satisfactory than the future they had planned for me. How would they feel as I turned my back on that? My father's reaction was unfathomable. My mother? Hard to tell. The antagonism that had seethed beneath the surface of our relationship in the year that led to my marriage had subsided without erupting and there was an uneasy calm between us. It was as though we had finished a passage of arms and, whereas nothing was concluded, something was over and done with. Odd as it seemed, I considered now that the impetus behind the events of the past year had derived not from the relationship between myself and my lover, but rather from an imperative impulse to have some kind of contest with my mother; if not an actual contest, a dialogue all the more violent in that it was indirect, never spoken.

I told them what I was going to do; at least, I told them what I was going to try to do. It was understood that in the event of a success, there were to be consequences that would be dealt with later. Not for the first time, they astonished me. They cut straight to the end of a discussion they didn't bother having and, in effect, they simultaneously advised me to cut my losses and go. They finished each other's sentences. They were in perfect accord. 'And count on us,' they said, more than once. 'Anything we can do to help.' I was shamed by their generosity and sympathy. There was a rider. 'Let this be an end of marriages,' said my mother. It was easy to submit. After a period – years – of thoughtless childishness, I was at twenty beginning to recapture the sobriety and lightness of my childhood self. I could remember how happy I was when I was focused and unshakeable and it was as though my parents knew this. Everything is redeemable if I get my scholarship. I have a second chance.

Chapter Twenty-three

Rehearsals with Herbert went on. Work went on. For the first time I was aware of the importance of having money and anxiously I scanned the BBC Repertory Company board to make sure that I had enough bookings to be kept on. I did all the presentation work I could get. There was no stage play to occupy me. Work on the novel was suspended. Life was being lived, not written about.

As Saunders advised, I made an appointment at the City Hall to talk to the Head of Education for Glamorgan County Council about the possibility of obtaining a grant for an acting course. The meeting was a disaster; I forgot Mr Haycock's name as I walked down the corridor to his office and wasted the initial five minutes mentally rifling through likely bucolic surnames: Straw, no; *two* syllables, Thatcher, Fielding, Snodgrass, oh give up. I hated asking for things and I especially hated asking for money.

To make matters worse I didn't really see why the local authority should give me another grant, but I could glimpse on his desk a letter in Saunders' writing and Herbert had doubtless called in a few favours, so Mr Haycock didn't reject my application out of hand, but he wanted me to explain how he could be sure of getting a return for his money. This being the first time he'd been asked to give money to a potential drama student, he was at a loss to understand how to calculate the end result. I told him that the outcome of an actor's training is impossible to predict. 'You seem very highly thought of,' he ventured, cautiously, indicating the papers on his desk, 'and you will not be needing a grant unless the Academy gives you a scholarship, which would indicate that it also thought highly of you.' 'There's still no certainty,' I replied and he seemed taken aback that I was not being more persuasive. When he pressed me to convince him that I had a good case I felt so intensely irritated that all I wanted to do was to end the meeting. I couldn't afford it, but I knew that I was going to scupper my chances of a grant within the next few minutes.

Before I got around to this something occurred that did indeed bring the meeting to a close and not in a way I would have chosen. 'I see that you married recently,' he remarked. 'Yes,' I replied, 'but I'm afraid . . .' and to my horror I began to cry. This was unbearably embarrassing for both of us. Councillor Haycock looked down at his large desk and my stifled sobs grew until, choking and gasping for breath, shoulders heaving, I gave way to a terrible fit of weeping. Shaking my head and gesturing an apology, I gathered up my things and left as fast as I could, making for the little park across the road from the City Hall where I sat and snivelled for a bit, appalled by my precarious emotional state. I dried my eyes and thought I would deal with it later. Nothing to do at present but apply a plaster to the inconvenient wound.

I did not in the least blame the local authority when I was informed that training an actress was thought to be inappropriate expenditure. I don't know why but I really didn't want that money. Now I had to make and save as much money as I could and hope that later on I would think of another way of raising funds. Oddly, for me, I was not at all worried about the practicalities of the enterprise.

December 1955 and the week of the audition was upon me. On previous journeys I had been guided 'across' London by other people; it was a noisy jumble of impossible-to-follow signs. Would I ever reach a destination on my own? I seriously doubted it, I had no sense of direction and was terrified of traffic, lacking the most basic of townee skills. Thinking back, I reflected that a trained dog would learn how to work the transport system with more ease than I had displayed, rooted to the spot like a rabbit, unable to distinguish words in the alien human roar that accompanied the terrifying sound of buses and cars and the distant under-the-ground trains. I had gone where I was told to go. Others had bought tickets, read signs, chosen escalators and platforms. 'How?' I marvelled, knowing that I was as spectacularly incompetent and vulnerably hopeless as a country bumpkin in Bartholomew Fair. 'Don't lose your money,' lectured my mother. 'Don't lose your ticket.' Every time she saw me she added another warning 'Don't'. She had no reason to have confidence in me when I had none. I thought I must compartmentalise my day; endure the trials and terrors of getting to Gower Street from Paddington, follow the map to the Academy, allow time for getting lost and probably robbed, then calm down, forget my surroundings and concentrate on the audition. Oh, please, let me concentrate as I never have before.

In the event, I concentrated so hard that London, the physical fact of the huge city, shrank to a room in a Paddington boarding house and a room in 62 Gower Street, the Royal Academy of Dramatic Art. When I went home I had nothing to tell of my journey except my recollection of the audition and my subsequent conversation with the secretary, Miss Brown, and even that had begun to assume a dream-like quality.

The Paddington bedroom had been as clean as a new penny and cold; multi-coloured, small, all-over patterned carpet (designed solely so as not to show dirt), fighting and defeating the refined hardly-there-at-all wallpaper and the pink satin upholstered stool, a daredevil piece of luxury in front of the walnut-type veneer of the low-fronted dressing-table with its big triple-mirror. I may have slept in it, but chiefly this served as my rehearsal room, and I moved the furniture and stood and looked dispassionately at my reflection in the middle mirror on the dressing-table, which could be tilted slightly so that I could see almost all of myself.

I looked as Existentialist as it was possible to look without actually applying the correct Juliette Gréco make-up. Tall, tiny waist, belted. Plain tight-fitting sweater; long, full woollen skirt, flat shoes. So far, so good. I didn't have a good coat in the appropriate style, but I wouldn't be wearing a coat so that didn't matter. The face was almost right. On the credit side, a faultless complexion (eczema temporarily at bay), regular features, dark red mouth, actressy and interesting at the same time. But the hair and the eyes . . . totally unremarkable; the former falling straight to my shoulders, clean but ordinary, whereas I would have liked it to billow, darker and thicker and more aggressive. The eyes were no more than nice eyes. I wanted big, mysterious, dark pools and had no idea how to achieve this without making myself look silly. I smelled of 4711, a Christmas present (rather more worldly than Yardley's Lavender). It wasn't exactly how I wanted to look, but it was going to have to do.

I went through my pieces several times (not too loud, just in case). I stood looking at myself. 'Are you any good at all?' I thought, quite calm now that the decisive moment had all but arrived. My reflection looked blank. I didn't have the remotest idea. I imagined the worst outcome. Someone – a man – would raise a hand and stop me and say something like, 'I'm sorry but you are not what we're looking for.' It wouldn't surprise me at all. I was shooting for the moon and prepared for the worst.

In the morning I went through my pieces again and then I was walking towards Gower Street, so contained in the little circle I'd manufactured around myself that I did no more than note in passing that the entrance was familiar; Mrs Lewis's medium had described it in detail three years ago. That didn't seem significant or even interesting; my attention was reserved for the interior: a smallish hallway, dark with a grand, wide staircase at the back. 'Not there, please,' said a tall, military-looking commissionaire figure in green livery, indicating a much humbler little staircase round to the right. As I moved through the hall I saw things that set my pulses wildly racing. There was a bust of George Bernard Shaw, who I knew had been involved in the creating of the Academy, a portrait of Violet Vanbrugh and on the walls great boards – they seemed huge – with names in gold letters. Those names! I was in a Holy of Holies. These were gold medallist actors and actresses who had trained here, in this very building where I was standing – Charles Laughton, Hugh Griffith, Barbara Jefford.

Then I was round the corner and ascending a poky dark staircase and being ushered towards a – lecture-room? ... studio? – that was, at present, a waiting room filled with people like me, hoping for a place. There didn't seem to be a 'type', I noticed gratefully. Some were very young, some were middle-aged, some were *very* good-looking, like people in a magazine, but others were plain and ordinary. I sat down and tried not to get distracted. I wanted to go through my pieces in my head, but I couldn't help hearing the conversations around and behind me. Oh, mercy, they sounded so *English*. I was painfully aware suddenly that for all my (thanks to the BBC) faultless pronunciation and for all my 'good ear' for languages, and notwithstanding the constant reading and writing in English, I was still thinking in Welsh. I felt like a foreigner and at the mercy of that wretched reflex common to my race that whispered 'English is superior'. It only took a second to readjust and say, 'No, it's not', but the fear and shame of that second were debilitating. Someone said, 'What fool would do the *Bible*, I ask you.' There was laughter and I closed my eyes and silently began, 'And Jesus went thence, and departed into the shores of Tyre and Sidon.' Herbert, have you got this right?

There were a lot of us, maybe fifty, waiting that day. When my name was called I crossed the corridor and was shown into a very big room with three large windows looking on to Gower Street. Some of them were darkened with what looked like leftover blackout material. The room seemed empty. Where I entered there was a 'stage' area – not raised, a few chairs and small tables, haphazardly positioned against the walls. Then I saw that at the far end, almost out of sight, four or five people sat behind a table. Someone must have indicated that I should begin. 'And Jesus went thence . . .' Oh God, I sounded too loud and these pauses were painful, I could only just hold them, but they were in my blood and the piece came out exactly as Herbert had rehearsed it. It didn't sound smart. It didn't sound *English*.

I moved a table and a chair and began the Willow scene, miming the hairbrush and table carefully and 'placing' Emilia in the scene. There was no possibility of going wrong, but my singing voice was a bit wobbly to my ears. 'Mine eyes do itch, doth that bode weeping?' To my surprise I *was* in tears. I finished and went out and back to my seat in the waiting room. Nothing happened for a while, no one was called, until an elderly woman in a brown felt hat came in and called my name again. The next applicant was called at the same time and crossed the hall to the big room, while the woman in the brown hat took me round the corner and said, 'Oh my dear girl.' I looked at her, puzzled. 'Is it possible for you to come back to do your scholarship pieces?' 'Yes, of course, but does that mean . . .?' 'Oh, no, yes – no, you *have a scholarship*, no doubt of that, but it would be good to hear your pieces.' I leaned against the wall. 'I've passed, then?' 'Oh, my dear girl, they – we are so happy that you are coming to us.' Tears welled in my eyes and she put her arm around me and gave me her handkerchief. It was the happiest moment of my life.

My mind registered nothing of my return to Wales. The letter came confirming that I had won the Maggie Albanesi Scholarship and was expected at the Academy in January. My parents were pleased. They were, I think, impressed. What were they impressed by? As much, maybe, by my success in getting there and back in one piece without losing anything or getting myself run over, as they were by my admission to RADA. This was a relief. It was uncomplicated, as though we'd *all* been wanting this for me and here it was. I didn't tell anyone about Miss Brown and myself sharing a hankie. I was not planning on any more public displays of emotion and, anyhow, I wanted this to seem ordinary, normal, to reduce the temperature. Herbert smiled and nodded and said, 'Knew it.' Saunders counselled careful preparation before entering into a life I had longed for, for so long. 'Think carefully what *sort* of actress you want to be. You might become an artist, who knows.' They both repeated that my troubles were not over by a long chalk. Saunders said and then wrote, 'You must learn to live on the knife-edge of insecurity.' I wasn't sure what he meant. I didn't think he was talking about financial insecurity. How could the insecurity he was meaning be a good thing? And why should I not become successful – soon? Herbert said, 'You have a long haul ahead of you,' and he grinned wolfishly as though it were a big joke to be relished. We'd see about that, I thought, and began my preparations for departure.

Chapter Twenty-four

Write a cheque for the remainder of the lease. Post it. Pack books. Divide china, ornaments, cutlery, linen. Pack, vacuum and dust. Arrange transport. Leave letter.

'Leave letter.' A shameful, cowardly item on the list. 'Divide china' – even worse. A scrupulous division of assets weighs little or not at all in the scales of fair dealing. Unwilling and unable to explain myself, tired of talking, I'd make my excuses by letter and quit the country, the marriage hardly begun, the obligations, the past.

I burn my unfinished novel, tear up my wedding photographs and, looking through my papers, keep only my exercise books with notes about acting; my attempt to understand Stanislavski's 'Method', a précis of Michael Redgrave's lectures on acting, by far the most helpful to me of all actors' observations. 'To act well and to act well repeatedly has to become an obsession,' I see underlined. My book of childhood poems, mostly in Welsh, written for Eisteddfod competitions seems to have gone astray and it doesn't bother me. Even the ones that won prizes were vastly inferior to the poems written by Dafydd Rowlands, the head boy at Pontardawe School, and now a 'grown-up' poet. There's a slim file of late teenage poems in English and I open it cautiously. I must have been pretty unhappy at seventeen:

> Consciousness of self returns
> Limbs sprawled in still abandon
> And a head that burns
> And burning turns on the? [*I seem to have
> had trouble with the adjective*] tormented pillow.

Pages later I seem to have reached for a watery oblivion:

A wreath of foam
A moment's peace
And then hear still the Life-yell underneath.

Oh, please. Obviously I'd decided that annihilation was pointless. There were *lots* of depressed poems and I made up a special bundle for the furnace, pleased that I was obliterating my younger, embarrassing self.

This time I was aware of the journey from Cardiff to Paddington. My mother insisted on accompanying me. She seemed different again, strangely sweet in her manner, and part of me was glad she was with me. Two small suitcases – very little luggage with which to be starting a new life: one raincoat, two pairs of shoes – one flat and one cuban heeled – two skirts, two blouses, two sweaters, plus my requirements for the Academy: really horrible black cotton tights that wrinkle, ballet shoes, leotard, dance shoes. All my smart, 'bourgeois', BBC clothes – stiletto heels, pencil-slim skirts, outside-broadcast long frocks – have been dumped. I felt I had to pare down and rid myself of bric-à-brac. Simplicity was to be the keynote now, I decided. I had to forget that I had ever been a professional actress, forget that I had rarely been out of work, forget that I'd had a responsible BBC job, an office, a secretary, forget my respectable 'prospects', wipe the slate clean and become for the first time a true student. Maybe my mother sensed this and it made her warm towards me.

As we pulled into Paddington she indicated the grubby backs of the houses and said, 'Well, there it is, let's see what you make of that.' She delivered this in a mild voice, at odds with the challenge of the remark. Her sense of occasion had led her to overplay the moment. She should have been high above Hampstead looking down at the dome of St Paul's, instead of sitting in a dingy train crawling along Westbourne Park Villas. I beamed reassuringly at her.

My carefully organised Welsh digs had fallen through; my prospective landlady fell downstairs and broke her leg. I was not displeased for myself. It was arranged that I should lodge temporarily in Earl's Court – and curiously with a niece of Richard Burton's whom I did not yet know. I felt dangerously indifferent and quite unable to take an interest in the practical arrangements. My mother came with me to Goodge Street and I was seized with concern for her and made her promise to stay put in the little café near the Underground station while I went over to RADA on Gower Street. We were to meet later and I told her

I would take her back to Paddington. All this to-ing and fro-ing seemed unnecessary, but I was terrified that she would get lost – or run over. After I had registered and been shown around the building, I hurtled back to the café to find my mother *returning* from Liberty's in Regent Street. How clever of her. London did not intimidate her in the least. To me it was as exciting and perilous as the Amazon jungle and I could not wait to wave my mother off and negotiate the journey to Earl's Court and sanctuary. Would they remember I was coming? Would they have changed their minds? Would they be out?

Earl's Court *was* a sanctuary; the girls were in, they did remember I was coming. They showed me the kitchen and my room and I retreated there, too exhausted and apprehensive to speak. They were music students, I gathered. One of them practised the same phrase over and over again. The Underground moaned somewhere around or below us, my meagre possessions were quickly unpacked and I was washed and in bed – for the first time I could remember without a book to read – listening to the alien sounds of this city that I had been dreading for so many years:

> Oh do not trust that wicked man,
> Be careful what you do-oo
> Tum tum tum *tum*
> Tum tum, tum tum
> He'll do the same to you

resounded over and over again through the small flat. I felt strange. What was it? The thought of RADA in the morning was exciting; would I get there in one piece – and on time? I'd get up very early. There was something else. I realised that I was smiling in the semi-darkness. (The streets of London could never be truly dark, I thought.) I was smiling because I had fallen in love and was deeply, unexpectedly in thrall to the city I had so dreaded. How could that have happened so quickly? As with all love affairs, there was little explanation and no arguing. This was *it*, all right. What a bonus! I fell asleep thinking of the corridors and staircases of RADA. Having no sense of direction, I had not retained any notion where anything was, where anything led. I'd have to start again in the morning. Light-hearted as I hadn't been for years, I fell asleep.

Chapter Twenty-five

On my first day I was in WC1 long before RADA opened its doors and I took a cautious walk round the neighbourhood. There were small hotels on Gower Street and one of them had a Welsh name. I had to find somewhere permanent to stay; what a luxury it would be to have a room here. However, I had already adjusted my wishes to suit my pocket and I knew I could not afford a cupboard in this part of London. I shouldn't waste time wondering how I would live after my savings gave out and I surprised myself by the ease with which I accepted this careless attitude.

I'd never worked so hard in my life. There were seventy-three new students, divided into three groups. The Gower Street house rose five floors above the street and there was also a basement where our lockers were housed. During the day we ran and ran and ran; up and down the building and also across the roof and down into the building that fronted on to Malet Street, behind and parallel with Gower Street. Unpunctuality was a cardinal offence and it was a nightmare running down to the basement after each lesson to change into the appropriate dress and get back upstairs in time for the next lesson – hundreds of stairs each day, taken two at a time, in terror of being late. Excuses were not accepted. At the BBC I had learned the hard way about timekeeping, but this was worse – there just *wasn't* time to get from A to B, change, and get back to C. In the theatre, they said, one would always be expected to be ready to rehearse at least ten minutes before time, so get used to moving fast. I would. I did.

The first week was especially fraught for me because I couldn't remember where anything was. I learned to identify a few people from my group and tried to keep them in my sights as I struggled in and out of tights and rummaged in my locker for books and shoes and tried not to give up on my appearance. Glamour was not required, but I could see that an undergraduate's total disregard for appearance would not be acceptable.

Each night I went home and only just managed to prepare for the following day before falling into a deep, dreamless sleep. I was in awe of the staff; some of them were in plays, some were celebrated, some were alarming, others bore famous names. There were seventeen of them and each one knew something that I wanted to know and was determined to learn. I was equally in awe of my fellow students; they were so *English*. I remembered Gwyn Thomas's observation of his first days at Oxford: 'I had landed on another planet and I had never seen such large, confident Martians. Some of them might have been on horseback but I never really looked up to find out.'

These people all seemed to have more skills than I; they were quicker and funnier and better at accents and much more graceful, some of them were dancers and didn't have to endure the torment of beginning ballet lessons from scratch. I was the worst fencer by far. And my voice was all wrong! In the space of a few weeks, I was reduced to rubble. I couldn't do *anything*. Astoundingly, I wasn't cast down. No reversal, no humiliation – and there were plenty – could extinguish my profound contentment. 'Keep up! Concentrate! Oh, for God's sake! The girl in the red shoes,' said Richard Ainley brutally and, as it happened, unfairly. There wasn't a moment of the day when I was not concentrating. I was *trying* with every sinew in my body. I had tried and succeeded in abandoning myself to insecurity. There was no plan in my head. On unfamiliar ground, I put one foot before the other and was happy. I was scared as well; it seemed to me that I might well be one of the many students to be sacked at the end of the first term. There were stories of a class of seventy, whittled down term after term until only ten remained at the end of two years. I refused to think what I would do if and when the worst happened in December.

Two weeks galloped by. Already, I could scarcely speak for self-consciousness. I couldn't even breathe. 'Toothpaste please and a packet of Kleenex,' came out as a scarcely intelligible gurgle. The whole weight of the Academy was thrown behind voice production. We did no acting. We had movement classes with Mrs Boalth, ballet classes, fencing classes with Captain Froeschlen and – a luxury – mime classes with Miss Phillips, which were the closest we came to acting.

The bulk of the time was taken up with voice, voice, voice, breathing, diction, musicality, audibility, control during extreme emotion, posture, rib reserve. It was like being in a nightmare without end. I couldn't envisage that there *could* be an end or that I would ever achieve a state where I would talk without thinking of twenty 'mistakes' I might be making. Miss Morrell, my voice tutor, was grey haired, fair and stern. Each time my turn came to speak a few lines aloud she listened, shook her head dismissively and quickly passed on to the next student. All my life my voice had been singled out for praise. All those years of filling auditoriums that held up to two thousand people had done nothing but iron in a dozen bad habits. Gradually, I let go of my home-grown 'techniques' and sank to the bottom of the class. I couldn't even tell *why* other students were right when I was so wrong.

It was fashionable to sneer at 'the RADA voice', partly because RADA had at times been perceived as a finishing school for rich young girls. In fact, there was no such thing as a RADA voice and within the last months the age limit had been raised to exclude sixteen-year-olds who couldn't think what they wanted to do in life. The long-time principal, Sir Kenneth Barnes, who had still been there to preside over my entrance audition, was yielding to John Fernald, the new principal. He combined the energy and confidence of a successful, practising theatre director with an attitude towards discipline that derived from his other love, the Navy.

RADA was transforming itself into a very tight ship, but the emphasis remained on vocal and physical technique, not self-expression. That suited me fine. I was desperate to know the 'how'. We were told that an actor's first duty was to be heard by everyone in the theatre. 'If they can't hear you, it doesn't matter how beautifully you're acting, it's a total waste of time.' Being heard was allied with being understood and that involved not only possessing a tongue that could rap out consonants at the speed of machine-gun bullets but also being master of a diaphragm strong enough to enable one to sustain breath over long passages. 'And then,' we were told, 'you have to have the industry to search out which are the key words in a speech so that you can highlight them while floating over the less important phrases. You don't want to *bore* the audience, do you?' God forbid – in the unlikely event that I would ever again be able to stand up on a stage looking like a normal person and think of ten things while being heard and understood.

I looked up my notes to myself that I had put together when I was an undergraduate – the only papers I'd kept – and actually all this RADA work was related to points I'd thought important, if barely understood then.

What is the secret of acting?

Voice, voice, more voice.

What is the secret of Lewis Casson's diction?

I took heart from the tiny scrap of text that read, 'Sir Lewis is not a Welshman for nothing.' Most important of all the lessons that my idol, Edith Evans, had been taught by her mentor, William Poel – there was a William Poel prize here at RADA. Hitherto I hadn't thought of him as a real person; he'd been a character in Miss Evans's life. He was long dead now, but he became a real person to me.

This was grind and drudgery and I embraced it, getting up at six every morning to go through the breathing and the diction exercises and then allowing myself a smidgen of Shakespeare before going to RADA to do more of the same until darkness fell. Not only did I fail to improve, I got worse. Around me I heard mutinous remarks about the soullessness of this process. Some even said they weren't going to bother with this phase, they were here to act, but I thought my soul would take care of itself and the acting would wait for me. I had to find out the *how*.

Chapter Twenty-six

I found digs! I began to feel quite a Londoner. Margot was a third-term student; she was beautiful with subtle make-up, hair that practically dressed itself into a chignon, and a modest, elegant wardrobe – so far above us harassed and dishevelled beginners. She put it about that there was room for two more students where she lodged. I went to be looked over by my prospective landlady. The Metropolitan Line took me to a part of London that was quite unlike any I'd seen. Dollis Hill seemed very far away and when I got off the train and followed the map to Mrs Styles' house I realised that I was in a bit of the city that must have been almost countryside before the coming of the Underground. The house, a white, rough-cast 1930s semi, was on the edge of open land. It didn't seem very big. Where would we all fit in?

I pressed the front-door bell alongside the front window. It was opened by a slim, well-dressed woman, middle-aged with formidably permed, neat grey hair and bright, darting, inquisitive eyes. 'No flies on me,' said her expression. I was meeting my first authentic Londoner, I realised, and I was fascinated. Her terms were reasonable: £2 19s for bed and an English breakfast, dinner and lunch on Sunday, no callers at the house, limited use of telephone, make own bed, in by a reasonable hour at night, use of lounge by invitation. She was brisk beyond belief and I was swept along on a wave of dos and don'ts. This was no motherly Mrs Lewis in Cardiff, but I sensed that she was completely reliable and I needed the quiet bolt-hole she seemed to be offering. Also, more and more, she was intriguing me.

When everything was agreed – on the double (I was to find that every moment of her day was accounted for) – I realised to my dismay that I was to *share* the double room at the back. Margot had the small middle room and Mrs Styles of course had the big front room. True, for a year I had shared a large study bedroom with Audrey at college, but I'd known Audrey for six years at school; sharing with a stranger was something else. It was too late to back out. I hadn't understood because I was too slow, and I was embarrassed to admit that now. I arranged to move in. This, I thought, was a real test of my translation from professional person with smart flat and (use of) chauffeur-driven car to humble student. It wasn't very glorious but it was a challenge, nonetheless. The tests in life, I reflected, were difficult because they were so undramatic.

My room-mate turned out to be part of the last intake of Young Things at RADA. She came from Blackpool and she was called Sandra. She was sixteen. She had a mink stole and a generous allowance. Her peroxided, blonde hair hung below her shoulders and she was lavish with lipstick and looked like a slight, baby-version of a Diana Dors or Veronica Lake. We had absolutely nothing in common and I became very fond of her. I was assembling a whole gallery of people who were as exotic and interesting as aboriginals.

How did I strike them at the digs? I fell into the role of 'good guy'. Margot, I gathered, was conducting a liaison that interfered with her student life and this was vaguely disapproved of by Mrs Styles. Sandra was sharp and knew how to stand up for herself. I marvelled at her nerve when she tackled Mrs Styles on the subject of catering arrangements. I don't know which of us was more aghast, Mrs S or myself, when Sandra said pertly, 'I really do think that I need a steak once a week.' I don't think I'd ever eaten a steak and, child of rationing, I didn't understand the significance or desirability of red meat. Mrs Styles was – almost – silenced. Recovering, she said, 'Listen, Miss, steak is a *man's* food. Women can't eat steak. They don't even know how to *cut* it. You have to watch a *man* cutting a steak to see how it's done.' 'I'll have to speak to my mother about that,' said Sandra, as she flounced out of the room.

'I used to give my hubby steak, of course,' said Mrs Styles. I didn't have the smallest feeling about steak, but I was enjoying the drama taking place in the breakfast room overlooking the back garden. Hubby had died, leaving Mrs Styles with two daughters to bring up; one was married and about to start a completely new kind of business. 'Launderette,' said Mrs Styles. New word. I understood that for a considerable outlay one could make a fortune quite quickly by providing people with the use of sophisticated washing machines (like my Auntie Hilda's at home) in a kind of shop where they could bring their dirty laundry. This was so 'London' that I hugged it to myself. The thought of washing one's clothes in public! (My mother had made me promise to post my small parcel of laundry to her at home.)

There was another daughter at boarding school and Mrs Styles augmented her pension by taking in lodgers and 'temping' (another new word). 'I go to the agency in Baker Street and I take what suits me, where it suits me and for as long as it suits me.' She was fearless. Her life was completely under control. Every so often she and a friend would make a trip 'up West' (another expression new to me) and there was never a sense that she was overstretched as she easily combined her 'temping' with her immaculate housekeeping, which included cooking three massive breakfasts and clearing up, before going for the Bakerloo train to the office and then providing three lavish dinners after her return from work, and if we weren't in at the appointed hour we were allowed to steam-heat the overflowing plates. Mrs Styles, after dinner, retired to the lounge to watch a little TV. Her very favourite performer was Liberace and she enjoyed him so much that we were invited to share the pleasure with her. Perched on the edge of the couch of a three-piece suite, I was astonished by him.

Somehow – how? – Mrs Styles had discovered that I was married and in her eyes this gave me a little status. 'It's all right for Siân to be a little late at night, she is a *married woman*.' The first time she made a remark of this sort I was aghast. This was my secret, I'd thought. Certainly, none of my fellow students knew and, ostrich-like, I refused to consider whether the paperwork on my admission revealed to the Academy that I was married. If so, no one mentioned it. I met Mrs Styles' comment with blankness. Sandra and Margot looked puzzled and I pretended I didn't notice. Would they tell anyone? I doubted it; we were all self-obsessed. At this stage we were barely interested in each other as people, each of us an insecure, confused and frightened single entity. 'I must be the only married female student in the Academy,' I thought miserably. This was 1956 and I couldn't deal with the shame of having run out on a marriage to embark on a course of action that could only end some day in divorce.

Divorce. I hadn't stayed around long enough to experience the shock-waves radiating from my grandmother's house and had left my parents to explain as best they could what I was about, and deal with the disgrace. It *was* a disgrace and I felt it keenly. Once or twice I thought I saw the outline of my husband in the shadows across the road from the doorway of 62 Gower Street as I emerged into the darkness of the night. I looked over my shoulder as I made for the Goodge Street Underground, and I wasn't sure. If it was him, he never spoke to me; was I imagining things? In fact, I didn't see Don again until we were divorced, years later. I was ashamed of what I had done and glad to be free, and ashamed that I was glad, and then I put it all out of my mind. There was no point at all to any of the pain and sadness if I didn't fully commit myself to this strange, new life. It was strange and I loved it. All of it.

I was devouring life in all senses of the word. I was living on a very limited budget – a living allowance of £4 a week from my savings, which only just covered my lodgings, my travelling expenses and obligatory theatre-going at the weekend (seeing everything from the Upper Circle) and snacks at the canteen at RADA during the day. Shopping, casual shopping, was a thing of the past; having to have a pair of shoes mended seriously upset the weekly budget. This was the first time I'd had to lead such a proscribed life and it didn't bother me at all. It was a small price to pay. Some of the students were much worse off than I and were bartending or waitressing at night and at weekends. All I had to do was work at acting, look at acting, talk about acting, read about acting, and I felt fortunate.

But I was hungry all the time. This was an unexpected consequence of my new life. In Wales I had been beleaguered, overworked, baulked, frustrated, uninterested in food and emaciated. Mrs Styles was providing me with more food than I'd ever eaten and I wanted more. The canteen sold cheap, fattening, stodgy food and, whenever I could afford it, I bought sticky buns and white, sliced bread and margarine. My clothes were beginning to strain at the seams. Was it happiness or insecurity that was changing my shape? I was exercising every day, walking as well, and, of course, running up and down stairs, but the regular meals and the buns altered me, and during the first term I became – if not fat – for the first time in my life, well covered. I didn't think it mattered and I liked the unfamiliar feeling of well-being and strength I was experiencing as the breathing and posture exercises imperceptibly began to take effect.

Going home to Dollis Hill for dinner I would, if I could find a spare sixpence, buy a chocolate bar at Baker Street. Standing in front of the vending machine I looked at the people on the platform and thought, wouldn't it be wonderful if one of them dropped a fiver into my pocket. It would make such a *massive* difference to the month and I resolved that when, if ever, I became a person of substance again I would do just that – hand a poor-looking student a five-pound note and quickly pass on without a word. The men around me wore raincoats over sports jackets and flannels. Almost all the women wore hats and gloves, and in the early evening the tubes 'up West' were full of well-dressed people in smart clothes on their way to the theatre or to restaurants. The women wore dresses and coats in stiff silk, and in cold weather draped stoles made of fur or wool interwoven with metallic threads around their shoulders. Nothing in my wardrobe was suitable for any part of the theatre but 'the gods'.

But I grew bolder and began to venture further afield on the Underground, becoming better acquainted with this city that had enchanted me.

Chapter Twenty-seven

Sunday was my day for walking. London in the Fifties was shabby. Willow-herb and buddleia flourished on open spaces that I learned to identify as bomb-sites. The new buildings, hastily thrown up after the war, were insubstantial and already looked run-down. Here and there, coffee bars were opening; they sold weakish coffee with froth on top and were regarded as infinitely smarter than teashops. The tables and chairs were flimsy with irritating little stick-like legs that stuck out at awkward angles and tripped one up. Sitting in a coffee bar was regarded as a bit of an extravagance and I felt middle-aged as I clutched my winter coat to myself and tried to shrink into the small space allotted to each patron in tiny, street-level rooms or mouldy-smelling basements. The floor coverings were alarming: lino-tiles in aggressively contrasting shapes and colours or (less often) carpet in brutal combinations of colours; purple with small orange and red jagged 'doodles', reminiscent of temperature charts on hospital beds.

I half liked the feeling of being in an up-to-the-minute place (there was no such coffee bar in Cardiff), while loathing the discomfort and especially the interior design that decreed that no two walls should be painted or papered to look alike and that ceilings should provide a further, brisk 'contrast' to the four walls and the floor. Gone were the days when doors and skirtings and window frames glowed magnolia-like or snow-white. A nice bright orange seemed to be the favoured colour. Perched there, dressed to look like my mother, I kept my opinions to myself and wondered if I'd heard correctly and the skiffle group that played at a time when I was safely home ready for bed in Dollis Hill could really be playing *washboards*? My mother still used a washboard, vigorously rubbing dirty clothes up and down the soapy corrugated metal surface of the board propped up in the sink, braced against her ribs. I couldn't imagine what a skiffle group looked or sounded like.

Occasionally, someone from my old life came to London and took me into a London that neither I nor my fellows at RADA could afford to penetrate. These restaurants – often hotel dining rooms – looked, I imagined, much as they would have looked before the war. There was no attempt to be 'new' or modern. The best thing a restaurant could provide was a return, or an attempt at a return, to the time of prosperity and plenty and fixed values in food, décor and behaviour. The grander the restaurant or hotel, the more successfully impenetrable was the veil that was drawn over the very recent rationing of butter, cheese, sugar and sweets and a shilling's worth of meat per person weekly. Thick, white-starched napery and heavy cutlery went a long way towards fostering the illusion that all was as before, before 1939. I felt at home; this was the London I had read about as a little girl and that I recognised from my mother's copies of *Plays of the Year 1933*. Steak and red wine were offered as the best treat possible and, indeed, I had never tasted anything so delicious.

When my friends and I decided to eat out – a lavish gesture – we ate snacks at an ABC or consumed 'as much salad as you can eat' at Lyons Corner House or paid 4s 6d for a 'proper' formal, three-course meal at the Montmartre in Tottenham Court Road where the food was only a smidgen better than canteen food, but what did we know about such things? The staples were breaded veal escalopes and spaghetti, cooked the only way it ever was in modest English restaurants, *thoroughly* boiled and drenched in thick, ersatz tomato sauce. The Spaghetti House off Tottenham Court Road was a cut above and was saved up for special occasions. Risotto came surmounted by a fried egg and was simply heavenly. When we were in funds, we went to Charlotte Street to eat Sunday lunch in the huge German restaurant, Schmidt's, and discovered the joys of dill pickle, sauerkraut and salt beef; they *were* genuine joys and must have been excellent by any standard, or the restaurant would have joined the other German businesses all over the capital and disappeared once the hostilities had begun in 1939. I always ate everything put before me, sitting up straight, elbows tucked into my sides and appreciating every bite.

Occasionally I was taken to Soho and I remember being shocked when, spending Sunday with my foreign diplomat, who was weekending in London, we popped into Gennaro's before lunch for a drink and I heard him say, 'Bring some little things – sausages – olives – salami.' 'Oh, just take a little, *leave* the rest,' he said in reply to my surprised expression. The idea of leaving anything was anathema to me and I thought, 'Oh, well, it's because he's foreign,' as I ate everything in sight.

Some time before I left Wales for good, he had taken me to the theatre when I was in London to do a poetry reading at the Arts Council. Terence Rattigan's *Separate Tables* (viewed close-up from the front stalls, a huge novelty) seemed to offer the same reassurance that the catering world did, maintaining that all was as it used to be and all was well. I wasn't totally convinced but I thought the actors were wonderful. Eric Portman was my favourite and there was a *huge* actress (too big, I felt) who was a Terry and consequently must be related to John Gielgud, and that was a thrill, so I forgave her her size. Margaret Leighton, the leading lady, was rather lovely but spectacularly thin, which for me counted against her in the believability stakes. I'd never seen, in life, a person so well dressed, so slim, so *unlikely* looking.

I had seen relatively little theatre in the West End. My mother and father had been to London to see *Waters of the Moon* in 1951 and *A Day by the Sea* in 1953, and although my father had slept soundly through both, my mother had acted them out, scene by scene, when she came home. I *felt* I'd seen both of the N.C. Hunter plays. There were performances that as students we simply couldn't afford to go to. Miss Morrell, emphasising that we had to have plenty of breath and *then* lots left over at the end of a speech, cited the example of the Bolshoi Ballet at Covent Garden when we were in our first term in 1955. 'This is the reserve of strength you need,' she said. 'The girls in the *corps de ballet* in *Swan Lake* exit holding one leg aloft. As they approach the wings, not only does the leg, held excruciatingly high, not drop slightly, it unbelievably actually *rises* slightly.' I passed the beautiful, inaccessible theatre in Bow Street, and stood to look at the photographs and marvelled at the wonders of discipline contained inside.

I was skirting warily around what I could see in the professional theatre, admiring aspects of it, doubting a great deal, listening to other people's opinions, being discreet, aware of the unattractiveness of student superiority. Once only was I completely enraptured and moved to think, 'This is why I'm joining up.' Wandering into a theatre only because there were plenty of available tickets, I'd seen *Waiting for Godot* and it had been the greatest experience I'd ever had in the theatre – except for my first ever visit to a panto – and I think I'd viewed it with the rapture and lack of comprehension of my five-year-old self in Swansea Empire. I didn't understand the 'story' either time, but I understood that I'd seen something rare and precious. Faithful to my favourite actress, I felt it would have been even better if Edith Evans had had a part in it. *Godot* apart, it seemed to me that the establishment was firmly in place in the theatre as in the other haunts of the middle class. I had come from a classless society, so the minutiae of English life and speech were endlessly fascinating to me.

My first term came to an end and I didn't feel I'd secured my position at the Academy. I'd been allowed to do one small piece of acting. We were given over to Richard Ainley (of the rough manner), who was the son of the great Henry Ainley, and he worked with us for the whole term on one scene from *A Midsummer Night's Dream*. He gave me Titania and for about seven weeks I prepared her encounter with Oberon, beginning, 'These are the forgeries of jealousy'. I pored over it, every day. Richard Ainley was alarming and unpredictable and he made me look at ways of acting the part that I would never have dreamt of on my own. I knew the play because I had played Helena some years before in the new Festival Theatre in Sophia Gardens in Cardiff, but now I began to think along bolder, more unconventional lines. Richard Ainley must have suggested to me that I capitalise on my height and my Celtic background to play Titania as a *big* woman, deeply in touch with nature, with a maternal distress over the upsetting of the natural order. 'I want *passion*,' he growled, 'not fairy footsteps.' All the pent-up energy of months went into that short scene at the end of term. I didn't know if it was good or very ill-advised. It was certainly committed. Some senior members of staff and the principal came to see the performance on a wintry afternoon in one of the big studios.

I wasn't sacked. That was my main joy and relief. Mr Ainley, the ogre, gave me a rapturous report 'notice' and so did the other instructors, except those in the Voice Department. I was informed that I'd been given another scholarship and was told to skip the second term and move into the third. It was the first indication that things were going to turn out well. I hadn't formed any close friendships during this first term. I liked and was intrigued by many of my classmates, but the drama of the events leading up to my departure from Wales, the tensions of the audition and my continuing guilt over the failure of the marriage had left me with only just enough energy to get my work done. I needed to be alone. I needed to recoup my strength. But I had become accustomed to working with my group and now I was to be separated from them.

I went home to Wales where the BBC welcomed me back to work part-time as a newsreader and announcer. I had to remember that when I was seventeen I'd lied to the Board and added two years on to my age in order to get taken on as an announcer. This was a bit inconvenient since I was a hopeless liar, and I gradually slipped back to my correct age and hoped I would be forgiven if anyone noticed. Saunders called me and said I was to go and see Nesta Harris at the Arts Council. In recognition of the work I'd done over three years of trying to establish a Welsh-speaking National Theatre, it had been decided to give me a bursary to study drama 'abroad', and I was going to be allowed to interpret 'abroad' as England. Everything was turning out terribly well and this was a huge help at home. I spent Christmas at the farm and newspaper reports of my 'success' were clipped out, if not remarked upon, and the irregularities of my private life were completely ignored.

Chapter Twenty-eight

In April 1956 my father drove me to Cardiff Station and we stood in the cold on Platform No. 2. Daily, for the whole of my first term at RADA, we had been reminded of the precarious nature of the acting profession, urged to bear in mind what bad luck as much as lack of talent could do for a career; that most failed. I had absorbed the lesson and my two small suitcases were witness to my continuing, cautious frugality. My circumstances had improved beyond recognition. A new scholarship would take care of my tuition and the Arts Council Bursary would look after my living expenses.

During the holiday the BBC had taken me back as a relief announcer and I'd done a little acting there as well. There was talk that during the coming summer holiday the Arts Council would ask me to play Saunders Lewis's play *Siwan*, a political love story about a Princess of Wales who had been raised and educated by Eleanor of Aquitaine. Herbert Davies was to direct. I was also being approached by BBC TV – fairly new to me – to try my hand at interviewing and presenting. It seemed as though I was going to be able to support myself during my training by working within the profession that I was preparing for. I could see that this was unusual, but it did not make me feel in any way special. In everything that mattered to me I was a novice with all to learn, and I longed to be on the train and on the way back to London and RADA.

My father, undemonstrative as ever, lifted my luggage on to the rack and nodded, smiling, the smile that never lost its power to derail me. 'Did they miss me?' I wondered. I could no longer tell. Their life seemed happy and complete, their circumstances better than they had ever been. I promised to write and waved at my father as the train drew out. He would drive home to the Vale of Glamorgan, to his dog and my mother and her newly acquired (mad) parrot and his piano and his oil painting and the interesting job and the good friends, but was there an empty space where I had been?

Paddington! Now it was like coming home. Dollis Hill was dearly familiar; Sandra was no longer with us and I had the back room to myself. Mrs Styles was as brisk as ever but I fancied she was glad to see me. Margot looked romantic and doomed and even more beautiful. I'd been working on my voice all through the holiday and I'd moderated my eating habits. Now Mrs Styles agreed to help me and promised not to mind if I didn't turn up for my evening meal. She felt sufficiently unthreatened by me to let me use the front parlour as a work room when she wasn't watching television. I felt a great deal more in charge of my life as I travelled to RADA the following morning. Gone were the days when every moment of every day was a trial.

If getting back to London had been good, returning to RADA was heavenly. I couldn't become accustomed to the consolation and liberation of being with people whose beliefs, aspirations and priorities were identical with mine. It was as though a huge weight had been lifted from my shoulders and not a day went by when I didn't celebrate the ease of this life. I had never been much of a 'joiner', but for the first time I understood why people became members of demanding cults and religions or made careers in the armed forces; there was something wonderful about never being at odds with one's surroundings.

My double remove at the end of the first term hadn't made me feel more secure; the 'sack' still loomed as an end-of-term possibility – (maybe my work last term had been a flash in the pan) – but I had learned to embrace this kind of insecurity and the absence of certainty seemed to add to my sensation of lightness and freedom. Last term I had been intimidated by my classmates. As for the seniors, acting in the Vanbrugh Theatre (in Malet Street, open to the public and critics), survivors of almost two years of winnowing out, they seemed to breathe different air from mine (and of course I reflected that they would have been breathing it properly, which was more than I had managed to learn to do in three months). Now I did at least feel that I had earned a little toe-hold in the Academy and I was sufficiently at home to look about me and take an interest in the other students.

There was one young man who stood out in the busy canteen because amid all the noise and the posturing he seemed to move in a little circle of calm and quiet. One couldn't help looking at him because he never seemed to do anything. I saw him play Dryden's *All for Love* in the Vanbrugh – he was a finalist – and on stage he possessed the same knack of absorbing interest and attention for no reason that I could discover; he wasn't actually *doing* anything. I didn't feel that I knew anything for sure, but suddenly I was certain that Albert Finney was acting really well; as well as anyone I had seen in the West End.

I found myself in a new group of third-termers (there were always three groups doing the same work but using different texts) and in the third term there was to be a little acting on stage; not in the beautiful Vanbrugh, gold and red, like a 'real' theatre with proper lights and scenery and a velvet curtain, even a Royal Box – we would be allowed there only if we survived to the final term – but in the 'little' theatre in the basement in Gower Street. It was small and shabby and very black, but it was a huge step forward from acting in rooms by the light of day with the traffic of WC1 roaring outside.

We were a mixed bunch in my group, some quite 'mature', which was a new departure at RADA. I didn't want to divulge my secrets, so I didn't pry into other people's private lives, but I knew that Gerald James had, at Christopher Fry's insistence, given up his job as Youth Employment Officer in Brecon and was, at the age of forty, embarking on this new career and working as a barman to support his wife and two daughters in Wales. He was short and rotund, and though his insecurities must have been as great as anyone's, he kept them to himself and watched over the younger ones with avuncular benevolence.

I made friends with Charles Kay and as time went on we began to partner each other in full-length plays. He'd given up a career as a dentist but still remembered the rudiments, which was a comfort to us both when I accidentally knocked out a piece of his front tooth, flapping my hands, heavy with jewellery, behind me while he pursued me across the stage before hoisting me over his shoulder and carrying me off into the wings. I towered over Charles and he must have developed muscles possessed by few actors as he strode about, night after night, in play after play, holding me aloft *and talking* at the same time. He and Edward de Souza had, whether they knew it or not, a steadying influence on me. I couldn't bear to speak of my failed marriage, but I felt that if they discovered my story, they wouldn't judge me too harshly.

My girl friends were Thelma Whiteley and Hélène van Moeurs. Thelma was from America and already spoke accentless English (with good breath control). She was calm and direct and wonderfully organised in work as well as in life. She got to know more about me than most and viewed my rather ramshackle life with incredulous amusement. What did I expect from people? I was all too ready for trouble and rather grateful not to be stoned in the street. Hélène, like the other two Dutch girls I knew, was a baroness. A compact and fearless baroness. Like me, she had been an announcer, so her English was first class (but I could see that Shakespeare in English was going to elude her for ever). Nothing could scandalise Hélène and she organised her love life, her sex life and her working life with the enviable precision of a general. Towards the end of 1956 we rented a flat together. Fredrik Öhlsson from Sweden made up the fourth in our little group and they provided a refuge for me later, towards the end of my time at RADA, at a time when my life spiralled out of control and I came close to a total breakdown.

But early in 1956 I was still safe in uneventful Dollis Hill. I became more and more fascinated by the students in my group and as the months went by those of us who survived became close in a way that was new to me. As an only child I had been reared to compete and win, and I now felt as though I'd used up my entire store of competitiveness. There was none left. But I was preparing for a life in a competitive world; it was considered important to be noticed, to make an impact, but as time went by and we watched each other struggle and fail and advance and fall back, feelings of affection and regard grew and grew, and there was nothing but goodwill. There was, between many of us, a deep, unspoken empathy that left no space for rivalry.

The hours became longer and the work harder ('You will rarely, if ever, have to work as hard as this,' we were told. 'Oh, thank God,' I thought) and I arrived at a depth of happiness previously unknown to me. I remembered, as an undergraduate, spending a week reading Kant's *Critique of Pure Reason* and, recalling the text, I thought now, 'we really are doing this *for its own sake*'. Unbidden came the thought, 'This will not last for ever and you will never again be happy in this way.' I wanted it to go on for ever, preparing to act, learning to act, thinking about acting, reading about acting, watching acting, all so that one could spend the night acting with no object in mind except doing it.

I didn't spend any time trying to decipher a RADA 'method'; there was always too much work to do. Voice production remained paramount even after we'd developed into some sort of recognised performers, acting full-length plays in the Vanbrugh. A good notice in *The Times* counted for nothing if Nan Morrell had caught a performance and spotted a lazy tongue or a flabby diaphragm. 'There is no point, Siân, in acting like an angel unless you can act like an angel eight times a week for maybe fifty-two consecutive weeks. *Breathe* and *support*. At this rate you'd be "off" in ten days, and we don't "go off".' 'What a nice performance that was, Siân,' said Hugh Miller. 'Nice, that is, if one were watching from the wings. *Sell it to the paying customers!* They're in the auditorium, all three tiers of it.'

Most of the teachers were unremittingly practical and they hounded us without mercy. Praise was rarely given. We, the girls at any rate, were allowed to stop fencing lessons after a few months but, along with voice production, movement classes went on until the very end of training. Amy Boalth had the awful job of getting me moving in the first place when I was like a block of wood, before I lost my sense of shame and embarrassment. ('The one thing an actor *cannot* be, my dear, is self-conscious.') Mary Phillips, neat, distinguished and quiet, was supremely watchful. She taught Mime and in her classes the unexpected happened. She observed small shoots of talent and unobtrusively tended them into startling bloom. From Miss Phillips I learned to be prepared, to wait, not to force the imagination (she also taught me to train my eyes to go for long periods without blinking and that, later, turned out to be very useful). Miss Duff, directing a third-term play, took things at a rush. 'Turn on your actor's keyboard! Come *along*.' Then, all too often, 'Oh dear, *donkeys* all.' I consoled myself with the thought that if I could survive Mary Duff's sarcasm, I could survive most things.

The teachers who were actually *in* plays were wonderful creatures, as were those who had worked with great writers or actors. Ellen Pollock, with hooded turquoise eyes, turbaned hair, dark tanned skin and draped in Caribbean colours long before such a look was fashionable, had actu-ally been directed by George Bernard Shaw. Little Nell Carter, who gave us our first-term Shakespeare classes, directing from an ancient prompt copy, had toured in Shakespeare with fabled Victorian and Edwardian actor-managers. John Fernald, the principal, was of course a very successful director (who'd 'worked with *everybody*'). Young David Giles came to direct plays in the Vanbrugh and Peter Barkworth came from his West End play to brush up on technique, and to my dismay he found plenty for me to practise (my least favourite exercise was having to give an informed, emotional reading of a Shakespeare soliloquy while walking round a rectangular table, holding a dainty cup of tea, without spilling tea or losing eye contact with the 'house').

When, to my amazement, I became reasonably adroit, I progressed to Mme Fedro's Movement class and, like most of her students, was enslaved by her, inspired by her and bowled over by her genuine glamour. She taught movement that enhanced acting – that conveyed feeling and ideas moment by moment. She 'gave' me my first big entrance when, in my final term, I played Magda by Sudermann, a play called *Heimat* (*Home*) in German. Magda was a successful opera singer who, in the play, returns to visit her narrow, oppressive home. The play hadn't been performed since Eleanor Duse and Sarah Bernhardt had both played the title role at the same time in London in the late nineteenth century.

By the time I opened at the Vanbrugh with all the London critics out front and a full house agog to see how I would acquit myself, Fedro had taught me how to walk like the opera star that was Magda, how to assume that I was the most interesting and glamorous person 'in the *whole of London*', she said firmly. Willie in the Wardrobe had shown me how to take off my buttoned gloves and trail my beautiful fur as though I had five more at home; Richard Carey had given me a *real* Sarah Bernhardt fan to wear (and shown me how to use it).

I made an overnight success and job offers flooded in, but I was taken back to the classroom and slowly and patiently the faults that had slipped by unnoticed in the excitement of a successful performance were laid out, examined and worked on. I was overwhelmed with gratitude for such care and attention. John Fernald, who had directed me, had been concerned only with the play and the part, but he handed me over without a qualm for technical debriefing. I should have been the happiest girl in the world, but there was a serpent in my Eden.

Chapter Twenty-nine

As though there was not enough work to do inside the walls of RADA, it was the practice to 'loan out' reliable students to professional and semi-professional companies. We rehearsed on Sundays and any evenings when we were not needed at RADA. The Tavistock Players had moved to the Tower in Canonbury, a beautiful Jacobean house that had once belonged to Sir Francis Bacon. There was an ancient mulberry tree in the garden and I was immensely taken by the beautiful, run-down, shabby neighbourhood. As I walked through Islington I thought that one day I would love to live in one of the broken-down Georgian houses I saw on all sides. Leaving Islington at sunset, sitting on the top deck of a Number 19 bus with an uninterrupted view down the hill to King's Cross with the fairy towers of St Pancras Station silhouetted against the pink sky, I 'printed' the view in my mind, where it remained, indelible.

I was to play the lead in *Les Justes* by Camus with two professional actors and, astonishingly, a friend of mine from my university days. Peter Gyngell, a fellow Philosophy student (and a RADA-trained student before that) who had played Othello, much better than I'd played Desdemona, and who had been sidetracked into playing *Les Justes* while preparing to go abroad to begin his new life with comput-ers. He was an interesting man and *Les Justes* was an interesting job. Our director was also interesting; all too interesting as it turned out.

Guy was smallish, intense and clever. Ever a sucker for brains, I was charmed at the first meeting. He had graduated from Oxford some ten years previously and I learned that his preoccupation had been docu-mentary film and that he and Lindsay Anderson had together won an Oscar for their first movie, *Thursday's Child*, but now he had assembled a portfolio of plays that he was going to begin trying out, with a view to moving into theatre production. *Les Justes* was the first of these plays and it would be seen by several West End producers. He had cast the rest of the company himself, but I was a kind of present from Gower Street for the crucial role of Dora, so I was anxious to prove myself.

I could tell that he quickly came to like his present and the play was a success, although it must have been a bit overwhelming; intensely written, intensely acted and intensely directed, not a smile from start to finish, it wasn't everyone's cup of tea. Guy and I began to spend time together, talking and talking in the Tower garden with its mulberry tree, and after the show we would drive down to the Embankment in his newly acquired car and sit looking across the river at the OXO sign, drinking cups of tea and eating sausage sandwiches that he bought at the little late-night tea and coffee stall nearby.

Not only was I never in for dinner, I was now getting back to Dollis Hill later and later at night. Guy couldn't believe that I lived in Dollis Hill. He couldn't believe in Dollis Hill. He had just bought a flat in Earl's Court, my first resting place in London, though he preferred to say that he lived in Kensington (which was just an inch away) and that, coupled with his snootiness about Dollis Hill, led me to think that he was a bit of a snob. By this time he could have revealed himself as an axe murderer and I wouldn't have turned a hair. I was *fascinated*. And it seemed so sensible and practical for an actress to take up with a director. For once I was using my head as well as my heart and I congratulated myself.

I could tell that Guy, having emerged from a difficult time when he had had to deal with consumption as well as a disastrously unhappy love affair, was not an easy person, but at that time I loved a challenge, and the fact that he had problems made him all the more interesting and appealing in my eyes. I conveniently forgot that I was a very inconclusively separated, young married woman with a string of failed relationships behind her, who had sworn off men for the foreseeable future and possibly beyond, and, needless to say, I kept very quiet about Guy at RADA. I had a feeling that the news of my involvement wouldn't go down well. I didn't know why, I just thought that it wouldn't.

Guy went abroad to make a film and I settled down to a more regular life at Dollis Hill, working hard and doing well at RADA. Charles Kay and I won a verse-speaking prize. It was reported in *The Times* and the following morning we both had job offers, to make a recording in a studio in Soho. Mr Fernald gave us the morning off and we bowled along to W1, hugely excited. The little doorway in Soho didn't look as though it led to much of a studio and we climbed the rickety, narrow

Georgian staircase to find ourselves in an almost empty little room with a curtainless window looking on to a ratty bit of backyard. There was a microphone, tied to the back of a wooden chair.

'Okay,' said an indifferent man, 'you for the recording?' We nodded. 'Here's your script,' he said, before disappearing into the next room. I looked at the first of about six pages. 'Hullo Chirpy,' it read – twenty times. I turned over. 'Give us a kiss,' repeated twenty times, took up the whole of page two. The bored face popped round the door. 'This is for the States, so not too Shakespearian. One of you take the intro, then divide it up however. In your own time. Leave decent pauses.' I took the introduction. 'Keeping budgerigars is FUN. Teaching them to speak is a BORE. Let us . . .' And so on. I hardly dared to look at Charlie and for the next couple of hours, leaving decent pauses and not too Shakespearian, we laid down the basis of good budgerigar diction in the United States.

Bored face gave us a tenner each as though he was tipping the cleaners and we raced down the stairs and round the corner before giving way to the pent-up hysteria of the morning. So much for the Forbes Robertson or the George Arliss – whichever prize we'd been so proud to win.

I went home at the end of term. My report arrived and to my relief it was good. I did a little work at the BBC as usual, went west to visit Meriel and my cousins and my grandmother, but not to Tŷ mawr this time. John, Meriel's husband had worked long and well at Tŷ mawr, building up the herd and improving and modernising the farm, and they realised that they could and should now move forward and upward, to a farm with richer land and no precipitous hills. Tŷ mawr had been in the family for generations. How would my grandmother respond to the suggestion of a move?

They agonised over the problem for months; my mother thought it too cruel to expect her mother, in her late eighties, to pack up and leave her birthplace that she had loved so long and where she had worked so hard. Meriel, ever more enterprising, thought it worthwhile suggesting. Everyone was astonished when my grandmother, having studied the business proposal and the deeds of the new property further west in Carmarthenshire, looked up and said in Welsh, 'Of course. It's wonderful. When do we go?' 'These women . . .' I thought again, admiringly. My mother misquoted from the Bible, 'What meat does she eat to grow so strong?'

So now I, sentimentally mourning the loss of my birthplace, went to Whitland to visit the new farm and saw my grandmother completely and happily translated to the big inglenook, still awake at 5.30 in the morning, still cooking, still cleaning twenty pairs of muddy shoes each day, still reading the Welsh Bible and the Welsh-language paper, *Y Faner*. Her only concession to her great age was that now she slept on the ground floor in the far front parlour. I noticed that Meriel and John and their son, Huw, home from school for the Easter holiday, all deferred to her in the most charming way as they discussed the running of the farm and the virtues of modernising.

Thelma Whiteley, one of my close friends from RADA, was spending the holiday in Wales with me, and my grandmother seemed politely bemused that two great, strapping young women should be idling away their time in London. A diploma in Dramatic Art made no sense to her at all, and why should it?

Chapter Thirty

Still in Dollis Hill. More than halfway through my course and progress had really slowed down. It had been noticed that I didn't stand straight and the doctor who looked after the bones of RADA students read me a stern lecture. I was given exercises and told to persevere with them or else I would lay up trouble for myself in the future, not least of all, vocal trouble. Oh, vocal trouble . . . The voice! When I read all those years ago in Cardiff that acting was 'Voice, voice and more voice', I had no idea that my life was going to be completely taken over by voice, voice and yet more voice. It was still unsatisfactory. I was very good at disguising my faults, but I knew that it just wouldn't do. On with the slow, plodding grind.

Guy was due back from location in Indonesia. London seemed empty without him and late at night on the day of his return I crept downstairs at Dollis Hill, took the phone from the hat stand in the hall and, feeling slightly foolish, sat curled up in the dark in an armchair in the front parlour, dialling his Fremantle exchange number and settling down to wait. I was half asleep when the ringing stopped and the familiar, rather precious, English voice said, 'Yes?' 'I just wanted to hear your voice say hello.' 'Are you in dreaded NW2?' 'Yes.' 'Be ready in half an hour, I'm coming to fetch you.' A few days later I collected my luggage from Mrs Styles, paid my bill in full and left Dollis Hill for ever.

Collingham Place, Earl's Court, and a very different life. Tentatively I played house until I realised that Guy had already made all the domestic arrangements and they were perfectly adequate. I had only to fit in. This suited me very well and I congratulated myself yet again for being smart enough or lucky enough to have fallen in love with a brilliant man who could also buy furniture, order curtains and carpets, equip a kitchen and cook! In Wales, these things constituted Woman's Work and I had never got round to mastering any of them.

My new life stretched ahead in a very agreeable way. Of course, Living in Sin was something to be reckoned with, a new misdemeanour ('Was it an actual crime?' I wondered). Guy wanted no truck with my schoolgirl nerves over what I perceived as an irregular situation, so I kept my worries to myself, said nothing to my family or my friends at RADA, and concentrated on the agreeable aspect of our life together. I loved to listen to Guy and he introduced me to a much more sophisticated world than any I had encountered before. Life at Oxford had been very different from life in the provinces, and his friends, a good deal older than myself, were, on the whole, establishment figures. I acquired a new reading list and mostly sat around listening and learning.

Things went wrong in a completely unexpected way. I had got out of the custom of concealing my ambitions and enthusiasms, and chattered away uninhibitedly about plays and parts I wanted to play and parts I was engaged on, until one day my seventh sense told me to stop. Months had gone by and Guy had driven me to Wales to pick up my books and bits and pieces of linen and china so that I would feel properly at home in the flat. Our situation had been presented to my parents as *a fait accompli*. They were not entirely happy, and when we drove away from the house I felt that I had burned several bridges. My London life was set and fixed with Guy, and I began to feel apprehensive as I realised that Guy's attitude towards the theatre was changing. The habit of a lifetime reasserted itself and I stopped talking about my working life. He'd made another film and I enjoyed visiting the cutting room in a Soho basement late at night, learning how to handle film and watching him edit. He dazzled me, still.

I was now in my final term, rehearsing *Magda*, and knew that it would be a significant test for me. As a final student I was to play in the Vanbrugh Theatre. It was a huge, difficult part and I was only too aware of the pitfalls ahead. With the press taking an interest in the revival, I knew I would be the subject of intense scrutiny. Herbert Davies made plans to come up from Wales to see the play. My parents said they might come as well. I knew that the Welsh press would be there and it seemed the English national press were going to cover it as well. For once I wasn't unduly nervous; the play had learned itself, John Fernald's rehearsals were superbly organised and everything rose to the boil at the right moment. The themes of the play were close to my heart: loss of home, exile, conflict between heart and career.

The reaction, however, took me by surprise. I could have left the Academy at that moment and started a career at the top of the tree. I was offered contracts, plays and movies; all the best agents wrote asking if they could represent me; artists wanted to paint me. I was asked to sit for cover photographs for magazines and endlessly the press wanted to interview me. It was a difficult situation for me as a student, especially since I had accepted the advice of John Fernald, rejected all the offers and decided to stay on at RADA and do another final term to make up for the term I'd skipped over earlier on. I played down the dramatic change in my situation, but it wasn't possible entirely to conceal it. From my fellow students I received nothing but generosity. The door was closed on the offers and the excitement. Journalists were discouraged and this suited me; I had no wish to publicise my separation or my relationship with Guy, and Guy was becoming increasingly edgy as my stock rose in spite of myself.

Gradually we became bogged down in ongoing, far-into-the-night discussions about the fitness and propriety of a life in the theatre. Guy revealed that he proposed to leave the 'business' altogether and intended to make a career in a completely different field, doing something – he hadn't decided what – more worthwhile, of more use to the world. I was aghast. These were themes I had been rehearsing all my life. Every boyfriend, every lover, my husband, Don, had all argued against the suitability, the worth of my chosen career, and all had tried to make me give it up. The arguments had varied in skill and intensity, but I had never seriously wavered. Now I couldn't face going through it all again. Guy was much cleverer than I was, much, much cleverer. He beat me in every argument, was by turns angry and tender, and I was in torment.

Magda came to an end and with it the brouhaha about comparison with Duse and Bernhardt. I breathed a huge sigh of relief at having come through. After the last matinée I was told I had a visitor. Peering out into the inhospitable cement stairway, I looked down at a very large red face looking up at me. 'I'm Robert Atkins,' said the face. 'I've got just one thing to say to you – *don't* go into the fillums,' and the famous former artistic director of the Stratford Memorial Theatre was gone, leaving me feeling as though I'd been given a very quick award.

I began to rehearse two small parts in *The Silver Curlew*, a musical, in which I was entrusted with a 'point' number (which seemed to define a song that didn't need to be beautifully sung). I was to play an ugly witch in the forest and a fairy godmother with the gift of beauty, which I would carry in a little jewelled box as I emerged from a christening cake dressed in a pretty frock and performing a little dance.

Guy was now pressing me to leave RADA after *Magda*. I came to the end of my defences and could no longer justify my chosen life. I had, by now, begun to believe that an actress's life *was* pernicious, that there was no possibility of combining an actress's career with a 'good' life. A psychiatrist friend of Guy's assured me that actresses were scarcely recognisable as normal human beings after the age of forty, when it was too late to hope for redemption. Guy sensed that he'd almost won and the endless discussions lessened.

I confessed my predicament to John Fernald and he was angry. He was enraged. I don't know what I had expected of him, but I was too dazed with unhappiness to realise that I was conveying to him Guy's contempt for *his* life as well as mine. John was deeply offended and demanded to see Guy. Meanwhile, I was ordered to concentrate on my work, remember my duty and think of my considerable debt to the Academy. Fernald wrote to Herbert and Saunders, and letters began to arrive by each post expressing outrage and completely failing to understand how I could possibly put a love affair before my career.

By now, I was ashamed of everything: ashamed of being in love, ashamed of having a career, ashamed of neglecting my career, ashamed of being unable to make paramount a loving relationship with another human being, ashamed of being too independent, ashamed of being feeble-minded. The heavy guns were mobilised and wheeled out to bring me back into line; Dame Sybil Thorndike summoned me to tea and lectured me kindly but forcibly about the nature of Service in the Theatre. Flora Robson was roped in to express sad resignation, but to confirm an actress's lonely lot. I couldn't work out what was right and I hung there, in pain.

The situation was slightly diffused by a bout of ordinary physical pain. Driving to a matinée of *The Silver Curlew*, in the throes of a weary argument after a sleepless night, our car struck a lorry in the fog in Paddington – or a lorry struck us. I was aware only of bouncing on to the windscreen and the huge, empty noise of metal striking metal. I came to on a pavement as a voice asked, 'She all right?' 'Nah, don't look it. She's a bit of a mess.'

I drifted off again and the next time I came to, on a cold slab, a young man's exasperated voice was saying, 'Oh damn and blast!' as he fiddled with my face. I opened my eyes and peered at him through what seemed to be a thicket of fine, black wires. I lifted my hand to my face and the exasperated one slapped it down gently. 'Lie still. Don't touch. I'm trying to sew your forehead together. You're very lucky you've got eyes, so just shut them for a minute, there's a good girl.' He stitched away silently, confiding to me that my jaw was back in place – he *thought*.

I opened my eyes again. He looked about twelve years old. 'Are you a student?' I asked. 'Never you mind,' he replied and did a spot more embroidery. I came to my senses suddenly. 'What's the time?' 'About two.' 'Oh my God. Excuse me.' I began to slide my legs off the trolley. 'Where are you going?' 'I've got a matinée.' 'Don't be absurd. I'm keeping you in. You're probably concussed and Lord knows what else.' 'Sorry, I'm off.' 'If you leave this building you have to sign a form discharging yourself.' 'Sure thing.'

I was on my feet and fishing for a pen in my bag that someone had put at my feet as I lay on the trolley. 'This is absurd,' began the young man. 'Sorry,' I replied, walking out of the room as steadily as I was able. The nurse, holding out a paper for me to sign, looked at my chest and I looked down to see my cream Viyella blouse stiff and brown with drying blood. 'Is my face clean?' I asked her. 'Ye-es,' she said, doubtfully. I had no wish to look. Instead, scribbling my name on the form and calling out 'Thanks a lot,' I left St Mary's, Paddington.

I was feeling decidedly odd but had the sense to button up my coat, hiding the blood, before hailing a taxi. 'Vanbrugh Theatre, Malet Street,' I said urgently. 'I'm in a bit of a hurry.' 'Are you all right?' asked the driver. 'Yes, fine,' I assured him and sank back into the corner of the soft leather seat, wonderfully protected from the outside world, which appeared in small foggy bits through the wedge-shaped back window next to my head.

At the Vanbrugh the show was about to begin. 'I'm here, I'm here! Sorry,' I called out before dashing into the dressing room. 'I'll need to see you later!' shouted an angry voice from the stairs. I got into my witch wig and costume, and laid about my face with a stick of green Leichner greasepaint. I suppose I was concussed because I didn't actually *see* my face as I got made up.

On stage, bathed in purple and green light in the dark wood, I squatted behind the huge cauldron and bobbed up and down singing my witchy song and it seemed to go quite well. Then I whipped back to my little corner and transformed myself into the Fairy Godmother. This time, it hurt rather to clean off the green paint and wipe the black from my teeth, and I noted dispassionately that my face looked odd. The young man's sewing had left a great deal to be desired; great black 'spiders' marched across my forehead and through my eyebrows. My nose was swollen and my lips were a funny shape. There were stitches on my chin. My whole face was turning a strange colour . . . 'Ah well, it can't be helped,' I thought calmly. I dabbed on a little more powder and made off for my place inside the huge christening cake.

'The Fairy Godmother with the gift of Beauty,' shouted a footman (Nick Smith, if I remember rightly). Tum TUM, tum tum, tum TUM, tum tum, went the orchestra. The cake swung open and I tried not to flinch as I stepped into the white and pink light and gritted my teeth as I determinedly set off on a circuit of the stage, keeping one eye on the cradle I was aiming for. 'If I can just make it over there,' I thought, 'I'll have got away with it.' I was so gone in the head I didn't even hear the laughter in the audience. In the wings, someone from Stage Management said, 'For God's sake, *do* something about your face – sequins or something.' I remember only going out between the shows to the chemist around the corner and buying Elastoplast, then down to Tottenham Court Road for purple sparkle dust and glue. Then, after my second outing as the witch that evening, I set to work putting Elastoplast across my forehead and gluing purple dust on to the strips. 'Pretty good,' I thought. 'You can't see the stitches at all. Well – just a bit.' I added a few more strips of Elastoplast to my cheekbones and scattered some more purple stuff here and there.

Did anyone sympathise? If so, I didn't notice. Certainly no one suggested that I should miss a performance, nor would I have wanted to do so. Everything hurt, but at one remove. I didn't even notice how my Fairy Godmother fared on stage that night and was next fully aware of getting off the tube at Earl's Court. If anyone stared at my face, rainbow bruised and iridescently decorated, or at my bloody blouse, then I was not aware of it and not in the least concerned. I felt rather pleased with myself. Guy was at home. I'd forgotten about him during the effort of getting through two shows. I couldn't quite bring him into focus and I certainly didn't want a post-mortem of the day. Not now. Not at all.

'Bath,' I said, suddenly quite cheerful. As I applied a match to the wrong bit of the geyser and blew myself across the bathroom, I lay on the floor and thought, 'Well, it could all have been a *lot* worse.'

Chapter Thirty-one

The same divine stupidity remained with me during the coming months and not once did I lament my ruined face, or fear that my career was at an end, or at the least, significantly changed. I came to my senses sufficiently to realise that at home I now occupied the moral high ground for a while. I figured that Guy must feel awful to have been driving the car in which I'd been hurt, grateful that I wasn't going to spoil his no claims insurance policy, and *sorry* for me. I was stupidly childish enough to think that maybe if I became a very plain actress I might appear to be more morally acceptable. Nothing much was said at home or at RADA. I postponed my showdown with Herbert and kept out of Mr Fernald's way at RADA. When he passed me in the corridor, he shook his head at my bent nose and jagged scars.

At the end of term, Guy decided that we should make a journey to Iona in Scotland. I was thrilled; I'd never been to Scotland and I'd read wonderful things about the islands in the West. Ever optimistic, I thought that everything was going to be all right, after all.

We drove to Scotland. It was a long, wonderful, cold journey. At Oban we took a boat that called at Rhum and Eigg and Muck, before depositing us on Iona. We made our way to the bare lodging house and went for a walk. Night was falling, but full darkness did not come, and the lilac light hung between us and the darkening stone buildings, and rough, grey, treeless fields with the black sea beyond. It was the same light that I had seen shimmering on midsummer nights in the Swedish countryside, but Iona was a world away from soft, warm, sensual Västerås. I went to my narrow bed feeling uneasy and all at once isolated.

After breakfast we walked again in the intense cold, and as we walked we began to talk, and the pit of my stomach seemed to fall away and my throat constricted as I realised that there was not to be an easy conclusion to our debate; I was not going to be able to charm my way to a compromise. We were both raw with misery and Guy was pushing for a resolution. Didn't this place make it easier for me to see how much 'better' life could be? How much better *I* could be in a different world? I longed to capitulate and be gathered up into a warm embrace of approval. The world I was being offered was attractive, and I was so in love and terrified as I felt myself free-falling away from the person that I admired, wanted, loved and feared. But I did not in fact have a choice. I couldn't leave the theatre. My world seemed bleak and as cold as charity, but it was my world and I had to find a way of living in it.

When he realised that I had made my decision and couldn't do as he wished, he grew cold and distant – partly, I thought, from pain. He wanted me out of his sight at once. There was no question that we should travel back to London together. I was to leave alone on the first boat and take a train from Oban. I thought my heart was breaking as I watched from the boat and the island disappeared from view. I had expected so much of this place and it seemed wrong that it should have served merely as a setting for an unhappiness that I had brought there.

I sat in the corner of a crowded compartment; eight of us squashed together for hours. Reserve fell away and the other travellers began to chat a little. A hard lump had lodged in my throat; speaking would have choked me. I looked sightlessly out of the window and struggled not to cry out. For eight hours? – nine? I averted my face and forced back the tears that were insisting behind my eyes. It was dark when we pulled into London and still I struggled to retain control of myself until the taxi drew into Collingham Place. I unlocked the door of the familiar flat and, dropping my suitcase on the floor, sank to the ground and wept.

Some time during the night, I shed my coat and shoes and went into the bedroom; then, still dressed, I climbed into the bed, sheets unchanged since they were ours from four long days ago. At daybreak I fell asleep, waking on what day and at what time I didn't know. The clock had stopped, I didn't wear a watch and it didn't occur to me to lift the telephone receiver to ask the operator the time. Tears had given way to fear. I knew there was no going back, but what had I done? I was following my instinct, but although it was strong enough to have forced me into this situation of extreme unhappiness, it wasn't *clever*; it wasn't telling me anything. I was left with no explanations and no certainties.

Self-preservation prompted me to think of food. How many days since I had eaten? But it was no good, I couldn't walk down the stairs and into the street. Instead I lay on the bed and the argument I'd been having with Guy began to repeat itself. I couldn't be sure that he wasn't right.

I couldn't be sure that I hadn't taken a fatally wrong step, turning away for good from intimacy and warmth and uncomplicated happiness.

Sitting on the bed, I feverishly picked through the theatre books piled up everywhere. Surely *somewhere*, *someone* had written *something* that would help me comprehend the nature and the reality of the world to which I had committed myself. Surely it wasn't the monstrous, pernicious, tawdry place of Guy's imagining, or the dark, secret home of the devil as my grandparents had believed? Obviously, it wasn't the place of uncomplicated happiness that I had understood and felt it to be. What was the price of admission? More than I had realised. Worse still, what was the cost of a permanent tenancy, and did I have the means to pay it? The questions remained unanswered and exhaustion led me to sleep again.

Waking, I put my coat on, smoothed my hair and ventured out. It was so cold, or was it that I was cold? I picked up a tin of baked beans, then, realising that I was going to begin crying again, I quickly paid for it and ran home. No, it wasn't home, not any longer. The tears flowed and I opened the can of beans and ate them cold from the tin. I felt a grim satisfaction that I could eat and cry at the same time. This was a good sign, and I undressed and bathed in cold water (I hadn't dared touch the boiler since I'd blown it off the wall), changing into clean clothes and ready then to start living. Leaving all my books and china and most of my clothes, I packed a small bag and, after telephoning my parents – in a quiet, and carefully neutral tone – I went to Paddington and caught the train to Wales.

Chapter Thirty-two

My family was tactful. I didn't have to explain that it was all over. It hurt me when well-meaning people who had learned the gist of my story consoled me with praise for having done 'the right thing'. This was not a story about being led astray by a bad person. I wasn't totally sure about the purity of his motives in his dealings with me, but Guy was a good person, and who could say what was the right thing to do? I was badly hurt and I kept quiet, scarcely speaking, grateful that I was being given time to recover before returning to London.

On my return Guy had softened sufficiently to find me a flat in Great Ormond Street. I felt better, but not better enough to go back to Earl's Court to pick up my things. I experienced a pang of regret only over my complete Charles Dickens, which I'd been reading and re-reading since I was little. It seemed better to move on with nothing. I liked the flat, in a modern back extension to one of the big Georgian houses. It was calm, uncomplicated, peaceful. On my first morning there I was awakened at 5 a.m. by the sound of several large vehicles starting up at what seemed to be the foot of my bed. Leaning out of the window that opened on to the little mews behind Great Ormond Street, I burst out laughing for the first time in months as I realised that I was living over a very busy, well-equipped garage that sprang to life at dawn. 'Every day?' I asked, weak with laughter. "Fraid so, miss.' I don't know why, but I felt immensely cheered, and within a week I was sleeping soundly through the noise.

Hélène and Thelma came to inspect my new living arrangements and were cautiously approving. They couldn't believe I'd been so 'stupid'. By now they knew the bare bones of the trouble I had been in at RADA. I loved their breezy dismissal of the anguish and their good-natured incredulity at my 'madness' following the run of *Magda*. I couldn't share their attitude, but it was a lifeline to normality. Guy also came to visit. I didn't know why. He said little but he stayed over, sleeping chastely on the floor. During the night I had a dream; the first dream that had ever woken me up, and it remained clear and entire in my mind.

Seated in an ornate cage-like lift (the sort I'd seen in France), I was dressed in my blue silk Act I *Magda* dress, playing a cello, very much in the pose of the Augustus John painting of Suggia. It was a brilliant scene: dark blue taffeta silk, gilt everywhere, rich dark shiny wood and the walls on either side of the lift brilliantly lit like the backcloth of an opera. As the lift began its slow ascent my dress began to unravel itself in strips, first the bodice and then the long skirt until, greatly shamed, I was left naked in full view of a large but invisible, silent audience.

I lay in bed in the early morning sun and went over the dream in my head; 'gilt everywhere', oh Lord, '*guilt* everywhere', 'shame'. This had to stop. Guy woke and I made tea. It was painful, preparing it exactly the way he liked it, because I knew, sadly and certainly, that I would never, could never again observe the little ritual or see him again.

A few nights later I was awakened by the occurrence of another vivid dream, or rather, a recollection of something I had never before recalled. I saw myself in the parlour of the house next to the one I had lived in until I was five years old in the little village of Dunvant, standing in front of a shiny oilcloth scroll that depicted two roads; one a broad thoroughfare with cafés and theatres and dance halls and people having a lovely time strolling down the road until suddenly they tumbled, very surprised, into the flames of hell at the bottom of the chart. The road from the middle to the top of the scroll was called the Narrow Way and people hobbled and struggled up its rocky surface in awful weather – no cafés or theatres – until they arrived – again rather surprised I would have thought, but I couldn't see their faces – on to a level plain in front of a huge rising sun where Jesus Christ (or God, I couldn't be sure which) stood welcoming them with outstretched arms.

I fancy that my parents weren't best pleased with my daily excursions next door to pore over the Broad and Narrow Way, which so enthralled me. The neighbours must have belonged to some obscure religious sect and they were delighted by my interest, but I viewed the scroll rather as one would read a horror story. I didn't want to fall into the pit, but I hated the rocky path of righteousness and didn't much like the level plain dominated by the oversized sun either. The only nice bit was the hanging about in dance halls and theatres, but, oh dear, those waiting devils with pitchforks . . . I thrilled to the horror at the bottom of the chart and never tired of peering at the awful details.

I lay looking at the ceiling, wide awake, half amused at the recollection and half appalled. The Broad and Narrow Way was a crude, simpler version of the sophisticated arguments with which I'd been wrestling for so many months, intellectually out of my depth but retaining a small piece of self-determination and just enough backbone to see me through – I hoped.

I missed Guy badly; I missed having a family life with him, but I hadn't spent all these years fighting the puritanism that seemed to have been bred into my bones in order to succumb now that I was over twenty. 'Take what you want and pay for it.' I went to work and began paying.

My face had healed, leaving me with deep jagged scars, a broken nose and a rather unstable jaw. It seems unbelievable, but still there was never a moment when I worried about my appearance or about its effect on my career. I don't know whether anyone believed this, but it was the case. My wayward voice began to come to heel! I wondered superstitiously if I was being given some kind of reward for good behaviour when I came to the end of a Shakespeare sonnet and Miss Morrell and I looked at each other, and for the first time in almost two years she nodded approval. Not for a single day had I stopped trying to be clear, unaffected, audible, flexible, unforced, musical-where-needed, interesting, intelligible, energetic, durable, strong. All I'd managed was strong, durable, audible and tense, dull, forced, rigid, unnatural and self-conscious. This was happiness, this easy stroll through a sonnet. Miss Morrell had been the bane of my life latterly; even other members of staff had begun to say, 'Well, you know, there's nothing *so* bad about her voice.' I won verse-speaking prizes for RADA, and within RADA was awarded an embarrassing number of awards. None of this had been signified to Miss Morrell and she'd kept my nose to the grindstone. Now, suddenly and unaccountably, I was through! Everything began to fall into place and my gratitude to my gorgon was limitless.

Deep inside I carried a thick, immovable layer of unhappiness, but it was overlaid with pleasure, joy and interest. My friends were wonderful to me. Charles Kay, Edward de Souza and Gerald James, always tactful, never prying, taking me 'out of myself', along with Thelma Whiteley and Hélène van Moeurs and Fredrik. We spent long hours drinking (very little) coffee in Ollivelli's café above the restaurant, and Gerald had tamed the greasy-spoon-café-owner on the corner of Goodge Street and Charlotte Street into letting us occupy the little room for hours on end and even buy meals 'on tick'. Gerald organised trips on the river on Sundays and we went to Kew and to Greenwich. We drank coffee in the Festival Hall café on the first floor looking out over the best view of London I'd yet discovered, and on special occasions went back to eat pasta in the Spaghetti House off Tottenham Court Road or a heavy German meal at Schmidt's in Charlotte Street. Edward organised us into more 'as much as you can eat' salad parties at Lyons Corner House in Leicester Square.

Food was still a necessary fuel rather than an entertaining part of life. Our eating habits seemed pathetic to the foreign students, especially to Americans. 'I'm going to die unless I eat some meat,' said an American student, Gay Gadbois, one lunchtime in the canteen. 'Come with me.' Gay looked as though she belonged to a different species: tall, glossy-haired and beautiful, with legs encased for work in shiny American tights and a leotard that never wrinkled. She had the air of one who had been reared on orange juice, cream and abundant meat.

We raced down Tottenham Court Road, I feeling very strange – it had never occurred to me to leave the building during the day. At St Giles Circus she strode into a café that was called a Wimpy Bar. I didn't know what a Wimpy was and refused one when she offered it to treat me – I'd already eaten a cheese roll in the canteen. I watched her as she devoured two hamburgers, flat discs of meat that weren't made of ham at all, squeezed into a large soft roll, ketchup provided in funny round containers shaped like a tomato. I'd never seen anyone so cheered up by a bit of meat and I shared her good mood as we tore back to work. The next time someone from my past life at the BBC took me to a smart hotel, I ordered beef and was appalled at the cutting and chewing involved in my shared piece of Chateaubriand, but very impressed by the Bearnaise sauce that accompanied it. A Bearnaise sauce sandwich would have been bliss, I thought.

All these outings and excursions were squeezed into a life filled with work. All day we laboured over mime and movement and improvisation, then began rehearsing until, at the end of the afternoon, we were given a few hours off before the evening performances in the Vanbrugh. I played some good parts in *The Three Sisters* and *The Three Daughters of M. Dupont*, and really small parts in other plays, enjoying those just as much. Even our theatre-going was limited; theatre-going was expensive and we didn't have many nights off. We heard each other's lines even when we were out, and grew close and wished each other well. We played old commercial plays like *Cry Havoc* and *Black Chiffon* in halls in Camden near RADA and in the open air in Russell Square where Act One was drowned out by the sound of taxis taking people to the 'real' theatre.

The Caucasian Chalk Circle played the Vanbrugh and also went to the York Festival. I was given the Governor's Wife and Lodovica, the Girl in the Hay. The nights were long and fine and we lounged about near the river and I began a flirtation with Fredrik. Gerald shook his head benignly. 'Just you wait my girl; soon, very soon, you're going to be swept off your feet by somebody – like a tornado.' 'I don't think so,' I smiled back at the Welsh wizard. I was only just coming to life again and a massive love affair was not on my agenda. Hans Haas was the curator of the Art Gallery at York. He took us under his wing and gave us a tour and a bit of a picnic. 'Education,' he said apropos of nothing in particular, 'is the impact of quality.' We looked at each other and nodded.

Chapter Thirty-three

The plan seemed to be to keep me busy so I'd have no time to get into any more trouble. I saw very little of my little flat (so small and so compact that it was actually termed a 'flatlet'). Not only was I acting in the Vanbrugh but I and another student, John French, were loaned out to a wealthy, mildly eccentric English gentleman who presented a Shakespeare play each summer in his beautiful garden in the country, near Newbury. At the weekend, on Saturday, if I wasn't needed at RADA, or very early on Sunday morning, Flair, the butler, would pick me up from Great Ormond Street and drive in a stately fashion to Berkshire, where Herbie, whose surname I missed completely, was waiting with his wife, Paulise de Busch, heiress to a huge soft-drinks empire ('Every drop of Kia-Ora, dear, is based on some kind of juice from the de Busch factory in Germany,' breathed an awe-struck house-guest-cum-extra-'walking'-lady) eager to feed us sumptuously, deliciously and get on with *Twelfth Night*.

When term ended I was packed off to stay at the country house, spending the week alone with Flair and the housekeeper and awaiting the invasion of house-guests chosen as friends only if they were proved capable Shakespeare actors. It was a charming motley crew of middle-class bankers and lawyers and retired diplomats, and my chum (Orsino) was Michael Vowden, who was 'something' in Shell but hated it and wished he'd stuck to acting instead. Herbie in his youth (he and Paulise seemed quite old to me) had been a member of the noted F.R. Benson Shakespeare Company. Marriage and the advent of all that expensive fruit juice had scuppered his career as a lowly, hard-working member of a touring company, but he loved Shakespeare and we all bent under his lash as he re-created the productions of thirty or forty years ago. It was an agreeable way of passing the early months of summer and I made my first encounter with the comforts of wealth. Food was delicious, unlike anything that I'd tasted except in France and Sweden, and comforting little snacks and drinks appeared unbidden at one's elbow. The famed fruit juice was much in evidence and I made the acquaintance of a long drink made of gin and heavenly German ginger beer. And the ice was *round* and the glasses were beautiful. We sat in the rose-framed outdoor dining room, protected on three sides, looking out over the lawns down to the stream with the sun setting beyond the trees, and I thought that my heart might be broken but I was loving every moment of this soft life.

Flair, the butler, drank. He approached actors taking their ease in the garden during rehearsal, picking his way cautiously through the summer air with a reviving drink sliding gently down the wobbly tray towards the reclining house guest. 'I believe your call is approaching, madam,' he would intone quietly as the guest snatched the falling glass. On weekdays when we were alone, he would open *The Times* and fill in the crossword, each clue no sooner read than solved. At weekends he merely read the crossword, then ironed the paper before giving it to Herbie.

I didn't much like acting in the open air except towards the end of the play, when dusk fell and the lights came up and the performance always drew to a beautiful close no matter what the deficiencies of the opening scenes. Michael Vowden was patient and wise when, unusually for me, I confided my troubles to him as we took walks in the comfortable well-tended countryside of Berkshire. He was one of the few people who didn't find my preoccupation with good and evil to be absurd.

As soon as the play was over, my face was finally dealt with. The representatives of Paramount Pictures in London were courting me with a view to putting me under a contract in the United States, though *Magda* was long gone. They sent me flowers and fruit and books on opening nights and occasionally took me to smart restaurants and talked of my life-to-be in Hollywood. Columbia Films also sent flowers coupled with business-like letters concerning seven-year contracts. It was assumed by my teachers at RADA that these overtures would be firmly rejected and I was quite happy to comply, never for an instant tempted by the offers. I was in RADA to learn to act in the theatre, and I agreed that although I had made a phenomenally good start, I needed a great deal more practice, and that I would only receive in the theatre. I wasn't being 'pure' or 'good' in this unusual situation for a student; I was taking what I saw as a common-sensical, practical stance. Saunders and Herbert agreed with Mr Fernald and my other advisors. 'But,' said one canny person, 'since they're so keen to do so, why not let them fix her face and her teeth?' The morality of this didn't trouble me at all and I graciously allowed Paramount to arrange a meeting with Sir Archibald McIndoe, the famous surgeon, who still continued to do wonderful work with maimed and burned ex-servicemen.

Sir Archibald was far more intimidating to meet than the movie moguls. He was polite and civil, but he was so obviously *somebody* that I was overawed and didn't make much of a job of explaining *why* I should have my face fixed. He declared that he wasn't interested in pret-tifying actresses and I didn't have an answer to that, concurring privately that mending my face – which wasn't so bad – came pretty low on a list of priorities that included burned airmen. He said he would be in touch and I was told later that he and Lady McIndoe would be drop-ping in to the Vanbrugh to see me perform. A week later I was told when to report to East Grinstead, where I would be kept for a week and my scars would be re-cut and re-stitched and my nose straightened and my jaw stabilised. Another bout of sublime idiocy took possession of me and I booked myself to make a TV appearance in Manchester two weeks after the operation and promised to be in Wales to do *Siwan* for the Arts Council immediately afterwards, turning up with the part learned so that I could join the production late and open a week later for me to be able to return to RADA in time for my second final term. Herbert sent me notes on the part and I studied it while rehearsing Viola in the country.

Michael kindly saw me off to East Grinstead and suddenly I was a little apprehensive. When I came to in the hospital the following day, heavily bandaged and none too comfortable, I had a moment's unease about my TV appearance, but the happy idiocy prevailed and I thought to myself that everything would probably be just fine.

It was – just – but any sane person would have been distraught at the first sight of the blackened eyes, bruised face and the new lines of (beau-tiful, even) stitches and the television job a mere six days away. I healed amazingly quickly and, looking normal again, took my leave of the great man. He said he'd resisted the temptation to give me a prettier nose and smiled for the first time at my confusion as I struggled to respond to that. No one looked twice at me in Manchester, and in Wales my appearance passed unremarked; I looked as I had looked before I took my header through the windscreen. I loved working with

Herbert again and acting with Glanffrwd James, Margaret John and Emyr Jones, who was fast becoming one of the best young poets in Wales. It was, I realised, a huge relief to be acting in my own language again. Welsh 'placed' the voice differently and I realised that I had never *had* a vocal problem when speaking Welsh. Saunders' words were wonderful, even coming so soon after Shakespeare.

Because I had been allowed to jump a term at the beginning of my time at RADA, I now 'owed' a term at the end. It was unfortunate that the correct psychological moment for me to leave was at the end of my first final term when I played Magda, which generated such excitement. It did not occur to me to do so. My gratitude to the Academy was too great and I was glad to do anything to repay my huge debt, so although I had completed the course and *Magda* had won me the Bancroft Gold Medal, I put my future on hold and returned to RADA to spend an extra final term playing *Hedda Gabler* at the Vanbrugh, then on tour in the provinces in England, and finally at the Duke of York's Theatre and at the National Theatre in Oslo. Mr Fernald had written out his thoughts on the play and the way he intended to direct it, and I read and re-read the play and the notes for weeks before we began rehearsing.

Charles Kay and I played a 'try-out' of a new comedy for a French author before I began the Ibsen. The play didn't work, but Charles and I had a hilarious time, he once again valiantly bearing me aloft as he tore in and out of a set of French farce doors. I'd played more with Charles than with any actor I'd known, and I was sorry that he wouldn't be appearing in *Hedda* and that he'd be leaving RADA – who knew when we would act together again? In the event it was to be over twenty years before that happened.

Fredrik Öhlsson – large, gentle giant – played Tesman, Donald Burton played Brack, and Edward de Souza played Loveborg. The words had learned themselves without my noticing and the three weeks of rehearsal passed smoothly. I had given up my little Bloomsbury home and now shared a large flat with Thelma and Hélène in West Hampstead. Fredrik – Fritte, as we now called him – and I were seeing a great deal of each other and he became a frequent visitor. Hélène took charge of my life, organising everything, making sure I ate proper meals and banishing me to bed early. I loved Thelma and Hélène and deeply appreciated their domestic and organisational skills. I took no pleasure in being 'hopeless' and tried to keep up my end and not be too much of a liability, but I think that on the whole they found it more relaxing when I didn't pretend to more efficiency than I actually possessed.

We opened *Hedda* and the play – and I – did well. Paramount and Columbia pictures were still in attendance, joined now by Sir Michael Balcon, who offered me a British film contract at Ealing Films. I was approached about doing a West End play before the end of term and turned down the offer. Out of all the agents that offered their services I was advised to choose Olive Harding of MCA to represent me. She seemed congenial, although I did find it odd that on my first visit to MCA at 139 Piccadilly she spent most of our time together talking about Peter Finch, whom she also represented. I was also made slightly uneasy by her rhapsodies over the beautiful life of one of her clients who had given up acting in favour of motherhood. She seemed very keen on motherhood; not something I had ever contemplated. I did a lot of nodding and met the men who ran other departments at the agency but I left feeling I almost preferred my Americans who actually said things like, 'I can make you a *star.*' Olive seemed to be saying, 'I can make you retire.' Not a good start, but maybe agents were a bit uneasy around actresses. Binkie Beaumont offered me a contract with H.M. Tennent Ltd, but I was told not to consider it as Tennent's was a graveyard for young actresses, who were made to feel less lovely than the young male actors.

Suddenly aware that this desirable life at RADA would shortly end, I began to have a few thoughts about what to do as opposed to what not to do. This pondering took place during a period marked by endless 8.30 a.m. jaunts to Mr Suk, the dental surgeon who was being paid buckets of money by Columbia Films to 'do' my teeth. Crowns or caps were all the rage, it seemed, the bigger the better. I went along with everything as usual. First one's own teeth were filed down to little stumps – this was lengthy and noisy but not at all painful – then temporary crowns were stuck over the stumps and one was sent out to face the world with strict instructions not to eat chunks of meat or bite into apples until the finished article was stuck on a week later (and still they came out in apples). I didn't enjoy any of this, but sitting there in W1 in the early morning gave me plenty of thinking time. Out of the blue, Mr Fernald called me into his office to put to me an unusual proposal.

The new career proposal went a bit like this. A very wealthy man wishes to invest in the Arts. He seeks advice and falls in with the idea that investment in the theatre would be interesting and amusing.

'Theatre' being a bit general, it is suggested that he should invest in a performer and instigate a little human experiment. For example, what would be the outcome if an actress with an embarrassment of offers were to find herself in the position of not having to earn a living? How would she then choose? Would her choices be better?

Douglas Uren was the rich man and he came along to the Vanbrugh to take a look at me, and when he subsequently offered me a contract by which he guaranteed me an adequate salary whether or not I worked, I was strongly urged to accept. I had no way of knowing if that really was how the offer came about, but I was intrigued by the unusual deal. It was a given at RADA and in many theatre circles that the cinema was not an appropriate place in which to come to rest after a theatre training and it had not occurred to me to question this. When Robert Atkins had said 'Don't go into the fillums', I had wondered why he should imagine I would do anything so foolish. Now I was immensely relieved to be able to put myself out of the running as far as going into the movies was concerned. Being under contract and spoken for would simplify my life no end, and also I liked Mr Uren, who was distant but friendly. I hoped that I would justify his rather eccentric venture. Why shouldn't I? I was firmly back on track with the hell of heartbreak in the past and my demons quietened, maybe conquered. There was room for cautious optimism.

Chapter Thirty-four

My friendship with Fredrik had blossomed into a romance, which was an old-fashioned way of describing what was for me a new kind of relationship. I wondered at the ease and the enjoyment, the lack of anguish, the absence of scenes, and thought it was possible that the fact of our both being obliged to communicate through the medium of a second language was moderating our words and consequently our behaviour. I had moved to Fredrik's flat in the Fulham Road in South Kensington. Thelma and Hélène came to stay at Christmas. We had such a good time that foremost in my mind was the question, 'When will it go wrong?' Fredrik would have to return to Sweden at some point; he had a good chance of working for Ingmar Bergman. He seemed able to envisage me living in Sweden and working in Swedish, and I just couldn't. 'It will be all right,' he promised. I didn't spoil everything by arguing, but I couldn't see how.

I had no trouble fitting into Fredrik's life, but I did have a problem fitting my clothes into his wardrobe cupboard. My benefactor had decided that I must be made to look more like a successful actress. No one trusted me to achieve this sartorial transformation, so the kindly and smart Noel Hood, one of my teachers at RADA, was deputed to take me shopping for an entire wardrobe. Equipped with a huge cheque, we set off for Knightsbridge (Harrods and Woollands) and the King's Road, which bristled with small, discreet 'Modom' shops staffed by elegant, frightfully grand elderly women who would have frightened me to death had I been alone.

Thanks to Miss Hood, by the end of the day I was, in theory, prepared and poised for any occasion and looked in all the outfits just like my mother would have looked were she to spend a fortune on clothes. Black and grey and violet were the predominant colours. The shoes, the handbags, the three-quarter-length gloves, were all the plainest and blackest, and the one frivolous item was an incredibly expensive hat; a huge cabbage rose tilted over one eye, a scrap of felt holding it, and a little flirtation of spotted veil just reaching the bridge of my nose ('perfect for easy eating,' I noted gratefully).

Almost immediately, yet another American film producer took the hat and me to the Caprice restaurant in Arlington Street. Without a hat one couldn't go to a smart restaurant at lunchtime and the same hat would bar one's entry at night for dinner. My rose clashed or toned in – I couldn't decide which – with the ruched red walls, lit by wall sconces disconcertingly fashioned from raised ceramic hands cut off at the wrist. 'Vivien Leigh's choice,' said my host. 'She *loves* hands.' Sitting up straight in my slinky black frock – wool crêpe, draped everywhere – squinting under a huge errant pink petal, I felt I was right at the centre of things. As usual, I ate everything I was offered and was hugely appreciative and paid no attention to what was being said about my movie career.

My agent began to smell trouble and so did I. We were set on wildly divergent courses (she was mad about films). Even she had to agree with me (though rather shakily), when after a cocktail-party outing for a new black, ballerina-length, silk frock with its tiny velvet bolero, small clutch bag and silk shoes, a representative of Revlon rang MCA suggesting that I might be suitable to be the Revlon girl and suggesting an indecently enormous fee, spread over five years. An actress accepting such an offer could kiss goodbye to a 'legitimate career' on the spot. Olive knew this perfectly well and would never have tried to persuade me to make such a mad career move. What shook her, I think, was the ease and *speed* at which the money was rejected. There must have been something mildly unnatural about such aristocratic nonchalance, coming from a sturdy peasant who was, on the whole, biddable. We rubbed along uneasily and my worries grew as the number of *Hedda* performances dwindled.

One day a week I was able to write and present a weekly TV magazine programme beamed to Wales from Manchester. This was television at its scariest; Meredith Edwards and I chatted and interviewed our way through an almost entirely unrehearsed programme, taking a keen, completely uninformed interest in pig farming or double-glazing or trombone-playing. One Wednesday the 'unusual pet' – a snake – escaped in mid-interview, which tested me somewhat, and towards the end of that particularly hectic show I glanced up at the control room window to see the director turned away from the control panel, head bowed, having given up the unequal struggle. The public was very tolerant. There was a feeling between audience and performers of all of us being in the same mess together, and a lot of the time it *was* a mess.

Well trained by the BBC, I enjoyed interviewing and talking to the camera, and now I was offered the first prestigious interviews 'in depth' on network television. These I accepted and they led to my being offered a more permanent job doing much the same thing. My agent, unaware of my past at the BBC, was puzzled but pleased – television was obviously going to be quite important and she didn't subscribe to the snobbism held in theatre circles towards this new medium. Realising that I was being sidetracked, I rejected all further offers to become a television 'personality'.

I couldn't work out why I felt so confused. The theatre seemed to be changing and changing quite fast. I had spent my life preparing and had now been trained at RADA to be a 'classical' actress, and that was what I wanted to be. The performances I had liked best had confirmed me in this ambition. The Shakespeare production that had most impressed me had been Tyrone Guthrie's *Troilus and Cressida* and my favourite performance was Paul Rogers' Pandarus in that same production, which put him on my private most-loved list along with Edith Evans and Ralph Richardson.

Richard Burton, with whom I played in Welsh as a student in Wales, was now a big star at the Old Vic, along with John Neville. Seeing *Henry V* from the gods I had been aghast, on a Saturday matinée, to find that I couldn't *hear* Richard at all times. Embarrassed and incredulous, I'd sat disappointedly through the play, which came and went fitfully, then suddenly, towards the end, Richard walked on to the stage in full Harry rig, gold and blue and resplendent, and there was a collective sigh of appreciation from the audience. Richard just stood there and *was* Henry V. Of course, they could doubtless hear more from the better seats, but even in the gods it seemed mean to whinge in the face of such beauty and splendour. All the same . . . what about Hugh Miller's 'Sell it to the paying customers – they're in the auditorium, all *three tiers* of it' and Michael Redgrave's 'To act well and to act well *repeatedly* has to become an obsession.'

I didn't know what to think. Much as I loved Shakespeare, the play I had liked most had been *Waiting for Godot*, but there didn't seem to be anything like that about, except maybe at the Royal Court. I'd been going to see the plays that were being produced there by the New

English Stage Company, run by George Devine. There was a great deal of talk about 'Working-Class' drama, 'kitchen-sink' drama. The massive success had been *Look Back in Anger* and some said that this had changed the face of the English theatre overnight. I couldn't make up my mind what I thought about this. It just didn't seem to me to be particularly working class or new; rather conventional in fact. And Jimmy Porter, the archetypal Angry Young Man, didn't seem to be especially angry. Cross, yes, and at odds with everything, but not angry. I'd seen working-class anger during a lock-out at a coalmine and that was a good deal more terrifying than Jimmy's bad temper. I couldn't help feeling that characters speaking with regional accents or 'lower-class' accents were perceived to be somehow more 'real' and genuine than characters who spoke with standard English accents. To a foreigner it all seemed to be part of the bottomless English preoccupation with class. Coming from a background where it was dangerous, certainly unwise, to assume that a working-class person was uneducated or illiterate, I was not completely won over by the excitement in Sloane Square.

The Angry Young Man had been popping up in novels since I was an undergraduate in 1953. John Wain's *Hurry on Down* was the book where I encountered my first disaffected young man and *Lucky Jim* had followed in 1956. In life he wore desert boots or sandals, checked, homespun-style shirts – no tie if humanly possible – didn't shave too much if he could get away with it and over his shirt he wore thick chunky sweaters or a shabby sports jacket, and the favourite choice for overcoats was the duffel. (Ex-army surplus shops were good sources of Angry Young Man clothes.) I fancy that the English weather prevented the more dramatic American rebel look (Marlon Brando in a singlet would turn purple in Nottingham). Also, it seemed to me that the Angry Young Men, the working-class heroes of English drama, were very specifically English and were the product of a British Act of Parliament, the Butler Education Act of 1944 which reorganised secondary education and introduced the Eleven-plus examination for the selection of grammar school pupils.

In America most people had more 'things' than we did; but they also had bigger problems. Over three-quarters of the population had television sets and washing machines and refrigeration and heating and cooling systems, but there were people who had nothing at all and, from a safe distance, we read with disbelief that less than a year after the Russian tanks had put down the Hungarian Uprising, Governor Faubus in Little

Rock, Arkansas, had used the National Guard to prevent black students from taking up their places at the High School. America was racist. That was a *real* problem. Hungary's revolt against communist rule was a *real* problem. England had a bit of a social problem.

In Britain, thanks to the Butler Act, my generation had been given access to higher education on a scale never before known; most of the students at my university or at RADA were dependent on grants from their local authorities. In England, Equality of Opportunity had, in many quarters, given rise to the misapprehension that we were witnessing the dawn of social equality. Not so in Wales. I remember my mother rather admiring Stafford Cripps for trying to deal with politics in ethical terms, until suddenly he went too far. As Chancellor of the Exchequer, he claimed he was dedicated to soaking the rich and creating equality. 'That'll be the day,' said my mother, dismissively, and switched him off.

London in the late Fifties was awash with young people who had been given admission to a society that hadn't changed since the time when they were excluded from it. They had to come to terms with a society in which the old order prevailed and the class structure stood firm against these post-graduates of the 'école de Butler', as we were sneeringly referred to. It was a hurtful discovery to find that the admission ticket led only so far, and for a disappointed young man the easiest course was to despise and ridicule the society that so effortlessly shrugged him off. This hero was a hurt misfit who felt he'd been misled, but surely he was offended rather than angry.

There were no Angry Young Women at that time, so there wasn't much richness for actresses to plunder. Even the clothes – the skirts so full they were restricting, and the petticoats – held us all in thrall. The lack of contraception except for married women – upon-production-of-a-marriage-licence – dictated our behaviour (the rituals of communion between the sexes were still quaint). Coming from a truly classless society but not expecting to find one in England, I was not cross or rebellious, but I was confused. There was a rush to portray people who didn't belong. I didn't 'belong', but it didn't bother me much and I didn't recognise myself in any of the plays I saw or read.

I was asked to go to the Royal Court for a chat and spent a depressing hour with a group of middle-class people in working-class disguise who told me a lot of things about the importance of the working-class point of view. The concept of the daring, strong, powerful, articulate working-class woman, familiar to me from childhood, was not, I felt, one that would fit in any framework devised in SW1, and to mention such a creature would be tactless. I was glad to get back to Fulham Road to listen to hard-working, working-class Frank Sinatra singing Nelson Riddle arrangements.

Chapter Thirty-five

Hedda had been going very well and now I looked forward to the challenge of taking her to Oslo or 'Ibsen's own country', as people had begun saying – ominous and somehow more important-sounding than 'Norway'. We planned to do a run-through on board ship, and Mr Fernald, who had served in the Navy during the war, was gleefully looking forward to combining two of his great loves – sailing and theatre. All in all, we were in a buoyant mood as we left Waterloo Station, I, hatted and gloved like a dowager. Bizarrely, I found myself being photographed by the press and waved off by a girl in a Welsh costume.

Our Company Manager (and my friend), Dot Tenham, had been told to brief me on the subject of clothes. I was to wear a hat to all daytime receptions, black court shoes and handbag, gloves to be worn at all times. Hélène, Thelma and I had spent my last night at home unpicking embroidered cherries from my new grey dress, bought specially but hurriedly for smart Norwegian gatherings. 'You look like a fruit bowl,' Hélène said, and set to work with scissors and pins to calm the party frock. I had lost interest in clothes, but I unpicked enthusiastically for something to take my mind off things.

The Swedish Lloyd ship bucketed up and down and I made the happy discovery that I was a good sailor at the same moment that I discovered the joys of *smörgasbord*. I had never seen so much food and all conveniently and decoratively laid out for easy and copious eating. We did rehearse on deck during a calm hour or two, but I think it was mostly for fun and it certainly didn't distract me from the joys of lurching around the dining room.

What with the food and my ability to take my mind off worrying things, I was quite unprepared for the attention I received in Oslo. I immediately fell in love with the look of the place, and I lay in my pretty blue and white room with its painted furniture and gingham cotton curtains, looking at the snow outside, from the soft depths of a bed, warm under a huge and thick, feather-filled something or other. It was like a super – oh, infinitely superior – eiderdown. No, it wasn't like an eiderdown, it was like the smell and taste of dill, novel and simply lovely. London was still post-war grubby and down at heel. Oslo and the air of Norway were unbelievably fresh and clean.

The first hint that I might be under a little pressure came when my dresser, who spoke no English, slammed me in and out of my costumes faster than I had ever before been dressed and undressed. Although it was our first run together, she was always there at my elbow or waiting for me at exactly the right moment, and for a while I admired her powers of intuition, until it occurred to me that, as a National Theatre dresser, she had in all probability dressed more than a few Heddas in her time and that this was a play as familiar here as *Hamlet* was in London. Hmm . . .

When opening night arrived, the director of the theatre came round in great good spirits to report 'a packed house, with *seven* Hedda Gablers sitting in the stalls'. Ho hum, I thought grimly, while responding, 'Oh, good!' with all the fake enthusiasm I could muster. My dresser and I looked at my reflection in the long mirror, I nodded a 'thank you' at her, and she put her hand on my arm and squeezed gently. Oh God, was she feeling sorry for me? This was no moment to start feeling small, so I indicated that I'd go down to the stage now, good and early, and have a bit of a stroll around. She accompanied me to the lift door and I gestured that I'd like to go alone. Punching the button, down I went. Although it was after the quarter-hour call, backstage was silent and in total darkness. I paced up and down a bit, wondering at the cold and the difference in backstage practice between England and Norway. In England the entire crew would be milling about and one would be able to hear the distant hum of a full house. And where were the other actors?

Having completed my private-calming-down-perking-up rituals, I ventured further down to the deserted prompt corner and peered through the curtain to see, to my horror, a completely dark and empty auditorium. I felt that I was inhabiting an actor's nightmare; any minute now someone would call me to begin a play I had never read, let alone rehearsed, and I would be in the wrong costume and then I would *wake up*! No, waking up was obviously not part of this nightmare and, picking up my skirts, I ran – not to the wretched lift – but out into a passageway and up the nearest flight of stairs. I would go back to square one and to my dressing room and start the journey again. What *time* was it?

Before I reached my dressing-room floor I came upon a brightly lit corridor with busy people – even to a foreigner they were recognisably stage-hands – bustling to and fro, then a reassuringly familiar set of double doors and, slowing down, I strolled through them to encounter a scene of un-Scandinavian, almost Neapolitan panic in full swing. I smiled reassuringly and pretended not to notice the shoulder-shrugging and head-shaking and eyebrow-raising as I walked slowly to my place. The play began and the rhythms of the perfectly constructed piece took over, the inner tumult of not being able to find the stage and the worry at being scrutinised by all those Hedda Gablers fell away, and I felt calm and almost passive as the story unfolded.

The curtain fell for the last time and we waited for the applause and prepared to take the curtain call in the one democratic line favoured in the days of *No Star Nonsense* (the title of the book by Peter Cotes). I felt faint with shock when the curtain rose to total silence. After what seemed an eternity, we were given a lengthy, conventional and hugely enthusiastic reception. The director of the Folk Theatre, whose family had been taking care of me, rushed backstage, elated at what he called 'A triumph'. 'But they didn't applaud for ages,' I began. He slapped his forehead and explained, 'If they *truly* approve they award you a silence.' Paranoia had taken hold and privately I thought that he was just saying that to make me feel better, so I braced myself for a long, difficult reception ahead. As it turned out it was a wonderful party. The Heddas, most of them, came to it and were gracious – as far as I could tell. There was a letter from the most distinguished Hedda of all, Agnes Mowinckel, summoning me to have coffee at her house in the morning.

At breakfast, I was told that the notices were nothing short of sensational. ('Don't forget you always get a lot of marks for being foreign,' reminded John Fernald on the phone, but I could tell that he was pleased as punch.) Accompanied by an interpreter, I set off to visit the great actress. Gravely she poured coffee and sat looking at me. I thanked her for coming to the play and for letting me visit her. She accepted my thanks and we had a somewhat stilted conversation. Maybe it was the language barrier, but I had a feeling that small-talk was not one of her specialities. Finally, she indicated the pile of Norwegian papers on the couch beside her. 'It may be because of your youth that they say you are one of the best. I am not sure what I think about that, but I would like you to know – and again this may in part be due to your youth – but I consider that you are one of the most . . .' – she paused and looked at me, then resumed – '*correct* Heddas that I have experienced.' I wasn't sure if this was faint praise or great praise, but I plumped for the latter and said lots of 'thank-yous' before I was released from the Presence and skipped off, feeling pretty cheerful.

The profits from all the performances of *Hedda* were to go towards funding a scholarship in memory of Jan Groth, a Swedish student who had recently died in a tragic accident while at RADA. His parents came to Norway to see the play and our meeting was restrained; they were part happy – happy that Jan's memory was being honoured – part sorrowful.

Back in London we continued playing in far less grand circumstances. The play and John Fernald's production were as sound as a bell and went well, no matter how unpromising the venue. The end of *Hedda* would mark the end of my involvement with RADA and I realised with dismay that I was worried and fearful. It would be difficult to imagine anyone with less reason to be apprehensive, but there it was and I couldn't help it. There were, I had realised, many things about 'the Business' that I had never liked or enjoyed: the competition, the malice, the genuine hard-luck stories – sadness at every turn. For two years I'd been protected from all those things and had conveniently forgotten about them. Now I dreaded leaving the safe haven.

Something happened that doubled my fears. One of the broadsheets picked up on the astonishing press that *Hedda* had received in Oslo and reprinted something of it, comparing our reception (and inevitably my part of it) favourably with that received by a far more mature and celebrated company from England that had played there earlier in the year. It was a piece of mischief-making, but it depressed me. 'Oh, there's the baby Bernhardt or was it Duse? Aiming to be the most popular girl in *Spotlight*, are we?' said a sharp-tongued guest teacher at RADA. Low in spirit, I began to dread seeing my photograph in the press. Flora Robson gave me her recipe for wet-white (to make the hands look beautiful on stage) and pointed out what I already knew: that the periods of riding high, when everything one touched turned, if not to gold then to something shiny, did not usually last long and should be, if not enjoyed, *used*. Easier said than done. I remember the overheard words from my childhood: 'She just isn't cut out for it.' What if they were right, after all?

Chapter Thirty-six

All very well deciding what *not* to do, but what to *do*? Where to go? Which way to jump? The Magic Offer, the one that, when it arrived, would proclaim itself to be the right, the only possible one, did not materialise, but destiny of another sort brushed by me one day off the Tottenham Court Road. It was like being afforded an accidental glimpse of something I was not meant to see just yet. A shutter opened on to a future scene. Without giving it a conscious thought, my system absorbed it.

Fredrik, Hélène, Thelma and I were on our way to the Spaghetti House for lunch and Fredrik paused to greet a friend who was accompanied by an actor who had left RADA before I enrolled. So this was the legendary bad boy who had spent the night asleep wrapped up in the Vanbrugh Theatre curtains, who was late to class, who actually drank during the day in the Gower Public House and who was now the shining star of the Bristol Old Vic, where he had been the second person in England to play Jimmy Porter, but who had already startled everyone with a *really* Angry Young Man performance when he played Hamlet. ('He actually *climbed* the proscenium arch,' spluttered a witness on his return to London.) Peter O'Toole was one of a group of gifted students who were still talked of at RADA (Finney, Pringle, Bedford, Villiers, Briers – the list was long).

Like most women, I have the gift of being able to take in every detail of an outfit at a glance. O'Toole looked as though he was wearing clothes unlike any I'd seen a man wearing. He had black, curly hair and blue, blue eyes set in a quizzical face. It was the expression of one who could hardly credit the evidence of his eyes. He looked like the Actor in Disney's *Pinocchio*. But that actor was a wolf, surely? We said goodbye and moved on. The wolf wore a green velvet or corduroy jacket, didn't he? And a neckerchief? Or was it O'Toole who wore the jacket and the coloured thing around his neck? I didn't turn to check and we went into the restaurant. I couldn't remember his face, just the wolf's face, an actor's face, though. Actor. Nothing but actor. In the time it took to look at the menu and order risotto with an egg on top, I wondered briefly when it would be that we would marry. Then I never thought about it again.

Not even when, about a year later, we met on the first day of rehearsal of a West End production of *The Holiday* by John Hall. It was still not time. The shutter remained closed as though it had never opened.

Instead of taking an acting job immediately, I left RADA and spent a month sitting still. John Fernald advised me to accept an invitation from the portrait sculptor, Dora Gordine, to sit for a head that she wanted to do of me playing Hedda Gabler. She had seen the play six times and chose to portray a moment from the last act just before Hedda shoots herself. Dora lived in an extraordinary house on a hill looking out on the tops of the trees of Richmond Park. Each morning I left Fredrik at home and caught a bus at 9 a.m. so as to be in the studio, on the dais in my wig at 10 a.m. Dora, who was Russian, fed me *kasha* seated in my chair and otherwise expected total concentration until 6 p.m., when I was released. I sat from Monday to Friday for four weeks. John Fernald had been right: sitting for Dora was a demanding but wonderful experience. While I sat silent and still, she talked about her youth as a young refugee studying under Maillol in Paris, about winning a five-year commission to sculpt the figures for the new civic centre in Singapore, and about spending all her money on semi-precious wood and white hand-woven fabric, returning to Europe by ship with the hold full of her purchases and no place to put them, no money left either.

Meeting Richard Hare was a fantastic piece of good fortune. He proposed, she accepted and together they built their house with materials she'd brought back. 'It'll fall down,' she was warned as she directed the builders herself. It stood, and when I was there it was like an enchanted fortress. On entering, shoes had to be removed and one took one's pick from the twenty pairs of carpet slippers in the hall, padding softly across the beautiful wooden floor, perfectly level so as not to jolt the trolley-bearing sculptures that were wheeled to the foundry where Dora cast her own bronzes. The first floor was an art gallery with huge windows, veiled with white fabric, and alongside the gallery Dora had built an enormous studio where she worked eight or nine hours a day. Their apartment was on the top floor, high above the trees, a smallish,

Russian set of rooms with half-moon doors and custom-made 1930s furniture, all made from Dora's blocks of wood.

She was tiny, with the severe countenance of a Bodhisattva. Watching her work with such ferocious concentration taught me something more about the labour involved in achieving anything. 'Education is the impact of quality.' The little tyrant was persuasive. How, I wondered when she showed me the figure, had she persuaded Edith Evans to pose in the nude for her?

Fredrik could no longer delay his return to Sweden and settled me into a little flat in South Kensington. He had accompanied me to Nottingham, where I was going to do a season of plays. The fact that I couldn't believe in our future together made the parting, when it came soon after, all the more sad. In my heart I felt that we were saying good-bye for good. Now, for almost a year, I bounced around at the whim of MCA, who were, it seemed, interested only in my future in movies or in the West End. I managed to squeeze in a few things that pleased me, and Olive was indulgent.

A while later I was told that this confusing, frustrating time need not have happened. The magical, the 'Right' offer *had* come, unknown to me. Sir Barry Jackson at the Birmingham Repertory Company had asked me to go and play a season there with a view to staying longer, and I would have begun by playing Lady Macbeth to Albert Finney's Macbeth. MCA, without consulting me, had rejected the offer, saying, 'We don't want her to learn reppy tricks.' When I learned this I was appalled. I left MCA and when they held me to my contract, I gladly paid them as well as my new agents 10 per cent until my contract expired.

At the same time as the rise of the kitchen-sink drama, there was a brief flowering of verse drama, and *The Holiday* was part of this move-ment. Actually, by the time we did *The Holiday*, verse drama was virtu-ally dead, so the production was more of an ending. O'Toole and I were to make our West End debuts in this play, presented by Donald Albery and playing brother and sister (we did look alike).

Once again, I was playing a part for which I was completely unsuited. It was a hard lesson, knuckling under and working on parts that didn't need anything that I had to offer. Difficult parts were easy – ordinary or bad parts were difficult, I realised. At one point Tony Richardson actu-ally said to me, 'Could you look as though you've just left Harrods?' Well, I could, but I didn't want to, and there was something about me that just didn't convince as a middle-class English, specifically Knightsbridge, girl. God, I hated those parts. Margaret in *The Holiday* made and poured tea, mixed and served drinks, was very good to everybody, spoke nicely and dressed quietly.

It was a remarkable company that set out on tour: Colin Jeavons, John Moffatt, Nicholas Meredith, Sylvia Syms, Mary Hinton, Jack Merivale and O'Toole and myself, all struggling with a play that was rewritten and rewritten, boasting a new title every so often in case that might help. The short, smart, pre-West End tour grew into a lengthy one, on what was called 'the disappearing circuit' as we trailed north into Scotland, where they *hated* us. I felt sorry for John Hall, the author, as he endlessly reworked the play, but I felt even sorrier for us as our audiences dwindled in the cold north.

John Moffatt played the central character of the victim, the outsider who commits suicide and makes everyone feel dreadful on the last page of the play. He was called 'Saxman' for ever such a long time and suddenly, in one of those all-too-familiar panic measures, word came that his name should be changed immediately to 'Jackson'. Why, I don't remember. Nor did the Company. That night we'd called John's character 'Jackson' for two hours and just before the last curtain, someone appeared centre-stage in the most dramatic moment of the play and said, 'Saxman's hung himself in the garage.' Who? What was that?

There was a long pause as the unfortunate actor's face changed colour and the tiny band in the auditorium stirred themselves into life. 'Who did she say?' 'Who's Saxman?' The S's resounded through the stalls. The whole evening had been rendered meaningless. Rocking with laughter, we all turned up-stage, shoulders heaving, and finished the play with our backs to the audience. It was the last straw. John Moffatt's face as he joined us for the curtain was a study. How he disapproved and how he wished he'd been on stage for the fun. Clive Exton, the playwright, was our stage manager, and he reported the lot of us. Back at the hotel, O'Toole and I ran into a few people who'd been at the play. 'We didn't understand *all* of it,' said a woman, trying to be nice. 'Ah well, y'know – *verse!*' said O'Toole airily and graciously accepted a drink.

Our relationship was, in a way, very proper; we just wanted to spend all our time together. I was introduced to the delights of drink, specifically Scotch whisky, and staying up late in bars chatting to the owners. We talked and talked and I listened a lot; I wanted to know everything

O'Toole had ever done, and over the course of seven weeks we covered a great deal of territory. I learned Irish songs and sang him Welsh songs and he played his guitar to me. One morning we woke at dawn, fully clothed, propped against each other where we had fallen fast asleep on my bed with a guitar between us; we were a bit embarrassed as we hastily parted. We were both involved with other people and that was just about the only thing we didn't talk about.

The tour ended with a long journey from Scotland to London. I wondered, but not for too long, how life would be now that we would not be spending all our time together. Not nearly so much fun, I thought. We stayed awake the whole night talking, and when we arrived in London I went home to a new flat I was sharing with Thelma, showered, borrowed a clean frock and went to the BBC in Portland Place where I was to record *Treason* by Saunders Lewis. Two versions: first English and then Welsh. The cast included Richard Burton, Clifford Evans, Emlyn Williams, Donald Houston and myself, playing a 'proper' woman for a welcome change. Richard was hardly ever there. Days went by and he sent messages saying he'd be with us soon. Emyr Humphreys, our director, squared it with the powers-that-be and we made ourselves at home in our studio on the sixth floor, writing letters and doing crosswords and taking long lunchbreaks.

Emlyn took me to a restaurant in Wigmore Street and we passed a hearing-aid shop – rather up-market – with a plastic orchid supporting the aid, making it look glamorous and desirable. 'Oh look,' he said, 'privilege to be deaf.'

He began to bring in a typewriter and sat with a glue pot and scissors and coloured paper, retyping his part and doing mysterious things with paper markers. Only the tap-tap of the typewriter was heard when Wolf Mankowitz put his head round the door, surveyed the silent Welsh gathering and withdrew, saying, 'Sorry.'

'Didn't get much of a welcome in *this* valley,' said Emlyn without looking up from his typewriter.

The commissionaire rang up to say that there was a lady down below for Mr Burton. 'Not here,' said Emyr. Richard was coming to the end of a protracted affair with a famous young actress and evidently she wasn't about to give him an easy exit. Day after day there were phone calls: 'I *know* he's there.' 'I wish,' said Emyr, wearily. Finally, the commissionaire called up to say that the young lady had left a letter for Mr Burton. Emlyn took the call. 'Bring it up,' he said, 'and bring a steaming kettle, too.' Richard, looking a little worse for wear, turned up eventually, and was charming, and performed wonderfully well in both languages.

I didn't actually talk *about* O'Toole, but he was much in my mind and I related some of the fascinating things he'd told me, for instance about his time in the Navy as a National Serviceman.

Me: Did you know that in the Navy – well, in submarines
   anyway – salt is called 'sea dust'?
Emlyn: Go on, it's not, is it?
Me: And butter is called 'slide'. Isn't that wonderful?
Emlyn: And what other wonderful things did Peter O'Toole tell
   you on this tour?

I went on to a backbreaking stint of live television, playing a huge leading part each month in what was a version of four-weekly rep but with infinitely more pressure. I rather enjoyed the pressure, but began to suffer from boils and abscesses, which would develop slowly and painfully during the three rehearsal weeks, then burst dramatically on the day of the dress rehearsal, leaving me weak but free from pain for transmission, and the whole miserable business would begin all over again. The boils, to which I attributed malicious human sensibilities, would occasionally get confused because we went into a small studio, in costume, and performed a short trailer, then, after transmission, we would turn up a few days later and give a repeat performance of the play. The boils didn't know where they were.

Back in London, O'Toole and I saw a good deal of each other whenever we were free.

One dreadful night, after a late transmission in Bristol, I revealed a confidence that had been entrusted to me by O'Toole, to a friend of his, a writer who I assumed would have been privy to the secret. He wasn't, and when O'Toole heard what I'd done we had a monumental row, standing outside the Royal Court. He was in a towering rage and we parted noisily – and for ever. I walked the length of the King's Road before I stopped shaking. An actor whom I knew gaped, astonished, as I passed by, sobbing fiercely and walking too fast to be stopped.

We were both due to begin rehearsing new plays. O'Toole was to do his first television, playing Gaudier-Brzeska, the sculptor. His play would be transmitted from London. Mine, *The Quiet Man*, was to be transmitted from Cardiff, and I stayed with Herbert while I was rehearsing. Herbert sympathised as I told him the sorry tale of how I'd lost 'my closest friend', as I described him. 'Hmm,' he said, looking at me over his glasses, 'and have you told Fredrik about your "friendship"?' 'I don't have to. There's no harm in it.' 'Oh, Phillips, Phillips, you're madly in love.' 'Don't be silly. Anyway, I'll never see him again.' And I believed that.

Herbert and I watched *The Laughing Woman* together. O'Toole was breathtaking. We sat silently in the front room, our drinks untouched, until the play was over. It was obvious that O'Toole had scarcely hit a mark from beginning to end and even the cameras were at white heat as they jostled with each other, trying to get in for a close-up of a left ear or a bit of nose. It was live TV at its most thrilling – dangerous, messy and immediate. I could hardly bear the thought that I wouldn't be able to talk to him about it. But there it was. I'd been really stupid and thoughtless and that was the end of it.

I did my play with Alun Owen, who was giving his last performance before becoming a full-time playwright. He was a good actor and in spite of my sombre mood we had a good time together and the play went well.

My parents were pleased to see me alone, as they thought, running a successful career as a consequence. 'You're better off,' said my mother as we ate our farewell lunch. She was pleasantly flushed as the phone rang all morning with calls from people she knew who had watched the play the night before. I could see that she was a mite surprised that acting was proving to be such a normal, full-time, gainful occupation and I could also tell that she was afraid I might mess it all up. 'It just isn't right for you – being married.' 'What, never?' I asked. 'Oh well – I don't know,' she prevaricated, unwilling to commit herself to anything too sweeping.

I had a feeling that she was probably right. Well, I had no wish to marry, and if my childhood picture of myself, living alone but doing what I wanted in life, was coming true, then I could manage that. It wasn't as simple as I'd imagined, but who ever said life would be simple?

Chapter Thirty-seven

London was cold and most of my friends were working out of town. I liked the new flat in Notting Hill Gate, the front room with its big ground-floor window overlooking Ladbroke Square, but I was glad that I was working non-stop. O'Toole was having an enormous success in *The Long and the Short and the Tall* at the Royal Court and each time I passed the front-of-house photographs on my way to rehearsal I thought, 'I must go to see the play' – but I didn't. Our falling-out had, I reflected, left me with a greater sense of loss and waste than I had ever felt in my life. But I was determined not to fall apart. There was a touch of grimness in my brisk day-to-day life, but I was, most certainly, all of a piece. All the same, going to the play was better postponed.

I awoke and wondered why. There was a noise of something at the window. I got out of bed without putting on the light. There was nothing to make me nervous; there was a wide area between my window and the front-door steps. Improbably, there was a face at the window and a tall figure perilously straddled the gap outside. I raised the window slowly, fearful of upsetting the delicate balance. Two hands plunged in and seized the sash-window frame and, with a heave, two long slim feet swung through and to the floor, and over six feet of O'Toole straightened itself cheerily and seemed to sketch a little bow. I wanted to applaud. It was *such* a moment, beautifully executed.

How could I have forgotten that this was going to happen? Like the shutter of a camera, the fingernail of a picture widened to confirm itself, then shut seamlessly as though it had never been. I was a pawn in this scene. As it happened, I could see that here was my brother, my lover, my child, my father – and most importantly, my equal partner, who loved and inhabited the world that I also loved. Everything made sense. Everything was turning out right.

'I've got a car. Coming for a cup of tea?'

'It's three in the morning.'
'So?'
'I'm in my nightie.'
'Put a mac on.'
'Why not.'
'Hullo you.'

Public Places

To my daughters, Kate and Pat, who have helped me and to those who helped all of us; the people who 'lived faithfully a hidden life'.

Acknowledgements

My sincere thanks to my editor at Hodder, Rowena Webb, and to my agent, Mark Lucas, for their good advice and support throughout. I would like to thank Peta Nightingale at LAW for the invaluable editorial suggestions and Stephanie Darnill, my copyeditor, who gave so generously of her time. Without Nina Humm, who not only can read my writing but has a firmer grasp of the chronology of my life than I, the book would not have come to completion. I owe her more than I can say.

William Corlett has been unstinting in his help and encouragement during a year in which he and Bryn Ellis have smoothed my path. In many ways I owe a huge debt to Thierry Harcourt for reading the book as it progressed and for being so candid in his opinions, as was Sarah Randall, who may know more about some aspects of my life than I do.

Bob Willoughby has been more than generous in allowing me to choose from his magnificent collection of photography taken in South America. I am grateful to my theatrical agent, Lindy King, for her forbearance when I was obliged to steal time from acting in order to write. Above all, I thank the friends who have stood by me during the past year – in particular Fabi Waisbort, the best sort of friend with whom to travel a difficult road.

They change their climate, not their lives,
who rush across the sea

Horace

Chapter One

March 1975

Naples Airport, and I'm frightened. Coming after the black winter months in London and the weeks of filming on the icy Suffolk coast, the March light of Italy is blinding me. And the noise is confusing me. London and its airport must have been busy, but I feel that we have emerged from near silence into this aggressive, light-hearted tumult. Years of disciplined dieting have left me stick-thin and as I shuffle the travel papers and passports and begin to worry about the baggage, I am aware that there's nothing much in the way of protection between my frame and the demands that are being made on it by this expedition. No ordinary journey for me or for the tall figure standing a little to the side, detached, aloof and rather grand but in fact carefully positioned so as not to be conspicuous and finding the place of maximum safety in this press of people. If I'm scared, he must be terrified. Not that he's show-ing it. Only a slight over-stillness and a too-studied air of relaxation betray him.

He is not supposed to walk more than a few steps, forbidden to lift anything heavier than a teacup. There is no certainty that he won't suddenly need the resources of a well-equipped hospital. I have on me the number of a helicopter ambulance service and the address of an approved hospital. His medical records are in my suitcase along with a letter from our doctor, Gerry Slattery. Don't leave London, they all said, the doctors who have become familiar to me these last months. And here we are in Naples Airport on our way to the San Pietro Hotel outside Positano. More importantly, we're on our way to Sr Carlo Cinque, the builder, architect and proprietor. We are the hotel guests from hell.

Left to me, we would still be safe in Guyon House, on Heath Street in Hampstead, just up the road from Dr Gerry Slattery and the Royal

Free Hospital (the umbilical cord attaching me to Men's Surgical has yet to be cut). As usual, confronted with the prospect of O'Toole standing alone against expert opinion and common sense and people who know what's best for him, I crossed the line and stood with him against Them. 'He's not an alcoholic,' they told me. 'He just drinks a lot.' When he became aggressive they always made themselves scarce, I couldn't help but notice. 'See you tomorrow,' they'd cry, trooping out into Heath Street as the first glass shattered. They have been very present at the hospital, looking grave and concerned.

The sense of the folly of this adventure and awareness of the responsibility I've taken on myself have kept me awake for a week past. And this comes at the end of the worst time in my life; standing vigil while he hovered between life and death, returning to an empty house only to change clothes and deal with the journalists anxious to verify the show-business facts of a life that they believed to be coming to an early end. They didn't try to hide what they thought and offered sympathy. Only Jules and Joyce Buck, our partners in Keep Films – our 'family' – knew what was really going on. We spoke briefly at night. They knew too much, feared too much, to be interested in chatting or speculating. Night after night I sat, alone, on our bed in the big, gleaming house. Manolita – much, much more than the 'daily' and one of the few people to know anything of our private life – had been there all day, cleaning as though she were banishing fiends, conquering illness with antique wax. She brought from her house little plates of food and left them in the fridge, and these small kindnesses were enough to tip me over into short, violent bursts of weeping, never a long, healing, outpouring of grief. There were too many moments every day when I had to assume a bright face; even the children and my mother, away in Ireland, and his parents, in a flat off Haverstock Hill, are not to be told how bad things are until the last moment – should the last moment come.

For a while I even fooled myself. 'All this is to be expected, I suppose,' I said to Sister in a sensible tone after a particularly bad night. 'It will get better, won't it?' Her eyes filled with tears and she looked away before leaving the room without speaking. Then I knew we were in more trouble than I had realised. 'Be prepared for the worst,' I was then advised, and during the next few weeks I forced myself, alone at home, to come to terms with the fact that the person dearest in the world to me was possibly never going to return to himself but would slide from this comatose state into his death and I would never speak to him again.

I had never before felt such grief. When the worst thing in the world happens, it seems incredible that one should be able to get up and bathe, get made up, phone for taxis, wish people good day and lie. Lie all the time. 'Oh, you're giving yourself a bad time,' said my closest friend, Ricci Burns, when we met in the street. 'Stop making a drama. He's going to be fine.' Oh Rick, if you only knew what it was like in that side ward.

Against all the odds one day, many weeks later, he opened his eyes in that side ward, ripped out his tubes and irritably demanded sustenance. The tubes were replaced and it was explained to him that he'd been 'really quite ill'. He didn't seem interested and quickly graduated to what we called 'flat' food – little pools of puréed who-knows-what. The family returned to London, the house grew light again, and not quite as gleamingly perfect. And he came home. 'I *told* you it was nothing too awful,' I said to everyone. Dr Slattery and the surgeons and Manolita and I looked at each other in mute fellow feeling. All our lies were coming true, but the shadow of death had come very close.

The question of drink was not broached. Gerry Slattery must have explained the score to him. Large quantities of vitamins and packets of something new and helpful called Valium were deposited in the house. O'Toole insisted that the bar – just opposite his large leather chair – was fully stocked and the wine cellar kept full. He just didn't drink. No discussion, no help required. It was an extraordinary turn of events. He'd always been bookish and an easy, fluent writer. Now he became a slow, painstaking writer of sonnets. I could not even imagine what went on in his head as he embarked for the first time since his mid-teens on a life of sobriety. My admiration for him increased even as I found it difficult to keep up with his frantic intellectual curiosity; everything was considered and questioned down to the most trivial newspaper stories. It was exhausting. Admiration and respect struggled with resentment. In the past I and the girls, Kate and Pat, could have done with a sober, present husband and father, but nothing that I could have said or done would have stopped him drinking. He stopped now to save his life – which is reasonable enough and thank God he has – but . . . but, I wish he could have stopped for *our* sake.

My mother, who had come to live with us in London after my father's death in Wales in 1962, flung herself into the role of matron; cauldrons of beef tea were prepared in the kitchen and she mastered the art of flat food. The children, aged twelve and fifteen years, learned not to lean on his stomach but otherwise enjoyed having a father captive in bed instead of one that dashed in and out of the house, worked behind closed doors, surrounding himself with people. I never talked to him of the time in hospital, but he must have thought I looked the worse for wear and after a few weeks he urged me to accept a job that I had thought I couldn't possibly take. Each night, scared, I called him from Suffolk and he, tucked up in bed which he referred to as his 'teapot', assured me that he was enjoying his life as a dormouse. Dressed as Mayflower pilgrims in a film made for American TV, we froze all day on the desolate beach and I returned to long, dreamless sleeps in the hotel. I discovered a tiny brewery that made exquisite beer. That and the fresh air began to repair me. I went home to my beloved dormouse.

'I need to go somewhere nice to recuperate. Not too much sun. Quiet. Nice.'

'Go? Where? You're not even supposed to be *up*. Not for ages.'

'I'll *get* up.'

'Categorically, NO. We stay in London.'

'Oh. Hello. My name is Siân O'Toole. I'd like to make a reservation. Is your hotel suitable for a semi-invalid?'

'Is there total privacy in your hotel?'

'How far is it from your hotel to the nearest hospital?'

'What do you mean, you're not even open yet?'

'I see, sorry to have troubled you.'

O'Toole's partner, Jules Buck, and I looked at each other in despair. We'd been on the phone for hours. North Africa, France, Italy, Austria. Nothing.

Then suddenly, 'Oh, we have *total* privacy – a suite hanging over the Tyrrhenian Sea. No, we are not open, but we will open for you and look after you like family. We will respect the ill-health and never make anything of it.'

Oh blessed, blessed Carlo Cinque. Just let us get to you quickly now. We are an odd little procession. I've got a porter and the bags are piled high on a cart, and he wants it to be the fastest cart in Naples Airport. I want to slow him down so that the third figure bringing up the rear can seem to saunter as though his mind were on other things. Each step is painful, I know. Tapping the porter on the shoulder, I shake my head and apologetically pat my chest. I don't have the Italian to say, 'Feel a bit woozy.' But, hands raised in comprehension, he nods sympathetically and we proceed at a regal pace and he keeps a brotherly eye on me until we reach the waiting car.

Good as O'Toole is at 'disappearing' in a crowd, people are beginning to recognise him and as I'm carefully eased into the back seat I try not to look at him on the other side of the car, nonchalantly negotiating himself into the seat beside me. I can tell it's a miracle of small, self-controlled, slow movements. The half-smile disappears once he's seated and we're pulling away from the curious crowd. I'm so relieved I could weep. As for him, I think that in the last forty minutes he's done enough acting to last the year and now we're silent and grateful that the pressure is off. Well, I am. Who knows the state of mind of someone who has been in what doctors call 'unacceptable' pain ('torture', I'd call it) and who is now, after a close brush with death, biting all the hands that have helped and fed him because he *must* try to return to what *he* thinks of as normal living. O'Toole on the ropes is beyond sensible help. Only crazy people can lend him a hand. No, not that. He needs crazy people who are also rational. Madness has to walk hand in hand with common sense to be any use to him. And that's my talent. It would be nice to say only great love can help in these extremes, but I don't think that's it. Fear and anxiety and grief have left me empty of soft emotion, but I can't see this person without seeing my shadow behind him. And I don't feel I exist without his presence, informing my voice, my behaviour, even when he's there only as an irritating grain in my shell and I'm forming layers of disagreement along with the shiny, graceful insights I get from observing him at what I think of as his best. Even after all these years, I'm not sure that I don't make up this state of mutual dependence, the 'oneness', this very special state that is never discussed. Maybe it only exists in my head, and that has worried me in the past; now it doesn't matter. We're on yet another crazy, possibly doomed journey.

There's a tiny chapel – hardly that, maybe a shrine – on the roadside. In a less anxious state the twists and turns of the Italian Riviera road would have left me a wreck, but today I'm not worried about my skin. Steps! Damn! Lots of steps! No one said anything about steps. The hotel is out of sight below us. How far below? Very slowly we begin the descent. If there are hundreds of these steps, we're not going to make it and this place will be impossible for us to stay in. So what do we do? There's a turn in the staircase and a lift-door appears in the rock. We step inside and descend, emerging into a lovely room – a huge foyer looking out at the ocean. There seem to be seven people to help us to our set of rooms, and the terrace, already flaming with bougainvillaea, does truly hang over the Tyrrhenian Sea (is this the 'wine-red' sea? It's lovely but about as wine-red as ink).

This feels like home. Are the Italians alone in their talent for purveying luxury in a way that has one reaching for words like 'simple', 'homely', 'unassuming'? Since 1970 I've spent almost five years building a house in Ireland and immediately I feel here much as I feel on the West Coast in Connemara. Even the ground under our feet is familiar; solid rock everywhere around, above and below. Who or what guided us to this place? I'm overwhelmed with a sense of good fortune. Maybe our luck has turned. Luck is important. O'Toole is lucky. Leaving him to potter around the rooms, I set about fine-tuning our life here. Breakfast quite early, big jugs of fresh juice mid-morning. No alcohol. The simplest of small lunches. More fresh fruit juice at the cocktail hour. Dinner as much like lunch as possible. The minimum of attention. Telephone calls only from my mother or Jules (and they won't ring unless there's an emergency). I unpack, and within hours his books and papers (O'Toole never attempted to master the art of travelling light when in 'civilised' surroundings) cover the tables in the enormous sitting room. My books are piled high in the bedroom. Carlo has raised the drawbridge for us and we are alone.

I've stayed in some of the loveliest hotels in the world, but never in one that met all the urgent needs and desires of the moment as did the San Pietro. As the weeks went by, we began to tackle the corridors and the steps to the foyer and the dining room. At first we were the only guests and it *was* like being in the West of Ireland. Service was impeccable but running through everything was a streak of idiosyncratic *joie de vivre* that was peculiar to Carlo. There was a St Bernard (suffering in the warmth of southern Italy) who came and yearned mournfully at the food on the table. Outside there were grumpy penguins living in and around the pool. The parrot in the dining room shrieked obscenities learned from the village builders. The builders . . . When we learned the story of the making of the hotel, I knew that we were right to feel at home. In the West of Ireland, before you build anything, you buy gelignite and you blast yourself a flat space on the granite. The boys cycle out to you with a bit of 'jelly' in the basket and, fag in hand, survey the impossible terrain; then they lay their charges and murmur, 'Better get back there now, missus', before the ground explodes. 'Would ya like a little bit of that over there blown off?' 'Mmm, I think a terrace looking out at the—' 'Sure thing. Better move back a bit.' Pow! And there's your terrace – just where you wanted it.

Carlo Cinque, who ran a successful hotel in Positano, thought he'd like a quiet place just for himself and, having bought the San Pietro chapel, perched on the edge of a cliff outside the town, he and a few of the village boys 'jellied' a bit of a ledge and, having cut some steps down to it, he built himself a few rooms and a kitchen. His friends kept borrowing them, so he blasted away another ledge and built a few more rooms, and on it went. Most wonderful of all (and if he was proud to tell this tale he never found a more admiring audience), when he decided that this was now a proper hotel and maybe should include access to the beach, he decided to make a lift through the cliff to the seashore hundreds of feet below. A couple of village boys came and surveyed the problem and quickly said they were ready to start. Carlo gave them the go-ahead and provided the explosives. (A less confident man might have feared for his hotel.) Off they went. One boy descended through the rock from the hotel ledge and the other ascended from sea level. They blasted away and one day they met – smack on target in the middle – and there was the elevator shaft. It's sad that this is an extraordinary story. People – understandably people in remote neighbourhoods – have talents and skills and don't question them. Closer to urban communities they lose their confidence and learn to bow to 'experts in the field', experts on building, parenting, meteorology, lift construction. Well, I hope nobody wages a guerrilla war in southern Italy. Those men are invincible, natural engineers.

We were told that we were too early, alas, for the annual, month-long visit of the famous Welsh actor Hugh Griffith and his wife, Gwnda (one specially designated member of staff would tactfully head him off as he made for the edge of a cliff late at night, glass in hand), but a few guests appeared in the dining room as time went by – charming, quiet Americans mostly. Carlo and they and O'Toole and myself began to meet for 'drinks' before dinner. Innocently, they would urge us to have a glass with them. Carlo never betrayed his anxiety at these moments. Nor did I. O'Toole was a model of tact and sweetness, saying he'd 'not been very well' and would have a fruit juice. They, worlds away from the hells we'd inhabited, said, 'Well, when we get home, there'll be no more wine, Fanta only, so we're going to have a glass *every night*.' Oh God, they were so nice and I loved the glimpse into their nice, safe lives. 'Why *not*?' we chorused, raising our glasses of fruit juice, and Carlo nodded, beaming.

Normally a sound sleeper, even in the most desperate of circum-stances, I lie awake in this Eden. James Herriot's books are making me laugh in the wind-down part of the day. Siegfried seems to be such an O'Toole character; I read aloud to him and he recognises his own maddening habits and it makes him laugh also, before he falls asleep. After that, with the lights out, in the profound silence I lie awake, listening. When I was a little girl I would creep across the landing to see if my parents were still breathing, but that was out of fear that I would be left alone in the world. This is different. I feel that if I don't stand vigil he might stop breathing after all. I fall asleep at dawn. Only the dark hours are dangerous. Exhausted, I fall asleep again after lunch. I think that my fears are concealed, but one day we decide to take the famous lift to the deserted beach. Entering the cave below we look around, admiring the arrangements, the bar that would operate in season. We stand there looking out at the sea, which looks different at close quarters, more real, less like a set. Above us rises the press of hundreds of feet of rock. My feeling of dread is profound and when O'Toole says, 'Well, I think we've seen enough of this', I gratefully get into the lift and return to the familiar warm, sunny lounge high above the painted sea. In our suite I climb on to the beautiful ornate day-bed in a corner of the sitting room – and sleep, and sleep. When I wake, O'Toole is sitting there looking at me. 'You were afraid, weren't you?' I nod, eyes full of unshed tears. 'Don't fret,' he says, stroking my head. Does he mean that there's nothing more to worry about? Does he mean I'm allowed to feel nervous about rocks? Does he mean he's going to be all right? I nod and resolve to try not to fret.

We now have a lovely pattern to our lives. We've so rarely had patterns. Rising, we have breakfast in the sitting room. (Who brings breakfast? I see no one.) Then we prepare for The Walk. It becomes a little longer each day. The hotel car follows us and at first we're lifted the last kilometre into the town. There we buy the New York *Herald Tribune* and sit outside drinking coffee and doing crosswords or playing word games. There are few people about. Then the car takes us back to the hotel and we lunch in the dining room. Now that visitors are begin-ning to arrive, the foul-mouthed parrot has been banished. Also the St Bernard (we know that he stands in the kitchen, drooling over the preparing of lunch). The penguins also have had to go. The hotel still doesn't look quite 'there' in brochure terms. It's the gardens, of course. Carlo and I go to Naples and buy hundreds of plants. (This time the road *does* scare me half to death.) Over the next week I spend a few hours a day digging and fertilising and planting, and *voilà*! There we are. Every suite has a beautiful, planted, fed and watered garden. By now, I almost feel I'm on the staff and I'm happier than I have been for a long, long time. One day O'Toole and I walk *all* the way into Positano. Triumph! We peer at Zeffirelli's villa down on the beach and hear stories of the goings-on down there. Nureyev hurling heavy objects down from road level is one I particularly like to contemplate. Having been around during the time of Rudi's worst excesses it doesn't surprise me in the least that he should have been thrown out of the villa. Though frankly, by O'Toole standards he's not so bad and I, for one, would never have kicked him out.

Life is calm, a bit like our early days in Connemara when we first acquired a small cottage and a little land. It's not so much having a time to think and reflect, rather it's inhabiting a space in which not to think at all. There was a time in 1960 in the desert when I felt like this. Nothing happened. Living closed down to existing, getting through the day, like a tree. Or a cabbage. Maybe there's something wrong with me. I love life at its lowest level. One thing is clear: I have never felt such love for O'Toole as I feel now. I was all loved out, slumped like a boxer, beaten in my corner. I thought I knew all the turns in this maze he and I inhabited and there was nothing that could dismay or surprise or delight me. Wrong. Where did it come from, this huge, even surge of love? Not from pity. I could never feel pity for such a dangerous, disruptive human being. Sympathy? No. I've never almost died, so I don't know what that feels like. Well, this is the place we've arrived at after so many exhausting twists and turns and stops and starts and ups and downs and false endings, and I've learned one thing: to accept what comes my way. I'm not going to try to work it out, the reason for this intensely happy time.

Chapter Two

Nineteen fifty-seven, when we first met, seems a whole lifetime away . . .

'Marry Siân and become a famous couple in the theatre.' Emlyn Williams talking over the supper table, Micheál MacLiammóir nodding enthusiastically. The two matchmakers smiled on us. We were in our early twenties and it was only a matter of weeks since, after a long estrangement following our first play together, John Hall's *The Holiday*, he'd appeared in the early hours of the morning at my window in Ladbroke Square and swung himself back into my heart and my life. No, he'd never left my heart.

Now, we were sitting in a dark nightclub arrangement that Clement Freud used to run high up under the roof of the Royal Court Theatre in Sloane Square. We raised our glasses, though the subject of marriage had never been mooted before and I don't think either of us was keen on the idea, and I was still married to Don, from whom I'd run off to come to London and RADA. For now, it was more than enough to be together. I was dazzled by him (and I could tell that he was fascinated by me). We knew from our time together on tour that we got on very well. We were good company for each other and had no trouble adjusting our living habits to suit each other. I'd never stayed up late, but I got to love it. He began to enjoy seeing the world in daylight hours – streets and parks as well as the dark interiors of bars. We shared erratic eating patterns, a love of music, singing, guitar playing, people watching. Our likes and dislikes chimed. The only slight difficulty was drink. Before I met O'Toole I had never even tasted beer or whisky.

On tour he had introduced me to Highland malt – single and blended – and I had liked small quantities of both. Beer and Guinness were utterly beyond my comprehension, but I realised that an appreciation of draught Guinness was pretty essential in my new life and I persevered, sipping the hated drink slowly during evenings when O'Toole drank his own age in the stuff. Everyone we knew drank so much; incredible quantities of alcohol were lowered on every conceivable social occasion. I was cautiously intrigued.

Drink apart, it was easy living together and with wonderful sex thrown into the mix it was ecstatic. He was still in Willis Hall's *The Long and the Short and the Tall*, his first big London success, while I played lead after lead in live television plays, also successful and making a great deal of money. We would meet in his dressing room after my rehearsal ended, before his performance began, and eat high tea together; the same meal every day. Huge plates of anaemic scrambled eggs on white-bread toast and mugs of tea, sent in from the workmen's café round the corner. While he did the show I would spend the evening watching bits of the play or looking after the new friends we were making, the people who flock to a new success. They were, on the whole, truly nice people, some of whom became part of our lives – people like Dr Slattery and his wife, Johnny, and R.D. Smith, the radio producer, and his wife, Olivia Manning, the novelist; but already I could distinguish between them and the people who came to devour, whose eyes lit up if he said something outrageous and unsayable, who became excited when he crossed the line between high spirits and being hopelessly 'jarred', as the Irish put it. I was made uneasy by them.

I became used to working really hard all day (fortunately I never had to sit down to memorise anything, lines sank in after a few readings) so that I was able to join O'Toole after the show, ready for whatever the evening had to offer. After the play the company would move back next door to the bar where a few hours previously they had been enjoying themselves as the 'five' was rung. Bowing to the inevitable, the theatre had rigged a line relaying the calls through to the pub – there wasn't much hope that the hard core of the company, Ronnie Fraser, Bob Shaw, Bryan Pringle, O'Toole, was going to leave the 'craic' and get into the theatre at the 'half'-hour call, which is given thirty-five minutes before the play is due to begin. The 'five' sounds ten minutes before curtain up and at that point they would straighten up and stampede for the theatre, pausing only to wipe their fingers under the hot-water pipes and rub the dirt on to their faces. It took them a matter of seconds to discard their clothes and pull on their 'distressed' army uniforms. A dab of Vaseline rubbed into the dirt and they were on stage, looking as though they'd spent a long time in make-up to achieve that diseased, desperate, jungle-damp look which the play demanded. They drove

Lindsay Anderson, the director, mad. The expert on army behaviour brought in to make them look like soldiers had a nervous collapse and left. I don't suppose any of them behaved as badly ever again, but they and author, Willis Hall, were unstoppable. Had they not been a triumph they would never have worked again. As it was – who argues with success?

A member of the company who did not racket around London was Peter's understudy, who was called Michael Caine. When O'Toole hurt his knee badly and was told he'd have to go 'off' for surgery, he refused flatly. 'What – and let Mick on stage?' he said. 'No chance, thank you very much.' It was a compliment from one good actor to another. Who knew what Michael got up to? He was focused, quiet and circumspect.

Observing the boys, I realised that in fact they'd all done a huge amount of work and that they were desperate to conceal the fact. I heard the story of the 'foreigner' in Dublin who suddenly realised to his nervous amazement that the men standing next to him at the bar were members of the international rugby team he was about to watch playing England. 'And they played a *blinder. And* they *won.*' Playing a 'blinder' was crucial. So was winning. The company's behaviour was a pose, and none of them believed you could just stroll on stage without preparation and be wonderful, but that was the impression they liked to give – no one more than O'Toole.

There was something else to it as well. I think there was a revulsion against the 'actorish' English actor who went home after a quiet day of organised rehearsal, had a small sherry and settled down to a few hours of 'study' after dinner; the sort of actor who appeared in well-made plays and led a middle-class life, as respectable as a banker; who, after the show, tied a silk cravat around his neck to protect his white shirt against the remnants of Leichner make-up, numbers nine and five. Plays were altering and the lads were going to show that they were the new breed of actor, born for the occasion; unconventional, bohemian, with no pretensions to belonging to the polite society of 'civilians'. No use expecting polite speech and middle-class behaviour from this lot. The Lord Chamberlain was being challenged to allow unheard-of words on the stage and they were the guys to whom such speech came naturally. Stage make-up was considered 'poncy'. It was all very understandable and rather attractive. Exciting, certainly. It was over-simple, and no actor who cared about theatre would have maintained a prejudice against the great writers and actors of the Thirties and Forties, but for a while in the late Fifties it was no bad thing to seem to be rebelling against everything that had gone before.

It was a mercy that we were all so young and in possession of endless energy. When the pub shut there would be a muttered conference and then a large part of the crowd would drift into taxis and cars and find themselves in basement flats in Paddington and Bayswater. How did anyone know where the parties were happening? It was all a mystery to me. These gatherings weren't recognisable parties either. 'It's just a piss-up,' explained O'Toole. I don't ever recall going further north than WC2. Hampstead was reserved for exquisite Sunday lunch around Johnny Slattery's kitchen table. She would feed at least six actors as well as her own family and it was often the only 'proper' meal that we found time to sit down to eat all week.

More or less the same fifty people found themselves together late at night several times a week; actors from the London shows. All the new Australian actors in town were there, arriving bearing crates of Foster's lager (Ken Warren from *Summer of the Seventeenth Doll* was a host several times a week). The actors were mostly young, those unencumbered by domestic life, and guilty young actors who *did* have families and went home at dawn to ruffle the sheets and take the children to school. There was always a sprinkling of actors from an older generation who were curious to see what was going on. Willis Hall was an enchanting leader of the pack. Describing a more sedate version of an actors' party, he said, 'Oh awful. You know – white wine in cups and young girls being sick.' There were very few rehearsal rooms, and companies moved from church hall to church hall – St Thomas's, St Luke's, St John's. One day Willis, checking his diary for the next rehearsal, shook his head and said without looking up, 'If I get knocked over they'll think I'm the fuckin' Pope.'

Robert Bolt was another nightly companion. He used to like to visit the theatre where his first West End play, *The Flowering Cherry*, was playing. Anxiously eavesdropping, he usually heard good, enjoyable things about himself. Not always. (One of his favourite remarks was a grumpy, 'It's all right, I suppose – if you like a great play.') I listened to his worries and didn't talk about mine, but I remember a night after I'd been to a party at the German Embassy (I did so many translations of German classics on television that I was on their guest list for years) and Robert and I were slumped, I in full evening dress. Conveniently forgetting that, acting on advice, I'd turned down three film contracts in order to become what people in those days called a 'real' – a theatre – actress, I moped a bit and shed a maudlin tear and said, 'I was sent for by Mr Vidor for a big movie and he's just DIED!' Robert, who'd been going on about the problems of being a writer, wrenched his attention on to my life for a moment and tried to console me. 'Oh my poor girl. Sudden death *does* seem a bit hard. But cheer up.' We both started to laugh at ourselves at the same moment and reached for another Foster's.

There were after-hours clubs. Jerry's, which I knew when Sean Lynch ran it (he later married the formidable and talented Annie Ross and they opened Annie's). There was the Kismet run by Raj and his father, just off St Martin's Lane. Jack's near Orange Street was approached through an unmarked door alongside a plain black window. This seemed to be harder to join than the Garrick; only death left a membership place open. Joan Littlewood of Stratford East held court there, and as far as I could make out they served only steak and baked potatoes. The Buxton was the jolliest place, situated in a quiet street behind the Haymarket across from the stage door of the Haymarket Theatre. I liked it because it was the only place where I ever got to eat anything (a lunchtime sausage and a scrambled-egg high tea left me ravenous by midnight. Tough, overcooked steak and frozen peas were the staple diet and so good). The Buxton was a bit more like an actors' restaurant of today, but there were no customers outside the profession and it had an illicit air about it. One memorable night in 1953, John Gielgud, newly knighted, and newly convicted of soliciting, squeezed his way through the crowded club. John was loved and revered in the profession, but few knew how best to deal with what must be an embarrassing time for the great actor. Stumbling, he put a hand on Emlyn Williams's waist to steady himself. Without looking round, Emlyn in ringing tones cried, 'Four months!' When the laughter subsided, relief and comradeship pervaded the room. Some time afterwards, looking up from his mail, O'Toole said, 'This is ridiculous. I've been thrown out of the Buxton for bad behaviour and someone wants to put me up for the Garrick – oh, sod them all.' And he binned both letters.

The fag-end of the night was my favourite part. Often still hungry, the two of us would walk down to the all-night tea-and-sandwich stand in Covent Garden and order huge white-china mugs of tea and hot-sausage sandwiches, which we ate sitting opposite Lloyds Bank, alongside Boulestin's great restaurant. Fortified, O'Toole would say, 'Okay. Now for a little climb', and he would scale the wall of Lloyds. The first time he did this I was terrified and tried to dissuade him. I was upset by what seemed to be mad, dangerous behaviour. In a remarkably short space of time, I came to accept the behaviour as fairly unremarkable – what did that say about the state of my mind? – and I sat nursing my tea, sitting on the low wall with the tramps who liked to hang around near the cheerfully lit stand, watching him as he negotiated the familiar footholds. He was sure-footed. And lucky. The regulars at the stall knew him as 'Pete' and gave him a little cheer as he finished the descent.

When it was time to go home, we would retire to our tiny room in Ken Griffith's flat in Belgravia, facing the side of the National Coal Board building. Ken Griffith and Doria Noar were like guardian angels to us and we lived for next to nothing in SW1. If Doria caught us standing still for ten minutes she fed us nourishing meals. We slept in a double bed which rested on about £75,000 worth of stamps ('Covers', as I learned to call them); part of Kenneth's passion for the Boer War. He adored and admired O'Toole and the feeling was mutual. He made me welcome, partly because I was a fellow countrywoman, but he had grave doubts about the union. When we were filming in Cardiff, he walked me round the Temple of Peace saying, 'You cannot marry this wonderful man. Understand, he is a genius but he is not normal.' I replied, 'He is the most normal man I've ever met.'

I meant it, but what did I know about him, this super-normal man? Something and nothing, and everything. He was Irish and he came from Leeds, from the same neighbourhood as Keith Waterhouse and Willis Hall and Albert Finney. His father was an off-course bookmaker – feckless, a drunk and occasionally violent. His mother struggled to keep the family afloat. A Scots Presbyterian, she loved the Catholic Church, its kindly priests and candles. Beautiful, with a low husky voice, she was given to quoting Robbie Burns and loved to stay up drinking tea – or preferably whisky – and exchanging stories with her children, O'Toole and his sister, Patricia. I could tell that both children were bright and I was baffled by parents that wouldn't have fought to keep their children at school. O'Toole's sister had made an early exit from the bosom of the family and set about making up for their lack of education by joining the Wrens. Later, having achieved a coveted job as an air-hostess, she had just made a brilliant marriage, and here was O'Toole, one of the brightest young stars on the London stage, via National Service in the Navy and two years' training at RADA. I had never been to the north of England, except on tour, and couldn't quite make out what his upbringing had been like. His father had come to visit when we were on tour, playing *The Holiday*. He'd arrived, looking dapper in a good suit and a sharp trilby, no overcoat against the cold, long Irish face like a fiddle, a lopsided half-smile and a permanently raised right eyebrow.

'Where are you staying?'

'I don't know – I don't know.'

'Any luggage?'

'No. Stop fussing. Don't spoil everything with *details*.'

He sat in the front row of the stalls and when O'Toole entered he raised his hand in salute. Outside the theatre as we made off for a drink after the show, he didn't refer to the performance but he pointed to the front of the theatre, at O'Toole's name featured prominently. 'Look at that,' he said. '"O" as big as a cartwheel.' He wasn't much of a theatre-goer.

I don't know what he thought of me. O'Toole's friends saw their free spirit being sucked into a conventional relationship and, with no special ill-will towards me, they tried to put a stop to it. I didn't mind. They weren't to know that we had a *new* kind of equal partnership and that the last thing I had in mind was domesticity – as alien to me as it was to him.

My friends, advisors, employers were equally appalled and bluntly said that he would destroy my career, that I needed taking care of and bringing on, and that O'Toole would trample all over me. They must be mad, I thought. We both love the theatre above everything. What can go wrong? For the first time in my life I am living with someone who respects me as an equal and he *will* look after me. Gradually, I lost my support system – the older actors and the directors and producers who were good to me dropped away. But work was still plentiful.

When I left RADA, MCA was the agency I went to, but, with their approval, I had signed an exclusive contract with Douglas Uren, a businessman who was interested in the theatre and chose to make an investment in me. He guaranteed me an income whether I worked or not. But I liked working – all the time. I realised that my private life would have to alter now and I was willing to adapt – sometimes in unexpected ways.

O'Toole looked at my wardrobe of good clothes and said, 'You look as though you're in mourning for your sex life – all this black and violet. Give it here.' It was late at night and it was raining as he gathered up armfuls of organza and wool, bags, shoes, gloves, frocks, hats, suits and, opening the window, flung thousands of pounds' worth of clothes on to the wet cobbles below. I had a momentary pang of regret but spoke only to say, 'But what will I wear?' '*My* clothes,' he said grandly, gathering me into his arms. I would have liked to retrieve my things, but the new woman in me thought, 'Maybe he's right. That's an old-fashioned way of dressing.' So we became the only couple in town who shared a wardrobe. Winter and summer we wore coloured cotton trousers and canvas shoes and lumberjack shirts and big, thick, knitted fisherman sweaters. I had to roll his trousers up, of course, which made me look like a waif (he looked like a handsome pirate). My next TV role was that of a sexy publican's wife who was no better than she should be, and after the show they gave me the skin-tight frocks and six-inch heels. So for months I veered between looking like a tart with a heart and the shrimp boy. I was so deliriously in love I couldn't understand why everyone around me was worried. 'You are going to ruin your career' was the constant warning. Indeed, it was as though he wanted to eradicate my life before I met him, but I was a willing accomplice.

The Long and the Short and the Tall ended, not having transferred well to the New (now the Albery) Theatre in St Martin's Lane, and while O'Toole began to figure out his next move I went on from TV play to TV play. It was the time of the single play when the writer was still king, so working in television was not unlike working in the theatre. Many of the plays were written specially for TV, otherwise we did stage plays barely adapted for the screen; three acts with thirty seconds in between to change clothes and re-dress the set. Everything that went out on the screen was live. It was pandemonium in the studio. If anyone got injured they were dragged out of the way. During a flu epidemic I watched a sound engineer faint and fall off his seat high above the studio floor, and since I was carrying around a bucket into which to throw up, I didn't have much sympathy to spare. In one play at this time an actor died on a set of a mineshaft and the rest of the company had to crawl over him, sharing his lines amongst them, until someone managed to extract his body. There were no rules to speak of. It was like travelling without a map.

We would rehearse for four weeks and after three weeks we'd get into costume and pop into a small studio, pose for stills and play the 'trailer' – live. Then we'd do the show and, having done it once, we'd have a few days off and then we'd go back into the studio and play the 'repeat' – live again. Prompting was out of the question. There was very little anyone could do to help. Being on screen alone when an actor was 'off' was a nightmare and we became used to ad-libbing – not very well in my case. I doubt if the watching audience was fooled as I sat there one night saying, 'Well, I thought that *GEORGE* would be here now. *GEORGE!* Is that you I hear on the path? Well, my goodness, there's no one there. I could have sworn that was *GEORGE's step*. Oh, *GEORGE*, there you are – darling, you seem out of breath.' (You bastard.)

Only people who never lived through these experiences talk of the 'wonder' and 'immediacy' of live TV. Immediate coronary, more like. But it was all we were used to and very early on I began to see that television was going to be the most powerful and influential arm of showbusiness. Many actors were snooty about it for a long time. Some of the directors had moved over from radio or the theatre and were pretty pedestrian, but there were also wonderful directors who were devoted to the new medium. When Sydney Newman joined the BBC he galvanised everyone and kept agitating for more boldness, more close-ups; he didn't want to see any more 'photographed plays'. 'Get *in* there,' he yelled at cameramen. 'This has to be a close-up.' When you think about it, it stands to reason that close-ups come in ones or twos. At that time I was doing a rather 'sensitive' play for a sensitive director who was petrified when Mr Newman came in to watch our final rehearsals. He looked at the five actors in the scene and, feeling he should be moving in, he whispered desperately to the camera crew, 'Come on boys, in you go. Make this shot – a *close five*'. The fallout was awful.

O'Toole was offered three short films made for television. *End of a Good Man*, *Once a Horse Player* and a little aeroplane drama with Patricia Neal who had quit Hollywood and stardom for life as Roald Dahl's wife in Great Missenden. (I'm not sure that he explained to her where Great Missenden was. She was a little nonplussed and, unbelievably, she was finding it hard to find work and quite glad of this tiny film.) When we went to stay at her house we had to pretend to be married or her housekeeper would have resigned on the spot. Oh, the Fifties.

One of these short films was chiefly remarkable for introducing into our lives a woman who helped provide the glue of our relationship, the Abbey actress, Marie Kean, who was moonlighting in London for her chum, director Charles Friend. Immensely struck by O'Toole, it seems she'd tactfully nudged him so that his acting might be rather more than less visible to the camera whose existence he didn't appear to notice much. He in turn was hugely impressed by her. He knew all about her work, and the Abbey Theatre, Dublin, was of course almost a holy place to any theatre-lover, let alone an expatriate Irish actor.

He introduced me to her at dusk near Victoria Station and before the evening was over we were a family. Older than we were, she was like a big sister, a big sister who didn't pull rank. A voracious reader, she had a prodigious memory for books and for people, and a humorous outlook on the world that was to make my life possible and was at the same time the undoing of me. I learned from her not to take personally the abuse uttered in drink. 'Sure, he was drunk at the time' was supposed to wipe out all hurt. Men, I learned, were given to excess and behaved like children 'when they had drink taken'. In *vino* was never in *veritas*. Drunken talk made no sense. Had no relevance. Women shrugged tolerantly and loftily in the face of masculine stupidity. Clever women never nagged. Clever women dodged the flying crockery and went away where they could get some peaceful sleep and never in the morning referred to the excesses of the night before. Clever women never made men feel guilty. I tried to learn these lessons. Up to a point they made my life tolerable. In the long run? I don't think the deception could be sustained.

A wonderful actress, Marie had a great love of food and drink and good company; something of a fine disregard for clothes and interior decoration (the minutiae of housekeeping passed her by completely). Shrewd brown eyes missed nothing and the lips could assume a threatening curl. I realised at once that we had come by our best friend. Somehow, then and ever after, she managed to love us both.

Chapter Three

Each Sunday for three years, I would take a train or fly to Wales from wherever I was acting in the theatre or rehearsing a TV play and present *Land of Song*, a programme of light music with links which I wrote and delivered in Welsh and English. English was not allowed in the charter for TV Wales and the West, but my bits of inserted English meant that we were taken up by the network and I spoke fast, hoping no one would notice which language I was speaking. The ratings were high and I was extremely well-paid. That sort of job brought in a great deal more than I could earn playing a star part at Stratford, for example.

One Sunday O'Toole decided to come to Wales with me. As usual the journey became complicated. I think we went by way of Bristol – never a good idea if one wanted to arrive anywhere on time. I managed to mislay my presenter's dress and did the show, after racing against time to write it, in my trench coat, hoping it looked more Left Bank French than desperate. O'Toole mingled with the extras for fun and everyone was charmed, at which point he said, 'Let's go to Dublin', and we adjourned to the small, almost deserted airfield that was Rhoose Airport until we found a plane that would go to Ireland. We were due to go West, the mythical West I'd been hearing about since I met O'Toole.

In Ireland we hired a car and set off – O'Toole confident, although he didn't have a driving licence and had learned to drive on holiday in the Swiss Alps. (Kenneth Griffith to O'Toole on a vertiginous road: 'I say, old son, you're doing very well, but should you be trying to change gear with the handbrake?') First we called in to see Johnny Slattery's brother, Dick Wilkinson, and his wife, Bridget, in their farm, Balcorris House at Santry. A day and night later we were still there. It was my first experience of Irish country house life and it was like being in a Chekhov play: the beautiful house in some disarray, a house full of drifting people (some never identified), rain, large meals with no discernible beginning or end, sad old dogs, cheerful old people, melancholy conversations and bursts of wild hilarity. Drink.

It was O'Toole who decided that we should move on. Too late to go West. (This was to become the first of many abortive attempts to go West.) What about going to Marie Kean's flat in Dublin? It was spring and the fields outside the farmhouse were yellow with thousands of daffodils. (Very un-Welsh that sort of farm crop. Could it be an Irish custom to farm daffodils among the cows?) We were given a carload of daffodils to take to the city. Arriving at Marie's, we hauled the flowers up five flights of Georgian stairs in the house in Lower Baggot Street. Marie had the ham and cabbage almost ready. She went back to the kitchen and, surrounded by daffodils, O'Toole clutched me and said, 'Have my children.' Without pausing for breath I said, 'Yes.'

Thank God for contraception, or I could have become one of those women with nineteen children clutching at their skirts. Our first child was no sooner suggested than conceived. Marie, the witch, claimed to know this the following day. Never having given obstetrics so much as a passing thought (I'd never held a baby or particularly wished to), I forgot about the consequences of the long, joyous spring night – illuminated, it seemed to me, by the shine of scores of daffodils, pungent with the smell of bitter vegetation, remembering only that I'd – well, what had I done? 'Plighted my troth' were words that seemed to fit the bill. 'Thrown my bonnet over the windmill.' 'Cast my lot with.' Now, had he said 'Marry me' I would have shuffled a bit and said, 'Oh I don't think you really mean that' and 'I don't really know about that' and we would have moved on to bacon and cabbage and Guinness and conversation and a simple, lovely night like any other, but the unwanted proposal didn't come. Not then. Not ever. And I began the one great journey that underpinned all the hilarious, foolish, reckless journeys that characterised our life together.

Five weeks later it dawned on me that I must be pregnant. I didn't tell anyone, especially not my agent at MCA, who grew restive as I turned down a long-term project. To do her credit, she was very satisfied with my contract with Douglas Uren, which freed me from the necessity of taking job after job, but I felt guilty now and booked myself up with a great deal of highly paid TV work and, as a nod towards what I should have been doing – theatre – I agreed to do a play for the reopening of the Hampstead Theatre Club with a translation of *Siwan* by Saunders Lewis, the great Welsh writer who had written for me and befriended me and helped to change my life by leaving Wales for London and RADA. James Roose-Evans was to direct this limited run and I figured the thirteenth-century costume would conceal my interesting condition. Someone would have to be told. 'Someone – sometime, please – soon,' nagged Marie. Yes, but not yet. O'Toole and I were both pleased but I could tell that no allowances were to be made for this happy event. Life went on exactly as before and I was lucky that so far I wasn't visited by any of the inconveniences of pregnancy. Rude good health persisted, unmarked by fancies, moods and morning sickness, or, should I say, rather, there were no symptoms which I was able to identify, but what power was it that made me so blessedly, stupidly unworried about tomorrow if not some kind of hormonal change? Any fool except me could see that it wasn't going to be possible to continue my present way of life; getting up early, working all day, staying up late, sleeping too little, eating when and if the opportunity arose. I didn't have to worry about smoking because no one suggested that it might be better to cut down, let alone give up. 'Relax, have a cigarette!' we all cried to each other; 'Have a drink!' And where were we to live? *How* were we to live? Would O'Toole help me with the baby? (That didn't seem likely, but one never knew.) When would I have to give up work? (Last minute, I thought.) When could I resume work? (As soon as possible.) What did having a baby cost? Did we make enough money? The months went by and few of these questions were formulated, let alone addressed, except for one. O'Toole took a short lease on a fourth-floor flat in Bryanston Street.

Before we moved, something happened that was to alter us both completely. 'People don't alter,' said O'Toole; 'they adapt. Or die.' Maybe. But make a huge, major adaptation and you end up pretty altered. Or so it seems. And if you *seem* altered then you *are* altered.

O'Toole's agent asked him to go and see a film producer called Jules Buck. I knew who he was because my agent had asked me to come and meet him at the MCA office near Hyde Park Corner. I couldn't confess that I was going to be too out of shape to be in the film, so I went along half-heartedly, wearing a really boring 'good' dress that I'd just been given after playing a middle-class character in *The Tortoise and the Hare*. (Already it didn't fit properly around the waist.) Mr Buck, very American, smoking a big cigar, wasn't mightily impressed, I could tell, and my agent was willing me to snap out of my lethargy and sparkle a bit. For the first and only time in my life I was asked to 'turn around'. I couldn't believe my ears. I turned on my sensible shoes, and felt the first spark of interest and amusement, which lasted for the short remainder of the meeting. (It was a dull part anyway, but I knew I'd never have to worry about how to play it. The part went to a sensible English Rose with a small, unpregnant waist.)

And now O'Toole was going to be seen for the same film, *The Day They Robbed the Bank of England*. Would he have to do a twirl as well? Or was it just girls? When he'd been gone for about an hour – just round the corner to Groom Place – the phone rang and Jules asked me to pop round as well. Jules and his wife, Joyce, were enchanting. I was ashamed that I had written him off in MCA as a crass American mogul. He was very funny and very Jewish. Joyce was the most beautiful and elegant woman I'd ever seen; sophisticated, witty and with such stories! Everything was going swimmingly, I could tell, and I was sure that O'Toole would be offered the quite nice part of the Irish 'boyo'. They were talking about Hollywood, telling hilarious tales about people who didn't seemed quite real to me, Olivia (de Havilland), John and Walter (Huston), Sam (Spiegel), Marilyn (Monroe), Dimitri (Tiomkin), George (Axelrod), Joan and Eric (Ambler), it went on and on.

Jules was part of the exodus from Hollywood to Europe as the studio system broke down. He and Joyce had just moved to London from Paris where they'd been working and sharing a life with Jacques Tati and his wife. This was almost too much to take in at one sitting. Hours went by. Joyce, ever the good hostess, provided a picnic dinner. Drinks came in huge, beautiful tumblers. The drawing room was the most lovely domestic drawing room I'd ever been in; clean and fragrant, dark walls, gleaming walnut and mahogany furniture, blissfully comfortable chairs, softly gilded picture frames and drawer handles, and bits of ormolu glowing here and there in pools of light. Joyce noticed my look. 'Twenty-seven sources of light,' she said. (It was the first of many lessons I was to learn from her.) I marvelled and settled down for more delicious small eats and stories.

It seemed a shame to come back to the present and O'Toole's part in the film. And it seemed a *real* shame when O'Toole, who didn't have any other decent options, grandly said that he didn't want to play the part under any circumstances. Horrors. Dismay. He would, however, consider the part of the upper-class English officer. Jules, who was very taken with the Irish Irishman – who reminded him of a former business partner, John Huston – was severely jolted. I nodded off, but at five o'clock in the morning I was nudged out of my chair and joined the other three in a toast to a new company, Keep Films – directors Jules, Joyce, Siân and Peter – and we toasted O'Toole's coming appearance as an English officer in Jules's movie.

Chapter Four

I settled into the flat O'Toole had found – a fourth-floor eyrie in Bryanston Street. Doriah helped me move. Before he began Jules's film, O'Toole had a good part in another film, *The Top of the World*, which was to be directed by Nicholas Ray. We expected a great deal as we went to meet him; he'd been married to Gloria Grahame and he'd directed *Rebel Without a Cause*. Like all visiting Americans, he was installed in a sumptuous flat in SW1 (they didn't seem to consider living anywhere other than Mayfair or Belgravia). He was oddly disappointing; distracted and unfocused. But he wasn't drunk – maybe he was ill? O'Toole met his director at the fag-end of an interesting career.

What had seemed a wonderful opportunity, playing opposite Anthony Quinn, quickly turned into a farce and O'Toole's mood blackened. Anthony Quinn was very honest with him. When O'Toole pointed out that his balaclava came down to his eyes and the frozen dirt covered the little bit of face visible between the cap and his beard, Quinn said, 'Listen kid, it's taken me twenty years to get to be first over the title. If you think I'm letting you loose on the screen with me, think again.'

It was a disaster of a job. O'Toole turned to Jules to get his name off. More and more we were turning to Jules. He was beginning to regulate our lives. For instance, income tax was something O'Toole intended to think about some other time. While we were living with Ken and Doriah in Dorset Mews, Douglas Uren and the accountants at my agents, MCA, saw to it that *my* affairs were in order and I was half horrified and half impressed by O'Toole's cavalier attitude towards law-abiding existence. His attitude towards most of the practicalities of life was nonchalant, to say the least, and Jules had a great deal to contend with. He urged O'Toole to acquire a driving licence for his car, and on a wet morning in 1959 the newly hired instructor drew into the mews and off they went, O'Toole a little hung-over but in great high spirits, brimming with confidence. He had, after all, driven in France and Switzerland, and London traffic held no terrors for him. Ken Griffith was apprehensive, and he was justified; in the few minutes it took to do a three-point turn and head out of the mews into Wilton Street, connecting with one of the pillars on the way, an executive decision was taken inside the car and the BSM official requested that he be brought back to the mews. O'Toole obliged, and as he got out of the car, the shaken instructor wished him a firm 'Goodbye', adding mysteriously, 'a wink is as good as a nod to a blind horse, sir'. O'Toole seemed surprised by the man's attitude and promptly forgot all about taking lessons. Instead, he bought an Irish driving licence for thirty shillings. Decorated with harps and shamrocks it was, surprisingly, valid in the UK. Then he made plans to buy a sports car he rather fancied. Jules was not happy, but for the present he turned a blind eye to motoring and set about dealing with the Inland Revenue and its neglected place in O'Toole's life, and he also turned his attention to the matter of my divorce.

In 1959 it was not possible to live in sin, as we were doing, and conduct a reasonable public life. Having a child out of wedlock, which we were about to do, was asking for trouble. Urgency was therefore in the air; but divorce was no easy matter. Three years of separation had to elapse before we could apply for one. Before that, there had to be proof of infidelity or unreasonable behaviour. Private detectives did a roaring trade; men and women were made to sit in bed with each other while a prearranged photographer burst in upon the bedroom scene, after which they accepted the cheque, donned their clothes and left, breakfast uneaten. My husband wouldn't (why should he?) give me grounds for divorce, nor would he prosecute me, so I was stuck with another year to go. A year too much, Jules decided, assuming, correctly as it turned out, that we would shortly be the subject of public curiosity and scrutiny. Having something to hide would make life impossibly difficult. I maintained a kind of lunatic calm and didn't worry about the arrangements. Jules's (now 'our') lawyers got me divorced by proxy in Mexico. The papers were signed and O'Toole and I were free to marry – in secret, of course – and we chose to be married in the only registry office in Dublin.

As usual there were cliff-hanger moments on either side of the ceremony. Fog at the airport and over St George's Channel meant that we only just made it to the registry office. One of the requirements made at the office was that we should have been, for some weeks, resident in

Dublin – O'Toole at the Wilkinsons' house in Santry and I, care of Marie Kean in Lower Baggot Street (Marie was our best man and Joyce gave me away), so when I launched into a breathless apology and, finger pointing heavenwards and circling, began, 'I'm so sorry – there was terrible fog—' O'Toole grabbed my raised hand, turned my index finger down and, rotating it, finished the sentence '. . . around St Stephen's Green'. He had the nerve to wink at the registrar. Too late I remembered the Irish method: be seen to observe the proprieties and do what you damn well please.

I had never enjoyed a wedding; this one didn't seem any better than most, but it was, at least, full of incident and quite wonderful in the early stages of the day. As far as I was concerned, O'Toole and I were indivisible. There was nothing I wouldn't do for him and he said as much for me. But a wedding? It seemed irrelevant and brought out the worst in both of us.

Three o'clock in the morning in a Dublin shebeen. O'Toole, great, diminutive actor Harry Brogan, Marie Kean, Joyce Buck and myself and the host sit around a scrubbed wooden table in a first-floor back. A child in his pyjamas sits half asleep in an armchair next to the fire. The lino is worn but was once patterned to look like Axminster carpet. No two walls are papered alike and any one of the patterns could easily be said to dominate anything near it. The ceiling of the beautifully proportioned Georgian room is papered blue, studded with gold stars. A sheet hangs on one window and a flimsy curtain gathered on a wire covers the other. The table has disappeared under Guinness bottles and there's a bottle of Jameson's whiskey as a nod towards Joyce Buck's superior status as an American. Harry Brogan loves Joyce Buck. I may be the bride but the early morning wedding is already forgotten and the star of the shebeen is Joyce.

We've just seen Harry on the stage of the Abbey. The moment we sat in the Circle we all fell asleep, the four of us waking in terror in that awful silence when there's a 'dry' on stage. Once they were back on track, we all fell asleep again. (What would you do on your wedding night but catch the show at the Abbey? It seemed reasonable to me at the time.) The party had been moving around the city since curtain down. There had been Breakfast at the Dolphin where the Irish gourmets were said to order 'Four tomato soups, four mixed grills, four large Irish and hurry up with the Irish.' God, I was hungry and glad to be in the Dolphin. From pub to pub we crossed and criss-crossed the city, gathering well-wishers, famous or just entertaining. Liam O'Flaherty recited a poem for me. For me? Not at all. This wedding ceremony didn't signify. It was just an excuse for a piss-up, but I didn't feel done out of anything in the way of ceremony.

Now there are just the five of us left standing – or rather, sitting around the table. O'Toole and I have to be back in London in the morning and it's decided that we really should go to bed. Harry, looking older with each glass of stout and not wanting to be parted from Joyce, says, 'Would ya like to go to the Ladies now? I'll take ya. My aould mother told me how to look after a lady.' 'I'm just fine,' she says firmly (what a test for a Jewish princess and how brilliantly she's doing). Attempting a different tack, he says, 'Have ya ever read *Ulysses* by James Joyce?' 'No,' she says faintly, 'but I think I'm in it.' We acquire two taxis.

Marie and Joyce sweep into the night and we set off to deliver Harry Brogan home. We aren't to know that, great actor that he is and fully deserving to be the centre of our attention on our wedding day, his party piece is to refuse to say where he lives. We drive around for what seems like hours and he grows more and more skittish and it becomes harder and harder to maintain the respect due to great actors, '*even when they're drunk, Siân*'. Finally, I think we may have tipped him out and returned to Lower Baggot Street. None of us can be called sober, but I develop a disdain for the tone of the evening and adopt a dignified *froideur* towards my bridegroom. Marie opens the door and I sweep in without a word. O'Toole follows, laughing sheepishly. 'I think she's a bit cross with me.' The phone rings.

Joyce: 'Siân, please, dear – come over to the Shelbourne and get some *sleep*.'

'No, I'm fine – really. Thanks. Goodnight.'

Putting the phone down, I turn into the bedroom saying (according to Marie), 'I might as well go on the way I'm going to start.'

Where is Jules? Back in London planning deals. Wise in the ways of our business, I doubt that he thought it worthwhile interrupting business to attend a wedding that, to outside eyes, seemed unlikely to last. Volatile young actor takes up with young actress. Same actor becomes an international movie star and *stays married* to the same young actress? Hardly.

★   ★   ★

Back in London, a married woman. Oh, this is good. Proxy divorces made in Mexico are not recognised by English law. I don't want to be finicky, but it seems to me that I may be bigamously married and there are those who have been known to take a dim view of bigamy. I don't like to complain; it seems mean-spirited after all the trouble people have taken over the arrangements. All the same, the sooner I'm properly divorced, the better. Getting divorced after the marriage ceremony could arouse comment, so how on earth are we going to manage that without attracting publicity? We manage it! I dress in a voluminous raincoat of O'Toole's and my mother's riding hat and use a Christian name, long abandoned but legal. We drive at dawn through the fog from London to Shrewsbury, missing death by inches as a four-ton truck screams to a halt in front of our wrongly overtaking bumper. It's so early and so foggy and so horrible that there's nothing to do but look each other in the eye and thank God that we're all alive. In court, the judge implies that Don is well out of this irregular situation, and he's right. We drive away and I am now legally an O'Toole person. It feels astounding and enlarging. O'Toole – ' "O" as big as a cartwheel', as his father had said.

If you put your mind to it, the press is easy to evade. Every so often we fail. When I was being made a Druid of the Gorsedd of Bards we had to take a taxi from the National Eisteddfod in North Wales all the way to London, I didn't mind the aggravation so much as the expense. I'm no longer sure how well-off we are. Media attention is pushing us into living like film stars – a taxi from North Wales, I ask you!

Finally I've given in and bought two maternity outfits. One dress – pillar-box red. One red-and-black suit and a present from O'Toole, a silk shirt covered in a design of playing cards. Nothing more eye-catching could have been devised. And I'm trying to lie low.

The fourth floor of Bryanston Street is lonely; horribly lonely. And the décor is pure Peter Jones – nicely painted or reproduction furniture, well-made shiny curtains. Blameless. Dull. If I hadn't observed Joyce's living arrangements I might have rather liked it. Now it's lowering my spirits. O'Toole goes off early for a gloomy day of filming in his balaclava with his back to the camera. He says he's learned from Quinn – they quite like each other – how to upstage on a film set. (Quinn is upstaging *him* of course at this point, but who knows when that little skill might come in handy.) There are polar bears who are dangerous and can't act and a Japanese actress who can't talk – or act. At night he comes grumpily home and sometimes he goes straight out again. Some nights he doesn't come home at all after work. I know what he's doing. He's leading the life we used to lead together, but now I'm the wife and not really eligible. Anyhow, I can no longer stand about in bars; it would look irresponsible and inappropriate. I acknowledge that I never much liked pubs and clubs anyway. I've given them a try and now I shan't bother with that life any more. But I don't mind O'Toole living it because it's what he's used to and he *does* love it. Occasionally after work, I call him a taxi to go to the Salisbury. Discomfited, he says, 'I can't have you getting me a *cab* to go on a batter.' Well, I can and I don't know why he should find that so hard to understand.

The Top of the World was to be followed by *The Day They Robbed the Bank of England*.

The question of his nose came up, and was dealt with very casually. Little did we guess the furore that would follow. The nose was kicked in while he was in the Navy playing rugby against the Swedish police team and every cameraman who had to photograph him had complained of the time involved in shooting around the bent gristle, lighting it out. So much easier to push it back and straighten it to where it was before. It didn't take a minute to do. The media outcry was incredible. I was disbelieving when I read that his 'character' had disappeared. His nose was now 'retroussé'. He had 'sold out'. His so-called 'friends' said it was symptomatic of his changing life. I was so sorry for him. I think he found it very hard to recover from this ill-considered cruel stupidity. What, I thought angrily, had two-tenths of an inch of gristle to do with talent? Other actors might have insulated themselves by moving into the company of equals only; O'Toole obstinately refused to do that. His obstinacy was ill rewarded. I felt nothing but contempt for those smart-asses who saw psychic value in a rugby-bent nose.

Left alone in the flat, I have time to take stock. I can't see the way forward at all. My agent isn't speaking to me, she's so fed up. There are jobs I want and I can't accept them. There are jobs I need and I can't go after them. Jules talks of a future framed around O'Toole's career, whatever that might turn out to be. It isn't acknowledged any more that I am an actress. I'm depressed and completely cut off from everyone I've ever known in my working life. I'd thought I'd show them how well this was going to work. Now, I have my doubts. But I don't want blame or sympathy.

When I see the stills of O'Toole in *The Day They Robbed the Bank of England* looking every inch an upper-class officer, I know he's made the right choice of role. It's not going to be a great film, but he's obviously going to be very good in it, and the film won't be bad either. I'm ignobly happy to note in the rushes that the girl's part is hopeless. O'Toole is behaving himself. His new partner is pleased. So am I.

I may be worried and confused and depressed, but I do love this man, that's the only thing I'm sure of. He comes home one day with a lovely red MG motor car, bought with his film money. 'Get your passport,' he says. 'We're off.' He's going to show me his favourite city in the world: Venice. We leave at once. The problems are left behind in Marble Arch in W1.

Chapter Five

Two weeks of refuge from London. The November weather was foul but neither O'Toole nor myself much minded the cold and the wet. We arrived in Mestre, outside Venice, and it was hideous. 'Just you wait,' said O'Toole gleefully 'you won't believe what you see.' Then, more purposefully, 'Wait here.'

'Why?'

'Just wait here.'

There was a limit to the amount of money that could be moved from country to country, but there was some kind of illegal scheme – something to do with petrol coupons – that enabled one to augment one's foreign currency and O'Toole had been told about it and was about to give it a try (I suppose). One of the things I most liked about O'Toole was that a great deal of the time I didn't know what he was up to. He didn't expect help either – just non-interference. I read my book while he trawled the bus station.

After a few hours he was back looking jubilant and I assumed we were in funds as we set off down the Grand Canal. Yes, it *was* all the things I'd been told and all the things I'd read, but O'Toole loved it so much and expected me to share his feeling that I soon became tired of enthusing and was hungry and cold, I began to feel a bit unwell and not a little grumpy. Naturally, we didn't have hotel reservations. 'Wait here with the luggage.' He was soon back having found us a lovely room in the Gabrielli Sandworth on the Riva degli Schiavoni. It was dark and wet but I realised that the window had the loveliest view I've ever seen, across the water to the campanile and cupolas of Santa Maria della Salute.

This should have been such a lovely night and it wasn't. I was six months pregnant. My body was letting me down somewhat in that I suddenly felt I'd like to go to bed, but O'Toole was so anxious that I should see and love everything that we walked and walked and walked

in the rain before subsiding into a restaurant where the warmth and the
food and the wine finished me off and I fainted away. I could hardly
believe that we were scurrying 'home' through the rain, up and down
slippery steps and I was actually crying with irritation and we were
having a row about Hy Hazell's *legs*! Best he'd ever seen. How could he
be so brutal as to prefer Hy Hazell's legs to mine? Grabbing a pillow and
an eiderdown I flounced out to spend the night in the bath, where I
slept like a lamb and woke feeling loving and happy, and when I looked
out of the window my spontaneous reaction of wonder and admiration
would have satisfied the most demanding lover of the *serenissima*. We
didn't refer to Hy Hazell or her wretched legs.

My great, abiding love for Venice didn't catch fire for years, but from
that first visit I was overawed and overimpressed and wanted more,
much more. I was glad to have a respite from my problems. O'Toole
was also escaping problems. After the huge impact of *The Long and the
Short and the Tall*, and the film work that followed, he was restless. Now,
after a few days in Venice, he said, 'Let's see if it's warmer down south,'
and, handing me the map, said, 'Let's go to Rome.' I'd never been asked
to map-read before. 'Turn right, here,' I said, and by late afternoon we
were heading towards Yugoslavia. (I think Rome was a left turn.) Soon
it was dark and we were high in the mountains on a horrible road, and
when we came to a checkpoint where soldiers with serious-looking
guns wanted visas (visas? What were they?), O'Toole reversed hurriedly
and thought for a moment. I knew what he was going to say. Extracting
a bottle of emergency brandy from the back of the car, he said, 'Wait
here. It'll be all right,' and disappeared into the darkness.

When he came back he had a sheaf of papers and he was smiling.
'Off we go,' he said, accelerating alarmingly, and we shot past the
waving, smiling soldiers.

'What did you do?' I asked.

'Just trust your uncle,' he said, smiling wolfishly.

What could he have been doing? Yes, I'd trust him to get us out of
any mess, I thought, but the journey over the mountains was unremittingly awful. Although I was ready to trust him with my life in a crisis,
I couldn't fail to notice that he was a terrible motorist. In the total darkness I could sense that we were perilously close to the edge of the road
and that the darkness beyond the road was that different darkness of
nothing but space. It stood to reason (I thought) that as we climbed, the
drop on our right became greater. Every muscle tensed, I sat bunched

up, stifling the squeals and whimpers that threatened to surface as we swung around the hairpin bends on that terrifying road. I longed for the drive to be over. Even more, I longed for it to stop for a bit.

My prayers were answered and O'Toole braked suddenly as, into the middle of the road, ran the first person we'd seen for hours. She was old and draped in black shawls, which rose and fell like wings as she waved her arms up and down. Satisfied that she had our attention, she darted to my side of the car and launched into an urgent torrent of what I supposed to be Yugoslav – or Serb – or Croat. Apologetically, I shook my head and she immediately switched to a violent mime, holding her head and rocking from side to side and moaning horribly. 'Oh my God, help me get her into the back,' said O'Toole, catching the urgency of the moment. It took us a few minutes to realise that we were failing to get her into the car, not because she was infirm and hampered by layers of clothing, but because she was putting up a spirited resistance. Discomfited, we stopped being good Samaritans and stood back from the lively little bundle of shawls, still wailing, but now wailing with a note of irritation. There was something we weren't comprehending and she was losing patience with us. Clutching her head with one hand, she pointed into the darkness with the other and took a few steps, gesturing to us to follow her. I realised that any fears I entertained that we might be about to be set upon and robbed was an utterly inappropriate emotion at this point in a promising and developing adventure. I was learning to strangle at birth these petty feelings of caution and prudence. It also occurred to me that while I was exhausting myself during the white-knuckle ride, O'Toole might very well have become *bored* as he flung the car around the turns in the road and to him this could well be an agreeable diversion. Briskly I brought up the rear of the little procession as it disappeared on to a rough path. Very soon we came upon another little group (more moaning) and I realised that the old lady wanted to load a child on to us. Obligingly, stumbling back to the car, we heaved the boy into the back seat and he was followed by a couple of men who got into the car, nodding approval and pointing at the road ahead. They wanted us to get a move on. O'Toole performed a racing start and we roared off, leaving the old lady in the darkness.

I couldn't make out if the boy had terrible toothache or acute stomach-ache. O'Toole concentrated on driving like a man possessed (I cannot begin to describe how much worse the driving became) and I kept an anxious eye on the passengers and they in turn kept nodding approvingly at me. We were doing the right thing. Whether more was required than making speed in the dark we had no way of knowing. As we approached a town the two young men leaned towards the front of the car, one head each side of O'Toole, and began to give directions, speaking very loudly and slowly in Yugoslav and making simple, clear gestures. The car was filled with a new smell – sweet and faintly rotten at the same time. What was it? We drew up at what turned out to be a very dimly lit, bare hospital and out hopped the men, half carrying, half dragging the boy. As they ran for the door, they made expressions of gratitude, more simple mime and much pointing vaguely in the direction of the heart. 'It was nothing,' we mimed back, shaking our heads from side to side, 'glad to be of use', and we pointed at *our* hearts. We felt a bit flat now that we weren't an ambulance any more, and when a couple of men in boiler suits carrying bags of tools (plumbing tools, I thought) indicated that they wouldn't mind a lift, we leapt on them as the most welcome of passengers and off we tore through the sparsely lit streets. I realised that we hadn't seen another car since we'd crossed the border. We were a novelty in our bright red MG.

The town centre of Zagreb was bleak; nothing much happening it seemed, not many people about, the few shops with lighted windows were uninviting (the window-dresser's art hadn't penetrated Yugoslavia). One of O'Toole's talents lies in his nose. Standing in a strange town, he turns his head this way and that, picking up little smells and sounds, like an animal, then he sets off, making unerringly for the best place to eat and drink or the only place still open after hours. Zagreb, however, had him nonplussed for a moment. Beaming, our plumbers directed us to what looked like a grand town hall. Entering from the gloom and cold outside was like entering paradise. There was no food in evidence but I felt there must be some, somewhere. Not having eaten since breakfast, I was ravenously hungry, but I forgot my empty stomach as I took in the extraordinary scene.

We were in what had once been the ballroom of a grand baroque hotel, which the People had taken over with a vengeance. Figures still in drab working clothes filled the huge, brilliantly lit room, drinking, dancing to fiddle music, having what could best be described as a knees-up. The story of our adventure as an ambulance and taxi service was told at once and we were immediately the centre of a large, noisy, extravagantly friendly crowd of workmen. An old lady in long skirts appeared and, clucking at my interesting condition, took me off for a much-needed toilette, shrieking with mirth as she showed me how to negotiate the hole-in-the-ground loo. It seemed rude to ask her to wait outside, so I peed as best I could to her accompaniment of more gales of laughter. 'Please, I have to be alone. I'm an only child. Intimacy doesn't come easily to me.' No. Instead I nodded at her toothless smiling face and, having washed my face and hands, launched into more 'How can I thank you?' behaviour. Bereft of a single word of Yugoslav, I developed a kind of Japanese mime; a little bow from the waist while indicating my heart. Rock-hard sausage appeared just for me. Delicious. I identified the sweetly corrupted smell which hung in the air everywhere as the smell of ingested slivovitz, divine corrupted apples.

A few hours later, excusing myself on the grounds of my advanced pregnancy – this time my bow was accompanied by a triple hand gesture; tummy to heart to tummy – I went to bed. O'Toole stayed behind to explore the true nature of slivovitz and to do a bit more taxiing, while I was shown to a room high above the celebrations, which looked as though they might well continue until morning.

Lying flat – *not* hurtling through the night, *not* expecting every moment to be my last – was negative pleasure enough, but it was augmented by the sign above the table, 'Your commands by telephone will be obeyed instantly.' I didn't want anything but I picked up the Bakelite receiver. Dead. I went to sleep smiling. This wasn't Rome, where we'd meant to go, but I felt very lucky to be here alive, lying flat in Yugoslavia.

Walking around town in the morning we saw that the theatre was as grand as the hotel. 'Better go and make ourselves known, then. They may give us "comps" for the show.' (Like all tourists we were short of money, in spite of the petrol coupon scam.) All we said at the theatre was that we, like them, were actors. There was someone who spoke a little English and he believed us and may even have thought that we were important actors (it could have been the effect of the car, which was still attracting a good deal of friendly envy), and with much handshaking (and bowing from me) we were told to present ourselves at the theatre and we would be 'passed' in to see the play that evening.

We felt underdressed when we were shown into a prominent box at stage level, but it was clear that no one was dressed to suit the splendour of the theatre and we settled down to enjoy the performance. Four and a half hours later we were still there, hanging on to the arms of our chairs, glassy eyed, stupefied with boredom. The play wasn't even in

Yugoslav, it was in an obscure Serbo-Croat dialect. It looked faintly fifteenth century. There were lots of children in the audience and they also looked a bit glum, but I could tell that the play was meant to be a comedy. 'I know what this is,' hissed O'Toole viciously. 'You know that one performance of some ancient bit of culture you have to give every year to justify the Arts Council grant? Well, this is *it*. The Serb equivalent of *Gammer Gurton's Fuckin' NEEDLE*!'

During the ensuing week, hurtling from country to country, we saw four plays. Three times the offering was *Boeing Boeing*, the most popular play in Europe that year. Probably the most popular play in the world. We didn't see any German theatre because O'Toole suddenly took against the thought of being in that country and we drove across it without stopping. Never in my life have I been so glad to see a veal escalope as I was when we got to Linz in Austria late at night. (Hunger was one of the leitmotifs of this breathless trip.) In Switzerland I developed violent toothache and O'Toole decided that the best dentists in the world were to be found in Italy and only the best would do for me. (I fancy he was thinking of barbers' poles and a long operatic tradition.) Useless to say that any old dentist would do, so after an evening of *Boeing Boeing* in Schweizerdeutsch, off we set for Milan. I held brandy in my mouth for hours until it grew hot and O'Toole drove and drove like a demon along these frightening straight autobahns. (He had never before encountered big, straight roads.) He got me to Milan in record-breaking time, slightly drunk, the pain all but banished by fear. After a lot of *'porco misere!'* and *'Bruto!'* and no anaesthetic because I was pregnant, the Professor of Dentistry put his knee on to the arm of my chair and pulled and pulled, encouraged by shrill cries from two admiring young assistant dentists. Finally, he reeled backwards across the room triumphantly, holding aloft a large back tooth.

O'Toole finished off the brandy – well, it had been a gruesome experience – and we turned the car towards Holland where Hélène (van Moeurs, my old friend from RADA) lived and where she was playing Molière at a theatre in The Hague. Apart from the terror I experienced all day in the car, I was loving the trip. O'Toole was loving the trip. He was the perfect travelling companion; each day was a challenge and a hilarious adventure. He was like a Pied Piper, collecting people wherever we went. No one knew who he was but everyone wanted to spend time with him and I was content to look on, but I was beginning to weary. The pace was gruelling and I wasn't making concessions to my pregnancy. I had never had many close women friends and now I thought that it was a good moment to have Hélène look over my new life, my new state.

The theatre at The Hague is so beautiful – like a meringue. It was, I was told proudly, 'the Stradivarius of Europe'. I was glad that we weren't seeing *Boeing Boeing* yet again, but even Hélène had to admit that Dutch is not the ideal language for Molière. The play sank heavily like unleavened dough and lay expiring on the beautiful stage.

We got into the car and (a by now exhausted) O'Toole drove from The Hague to Hélène's home in Amsterdam. Hélène – sturdy, strong, fearless and practical – silently climbed the stairs to her flat. 'Does he always drive like that?' she asked as I joined her in the kitchen. 'Ye-es,' I replied guardedly.

'He should never drive *anything*', she said. 'He's *lovely* but I thought we were going to die on that journey.' In a way I was relieved that she felt as I did; I had begun to think that I was being feeble-minded and wimpish out there, on the road. On the other hand, her reaction told me that I had a genuine problem on my hands. I didn't drive and I was terrified of cars and now was at the mercy of a terrible driver. 'You put a stop to all this,' she said briskly, chopping vegetables. I looked at her – so reasonable – and thought I couldn't begin to explain that it was completely outside my remit in the relationship to 'put a stop' to anything. 'And another thing,' she said. 'You should be resting and eating properly.' 'Oh it's okay. I do normally,' I lied.

After supper I went to bed, uneasy. Our life together would be lived very much at O'Toole's pace. I had played fast and loose with so many men that it was a huge relief – and a lifting of responsibility – to be involved with a man whom I could not hoodwink. There is something so attractive about being wholly known with all one's faults and vices, and now it was a huge relief to be seen through. I couldn't at the time see how childish and truly irresponsible I was being. The idea of female service and support to men had been taught only too well in Wales, and the childish part of me felt this to be right and proper. The Ireland I was beginning to know was male dominated as well. The idea of a wife with a career, demanding rights, was laughable in the Fifties.

I lay there in Amsterdam and saw that if things went awry over the birth of the baby and my ensuing life, then the problems would be largely of my own making. Hélène made a supper dish which I have never forgotten. Here's how she prepared it. Chop and cook every root vegetable you can lay your hands on (making sure you have carrots and swedes to make the final mixture pink). Vigorously mash the whole thing and pile it high in a large shallow dish. Make an indentation at the top of the pyramid and into it place half a pound of butter . . . eat.

Then go to bed and try to worry about your life and career. Sleep will soon take over.

Chapter Six

Safe in London again. A mere two weeks have elapsed. So much has happened, but the wonderful journey has done nothing to solve our problems. There's a Welsh poem that ends '*A groeso fôr, Ni newid onid air.*' ('Crossing an ocean only gives you a change of air.')

I sense O'Toole is profoundly dissatisfied with almost everything that has happened since Willis's play. The movies he's made have proved mildly interesting, profitable in a moderate way, but they were not what he wanted. The ones he did want have not come his way. There isn't a good play on the horizon. We have a rare council of war and decide that the best thing would be to go back to the beginning and restart in the theatre. Almost at the same moment there's an offer from Stratford for him to play Shylock and Petruchio and Thersites in Peter Hall's new company. It's so obviously the right thing to do that I can hardly believe our luck. I don't know what Jules thought of his partner's decision to disappear to Warwickshire for six or seven months, but he's extremely graceful when we all meet for dinner. About a week after the offer is accepted, I do a very delayed double-take and think, 'But how will *I* manage in Stratford?' The baby will be born at the end of February before the opening of *The Merchant of Venice*. I would hope to go back to work in the spring, but Stratford? Notoriously difficult to live in, I'm told. How will I manage? And O'Toole's salary will be low – but then I have an income and a reasonable bank balance. But is having a baby within the terms of my contract with Douglas Uren? My agent is already cool towards me and I no longer have a single friend or advisor to turn to. And where will we live? Pregnancy is making me feel completely powerless. My body, which has never let me down, seems to belong to someone else. And I'm lonely. I'm not accustomed to being isolated from people, but my life with O'Toole is absorbing all my energy and excludes everyone I've ever known. There is no question in my mind that my loyalty should lie with him, but it does seem hard to have to cut my ties with everyone else. I see no one. I begin to draw close to Jules and Joyce Buck. They are my new family. Denise Sée, the company lawyer, becomes a valued advisor – but she's not principally *my* advisor. Nyman Libson is to be our accountant. He and his wife and family, Sue and John, are to me the impossible-to-attain perfect family. Again, they are to be O'Toole's advisors, not mine, but I like them all, on sight. When I'm with them I admire them so much that I lose all confidence in *my* family life. Brutally, I don't have a family life. It's fashionable in our circle to despise uxoriousness, domesticity, bonds, ties, fetters. We're standing in some kind of no-man's-land, me and my unborn baby, because motherhood is suspect as a shackle on the masculine genius/worker/provider. Cyril Connolly's 'sombre enemy of good art – the pram in the hall' is familiar to all of us.

Before Stratford I do Saunders Lewis's play in Hampstead. It's well received but in translation it just doesn't work as it does in Welsh. 'Lovely Siân recalls the days of Mrs Pat', says one big headline, but I know that Mrs Patrick Campbell played Hedda at the Hampstead Theatre when she was fat and truly past being convincing! (Still, no one seemed to notice I was pregnant.)

One television play and then we're off again! Where? O'Toole wants us out of the flat in two hours. It's late. Why? Never mind. It's an adventure. I never really liked this flat. But where to go? My mother's brother, Davy, newly widowed, has a house near my old family home, Tŷ mawr farm. We can go there. I call him and he seems glad of the prospect of our company. Another journey through the night, this time from London to West Wales. No autobahns, thank God. As we climb in the dark towards the Black Mountains, I roll down the window and take deep breaths of the air, which is different from any other.

Gwaun-Cae-Gurwen.

This is going to work out very well. O'Toole, in preparation for *The Merchant of Venice*, is reading the whole of the Old Testament – two fields away from Tŷmawr farm, where I was born, where my grandmother, Mrs Thomas, Tŷ mawr, read the Good Book every day and was said to be able to write out the whole of it from memory. I'm not a good cook, but neither Davy nor O'Toole are gourmets, so I make very ordinary meals and sit reading at the table in the house on the Betws Mountain and watch Davy dealing with school and local government work and O'Toole in the other armchair, burying himself in the family Bible. Our evenings are long and silent and agreeable.

The best bits of our life together, like these months in the country, could not be imagined and would not be credited by people who see us out and about in London. O'Toole's friends wouldn't believe the sort of life we lead when we're alone. We keep it to ourselves, like life in a Persian garden – secret and unseen.

My tutor from university days, Moelwyn Merchant, is free to discuss *The Merchant* with O'Toole. We visit him near Caerleon and the men talk Shakespeare line by line and we women talk obstetrics. Is it being pregnant that excludes me from everything interesting? I hate Women's Talk. I'm sure that having a baby will be a breeze and there's nothing to talk about. I want to talk about Shakespeare. I feel mutinous.

And yet I have more fun with this Irishman than I've ever had in my life. One night he decides to cook dinner – he's never been known to cook anything. 'Oh yes. I can make French toast. The best French toast. Just leave me to it.' As the stove explodes into flames and we wrestle it, covered in blankets, out of the house on to the mountainside and the entire kitchen needs repainting and we have no supper, the three of us stand in the flame-lit cold garden and rock with laughter. It's been sad in this house since my Aunt Maya died. It took this conflagration to restore life and ordinary happiness, and it took O'Toole to light the fire. He has an invincible drive towards joy and life.

My uncle has to go to Westminster on Council of Wales business and we volunteer to drive him to the station in Neath and pick him up a few days later. We set out after dark to collect him and on the hill to Rhyd-y-Fro the car goes out of control on black ice. This is it. We're in an uncontrollable spin. I remember from my schooldays that there's a big drop on the right. For what seems like miles we career from right to left and I pray that we shan't meet another car. Finally, we crash into a bank and come to a halt. When we pull out we have a young sapling embedded in the back door of the car. 'Whew! That was close,' says O'Toole, cheerily, 'but if we get a move on we'll still be on time.'

Through the moments of danger O'Toole said, 'Put your feet on the dashboard. Keep calm.' And I said, 'Don't worry about me, I'm all right. I'm prepared.' And I *was* prepared and I was not frightened. And he *did* get us out of trouble and we *were* in time for the train.

Davy, when he gets into the car along with the young tree, splutters, 'What—?' 'Oh, just a little tap,' says O'Toole, and Davy beams, reassured, as he leans away from the buckled door. How does O'Toole do it? Davy would have wanted an explanation from anyone else. He also is under the spell. It's no wonder that my family feels about O'Toole much as I do. Who wouldn't? He says the awful, confronts the impossible and shrugs it off as though it were nothing. He doesn't *care* that his car is ruined and that he can't buy a new one. His priorities that night of Davy's return were to avoid getting us killed and then to meet the train on time. Both were accomplished and he was contented. And so were we.

The family has moved away from Tŷ mawr on the Betws Mountain to the richer lowlands further west. My parents now live in East Glamorgan at Dyffryn House. It seems odd to look up the Betws across the meadows at the farm where I, my mother and my grandmother were born and to think it belongs to someone else. I don't mind that. It never was technically *mine*, but it is mine no less now than when I inhabited it. Property is a mystery. There are things I own that don't feel mine at all, but some things are mine for ever.

The new farm is in Whitland. When the proposal to move was put to my grandmother, John and Meriel, my uncle and aunt, expected it to be the beginning of a long period of persuasion, emotional and painful. Elizabeth – Mamgu, my grandmother – sat in the house that her grandmother had built and looked at the business proposal, and having thought for a bit said, 'So, when do we move?' When she drove away, almost ninety years of age, she looked straight ahead.

O'Toole is taken down to Whitland. The farm is set in beautiful countryside, gentler, easier, more profitable than the slopes of the Betws above Gwaun-Cae-Gurwen. The house is a traditional long-house, at one end is a room with a deep and high inglenook, and that is where my grandmother sits. O'Toole and Uncle John and some of the boys sit up late in the 'top room', drinking whisky. John and the boys are up and about early, back at work. So is my grandmother, whose life is geared to six o'clock milking by hand (days long gone). When O'Toole descends at ten o'clock, she greets him in that intimidating way, each English word weighed and considered, 'Good day to you.' She's slightly wrong-footed by her lack of English, which is lucky for him, and never having encountered suede, she has spent quite a while trying to get a shine on his desert boots. Almost blind, there is very little she can do that is useful, but she has to do something – something now reduced to washing up and cleaning the seventeen muddy pairs of boots and shoes in the kitchen corridor every morning. While O'Toole sits at the table, I quickly cook us a Welsh breakfast and put both plates on a corner of the big table. I'm about to sit when her voice emerges from the semi-dark of the inglenook. 'Siân! *Tend* to Peter.' I realise that she expects me to serve O'Toole – pour tea, cut bread and wait on him before I give myself breakfast.

His eyes light up with amusement. It is inconceivable that I should disobey her, nor would I wish to challenge that touching certainty in her voice. She knows how things should be done. But this is a woman who ran a farm while her husband gossiped, and whose mother knocked her drunken husband down the stairs to his death. They are fearless and frightening these women, but part of their strategy seems to be that lip service should be paid to the god-like quality of Man. As I stand between Mamgu and the table, I can see the funny side of this breakfast ceremony, but I don't want to carry her teaching into my life and times, not even as a joke. I don't want to bend the knee – but then, I can't run a farm either. I feel lost between two worlds.

Chapter Seven

January 1960 and I was almost at the end of my pregnancy. O'Toole and I finished taping the Saunders Lewis play, *Siwan*, this time for TV in Wales, and then we moved to Stratford-on-Avon. Dr Slattery had referred me to a doctor in the town. I made myself known to him and I liked him. He was reserved and quiet. I had been booked into a cottage hospital. We were to live in 'Mount Pleasant' (promptly re-christened 'Mount Unpleasant' by O'Toole). It was the house occupied during the 1958 season by John Osborne and Mary Ure (and a right nasty time *they* had there, I was told). We hoped we would have better luck with it.

It looked all right; a big double-fronted Edwardian house, two storeys high with a grand porch, almost a *porte-cochère*. There was a lawn at the front and a rough private lane that led down through the fields to the road into Stratford. At the side, the drawing-room side, there was a huge dilapidated conservatory. I loved the drawing room – big, with huge, comfortable neutral-coloured sofas and armchairs and a large stone fireplace. There was a big dining room (the table seated about twenty people), a somewhat gloomy morning room furnished with reproduction oak furniture, and at the back a big 1950s kitchen. The master bedroom and its bathroom were lovely – windows south and west like the drawing room below. There was another bathroom and two bedrooms, and out at the back there was a stable wing, which would be taken by someone else in the company. I wondered nervously who my close neighbour would be. I didn't notice the door at the back of the big front hall. Fool that I was, this was the door leading to the most important object in my life for the next six months. The door led to the cellar, and the cellar contained the Boiler, the monster which had to be fed with coke before we had heat or hot water in the rooms above.

We didn't have much in the way of possessions, so I called a taxi and went into town to buy extra china, linen and cutlery. Meriel, my mother's sister, had sent me lovely bed linen, and my mother sent me a superb Welsh throw. I looked at the immersion heater in the bathroom and wondered how to live economically in what was a very big house. What did it cost to run a house? Damn it, why didn't I know these rudimentary things? I was heavy now – and resenting it – but, finding the cellar, I started shovelling coke. O'Toole was going to start rehearsing at any moment. He had discovered that there were two or three more possible Shylocks standing by in the wings in case the wild Irish boy didn't come up to scratch. Could this be true? If so, the pressure on him was awful and I decided he didn't need to know about the coke boiler. (But *was* it true?) Now I was alone most of the time. The boiler was a monster and all my worries about the impending birth and my inability to run a house were centred on the problem of getting the elderly central heating system to work properly. I didn't know anyone here in Warwickshire – and there were no neighbours. My family was a long way off and anyway, I wanted to be able to stand on my own feet. There was no one to help with the cleaning. With the confidence of the healthy and ignorant, I was not in the least worried about giving birth, but I was terrified that I would not be able to run our lives once the baby was born. Would I get the food right? How did you tell the difference between a cry of hunger, a cry of pain or a shriek of bad temper? I was painfully aware that I had never spent *five minutes* in the presence of a baby. Would I be able to keep the heat and water going? Would everything come naturally?

Feverishly I read my Dr Spock over and over again. We didn't have any prospect of help with the house or the baby, and I tried to give myself a crash-course in housekeeping. Marie Kean in Ireland sent me a large hard-backed manual on domestic science, and it quickly became dog-eared and dirty with furniture polish, detergent, cooking fat and blood. My hands were covered in small cuts. Apprehensive and clumsy, every time I began a simple task I cut myself – on sardine tins, chopping knives, the shovel in the cellar, blades of grass.

Alcohol had always been a major factor in our life together and, coming from a non-conformist, teetotal Welsh background, I had been charmed by the guilt-free, amusing nature of drinking-to-excess as practised by the Irish. There was something so wonderfully un-English, un-Welsh and un-Scots about Dublin society, where if you needed to see your MP you called round to his favourite bar, after hours, where he was busy getting very drunk. Everything functioned but there was a refreshing absence of bureaucracy and a totally un-British attitude towards life. And how merrily I laughed when I learned that the process of casting a play in Ireland began with the question 'Is he all right', 'all right' meaning back in circulation after a spell in hospital, drying out. The funny stories about drink were legion and no one enjoyed them more than I.

From being only a part of life, enjoyed in an endless festive atmosphere, drink became a dominant factor in my daily life. And I was alone now, no partying friends making jokes, and suddenly I was vulnerable and afraid. I was surprised but not shocked to find that my free spirit, my equal partner, expected me to take care of myself, clean the house, wash and iron and provide meals and be on parade when needed. This was the standard male expectation at that time. And I was faintly ashamed that I was so ill equipped for the job. I *was* taken aback, however, when I was told that the baby, when it arrived, was not to interfere with my husband's work. That *wasn't* what I'd expected at all; I think I'd rather hoped that I and my baby would be the centre of admiring attention (it's possible that a cradle with muslin drapes featured in this fantasy). Now our roles in life were made separate and strictly defined, and I mentally revised the scenario of my life within wedlock. I couldn't begin to think where *my work* fitted into this and there were no discussions on that subject. I made meals at night and threw them away uneaten before I went alone to bed. Sometimes there'd be a dawn demand for something to eat; more often I would wake to find O'Toole asleep in an armchair, an overturned glass beside him. I looked out to see if the car was all right and wished I could take an axe to it. His driving when drunk had become my chief worry and source of fear. I tried not to think of the journey from Stratford to Mount Unpleasant. Every night I tried and every night I failed.

Stratford, the marshy graveyard of showbiz relationships. On Monday mornings the platform at Leamington Spa was damp with the tears of furious actors' wives, returning to London tight-lipped and red-eyed after a ghastly weekend. I couldn't leave. And I didn't want to. I was damned if I was going to join the list of Stratford casualties. Stubbornly, I resolved to find a way of living through what was shaping up as a testing time.

What happened next would have defeated me utterly had I not been so near to the birth of the baby and had I not thought – rightly or wrongly – that O'Toole was beside himself with nerves and worry. I was aware that his professional future depended on this performance as Shylock. There had been a few setbacks and missed opportunities, and his drinking habits had led to a few hilarious and possibly damaging episodes. The bottle of whisky that fell out of his overcoat pocket as he sat down to talk to a producer, Cubby Broccoli, who wanted to see if he might replace someone with a 'drink problem' (at that time only Americans talked of drink as a 'problem') had added to a burgeoning legend. Now, he needed this job and needed to do it well. He was prepared, maybe over-prepared, but he was still unconvinced that he had the confidence of the management. His moods became darker and his drinking became more dangerous. Every morning he pulled himself together. Doubtless the knowledge that he believed he was being watched made matters worse. I was completely on his side even as he tried to push me away. My admiration for him as an actor was enough to withstand the anxieties and miseries of this life of insecurity.

When drunk he was savagely critical of me and my ego was taking a severe beating. When he imitated me, I could see there was some truth in his cruelty, but I recalled Hélène van Moeurs at RADA, out of patience with the psycho-babble of the day, saying, 'Ego? Little ego? To hell with ego! If my ego is so little and so feeble, it can go and take a running jump. I'll do *without* my ego.' I resolved to banish *my* ego, batten down the hatches and sit out the storm. Is it possible that you perversely push away your support just to test how sound it is? I felt he was doing that to me, trying me to the limit. That was the only inter-pretation of events which made sense to me, but this may have been my way of justifying my acceptance of a situation in which I was learning not to answer back, not to argue, not to defend myself. Sobriety brought wonderful interludes of repentance and irresistible charm, when I believed myself supremely loved and needed, but when I was made to feel like a useless encumbrance, I believed that just as fervently. I was living with the good cop and the bad cop in one person.

Meanwhile O'Toole justified his erratic behaviour towards me in the most unexpected way imaginable. He was the last person I would have expected to take the high moral ground over anyone's behaviour, let alone mine. Now he did just that. I had never made a secret of my past or made anything much of it either, never having had to live among people who subscribed to the Fifties double standard for men and women. The thinking of the time was that nice girls 'didn't'. Girls didn't really enjoy sex. Casual sex was fine for men but out of the question for women. Women were, by nature, monogamous and men were naturally promiscuous. Lest all this should seem to be something left over from Victorian times, biological arguments were produced to show that women were chaste in order not to become accidentally pregnant and men were promiscuous in order to ensure the continuation of their genes. Women were either Madonnas or Whores of Babylon. The idea that girls might have sex because they liked it, or for affection, or for fun, or for company, or out of boredom or loneliness was not entertained. If they did it, they were Bad. I had lived a life of carnal pleasure outside wedlock, completely guilt-free. Now, as the weeks went by, I came to accept the fact that my position was fairly untenable – in fact I had no position at all. In between whiles there were passionate reconciliations, but I lost my spirit and doubted that I would get over this. I was disenfranchised and very little trouble to live with. A quiet girl.

This is how I saw things in early 1960, but I was pregnant and I was living – trying to live – a new, different life and perhaps my view was distorted. Even then I could see that my wish to keep up appearances *was* ludicrous and O'Toole was right to despise my petit-bourgeois desire to keep our problems secret. When he was drunk he publicly exposed his view of my character and at that time I couldn't endure the humiliation. The best I could do was to remain impassive, but it was a very long time before I learned not to care what people thought. At that time I cared desperately – I wanted a private life, lived privately.

February was the longest month that year. I saw no one, spoke to few. My parents occasionally telephoned and we talked about immersion heaters and heat conservation and the boiler. O'Toole's big sister, Pat, who lived in a rich suburb of Birmingham, called and offered to help. She had married well and was living the most comfortable and orderly of bourgeois lives; a life I wouldn't have admired or wanted until now when, insecure and adrift from the certainties of my life, I envied her the calm, the certainty, the regular meals, the rock garden, the rose beds, the expensive reproduction furniture, the dogs, the housekeeper, the attentive husband who left the house and returned at the same time each day. I didn't want her or anyone else to visit me and see or hear what my life was like. It hadn't taken long for my Celtic guilt and pessimism to rise to the surface, and I now felt that I was to blame for everything that was happening to us. All the attitudes I had despised as hypocritical or retrogressive reared up to mock me. I had been wrong all along about everything – especially my instincts. Seeing that I was low in spirit, Pat took matters into her own hands and in a rather feudal manner drove her housekeeper over to Stratford and left her with me for a few days.

Austrian Gertrude quickly took charge and for a while all was quiet and the smells of comforting middle-England meals soothed me more than any kind words could have done. I watched her moving around the big house, taming it, and felt admiring and inadequate. After she left, I found myself alone again, but now the house was orderly and well stocked with food and cleaning material.

Before I had time to become anxious again – the baby was due in a week's time – I fell ill with influenza. I didn't know where O'Toole might be and I could no longer climb the stairs to bed or descend to the boiler, so I made a bed on the couch in the drawing room and lit a fire. I don't know how long I lay there, alternately shivering and perspiring, but one night after dark fell I awoke to find my doctor in the room rekindling the fire. He'd become worried because I hadn't kept an appointment and, failing to reach me on the phone, he had driven up to the house, and when no one answered the door he'd peered through the drawing-room window and, seeing me lying on the couch, had broken into the house through the crumbling conservatory. I was too ill to eat and he left me with plenty of water and a roaring fire and went away, saying that he would be back in the morning. In the morning, miraculously, the flu had gone away as abruptly as it had arrived, and slowly I got up, bathed, washed my hair and began to tidy the makeshift encampment in the drawing room.

Unexpectedly, O'Toole appeared after work and was sweet and solicitous and made me sit down while he cooked supper. I was astonished by his reappearance and sat there meek and vacant in the morning room; a room I would not normally sit in, it was so dimly depressing. I was given an enormous overcooked fry-up and it was one of the best meals I've ever eaten. Some things do come naturally to one and suddenly I knew that I felt different. O'Toole's timing had not deserted him. He'd come home just in time to drive me to the hospital to have our baby.

Chapter Eight

I've always felt apologetic towards my daughter Kate, not least because her birth was one of the most humbling and in a way annoying experiences of my life. It was unlike anything I could have imagined and it *hurt* and my physical well-being, my athletic body was useless to me. I simply couldn't get the hang of what was going on. Whatever it was, it was out of my control and I didn't like it. Lying alone, cold and fractious on a trolley in a hallway, I grizzled quietly to myself, a passing nurse flicked my shoulder with the back of her hand and said sharply, 'Come on, come on. Pull yourself together.'. She gave me the mouthpiece of a gas and air machine, and left me to 'pull myself together'. And I would have done had I been able. Rubber nozzle over my nose and mouth, I breathed deeply again and again before I realised that there was nothing but stale air in the machine and that the situation was getting nastier very fast. I didn't really want to see Miss Brace-Yourself of 1960 again, but she reappeared with a colleague and they wheeled me out of the sad, dark corridor into a warm room with a very bright light overhead. I lost track of time. The pain worsened, the light grew brighter, brighter, and then became completely white until the room was all brilliance and the light made a loud buzzing noise in my ears and I fell into blackness.

Waking up in bed in a ward, I thought I must have had a baby and I waited for someone to bring me a cup of tea. 'The best cup of tea you'll ever have in your life,' I'd been told. Ordinarily I didn't like tea, but I really wanted this cup of reward-for-having-a-baby tea. When it didn't come I thought, 'Well, that's just about typical of this whole experience.' As soon as I was able to sit up and look about, someone came and I was told that there was nothing to worry about but there was some complication about the baby's blood, which had to be changed. It seemed as though that was a lot to worry about and I lay there miserably. There was no way of demanding information. Demanding anything was out of the question in a 1960 hospital, but one had no reason to fear that best efforts were not being made on one's behalf. After what seemed an age, they brought me my baby. I looked at her, completely separate, already getting on with her life, and I wished I could feel that I'd *done* something. I wished I hadn't fainted before she was born. I felt as inadequate as I'd feared I would. I didn't know how to feel or what to do next. I held her and she seemed pretty solid. Whatever happens, I thought, I'm going to rear you properly. I didn't feel emotional. Just very, very determined.

There was a gypsy girl in the ward (a gypsy with no husband; how low can you get?). She and I were the only ones with no regular visitors at visiting time. (Visiting times were strictly ordained and maintained.) I tried to sink down below the sheets and pretend to be asleep lest anyone should come over and be sympathetic. Roy Dotrice's wife was right opposite and I didn't even want Roy's pity at that time. Just once O'Toole came in at the right time bearing a white television set! Televisions were still out of the ordinary and we couldn't watch this one – there was no aerial. It sat in a corner, silent and glamorous. One night, when all the lights were out, I awakened to hear the sounds of drunken revelry from the grounds outside – O'Toole and a car full of actors had left the pub or the party to come and serenade his daughter. Hoping no one would wake up and complain, I lay silently in the dark, looking at the ceiling until they went away.

I didn't feel very well. Sister said I was to feed Kate, as we decided to call her, in a small side room where I could be alone. Sitting there one afternoon, I overheard my doctor talking to the Sister. Referring to the gypsy girl and me, he said, 'Keep both of them in. Neither has a suitable home environment.' I'd read that tension was bad for breast-feeding, so I tried not to tighten my grip on Kate as she lay there. I couldn't look at her for shame. I had no suitable home for her to live in.

A few days later in the ward, we were both in better shape. The breast-feeding – so important to get right – was on track at last and I felt notably less of a failure. Kate looked quite wonderfully normal and even amusing. '*Kätchen lumpen*', I called her to myself: little lump of a Kate. Child of Stratford, she's called Kate, not Katherine, for Shakespeare's Shrew; she is 'Kate, sweet Kate, the prettiest Kate in Christendom'. O'Toole was due to play Petruchio after *The Merchant* opened and Peggy Ashcroft would play the Shrew. Before that, in a month's time, I was going to play Kate in another *Shrew* at Oxford.

Many of O'Toole's friends became fathers round about this time and the preferred names were Kate and Emma. As I looked at my Kate, a ladybird flew through the open window and came to rest on her shawl. I love ladybirds and in my shaky state I took it to be an omen – she was going to be all right. I hardly liked to think 'What about *me*?' No matter where I turned, this was not a 'me' time. But it was my deep-submerged question.

My experience during our winter weeks in Stratford had been so unnerving that I was anxious to resume what was to me the security of working life. I was able to do television plays until four weeks before Kate was born and then, four weeks after her birth, I would go back to the theatre. I would start rehearsing *The Taming of the Shrew* in London. Kate would come with me. I didn't know how to organise this, but Ken and Doriah were letting me stay with them during the week and I would return to Stratford at weekends until I was ready to open at Oxford, when I could commute by taxi each day. If anyone thought this was a mad plan, not a word was said. It was up to me to pull myself together again and I was silently determined to try.

The cry of all new mothers – 'What did I *do* with all the time at my disposal before I had a baby?' Mount Unpleasant has become a school where the sole subject is Reality. Indulgence is a thing of the past. Every moment is taken up with learning how to take care of another life, and the demands change every week. Armed with Dr Spock's book, I am efficient and determined to prove I am when the nurse comes visiting. I pass the test; the breasts are working like clockwork, Kate is functioning smoothly like a little engine, but there is something wrong here. I am so anxious to get everything right that there is little room for spontaneity. Housekeeping is still a monstrous, alien task. Now there are visitors to see to as well, and even if they only want cups of tea, rushing between the sink and sitting room, cutting bread and making sandwiches, keeping my eye on the clock for Kate's next meal, exhausts me. Washing up, cleaning, tidying the sitting room against the next wave of guests, running down to the cellar to feed the boiler, hand-washing clothes (no washing machine), ironing (what is the secret of the knack of ironing? If I do it the *Good Housekeeping* way, I shall have time for nothing else). All this is unwelcome activity and, try as I may, I don't like it. I don't like it because I'm not good at it and practice isn't making me better. I love Dr

Spock because he makes me feel successful. I hate *Good Housekeeping* because it makes me feel a failure.

Meanwhile the tension heightens. Only a few weeks to go to the opening night of *The Merchant*. Occasionally, some of the actors roll in, ostensibly to see Kate, actually to settle down, drink and gossip or worry aloud about their jobs. One night I go up to her and someone has dropped hot ash on her foot, and I'm so full of bile I find it very hard to be civil to these genial fellows. They seem to inhabit another world; carefree, jokey. I'm jealous, of course. This was *my* world. Well, now it isn't. Maybe it won't ever be mine again. Soon I'll go away, but I don't want to leave O'Toole alone here; it isn't much of a home but in my absence it could disintegrate completely.

My mother-in-law comes for a brief visit. We haven't met since I visited Leeds as the Girlfriend. I'm struck again by her good looks and her beautiful, whisky-soaked, 'Tallulah' voice. Desperately trying to be the good daughter-in-law, I go along with everything she suggests. It's really difficult not to react when she urges drink on her son. I can't understand why she doesn't know that 'Just one more small one, son' can be the beginning of the end of an evening. When it comes to breast-feeding time, she sits in on what has hitherto been a private occasion. 'I worked in a hospital you know.' Beside myself with misery, I grit my teeth and submit as she seizes my breast and rearranges it. O'Toole, re-entering the drawing room at that moment, sees this piece of intimacy and roars his revulsion. Doors slam and the car is heard roaring off. He won't be seen again for some time, certainly not until tomorrow. His mother shakes her head, disappointed to be left with me and an empty whisky bottle. Too late, she shrugs and backs off. Thank God for the beautiful white television set. We watch everything, including the 'Interludes', periods when a potter's wheel slowly revolves to the accompaniment of gentle music.

After a few days she leaves and O'Toole returns, and we are reconciled happily. His mother thinks he doesn't care for me. He doesn't when she's around. When later, his father arrives we have an easier time, but Patrick Joseph is not my cup of tea. We go on what is for me a mind-numbingly boring visit to Warwick races and I win money and he winks and says, 'Another sucker born.' (I don't think so, sir.) When I look at him I see the man O'Toole has told me about. The father sitting the little boy on the mantelpiece. Arms outstretched, he says, 'Jump, boy. I'll catch you. Trust me.' When the child jumps, the father withdraws his arms, and as the child falls to the floor, he says, 'Never trust any bastard.' O'Toole thinks this is an admirable story. I find it despicable, so I can't warm to the man. He *is* charming, in a way, but I would hate to be his wife or child.

Producing a baby has done nothing to improve my status at home. I don't know why I had been so sentimental as to think it would. Most people become embarrassed when my public trials begin, late at night. I'm not sure they believe what O'Toole says about me. Much as they like and admire him, they think he has a 'bad' side, a side that creates chaos and confusion and madness, and I, as the closest person to him, come in for the bad as well as the good. Only he and I know exactly what the dialogue is about and we do not fully understand the struggle between us. Those who don't like me rejoice. A childhood friend of his comes to visit and is hateful. Even at our worst, O'Toole and I are close, and the friend feels I've usurped a special place to which I have no right. One night, when O'Toole has finished abusing me and collapses into a deep sleep, his friend looks at me across the drawing room and, picking up from the coffee table the big salad bowl full of uneaten, dressed salad, smiles as he slowly empties the oily contents on to the pale green carpet. I can't defend myself. I can't complain to O'Toole because I know he wouldn't dare to take my part against this free spirit – the 'poor' artist, from his past life – the person who belongs to a world that he may be about to leave for success and fame and money. The friend picks up the half-empty bottle of Scotch and, still smirking, saunters to his bed in the guest-room. I want to garrotte him. I am left to pick up the lettuce leaves and wash the carpet and fetch a rug to cover O'Toole, asleep in an armchair. I am not sad but full of loathing, loathing for O'Toole's servility towards his friend and for my own inability to jerk the situation into normality and reason.

Chapter Nine

Kate was four weeks old and I was rehearsing the *Shrew* in London but was home in Stratford for the opening of *The Merchant of Venice*. The season had already opened with *The Two Gentlemen of Verona*, which was not bad but no great success either, so a great deal depended on this second play of the first Peter Hall season. And suddenly the wild Irish boy lived up to the worst expectations and disappeared into the Warwickshire air. Where was he? It was very simple, though shamingly no one at the theatre thought to ring me at home in Mount Unpleasant. He did what few people would have expected: he went to bed. Knowing how tough he was under his somewhat ramshackle, airy-fairy manner, I didn't fear the worst. He'll play, I thought. Occasionally, he took a cup of tea, mostly he wanted to be left alone.

When the theatre did begin to ring the house, he refused to take the calls. 'He's not feeling very well,' I said, unconvincingly. Undeniably, he was under stress – and he *was* only twenty-seven – but in the back of my mind I wondered whether or not this behaviour wasn't due to what he saw as a lack of support and confidence from the management. I had a faint suspicion that he might be thinking along the lines of 'You want to field someone else? *Four* someone elses? Go ahead. Do it.' The house was quiet. Kate, whom I was beginning to think of as a true theatre child, was amenably good-tempered in her cradle at the far end of the drawing room.

Opening day tomorrow. I have to arrange some kind of party here at the house. Jules and Joyce will come before the show and Mrs O'Toole will be at the performance. I'm working on the assumption that he *will* play, and I wash my hair and look out an old pre-Kate frock and ask the Shepherds at the local pub, The Dirty Duck ('The White Swan' to the Brewery), if they will look after Kate during the performance.

The day of opening night and by now the calls from the theatre are coming here thick and fast. O'Toole is still in bed, not speaking. I wish I knew what he was up to. I clean the house and see to Kate. No food is required in the bedroom. There are moments when I could take a club to him, but the minute anyone complains about him I become his chief defender. Jules and Joyce arrive. It's teatime and the situation is becoming critical, to say the least. Now, thank God, Jules will take all the phone calls and we will take turns to visit the bedroom. On one of my visits O'Toole extends a hand and says softly, 'Come to bed, girl.' I do and we are reunited after the long arid weeks since Kate was born. I dress and go downstairs. Jules goes up and I hear him saying, 'Listen, kid, if you're not going down there, *I'm* going to play Shylock and God knows, all I've got is the nose for it.' Suddenly, all is laughter and bustle and excitement and 'Where are my clean clothes?' 'How about a cup of tea?' 'Where's the car?' 'What's the time?' 'For God's sake everyone, get a *move* on.' And he's gone. It's almost time for the performance. We look at each other, Jules and Joyce and I. It's their first O'Toole experience. We're perched on a cliff edge, danger passed, giddy with relief. But what comes now? 'Let's go to the theatre,' says Joyce.

Theatre at its best, that April night, 'One of the great nights in the theatre' they called it. Those of us who were there in Stratford looked at each other, smiling, knowing that this was a night to cherish for a lifetime. At the wild curtain calls I sat in my unbecoming dress, tears rolling down my face. Whatever it cost, and now I had no illusions as to the price of life with O'Toole, I was going to do everything I could to help cherish this talent. Joyce nudged me. She was in full, beautiful, glamorous, first-night mode. 'We have to go back. He'll be *mobbed.*' Child of Hollywood, she was used to high excitement, not realising that by English standards this night was an extraordinarily heightened occasion. Backstage I had a brief moment with him alone. He was laughing. Clutching me with make-up-encrusted hands, he whispered in my ear, 'You're not going to believe this. Peter Hall was the first in here and he said, "We're going to be the youngest knights in the history of the theatre." Is he completely mad?' I went to pick up Kate from the Shepherds, got a taxi back to the house and settled her for the night before greeting the guests at the party I'd hastily organised.

I tried to put a brave face on it as they asked, 'When will Peter be here?' I didn't think he would be home for some time. This was going to be Hamlet without the Prince. His mother was inclined to make a drama out of his absence and I spent some time reassuring her, telling her lies she didn't believe, and she didn't help me by pretending to believe. I was nonplussed and caught off-guard, had no answer when a guest, non-theatrical and a stranger to me, enquired, 'Aren't you jealous? He could be anywhere, with *anyone*.' It didn't seem to be the moment to unravel my feelings, not even in the cause of polite hospitality. I filled her glass and moved on, smiling. She was insensitive, but I had to accept that she voiced a question that must have been present and unspoken by many of our acquaintances.

I would have been astounded to have seen him on this of all nights, handing round the canapés on his own Axminster, surrounded by admiring, well-dressed guests. At the same time, I would have liked him to have wished to share the moment with me in some way, but it was his moment with no obligation to share it. I knew him well enough to know that he had a need as keen as a need for food and drink to be abroad, alone, obliterating the tensions of the weeks of anxiety as he had geared up to prove himself in this great part and earn his place in the front line of actors. For all his bravado, the understandable doubts and misgivings of those around him had kept him on the rack. Knowing nothing of science, I imagined that his system must be poisoned and curdled with leftover adrenalin churning around inside him with nowhere to go. Eventually, he would reach the point of oblivion and collapse somewhere. That worried me only in so far as I was concerned for his physical well-being. I wasn't jealous. Unless I had made a massive misjudgement, there was nothing furtive or squalid in his character, and however outrageous his behaviour he retained a certain style.

Standing in our drawing room with the party subsiding gently around me, Kate safely in her crib upstairs, I dealt with the smallnesses of opening night, passing food around, pouring drinks, promising to pass on congratulations, laying aside the presents and cards, and when everyone was gone and the big house was quiet, I cleared up and washed up; tired, cross at being left alone at home, proud of his great achievement, glad to have got through the day and resentful to be the prey of so many conflicting feelings. '*Tout savoir est tout pardonner.*' Too much *savoir* puts one at a terrible disadvantage. It might be healthier to be able to look at things solely from one's own point of view. I put myself to bed and listened to Kate making small animal noises as she slept. I could hear her father's great voice in my head.

At this time O'Toole composed a song and would sing it, smiling. 'A sweet crime I sing you, a sweet, sweet crime. There's a dainty way to rape and a sweet way to kill, but I know something still.' Love and destruction walked hand in hand that spring.

Chapter Ten

For me it was wonderful to be at work again. I was lucky in Frank Hauser, my director, and even more so in my leading man, Brewster Mason. Large, good-humoured and self-assured, he had what was in those days an original approach to the relationship between the Shrew and Petruchio. Eschewing the paraphernalia of the war between them – the whips, the threatened violence which had characterised the famous 'wooing scene' – he said to me, 'Just establish yourself as a shrew – for whatever reason you choose – but when you come on for our first meeting, fall in love at first sight and I'll do the same and we'll see how we go.' I enquired nervously about the laughs, the funny 'business', and he shook his head and said, 'Trust me. No business. Let the play do the work. It *will* be funny.' Even Frank wasn't sure about this and I was only three-quarters convinced and very nervous. Only Brewster maintained his god-like calm, making time to put me in his car and run me home at lunchtime to breast-feed Kate in Doriah's flat in Belgravia.

My part was very active and after four weeks of vigorous rehearsals my milk dried up. Dr Slattery had wanted me to breast-feed for four weeks and now I'd done eight, so I thankfully moved Kate on to formula feeding and life became a great deal easier when I returned to Stratford and prepared to open the play – which worked like a dream! As the wooing scene approached, I suffered a moment of terror; no props, no business, nothing but the words and a rather bare stage. Almost immediately I heard the first big laugh – another line and a huge laugh – a riposte and a roar of delight from the audience. The play really does work on this 'straight' level. Who'd have thought it? Not I. Thank you, Brewster.

We came in for a good deal of admiring attention from the academics in Oxford and from the press as well. Full houses always. Bianca was the gorgeous Samantha Eggar who had the most exotic beaux imaginable (Graham Greene seemed to be one of them or am I dreaming this?).

She wore tattered jeans and cowboy boots and her boyfriend (Dandy Kim, renowned in the gossip columns – or am I dreaming this too?) picked her up in a jeep. What chic! No one else drove a jeep rather than a racy car. We shared a dressing room and she was forbearing about my taste for vinegar and chips. O'Toole was wonderfully admiring, especially lovely to Brewster, and asked if he could 'nick a few readings'. Brewster, charmingly flattered, said, 'But of *course*.'

It was great to be back on stage in a wonderful part. Ted Hardwicke, O'Toole's close friend from Bristol, was in the company. Sometimes he drove me back to Stratford in his Morgan, and even *I* could tell that this was a special car and that he was a wonderful driver. He was also a lovely man, discreet and tactful. Son of Sir Cedric Hardwicke, an international movie star, he must have been accustomed to the very grand side of showbusiness but maintained an impeccable, unassuming charm. I would say that he was more talented than his famous father, but I don't think he'd be glad to hear that. He told me stories about his time at Bristol with O'Toole when they used to entertain the talented young cub reporter Tom Stoppard (not so long ago, Tom Straussler) in their humble dressing room. They played the smallest parts in their first year and invented fantasies about their unimportant characters. The road sweepers or footmen or ostlers which they played were actually the true leading parts in the plays in which they appeared; they only *seemed* to be unimportant. Occasionally the fantasies threatened the balance of the play and they were threatened with suspension if the 'complex business' they invented for door opening or floor sweeping or coat hanging wasn't cut out – *at once*. They'd spent an enviable three years acting together in the same company.

The atmosphere at home had become difficult as we approached our opening of the *Shrew*. I think O'Toole got scared for me; maybe he feared I was not as good as he would have wished me to be. I turned up for rehearsal one day wearing dark glasses to hide my eyes, red from a night of wakefulness and weeping. Frank was cross and shouted, 'For God's sake, take off the glasses!' As I did, the company grew silent and looked away, embarrassed. Nothing was said.

During the run I experienced a disturbing and revealing incident. The night had been endless with accusations and inquisitions. When had these interrogations begun? Long after we'd first met, after our long months of exploratory conversations where we had told each other everything we could think of about ourselves! I'd never talked so much in my entire life and I'd never been as open and honest with anyone. Discovery, marriage, houses, cars, a baby; it was as though it had been too wonderful, too exciting, too fast, too easy. Within a couple of months of Kate's birth, everything began to come apart. What price now my belief that I was right to throw in my lot with O'Toole? What price my self-confidence in my own way of running my life? What about my rejection of the narrow morality of my non-conformist upbringing and my self-belief as I did what I pleased on equal terms with men? Hadn't I been proved right as my behaviour led to this wonderful union with the unconventional, totally lovable man? It was as though one day my husband made a huge, delayed double-take and found my past behaviour no longer just appalling but utterly unacceptable. Gradually, I came to see myself in the same, poor light. I was completely alone in that house, in that town, and ashamed and frightened, and only occasionally moved to answer back or to apply reason to the situation. Part of me didn't believe in his change of heart, but part of me was heartbroken to be the cause of such blackness in O'Toole and such unhappiness in both of us, and also, after Kate was born, to be responsible for bringing her into such an agonised home.

On this particular morning in early May, when usually O'Toole would have been expected to fall asleep, the row continued until it was time for me to leave for the Oxford theatre to play a matinée. There was silence – maybe he had gone to sleep somewhere. Mindlessly, I set about packing Kate's luggage for the day. The taxi arrived and I began to load the boot when I saw the driver's eyes lift and his expression changed. Looking over my shoulder, I saw O'Toole on the leads of the roof. There was silence all around. I couldn't read his expression but he looked – well – spectacular and impressive. He swayed precariously. I was aghast but it didn't occur to me to stay. I *had* to leave within minutes or run the risk of missing the matinée. Running into the house I called the only person I could turn to, my doctor. He promised to come over immediately. I got into the back of the taxi with Kate and said, 'Drive off, please.' Sitting there, looking straight ahead, I began to close my mind to the happenings of the night and the nightmarish scene I had just left. I was conscious of my lack of a 'normal' response; it was as though the effort of living with extreme behaviour was numbing my reaction. I thought ahead to the theatre and the prospect of doing two shows. Kate would stay with me in the dressing room, as usual, until I would hand her over to the wardrobe mistress as I went on stage. I felt a flicker of anger against O'Toole. It just wasn't fair. Living from day to day was proving exhausting and almost impossibly difficult *and* I had a job to do. I needed help and felt sabotaged at every turn. I couldn't sustain my anger. 'It's your fault,' whispered a voice in my head, and how could I ignore the fact that O'Toole himself was in torment. 'Life isn't fair' was one of his often-repeated remarks and I was slowly learning the truth of it. But clear in my mind was the conviction that I had to do my job meticulously with no concessions to my hopeless state.

We gave two good performances and, briefly, unbelievably to an outsider, I was very happy. On my return home I found the house in darkness. I hadn't been to bed for two days and once I'd settled Kate for the night, I fell into a long sleep. When I awoke, O'Toole was home. We didn't speak of what had occurred.

Kate was now approaching five months old. I was still nervous of child-rearing, had worn out one copy of Dr Spock and was into my second, but my life was transformed by the advent of Lonnie Trimble.

Our house in Stratford had become a kind of ramshackle hotel for people who wanted to see the plays and stay over. Working closely with the tourist industry, British Railway timetables made it impossible for people to see a play at Stratford and get back to London again on the same day, so our spare beds and couches were constantly occupied and once, in fine weather, there were makeshift beds on the lawns, as well. O'Toole was lavish in his offers of hospitality. More often than not he wasn't there to attend to his guests, and very often I had no idea who they were and hadn't been warned to expect them. I muddled through the day from one nightmare meal to the next. His salary of £45 a week was going nowhere towards covering the cost of this generosity. The laundry alone was a major problem, and I learned how to remake beds with roughly dried sheets, plugging the iron in at the bedside and ironing only the top of the sheet where it turned over. Fortunately I had my weekly income from my contract with Douglas Uren and had money left over from my pre-marriage days with which to help subsidise our life. Even so, it was a bit worrying.

Kenneth Griffith, most blessed of guests, arrived and solved some of my problems. He had made the acquaintance – I never discovered how – of a young, black, ex-marine from Atlanta, Georgia, one Lonnie Trimble who, having tasted life in the Navy, found it impossible to resume segregated life in the South. He was in England with no job, no work permit and needing some kind of humble employment for three years so he could become a legal resident and fulfil his ambition of becoming a chef.

Me: 'Well, Kenny, thank you very much, but I sort of thought that I needed a *nanny* right now.'

Ken: 'Yes! And *he's* your *man!*'

Well, why not? He could read Dr Spock as well as I and he could cook a great deal better than I could, so it had to be a good move. It worked well in another, more subtle, way. I suspected that O'Toole was feeling half-guilty about the changes in his life; acquiring a wife and child was bad enough, renting a big house was a bit worse, employing a *servant* was beyond the pale. Which is why Lonnie was perfect; he was no man's servant. In his head he was already the boss of a catering firm. He wasn't an early bird either and I took him a cup of tea to awaken him in the morning. Oh, but he was fearless in the kitchen; an unexpected twenty people to supper brought a happy smile to his face. Faced with the usual request for a 'cup of tea and something on toast' from O'Toole, he sulked. Possessed of endless patience, he played with Kate; she emptied a box of matches and he picked them up. She emptied, he picked up. She was in heaven. We did the marketing together (it had never occurred to me before that you *planned* your meals and bought everything in one fell, weekly swoop). He was six foot four and jet-black and beautiful. In the crook of his arm he held Kate in her beautiful white shawl, which Sidney Poitier had unexpectedly sent me after we'd met at dinner one night in the White Elephant in London. 'All very well,' sniffed a Stratford housewife in an audible whisper in the greengrocers. 'It's the *children* that suffer.'

Under his easy, masterful control the house assumed a semblance of normality. Now at least there were two of us ranged against the chaos. When times were bad between O'Toole and myself, he became an invisible presence in the house; to all intents seeing nothing, hearing nothing. It must have been an outlandish solution to his immigration problem. I could only hope that it suited him as well as it suited me. We didn't discuss it. He arrived in time to prevent a total collapse on my part. The scenes and inquisitions that had murdered the weeks before Kate was born resumed after her birth and I sank deeper into despair. I had never heard of post-natal depression; my books hadn't mentioned it. Babies, as far as I knew, arrived bringing good cheer and happiness unconfined, but I was getting more and more unhappy.

One night after hours of more close, drunken questioning about my past – and yes, he was now right to doubt my veracity – I was lying with a will about everything. My instinct to tell him the truth had brought me nothing but trouble, and pins under my nails would not drag more confessions from me. The table overturned, doors slammed and the car raced erratically down the long drive. I walked out of the house reeking with fear and suspicion and noise, lay in the wet, long grass on the untended lawn in my nightgown, unable to stay inside. It was almost dawn but I didn't feel the cold. My wish was to get ill and die. 'Let me just *leave*,' I wished. Even as I made the wish I was shocked by my cowardice. Incapable of killing myself, what did I want to happen? That the harmless damp should carry me off while I wasn't looking? Desperate as I was, I couldn't bear to be so feeble. I sat up. It was quiet; in the distance the lights on the road led to Stratford, the theatre, actors, my past life, the only life I knew how to live. As dawn broke I heard the country noises around me and I returned to my senses. I looked at the house, the scene of more misery than I could have imagined possible. Kate was inside, sleeping in her basket. What was I thinking of? So long as she was there, I would have to be there. Getting up, I returned to the house and sat on the floor, leaning against the wall, waiting until she woke. I might have forfeited my right to what I had imagined was my due as a wife and mother – protection, tenderness – but all her rights as a daughter shall remain intact, I swore to myself.

I don't recall O'Toole hurting anyone when drunk. He broke things and made a great deal of noise. I didn't fear for myself, but the noise and the destruction terrified me. I hadn't quite acquired the knack of never answering back and sometimes, unable to resist speaking up for myself, I would add fuel to the flames. When he erupted out of the house, running in bare feet into the dark across the Warwickshire fields out of sight, beyond the lights of the house, I stood alone crying tears of rage and helplessness.

My nerve was gone; a raised voice, a loud noise – nothing much in themselves – these were enough to frighten me. Sitting alone, trying to find a solution to my helter-skelter home life, I did the stupidest thing imaginable; for the first and only time in my life, I called my parents in Wales and asked for help. My father had retired from the police force, and he and my mother were running a further education house in the country outside Cardiff and enjoying the work and their pets and hobbies and generally living a more comfortable life than they'd ever had before. I had not lived with them since moving on to university, but I visited as often as possible and they were completely charmed by O'Toole and impressed by his talent. Of course, they were ecstatic at the arrival of a granddaughter. The consequences of my phone call were appalling. My father, realising I must be desperate, believed me to be seriously at risk and, hundreds of miles away and powerless, he collapsed. It was left to my mother to find a friend, Joyce (director Herbert Davies's wife), to accompany them on the long car journey from Wales to Stratford. When O'Toole, sobered, learned what I had done he was angry and appalled; it was the first time that an outsider had been allowed into our private torment. There was nothing to do but wait for them to arrive and for once he said little. He seemed contemptuous that I'd felt the need to lean on someone else. I didn't know what to think. I had lost all sense of self, all sense of pride in myself. I doubted my motives, my abilities. And yet, I was sure of my duty as a mother. And there were moments when I thought I couldn't be as bad as I had come to believe. Was *everyone* out there, in the world beyond the lawn and the field to the road, virtuous and good? I thought with envy of the company in the town, going to work, going to the pub, having fun, misbehaving – and all in some way acceptable to O'Toole where I was not.

My parents and Joyce Davies arrived and there was a good deal of shuffling of feet and tea making. My father looked awful. I felt guilty all over again. For the first and only time there was a proper 'family' talk and I didn't much like it. I had to confess all over again bits of my past in order to explain why O'Toole was so angry with me. I remembered my friend's sister being expelled from chapel for sexual irregularity and felt much as she must have felt. People went away in pairs, regrouped and whispered. I just sat there in a pool of shame. Finally, all five of us sat together and the consensus of opinion seemed to be that 'We all make mistakes' – we now had to 'Go forward'. I wasn't too sure whose mistakes we were talking about, but I felt it was better not to enquire. We seemed to have arrived at a measure of calm. O'Toole had some time off from work and he announced that my parents were going to take Kate to Wales for a week and he and I were going, at last, to the West of Ireland. This was the most unexpected outcome. O'Toole charmed them all over again. I would never be able to forget the events of the last few days. I didn't expect anything good to happen again, but everyone was now smiling and making sandwiches and everything was behind us, it seemed. I was unbelieving, but I was relieved to be out of trouble, even if just for the moment. O'Toole was adorable to me, as only he could be, and he was taking me to the West – the precious, mythical West he'd talked about so much, the home of the troublesome O'Toole clan, I was told, after they'd been banished by Cromwell from the eastern side of Eire. I was back in favour. I was forgiven. Why? For how long?

Jules's film, *The Day They Robbed the Bank of England*, was due to open in London in a few days and we were to go to that after our visit to Ireland and before I returned to Wales to pick up Kate and resume life in Stratford. I couldn't quite believe what was happening. Had I done the right thing after all by calling in my parents? My father's face was bitterly changed. I didn't know what he'd said to O'Toole, but it was evident that the episode had cost him dear. His worst fears for me had almost come true. His expression haunted me. Even as he smiled and joked and said how pleased he was to be taking Kate to Wales and was glad to assist, I could see fear and defeat in his eyes. I recognised his look because I now had been taught fear and defeat. I was an unworthy wife, an uncertain mother and a troublesome daughter. My theatrical vows were neglected and broken. He never lost the look he wore that day and that was my gift to him, the man who would never harm me.

My mother, harder, more realistic, didn't address the problem, the discussion or the resolution. She took me aside, looked at me, and said in Welsh, 'Understand, if you want this to work – and for Kate's sake you must make it work – from now on you're going to have to stand in a very small space.' The unspoken question, 'What are you going to do?' hung in the air. I knew she was right. I had seconds in which to think as bags were packed, the fridge was emptied, doors were locked, cars were loaded. I didn't look at my mother or answer her. O'Toole was looking at me, smiling. He held out his hand and I could no more resist him than stop breathing. I waved goodbye and with a lightness of heart that comes from doing the inevitable, if doomed, I took my husband's hand.

Chapter Eleven

After all that O'Toole had told me about the Eire beyond Dublin, I was nervous when we arrived. What if he'd exaggerated? What if I couldn't enthuse? But, like Venice, everything was just as it had been described and at the same time better. The weather alone was wonderful to me and assuaged a homesickness I never dared acknowledge. It was weather Celts are used to and love; damp, unpredictable, changeable, unreliable, enlightening. Jack Yeats, the painter, talking of the problem of painting in the West, said, 'The light has legs,' and everything does change even as you look at it. In the West, the countryside is a mixture of the lush – the Gulf Stream nudges past the coastline, cabbage palms intrude exotically, fuchsia hedges riot around the brutally barren little fields – smaller than one could imagine – bounded by lumps of granite. Cromwell, consigning the native Irish to the West, sent them 'to Hell or Connaught'. Coming from farming stock I was appalled by the agony of farming this landscape, which looked at times like the far side of the moon. And the people – this was a foreign land and it was home to me. As a Celt, I was used to listening to stories, hearing people sing for enjoyment, wasting time talking, but these people were something extra, something from a past I'd only been told about. The gift of storytelling, now barely a memory in close-to-England Wales, flourished here from acknowledged spielers to your neighbourhood grocer or the bus driver. Language was supreme. I remember that in London, O'Toole and I were one night trying to find the Stratford East Theatre. Hopelessly lost, we stopped a local East Ender who turned out to be an Irishman. He directed us, 'You go down that road until you come to nothin' at all and you turn left.' Thanks for nothing. Going 'down that road' we came to a bomb site, which was *'nothin'* at all' when you think about it. So we 'turned left' and there was the theatre. At the time I thought that man was a poet. Now going West, I realised that he was just an Irishman.

Coming to a crossroads we saw two men, *not* hitching a lift – nothing so vulgar – they were looking expectantly in the direction in which they wished to go. We stopped and they got in, my first Irish countrymen: the tall, serious, thin one in the front with O'Toole, and I hopped into the back with the small, cheery, fat one. (How did I know to give up my place to the natural leader?) We drove in silence for a while and O'Toole asked his passenger if he'd ever been in England. 'Yes,' was the taciturn reply. My small, fat friend dug me in the ribs. 'He was in Dartmoor and Pentonville.' Oh, gosh. 'Yes, he was trying to shoot policemen and, needless to say, he missed.' We both heaved with merriment in the back. The tall, thin, would-be murderer asks, ruminatively, 'Have you ever been to Brighton? When I left Pentonville I went there. Beautiful. England is beautiful.' I didn't really know what to say to that. They got out, thanking us in a sprightly, somewhat Japanese way that I remembered from Yugoslavia – a touch to the heart, the head, and then open the palms and bow from the waist.

In the Great Western Hotel in Kerry, as we sat in the garden, the bartender approached us unsteadily, tray tilting perilously away, he treading the lawn carefully as though he was negotiating very long grass. 'Bin and Binjer Jeer?' he intoned sonorously as we clutched at our falling glasses of gin and ginger beer.

I love, I love, I love this place. I want to live here. I think this is what Catholic Wales was like before Non-Conformism laid its hand on it. That's unfair. Non-Conformism has done so much to save us as a nation, made us remember we are different from a nation that has a ruler wedded to the Church of England, it's sent us underground, which produces another kind of strength and energy. But the joy of this place, the lack of shame, is overpoweringly attractive. It is with difficulty that I embrace my husband at times, but I unreservedly adore his country, the things that made him. He may not have been born here, but he is a boy from Connaught.

Another time, we sit in Frank Kelly's pub, Kings, on the square in Clifden (the centrepiece of the square is a half-submerged concrete public lavatory). As we drink our Guinness – 'Takes forever to draw, half a minute to drink' – a long-faced man asks, 'Are you here for the funeral?' 'No,' I say. 'What funeral?' 'Peter O'Toole's daughter.' 'Oh, my God.' 'No, Peter O'Toole. Peter's daughter.' 'Sorry?' 'Peter O'Toole. Peter's daughter's funeral.' 'Oh, I see. Yes.' Looking around I see that I am surrounded by men who look exactly like Peter O'Toole, long faced, blue eyed, thin, almost skeletal, tall, beautiful in a Sam Beckett sort of way. This is O'Toole country. I want to live in it.

How could I have imagined a mere two days ago in Warwickshire that I would be sitting here in Ireland totally happy with my decision to stay married. I didn't just marry O'Toole, I married a country, and I am ecstatically happy with my decision. This country is part of my child's inheritance, she is half Welsh and half Irish. I'm proud to have made her this.

And looking at these poor little abandoned farms – hearing stories of people's grandmothers found dead, lips stained green from eating grass – I dimly understand something akin to the Welsh experience, the fear of something beyond poverty, the total annihilation of one's right as a human being. Is the dread bred into his bones as it is into mine? If so, we have a difficult time ahead. How can the blind lead the blind? In a relationship, opposites are better. When he says, 'I'm done for', I think, 'Yes, of course you are.' What use is that? I think I see his truth and he knows more of my truth than anyone. We are completely 'suited', and we have such a chance of riches. He buys me a red-dyed bawneen jacket. If only we could stay in Ireland. This is the land of lost content for me, which is absurd because I encountered it only yesterday.

We lingered too long and now we had a wild race against time to get to London in time to change at Dorset Mews and get to the opening of *The Day They Robbed the Bank of England*. My hair was a windswept disaster and I didn't have time to get made up and I vowed I wouldn't again be such a good sport. I looked awful.

The film was very well received and O'Toole was first rate as the English officer; it wasn't a great part but playing it was a good move, I thought.

It was a better move than I could have imagined.

Back to Stratford. The trip to Ireland and the opening of the film have had a miraculous effect on our home life. We're happy. The days get longer, the elms and laurels round the house stop dripping, everything lightens. Lonnie cuts the lawns. Max Adrian has now taken the stable block, and the moment I meet him I recognise a lifelong friend. He becomes Kate's baby-sitter or rather she shares his bed when he's resting. With Lonnie on board, I no longer dread the guests, and the rickety domestic arrangements seem bohemian and amusing rather than desperate and slovenly. And what guests! Celebrities come and go. Sometimes

Lonnie is the only person to see them. Anthony Quinn arrives for the weekend from America, the current girlfriend in tow. He dosses down in Mount Unpleasant very gracefully and more or less ignores his gorgeous companion who sits in the drawing room and sobs for the entire week-end. Tactfully we also ignore her, walking round her armchair and leav-ing cups of tea within reach along with fresh boxes of Kleenex. He decides to take us to dinner and as I call the only decent restaurant he hisses, 'Book it in my name.' I call this restaurant at least once a week, but I oblige him. 'Who?' says the Warwickshire lad on the phone. 'Anthony Quinn.' 'Anthony what? Can you spell that.' 'Q-U-I-N-N.' 'Is that Siân?' 'Yes.' 'Well, why didn't you say so, girl.' I replace the receiver and he smiles across the room. 'Got a good table, huh? Always pays to *use* the name.'

Elizabeth Taylor wants O'Toole to be in a rather dubious version of *Anna Karenina*. We've read it and it's horrible and O'Toole has turned it down, but now Eddie Fisher is despatched to Stratford to woo him afresh. Just for the fun of it, O'Toole nips up to the Dorchester for talks, wins £100 from them at poker and buys a new set of clothes, and having thrown his old ones away comes home looking gorgeous like a peacock. No *Anna Karenina* of course. Everything is fun. He's inun-dated with illustrious visitors, but the only solid job offer on the table after his colossal success in *The Merchant of Venice* is a schools' broadcast for the BBC. We both vow that we'll try to remember this. Huge successes are more often than not followed by absolutely nothing.

I am approached to be in a play with Gladys Cooper and that is hugely tempting, but just for the moment I feel I have a chance to mend my life with Kate and O'Toole and I decline. O'Neill's play, *A Moon for the Misbegotten*, at the Arts is more seductive still, but now we are getting along so much better I will stick out what remains of the season in Stratford and fill in with radio and television. Now, unac-countably, life is good; I'm a good Irish wife; Marie is here; I feel useful in Mount Unpleasant. I'm living again with the man I married and he is the only person I can imagine living with.

Now most nights Kate and I are invited to supper after the show in one of the two restaurants in the town. She is an amazing child and sleeps in her basket under the dining table. (In the theatre at Oxford she slept in a skip in the Wardrobe.) I don't think she ever utters a sound when she's out for the night. We don't go to the parties, of course, but at least I hear about them now and I feel a little as though I'm part of the season.

Patrick Wymark comes calling and when he gets drunk, he puts classical music on the record player and conducts an imaginary orchestra for hours on end. He reassures O'Toole, who at twenty-seven is playing Petruchio to Peggy Ashcroft's fifty-two-year-old Kate, that she will *give* him more than any other actress alive. She has a reputation for being predatory towards her leading man and I can't help but feel nervous that she will be *too* generous with her attentions. But I remind myself that, at fifty-two, she's ancient and past such follies. She invites us to tea at the lovely house she's rented outside Stratford – strawberries and cream on the lawn. Hanging in the hall is her Vita Sackville-West-type hat and raincoat. 'I walk to work,' she declares briskly. I'm afraid she *does* look struck by O'Toole, but I don't think it's anything for me to worry about.

Sam Wanamaker and his wife invite us to tea as well (I hate tea, but I like these invitations – they're a Stratford institution). They have a wonderful half-timbered house and beautiful garden. There are young girls – daughters? – in the kitchen, but they don't join us. Kate's Moses basket is placed on the lawn, and when I turn to see if she's all right I see her covered in blossom from the tree above. Her arms are raised and she's smiling in the soft pink shower. No one remarks on the sight, but we all smile and the picture is engraved in my mind as *the* picture of my daughter as a baby in Warwickshire.

These were the more sedate aspects of our intense social life. The parties I didn't go to sounded a lot of fun. Jackie MacGowran was in the *Shrew* company. He was one of the most famous Irish actors working in England at that time and 1960 was the height of his excess, the watershed of his drinking life. (At the end of the season he checked into a drying-out clinic under our former flat in Bryanston Street.) In his apartment in Stratford there were two goldfish called King Lear and Cordelia. During a party, in the early hours of the morning, Jackie slipped out of the sitting room and got busy with the frying pan. He re-emerged, ashen, saying, 'Jayses – I feel like a fuckin' cannibal. I've just eaten King Lear and Cordelia.' He'd had them on toast.

Dinsdale Landen and his beautiful wife, Jenny, woke one morning (at her insistence, 'There's someone in the room, Din.' 'Oh, don't be silly, darling') to find a damaged car, *in* their very damaged bay window. There was an explanation for this, but at the time it escaped a hungover Dinsdale. There was so much bad behaviour during this season that people flocked to the town to see what this outrageous bunch of actors were getting up to. Mercifully, on stage, they were wonderful, but it was touch and go at times. The Shepherds who ran the Dirty Duck were invaluable allies in times of crisis. One day Jackie MacGowran before a matinée, blind drunk since the night before, said in the Duck, 'I can't go into the theatre in this state – I'm a disgrace to my profession.' He was on a warning so it was imperative that he should play the matinée. 'Look, Jackie,' said Dinsdale, 'put your clothes on back to front and they'll think at the stage door that you're coming *out*, not going *in*.' 'Right, aould son,' said Jackie, beginning to take his clothes off. O'Toole mixed him a 'cocktail' of beer, mustard and tobacco from cigarette ends, guaranteed to make anyone throw up. Jackie drank it down, shook his head and said, 'Great, aould son, great!' and proceeded to put his clothes on back to front. He played the matinée and never threw up.

The Stratford *Shrew* was a joyous production (Peggy carried Kate on at one matinée) and with other actors it went on to enchant London audiences, but it had had a difficult birth. John Barton's production was set in a winter-gripped Italy. The company was encased in furs and wools (a bit at odds with the text). There were endless stage revolves and the difficult part of Biondello was played by a child. Peggy had decided to play Kate as a stroppy, angry, militant suffragette (shades of the CND demonstrations of the time). Came a night when Peggy shut herself in the dressing room in tears of despair and refused to come out. Rehearsals were abandoned. The following day, the furs and wool were jettisoned and the wardrobe department raided for sunny Italian clothes, the revolves were halved, Dinsdale replaced the child, and O'Toole persuaded Peggy to stop being Major Barbara and just come on and fall in love with him. She did and she was sensational. It was odd, seeing her do the 'gags' that Brewster had worked out for me, but she did them so wonderfully that I was forcibly reminded that, in acting, it doesn't matter who *gets* the idea, it's how well you *execute* it that matters. She was heavenly and seemed younger than her Petruchio, who was more than young enough to be her son. The opening-night performance was a great occasion, but I didn't organise a party. The tense opening of *The Merchant* – the party without O'Toole – meant I never again expected an opening night, mine or anyone else's, to be pleasurable, or fun. But I was happy he'd 'done the double', as his bookmaker father would have said.

Chapter Twelve

Ordinarily, I would have been disappointed that the proposed foreign tour of the Oxford *Shrew* was cancelled, but, given the volatile state of my domestic life, I recognised it as a piece of good fortune. I was far from giving up my efforts to redeem myself in O'Toole's eyes, but part of me just wished for a miracle; a change of heart on his part. The likelihood that he would turn round and agree that he was over-reacting to my 'past' – which was no worse than that of most of the actresses he admired and respected and which had never been concealed from him – receded as the weeks went by. Every so often our bubble of normality was punctured by scenes of appalling verbal abuse and these were to continue at unexpected moments. I realised with regret that in his eyes I was not a woman deserving of respect. There wasn't a stage play on offer that would not keep me away from Stratford for unacceptable periods, so I began to consider television plays again.

Wilfrid Lawson was one of the greatest and most revered actors of the first half of the twentieth century. A driving accident in Hollywood had left him with a legacy of ill-health and he continued throughout his life to be a spectacularly heavy drinker. He was a great actor and it wasn't his fault that subsequent generations strove to emulate his drinking exploits and his outrageous behaviour as well as his talent. When I was considering a play by Kenneth Jupp, *Strangers in the Room*, O'Toole happened on the proposed cast list and said, 'You *have* to do this play. It's the chance of a lifetime to act with Wilfrid Lawson!' Richard Pasco, Donald Houston and I were the leading players. Mary Ellis was going to appear and Wilfrid was to play the relatively small part of my grandfather. It was a good play, but I went into it as a designated handmaiden to the great Wilfrid. 'Look after him,' said O'Toole sternly. 'Whatever it takes, DO it.'

I did. Wilfrid, playing a part that absorbed less than 10 per cent of his ability, reined in his astounding talent and behaved meekly during rehearsal. The producers were on the alert for the smallest backsliding into drunkenness. Mary Ellis loathed him and his reputation, and *still* he was adorable. Remote and unfathomable – but adorable.

During rehearsals I had an urgent dental appointment and Wilfrid offered to look after Kate! (As usual I had her with me in her basket in London.) I couldn't believe this – I was so in awe of him and he was completely undomesticated. 'Where will you be?' I asked. 'At the Kismet,' he replied. The Kismet – the afternoon drinking place in Cranbourne Street, peopled by drunks in between licensing hours in the pubs, where the owner, dear Raj's father, cooked delicious but dubious curries in the rudimentary kitchen over a blackened stove. Never had a baby graced these premises. And a baby in the charge of Wilfrid Lawson? No. Yes. Why not?

I went to the dentist and rushed back to the Kismet and . . . Wilfrid and Raj's father had looked after her beautifully, so we stayed on for more convivial hours, but even O'Toole was taken aback when I told him where Kate and I had spent the afternoon.

After that I was Wilfrid's willing slave and when we went to Manchester (without Kate) for the transmission I was the first person dressed, packed and in the foyer of our hotel when Wilfrid was evicted for roaming the corridors in the night shouting for 'Aggie'. I knew that 'Aggie' meant something to Wilfrid. She meant nothing to anyone else. There was a story of him going to Germany to do a television show. In his scene he had to say, 'Kneel, serf,' and then proceed with some faintly ridiculous speech. The lines escaped him. 'Kneel, serf,' he intoned, then, searching around for a suitable continuation, he went on, 'I have fought with Aggie' – long pause – 'the one-eyed Dane' – pause – 'several times' – pause – 'recently.' 'Cut!' said the horrified director in hushed tones. Wilfrid turned to his equally shocked fellow actor and murmured, 'That was a close shave,' pleased to have got away with something. He wasn't aware of being dismissed from the show and sent home to England. Who was 'Aggie'? Now she was here in a Manchester boarding house. I wouldn't have dreamt of abandoning Wilfrid and we taxied around until we found an Aggie-proof boarding house. The landlady liked him on sight. He kissed her hand and we were given lovely rooms and special breakfasts.

He repaid me by trying to give me a few acting notes. One of them: 'That big scene – don't play it like Lady Macbeth; it won't stand it. Never impose more weight than a scene will take. That's showing off.

Never show off.' When we came to transmission day for ABC television (the Aerated Bread Company, Wilfrid called it), he fell off the wagon. Chlöe Gibson, the director, was incensed. Mary Ellis was beside herself and Wilfrid stole every scene he was in; drunk but great. I sat on the arm of his chair (he was my grandfather) and acted away, laying down yards of text while he made holes in his biscuit with a pencil he happened to have handy. Even I was fascinated by this bit of business and I realised that my fascination with 'characters' and my slavish admiration for good actors was not going to be a help in my career. He was drunk as a skunk and all I wanted was for him to get through the show. As though he needed my help.

I was asked to join the Royal Shakespeare Company for its move to London and the first Aldwych season. I hadn't been on stage for a couple of months since *The Shrew* just after Kate was born and this seemed to be a gentle return. They were the dullest parts I'd ever been asked to play but I so wanted to be in the company. Events at home overshadowed this small decision. David Lean had seen *The Day They Robbed the Bank of England* and decided on the spot that he wanted O'Toole to play Lawrence of Arabia. Sam Spiegel – no admirer of O'Toole's – offered it to many other people including O'Toole's friend Albert Finney – who, it seems, turned it down because he didn't want film stardom at that moment – and Marlon Brando, who turned it down goodness knows why. David's choice was always O'Toole. Sam desperately went on suggesting other actors, *any* actors. O'Toole went to London to do a test, the same test that Albert had done. His partner, Jules, an old adversary of Sam's, insisted that he test in uniform as well as robes. He looked great in both. David's instinct was confirmed and even Sam had to capitulate. O'Toole was undeniably Lawrence.

'It'll be a six-month shoot,' said Sam. Jules warned that movies on this scale took twice as long as scheduled. Sam insisted that it was a six-month job. O'Toole's contract with Stratford ended in the autumn with *Troilus and Cressida*, but he had expressed a wish to play *Becket* by Anouilh in London the following spring. He and Peter Hall went to the States to see Anthony Quinn in the play on Broadway. It was O'Toole's first visit to America and he fell in love with New York. For a city boy it was *the* city above all cities and it became his favourite playground. As a country girl, I wasn't sorry that he liked to visit it alone.

He was morally committed to *Becket*, five or six months away. Also on offer was the biggest film opportunity of the decade, which should end in five or six months. When Sam Spiegel reluctantly gave in to David Lean's insistence and announced the casting of O'Toole as Lawrence, there was consternation at the theatre. O'Toole was characterised as a traitor to his profession. Life at home descended again into chaos. The brief interlude of shared days and meals eaten together was over. I lost my precarious happiness. Sadness, which I didn't think to characterise as depression, crept closer and coloured the days and nights grey.

I could still take my pick of the best television on offer, but my confidence was at rock bottom. O'Toole despised radio and television, media in which I'd grown up. Welsh-speaking theatre was, to him, not theatre at all. The Welsh were completely outside the mainstream of 'real' life and art. I took him to meet Saunders Lewis in Cardiff. During lunch at the Park Hotel, he told Saunders this; Saunders took it badly and rushed out of the hotel to disappear from my life for five years. I thought that if he dared to treat our greatest Welshman in this way, there was nothing he wouldn't dare to do to me. At the nadir of my life at this time, the BBC came to Stratford to film a day in the life of one of the 'bright young hopes of the British Theatre'. My agent said I *had* to do it. I slunk out of the house and spent the day walking around Stratford being interviewed in scenic spots, smiling, looking confident, talking about my 'exciting life' and my 'glittering future' and wishing I were dead.

Peggy Ashcroft summoned me to tea and lectured me on O'Toole's folly in 'selling out'. Surely, she said, I could use my influence to make him see sense and play Becket for the RSC rather than Lawrence in the movie. Much as I admired her, I felt unfairly invaded. She was so enviably in the right, and at the same time so comfortable, so successful, so middle class, so English. I wondered whether she had ever been asked to refuse the chance to become an international movie star, in a great part, written by a wonderful writer, directed by one of the best living directors. Given my training and inclinations, I agreed with her and, asked to choose, I would have accepted a play rather than a film. But the world had changed and was changing very fast, and in my heart of hearts I feared that my recent choices and the one Peggy was advancing were mistaken. And I wondered if she had any idea how little influence I wielded. Aloud I said that I felt it would be wrong for me to try to influence events. We parted frostily. I didn't want to alienate the great woman, but even at a time of resentment and fury with him, my loyalty to O'Toole was absolute. I couldn't discuss him. Not even with her.

Our life spiralled further out of control as his professional problems grew more oppressive. He was being made to feel guilty and unworthy by day, and at night he had the responsibility of two major parts and was on the receiving end of a huge amount of adulation. I felt that I and Kate and the house were just too much for him to deal with at this time. Had there been no love, no need on his part, it would have been easy to turn aside and wait for his life to return to something approaching normality. As it was, there were times when he clutched at me as though his life depended on me. And there were times when he couldn't bear to look at me and I had neither the years nor the sense to know how to find a balance. All too often now I found myself accepting his view that my behaviour before I met him was something for which I had to atone. Marie Kean was the only person who was allowed to witness the worst of these scenes. On a brief visit she tried to make light of things for my sake. 'Look now. He can't have expected you to live like a NUN until you met him.' 'But he *does*!' 'Not at all. He's just having a bit of a bad time and it's up to you to put up with these Moments of Truth and it will all blow over.'

The Moments of Truth, as I learned to think of the hours when my character and morals were scrutinised and found wanting, grew more frequent and one night, more intense, more anguished than ever before, I decided that I could no longer continue to live in this fashion. As the car hurtled down the lane, I looked about me and vowed that I would never again spend the dark hours in this house, which had become so hateful to me. I assembled Kate's things and packed a suitcase for myself. For the remainder of the night I restored the house to perfect order, working mindlessly until the sun was high in the sky. I bathed and called a taxi.

It was a couple of days since I'd slept, but I wasn't tired. I fed Kate and took Lonnie a cup of tea. On a deep level and beyond expression, I was angry. I couldn't work out the consequences, but I knew I had to leave Stratford, taking Kate with me.

It was a beautiful morning. I sat on the front step and thought I must be slightly deranged to be so happily affected by a perfect English summer morning, looking at a view Shakespeare might have seen.

There had never been a moment in my life where my concern with my own affairs couldn't be entirely diverted into pleasure in my surroundings. That *must* be a kind of madness, I thought, not for the first time.

It was barely more than a year since I cocked a snook at everyone as they predicted that I was embarking on a course that would ruin my life and my career, and if I'd laid about me with an axe I couldn't have made a better job of fulfilling their prophecies. The stupidest thing I'd done was to allow Keep Films, at O'Toole's urging, to buy me out of my highly unusual and good contract with Douglas Uren. I had hoped that ending the contract would help our situation, but all I'd achieved was to place myself in a very vulnerable position. I had to take a job as soon as possible. I was short of money.

The taxi was late, but the best imaginable house guest appeared. Gary Raymond, slightly taken aback to be given a pram containing Kate and asked to wheel her around the lawn for a while, obligingly fell in with the unusual social arrangements. He'd been at RADA with O'Toole and had made a name in movies almost immediately (he'd just appeared in *Suddenly Last Summer*). Much too gentlemanly to ask questions, he helped us into the taxi when it arrived and I left him in Lonnie's care to enjoy the delights of Stratford, a place I devoutly wished never to see again. I reminded myself that I shouldn't make too operatic an exit since I would have to return to rehearse *Malfi* and *Ondine*, the plays which would open the RSC season at the Aldwych in December. How I would organise that was impossible to imagine. For the moment I should content myself with the mundane business of finding shelter and quiet and getting some sleep.

Ken and Doriah's mews in London provided all that. I saw no one except Jules and Joyce briefly. I had cut myself off from everyone I had ever known and now I was much too proud to look them up, admitting I'd made a terrible mistake. Jules and Joyce were sympathetic but I reminded myself that they were in business with O'Toole; the three of them were about to take off on the exotic journey that is the beginning of a great career. I would probably have no part in this; already I felt part of the past. I don't know how people like Ken and Doriah preserved their integrity — discreet and unintrusive, they found it possible to shelter me and Kate without for a moment taking sides or even wanting to know what passed between me and O'Toole in Stratford.

And what *had* passed? Nothing that made any sense. O'Toole found it intolerable that he was not the first man in my life and he found my past beyond pardon. I found it intolerable that I should be blamed for having a previous life and then I came to blame myself for it as well. Was that really what made our lives so dangerous and hideous? Looking back, the only reality was that we were hurting each other beyond reason.

Chapter Thirteen

I spent a few weeks hibernating in London. Returning to Stratford to rehearse the new season was difficult. I found lodgings in a quiet back street and my landlady took care of Kate while I was at work. I ran home at lunchtime to feed her and returned home as soon as rehearsals were over, taking care that I was not followed. For two weeks I remained hidden. At night I sat in our room, reading, but inevitably in the end I was followed and found and O'Toole insisted that I be moved to his sister's house outside Birmingham. From there, I could commute to work every day and his sister's housekeeper would look after Kate. I felt like a Victorian serving maid who'd got into trouble and whose life was being organised by the Young Master. Had I had only myself to think about I wouldn't have agreed to any of this, but I was now a mother and, good as my landlady was, my digs weren't ideal for Kate. I sat on my single bed and looked at her in her basket. What right did I have to subject her to this improvised existence, which was the best I could muster? I had to admit that O'Toole's arrangement was better for her. I'd spent all my savings on that profligate season at Stratford and, my contract terminated, I now had no private income, only what I earned each week.

My brother-in-law, Derek Coombs, and his wife, Pat, were generous and tolerant. Their house and its comfort and security had an alarming effect on me. Arriving, I sat at the end of one of a pair of seven-foot couches and burst into tears. For two days I sat there and wept, rising only to see to Kate. I couldn't stop crying. The warmth and the comfort debilitated me completely. Derek and Pat looked in from time to time and just let me get on with it – whatever *it* was. Later, Pat said she thought I would never stop. She drove me to the train each day and picked me up at night and I marvelled at her kindness (I still do). She must have had better things to do with her time. I thought that my world had come to an end, but Derek and Pat didn't

seem to understand this. I thought that if these good people understood how 'bad' I was and how my badness had led to the destruction
of my life, they wouldn't want me under their roof. Sitting on the train
to Stratford I wondered how on earth I had come through life before
O'Toole with no carnal guilt. Now, I felt guilty about everything I'd
ever done or felt.

Not only guilty but scared. Scared because not only was I heartbroken and sad, I was incompetent. All my life, through bad and good,
I had been able to perform. Now, suddenly, at the beginning of this
engagement with the RSC, I couldn't act. The prospect of walking on
to the rehearsal set was terrifying. The prospect of 'doing it' in front of
an audience was so terrifying that I couldn't entertain it. Was this the
thing I'd only read about – stage fright – or was it life fright? To whom
could I turn? There was no one except O'Toole and he was the prime
'fixer' and solver of acting problems. When he called me to see how
Kate and I were doing, I slipped in an acting question. He responded
immediately and effectively. Sensing I was in trouble, he told me to call
him with a progress report. From that time on we talked acting every
day. My tormentor had become my saviour. Wouldn't it be nice, I
thought, if we could solve acting problems all the time? We seemed so
hopelessly bad at everything else.

We didn't meet. I was informed by Jules that O'Toole had rented a
mews house into which I and Kate were to move when the company
moved to London. What did this mean? Did it mean that we would
resume life with O'Toole? I couldn't ask.

One November morning weeks later we *did* meet. He met my train
from Birmingham and drove me to the theatre where I was rehearsing.
Parking the car, he said. 'Bit of a problem. I'm to be taken to court
because Anouilh is allowing *Becket* to be performed only on condition
that I play Henry.' It was odd to be sitting so close to him. Reluctantly
I acknowledged to myself, looking at his left shoe and his hand resting
on his knee, that I loved him as passionately as ever. Focusing on his
problem, I said, 'I very much doubt, saving your presence, that Anouilh
has ever heard of you.' He looked at me for the first time, my conspira-
tor, and an evil Irish smile suffused his face. 'Hmm,' he said. 'Maybe I'll
just nip over to Paris.'

In Paris, it seems that John Huston's mistress at that time, the
wonderful actress Suzanne Flon, also a friend of Jules and Joyce, took
him to see Anouilh, who said, 'I am enchanted to meet you but who

are you?' Anouilh wrote a letter saying he did not care who played the part and by 10 November O'Toole was free to play Lawrence of Arabia.

We opened *The Duchess of Malfi* at Stratford while I was still living in Birmingham. Max Adrian, with whom I played my erotic scene, making love on a tombstone – he in Cardinal's robes – was a tower of strength. Stephanie Bidmead got me through the worst of my stage fright. O'Toole was wonderfully supportive on the phone (the house in Stratford had been given up and he was in London). I don't think I was very good, but my sights were so lowered that I was grateful to be 'on stage', picking up my cues, making sense. It was the lowest point in my professional life, but at least I was practising my profession – and that was something.

Why was I so passive about my living arrangements? The stuffing had been knocked out of me, but I couldn't understand how I'd been brought so low, so fast. There must have been something in me – some infection at the core – that lay there waiting to be exposed, biding its time to spread through my system. O'Toole was the only person close enough to me to probe that core, and his terrors happened to chime with my failings. We clung to each other like drowning people, incapable of helping one another, unwilling to let go. We both had an instinct towards health and we kicked away from each other, only to return for another possibly fatal embrace. But health lay in being together as well. Parting for good was inconceivable. It wasn't an option for me nor, it appeared, was it for him. I don't think I hoped for happiness, but I couldn't stop trying for resolution. Ken Griffith's words came back to me: 'Do you really think you can sustain being Mrs Edmund Kean?' I loathed the romanticism, rejected the exaggeration of the notion of the wild, doomed genius. But, all the same, I *was* hitched to an acting genius, according to some, and I *was* attempting the impossible.

When *Malfi* opened, the roller-coaster life at Mount Unpleasant had taken its toll and I was very far from being the healthy, optimistic, confident young woman who had arrived in Stratford at the beginning of 1960. I was doggedly following Hélène's dictum, and managing without my 'wretched little ego', but it was hard to get through the days. I had no idea what life held in store for me. Was I to live in our London mews house alone? Sometime soon O'Toole was to go to Arabia to acclimatise; learn to ride a horse, a camel, stay with the

Bedouin, who were going to make a major contribution to the making of the film, learn some Arabic, get fit.

I was astonished to read in the newspaper that his contract stipulated that each month I, his 'cherished' wife, should be provided with an airline ticket to visit him in Jordan or wherever he might be filming during the making of the film. What did that signify?

We moved to the Aldwych Theatre and after *Malfi*, the company opened *Ondine*. Peter Hall's wife, Leslie Caron, was the water nymph and was ravishing, but the play, like most of the French plays I was ever in, didn't travel well. What a company it was, though. Peter Jeffrey, Ian Holm, Gwen Ffrangcon-Davies, Eric Porter.

So I returned to London to a little mews house in Hyde Park Gardens, a house rented for a year by our company, Keep Films. O'Toole was in residence and charmingly anxious that I should approve the arrangements. Bemused, I settled in. It was as though the previous eleven months had not occurred. I was wary and faintly disbelieving as he took me out and we posed for magazine and newspaper features. My new helper – Swedish Marianne – was installed, Kate was promoted to a bigger cot and it seemed insane to embark on questions and recriminations. I wondered if I would ever lose the mistrust that had lodged in my system. I ignored it and faced forward, undeniably happy again.

Lonnie had moved on to a job cooking for the American boss of Pan Books just around the corner. It was a hectic job; he was all the help there was. He wore three uniforms in rapid succession each day. One for cooking, one for cleaning and one for serving drinks. On the evening of a dinner party, when the front doorbell rang, he ran to answer it, tearing off his white cooking jacket and replacing it with a dark one as he majestically opened the door and took the coats. He served drinks wearing white gloves and from time to time hurtled back to the basement kitchen to keep dinner on track, tearing off his upstairs jacket as he ran. White gloves were replaced for serving at table. Occasionally, English food flummoxed him. One night the telephone rang at 7.00 p.m. and an anguished voice said, 'Siân! Siân! Hurry! Hurry! Tell me, what is this mint sauce they're talking about for the lamb. Is it meant to be hot or cold?'

Domestic life was sweet and calm. Even when Marianne dropped all O'Toole's precious 78 rpm jazz recordings and couldn't look up she was so horrified by what she'd done, O'Toole shook his head tolerantly and said, 'Accidents.' His behaviour was unnervingly benign. Then, a few days before Christmas, he went missing. I was upset but not as worried as I would have been a few months earlier. All our cars had been wrecked or abandoned, and he was no longer driving, so I had no fears for his safety. It was dismal preparing for a Christmas that might or might not happen. I trundled up the Edgware Road in the winter dark with Kate in her pram, assembling a small tree and coloured lights and presents and food. On Christmas Eve I said goodbye to everyone at the theatre and returned apprehensively to an empty house. Marianne left and Kate and I were alone. Obviously he wasn't coming home. Was it worth preparing a Christmas lunch – the first I'd attempted? Before I went to bed the front doorbell began ringing insistently. There was a great deal of noise in the mews and O'Toole was at the door, laden with presents for Kate, beaming with pleasure, so pleased with himself and pleased to be home that I didn't have the heart to spoil everything by pointing out that he'd been gone for days. After a bit he said, 'Have you looked out of the window?' 'No.' 'Why don't you?' There, sitting perkily outside the house, was a powder-blue Morris Minor car with a huge ribbon around its middle and a massive bow on top with a banner reading: 'Happy Christmas Siân, with all my love, your Peter'.

I struggled with a confusion of emotions; guilt for having thought that he wouldn't be home for Christmas, pleasure at being given such a magnificent present, and fury at being given a present which he must surely know I wouldn't use. When I was at RADA I had been involved in a traumatic accident which had led to a spell of reconstructive surgery. My terror-soaked experiences in O'Toole's cars when he drove when drinking, in Stratford, had left me with an abiding fear and hatred of the combustion engine. But it did look lovely, sitting out there, motionless. The atmosphere in the room became positively Dickensian as we hugged our good fortune to ourselves. The fire glowed, Kate beamed, my recipe book was open at the page reading 'How to Cope with Christmas'.

The days that followed were happy until O'Toole, deciding that he would like to bid farewell to Bristol before leaving for Arabia, borrowed 'my' car and, while I went back to the Aldwych, drove west on his sentimental journey. In bed after the performance, I was awakened by the phone. 'Is that Siân?' 'Yes.' 'Ah, well' – West Country voice – 'now I'm very sorry about this but I'm afraid we've had to lock Pete in the cells. We thought you ought to know.' 'We' was the constabulary. Jules, awakened in turn, promised me that he'd take care of things. He rang me back to say that O'Toole, much the worse for wear, had absently driven 'my' car, full of actors, into the back of a police car, which in turn was full of dozing policemen, who weren't best pleased. He was processed through the court with the minimum of fuss and the maximum of despatch and packed off home by train. I never saw the car again and I was pleased about that. On this occasion it truly was the thought that mattered.

Chapter Fourteen

There was excitement in the small house as O'Toole prepared to leave England in the early part of 1961. The film company had set up an office in Amman in Jordan, and another, the home office, in Mayfair in London, and mail was sent to and fro in the company bag. Filming was not due to begin until May, but the preparations were well under way. The King was firmly on board as an ally and had placed the army and his own Bedouin desert patrol at the service of Horizon Pictures. I was told that O'Toole would be sent into the desert and would be completely out of reach of the phone or letters for long periods. We had been enjoying a wonderful time and I didn't like the thought of being separated for so long, but in a way it was fortunate that we had endured that time of misery at Stratford. Being apart was not going to be much fun, but it wasn't as bad as parting unhappily or even living together unhappily. The alcohol consumption had already been reduced drastically; in Arabia drink would have to be banned completely except for the odd infrequent break in Beirut, the nearest fleshpot. The heat at times would be over 120 degrees and we learned that it is impossible to live and work in that heat encumbered by a hangover.

This piece of information was part of a comprehensive briefing that took in manners and morals as well as food, drink and hygiene. O'Toole was reading everything that had been assembled for him; Lawrence, his campaigns, the geography of Jordan, religion, the background history of the 'fertile crescent', and we were meeting people who were involved with Lawrence himself. Anthony Nutting had been appointed advisor; an expert on Middle East affairs, he was a wonderful source of information and good gossip. Lunch with Captain Basil Liddell Hart at his house in Medmenham brought home to me the scale and nature of this job. Even to me it no longer felt like a job; this was the biggest adventure of a lifetime. Making a movie on this scale was a bit like mounting a military operation. I was aware that, David Lean apart (his confidence in O'Toole was absolute), there were doubts again about the maverick Irishman. Would he be able to submit to the unrelenting discipline, the physical hardships that awaited him? Did he have the strength of character? How would he manage, hundreds of kilometres from the nearest water let alone a welcoming bar? Did he have the 'right stuff' in him? The whispers were incessant. It was Stratford all over again. I had no doubts at all. I knew how hard he drove himself when he was working. I also knew that he wanted this film and all that it would bring. Jules, knowing as neither of us could that O'Toole's life was about to change completely, asked O'Toole suddenly one night, 'Do you *want* this? *Really* want it?' There was no need to answer yes as their eyes met. In his words, he wanted it so much he could taste it.

I buried any nervousness I may have felt about our future and joined in the excitement. I was ashamed to admit even to myself that the future frightened me. I was not at all sure that *I* wanted all this. I was not even sure that I would have a part in it. I was not sure that I liked the film world. I didn't voice any of these doubts and braced myself against the trial of the coming months which Kate and I would spend alone. 'Months?' said someone. 'This picture is going to take over a year and then some.' My heart sank. Smart restaurants, interviews, photo sessions, eight shows a week at the Aldwych for me, and too many people packing into our small mews house, an endlessly ringing telephone, happy noise – and then silence. He was gone. It was as though he'd taken all the colour and light with him. For a week I mourned and moped and grieved, then I began to look about and realised how very fortunate I was in my job, in London, in Hyde Park across the road, in the shops of Connaught Street, in my lovely bedroom in the front with Marianne and Kate tucked in at the back, but I couldn't even imagine what the desert was like. What his new life was like.

Naturally, during the bad times at Stratford my eczema, which I had suffered since childhood, had raged out of control and I'd developed abscesses inside my ears. At the theatre this was a problem. I was getting over my bout of stage fright, but many nights at the Aldwych I couldn't hear anything much; it was like acting in a thick fog. My friend in the company, Stephanie – Steve – Bidmead, who, having had health problems of her own and overcome them, recognised a fellow casualty and took me under her wing. She made coping with the deafness into a game. On stage or watching me from the wings, she would raise an index finger a mere centimetre and that meant 'speak up' and lower it fractionally to mean 'stop shouting'. Once I had arrived at the correct pitch, she'd give me a big wink and get on with her own performance. Gradually, I learned to tell if I was too loud or too soft by the feeling in the resonators in my face, but without Steve I don't know how I would have survived the early months of 1961.

The first wonderful letters had begun to arrive from Jordan. I read them over and over again, sometimes I read them aloud to Kate, who looked benign and indifferent. I pinned a photograph of her father near her playpen. This was foolish, I know, but I was not quite sure how to behave and I was also sure that Mr Spock didn't tell me everything about babies in general and Kate in particular. I sang her the song that O'Toole composed for her and used to play to her on his guitar (the only thing which had survived Stratford unbroken and which had now been packed and sent to Jordan).

> Why do I laugh? Why do I sing?
> Why is there music? Birds on the wing?
> Kate is charming
> Kate is charming

Who knows? Maybe she recognises it, maybe not. I'm not sure of anything. Looking back at my younger self a mere year ago I cannot believe that I was ever so confident, so sure of myself. Now I'm uncertain of everything and, in particular, unsure of my own ability. It seems that once one's confidence is destroyed, nervousness seeps into every area of existence. I look at Kate and she looks back at me and I wonder am I doing right by her? We're a bit like a couple of comfortably installed hostages. I've learned to organise and manage, and we share an orderly life but a life lacking in spontaneity. There is nothing to indicate when my period of atonement for my past might end – maybe never. I have overcome the pointless fits of frustration at not being able to do anything to put matters right. My childhood dream of having done something so bad that it is unpardonable and unforgivable has come true, and all I can do is to ensure that I lead a life which is, and is seen to be, beyond reproach. My old, pre-O'Toole life is as though it never was.

I have a few new, permitted friends and acquaintances; Jules and Joyce keep an eye on me, Derek Bowman, a journalist on the old *News Chronicle*, comes round and patiently picks the bits of ham out of the omelettes I absent-mindedly make for him. Tom Stoppard, an old friend of O'Toole's from Bristol, temporarily fills the space I like to reserve in my life for the person-a-million-times-cleverer-than-I and brings me out-of-print books. He's going to be a full-time writer. John Libson, our accountant's son, soon to be an accountant himself, rescues me from the ladies' seminary I've created for myself and takes me for spins and Chinese meals. He, also, is a lot cleverer than I am and solves domestic problems as well as fiscal ones. Stephanie Bidmead stays over sometimes and we talk about everything except my private life. I don't think that she knows O'Toole at all. If she does, she never mentions him. Then – heaven sent – Marie Kean arrives from Dublin to do some filming in London. Now we're four girls in this little house. Marie and I step out after the show at night and within days she raises my spirits. I doubt that I'll ever again be as high-spirited as I once was, but this will do to be going on with and I thank God for Marie, the funniest woman I know.

As the season draws to a close, O'Toole begins agitating for me to end the engagement. Understandably, since the Royal Shakespeare Company took him to court over *Becket*, he's taken against Stratford in a big way. This is a shame and inconvenient for me. My natural 'home' is obviously in the theatre and my natural place in the theatre is obviously within a permanent company. It is equally obvious that to make my life in the Stratford company would be regarded by O'Toole as totally disloyal, almost grounds for divorce. I don't know how I'm going to proceed, but I do know that I have to finish at the Royal Shakespeare, go to Jordan (which I want to do), and only then come back and worry about my future. The values of the Forties and Fifties still prevailed in the Sixties, and it would have been unacceptably disloyal of me to have defied my husband and thrown in my lot with people whom he regarded as enemies at that time. My mother had told me that I would have to stand in a very small place to make this marriage work and I was prepared to do that, but I was quite unprepared to give up my work. I would try to have it all.

I have changed agents and am now represented by John Redway & Associates, but I am being held to my contract with MCA and am paying two lots of 10 per cent on every job. O'Toole is going to be paid £19,500 for making Lawrence. The other actors will make a great deal more, but Jules says this is all fine and all is going according to plan – whatever that is. He doesn't say. My RSC salary is completely swallowed up by the cost of employing Marianne, the nanny, and the cleaner who comes with the house. During the day I'm able to do radio work and I make commercial recordings of plays as well, so I get by, but I do have to keep working.

Alarmingly, people assume that I don't need to work now that I'm a 'film star's wife'. They also assume I might not *want* to work and that if I do, I'll want to do only very smart work. These are problems which I had not anticipated. Even more worrying is the attitude I detect in my own camp. Keep Films, our company, is establishing itself; accountants, bookkeepers, lawyers, secretaries are being assembled. Naturally, everything exists because of O'Toole and everyone's effort is directed towards his work and well-being. I am very much a willing part of this team and I can see that my co-operation is essential to the enterprise, but I am mortified to realise that my work hardly figures. It's as though my life before Stratford is completely wiped out. I'm known as a wife on a difficult assignment, a mother and – oh yes – an actress. Sort of. (Nice for me to have something to do in my spare time now that O'Toole's away.) Jules, who is genuinely fond of me and whom I like hugely and depend upon hugely, is heard to say, 'It's all right for her to work so long as it doesn't get in Pete's way and so long as he isn't embarrassed by her.' This is crushing, but this is my life now and somehow I shall have to find a way of surviving as an actress. To protest and to demand a toe-hold of my own would be perceived as grotesque and graceless. This is 1960 and women – wives – are meant to be helpmeets, not strident nuisances. And this *is* a great, important and testing time for O'Toole and I *do* want to help. In the back of my mind I harbour the hope that, when he is able, and if ever he is able to accept the fact that I was not a virgin bride, O'Toole will be my ally and help me out of this difficult situation. He may disapprove of my past but he does also love me, and to others – never to me – he is extravagant in his praise of me. Michael Langham says that when he was thinking of mounting a production of *Cyrano*, O'Toole, approving my casting as Roxanne, wrote: 'Her voice is a great bell that rings in my heart.' To Marie he said, 'I'm marrying the best young actress in the country.' This astonishes me. I feel like a goose girl with bare feet over whom O'Toole has thrown a beautiful cloak that hides the rags underneath. I may have to buy my own shoes.

Ondine at the Aldwych comes to an end. The parts I've played have not suited me much – or rather, I don't feel that I've been able to do anything with them. For many reasons the season has been an uphill climb all the way. I'm not sorry to come to the end of it, but I am desperately sorry to leave the company. Two memories of the play: exquisitely beautiful Leslie Caron in the title part, and the night when, processing as part of the Court up from the orchestra pit, on stage right and moving diagonally up stage and off, stage left, I felt my fourteen-foot train (suede, trimmed with fur, designed to look like velvet – don't ask) to be more than usually difficult to negotiate. Looking back I saw my mother, the Queen, in the person of Gwen Ffrangcon-Davies, on her hands and knees on my train, myopically peering at it in a puzzled way and presumably wondering why the stage cloth was moving. I dragged her about thirty feet, but she seemed none the worse for wear when she was helped up in the wings. (Not a titter from the respectful audience.)

Kate has been taken to Wales to stay with my parents, who are delighted to have her all to themselves. With a few pairs of trousers and a ladylike divided skirt and a sun dress for private wear and a few pairs of long-sleeved garments so as not to offend anyone on the street, I'm heading for the Middle East. I've been reading all O'Toole's research books, but I don't really know what to expect.

Travelling in a nice new American tweed suit, I walked into a wall of heat in Amman Airport. Exhausted and overpowered by the heat, I immediately fell under the spell of Jordan. The flight had been endless. Hungry, I looked longingly at a street vendor's tray of pungent food. 'Uh-huh,' said the Columbia official as he followed my glance, 'never. Not ever. Asking for trouble.' The car bumped along what was little better than a dirt road, and we drove to the best hotel in Amman, the Philadelphia, a ramshackle affair with flimsy doors and furniture – but still those wonderful spicy smells everywhere. And the sounds! Chaos in the street below and on the radio, music that seemed to go on and on and on without a break. 'Ghastly din you can't get away from,' said my American escort. I looked at him in his beautiful jacket and slacks and polo-necked cotton shirt, shiny shoes, manicured hands, and thought he must be having an awful time since he didn't seem to like anything about the country. I couldn't wait for him to leave. Before he abandoned me for the night – in the morning I was to be taken south to Aqaba where O'Toole was based – he pointed out the Royal Palace on the dusty hill, one of the 'jebels' I'd been reading about. It was an undistinguished, squat, sandstone house, and on another hill there was a biscuit-coloured piece of suburbia where Columbia Pictures had made its home.

Left to myself, I leaned out of the window (arms covered in case anyone looked up) and marvelled at the scene below. There didn't seem to be a rule of the road, or if there was, no one observed it. The men in their robes looked exactly like the men in every drawing I'd ever seen in childhood Bible classes. I'd never been in a place where everything matched up to my mental picture of it, but I couldn't have known what the sound would be like, or the smell. I don't know how long I hung out of my window before the muezzin began to chant and the wonder was complete.

Reluctantly, I withdrew into the spacious, ugly room and began the long struggle to summon room-service and, having eventually raised someone, to order some food – *any* food – and then to get it delivered. When eventually it came it was nothing like the delicious concoctions sold on the street. This being the best hotel, the food was a muddled attempt at European hotel food, but nothing could lower my spirits and I ate the grey meat and watery boiled vegetables, then bathed in tepid water and, lying on top of my artificial silk bedspread, fell into a deep, contented sleep.

In the morning I woke early, dressed and hung out of the window until the company car arrived to take me to Aqaba. Breakfast was a bit of bread left over from dinner. I couldn't face another struggle with room-service. It became hotter and hotter as we descended to the southern coast. The heat in the car was almost unbearable. The heat outside was just as bad. We passed no other traffic; occasionally I saw a little cluster of small dried mud-coloured houses that looked as though they'd been assembled from a child's outsized building kit. When I saw a few Bedouin on their camels I swallowed hard and pointed. The driver nodded, bored. I almost burst into tears; I had never, ever seen anything that looked so totally *foreign*. Everything, every single thing that was happening, was intoxicatingly new and unknown – maybe unknowable. By the time we drew into the tiny settlement that was Aqaba and bumped along the track to the Columbia Pictures encampment on the shore of the Red Sea, I already felt in some way altered just by being in this place. I wasn't concentrating on myself and certainly wasn't ready for what greeted me.

Chapter Fifteen

Aqaba – a dirt track through a sketchy village, then, slightly apart, a military-style compound; a dining mess, a few hastily thrown-up rooms around a cement yard on a beach bordering the Red Sea, rudimentary lavatories, showers and a few un-smart trailers. The film was in pre-production, O'Toole was one of the very few actors present and he'd been installed in a trailer. There was very little room. The walls were completely covered with sheets of paper on which he'd handwritten useful Arabic phrases and a daily addition of ten words to a growing vocabulary. One end of the trailer was filled by the oversized bed. There were no home comforts, but there was Arabic, Arabic everywhere, then books, papers, and a little ledge holding soap, towels, toothpaste and brush and bottles of Ambre Solaire. I had very little luggage and I found a small cupboard where I could stow my things. O'Toole was wearing long boots, trousers, cotton shirt and a belted cotton robe, his camel-riding gear. We were both shy and tentative as we greeted each other. He looked extraordinary, a thousand times fitter and healthier than he'd ever looked; his eyes were clear and for the first time in his life he was tanned, his curly black hair had been straightened and bleached. He looked – I couldn't quite think what he looked like. Then it came to me. He looked like a movie star.

Someone brought us tea. The heat was stifling. He began to pass on to me the lessons he'd learned about how to live here and in the desert where he would take me soon. He'd been living with the Bedouin camel-patrol as they travelled around the desert and, clearly, he'd formed a great attachment to them and their way of life. It sounded wonderful to me. He described the nights sitting outside the black tents, grateful for the cooler air after the horrendous heat of the day. They would sit, leaning on their saddles, still holding the sticks they held in their right hands while riding. Total silence, except for the occasional noise made by a sleeping camel, and no conversation, unless someone had something useful or amusing to say. I couldn't quite imagine the absence of small-talk. Silence in society makes me feel uneasy. They would draw mean-ingless patterns in the sand with their sticks and the patterns looked like exquisite Arab calligraphy.

Enthralled, I forgot the heat and my inappropriate clothes. When could *I* go to see The Boys, as he called them? The atmosphere changed at once. 'Maybe not at all' was the reply. It was a totally male society. Women were never seen. I began to wonder where I would fit, even temporarily, into this new life O'Toole was experiencing. He contin-ued to talk about these wonderful people, their skills, their hospitality, their code of honour, and I realised with dismay that we were moving into the familiar territory of my *lack* of 'honour'. It wasn't possible, was it, that we were reprising the awful, circular debates of our wretched months at Stratford, debates that I had assumed to be behind us for ever. Exhausted and incredulous, I couldn't think of anything to say except 'Well, shall I go home then?' I sounded cheap and chippy. 'Maybe that would be best,' was the reply and O'Toole slammed out.

I sat there in the little oven of a trailer. I had loved the journey, I loved what I'd seen of the country, I longed to go into the desert, I longed to be reunited with O'Toole. A part of me had now become so accustomed to failed expectations, to finding that nothing turned out the way I expected it should do, that I didn't waste time crying. I began to puzzle out whom I should talk to in order to get a car back up the length of the country north to Amman. The door opened, O'Toole entered, and swiftly, without speaking, we fell into each other's arms and laughing and crying we started all over again. It was the beginning of one of the best times of my life.

I'd thought I was a brisk creature of damp and cold, changing skies, winds and mountains, and now I'm gladly ravished by the baking, dry, unbearable heat, the cloudless skies, the slow pace one has to learn in order to survive the long day between dawn and sunset. O'Toole gets us both up at five in the morning and we drink sweet tea with mint and shower and dress and tidy our tiny living space before the heat begins. We lie in the sun for ten minutes only; the rest of the time we stay covered up like the Arabs. Nevertheless, very quickly, I become brown and my hair bleaches itself. I've never looked like this before.

Gradually I meet the huge unit. Phil Hobbs, the location manager, has built a large village here; some of the men already dislike the climate and the lack of comfort (with much more hardship to come when filming starts) and they begin to ask to be sent home. The airlines are doing a brisk trade. It seems to be the luck of the draw; hating this place or loving it. There are very few women here. Barbara is the continuity girl and she's already up to her eyes in work. The most colourful members of the unit, the property master and his brother, Eddie Fowley and Dave, live slightly apart from everyone else and Eddie has his wife, Doris, with him, but she is never seen except at night when Eddie returns from the day's 'recce'. Leila Lean, David's Indian wife, is installed in one of the concrete bunkers, windows shaded against the light. She's brought over a hundred saris with her and a huge, stringed instrument irreverently referred to as the 'joke banjo'. She doesn't emerge during the day. David has already gone into the desert and doesn't return to base.

Eddie Fowley is an amazing man. Blackened by the sun, stripped to the waist, he's ready for anything. I'm told that he's the man who built *and blew up* the bridge on the River Kwai. He has a large truck and no matter what outlandish request is made to him, he lifts his head belligerently and bites out a command, 'DAVE! In the *TRUCK*!' He speaks in capital letters and he's never been known to be found wanting. David Lean rightly treasures him.

People in these early stages are still trying to shake down into some bearable kind of life together, getting ready for the long, hard haul. I've never been on a location like this (I don't suppose there *are* many movies planned on this scale). The problems are mind-boggling; I listen in the mess as they begin to discuss the question of trucking water, daily, hundreds of kilometres into the desert, some of it uncharted. How much water is needed by each person daily? Canvas villages will have to be erected, latrines dug, field kitchens built at speed. Huge quantities of salt tablets are flown in and every table has a big jar of them along with the HP and ketchup. If you forget to take regular handfuls, with no warning at all you gently keel over as you stroll along. Sweat dries even as it's produced and sometimes one is so dehydrated that three tablespoons of salt in a glass of water have no taste at all. Occasionally we walk into the village proper. There's nothing much there, but there is a lean-to café and we begin to eat forbidden local food – it's delicious – much nicer than our British-style canteen food. Leila Lean accompanies us and is grateful for the change of diet. We suffer no ill effects. The unit doctor shakes his head reprovingly. There is a Mayor of Aqaba and he sits outside his run-down house looking across the bay at the Jewish settlement, another small village, Eilat, which seems to be full of builders and – especially – electricians. It changes daily and one can just make out that they're building and installing lighted signs. It's odd to be sitting on this side of the bay, one mile and three or four hundred yards away from the Jewish side. Barbed wire divides the two places, the divide is mined, I'm told, and the stretch of no man's land is patrolled by soldiers in long frocks and bandoliers. What is the Mayor thinking as he sits hour after hour playing with his beads and glowering moodily across the bay? He's a bit jealous, I'd say.

Sam Spiegel, the producer of the film, is, of course, Jewish and his yacht is moored in the bay. He daren't come ashore, which pleases David Lean no end (no interference). There's trouble when the rumour is put about that this is a Jewish film with a Jewish unit. King Hussein comes to the rescue and drives into the desert to address the army and especially the camel-patrol – his special 'boys' – and says he is entrusting the safety of the enterprise to them. They adore him – this is like watching Henry V on the eve of Agincourt – they'll do whatever he asks them to do and it's pretty plain that he loves them, as well. It's very unlike home.

The King is sophisticated. Sam tries to be smart. When the concept of Ramadan is explained to him, he nods sagely and says, 'Ah yes. Just like our Lent.' The King is kind enough to pretend he didn't hear.

O'Toole and I on a rare visit to Amman are invited to the Basman Palace. It's very, very modest. Not pretty. We sit in large British-style, uncut moquette armchairs and are mightily impressed by the King, who is small with a bass voice and a wonderfully handsome head. I reflect that he's lucky to be a king, not an actor; it would be such bad luck to be so handsome and so much smaller than the most petite of actresses. People – not just the Bedouin – love him. Over and over I'm told how brave he is; recently he had his appendix out without anaesthetic and walked out of the operating room. I'm suitably impressed.

Not long into Operation Lawrence, the King takes a fancy to the chief telephone operator at the production office. John Sullivan, the charming, good-looking head of stunts and O'Toole's stand-in and companion, steps out of the romantic frame and, within the year, Miss Gardiner becomes Queen of Jordan and the phones never really work properly again. It's a bit like Alice in Wonderland here. Anything can happen.

Finally, I'm to meet the Bedouin – not in the desert – on a piece of scrub behind the little town. O'Toole and about six Bedu are practising with their camels. Racing camels are called *thalools*. They go from zero to thirty miles an hour in under a minute. The motion, I'm told, is almost impossible to understand, and being a horse rider doesn't help because the camel rocks forward and back and up and down and you don't know what to do for the best. We do a lot of greeting and bowing. I'm decently covered and wear a divided skirt and desert bootees and socks. They seem very jolly – full of jokes – and contrive to look blood-thirsty as well, hung about with guns and bullets. I understand as they gesture towards me and one of the camels that I'm being asked if I'd like to try riding. Shooting a glance at O'Toole, who is good-humouredly non-committal, I say, 'Why not? Well, of *course* I want to try.' It seems polite. They show me how to lock my legs around the pommel, hand me a whip and up rises the camel.

Well, this isn't too bad. It's rather lovely, being so high up, trying to get the hang of the motion as the beast begins to walk on. I look at them for approval; they nod. We're all in a good mood. Stepping forward, the man who seems to be the leader lifts his whip and, smiling broadly, gives my camel a brisk crack along the backside. I can only just hear the beginning of merry laughter behind me. I'm rocking at speed forward and back, hitting the big wooden 'nails' of a pommel front and back with each horrible movement. Lurching up and down and side-ways, I land just to the left of the saddle, then to the right. This seems to go on for ever before I fall off. Well, no, I *don't* fall off, I hang upside down, my legs and feet are locked, and I know that so long as they stay locked I can't *possibly* fall off, and no power on earth is going to unlock my legs. I thank God quickly for all those years of training at gymnas-tics. I may be hanging upside down but I'm staying calm. But where are we going? I lift my head slightly and see that we're heading in the direc-tion of a lot of barbed wire. Land-mines? No man's land? This is not good. I'm thinking what to do when I sense another camel tearing along and overtaking me. The rider begins to beat my camel about the nose and she begins to turn in a circle, and turning, decelerates, eventu-ally slowing down to a walk. I'm able to hoist myself back up into the saddle. The rest of the company has caught up with us. They're still laughing! I nod and smile and roll my eyes to heaven. I can see that this is one of the funniest things they've experienced in days. Too late, I remember – they love practical jokes. Down goes the camel and off I get, very shaky in the legs. 'After all that, would you like to go back to the trailer?' asks O'Toole solicitously.

'Mmm – maybe.'

'You all right?'

'FINE.'

'Okay, then.'

A small jeep is summoned and I bump back into camp. Blood is now seeping through my shirt front and back, and I stand in the shower to peel it off. Half a bottle of Dettol and a tin of lint and plasters later, I'm as good as new. And when after lunch O'Toole sees my torn midriff and back, I'm able – truly – to say that I'm just fine. Actually, I'm more than fine. I feel I've passed some kind of test. I'm having the time of my life.

Thanks to The Boys, O'Toole is now a really good camel rider. I'm overcome with admiration. No one prepared him for all this at RADA. He's learning to keep his eyes open in the blinding light of the sun. They're pale blue and sensitive to light, and all he wants to do is scrunch up his face and close his eyes, but that isn't going to do. I can see why he's so fit – this is like being in the army except the hours are longer and he'll have to wear a bit of make-up. The day arrives when I'm to be taken into the desert to the black tents. We pile into a jeep with enough cigarettes for us both, a shovel for going to the loo and a straw mat for digging out when we get stuck, a compass, and off we head into the desert.

Hours go by. He's becoming used to this terrain; we're miles away from Aqaba and I don't see how he knows where to go, there isn't a road. Occasionally we get bogged down and have to lay down the mats in order to get started again. It's incredibly *clean* here. When we stop, the silence is profound – no birds, no insects, hardly a breeze today.

Suddenly O'Toole nudges me in the ribs. There, ahead in the distance, is the most romantic scene imaginable: in the middle of nothing, the long, low, worm-like shapes of the black tents – woven wool with rugs hanging from the 'roofs'. Camels are lying alongside and they *do* look like moored boats, necks raised like elegant prows. As we approach, Getaifan Abu Tai (the grandson of the great Auda, played by Tony Quinn) emerges, dropping the door flap behind him. The women are inside the harem and we won't see them. We're invited to sit, and leaning against the large camel-saddles on the ground, I fondle a pommel, exploring the large, flat head of the nail-like shape, which crashed into me not so long ago. Greetings are elaborate and take a while. Then small cups of tea are prepared, sweet, sweet tea with mint, '*shai ma nana*'. I've learned the basics, '*hamdilla*', '*shwkran*' and '*afwan*', and nothing else. We sit under a black awning, shaded from the sun, and are joined by three or four men, all in full fighting rig.

The men have become fascinated by some of the paraphernalia of film-making. Mascara has become a favourite toy, little mirrors also. Laying down their rifles, they peer at their eye make-up admiringly and laugh with pleasure. Occasionally you see these fierce-looking soldiers stroll hand in hand past the tents where the wives and children remain out of sight until the strangers are gone. It looks unselfconscious and totally charming. And here's the famous social silence I've been hearing about. We smile at each other – the formalities have been observed and we lapse into quiet. They draw patterns in the sand with their canes. I find I'm doing the same with my index finger. At first I have a real compulsion to fill in the pauses, but once the pause is beyond help there's scarcely any point. Occasionally, catching someone's eye, I exchange a smile. Intermittently, someone does say something – there isn't necessarily a reply and the silence continues. Once I've become accustomed to this I find a wonderful state, a state of wakeful relaxation. Nothing need happen, nothing needs to be said. Hours go by and we finally take our leave, return to the jeep and make for the long drive back to camp. I realise that now *we* are hardly talking to each other either.

Night falls and the sky above and all around seems to dip below the line of the earth. I've never been so aware of the night sky and the stars and I wonder if I might be able to stay overnight out in the desert some time. We have supper and I go to bed. O'Toole works on his vocabulary while I try to assimilate the experiences of the day. One thing I realise now is that the desert Arabs are a good deal more sophisticated and tolerant than their small-town brothers. In the heat I took off my jacket, revealing a very short-sleeved bodice. No one batted an eyelid.

This was the first of many visits to the black tents. Much later that year we sat for hours with Getaifan and his friends, and after we'd made the long trip back to base camp by jeep there was a flurry of activity and shouts in Arabic. Looking out, we saw Getaifan, who'd galloped after us on his camel. While we'd sat there with him, his wife, inside the tent, had silently given birth to a baby – a girl. He wanted to know if he could name her after me. Later, on a rare break, O'Toole and I made for Beirut and in the gold market we bought Siân Abu Tai, Auda's great granddaughter, a gold chain and we hung a ruby on it. On our return we gave the chain to Getaifan to give to his wife, and when we next visited him he beckoned to me to come inside the back tent. It was an honour to be allowed into the women's quarters; dark and cool and hung with bright carpets and shawls; Siân was produced and unwrapped from yards and yards of swaddling clothes, and there was her necklace, fastened round her belly with the ruby nestling in her navel.

That was the only time I was allowed inside the black tent. I was, however, invited to a Mansaf. O'Toole, who was acquiring Lawrence-like status in the desert, was asked to settle a blood feud between two families. We sat for hours in the shadow of the ruin of a Crusader castle while our interpreter did his best to guide us through the byzantine complexities of this ancient family row, and when everything was settled to everyone's satisfaction, as darkness fell, a huge fire was lit and a sheep was killed and cooked, and we ate it – *all* of it. I was ravenous and it was delicious – *all* of it. Meat was a rarity and we felt very privileged to be allowed to share what was truly a feast.

The first day of shooting arrived. The long preparation came to an end around the time of my birthday in mid-May. I accompanied O'Toole and the unit into the farthest reaches of Jebel Tubeiq. Here and there are faint traces of eighth-century settlements. It is vast; one of the most inhospitable, awe-inspiring places on earth and, on the face of it, a mad place in which to try to shoot a movie. We received a message to join Eddie Fowley, with rough directions as to where we'd find him. After a long bumpy drive, we came upon the truck in the huge empty landscape. Eddie had produced a roll of plastic 'grass', a table and striped umbrella, yellow paper daffodils – the Welsh emblem – and he served us 'cocktails' of fruit juice in glasses with little parasols and glacé cherries, all produced from the famous truck. I had been there for a month and now, when filming started, I went home, riding with one of the unit members on an errand to Amman. We got lost, we got stuck again and again, and eventually reached the road that ran north–south through the country. Amman seemed incredibly noisy. I spent the night there and when I started a rare headache, prompted by misery at having to leave, someone sent out for some pills. When I got home to London, Jules called me and said he'd just got a bill from the production office: 'Mrs O'Toole – one packet Aspirin'. We paid up.

Chapter Sixteen

Back in London I missed O'Toole terribly. Picking Kate up from my parents' place in Wales, where they'd all had a wonderful time, I brought her back to Hyde Park Gardens.

Jules had decided that we could now afford to buy a permanent home in London; our situation had stabilised to the point where we both wanted to put down family roots. Lying on my couch suffering from flu, towards the end of the Aldwych season, I'd received a visit from Henry Woolf, a friend of O'Toole's from Bristol. He had presented what must have been the first performance of any Pinter play at Bristol University, so I credited him with impeccable taste. I couldn't stir myself to go house-hunting and play in the theatre at night, and I asked Henry if he would mind taking the house agents' lists and begin looking for a suitable house. After a few days he came back saying, 'Now, I know your top price is £8,000' (that was the price of a house in, say, Little Venice) '. . . but I've found a house which is *£14,000* and needs *everything* doing to it and you *have* to buy it.' I went to see it. It was inconvenient, big, needed years of 'improvements' taken out, but it was beautiful and Henry was right, we *had* to have it. It dated from 1740 and was built on five floors, all listing slightly to starboard. There were big cellars that ran under Heath Street and it had been one of the group of five Hampstead houses where felons could be 'secured' overnight, before police stations were established. Ownership would give us grazing rights on the Heath. The top floor was level with the top of St Paul's Cathedral and there was an uninterrupted view, almost unchanged since the eighteenth century, down past gardens and small suburbs to the City. The view decided me. Promising Henry that should he ever need it, one of the bedrooms was his, I put in a bid for £13,500, which we didn't have, and dumped the problem of paying for it in Jules's lap.

O'Toole wrote wonderful letters from the desert – I wished I were there (maybe I would never return, I thought). I had left the RSC, as requested, and got myself a West End play produced by Peter Bridge. It was called *Lizard on the Rock*, written by John Hall, and was due to open in the West End in seven weeks' time and who knew when it would end? It didn't occur to me to take time off. Harry Andrews and Anthony Oliver were my leading men, and it was a lovely company throughout that pitched in to help me when we went on the road, and Kate – eighteen months old and now walking – came along as well, as did Marianne.

Kate had a badly 'wandering' eye, so she wore patches and thick pebble glasses and had to endure her daily eye exercises. All the actors were careful with their language when she was around, solemn and adorable-looking with her owl-eyes.

However, on our last week on tour we walked into our bedroom and the first thing she did was to go over to the bed and test it for the quality of its mattress. 'Good,' she approved and then, dropping her little toy satchel, said cheerily, 'Oh fuck,' as she picked it up. Not a very good start, I thought. I looked at her, busying herself with settling into the room, and thought regretfully that maybe we should abandon the 'born-in-a-trunk' existence and establish a more conventional life and vocabulary for her.

The house is bought! I don't even *ask* Jules how he managed it. Joyce will help me 'do' it while I'm in the play. O'Toole will come home for a break in September and I'd like at least a part of it to be ready for him. Meanwhile our lease is up at the mews and Marie Kean – who is working in London – Marianne, Kate and myself move temporarily to an apartment in a large building on the Edgware Road. It's hot and the noise with the window open is deafening. We keep it shut and swelter. I tread a path between the Phoenix Theatre, Heath Street in Hampstead and this very strange building on the Edgware Road. It *looks* quite grand but there's something odd about it. The corridors are spacious, the elevator doors elaborately decorated, but one morning the whole of the front large elevator has been removed and is lying across the corridor. There *was* a bump in the night, but now there's no one about. It's a bit like being on a sinister movie set.

The play has not, alas, been well received. It's the tail-end of a verse-revival that began with Christopher Fry and continued with T.S. Eliot. The action takes place in Australia and as usual I have to toil away extra hard to achieve a tolerably presentable accent. Australians who see the play say, '*You* are what we sound like! People always exaggerate the sound of Australians.' My friends with good accents seethe.

As Heath Street was built and lived in for a long time by a family called de Guyon, I rename it 'Guyon House'. The last owner was the writer, E. Arnot Robertson, whose best-known book was *Ordinary Families*. Happily married to her sailing husband for the whole of her adult life, when he died it's said she lost her will to live and her death was unhappy. The price of the house reflected this sad event. The dining room and the master bedroom are lovely, the stairwell is beautiful, but every other room (and there are lots of them) is a bed-sitter with a Baby Belling cooker and a sink. I keep meeting actors who've lived in the house. It's a piece of old Hampstead and in a way I'm rather reluctant to start dismantling and clearing it out, restoring the fireplaces and making up-to-date bathrooms.

The kitchen, which lets on to the garden, has the same beautiful bowed wall that rises almost to the top of the house, and every deep window ledge, three to each floor, is piled high with bundles of letters and I long to start reading them but don't. One day when I go up to measure something or other, Mrs Robertson's son is building a bonfire in the garden – a bonfire of letters. Now I wish I'd stolen just one bundle.

Restoring the house is going to be a massive job – expensive as well. I wonder how long it's going to take me. 'Six months?' I enquire. Joyce Buck, who is going to help me, looks at me pityingly. 'It takes about five years to do a house like this properly.' Five years? Nineteen sixty-five before I'm through? I can't believe it. I questioned my other mentor in matters of building and decorating – Ricky, John Huston's wife, who has just spent an age 'doing' St Clerans near Galway, one of the most beautiful houses in Europe, where I holidayed before Kate was born. She looked at Number 98 and said, 'You should be through in five years.'

As usual, I hadn't thought through the practicalities of what I was up to. Now I began to learn about plumbing – *American* plumbing, plumbing that *worked* – wiring, lighting, how to recognise a good bit of furniture at the bottom of a pile of rubbish, learning what needed to be fixed, who could do the fixing, who was best at making lined, interlined, weighted curtains, where to find the best lamp makers, lamp*shade* makers. There was a never-ending list of things to be learned. And if something wasn't right, whereas my inclination would be to say wearily, 'Oh, I'll put a plant in front of it; it won't show,' Joyce made me take it back and have it redone. Ricky Huston even criticised the look of the forty door hinges I'd bought, and I had to take them all back and start another search for the perfect hinge. I was grateful for all the help and all the lessons, but I was completely exhausted all the time because I was acting, as well.

Marie, Kate, Marianne and I moved into the house in despair that it would ever get finished. There wasn't a window that closed or a door that locked, but none of us felt nervous; NW3 was a civilised, safe place. The nursery was finished – a beautiful Vie Bohème apartment at the top of the house, furnished, carpeted and curtained with a new bathroom and kitchen and sitting room and balcony and the view to St Paul's. Kate and her nanny, Marianne, were installed in style, while Marie and I put our beds in adjacent rooms on the floor below and camped out. The play was over but I was still busy, now doing television. One morning – having done a gruelling, taped performance of a Shaw play with Cyril Cusack and Alan Badel at Granada the night before (it cost a fortune to stop the tape so you had to try to keep going), I was awakened in my empty room in Hampstead by Joyce saying, 'Come on, come on! We're supposed to be in the Fulham Road looking at dressers in forty minutes.' I moved in a daze from antique shops to little basements full of promising treasures, to rehearsal rooms, to studios.

My best moments that summer were spent at the BBC in Portland Place. Martin Esslin was presenting modern European plays and I was in quite a few of them and made my first acquaintance with Genet and Ionesco and Marguerite Duras. I couldn't believe my luck when I read that I was to play *The Afternoon of M. Andesmas* with Ernest Milton. We had a wonderful time together and I couldn't get over that amazing voice, which I'd heard imitated by so many actors. *There* it was in the flesh and I was talking to it! He'd taught O'Toole at RADA, where he was adored by all the tearaway, young actors. He was a wonderful actor himself and had been an exquisite young man, but, old now, he was undeniably, incredibly 'mannered'. O'Toole had seen him outside RADA in Gower Street chasing after a bus, crying, 'Staap! S t a a p! You're killing a genius!' I was very nervous around him at first, but in no time at all we were sharing Chinese meals – still a bit of a novelty for me – in a restaurant on the first floor of a building above Boots in Piccadilly Circus. I'd always been fond of the company of elderly gentlemen and he came high on my list of Fascinating Old Men.

Life was good in Guyon House. The fine weather meant it didn't matter that the whole place was in uproar. Kate had her lovely flat and the rest of the house was an adventure playground for her – the garden was a wilderness and we began to explore the little streets behind the house. I bought a little boat for us to sail on Whetstone Pond. There was work to do at every turn, but there was also calm, and Jules and Joyce saw to it that Marie and I saw a bit of high life as well. We were taken to the new White Elephant restaurant in Curzon Street – opened, so it was said, so a few prominent actors, Albert Finney among them, could dine in style *without wearing ties* (extraordinary in 1961). Life was changing; there was a wave of Italian restaurants. The owners and *maître d's* became as famous as pop stars, Leslie Linder at The Elephant, Mario and Franco in Soho and later all over the West End, were the top of the heap.

I was changing a little as well. I realised that my clothes weren't good enough for my social life. Marie laughed sardonically when she recalled how in the early days of our relationship with Jules and Joyce, I got 'decked out', as she called it, in my only 'good' dress, a white shirtwaister from Jane & Jane with ropes of beads from a department store and high-heeled gold shoes from Pinet. As I arrived at the Bucks' front door, Jules greeted me warmly and innocently called up the stairs, 'Joyce, don't dress, honey.' I felt I'd better do something about my appearance, but it wasn't easy. My head was faultless; my producer, Peter Bridge sent me to a new salon in Bond Street, owned by Vidal Sassoon, for a haircut and colour job for *The Lizard on the Rock*. Vidal chopped off my perm and I emerged with dark red hair. (The author had specified smoky and I couldn't quite work out the connection, but Vidal Sassoon was extremely confident and no one dared to argue with him.) I now had straight hair. Oddly enough, it looked just like that of my first form mistress, Miss Inkin, the person I'd most wanted to resemble when I was a little girl. (She *had* been ahead of her time in those days of upswept rolls and permanents.) Joyce Buck took me to a tailor, who made me some plain dresses and jackets. I bought *plain* brown court shoes from Pinet. A *plain* black bag from Hermes, *plain* gloves from Harrods. Then, I discovered, at Liberty, clothes that I really liked; American clothes by a designer called Bonnie Cashin, wonderful, soft, unlined tweed, piped in coloured suede; canvas sports clothes, piped or edged in leather; swingy leather coats; cashmere sweaters with hoods; bean-bag caps in wonderful colours. I wasn't dressed '*up*' but I was *well-dressed* in a way I liked. Evening clothes would just have to wait until I had more time and more money. Money was a bit of a problem. Every cent I earned was going into running the small household of women and dressing myself and taking taxis, a vice I wasn't to cure for many years to come.

One morning, as I was nervously setting out to make a recording of *Measure for Measure* with Eric Portman, I opened the morning post to realise that I just couldn't pay all the household bills that month. I stood at the top of the big house and was suddenly appalled by its size, and by the number of workmen scrambling around in it. Kate and Marianne sat at the breakfast table. How had I imagined all this was going to be maintained? I called Jules and, to my astonishment, he was completely unfazed and mightily reassuring, and he said, 'And, of course, you should have an allowance.' Well! He – or rather, our office – would take care of the major building and decorating expenses and I would receive £60 a week with which to run our lives. I was completely enchanted and never thought to change that magic sum of unearned money which came my way henceforward. For the next twenty years I spent £40 on the house and each week I kept £20 of it for myself and thought myself very fortunate.

At work that week I was rather depressed. Eric Portman gave me his terrible cold. I *had* to show up, but he didn't always show up, and I lay under a grand piano nursing my temperature. Fortunately, I'd played Isabella in *Made for Measure* at RADA, so I knew it quite well. When he did come to work, he gave the impression of being overwhelmingly sad and I was glad when the job was over. Not for the first time I reflected that doing a part more than once was really difficult. If one had been – or thought one had been – good the first time round, one was very loath to alter the 'good' bits to suit a new production. If one hadn't been good in the part there was a feeling of desperation in the effort to get it right the second time around.

Months had gone by since I'd left Arabia. O'Toole and I had kept up an intense correspondence, but we longed to see each other and he arranged my return. I took Kate down to my parents in Wales and left London as soon as I could. I was to fly out with Anthony Nutting and go straight to the canvas village in El Jaffre. El Jaffre, the huge, mercilessly hot plain, which made Tubeiq seem almost hospitable by comparison. My parents were overjoyed to be getting Kate again, the building works were coming along nicely, and Joyce was spending a large part of every week in Hampstead overseeing the Irish team of builders. She never bought a spoon or a cushion or a table without taking me to see twenty spoons, cushions and tables and making me choose. I don't know where she found the patience. Slowly, I learned from her and soon my choices earned an approving nod from her. I was a good pupil but she was a wonderful teacher.

This time round, the Middle East was even more enthralling than I'd remembered it to be. Many members of the unit had disappeared, but the stalwarts were very much in evidence, thinner, more weather-beaten, and more determined than ever to see this film through to the end. O'Toole was more assured and he looked magnificent. He'd been having daily master classes in film-making from David Lean. (This job must be the equivalent of twenty ordinary ones.) Still there was A.G. Scott (Scottie the Hair), successfully translated from Mayfair and in charge of the bleaching and straightening, still dapper and well-dressed; Charlie Parker, head of make-up, still cussing and feuding, being brilliant and impossible at the same time; Eddie and Dave Fowley, indomitable, calm as though they were making a film on the back lot at Shepperton. Leila Lean was banished alas – her concrete bunker, never visited by David, was now occupied by an actor. We also were installed in a bunker at base and O'Toole had acquired a kind of 'body servant' Shwfti (what was his real name?). He would say, craftily, 'Shufti – *Mufti-Klefti*' (I see – I steal). It was hard to make life comfortable, even in a small way, and Shwfti would 'see and steal' little things to make our life cosier. He was a handsome boy, adept at killing vermin and keeping his eyes and ears open. Little happened in the camp that wasn't reported to O'Toole by Shwfti. He didn't travel into the desert and then I was glad of a reprieve from his constant twenty-four-hours-a-day presence, serving us, spoiling us, organising us, guarding our door day and night. O'Toole didn't seem to notice him, but I was always aware of those inquisitive little brown eyes intent on interpreting our smallest change of expression. There were times when I couldn't accompany O'Toole to work and then, to get away from Shwfti, I would sit on the deserted beach reading or playing the guitar. If I was very still I would quickly become surrounded by hundreds of tiny sand-crabs. A deep sigh on my part was enough to make them disappear in two seconds. Eilat, across the bay, was pushing upwards; each night one could see more neon signs than before. The climate here on the Red Sea made life difficult, so they must be spending a fortune on air-conditioning, unknown on this, the Arab side of the barbed wire.

One day as I watched the filming, we were all crouched under umbrellas or in the shade of trucks while O'Toole, dressed in heavy khaki, sat mounted all day in the intolerable heat doing the same scene alone, time after time after time. No one knew *why* it was being retaken. No one could ask. The director was always God. I've heard that, great though David was, he liked to enhance his power by breaking down his leading actors, and when they were broken, build them up again so they became grateful or dependent. No one moved in this vast, silent landscape, but I saw a few of the old hands exchange knowing glances. It did begin to look as though this was O'Toole's day for being broken down. I sat there under a truck knowing that O'Toole was *never* going to be broken down in this way. Calm and contained, he turned his animal and walked back along the camera track and waited patiently for the word 'Action'. Each take was faultless. Scotty looked pained. Even Charlie was subdued as he checked the make-up and walked slowly back to the unit, so far away from that solitary figure sitting alone in the hateful sun. Some eight hours later there was a simple word: 'Wrap'. It was the end of the day's work. O'Toole slid down from his horse and walked stiffly towards his jeep, parked in the distance. Everyone looked depressed. It had been a murderous day of unspoken conflict. Suddenly, I was compelled to run after David walking back to his vehicle. I didn't know him – I had hardly ever spoken to him. 'What in the name of God was all that about?' I demanded. His handsome face contorted as he replied, 'Actors! Actors! They have the easiest job going. Who gets here first in the morning? The technicians! And who gets the glory? Actors!' There was nothing to say to that and anyway I was now appalled by my cheek in ticking off a genius. We walked away from each other and I joined O'Toole in his jeep. He didn't ask what had occurred between me and David and I didn't tell him. I put my arm around his shoulders. Two things were clear to me suddenly. I couldn't bear to see him being badly treated, especially not at work where he was entirely correct in his behaviour, and second, he had put me through so much that I had no fear of anyone. I had heard him say, 'I've been worked over by experts'; well, so had I now. No one would ever be able to try me as he, the expert, had done. But now it was just a matter of getting through the evening quietly before he had to resume the fight tomorrow.

On the morrow, there was no fight. Work flowed enjoyably. David and O'Toole were sunny and the unit blossomed. Showbusiness . . . When I was last here I was asked to help Maurice Ronet (the French actor who was to play Ali) with his English. David wanted him to play a scene on camera with Omar Sharif – newly arrived from Egypt. What no one knew was that Omar was to be looked at for the part Maurice had been engaged to play. David loved Omar and Maurice was dismissed (with $30,000, I was told. Seemed like a *lot* of money to me). O'Toole christened Omar 'Cairo Fred' and they were by now firm friends. They were the constant elements in the picture, but all the big stars arrived to play supporting parts and O'Toole said he felt like a boxer waiting in the ring for the new heavyweight champ to show up. Anthony Quinn arrived and borrowed my eyelash curlers. He was on the run from a buxom blonde who pursued him all the way to Aqaba, God knows how she managed it. (I'm not sure that she didn't eventually succeed in getting him to the altar.) Things were altering at base. It was becoming clear in the film world that something extraordinary was going on and visitors began to arrive, never staying for more than a few days, with the notable exception of George Plimpton, who actually tried riding a camel.

Out in the desert everything remained inviolate – David saw to that. He and Barbara, the continuity girl, were, by now, living together. He and Barbara and Freddie Young, the brilliant lighting cameraman, formed part of a private nucleus in the huge unit. John Box, the designer, was another member of the closed circle. Every time I was around John I would pick up the crumpled drawings he discarded and threw away – wonderful drawings and watercolours which I straightened and ironed and packed away for framing at home.

There were wonders every day which I could hardly believe. In El Jaffre, the route to work was signposted by mirages, which never changed from day to day. The jeep travelled mile after mile over the chalk-white ground 'crazed' from the dry heat, and when one saw 'Westminster Abbey' up ahead, one bore east until one came to 'The Lake' and turned north past 'Dickins & Jones' until one saw the real trucks and the real location. The landmarks remained constant, more real than reality. The silence of the movie set was always alarmingly wonderful. Everyone strained not to allow any of the detritus of our living arrangements to escape. A single paper cup rolling away across a virgin distant sand-dune to be retrieved on foot was enough to stop work for hours. David and Freddie squinted at the sky and waited and waited for everything to be perfect, while Sam Spiegel became mad with fury at the measured pace of filming. And, of course, he couldn't come into Arabia to see what was going on. David smiled evilly and sat in his chair happily waiting, waiting.

We took a short break in Beirut. The morning after we arrived in that most glamorous of cities, I leaned out of my hotel window and in the street below two men from the surrounding hills shot a young girl, a family member who'd brought disgrace on them by descending to a life of sin in the big city. 'What'll happen to them?' 'Nothing, it's their right.'

The Middle Eastern correspondent of the *Daily Mail* was someone O'Toole had known on *The Yorkshire Post* and we were invited to a drinks party in his flat. We passed a very pleasant hour or so and only afterwards did I have reason to remember a quiet chap we'd been introduced to that night – Kim Philby. It was unsettling, being in a city, and I was glad to return to the desert. When I left Jordan this time I knew that I was unlikely to return. I realised that I'd rarely been happier, anywhere.

The month in the Middle East had gone by very quickly and I missed O'Toole, but equally I missed the smells and tastes of the Middle East, and I missed the never-ending music incomprehensibly going on and on – and on. I didn't need reminding that if I wasn't married to O'Toole and if he didn't wish to have me with him, I would never have experienced this adventure. I did, however, have an unexpected legacy from Arabia when I was suddenly presented with the ultimate in what I called Petruchio's servants, people who were undoubtedly good at something, but absolutely useless at what they had been engaged to do. When O'Toole finished in the desert, he determined to *do* something for Shwfti and contrived to send him to live with me and Kate and Marianne. To what end I had no idea. The house didn't suit him, our meals didn't suit him; he slept in Kate's small bedroom with a scimitar under his pillow. After the show I would return to find the small sitting room out of bounds to me as he lay, unsmiling, smoking on the hearth rug. His cigarettes smelled strange. One day, before a matinée when I'd cooked and cleared away lunch, I said, 'Shwfti, during the afternoon could you please wash the dishes for me?' He looked up from his favourite spot on the hearth rug and made no response. Holding the look between us, he slowly closed his hand on the wine glass he was holding and red wine and blood trickled down his wrist. There wasn't time to stop and discuss this new development in our relationship, so I left for the theatre without another word. After that, mindful that to him I was a mere woman, I was tentative in my dealings with him. He began to explore London. I had no idea what he got up to, but was relieved when a few weeks later he was picked up in Soho, arrested for drug dealing and deported. He was never mentioned again, the scimitar was tidied away and we repossessed the sitting room, which smelled once again of Virginia tobacco.

The Hampstead house is progressing. Life is changing rapidly. People are taking an excessive interest in us as a family. One day I walk into an empty second-floor room in Guyon House and find a journalist and a photographer poking about in a cupboard. The phone rings all the time with requests for photo sessions and interviews. The house, we are agreed, is not to become the subject of magazine layouts. For one thing, O'Toole has begun to acquire art and the last thing we want to do is advertise to burglars that this might be a likely place into which to break and enter. Also, we want Kate to have a private life untroubled by publicity. Columbia Pictures' publicists are jumping up and down with irritation. I now have enough of the house done for O'Toole on his return to have a room in which to talk to people, a room with a bed where we can sleep, a front door that locks, and for meals we'll just have to use the nursery kitchen or have picnics. Mercifully, food does not loom large on his domestic horizon.

On 28 September Sam shut down the production of *Lawrence* in Jordan. David was dismayed; there were many wonderful locations, Petra included, that would never now be used. And the charge at Aqaba would be the charge at – well, somewhere in Spain. The suspension of business was all to do with money and – contrary to popular belief – had nothing to do with screenwriter Robert Bolt's imprisonment; he was jailed in September 1961 after a CND demonstration in Trafalgar Square. It wasn't a horrible experience being jailed as he was in an open prison, but they wouldn't let him write, so it wasn't very convenient and, besides, Sam wanted Bob at his beck and call. He tried to persuade Jo Bolt, Robert's first wife, to cajole Bob out of jail. Little did he know that Jo had conceived a rich and abiding hatred of him and his way of life, and what it might do to their life (hers and Bob's). Finally, Sam convinced Bob that the entire unit would be thrown out of work if he didn't allow himself to be sprung. Shoulder to shoulder with the workers, Robert allowed Sam to secure his release and I don't think he ever got over the mortification of realising that he'd been 'Spiegelised'. His release was convenient for Sam and that was all. It earned him Jo's contempt and made him feel thoroughly guilty. Meanwhile the picture closed down in Jordan simply because Sam wanted it moved.

Activity at the house accelerates as O'Toole is expected home for a break. Everyone is feeling the strain. I desperately want him to be pleased with what I've done. This is our first real home and after a bad start our life together has moved, imperceptibly but surely, into calmer waters. And I've made a friend. (Marie doesn't count. She is more like family.) During the run of *The Lizard on the Rock* throughout my visits to Vidal Sassoon I'm looked after by a young man; years my junior, still in his teens, but almost from our first meeting I sense that Ricci Burns is a friend – a potential friend anyhow. The changeable circumstances of my life make me slow to admit anyone beyond a certain point, but I suppose only children always have their antennae out for potential brothers and sisters. Ricky feels like a potential brother. He seems to read my mind. He makes me laugh. He's smart where I'm naïve. He has a terrific sense of style. He's brutally honest with me but he's on my side. I'm immensely cheered to see him always. I think I'll keep him to myself for a while.

The homecoming is a stupendous success. The bags are laden with robes and coffee pots in three sizes and brass pestles and mortars for crushing cardamom seeds for future Arabic coffee (never made). There's beautiful, bad-quality glass that breaks almost at once. O'Toole is bigger and handsomer than ever – he looks absurdly fit and if Kate doesn't really know who this is, like the rest of us she's fascinated and excited. We all want to touch him. The builders have stayed behind and share a glass of champagne with us as everything is inspected and admired. I have a feeling O'Toole at this moment is taking in little if any of the detail of plans for the rest of the house, but we're all pleased and happy. What must it be like for him to be back in England after all these months and still only halfway through this huge job? There's a break of at least four weeks and he'll have to keep everything bubbling in his mind in spite of the long pause and the inevitable distractions of London life.

After a few days' rest he begins to examine the house more closely and he falls in love with it; I can tell. Because of the complications of replumbing the old house, we've had to push many of the central heating pipes that festooned the dining-room ceiling up into the room above and Joyce has had the notion of building a platform over them. This becomes the 'stage' and the room becomes the actors' Green Room. It's also known as the Marcus Luccicos room and there is a plaque on the door commemorating the character in *Othello* who is mentioned once, never appears and has no lines. Already it's the most used room in the house.

With one or two hiccups, he and I have been getting on better than I could have imagined during our Warwickshire life. I had not dared to hope that we could be as happy as this and the house seems to set the seal on this exciting, light-hearted phase in our life together. He runs up the ninety-seven stairs several times a day, revelling in the beautiful eighteenth-century stairwell. We have an uncomplicated month together, the three of us, and then it's time for him to leave again. I tell myself that this is no more difficult than the life of hundreds of servicemen's wives. If I want to work and let Kate have a settled life then I have to learn to deal with separations.

When he resumes it is in Spain and as soon as I am able I visit him in Seville. My mother takes care of Kate again. Now he's surrounded by actors – Claude Rains, Jack Hawkins, Alec Guinness. There are infantile, highly enjoyable unit jokes based on the 'th' sound in the Castilian dialect. They stay at the Alfontho Trethi, and Alec Guinness, encountered in the street on Sunday morning and on being asked where he's been so early, replies sonorously, 'Confethione'. They're all happy to be acting in the interior scenes. The unit, after the rigours of Arabia, is ecstatic to be what they call 'ashore'. Sherry is a penny-halfpenny a glass. For ten shillings (fifty pence) you can eat as many prawns as you are able and finish the evening blind drunk as well. There are a few catastrophes at work; men in the grip of ferocious hangovers fall off ladders and are sent home. Only the wild men on the unit regret the hardship and the beauty they've left behind in Arabia. I feel that David Lean is one of them.

O'Toole can see now that the film is going to absorb two years of his life. This is an unusually long time and the strain on him and indirectly on me is considerable. He is having to maintain concentration and immaculately good behaviour while coming to terms with the fact that his status is altering by the month and that the rewards – or recriminations – lying in wait are, in the world of entertainment, huge. I have a foot in two camps and make a quick adjustment to a way of life that will persist; one that combines the extremely ordinary business of shopping and cleaning and stripping and mending furniture and spending my hours in very unglamorous theatres and TV rehearsal rooms with occasional well-dressed, chauffeur-driven forays into a much grander sphere. Mrs O'Toole is treated very differently from Miss Phillips. I learn to take it as it comes. Ever a realist, I am not bothered either when people jostle me out of the way in their need to get near the rising star. I did object when little Gina Lollobrigida actually put her stiletto heel through the arch of my foot in her hurtling frenzy. Unrecognised and unacknowledged, some moments later in O'Toole's dressing room I handed her a quadruple single malt whisky and watched happily as, gulping unthinkingly, her eyes began to roll, and I took a malicious delight in reading that she'd been unable to turn up for work the following day because of a 'virus'. Ordinarily, I was all sweetness and understanding, but she managed to get on my nerves.

I can hardly believe that, in spite of the unusual circumstances (or maybe because of them) our life has become so harmonious. Our times together are both hilarious and tranquil – not for a year had there been a mention of my Past. Did that mean it was forgotten for good? I didn't dare to relax my guard completely, but nor did I allow the small fear to spoil the present. There is no one else I would prefer to be with. We talk and talk and talk again as we used to. That was what I missed most during our estrangement, the interrupted conversation. Of course, now from time to time our conversations have to continue on paper, and he writes such wonderful letters that I am almost reconciled to the separations. Some of the letters are written in pencil and the writing grows faint with re-reading.

No Christmas leave for the *Lawrence* unit. I have work to do and I take Kate to Wales and try to be cheerful for her sake. We do eye exercises daily, but the eyes are not improving. It hasn't been nearly as much fun, working on the house in the cold and dark of winter. Marianne has left for home and I embark on a series of mostly awful nannies. Now that we're becoming famous, some girls come for the interview just to have a look at the house; one stays overnight and is gone when we wake in the morning. Because of the lack of good help, leaving home is becoming a problem and much of my TV work is at Granada, Manchester, which has the most adventurous TV drama department in the country. I worry all the time and hurry home the minute work is over. All the young mothers I meet tell me horror stories about unreliable nannies. I don't really know how long I can go on like this and I think I am going to have to work only in and around London. Before that I solve the problem temporarily by asking my parents to take Kate to Spain to visit her father. They can all holiday and I can go on working without having to worry about child-minding. When they go south to Marbella, my father, handsome still, has a lovely time at a bullfight with glamorous April Ashley, later Lady Rowallan. O'Toole didn't spoil everything at that moment by telling him – as April herself would have done, given time – that she had begun life as seaman George Jameson. April – a really good sort – was adorable and put herself out to entertain my unworldly father.

Later in the year I spent a few weeks in Almeria, where Columbia filmed the charge at Aqaba. O'Toole and Omar had rented a frightful house full of hideous religious objects; there were figures of saints with seeping, lit-up bloody wounds, a sacred heart that pulsated. Every classical statue in the house had its sex organs removed. Living there was unnerving. Robert Bolt was the brightest presence. In spite of the rigours of working for Sam – and he did hate being 'Spiegelised' – he maintained his good manners and his good sense. His marriage was in difficulties, however, as was Omar's, whose sister had come to join us in Nightmare Towers. There was a strange mother and daughter duo there as well, the sort of people who trail around in the wake of film crews and one is never quite sure how they pitched up or why. The Twist had begun to sweep the world and everyone in the house practised it day and night. The noise was deafening, and that and the lack of privacy made me long for escape, which we did briefly to a charming little place called Torremolinos. Sitting in a restaurant on a cliff, we saw a British ship sail in. Taxiing down to the coast, we waved and waved until someone sent a boat for us and we had a lovely afternoon and evening in the bosom of the Navy. What is it about sailors that makes them the best of all hosts?

I didn't want to leave O'Toole, but I was glad to leave the overcrowded house in Almeria. With the exception of the trip to Torremolinos and meeting April and catching up with the Navy, it hadn't been a successful visit. O'Toole had been distracted, or tired or worried or bored, who could tell? Any of these would have been understandable, but I had not yet learned to stand apart emotionally and I was hopelessly affected by his moods. Now that we had become so close again I could not bear the occasions when we were not of one mind and heart. He was as bad as I was; absurdly possessive and jealous of my attention. My unthinking, polite response to another man, no matter how unprepossessing, caused him distress, so I learned to tailor my behaviour to the occasion. It wasn't difficult.

I'm told that Columbia Films is spending millions of dollars on O'Toole's publicity. Can this be true? It seems an incredible amount of money. Jules is convulsed with mirth when we discuss this. 'What's so funny?' 'Never mind, kid.' I *do* mind. It's lonely once Kate has gone to bed. Marie has gone back to work in Dublin. Almost all the Irish actors I know have a cut-off point beyond which they do not care to stay in England and three months is the most that Marie seems able to endure. Alone in the building site at Number 98 I keep busy, acting in television. There isn't a commercial play I like and the Royal Shakespeare Company is now out of my reach. People say, 'You're always busy. You're so lucky.' No, I'm not. There is a world of difference between being courted, chased after, getting first bite of the cherry, and keeping busy, mopping up the crumbs that fall from the big table. I think – no, I know that during the last year or two I've missed some big chances and have missed them because of my character, or a lack of it. Will I get another chance? I doubt it. Life isn't that sweet. The best I can do now is to persist somehow. Nothing will make me give up that first childhood resolve to be an actress, but I'm going to have to be a quiet sort of actress. It may be that I shan't succeed in being any sort of actress at all, but I'm going to try. I see clearly that all the career mistakes I have made I would probably make again, so I have to accept that my life is going to be problematical and the problems are of my own making. This doesn't make me feel better.

Chapter Seventeen

Because of work and my need to be at home with Kate, I didn't visit O'Toole when the unit moved for a brief time to Morocco. I wasn't to see him again until he returned to England – we were reunited in the early autumn of 1962. The foreign locations are over at last. The remainder of the film will be shot in England. There's been a stupendous homecoming – the hall looks like a souk, he's been shopping in Morocco. There are piled-up carpets everywhere, one of them so big it will only fit into the big, empty first-floor drawing room; there are robes from Ouarzazate, and Kate and I sit there covered in luxury, speechless. 'God has come home.' It is heavenly.

Joyce and I have made a ravishingly beautiful bedroom on the first-floor back; walls upholstered in rough grey and off-white silk fabric, dim gilded lights, dull, gold-curtained windows, a beautiful Louis XIV desk in the Georgian bay – she's made me walk all over London for six months before settling on this one. I've found there is a 'fair' price for a good piece of furniture. There's no such thing as a bargain, but some pieces are marginally nicer than others, marginally cheaper too. I've looked at scores of desks, including the supreme examples at the Wallace Collection, and this is the best one going at £400, and I'm so keen on it I pay for it out of my most recent fee. It's almost an object of devotion for me; dark red wood inlaid with dull metal strips, the top pulling out to seven feet wide. I lie in bed and look at it and wonder at it, so plain and so beautiful. In a junk shop just off Gower Street I acquire a Louis XV chaise-longue in bad shape and have it done up, and with a couple of plain English eighteenth-century night tables at the bedside and plain lamps and a huge, spectacular bedhead made out of a semi-circular picture frame picked up on a pavement in the King's Road for £40, mended and upholstered with a pad covered with the wall fabric. I'm in the perfect bedroom business all right. Once inside that door there is total tranquillity. He's *got* to love it. He does.

Our bedroom sits behind the first-floor drawing room, which is a big empty shell. There's no money left to do anything to it at present. I can't mess about with the structure of this pretty house to produce an en-suite bathroom (so desirable these days), as it would destroy the proportion of the first floor, so our bathroom is on the second floor and it's quite beautiful – but it does involve a run up the stairs. O'Toole decides that he'd prefer his own bathroom, which means running *down* the stairs to the newly made ground-floor shower room. We've shared so little domestic life together and I realise that he doesn't see me getting made up and I don't see him shaving, and this seems just fine to me. In many ways we're too close for comfort and this bit of apartness is welcome. The happiness of our time together in Jordan, in the Lebanon and in Spain was no illusion. In grey, damp Hampstead I can tell that we have turned a corner and we are truly happy.

Elated by our good fortune, we decide to have another child and I become pregnant at once. (Thank God for contraception, I breathe, yet again.) I am still unsure what the future holds. The film is not finished and already our life has changed utterly. We're invited everywhere but we don't go anywhere much. Every day there are requests for interviews, photographs; hardly any are granted. We lead a quiet life with very occasional forays into society. People come to us.

It was at home in Hampstead that I first met Rudolf Nureyev. He was presented to us by the writer, Eric Braun, as a brilliant, homeless waif. 'Not quite,' I thought as the slight figure pursed his lips dramatically and raised his hand to his heart and *retreated* a few steps, instead of advancing to take my hand, outstretched in greeting. He struck a pose, standing in the Green Room with his back to the window overlooking New End Hospital's Men's Surgical. 'The kind of woman who gets me into trouble,' he said to the interpreter, throwing his head back and watching my reaction, which was to smile, shifting my feet awkwardly. I wasn't embarrassed for me. I was embarrassed for him; he was too theatrical by half. Nureyev swooped forward and kissed my hand and, at that moment, the door opened and O'Toole entered. Rudi dropped my hand like a used hankie and it was *his* turn to smile and shuffle and come over girlish as he fell under the scrutiny of a pair of eyes every bit as potent and confident as his own. We knew next to nothing of the ballet and meeting Nureyev was like encountering an exotic, amusing animal – a bit of a show-off.

Nothing could have prepared us for our next meeting after he had rapidly become the huge star and partner of Margot Fonteyn. One didn't need to know anything about the ballet to realise that he was phenomenal. One didn't need to like ballet to love watching him, much as one could be enthralled by watching Cassius Clay in the ring while knowing nothing and caring less about boxing. Rudi conquered society as well as the theatre, and the way in which he exerted his social power was a measure of a rapidly changing social structure. Young Turks could get away with anything in the Sixties.

At a dinner given in Belgravia there was considerable excitement among the ladies because Nureyev was due to come on after a performance. It was a cold night of frost and snow. He arrived when we were still at the table, he swathed in woollen scarves and sweaters and carrying a duffel bag full of dirty practice clothes, which he dropped in the dining room, making for the drinks tray and picking up a small-ish bottle of plum brandy, which he lifted to his lips. The large throat opened and relaxed like a singer's and he drained the bottle in what seemed like seconds while we all watched in silence. The room was, not exactly frozen – everyone was too delighted – but it was halted, wrong-footed; there were glad cries of welcome, some only half uttered; people had begun to rise, but didn't know if they should continue. Rudi's next move completed the confusion. He seemed to levitate on to the table and, slightly smiling, he danced down its length, sure-footed and dignified, extending his arms and deftly but forcefully lifting off a postiche here, a topknot of ringlets there. The cries of alarm and anguish were overlaid with uncertain laughter. The ladies were going to love and appreciate him no matter what he did to them. I wondered what O'Toole – no stranger to the outrageous – was making of this new Rudi. Margot had also arrived, perfectly groomed, smiling and imperturbable as though Rudi's behaviour was the most natural thing in the world. I was pregnant and wearing a heavy, green Dior velvet dress and jacket, trimmed at collar and cuffs with heavy jet beads. The heat and the excitement proved too much and as I stood chatting to Margot I knew I was going to faint, faint right on to her, squashing her flat. As I began to fall, I felt someone catch me and when I regained consciousness I was floating in a stair-well and I realised after a moment that Rudi was carrying me above his head. He was drunk and I weighed a ton, what with the unborn Pat and yards and yards of expensive Christian Dior, lined, interlined and beaded. There seemed to be a little procession. O'Toole and Margot followed us and they in turn were followed by a few ladies who, slightly unnerved, decided to leave us in a very pretty nursery, upholstered and curtained in pale, grey *toile de jouy*. I recovered and we chatted for a while until Rudi began to throw up violently. I don't think he missed a wall, a chair or a piece of carpet. Margot and I looked on while O'Toole came into his own. The great dancer was as drunk as a skunk and needed to be packed off home. Rudi wanted to curl up and sleep. 'Come on, mush,' barked O'Toole, 'you can't sleep on the town hall steps. Here we go,' and seizing him by the legs he began to bump him down the thickly carpeted stairs. Rudi seemed perfectly happy with this method of descent, but in the hall below there were anguished cries of 'Be *careful* with him', 'Take care of his *feet*.' 'To hell with his fucking feet,' muttered O'Toole as Rudi giggled to himself, and louder, 'Just get us a cab.' As we negotiated the icy pavement, the assembled diners called out with more pleas for caution with the precious feet. Margot and I tiptoed behind the ungainly, slipping, lurching couple ahead. Rudi was angelic in the cab; smiling, well content with his evening, delighted to be looked after so glamorously, wanting to kiss us all.

O'Toole and he went out on the town alone sometime later when the Twist was still at the height of its popularity. In Al Burnett's club they were dancing with a couple of hostesses and O'Toole heard the rather bored girl, gracelessly twisting near Rudi say, 'Are ya Polish?' 'No!' growled Rudi, concentrating on a very muscular bit of twisting. 'I am *Tarrtarr*.'

Sam had ordained that the film be ready for public viewing by December! David was inclined to argue that this was completely impossible, but Sam had craftily secured a Royal Première and since the Queen would attend, it had to be ready. A royal opening was important for the success of any movie. David was once a brilliant editor and *he had* a brilliant editor, Ann Coates, working with him now, but a large amount of the editing had already been done as he shot the film. He would, for example, cut in the camera to make it impossible for anyone to alter his concept. One day he asked O'Toole to casually move the cigarette to the 'wrong' hand during a scene which had been requested but which he didn't want used – the continuity was broken and the scene became useless. Even so, it was a mad rush and he moved a truckle bed into the cutting room and stayed there day and night.

I went to work on a modest TV film at Elstree, *This is Not King's Cross*; Michael Craig was one of my leading men. He drove a Jaguar and, sensing I was under some pressure, he kindly named himself 'Radio Jags' and became my personal cab company, picking me up in the morning and returning me to Hampstead every night. O'Toole was now fully occupied doing press and publicity. Jules still seemed to be nursing some private joke as he organised O'Toole's busy days. I joined Jules and Joyce and their daughter, Joan-Juliet, and Peter at night after my rehearsals. I went home to bed alone. I wasn't really a part of the circus. Not yet.

December 1962 and the only London pea-souper I remember. There must have been others but I didn't notice them. When we worked in North London, I rose early and walked from Heath Street to rehearsals at Swiss Cottage, clutching at the walls, unable to see my hand in front of my face. Sound was so muffled that one collided with people before becoming aware of another presence. Cars veered dangerously and silently on to the pavement. It was frightening but everyone was imbued with the spirit of the Blitz. Mich Craig slowly, slowly, drove me home at night. I had a beautiful brown woollen robe that O'Toole had brought me from Arabia and one night I went upstairs when it became obvious that he wasn't going to be coming home for dinner and lay on the bed reading until it was time to take off the big robe and go to sleep. No O'Toole. I was only a couple of months pregnant, but I was thankful for quiet times. (A non-appearance at dinner and no phone call didn't rate highly as a bad time.) I fell asleep and at five o'clock in the morning I was awakened by the telephone, always on my side of the bed. I looked around. Still no O'Toole. Picking up the phone I heard Uncle Davy's voice. In Welsh he said how sad he was to tell me that my father had just died in a hospital outside Cardiff. To my shame and surprise, I realised that I was feeling a flood of relief, before it was followed immediately by acute grief. I put the phone down and sat on the side of the huge bed looking at the wall. Cold, I pulled on my heavy robe. As I sat there I realised that I had spent my life worrying about my father. He had probably done the same for me. Neither of us had been able to do much for the other. He may have heaved a sigh of relief when I married O'Toole and became his responsibility (as men of that generation would think) and now, for a second, I had breathed relief and release. I felt bad, but I could understand why that feeling had come for a moment.

What to do now? I didn't know where O'Toole was and it was a measure of my acceptance of his need for freedom that I had no idea how I might reach him. He didn't carry identification, or keys, and hated to be contactable. I wasn't sure if this was a pose or a genuine wish to maintain a measure of liberation in a life that was becoming more and more constrained by approaching fame. Whatever the reason, this behaviour was part of the rules of the house and I didn't have too much trouble incorporating it into my life, though I did have mixed feelings when roused to respond to his insistent ringing on the doorbell in the early hours. But even then I thought there was something rather touching about his being so sure of his welcome. And I *did* always feel welcoming.

Now, calling Michael Craig, I left it to him to inform the company that I wouldn't be at rehearsals for a day or two and he volunteered to drive to Hampstead and get me through the fog to Paddington. I packed, went to the nursery to talk to the nanny and make sure that she could cope for a while; played with Kate – she had been adored by her grandfather – and I felt sad for her, unknowing that she'd lost a great, tall, handsome supporter from her little corner in life.

Mich Craig picked me up. I wrote a note to O'Toole and left for Paddington, Michael driving through the white wall of fog, to begin the long train journey to Wales. Oh those train journeys packed into claustrophobic compartments; no buffet, very little heat, no privacy. My father's death was such a shock I couldn't truly confront it. He'd been unwell and I'd brought him to London where Gerry Slattery had arranged a meeting with the Queen's heart specialist, a Welshman. 'Don't worry,' he'd said. 'Live normally, eat and drink whatever you'd like. Don't fuss.' 'There you go,' I'd added, briskly, willing him to be well and strong and willing him not to be ill, willing him not to die. 'Don't *fuss.*'

Lawrence of Arabia was due to open in a few days. Would I be there? O'Toole had bought me a dress in New York and amazingly it fitted; Joyce Buck had organised a coat to go over it. Ricky Huston had loaned me a reliquary to wear as jewellery and Ricci from Sassoon would do my hair. How? Where? I didn't care.

My mother was in black, observing the formalities, sitting alone while people came to pay their respects and talk of my father. I'd never seen the Welsh ceremony before and I was faintly and irrationally irritated by the formal demonstrations of grief. My mother *had* to look sad all day. There must have been moments when she would have liked to smile – but no – all was unrelieved gloom. Davy, her brother, was there, making arrangements and suddenly, out of nowhere, there was O'Toole. I was overwhelmed with relief. I adored him in the role of rescuing cavalry.

He'd found my note and, abandoning Columbia Pictures and the publicity machine, had hurtled down to Wales by taxi. His arrival changed everything and everyone for the better. My mother cheered up and resumed a little light cooking. Davy and O'Toole went to the pub and Davy looked uncharacteristically cheerful when he returned. Funeral arrangements speeded along, interspersed with little drinks (normally, unheard of), and then he was gone again to London. Before leaving he told my mother and Davy that I was pregnant, and that also helped to alter the atmosphere for the better. I arranged with my mother that as soon as she felt able, she should come and live with us in London. I didn't doubt that O'Toole would be generous hearted enough not to question this decision and I was right to take his generosity for granted. He could be awful but he wasn't mean and at moments of crisis he displayed a shining grace that lightened all around him.

December 9 was the day of the funeral and I was overcome with grief afterwards. Icy cold, I went to the railway station in Cardiff and sat bolt upright during the three-hour journey to London and the première of *Lawrence of Arabia*. Jules had told me to go to Claridge's and there I found him and Joyce and Joan-Juliet and O'Toole and his sister and Derek, her husband. My clothes were there in the suite and so, blessedly, was Ricci, who washed and fixed my hair, tweaked my dress and chivvied me into presentability. We went to the movies and in my sad state I didn't see an inch of the film. The Queen was there, but as a wife I wasn't needed in the line-up so I was able to slump a little. Afterwards, it seems there was a party for about five hundred people. I don't remember it at all. But I do remember going to Tony Nutting's lovely house in Chelsea and sitting there until dawn when, leaving the group, I walked alone into the street and got a cab home. The fog was over. I bathed and changed my clothes at home and was picked up by Mich to go to Elstree to start filming.

I didn't see O'Toole for days; I was putting in long hours at the studio and he became the hottest young property on two continents. I knew that life had changed yet again, but everything was happening at two removes from me – and anyway, there was a show to do.

Chapter Eighteen

Guyon House is reorganised to accommodate my mother. She will have the second-floor front as a bed-sitting room and her bathroom is almost en suite. (This house is always going to be slightly cockeyed.) Kate is delighted she'll be one staircase away from her Mamgu (specially dear mother – the Welsh for grandmother) and I am delighted because now I'm going to be able to leave home and go to work without fear. (Since Marianne's departure to Sweden I've been glued to NW3.) On the other hand . . . I bid a mental goodbye to the kitchen; my mother will want to take over. But on the other hand, I can't cook well and don't much like it, so why *not* hand over? On the other hand, am I going to enjoy resuming life under my mother's thumb? But we haven't lived together since I was sixteen – I'm grown up now and this is a big house, there's room for us all. On the other hand, she's never witnessed anything like O'Toole's drunken rages (no less alarming for being less frequent) but I don't intend that she shall, neither she nor Kate. (I add green baize-lined double doors to the list of work for the builders.)

Christmas is approaching, our first Christmas in Guyon House. My mother arrives. She's sold her furniture and almost all her possessions. 'Good!' I nod breezily and set about settling her in. She adapts to London life without missing a beat. Lying awake at night, thinking of her on the floor above – also lying awake? – I wonder, have I done something wonderful for her? Or have I asked her to do something incredibly difficult? I'm three months pregnant and selfish and I don't dwell on the problem. There are no cosy chats. Not that we ever had any. The Christmas holiday is here and we have immaculate Christmas and Boxing Day dinners and lunches – organised by Mamgu of course. The kitchen holds inexhaustible reserves for all who are invited or who drop in or pass by. The turkey is perfect, the puddings are my mother's vintage puddings made last year. O'Toole is not given to family occasions, but even he goes along with this perfect festive regime. Kate bangs her turkey bone on her plate at the huge dining table. There's a massive fire in the newly uncovered eighteenth-century fireplace. The big tree shines in the hall. But I don't allow mourning. I miss my father so much and don't know how to express it, so I don't allow *any* expressions of grief. I cannot bear to talk of him. My mother, still dressed in black, smiles and cooks and greets strangers and becomes 'Mamgu' to everyone. We don't speak of my father. And I know I'm failing her.

My pregnancy is beginning to show, so I find a clever dress and do a television play with young Robin Phillips, feeling a bit too old to be his lover. It's the first time I've ever felt like that. Time is knocking on. I'm almost thirty and that seems so old. Robin wasn't very happy and it didn't surprise me to learn that he became a director shortly afterwards and directed Maggie Smith's glittering seasons in Canada. Just at the moment Maggie is involved with O'Toole and Marie Kean in London, preparing a reading of Sean O'Casey's *Pictures in the Hallway* (this is O'Toole's response to international superstardom). Arriving to rehearse at ten o'clock and finding the door open, Maggie drifts in past a builder or two and finds herself in Marie Kean's bedroom where the great Irishwoman is discovered fast asleep in a gold lamé evening gown. Maggie's day is made, I think. She's wreathed in smiles and Maggie, wreathed, spreads the smile over a half-mile radius.

When I am too heavily pregnant to work, O'Toole decides to do a play in the West End. *Baal* by Bertolt Brecht, his first appearance in London since the ill-fated *Oh Mein Papa* and *The Long and the Short and the Tall* in the Fifties. And O'Toole is not going to take a fee. 'How good,' they say. I wonder about that. I feel that such a magnificent gesture really undermines people who have to make a living in the West End. After registering my protest and seeing it ignored, I shut up, but I'm disturbed. I suspect that O'Toole's altruism is tinged with guilt. Being a movie star is perceived in this country to be in some way a disgrace. Albert Finney turned down Sam's offer to play Lawrence because he didn't want to become a movie star. (He went on to make movies for Woodfall Productions, nevertheless.) There's something about success that is regarded with suspicion and the received wisdom is that movies are not for 'real' actors. But I can see that our world is changing – it has changed. (And do these self-appointed critics have any idea how *difficult* it is to become a movie star?) I'm worried that Jules is being too accommodating when every fibre of his being must be screaming, 'No Baal! No dirty leading man in filthy rags singing dodgy songs in a not too successful Brecht play.' Instead (and probably wisely) he says, 'Sure, play it until the next movie. Sure, do it for nothing.'

The next film? Finally, I see why Jules had been chuckling to himself at any mention of O'Toole's future. Wise, from their years at Fox, to Sam and his wiles, Jules has somehow slipped past Sam and Columbia an agreement for O'Toole's services that does not extend beyond *Lawrence of Arabia*. On the day when Sam tells O'Toole that his next four films will be X Y Z and A, Jules says, 'I don't think so.' Sam explains that over the next seven years O'Toole, like Omar, will play whatever he decides he should. 'I don't think so,' repeats Jules, softly. Lawyers and vice-presidents open files and scrutinise O'Toole's contract with Columbia Pictures beyond 1962. 'Hell let loose' is a mild way of describing what happened next. People were fired. People hastily resigned. Well into their million-dollar campaign, they realised that they were promoting an actor they didn't 'own' and, what was worse, they had to go *on* promoting him for the good of the movie.

Jules and Sam were old hands at the game of dog-eat-dog, but Jules had scored the revenge of a lifetime. Knowing the background, I couldn't do anything but salute Jules. I had never doubted his business sense, but I was bowled over by his capacity to wait for his cooled revenge.

Jules and Sam had been partners in Horizon Pictures, which had produced *Treasure of the Sierra Madre*. As young things they had seen their furniture dumped on the pavement for non-payment of rent. John Huston (the third partner) had gone out hustling for production money. Joyce Buck's father had sent a cheque to ensure that Kate Hepburn continued on into the jungle for the shooting of *The African Queen*. Their association had been long and eventful. All the same, I was slightly worried that Jules – like all of us involved in the family firm – was over-charmed by O'Toole. Much as I adored him as a man and revered him as an actor, I was well aware that O'Toole could be horribly wrong about many things. It wasn't easy being the one person who would risk telling unpalatable truths, and I had a feeling that no one would ever compete with me for that job.

Baal – well, worth doing, I suppose. I wasn't sure. It was, like all O'Toole's projects, fraught with dramatic incident. His dresser, on the night of the dress rehearsal, screamed, 'This show is cursed', flung the clothes on to the floor and fled into Charing Cross Road, never to return. The beautiful Jocelyn Herbert sets were changed by a gauze 'wipe' that traversed R to L and L to R and took for ever to move, so the play lasted almost five hours. In the middle of it all O'Toole summoned George Devine to come and 'fix' it, ignoring the director's feelings. What a time they had! George Devine (who ran the Royal Court) and Jocelyn Herbert were lovers, the director had to be shunted sideways – it was exhausting just listening to the backstage drama. They opened and everyone fairly hated the play. A large portion of the audience slammed out each night crying, 'Disgusting'. But – was it all worth it? O'Toole looked awful on stage, which he wanted to be as a change from the beauty of Lawrence, but why, I wondered? The public isn't in the least bit interested or impressed by versatility. Marie and I went to the opening and nodded our approval of best efforts, but we both wondered, why bother? The play opened on 7 February and had to close at the end of April to accommodate the beginning of O'Toole's first picture as a co-production between Keep Films and a big outside company. The chosen film was *Becket*, based on the Anouilh play he had not done for the RSC.

May. *Becket* begins with Richard Burton. I haven't seen him or worked with him since I first took up with O'Toole after I left RADA. He's now involved with Elizabeth Taylor and against everyone's guess and wish has left his wife, Sybil. Of course, Elizabeth represents the great uncharted sea of superstardom and Richard has always wanted to be a superstar – a *wealthy* superstar. There's a story of him – a favourite of Daphne Rye, the H.M. Tennent Ltd casting director – at an all-night party, sitting in a circle of young things who were asked to declare their ambitions. 'I want to be the greatest Juliet since Ellen Terry.' 'I want to play Hamlet as it has never been played.' 'How about you, Richard? What do you want to be?' The reply was simple. 'Rich.'

Thanks to Elizabeth, he is now going to *be* rich. Very rich. They both come down to the pub near Shepperton Studios and eat more food than normal people can imagine putting away. I'm a healthy eater (to say the least) but Elizabeth Taylor's food consumption leaves me standing . . . 'Those fat pigs,' snarls Kate Hepburn in disdain at such indulgence. I don't know. A part of me admires that kind of robustness. Another part sides with Miss Hepburn; such unbelievable self-indulgence *can't* be right – or can it?

Richard seems sheepish but rather pleased with himself, I think. Not sure where he stands with us in his new role. Nor am I. As his wife

Sybil's husband, he would have fitted perfectly into our life, but now? O'Toole senses that I am holding back rather and doesn't push to accept many invitations to the Dorchester or anywhere else.

Elizabeth and Richard are at the height of what is called the 'Scandale'. They seem to love the notoriety and the publicity. One night, Elizabeth wants to go to a theatre in St Martin's Lane. We arrange seats. Elizabeth is very small. She wears a huge, turquoise turban. Word spreads (how, I wonder?) that the Seductress is at the theatre. In the interval we arrange drinks to be served in the manager's office, front of house. 'No,' she cries to our horror, 'we're next door to the Salisbury. Let's go to the pub now!' St Martin's Lane is fairly heaving. Someone clears a path. All they can see is a turquoise hat. 'Oh,' cries a woman, 'the bitch! I'm so close, I could spit on her.' Unaccountably, Elizabeth finds this charming. She beams. 'It is so awful,' she says winsomely to O'Toole, 'not being able to go anywhere in peace.' 'It might help a bit,' O'Toole replies tartly, 'if you took off that fuckin' turquoise busby.'

There is something wonderful about her appetite for being noticed. Richard? No, I don't think so. He looks faintly embarrassed. But it's so obvious that he's willing to pay the price of fame. O'Toole may be disconcerted to be confronted by Stardom in its complete, unacceptable – but true form. He can have this, if he wants.

In 1967, very generously, they offered to take the children to stay on their yacht *Kalizma*. Over my dead body, I thought; it's hard enough trying to bring them up sane in NW3, never mind on a luxury yacht.

The same year, quite by chance, we flew to a film festival together, a beautiful festival in Taormina in Sicily where the Italian Oscars are given out. There was a confusion over tickets and Elizabeth snapped her fingers and got some boxes produced out of nowhere and the four of us cluttered up the front of the first-class compartment. We drank champagne all the way to Italy (I was right to avoid them, it was impossible not to behave excessively in their company). Elizabeth was very good natured. Richard was – Richard, and I remembered that even *reasonable* behaviour on the part of royalty or celebrities is translated into *wonderful* behaviour; the expectation is so much less, I suppose. When we got off, Rich and O'Toole and I looked dishevelled and blowsy. Elizabeth, who was royally drunk, looked stone-cold sober and the photographs reflected this. 'Camera cleans her up,' said Richard philosophically.

At Taormina all the film stars were mobbed by screaming crowds. We stayed in a pretty and very uncomfortable hotel. Staying in the rooms (formerly monks' cells) was out of the question and in order to do some sightseeing and visit restaurants, we braved the boisterous fans who never left the front courtyard. After a day or two they grew bored with the stars and life was very pleasant for everyone. Richard and Elizabeth, on the other hand, remained closeted in two tiny rooms where they sat squashed in with their hairdressers and assistants. 'We're not going out till The Night,' said Richard. 'By then, they'll be MAD to see Elizabeth – it'll be a riot.' He was deadly serious, I realised dismally. He was right, of course; Elizabeth, the only star who hadn't been seen, was nearly killed by the pent-up enthusiasm as she left the hotel. On The Night, Richard said, 'Watch this, it'll be a sensation. The light will go on *there* but *she* will come in *here*.' We were in a Roman amphitheatre – rubble everywhere 'backstage' – the auditorium, beautifully lit by candles issued to the audience as they arrived and then sat with their backs to the ocean. O'Toole was suitably, sincerely grateful in bad Italian. My friend, Silvana Mangano, brought a loving house of fellow countrymen to their feet, striding on casually and exiting smartly, then Elizabeth was introduced and didn't appear – didn't appear – didn't appear – and finally she was picked up in a light in the wrong place, picking her way through the uncleared rubble to the podium. It seemed a lot of trouble for very little return.

Much later, Richard and I sang some Welsh songs. A minor princess who seemed to be setting her cap at him was not best pleased. Elizabeth suddenly summoned him and we exchanged a wry smile. 'Mabel calls,' he said. One thing I remember about Elizabeth was that she had a terrific voice, clear and incisive, always interesting, no affectation. Richard and I had other, sadder, meetings as he lost his robust constitution and the years of excess took their toll. But he got what he wanted: 'Take what you want and pay for it.' Didn't he just!

Kate is three and already, as my mother says, she is a 'bit of a character'. She wears her round, metal-framed glasses with a forbidding air, peering suspiciously at the world, pinning my mother to her chair with demands to be read to. We're heartily sick of *Ant and Bee* and *Janet and John* and I begin to read her poems and stories that I find entertaining. She tolerates almost everything – even the fourth leader of *The Times* – but remains loyal to *Ant and Bee* in particular. Between us, my mother and I run the house. Manolita, the daily help, comes every day and cleans and mends and helps organise our lives.

Becket is a long movie and is being shot at Shepperton. Peter Glenville, who has a sound theatrical pedigree, is having no trouble at all with his stars, O'Toole and Burton. The press tries to create stories of tension and potential mayhem, but even they have to give up in the end. The journey from NW3 to Shepperton is long, so the weekdays are calm; O'Toole leaves in the early hours of the morning and returns late with barely time to greet everyone and have dinner with me in the Green Room before going to bed early. Saturday is a bit of a lost day when he sleeps and sleeps, but Sundays are enchanting and we all lunch in the dining room before O'Toole and I take a walk around Hampstead and then sit and read until it's time to prepare for another hard week. Quiet, dull and totally happy, those months.

However happy I am, I feel I cannot forget the circumstances surrounding Kate's birth and I make up my mind that I am going to protect myself and the next baby from the remotest chance of drama and over-excitement. How to contrive this? Marie suggests that I come to Dublin for the birth and everything falls into place. Having a child on Irish soil will compliment O'Toole and put me beyond his reach at the same time. It works! Everyone – except my mother – is happy. It's seen as a charming gesture, but it's actually self-preservation on my part. So, three weeks before Pat is due to be born in June, I fly to Ireland and move into a back bedroom in Marie's flat at Lower Baggot Street. She's booked me into the Stella Maris Nursing Home (staffed by nuns) and Declan Meagher, a friend of Dr Slattery's, will be in charge. I'm told to prepare a bag and the list includes a bottle of chloroform and a large pad of cotton wool; I find myself packing for myself a pair of white silk pyjamas of O'Toole's. I may be wanting to do this my way, but I also need to feel close to him and wearing his clothes will help me, I know.

The June days are perfect and long. Marie cooks wonderful meals (the Irish potatoes in June are heavenly). I lie on my bed high above the Dublin rooftops and I think I may never have such a relaxed time again. Marie is at work at the theatre, but her flat is lined with books so I read and read and read and look west out of the window. Joan Huet, a friend and stage manager, and Marie and a couple of the boys from the company decide that maybe we should speed things up a bit (I might sit there, reading and dreaming for ever). 'Into the car,' they cry. 'Off to the Wicklow Mountains.' Joan brings her stage manager's stopwatch. In the mountains we stop here and there. 'Small gin for the lady,' say the boys.

I scarcely drink but gin and orange doesn't taste like alcohol at all. After a few hours of bumping around the country roads, I feel a twinge.

'Oh Jasus – great,' they cry, relieved, and we speed back to town, Joan recording twinges on her stopwatch. When we reach the Stella Maris, she confers with the nuns while Marie and the boys bring my little bag up to my very nice room – two beds (bathroom en suite). 'Ouch,' I exclaim at the next small twinge. 'All right. Everyone away now,' says an adorable nun. 'Did you feel a little pain? Aren't you the good girl? Here!' And drenching a pad of cotton wool with chloroform, she plants it on my face.

I'm told later that Declan shot across Dublin for the birth and, as an ex-Irish Rugby International player, was nonplussed to hear the unofficial Welsh Rugby anthem issuing from the prone, unconscious body beneath him. '*Sospan Fach, yn berwi ar y tân, sospan Fawr, yn berwi ar y Ilawr.*' 'I didn't know,' he said, 'whether to pass the baby or score a try.' All unknowing, I woke up in O'Toole's silk pyjama top. 'You've got a beautiful baby girl,' said the saintly (I'd elevated her) nun. 'Oh, thank you. How nice,' I replied and looked at the perfect, pink happy bundle. Could anything be more perfect than this? This is the way to have a baby, I thought, as I drifted off to sleep again.

I woke up to find great excitement going on. O'Toole from England had ordered champagne and Guinness – enough Black Velvet for the city, it seemed, and the city was turning up. The bath was out of commission because it was full of ice and champagne. The room was full of Irish actors. I regarded the assembly calmly. I've done this my way. My baby was calm and untroubled and I was calm and untroubled.

So, Kate was born in Shakespeare's country but Pat has been born on Irish soil and I feel I've managed things very well. Jim Fitzgerald, a lively young director, drops in for a drink. Pat sleeps resolutely through the incredible din. Jim feels a little tired and says, 'D'ya mind?' as he rolls into the other bed in the room. He's still there twenty-four hours later. 'Ah, the craythúr,' snaps Marie, irritably. 'Who cares?' I say. The nuns just smile.

O'Toole arrives. Jules and Joyce, also Peter Finch; various nobs. I'm concentrating on Pat. She is a miracle baby. I wonder if her manner reflects the way she was born, women only, no problems at all. She's easy. I'm easy. O'Toole leaves and returns to *Becket*. On my bed is the script of the movie. They need an actress who can speak old Welsh, find appropriate music, sing it and play the gittern at the same time. What kind of competition did I have to beat off to get *this* job? Yes. I'll do Gwendoline when I get home. But it's not a great part.

Robert Bolt sends me the script of his new play *Gentle Jack*. Again, it's not a great part, but Edith Evans will be in the play. I have adored her for so long and nothing would give me greater pleasure than to sweep the stage so I could watch her – so, Yes! Of course I'll do it. Dame Edith . . . Can she be as wonderful as I think she is?

I feed Pat, who is completely content and untroubled. Jim Fitzgerald wakes and says, 'Oh Jasus, where am I? I'm late for rehearsal.' He's a day late.

Marie makes me get up and get out to Bewley's for a coffee. I don't feel so good. Give it another day, she says, and then she puts us on a plane to England, where there's a *proper* nanny. The first ever for me. Elizabeth de la Cour Bogue has arrived via Jack and Doreen Hawkins, almost snaffled by David Niven and then Lauren Bacall on the way, but she's OURS! Young, smart, upper-crust, great with horses as well as children. What have I done to deserve this? Doreen Hawkins, I bless you for ever. And Mamgu is in residence. And there's a crib swathed in pink. And there's a grim, cross-eyed, three-year-old sister. When she's seen holding a pillow over the baby's face with a pair of scissors in her hand, I think The Baby (even I can see 'The Baby' is a term of opprobrium) should be moved three floors down out of Kate's reach. Poor Kate, who had such a horrible birth and who has gone through so much already – has she any vague notion how she's been seized and rescued and re-seized and moved from pillar to post? And now here's this blissful creature who has never known a moment's trouble.

When Kate was born she was one of many children born to Royal Shakespeare Company members that year – all girls. Someone asked if my husband minded not having a son. I – so completely sure of my welcomed and treasured existence in my parents' lives – was amazed at such a question, but, when I remembered it, much later, I put it to O'Toole. As I expected, he was as amazed as I and said that a houseful of women would suit him very well. When Pat was born, again I heard a sympathetic 'still no boy'. O'Toole and I looked at each other in mute amusement. What is this obsession with boys? Our friend Robert Shaw longed for a son and went on producing child after child until he succeeded in getting a boy. Such persistence was a source of wonder and amusement to O'Toole and we decided that two children was enough and so the houseful of women was established. When Pat was brought home from Dublin, Guyon House was up and running and it was much, much easier to ensure that O'Toole was not aware of the noise and tumult that a baby trails in its wake.

An infrequent visitor to the nursery on the fifth floor, he came up with me one night very late to see Pat in bed when she hadn't been too well. He was charming and she was charmed. Days later she asked me, 'You know that man – not the one with the beard, the other one who came to see me – who *is* he?' It had never occurred to us that his infrequent presence in London, coupled with the constant changes in appearance, could be so totally confusing to her. After that I made sure that I scattered around stills of their father in whatever new persona he had adopted for the current movie or play. These misunderstandings evaporated as the girls grew older, but even so, Pat didn't exactly distinguish herself at her primary school by claiming that she knew the Bible *very* well and that it was a movie, starring her father.

Chapter Nineteen

Becket continues without incident. O'Toole and Burton have both vowed to stay on the wagon. There's been no trouble and then one night they both fall off the wagon at the same time and meet up in some horrible dive (there are few pretty dives in 1963) and, partly appalled and penitent, go home for an hour or so and turn up on time for the first scene of the day, still drunk and hanging on to each other. They do a good day's work, but the lapse has been noted.

I turn up to do my scene – quite complicated with all the music – but it goes smoothly and quickly. They incorporate my music into the theme of the movie. I go home to the girls.

Pat O'Toole continues to be the dream baby. Blonde, serene, she lies outside in the garden at Number 98. I, my mother and Liz, the nanny, dote on her from a distance. She makes no demands. She smiles, the sun shines. Life is deceptively easy during the summer months. She's called Pat because I'd got it into my head that she was going to be a boy called Patrick and when they asked me her name in the nursing home, I couldn't think of anything different.

Soon it's time to start work again. *Gentle Jack* will now include Kenneth Williams, who is a great friend of Robert Bolt, and Michael Bryant, one of the best actors in England. It's a very classy show. Robert comes to stay with us while we rehearse. On the first day we're required to wear hats and skirts and gloves. Trousers are allowed on day two, thank God. Robert is conceiving a real dislike of the Dame. It's true that she hasn't read the play. It's true that she's demanding that Hardy Amies should design her a ballgown in stiff taffeta for all her daytime scenes in the City office. No one dares question her about this. They all moan in private. She sees that there will be rostra, six to nine inches high, here and there. 'I can't possibly act on those,' she cries. 'I'll have to wear slippers.' Carpet slippers and Hardy Amies frocks. No one dares comment. 'You seem very relaxed,' she accuses me in a cross voice. I'm petrified and I'm trying to *act* a relaxed, upper-class girl. I shake my head. She glowers. Gretchen Franklin learns that I'd like to improve my tap dancing. 'I'll teach you,' she offers. And does, until the Dame tracks down the source of the noise. No more tap. I have a passion for oranges. She hates oranges. No more oranges in the theatre.

But the Actress is everything I'd thought she might be. All day at rehearsal and every night during the run I stand and watch her and I can't see what she's doing. She gets laughs and I can't see how – there doesn't seem to be any preparation – no special light, no good place, no clean 'feed'. She just gets a laugh if *she* thinks it's a funny line. If she doesn't understand something, she says it with no expression at all. She never 'helps' the dramatist, never papers over a crack in the script. Faced with a bit of bad writing she suspends her acting until the moment is over and then carries on. The behaviour is aristocratic.

Producer Binkie Beaumont is brutal to her when the play does badly on the road. In the broad alleyway to the stage door he barks, 'Come on, come on,' after a performance in Brighton. 'Do your magic! Pull the play together.' What a hope! He should know her better than that.

We play Brighton for a month. She and Kenneth Williams stay at the Royal Crescent, traditionally the stars' hotel. I stay in a suite at the Albion and have the girls there with me a great deal of the time. When Dame E. and Kenneth go home, they share a miserable wilted salad and as they go up in the lift the friendly night porter nudges the Dame in the ribs and says, 'Enjoy your grub?' According to Ken, not once does she acknowledge his presence.

In the wings, at night, she stands, smoothing down her taffeta dress, making a horrible crackling noise and muttering to herself. She fairly *hates* this play. They told her she was playing a modern-day Elizabeth the First. Well, of course, her part is nothing like that at all and she hasn't read the other bits of the play. 'Remember *Nina*,' she says to no one in particular (*Nina*, a play few of us had seen, was a great failure and she left it on a stretcher), rustle, crack, rustle. Norah, in the prompt corner, hisses fearlessly, 'Please, SHUT UP, Dame Edith!' She smoulders a little and then resumes the crackle, rustle, crackle, mumble, mumble, until she has to enter in her carpet slippers and grand frock. I'm more enslaved by her than I could have thought possible. Robert cares for her even less than before. When she died, he happened to be staying with us and I said, 'Look who died!' Eulogies were pouring in.

Robert looked at the tributes in *The Times* and delivered his own, terse, obituary: 'Well, she was no use to me.'

In Brighton – it being almost the Christmas season – there's a misconception that *Gentle Jack* is a children's show about Jack and the Beanstalk (grand managements like H.M. Tennent Ltd don't think that they need to advertise or let the public know what to expect). When a dog is disembowelled quite early in the play, the hatred wafting across the footlights is palpable. Occasionally people tut-tut at us in the street. This doesn't augur well for London.

While I was rehearsing *Gentle Jack*, O'Toole accepted an engagement in London, which he'd be able to fit in before going off to shoot *Lord Jim* in Cambodia. It was to play Hamlet in the Laurence Olivier production of the play, which was to open in the National Theatre (housed at the Old Vic). Before we opened on tour in Brighton, I attended the first night. It was a huge occasion, a landmark in the British theatre. As I took my seat in the stalls, I felt all the symptoms of acute stage fright. Bob Bolt took my hand and gave it a shake, but I couldn't respond; my tongue had stuck to the roof of my mouth and I could only nod in answer to his encouraging 'Come on, girl, it's only a play.' It *wasn't* only a play (and he didn't believe it either). It could have been worse, I reflected. A few months previously Larry had asked me if I would like to play Ophelia. I was speechless and O'Toole had spoken for me, saying that they ought to cast someone really young (I was thirty at the time – no juvenile). For a moment, just a moment, I had felt dashed (and Larry looked quizzical), but within minutes I thought that I had probably been saved from myself. I was *not* a juvenile, but would I ever have turned down such an opportunity? Now I sent up a prayer of gratitude that I was not backstage, coping with my own terrors and worrying about O'Toole as well. Even so, sitting out front was a nightmare; the play and the building were bedevilled. Buses thundered past the side of the unfinished building swathed in tarpaulin and this *Hamlet* was a pale shadow of the performance O'Toole had given at the Bristol Old Vic in the mid-Fifties. Sean Kenny had made a lovely set that rarely worked. Only too often the company climbed down from the lofty bridge that hadn't met in the middle and continued the performance on the flat apron in front of the safety curtain. Since they were giving these performances uncut (nine hours on matinée days), some of the evening performances interrupted by technical glitches were interminable. The public didn't care. They flocked.

Larry seemed intent on making O'Toole look like a clean, well-dressed, young master. O'Toole went along with everything – pudding-basin haircut, Lord Fauntleroy collar. Larry wrote him god-like notes and letters. 'My son, in whom I have such pride . . .' Some temporary cleaner swept these into the bin and I got the blame. I thought O'Toole was badly served by Larry and for once he was too obedient by half. But it's very hard *not* to be subservient around one's idol.

When we arrived in London the critics savaged *Gentle Jack* and Robert was terribly upset. He'd thought it was his best play. We played on while *Hamlet* closed and O'Toole prepared to play the lead in the film of Conrad's *Lord Jim*. Jean Simmons and her husband, director Richard Brooks, and their children had come to lunch at Guyon House to talk about the project before leaving England. 'No script to be seen until we've started shooting,' said Richard Brooks. The Conrad novel was a wonderful subject, but I couldn't quite believe that O'Toole was breaking his cardinal rule: no script, no deal. Jean Simmons looked as harassed by domesticity as I. Our children got wet and dirty in the garden. My mother beamed at the Jean Simmons she saw in her mind's eye, not the tired mother scraping mud off small wellington boots.

It was time for O'Toole to leave (for 'the high China seas' I read in my atlas) and I would be able to join him there as soon as I was free. Pat was thriving, Kate was at kindergarten (and already her life was an endless round of parties). I'd grown to enjoy the long period of home life, only rarely threatened by alcohol owing to the daily pressure of work, and I didn't want it interrupted, but this was a pointless regret and I didn't even voice it. It was easier to deal with these separations if we didn't have farewell scenes.

While I was playing *Gentle Jack* I accepted, as a day job, my first 'real' movie, *Espionage*, albeit made for TV, and the first made for TV in the director's long and fascinating career. 'Oh, you'll have an *awful* time,' said his contemporaries. On the contrary, Michael Powell and I found ourselves working together extremely happily. The great Powell and Pressburger days were behind him, but films like *The Red Shoes* and *Peeping Tom* were fresh in people's minds. He and Anthony Quayle, my leading man, between them gave me a month's seminar on movie acting and it was the first really interesting job I'd had in about two years. There was an actor in the movie whom I found dazzling. Marie knew and admired him also and we used to inveigle John Wood round to

Heath Street for sketchy suppers, lots of drinks and tons of adulation, which just slipped off his back unnoticed.

Michael Powell took me under his wing and began to make plans for a movie future for me. But he'd fallen on hard times himself and none of his projects for me came to fruition. I sensed that he was whistling in the dark, but I felt very privileged to get to know him and his wife and talk, talk, talk about films in his flat in Melbury Road.

Dame Edith, who wasn't good at names, usually addressed me as 'Mother-of-two'. I feel like a 'mother-of-ten' and I'm a full-time daughter again, but finally I've had to learn how to run a house properly – even I can tell, however, that I'm very tense and over-anxious. There are lists everywhere; menus for the children, menus for us, notes to the daily, memos to myself and just about anyone I see who passes me on the stairs. And I feel I would like to be four wives – four separate wives: one, sleeves rolled up, seeing to the nuts and bolts of daily life, doing the odd bit of carpentry and furniture removal; one for dealing with the delicate, personal secretarial work that can't be handed on to an office; one for fun; and one for going to the hairdresser, the dressmaker, the chiropodist, the manicurist and looking smart, and entertaining like a lady of leisure. Then, there's Miss Phillips, the Equity member, to accommodate somehow. I'm keeping a tight grip on things but every second of every day has to be accounted for and I'm losing even more weight and on my way to becoming 'thrillingly thin' as my friend, Debbie Condon, describes the emaciated, model-size figure I had never thought to possess. Deb is a beautiful American supermodel, married to our friend, playwright Kenneth Jupp, and we spend what little time off we have with our friends and business partners, the Bucks – including daughter, Joan-Juliet – and Ken and Deb Jupp. I keep two diaries, one big desk diary and a small Hermès agenda, which I carry around. Ah, Hermès ... Yes, life is becoming very 'Gucci, Pucci, Cucci', as I heard a disgruntled husband mutter while he trailed up Bond Street behind his busily shopping wife. The diaries intimidate me at the beginning of every week. Kate's eyes require constant attention, the patches have to be moved regularly from eye to eye, so every page bears a note saying 'Left', 'Right', 'Both for a bit', 'Check-up, Mr Wybar' (Mr Wybar, the saintly oculist of Wimpole Street, is the man who features most regularly in my diary, accompanied by Mr Cuthbertson, the equally venerated dentist). The travelling is tiring even to read about. The lists read like incomprehensible gibberish within weeks of being written.

1964: Feb. Close play. Girls on holiday with my mother. Fly to Cambodia 26th. *Lord Jim*. Move to Hong Kong 28th. Depart to Japan by 3rd March, Kyoto on 5th. 11th: opening of *Becket* in New York – organise hair and dress. Party P. Glenville. 13th March leave for London. Children. Kate to Mr Wybar. Work on drawing room. Learn lines. Be in Manchester 17th March. Film in Southport. Sleeper to London arrives 5.30 a.m. Dinner Ken and Deb. April 3rd *Tom Jones*. April 10th Bermans and Wig Creations. Costume pick-up. Ireland. Soup Bowl Restaurant, Molesworth Street today. Girls to Marie Kean – and so on and on unremittingly.

The circus moved on when O'Toole went away on location and life at the Ladies' Seminary settled into a quieter rhythm. There were seven of us, sometimes eight: my mother, Elizabeth, the nanny, Manolita, the treasured daily housekeeper, Pilar, the au-pair, Marie Kean, Kate and Pat and me. During the year I did more television and began another play for the West End. Out of the blue I was asked to do a play, *Hogan's Goat*, on Broadway and declined at once. I could see that there were several ways of organising family life, given our circumstances. More and more movies were being made on location and more Americans seemed to be based in Paris and Rome, so the chances were that O'Toole would work away from home in Europe. Many actors liked to travel their 'homes' – wife, children, nanny, secretary, friends – with them. O'Toole firmly rejected this. Some mothers, when they travelled, took the children with them, bringing a tutor if necessary. My mother and I between us decided that the girls' life should retain its own routine, regardless of our activities. I would try to work around their lives. They were not to go away to school and that way O'Toole would be able to see them whenever he was at home whether it was term or holiday time. My going to New York while O'Toole was in Europe was out of the question. The New York producers and my agent were put out by my continuing resistance. Finally they wrote testily, 'You know there is an actress in America who is *longing* to play this part.' 'Well, I'm afraid you'd better give it to her then.' So, Miss Faye Dunaway got her first Broadway break and very good she was, too, I was told.

Instead, I did a French play with my friend, Max Adrian. It was a fantastical work by Marçel Aymé, translated by Kitty Black, and it was the first of many French plays I was to perpetrate over the years – all flops – but I liked them and *Maxibules* was one of the most spectacular failures. No amount of work in rehearsal and on the road could make it acceptable to the English audience. After a faintly improper (for 1963) scene I had to say 'I'm disgusted.' 'So are we,' came a cry from the upper circle. 'And I'm going home,' I continued. 'So are we!' replied the self-appointed critic in the gods.

As the curtain fell on opening night, someone hissed, 'Don't take the rag up again, for God's sake!' 'Nonsense!' barked Max – heart of a lion – 'Take it up!' He held my hand tight as we got the bird; my first experience of being booed and hissed. They threw money at the stage. Four days later we were off, but I'd had a lovely time working with Max and I *still* liked the play.

The television play was more successful. It was a very interesting piece of work, *The Other Man*, by Giles Cooper. I played opposite a reserved, young John Thaw and Michael Caine, and Granada generously allowed us seven weeks in which to rehearse and film the play. On the long railway journey to Manchester, Michael – also quiet and rather self-contained – outlined his strategy for the next stage of his career, at the end of which he said, 'Within a year, I'll be in movies in a big way.' I nodded, doubtfully. I didn't question his ability but I didn't see how he could be so sure of a thing like that. Just over a year later I noted that he'd been absolutely correct in his strategy and in his prediction.

One night while I was doing a stage play on tour in Guildford, the well-known agent, Harvey Orkin, took the train to see the show and travelled back with me in our car. Before I dropped him off in the Fulham Road, he handed me a script and said, 'Read this, I think you'll find it funny and you'd be very good in it.' It was days before I got around to reading the screenplay and when I did I found it brilliantly funny. I'd never heard of the author. The part Harvey wanted me to look at was fine, but the men's parts were wonderful. Harvey wasn't my agent and I didn't know him very well and I wasn't sure what he thought I could do with the script. When I showed it to O'Toole his eyes lit up. I was so pleased he agreed with me – it *was* brilliant. When he took it off to our office, which Jules had set up in Belgravia, I hoped that he would like it as well. O'Toole would be wonderful in the leading part and I wanted to be in such an original movie. The author was invited to London and I was intrigued and enchanted to open the door to a small, droll, shy character who settled cautiously into a corner of the big couch in the Green Room and was sufficiently moved to pull himself together to pay me a compliment on my dress as I brought him tea. Good. He liked me, and he warmed to me even more when I complimented him on *What's New Pussycat?*, which is what he'd called the script.

O'Toole entered the room and the cosiness was at an end. 'All right – thanks,' O'Toole smiled and nodded affably but firmly at the door. Evidently I was dismissed. I said goodbye, hoping I looked as though I had lots of other interesting things to do, and went up to the nursery. I was a bit put out, but even more I was bemused. For someone to be flown across the Atlantic for a chat was wonderful and extraordinary. Less wonderfully, I never saw Woody Allen (for he was the short, shy American) or the script again and was never told what had been discussed over tea.

As the weeks went by I realised that our company, Keep Films, was actually going to co-produce *Pussycat*. During a meeting one day I gathered that 'my' part was going to be offered to someone called Capucine. I was mortified at first, but I did appreciate that O'Toole loathed nepotism and it was a measure of his slightly cockeyed respect for me that he strenuously avoided doing me any professional favours. (I saw a photograph of Capucine; she was *incredibly* elegant!) We never discussed this development of casting and I confined my interest in the movie to events in the production office – drama enough.

Because of the attention of the paparazzi, and an attendant court case, O'Toole insisted that the movie he was shooting in Rome be moved to France and so began several years of filming in Paris. All the movies were co-productions with our company, Keep Films, so we kept an apartment at the George V, and Jules and Joyce and I flew to and fro as though we were bussing to Putney. O'Toole built up his art collection and I bought my clothes from the big houses and there was much pleasure in our life, but it seemed to me that my hold on my place was so precarious that, like a mole in the night, unacknowledged even to myself, I began to build a little power for myself. Rather pathetically, it took the form of making sure that I myself remained extremely thin; ultra-fashionably thin. Anorexia or bulimia was totally alien to my healthily greedy appetite, but discipline was second nature to me and I now put myself on the strictest of strict diets. Eating only in the best restaurants in the world, I read the menu, looked at the elaborate food, and ate a lamb chop or a piece of fish and a grapefruit every day for lunch and dinner. Sometimes I drank wine, mostly I drank water, and I was so thin that I was much in demand by designers to model their clothes. I was flattered to be asked and, more to the point, bought my grand clothes cheaply at Dior because I was exactly the same size as their German house model, Christine, and at the end of the season I could buy the clothes she'd been wearing during the shows. I don't think O'Toole even noticed my strange eating habits or my clothes; if he did, he never remarked on them, but being thin – never giving way to temptation – made me feel stronger and more in control than I actually was.

Of course, I was addressing the wrong problem in the wrong way, controlling the wrong thing.

Chapter Twenty

During this period O'Toole found a way of 'remembering' my birthdays, our anniversaries and Christmas presents. 'Let me off the whole thing,' he said. 'I'll give you things to cover all occasions.' And he did. He'd begun to collect Etruscan jewellery – wonderful, intricate objects, unbelievably crafted before magnification. Most were things to look and wonder at but some were wearable – just. The gold was unalloyed so a chance bump in the night could seriously damage one's favourite bangle. I was happy with this arrangement; there was no suspense about one's birthday being forgotten, no marking of the anniversary – and Christmas? Well, one less thing to worry about at that time of year could only be to the good.

On Joyce's advice I took my Etruscan collection to Mme Claude de Muzak on the Left Bank in Paris, who made beautiful, gunmetal-bound vitrines. I took a few of the more robust-looking pieces to Boucheron to be fixed for wearing. The workroom there refused to touch them because they were afraid of destroying them. The man I talked to there asked me if I minded that he'd shown the collection to someone at the Louvre. 'Well, heavens, no, why would I?' I asked. 'No, you don't understand. This is something that should *be* at the Louvre.' 'Oh dear. Yes, I see.'

'O'Toole, do you want this to go to the Louvre – I don't mind, really?'

'Do I fuck? It's *yours*. Take it home.'

And there it sat in the drawing room for years and as the years went by there were more and more vitrines. They were so beautiful and they were mine. I couldn't quite believe my good fortune.

But those years in Paris were such a time of unbelievable beauty; beautiful things, beautiful places and acquisitions. The paintings were lovely: a quiet Bonnard for the wall opposite our bed, gorgeous vivid Bro's for the entrance hall, a Braque for the drawing room. The drawing room at home was ravishing. Most of our Jack Yeats' paintings were hung there and we had seven big oils; the weakest of all (according to our friend, art dealer, Leslie Waddington) was the one I liked best, *False Morning Promise*, a clown on a raft sailing into heaven knows what sort of day. Milton Avery, the American, was the painter I best liked to live with. O'Toole bought a few, lone seagulls on a grey American coast. Jules and Joyce gave us a lovely grey bird against a blue sky as an anniversary present. I looked at it in the front study every day and loved it more and more. My only outright possession and my favourite painting was one that O'Toole gave me one Christmas when he had missed six planes from Orly to London (in all fairness the distance from the bar to the gates was, in those days, enormous). Lionel, the chauffeur, and I went to the airport at lunchtime and waited in vain – came home; went out again, came home – and so it went on all day and finally the children went to bed and so did my mother and dinner was thrown out and Lionel went alone to the airport. Late at night a very vague O'Toole was delivered to the front door, apologetic and not very well but clutching a smallish parcel, which was my Christmas present. When I saw it all was forgiven. It was a painting by Paul Klee. Called *Little Hope*, it was a small, sad face painted on burlap in 1939. I couldn't believe that I could own anything so extraordinary. Every day after that I unlocked the drawing-room door and snatched a look before locking up and going about my day.

Joyce Buck was a wonderful companion in Paris. She and Jules and her daughter, Joan-Juliet, had lived there for years – part of the time as neighbours of their colleague, Jacques Tati, when Jules was producing *Mon Oncle*. (He introduced Jacques Tati to America.) Jules hadn't even got to the point of pronouncing 'Peugeot' properly, but Joyce had taken the whole thing very seriously and had learned French, and young Joan-Juliet to all intents and purposes *was* French. When we came to Paris at weekends, Joyce took me around art galleries and antique shops and framers, restorers, carpetmakers – I saw aspects of Paris I would never otherwise have seen. At night we went to the smartest restaurants – lamb chops and grapefruit for me – the newest night clubs (hell on wheels) and one night, I cannot imagine why, Joyce and I – so correct, so controlled, so proper, so not wanting to get our hair messed up – went madly out of control, got drunk in a Russian restaurant, danced all night like dervishes, while our bemused husbands sat, mournfully patient at the bar, looking on. One of my (four) hairpieces fell off. I kicked it into touch without missing a step and cried, 'Leave it! The waiter will get it.' 'Is she often like this?' asked a tired-out and sympathetic Regine, queen of the nightclub scene. 'No,' said O'Toole, puzzled and truthful. John Shepbridge, the producer, danced with Joyce – watched by an unbelieving Jules. 'Oh John,' she said the following day, 'was I dreadful?' 'My dear,' said John, 'I don't remember a thing.' Joyce, who did remember dancing lewdly, said to me, 'There *are* good guys. They're the ones that say they don't remember a thing.'

During the late Sixties especially, O'Toole spent a great deal of time filming in Paris, but my attention was mainly on life at home with the girls and my work in London. I do remember learning that my hero, Hugh Griffith, had been fired off *How to Steal a Million Dollars*, one of the films we co-produced during this period, after persistent bad behaviour, culminating in a naked stroll down the corridors of the George V with 'Don't' struck out and 'Do' substituted before 'disturb' on the card he held in his hand. What is the matter with these film people? They themselves are *so* badly behaved, so cynical, so seriously amoral. An inebriated, naked stroll down a corridor doesn't seem to me to warrant dismissal. In one of the movies, beset with problems, almost the least of the problems took the form of a leading actress who, having completely flipped her lid, was discovered up a gantry with slit wrists dripping blood on the upturned faces below. Deprived of alcohol, she'd been drinking Eau de toilette and had to be coaxed down and packed off to hospital. The more I saw of the movie world, the more astonished I was at the nonsense people got away with.

Audrey Hepburn (in *How to Steal a Million Dollars*) was so lovely. She was surprisingly tall and when we were introduced I was shocked to feel her tiny, fleshless hand – like a bird's claw or a small cat's paw. She lived a life of iron discipline that made me feel self-indulgent, watching the rushes twice; once alone and once with her make-up man, making notes; filming from noon till seven or eight p.m., eating only a little dry salad then going through every still photograph taken during the day (hundreds), rejecting all that weren't flattering, then home to the hotel, alone, for a little more dry salad and back to the studio in the morning for more rushes, more consultations and two hours in make-up before the day's work began. I realised that she was a woman playing a much younger girl and that the work behind this successful deception was enormous and gracefully embraced. It wasn't vanity on her part, it was attention to business. I didn't much like her husband at the time, Mel Ferrer. He installed her in Paris, sent her out to work and decamped, all over Europe, having, as far as I could see, a fine old time.

When *What's New Pussycat?* was being shot, I spent my time at the George V and went sightseeing each day rather than go to the studio too often. Romy Schneider was a pillar of professional good sense, but I couldn't warm to Capucine, who was playing 'my' part, though she was perfectly amiable. I thought she was a little dull. It was difficult to see how the director, Clive Donner, managed to keep the whole thing chugging along on schedule. The stories we heard told in the office back in London were alarming and Peter Sellers, whom I revered as an actor, went down rather in my estimation. Since his heart attack he was uninsurable and after the financial disaster of *Cleopatra* caused by Elizabeth Taylor's near fatal illness when she was shooting in England, film companies were very aware of the dangers of employing actors who were not in good condition. O'Toole, also a huge admirer and sympathetic to his plight, had pushed and pushed for engaging Sellers, and finally the company had agreed to take the risk. At this point Peter Sellers, 'agreeing' to do the film, which he desperately needed and wasn't wanted for, said he would only do the movie if he was given first billing over O'Toole. Executives reeled back, laughing feebly at this piece of madness, and were totally nonplussed when O'Toole calmly told them that he didn't give a damn and Sellers was to be given anything he asked for. Jules was fit to be tied and even I thought it was a bit over-casual, but O'Toole refused to discuss the matter. So P. Sellers was given everything he demanded and he got top billing. Then, when they started shooting, he took against Woody, throwing out huge chunks of script and wiring music-hall entertainers in England for gags, which were then inserted into his scenes. I was disappointed to see that O'Toole condoned this behaviour. They refused to rehearse with Woody Allen and I don't think Peter Sellers ever realised that he was dealing with a comic talent every bit as great as and even more complex than his own. Clive juggled the personalities and managed to run a very efficient, hardworking unit and produced a funny film.

Sellers came into my life some years later when O'Toole was filming *Man of La Mancha*. He pitched up in O'Toole's suite of rooms at the Excelsior Hotel in Rome and installed himself on the sitting room couch. He was having personal problems so he was depressed and couldn't return home to England because of taxation problems. Tiring of his guest, O'Toole urged him to go and stay with me in Hampstead, where he could be hidden from the Inland Revenue and would find the study day-bed much more comfortable than the Excelsior couch.

Our house, when O'Toole was away, centred around the activities of the girls; their diary was crammed with dancing classes, parties, visits to the dentist and oculist, homework, tests, sports and holidays. (I was amazed that they could fit so much into each day.) Now, we were told to expect the movie star and his chauffeur. I myself was also busy, so my mother made a wonderful boeuf bourguignon, which would only improve as the hours went by, and we awaited the arrival – time unspecified – of the Sellers team. When the doorbell rang I rushed for the door and saw more Louis Vuitton luggage than I had ever seen outside an antique shop (at that time there was no Louis Vuitton shop in England and it wasn't widely familiar). This was not luggage for a short stay I thought, with a sinking heart, as I yielded up my study and day-bed. When '*Boeuf*' was mentioned, the two men started back, 'Didn't Petey *say* I was a vegetarian?' said Peter. 'No dear Petey didn't,' I said grimly. 'Well, he may have done,' soothed Mamgu. 'It's not a problem.' As we tore down to the basement kitchen she wailed in Welsh, 'What do vegetarians eat?' 'Vegetables,' I snapped. Liz the nanny and I plundered our big cellars under Heath Street, returning with mountains of carrots and cabbages and potatoes and onions. 'Okay Siân, you upstairs to give them drinks and keep them distracted,' ordered my mother, back in charge. 'Liz, start peeling and fetch someone to help you.'

Within an hour Peter Sellers was exclaiming over the best home-made soup he'd ever tasted. 'Can I have this every day?' 'Of *course*,' said my mother, sweetly. Downstairs Liz and the au-pair and I cleared away mountains of peelings and began assembling the next day's pyramids of vegetables. When my mother came down, beaming, I held up a large cauldron and pointed at the dregs. 'What's that?' (In Welsh) 'Bones.' 'Vegetarians don't eat *bones*.' 'You can't make soup without bones.' I gave up the unequal struggle and for a month Peter Sellers thrived on what he thought was vegetable soup, and, glumly picking my way round the L-V trunks, unable to use my phone or get at my books, I thought, 'Oh, what the hell, it won't harm him.' Like many great comics, Peter was not much fun at home. He was depressed. At night, I would let myself in and try to tiptoe past the study and fly up the stairs unnoticed. On the nights when I was waylaid, we would sit in the Green Room

382

next door and Peter would talk of himself, explaining to me how impossible his life was and how sad. He had made a film with Sophia Loren and conceived an unrequited passion for her. Listening to him I couldn't believe that anyone so smart in his own field could be so stupid as to misunderstand the situation so utterly. How could he imagine that a practical, ambitious woman from a poor background – protected by Carlo Ponti, her powerful, film-producer husband who devoted his life to promoting her career – would, for a moment, consider endangering her position for a romance with a mere actor. I wasn't much use to him and I didn't become a close friend. As soon as I could I left the house and joined O'Toole at the Excelsior in Rome. The girls came to Rome as well and O'Toole laughed evilly when I arrived, worn out by my house guest and his self-preoccupation. 'How *could* you?' 'Ah, get off. Don't make a fuss. There's no harm in him.'

Naturally, Mamgu became a confidante of Sellers and got to like Bert, the chauffeur. Peter had embraced an Eastern religion, we supposed, and she didn't much like the Eastern scrolls hanging over the bookshelves or the chanting which filled the ground floor from time to time, but she liked looking after him. I stayed away until he was gone.

I'd been bumping up against famous people since I was a girl, so it wasn't exactly difficult having to live with celebrities and I knew enough not to expect them to be fascinating when they were off duty, but alas, many huge stars were really heavy-going. There is a kind of self-absorption that infects their behaviour and makes them less interesting than they might otherwise be. I'd been raised to have respect but not to be 'a respecter of persons' and I couldn't shake that off. There were glorious exceptions. I loved my time with Wilfrid Lawson, I would have given anything to know Ralph Richardson better, the time I spent with John Steinbeck and his wife, Elaine, is indelibly etched in my memory, as were the few evenings I spent with Jacques Tati and his wife. Laurens van der Post was even better than I could have imagined from reading his books and I was perfectly happy to be a kind of third handmaiden on the left for Edith Evans because I admired her so much.

Kate Hepburn, whom I first met when she was filming *Lion in Winter*, was interesting and in many ways admirable, but I couldn't help feeling envious of the way in which she seemed to have her life organised so as to have things all her own way. Her seemingly simple life was in fact kept oiled and running by retainers of long standing. Her companion ('Phy-lisss!' would go the shout whenever she wanted anything) travelled with her and organised her living arrangements. She wore gorgeous, glamorous clothes all her life until, cleverly, realising that, no longer youthful, she couldn't compete with young actresses, she devised a marvellous uniform; colours of beige and red, black or white; slacks and smart gifted or purloined men's sweaters or jackets. Her years with Spencer Tracy suited her very well – a wife with none of the wife's boring jobs – and she admitted as much to me. When O'Toole, who was very smitten by her glamorous, unusual presence, was moved to say, 'My God – if I was thirty years younger I'd have given Spencer Tracy a run for his money', we looked at each other, slightly cross-eyed, wondering which of us had been more insulted; Kate for being considered too old to be desirable, or me, who, all things being equal, would have been discarded in favour of a young Kate. It wasn't something to be thought about too closely, so we both smiled sweetly. When, in 1970, Kate was playing in Coco, the musical, in New York, O'Toole and I dined at her house before leaving for South America. As we left, she grabbed me by the arm and hissed, 'You let him push you around – stop it. I'm spoiled. *Get spoiled!*' I nodded, smiling, and thought I'd like to see her try getting her own way with O'Toole, were she thirty years younger. Not a chance. I remember her as spoiled and selfish indeed, but what wonderful common sense she had. And she took what she wanted and paid for it, and, I would hazard, has rarely had occasion to regret her choices.

On the whole, O'Toole kept me out of his professional life. Very few people were invited to Guyon House. We gave the most two large parties and one tiny Christmas morning cocktail party, distinguished only by a very woozy Robert Stephens falling right through a rather nice chair. He was living with my friend, the remarkable and beautiful Pat Quinn (whose mother I played in Shoulder to Shoulder, the TV series about the Suffragette Movement). They married subsequently and were perfect for each other. An Irish friend of mine went to them for lunch one day and round about teatime Pat – not quite herself – served some meat, then a little hors-d'oeuvre, then a pudding, then said, 'Oh God, I forgot the veg,' and left the room never to return. 'Please excuse Patricia,' murmured Robert. 'She's frightfully unhappy today.'

It was so mightily encouraging when Robert made a return (almost from the dead) to play Falstaff and get knighted. The most extraordinary things happen in our profession. I'm sure Anthony Hopkins would agree that he was, in 1978, the least likely candidate for international superstardom and respectable knighthood. Then he went to America, made some awful movies, temporarily renounced the theatre, nearly killed himself in a car, joined AA, and became one of our senior, respectable ennobled actors. Hepburn was one of Tony's first mentors in the movies. O'Toole, against the wishes of the American producers and the casting director, had insisted on engaging him for *Lion in Winter*. (John Castle was another of his 'finds' and Nigel Terry also – a remarkable, very Cornish actor.) When Tony played his first scene with Kate, she took him by the shoulders and turned him away from her. 'There's the camera – over there. It needs to see you.'

Most of the actors I knew and liked were people I'd worked with, but one actor, very close to O'Toole, became someone I treasured although we never worked together. Donal McCann was hugely talented. The son of a sometime Lord Mayor of Dublin, he'd been raised in the Big House and during his childhood had suffered an enormous tragedy. Entrusted with his younger brother's safety on the way to school, he'd looked away for a moment and his little brother had darted into the road and was run over. Donal never recovered, never escaped the demons that pursued him after this, and he drank to excess for much of his adult life. He and O'Toole played *Godot* together many times, learning it holed up in the Shelbourne, sleeping in twin beds and working every moment that they weren't sleeping. They were wonderful together in the play, with Niall Tóibín playing Pozzo. One day Donal came to visit O'Toole in Guyon House. His chum was spending the day in bed and not even for Donal could he be disturbed. We sat together until lunchtime and Donal refused to come to the dining room to eat. I returned to the Green Room after lunch with the girls and we sat there as darkness fell. By this time Donal was into his second bottle of vodka and I, sipping cold tea, was getting sleepy. Nodding off, I jerked awake to dimly make out something odd about Donal's silhouette as he sat on the Green Room 'stage' with his back to Men's Surgical beyond the garden. He was on fire, having dropped his cigarette into his curly black hair, which he was in the habit of teasing with his right hand as he talked. I crossed to the drinks tray and, picking up a soda siphon, turned it on to Donal and put out the fire on his head. He blinked a bit and held out his glass for a refill. Years later, when I was on location in Dublin, a slim athletic figure darted across the road and embraced me. I could hardly recognise the teetotal Donal. His work, which had always been good, became even more wonderful.

The Steward of Christendom at the Royal Court, not many years before his untimely death, was a never-to-be-forgotten piece of acting.

Godot is one of my favourite plays and McCann and O'Toole surely approached the intention of the author. The author . . . Sam Beckett. So beautiful, so vain. Blind as a bat and didn't wear glasses. Exquisitely dressed in cashmere polo-necks and soft tweeds. A cross-Channel swimmer. And an opinionated bigot in some ways, I thought. I sat in a flat in Manchester Square and listened to Beckett and O'Toole, fascinating and good-looking, as they became drunker and drunker, and through a haze of tiredness and boredom I heard Mr Beckett say, '*Godot* can never be filmed. No film with dialogue has *ever* succeeded. Buster Keaton is the only film actor worth considering.' Sitting there, slightly outside the adoring throng at the great man's feet, I thought, 'Oh puhleez. Give me a break' and, aloud and unheard, said, 'Excuse me,' and left. Standing in a fog-bound Manchester Square I began to laugh as I searched for a cab. Here I was wandering around WI on my own because I was bored to death by a great playwright who I thought was talking rubbish about the movies.

In 1966 I worked for Sam, and it was an extraordinary experience. Jackie MacGowran came to my dressing room at the Vaudeville Theatre where I was halfway through a long run of *Man and Superman* with Alan Badel. He was carrying a copy of *Eh, Joe*. 'We'll do it at the BBC,' he said. 'You will speak the "play" – a monologue lasting twenty minutes. You won't be seen and the camera will remain on me throughout.' What a lovely, easy job, I thought as I agreed to go the following Sunday to a flat on Haverstock Hill and work with Mr Beckett himself. There were very few preliminaries and I began to read for him. It wasn't an *easy* read but I thought I was doing quite well until, after about ten minutes, I caught sight of Sam's face contorted with what looked like pain. I ploughed on and when I'd finished there was a long silence. Then, 'I don't know where to start,' said Sam, faintly. I was too sorry for him to be upset on my own behalf and I urged him to be as brutally frank as he wished and please to believe that if he *told* me what he wanted I *would* be able to deliver it to him. I don't think he believed me. It took two weeks of grinding work to get the twenty minutes anywhere near what Sam wanted. He banged his hand on the table like a metronome; three beats for a full stop, two for a colon, half for a comma. Three speak, speak, speak. Half speak speak. Two speak stop. I gave up trying to interpret the monologue and learned it like a piece of music, hanging on to that text like a stubborn dog with a bone. Finally came the moment when Sam nodded from the control cubicle. Michael Bakewell, who was producing, and Jackie, who was hanging about looking anxious, both looked relieved. I had a bit of time to spare before going to the theatre and I asked Sam if I could try another take; one for me. He shrugged but maybe he thought I'd earned a small favour after all we'd been through, so off I went, hoping that enough of Sam's rhythms had become second nature to me because I wasn't thinking about them on this take. When I'd finished Sam said, '*That's* what I meant all along,' and I could have hugged him except I didn't dare. I could quite see why whole companies had gone on strike during rehearsals of his plays and refused to work if his time-beating hand wasn't removed. But I was glad I'd hung on; it had been quite an experience to remember. Patrick Magee and Jackie MacGowran and Billie Whitelaw were Beckett 'naturals', the rest of us had to work quite a bit harder. And there's nothing quite as wonderful as having the author around. What would it be like to be able to pop up to Admin to ask Shakespeare what exactly did he mean on page 32?

A pattern of sorts emerged. O'Toole's work took precedence over everything. His large office in Belgravia presided over by Jules was organised so as to keep him busy as much of the time as possible. Jules, who had spent his earlier life with some of the major players in the movie business, had a theory that work was the only thing that kept some of the more 'highly coloured characters' sane. And much as I would have liked to have been able to have more of O'Toole for myself and the family (maybe even to take a holiday), I had to admit that Jules might be right. While he was preparing for a big movie, O'Toole was an angel; hardworking, moderate and a benevolent presence in the house. When he was actually filming he was quiet, self-disciplined, a little 'absent' even when at home. Once work was completed, very often after a six-month work period, he became a different person, erratic and unpredictable, turning night into day. Then he would sleep and sleep and wake penitent and chastened and spend days being attentive and charming – overwhelmingly charming. I never saw anyone fail to forgive him completely, no matter how badly they'd been hurt, and I was as susceptible as any of them. This roller-coaster life would continue only until his attention was engaged by a new job and then quiet times would be resumed. It was my good fortune to love and be loved by this extraordinary man, and it was my deep misfortune to be as incapable as the next person of expressing my anger at his unfair, unjust behaviour. No one else in my private or working life had ever been able to treat me as he did. I was part of a huge conspiracy directed towards protecting O'Toole from the painful consequences of his behaviour. It didn't make me feel better that bigger, stronger, cleverer people than I shared the urge to protect him.

Walking out on him was not an option. Unbelievable as it may seem, life in Guyon House was happy; it was a big house and the children, my mother and Liz led busy, enjoyable lives in very comfortable, beautiful surroundings. They took holidays in Ireland in a cottage we had acquired in the Sixties, and we began to plan an Irish home, on the large piece of land O'Toole had bought. Taking a meat-cleaver to all this seemed pretty selfish. And there was so much of our life that I loved. Trying to figure out how to proceed, I decided that the only truly awful thing that could happen to me would be for me to become sour and resentful. I had *truly* to get over my feelings of hurt pride. I also had to stop identifying with O'Toole, feeling embarrassed or guilty when he behaved badly in public, and above all I had to learn not to accept as truth his icy criticism of me as – when drunk – he ordered me out of the car or restaurant or our house. 'Who owns this house?' was the frequent Dr Jekyll challenge. I never liked to point out that we owned it jointly. On the whole – with a few mutinous lapses – I managed to embrace survival strategy and in the process I became harder and rougher around the edges, but it made the bad times bearable. Someone asked me, 'How do you manage to combine your busy private life with your career?' O'Toole answered for me, 'She doesn't have a career. She has jobs.' No, I thought, but let the moment pass without comment.

I didn't show my hurt over my summary rejection from *What's New Pussycat?* and I got my reward almost at once. A few years previously I'd been asked to be in *The Night of the Iguana* by Tennessee Williams. Vanessa Redgrave, who'd made a *very* good start to her career and had great support from her husband, Tony Richardson, was to play Hannah Jelkes and I was asked to play a part I was totally unsuited for – Maxine – the character that Bette Davis had played when Margaret Leighton had done the play in America. I fell completely in love with the role of Hannah and felt bitterly frustrated not to be asked to play her. I was so right for the part. So was Vanessa, of course, but that wasn't my concern at that moment. I'd turned down the offer and in the event the production didn't take place. Now the play came to me again; Richard Shulman and Philip Wiseman had acquired the rights and were going to mount it in Croydon. Croydon . . . the Ashcroft Theatre in the Fairfield Halls complex wasn't exactly the most appealing of theatres. I said 'Yes', of course. I just wanted to play Hannah Jelkes, but it was a damned shame that it was going to take place for such a short run in one venue.

I'd seen the movie of *The Night of the Iguana* with Richard Burton, Deborah Kerr and Ava Gardner, and hadn't thought much of it. It was given wisdom that once a play had been filmed it could not be mounted as a West End production, so I was lucky to get Croydon. And I would be able to commute.

As I read the script I realised with dismay that it wasn't the same script I'd read when Woodfall Productions held the rights, before the film was made. The cuts really bothered me and I began to ask if I could reinstate bits of the play that for no reason I could see had vanished. I became a terrible nuisance, bargaining for a line here, a speech there. Philip and Richard were patient but firm – we *had* to perform the new version. Gradually I discovered that some of the cuts had been made at the insistence of Bette Davis, who hadn't been too happy with the way her part was received as they began touring (Maxine just isn't as good a part as Hannah). Tennessee, I was told, was obliging beyond belief, chopping away at his play with a will. I was astonished; the playwrights I'd met were touchy about altering commas, let alone brilliant chunks of text. Temporarily deflated (I'd seen myself as the author's champion), I began rehearsing the new version, but as the weeks went by I began to slip back the bits I couldn't bear to be without and Philip turned a blind eye.

This was the best part I'd been given for years and I became over-enthusiastic and probably tiresomely obsessed by the play. Philip Wiseman, a quiet, bookish American in English tweeds, was a marvel of discretion. Somehow he reined me in – he admitted afterwards that directing me was a bit like handling a jumpy, highly strung race horse – and we arrived safe and secure at our opening night. I fell in love with the Ashcroft auditorium. Philip had 'placed' the production so well in it that it felt wonderfully comfortable. I enjoyed going to the stage in a lift that also carried boxers or wrestlers (half-dressed muscular men, raring to hit something) on their way to the sports arena. It was very relaxing to be in a dressing room that totally defied one to pretty it up.

There were half-pint glasses of half-drunk beer on the dressing table with its layer of dust and grease. I didn't even bother to make a 'place' for myself. I don't know if anyone sent flowers; they certainly didn't make it to the dressing room. Mark Eden was the Reverend Shannon and I was lucky again that he also possessed the temperament of a gentleman. As I nagged and altered things and rehearsed and re-rehearsed and over-rehearsed, he got on with his own work and helped me where he could and resisted what must have been a justifiable temptation to take me by the shoulders and shake me until I quietened down. I think I was as much of a nuisance as is possible to be within the walls of a theatre.

On opening night the play went wonderfully well. The following day I got up early and went off to model some clothes for an Irish designer. I was in the middle of a long photographic session when Philip tracked me down and asked me if I'd seen the papers. No, I hadn't (I hadn't thought the national press would come to Croydon). 'Well,' he went on, suppressing what even on the phone I could tell was huge excitement, 'we have rave notices across the board and our pick of five London theatres into which to transfer. Be at the theatre early and we'll talk.' I went back to my photo session more thoughtful than excited. Already I was worrying about the transfer; would our show work as well outside the confines of what had become to me the 'dear Fairfield Hall'? The phone went again. Audrey Wood, Tennessee's agent, sent a message of congratulations and said that 'Tom' (Tom? I didn't know that Tennessee wasn't called Tennessee) would be coming to London for the West End opening. Back to the clothes and the posing. 'Chin down, eyes up, button the jacket.'

Eventually I'm through and dash home to see the girls and then take the train to Croydon. The journey gives me time to think. My mother says the phone has been ringing all day with requests for interviews and photographs, the house is full of bouquets; she's quietly pleased. I feel odd. It's four years since I was the subject of this kind of attention and something has happened to steal the joy from the moment. I feel – what? Apprehensive. A bit of me seems to have broken and I don't have the confidence to enjoy all this fuss. It's as though I'll wake up to find that a mistake has been made. 'Not you! Whatever made you think we meant you?' And what if it *was* a kind of mistake last night at the theatre? What if I can't do it again? Keeping these fears hidden I put on a brave, bright face and join the high-spirited gathering at the theatre. It is wonderful for Richard Shulman and Philip and I'm genuinely happy for them. We'll choose a theatre tomorrow. What larks! I'm glad to get to my dingy dressing room and put on my dingy clothes. The only way I can maintain my equilibrium is to think about nothing but the play from now on. Let the rest wash over me. See to the children. Attend to the play. This unexpected turn of events has thrown into sharp relief how badly I've reacted to the events of the last few years and how low I've been brought. For whatever reason I've arrived at a state of mind where I cannot feel that anything I do is of any consequence whatever and I'm worried how this success might affect my relationship with O'Toole. Might this change? If it doesn't, is it something I might be able to turn to my advantage? Or will it always apply a little brake to my efforts?

Chapter Twenty-one

Playing eight times a week really suits me. Many of my friends hate it and they hate being in a run. Not I. To me there is no greater pleasure than steering a good production of a good play through the different circumstances that occur each night. Each night is different and not different. Flops are another matter. I've had more than my share and can get fed up with a bad play in a week, but even then, there's a kind of perverse satisfaction in getting a bad job done well. I've been stage-struck since I was six, and sat in Swansea Empire watching a panto-mime. Will I go on feeling like this for ever, I wonder?

At the moment I'm as happy as can be, ensconced in the Savoy Theatre. Tennessee – Tom – did arrive and stood on his seat in the front row and overdid his enthusiasm. Richard Condon (the novelist and Debbie Jupp's father) rushed a massive basket of flowers down the aisle and had a noisy row with an usherette who wouldn't let him hand it up to the stage (for fear it contained explosives?). There were flowers everywhere and I remembered that on my last opening in London, just a few months ago, someone had thrown copper coins on to the stage and there had been the noise of booing and hissing, rather than cheers.

Nothing had happened to alter my reservations about opening nights. I'd worn a nasty, mustard-coloured old frock to work so that I wouldn't be tempted to go out to celebrate afterwards; straight home as usual, a relatively early night and up early with Kate. Later, when the play settled down, I began going out to parties with my new best friend Tom, but I think I was a bit of a disappointment to him as a date. My neuroses were far too well submerged and I could have only a flimsy grip on his attention. As we entered a room I would watch him as he prowled around for a while before homing in on someone who, a surprising number of times, would turn out to be in the throes of a breakdown, or recovering from a failed suicide attempt or about to do something disastrous. Nose to nose, they would chat for hours.

On other levels, we got on very well and corresponded from time to time after he returned to America. He sent me a poem he wrote for me. I got to know Audrey Wood, his agent, as well, and they sent me all his new material for many years to come. I admired him above all the authors I knew, so I suppose that predisposed him to like me too.

Soon after we opened, O'Toole returned from France where he was filming and when he came to see the play he was generous about my performance. To Ken Jupp he said facetiously, 'Blimey, they'll be calling me Mr Phillips in a minute. I'm off!' and hopped back to Paris. When the film finished he went into rehearsal for a new play by David Mercer, *Ride a Cock Horse*. It was long, very long, and had a difficult shape. In two parts, it consisted of six duologues between the hero and his wife, his girlfriend and his older mistress. It was a marathon part for an actor. It was also, I was given to understand, a '*pièce à clef*' about well-known contemporary writers. It was so well written and so depressing. (My life, in comparison, seemed peachy, I thought gratefully.) The ladies of the company were Wendy Craig as the girlfriend, Barbara Jefford as the wife and Yvonne Mitchell as the unhappy mistress. Rather them than me, I thought as I made my way to the Savoy.

David Mercer began to visit the house to work with O'Toole. A great deal of alcohol was consumed. Then, when O'Toole began rehearsing and cut out the drink, David would arrive and drink alone, and finally O'Toole would retreat to the bedroom to work, leaving my mother to cope with the brilliant but very touchy playwright. I, thank God, was out of reach at the theatre. My mother spent hours listening to David talk about his parents, so one night when he arrived dressed in a railwayman's overalls, mourning the death of his railwayman father, my mother ministered to him and finally he spent the night on the Green Room couch. When it was revealed later to her that his father was in fact alive and well, my mother – endlessly patient – was *almost* annoyed with him.

Between shows at the Savoy on matinée day. A knock and then the door opens before I can say 'Come in' – O'Toole, followed by Michael Codron the producer. Drama. At rehearsal, they've lost (or shed) Yvonne Mitchell. Can I open in Nottingham next Tuesday? I open my mouth to say 'But what about my play?' and they say they'll buy me out of the last two weeks of the run (Bernie Delfont, a friend, is one of the producers). I don't want to miss two weeks of *Iguana* but it doesn't occur to me to deny O'Toole. Also, it's a challenge. I don't like the

David Mercer play and I don't think that, at my age, I'm very well suited to a part based on Penelope Mortimer in a bit of a decline. All the more reason to try, I think perversely.

So I'll travel to Nottingham the day after I close Tom's play on Saturday and open on Tuesday. 'When will I rehearse?' O'Toole considers. 'Well, now, let's see. Learn it and go over the moves with the stage manager and we'll rehearse you *after* we open. We have four weeks on the road.' Heavens – this *is* a challenge. I've never opened a play without rehearsing it. It's an endless part; two duologues of over half an hour. If I pull it off, O'Toole will be so grateful. And I'll be doing him a favour. Michael Codron is strangely silent. I wonder if this is O'Toole's harebrained idea and he doesn't like to object. We're all going along with the idea. Gordon Flemyng, who had made such a good job of directing the TV play *The Other Man*, which I did with Michael Caine and whom I introduced to O'Toole, is directing the Mercer play. I didn't know he worked in the theatre at all.

Nottingham is a nightmare. O'Toole has decided that we will only play the biggest of theatres and, confident of doing good business, he will clear all production costs before we come into town. There are banners reading 'O'Toole' all over the streets and the run is completely sold out before we begin. I've never seen anything quite like this and I've played with some of our biggest theatre stars. I learn my lines and write down my moves from the prompt copy. I share a suite with O'Toole but hardly see him. He's deeply involved with David Mercer, who is drinking heavily. Every night we have dinner with him and Gordon in a private dining room in the hotel. I still haven't rehearsed. I haven't dried on stage and I haven't stood in the wrong place, but I haven't the faintest idea what I'm doing. It's utterly horrible. The little bit of confidence that grew during the months of success at the Savoy drains away now in the first week of playing *Ride a Cock Horse*.

They cut chunks of the play. Every night the stage manager comes round at the half and says things like, 'Take out pages twenty-four and twenty-five, the top of forty-five, two lines at the bottom of fifty, this section on fifty-one.' I barely know the original text, learning cuts every day as well is torture. The play is down to about four hours long. Now O'Toole declares, 'Go faster. Top all the laughs and let's see if we can't cut fifteen minutes by playing faster.' 'Topping' laughs means coming in at the crest of the laugh and moving on smartly; it's a struggle, in a huge theatre, to be audible without shouting when you're speaking over a huge laugh. We all manage. Floundering about a bit, I catch O'Toole on stage looking at me quizzically. 'Are you going to *do* it like this?' he mutters sardonically in the middle of the scene. I'm fashionably flat-chested. Message from the management: 'Get her some falsies.' This is hell.

'When do I rehearse?'

'Tomorrow.'

'Oh, thank God.'

At seven o'clock I wake, alone, in the suite. At nine-thirty a.m., walking through the foyer to go and rehearse with O'Toole, I meet him and Gordon Flemyng coming *in* after a night on the town.

'Hello, darling, where are you off to?'

'To rehearse with you.'

'Ah, sorry about that, darling. Bye. See you for a spot of late lunch?'

Each day I go to the theatre and go through my lines, but I'm no nearer playing this part properly. I hate this play now. I hate the dinners at which D. Mercer gets drunk then gets on the hotel phone and recites soliloquies from it to someone who must be driven mad. It's all so depressing. But the money is flooding into the box office. Who is in charge? 'I'm going to complain to the management,' I think and then, remembering that this is a co-production with Keep Films, I realise I *am* the management.

The torment continued. Being confused, nightly, in front of thousands of people may not rank high in torment on a global scale, but it *is* major nastiness on a personal scale. Gordon, the director, managed to avoid me, Barbara and Wendy had their own problems and O'Toole never did rehearse with me. We opened to a sold-out, limited run in London. The big Piccadilly Theatre seemed quite cosy after our huge touring theatres. Production costs had been paid off. I supposed that, as usual, O'Toole was not taking a salary. I don't know how the play was received by the critics (I'd recently stopped reading reviews), but it was a huge commercial success. People – Kenneth Tynan notable among them – came again and again. I hated every minute of it. O'Toole and I had completely different timetables. I would rise early, see the girls, see to the house while he slept. Seething with resentment, part of me longed to have a huge row with him. Who else, I wondered, would treat me with such colossal disrespect? No one I could think of. But he was marvellous in the play and he loved it and he had a huge job to do each night: how could I have a row with him? And if I did, how would he torture me on stage? I didn't delude myself that I was smart enough to cope with an angry O'Toole, certainly not in front of a packed house. Each day at five o'clock I would eat a plate of scrambled eggs, go to the West End, walk about a bit, go into the theatre and go up to my dressing room, call home unnecessarily to check everything was still all right, throw up, get made up, do the show, afterwards descend to dressing room Number One if we had mutual friends in to see the show, occasionally I would go to dinner (always if the Bucks or the Jupps were around). The rest of the time I went home alone. It was odd. And faintly embarrassing.

And yet O'Toole gave me one of the best opening-night presents I ever received. He remembered that, many years ago, fleeing from a failed relationship, I'd had to leave behind my mother's complete set of Charles Dickens, which I'd been reading since I was a little girl. He bought me a lovely edition of the complete works. The boxes were delivered to my room just as I was throwing up and hating him, and I was overcome with gratitude and love and misery all at once. Fancy his remembering something that had happened so long ago. Fancy his knowing how much I missed those books. He always knew things about me that no one would guess at.

It felt as though the whole town flocked to Dressing Room One. One regular visitor – and he didn't even watch the show – was Robin Douglas-Home. He irritated me hugely and was for ever insisting that we should go with him to a gaming club in Mayfair. O'Toole, son of an unsuccessful gambling bookmaker, liked gambling, but had successfully disciplined himself not to indulge. Week after week, day after day, Robin Douglas-Home haunted the theatre and, finally, we went with him. I watched, impassive, while O'Toole lost almost £10,000 in half an hour. We smiled and accepted a glass of champagne and drifted into the night, still smiling, but I couldn't speak for fury.

The play and O'Toole's pace of life are taking their toll. He begins to bleed from the nose on stage. Night after night there's blood everywhere, but the audience doesn't seem to notice. I never cease to be amazed at what the audience simply doesn't see. No one can understand why he's losing blood every night, but Gerry Slattery says it's time to stop. The play, which is only slated for a limited run, could actually run for ever, but everyone has been paid and a profit has been made so it's decided to close the show two weeks early. There is a God, I think. I'm just about as low in spirits as it is possible to be. One of my teachers from RADA and a friend of O'Toole's as well sees that I'm in a bad way despite the bright smile after the show. The following day he sends me one of my unread notices for *The Night of the Iguana*; only months ago W.A. Darlington, the senior critic of the *Daily Telegraph*, it seems, had written, 'If she never acts again she has proved she is a great actress.' I look at it in stupefaction. I feel that I've now spent months acting badly and doubt that I was *ever* any good. The review gives me no consolation. Going about my daily business – dealing with the domestic details of our life, occupying myself with the children, listening to my mother and my treasured daily help, Manolita, writing letters for O'Toole – I am well aware that the way I do my job doesn't matter to anyone except me. But it does matter terribly to me whether I act well or badly.

We never worked happily together, sadly for me. *Ride a Cock Horse* was a push-push experience – all bad, but usually there were good aspects as well as painful ones. *Goodbye Mr Chips* was an example of a pull-push engagement. I was cast in a roundabout way and felt that O'Toole was not pleased that I'd been given the part of Ursula Mossbank (which Terence Rattigan based on Tallulah Bankhead). I spent some time during the student riots of 1968 in Paris, marooned in the George V with Herb Ross, who was to direct the film, and Nora Kaye, formerly a prima ballerina and now Herb's wife and collaborator. We got along famously and Herb asked me if I'd like to be considered for the part of the actress – along with half a dozen of my contemporaries. When we were able to return to London, I duly presented myself at the studio and read for Herb, who had never seen me act. He gave me the part and, to our dismay, when we came to film the party sequences, O'Toole declined to rehearse with me, leaving me to walk the set with Herb and with Ossie Morris, the lighting cameraman.

I retired to my dressing room and stayed there alone, going over the scenes until I knew them backwards, sideways and upside down. I was terrified of the ordeal ahead but determined not to be found wanting. Called to the set, I sat on my own, waiting. O'Toole sat alone, some distance away. Afterwards, Herb said it was like sending into space astronauts who didn't know each other. He was nonplussed and I didn't know either why O'Toole behaved as he did. I guessed that maybe he was overwhelmingly concerned that I might not be any good and simply couldn't deal with his nerves. But that was my guess. In the event the scenes worked like clockwork without the usual preparation, and despite the complex set we 'got' the scenes in one take. 'What was that about?' asked Herb. I shook my head, as mystified as he was. No mention was ever made afterwards of the tensions of the day. O'Toole was affability itself when he returned home. I loved watching him work on that film and thought that he gave a great performance in a so-so movie. When he was made up as old Mr Chips, I looked for him in the canteen and, not recognising him, walked past him. He made a lovely old man. We rented a house in Cerne Abbas in Dorset where the bulk of the film was shot and the girls and I spent wonderfully happy weeks there.

Trials, like the hateful first day of filming, served me well in the long run. There was very little I couldn't handle and very few actors who scared me, however 'difficult' their behaviour. Surviving O'Toole in a bad mood made me very self-reliant. When in 1970 I came to work with Rex Harrison on *Platonov*, I was aware that he had a fiendish reputation for being ungenerous, to say the least. His behaviour didn't alarm me at all. Interestingly, in Wilfrid Lawson's opinion he had the edge on his contemporaries: Sir Laurence and Sir John and even Sir Ralph. 'Took the wrong turning,' Wilfrid said sadly. Rex's rages were apocalyptic and strong men paled as he tore a phone from the wall one day and threw all the furniture off a set he didn't particularly like. Watching him, I could imagine what a great Lear he would have made. Knowing him to be ruthless in appropriating whole scenes for himself, I was determined not to be eclipsed, and once he saw that I had more than done my homework and that I wasn't frightened of him, he let me 'in', and although it was always as dangerous as acting on sheet ice, acting with him became truly thrilling and rewarding. I admired him almost more than anyone I had ever worked with.

Chapter Twenty-two

Meanwhile, our domestic life was going through one of the welcome, quiet periods. O'Toole and I were working hard and my mother became the point of refuge for neglected guests. O'Toole was lavish in his offers of hospitality and equally protective of his working time (easily bored, as well). People would arrive and find themselves adrift and alone in the Green Room. A great deal of the time I didn't know who was in the house, and if I returned late from the theatre to find a party in full swing I shot through the hall and up the stairs to the bedroom before my presence was registered. I really liked getting up early and seeing the children in the morning.

My mother actually enjoyed staying up and talking, especially to the writers. For instance, she was the one who scooped up and took down to the big kitchen a figure that I'd stepped over in some exasperation as I left with Kate early one morning. He'd obviously been asleep on the hall floor for hours. I called her later to find out who the derelict drunk was. 'Oh a lovely boy,' she replied. 'Yes, but who?' 'Wait a minute now, James – James Baldwin, that's it. I've just ordered his books from the High Hill Bookshop. He's had a wash and eaten a good breakfast. *Brilliant* man.' She guarded O'Toole's privacy ferociously and was known as 'The Dragon' by some of our more frivolous friends ('They've got nothing but time to waste, that lot,' she sniffed). I felt a little faint one day when I heard her on the phone saying, 'No Sir Laurence, I'm afraid it is *impossible* for me to disturb Peter. He is *working*.' 'No' (more emphatically), 'it is *impossible*.' 'Mummy, are you sure about that?' She turned, wide-eyed and shocked. 'He's *working*.' She worshipped him and the two of them would sit up late into the night playing Scrabble and talking, talking. She got rid of our cook and catered for his every whim – surprise lunch for eight, midnight snack for him, endless pots of tea at all hours, breakfast for people who hadn't been to bed.

It was a big house and because of the increasingly valuable art collection, it couldn't be left empty. Even so, with constant vigilance, dozens of internal locks, alarms and bars, we were still burgled twice; once very audaciously through the bars at the front of the house, well lit by a lamppost in Heath Street. It was a rather Hampstead-type break-in: the (very slim) burglar left with a valuable painting cut out of its frame, leaving behind a comb and a bloodstained copy of that week's *New Statesman*.

Good daily help was crucial, but finding it wasn't my great talent, especially as I tended to muddle up the people I'd interviewed. I must have been more dozy than usual the day I engaged Miss Statema; Dutch, almost six feet tall, stately in sombre clothes. 'What d'you think, Mummy?' Mamgu, who would have been the one to perceive the softer side of Genghis Khan, enthused, 'Wonderful choice. Immaculate.' When Miss Statema became ill, almost at once, my mother tore down the hill to her basement room, bearing flasks of hot soup and home-made bread, and Miss S. was back at work in no time, but looking subtly different. It was the clothes! No longer sombre; many shades of pink and the apron had been discarded. She looked almost modish. The following week she appeared in a dated but very dressy light wool 'afternoon frock' and the following week I was halted in my tracks in the front hall as she sashayed by in a lilac taffeta dress with a sweetheart neck and puffed sleeves, ballerina-length skirt, the ensemble finished off with elbow-length lace mittens and silver, open-toed dancing slippers.

She had a bad habit of throwing away a Hoover bag every week and I'd narrowed my good housekeeping down to the task of curing her of this wastefulness. Now, not quite daring to remark on her sartorial tribute to Christian Dior circa 1947, I overtook her, stood barring her way at the top of the stairs to the basement, and began, 'Em – Miss Statema, once again I must *insist* that you reuse the Hoover bags.' Towering above me malevolently, she stretched her right arm out behind her and, swinging it round, whacked me accurately across the face. As I reeled sideways into the (mercifully) closed door, she drew back and waited, strangely serene, as I gathered myself sufficiently to say, rather feebly, 'Em – I rather think you're going to have to – er – leave.' She nodded graciously and swept out saying, 'Send on my National Insurance Stamps.'

Determined not to share the house with any more sinister people, my very next choice was a small, round and cheerful, apple-cheeked woman who looked down to earth and healthy, as though she worked out of doors.

O'Toole was reading in the ground-floor study, so I asked her to work very quietly as she moved around the hall and Green Room. She nodded cheerfully. Descending from the nursery that afternoon I heard the lusty strains of music from below. 'Come and join us! Come and join us!' she sang, and as I peered down the stairwell I could see her, duster in one hand, bucket in the other, not doing much in the way of work, *marching* up and down outside the study as she sang. Running down the stairs, I hissed, 'Hush! Hush!'

'Oops,' she beamed and disappeared down to the basement. I knocked on the study door and went in to apologise. O'Toole was sitting in his wing chair and looked amused. I joined him and while we chatted, our new daily left by the front door, and as we glanced out of the window we saw her put down four bulging plastic bags and open up the doors to the big dustbin enclosure. She began riffling through the bins, singing to herself. I opened the door. 'Where exactly did you say you lived?' 'Oh, here and there,' she said breezily. I realised I'd employed a lady tramp who'd fancied a day or two indoors.

Mostly I left the interviewing to my mother and it was she who found Manolita, one of the nicest women I'd ever met. We became close; she did her job perfectly and a lot more besides, and I became godmother to one of her children. We never discussed anything personal or intimate, but she knew more about my life than anyone else in the house. Her discretion was absolute and I was grateful for her.

I used to tease O'Toole for acquiring what I called 'Petruchio's servants', charming, feckless people, hopeless in any job. Now, *he* got lucky as well and in fact the whole family benefited when Lionel Bryant was appointed as O'Toole's chauffeur.

One of his previous jobs had involved driving Montgomery Clift while he was filming *Suddenly Last Summer* and rendering everyone mad with confusion and exhaustion (and a young O'Toole was interviewed with a view to replacing him, should he fall apart completely). His drivers came and left on a regular basis. He never went to bed. He never told them where he was going – or why – or where he might be going next. They hung about all night and sometimes all day and, overcome with fatigue and deafened by wifely complaints, they resigned. Young Lionel Bryant heard the horror stories at the prestigious car hire firm where he worked and became intrigued by the challenge. He liked

Monty Clift's acting so why not have a go, he thought, and volunteered his services.

Warning his wife, Margaret, not to expect him home much, he told her, 'I'm going to drive Monty Clift and I'm not quitting.' And he didn't. Monty, with a drink or two taken, liked to travel lying on the floor of the limo with his feet out of the window. This raised eyebrows as they pulled up at smart restaurants, so Lionel always shot round to open the door, addressing him as 'Sir', daring the doorman to be disrespectful. He liked to tease at five o'clock in the morning, going round and round in the revolving door of the Dorchester. No one could use the door; he was impossible to catch. The staff liked him and were tolerant. Lionel found him to be as congenial as his acting was wonderful and, enduring nights in the countryside tramping through fields, looking for 'cows to stroke', he stayed with Monty and grew to like him more and more. He didn't quit, but Margaret Bryant was rather pleased when the movie finished and Monty went home to America. Driving Judy Garland, he felt sorry for what he saw as her underprivileged children and gladly spent days playing with them in Battersea Park. 'But you know, the little girl – she never talked. Just sat in the back of the car, singing, singing all the time. Drove me mad, all that singing.'

Now some benevolent act of fate directed him to us. It was Jules who engaged him and it was the most perfect piece of casting he ever accomplished. He was part of our family for thirteen years. He was O'Toole's driver, but when O'Toole was away he drove me or Mamgu or the girls (Liz, the nanny, had her own car). A Leo, he was an organiser and a bit of a bully, in a quiet way. No use getting into his car and saying 'Shepperton'. He really needed to know why Shepperton? Was it a nice visit, or an ordeal? Did we need to be dead on time or keep them waiting a minute or two? And how was I feeling? I learned to tell him what the day held; how easy or difficult it was going to be; and then he would work it all out and it would always be to perfection. I was surrounded by Leos: Jules, O'Toole, Lionel, Derek Coombs (O'Toole's brother-in-law), and they all had to be top dog.

Lionel wore Rolls-Royce livery at times, but he knew I was unimpressed and cared nothing for cars. I overheard him outside my dressing room at Pinewood, standing next to our brand-new Rolls. 'So, what's the Boss's wife think of it?' asked his friend. 'Her? All she wants to know about a car is "Where's the ashtray?"' He was like a brother to me and loyal to O'Toole and fond of my mother and protective of the children. Sometimes, when O'Toole was hard on me, these feelings were in conflict with each other and reconciling them put years on his life – literally, sapping his strength. While he remained at his post, I remained at mine. Does this seem absurd to outsiders? I suspect that only Lionel and I would fully understand the situation.

My mother, Manolita, Liz and Lionel formed a protective shield around me. I might have had difficulties at work, but I had more security at home than I had ever before experienced and I had no fears for the girls. Even so, I never forgot the need for caution and I took nothing for granted. The balance achieved was delicate and I prayed we could all maintain it.

Chapter Twenty-three

At last, the closing night of *Ride a Cock Horse*. I've been writing lists for a week at home and I've packed the bags and they're ready at the theatre. During the last show I clear out the dressing rooms. Lionel drives O'Toole and me to Heathrow and we catch a plane to Venice – just the two of us for two weeks. All the ugliness of the preceding months drops away and we move on to a level of total harmony, total happiness. His nose stops bleeding. I stop throwing up. We beam at each other, hold hands. This is what our doctor, Gerry Slattery, calls 'Time out of life'. But surely this is the problem. 'Out of life', above the humdrum, on journeys, in crisis, in danger even, we are in perfect accord, and happy, ecstatically happy a good deal of the time. Faced with ordinary life, surrounded by people and obligations, we become stiff, disjointed, dysfunctional, resentful. Nervously I put in a bid – can we try to make work a *part* of ordinary life, not something divorced from everyday life? He looks at me with those old eyes and nods as though he knows what I mean, but that's as far as it goes. He knows how hurt I am, how much I've hated him over the last months, and effortlessly he makes it all better. I don't understand his magic. So how am I ever going to make sense of my life? I don't think anyone could ever know me the way he does and I do have this urge to be wholly known. So does he. We know things about each other that we never articulate or share with anyone.

Cold, misty Venice. Unpoetically I think of it as the great poultice; the badness is drawn out of both of us, everything is healed. I grow smooth and soft and stop protecting myself.

Familiarity with Venice has bred more and more love for the city. We have been coming here every year since we met. This time we've brought James Morris's book on Venice. We walk all day carrying his book and find Othello's tomb, with strawberries carved on it, and as we approach the district called the ghetto (I think the word *getto* means metalworks), we hear the clink, clink of hammer on metal. One morning we meet a lovely American (there are very few visitors in this weather) and he says would we like to explore the lagoon with him? Of course we would, and we set off in a small boat to look for the island where the dug-up bones are put when the city graveyard is full up. 'It doesn't exist,' we've been told. Following a slim Edwardian guidebook, we cross and criss-cross the lagoon, finally bumping up through the mist into a bank of reeds. Pushing in, we reach solid ground and, in the silence, hear the rustling of tall dry reeds stuck here and there with bones. It is an island of dry bones pierced by grasses. Sam Beckett talks of a 'bone orchard' and here it is. We don't want to walk on the bones, so we push off again into the mist, cold and silent and glad when we get 'home' to the bar of the Danieli hotel, where we're staying, and the company of Gastone de Cal, the head barman, who has now become a friend.

We're building a little family in Venice. Gastone began it all and introduced us to the four-star gondolier of Venice, Gino Macropodio. He's doubly endeared to me because he has a wonderful tenor voice; Welsh tenors sound like Italian tenors and Gino makes me feel at home. We sing duets. Then we meet Gastone and Gino's friend, Buzz Bruning Jr, who is American but has become a Venetian resident, owning a house next to the Frari. He is writing a cookbook with his friend, the Cavalieri, who is a great gourmet and a war hero. We all dine out with the Cavalieri's sister, Maria, who is in her late seventies and is hugely admired by all the young men for her sprightly gait and terrific appetite. 'Look at her eating,' says Gino to the young waiter. They gaze in fond admiration as tiny Signora Maria tucks into a dinner that would satisfy a bricklayer. Sometimes Norma, Gastone's wife, brings their little children along for dinner as well. Each night we are three or four generations at one table, all having a good time, enjoying each other. A generation gap is maybe the first sign of a sick society.

Gastone, Buzz and Gino finally introduce us to their friend, the Great Toio, 'Toio Piazzetta' as he's known. He has a restaurant on Giudecca – a restaurant? It's a room with one table and the people at that table eat whatever it is that Toio's wife and mother-in-law are cooking for the family in the room beyond. Toio feels that he was meant for greater things and at night he escapes from the bedroom window and makes for the piazzetta next to St Mark's Square, and there he spends his time hanging out with his friends, moving slowly from bar to bar. He doesn't speak Italian, only Venetian, and even Gastone and Gino have trouble understanding him. I spend entire evenings sitting next to him, desperately trying to get the drift of the stories he tells – he never stops talking. Many of the stories are to do with the war and bunkers. The minute we hear 'bunkers', pronounced 'Boonkerrs', we know we're listening to a joke, and in time the word is enough to start us laughing – which inspires Toio to tell *more* funny war stories. Never in my life have I spent so many hours genuinely laughing at stories I don't understand at all. Dear, exasperating, rotund, bellicose Toio.

For years, as I got to know the city, I felt more and more that there was a deep reserve within the Venetians, and even O'Toole, usually adept at nosing out secret places, admitted that there was something he could not penetrate. It was as though, overrun by and living off tourists, the city with its great past resolutely kept something of itself to itself as at the same time it entertained, cosseted, cheated, spoiled and took advantage of the hordes that invaded it except in the depths of winter; hordes without whom it could not live. In a city where the inhabitants live with an awareness of the past ('So we all clubbed together and built this.' 'When was that?' '1732.'), tourism must be a bit of a comedown. Our feeling of being politely excluded lasted until our visit following the close of *Ride a Cock Horse*. It was winter. We flew to Venice, but in fact we were diverted to Milan, landing in torrential rain. There, we were put on a bus to Venice and when we arrived – it was still pouring with rain – the driver said, 'Okay, everyone back to Milan. You cannot go into Venice.' O'Toole looks at me and jerks his head towards the exit. Without hesitation I make for the door. 'No, you cannot disembark. There is nowhere to go.' 'Thank you. All the same—' pushing forward. 'No, madam. I must insist.' 'Keep going' (O'Toole from behind). 'Frightfully sorry, I have to get off. Thank you, goodbye. Just need the bags.' O'Toole, following, stuffs a bundle of notes into the driver's hand and he releases the bags from the hold.

Well, here we are. It's so quiet, unusually quiet, in Mestre. There's a lamp outside a deserted building and underneath it we pile up the bags and I sit on them. O'Toole gives me a book and says, 'Look after the bags and have a read. I'll be back. Just wait.' I read. It's still raining. When he returns – there is still no one about – he says, 'Okay, I think we're on,' and we manhandle the luggage to a jetty, which is in pitch darkness. The bags are loaded into a little motor boat. We speak in whispers. Why? Off we go. Why does the trip seem so strange? Well, for one thing it's dark – totally dark. It is the middle of the night, but there are no lights at all. We go down a deserted Grand Canal and encounter no other traffic. Here and there windows are lit by candle-light. This is a view of Venice no one has seen since the nineteenth century; Venice lit by candles alone. We turn off the Grand Canal and see a bridge ahead. The driver turns round and motions to us to lie down. Obediently, we lie down on the floor. So does the boatman. He cuts the motor and as we approach the bridge, which seems danger-ously near to our heads, he lifts his legs and begins to 'walk' slowly along the underside of the bridge. He gestures to us behind and we follow suit, pushing the boat down in the water. We have to 'walk' with bended knees and, emerging the other side, we straighten up and look at each other. The boatman raises a thumb. We nod. What on earth is going on? We're in a dark, empty stretch of water and there are *things* bumping into us. What are they? As we approach the Danieli Hotel I realise that we are working our way through broken masonry, bits of timber, and drawing close to an unfamiliar-looking jetty. It's the top of a balustrade and there, back-lit by a huge, flickering candelabra, is the massive bulk of Bruno, the doorman. He looks amazed and, arriving at the boat, lifts me over his head and, reaching the top of the mahogany reception desk, he sets me down on it and returns for O'Toole and the baggage.

The Danieli is under water. I walk along the top of the desk and begin to hop and skip through the flooded foyer on stepping places made of pieces of furniture. Gastone de Cal, the head barman, hasn't gone off duty and is standing on a little island of tables, looking amazed and overjoyed. No one has managed to get into Venice for twenty-four hours. Traffic is not allowed on the Grand Canal after dark. There are no guests in the hotel, they've all left. What do we do now? 'Have a drink!' Normally, O'Toole would be only too glad to sit down and celebrate our feat in getting into the forbidden city. Tonight – this morning – he can see that things are bad; the staff are trying to save the ground-floor furniture. 'Come on, Siân,' he says. 'Get some wellies. Let's get to work.' They find waders for us and we spend the next few hours carrying chairs and tables up the main staircase, rolling up the stair carpet and hoisting everything that can be moved up to the first floor. I never had such a good time at the Danieli as I did that night. Finally, at dawn, we take our pick of the empty rooms. Gastone explains that we'll have to move from bathroom to bathroom as there's no plumbing and there's no electricity and are we *sure* we want to stay? Are we sure? What could be more fun than to camp out in this beloved, familiar, romantic hotel.

We've been coming to Venice for years unremarked among the glitterati of the world, avoiding high society and any occasion remotely smart. Now, we are famous in the nicest way. Wet and shabby in our waders, we seem to be the only guests in the city. As the water subsides we have our own brooms and we help sweep out the filth from Florian's and the little shops around St Mark's Square and, finally, after years of being visitors, we discover real, hidden, secret Venice. It's a rich reward for a bit of discomfort and no running water. The Venetians let us in and we spend weeks of pure pleasure, getting wet and dirty and sitting in people's back parlours and being entertained in their favourite wine shops, far off the tourist track. All our new friends are 'experts' on their city and we're dragged to and fro, sightseeing all day long from the eye-opener of grappa first thing in the morning to the nightcaps at the Danieli.

A member of the hotel staff who has become a companion and guide in his off-duty hours shows us paintings, dirty and unlit, in small churches where he produces a torch so we can stand and admire silently with him. He's as proud as though he were the painter. We go into little bars serving food, which we have passed by dozens of times on earlier visits. 'No tourist has ever walked in here. Good wine – *our* vineyard.' The wine is alarmingly robust but very welcome in the cold morning air. It's also purple and stains our tongues and lips an ineradicable, lurid but rather fashionable Mary Quant colour (it looks better on me than on O'Toole, who looks as though he's in some louche Carnival scene). Our friend's father is a painter – a very special painter. Sworn to secrecy, we visit his studio in an unremarkable apartment in an unfashionable street. The sprightly, elderly Venetian is busy grinding his 'colours'. All around are astounding eighteenth-century paintings. After a few hours of sitting around and admiring and drinking tiny beakers of wine ('I know the vineyard – very good', I read in our good guidebook that the Venetians don't drink; I'll be lucky to get home with half a liver intact), and after a spot of lunch – blissful home-made pasta with tiny, almost transparent, brownish shrimps (I also read that Venetian food isn't up to much!) Sr X confides that his business is forgery.

This doesn't pose an artistic problem for him as it does for many forgers, who feel their 'own' art, just as skilled, is unappreciated. He lives for paintings, loves Guardi, in whom he specialises. 'It's only embarrassing,' he says, 'when I have to go to authenticate something for a museum, sometimes in America. I see it is mine' and I hate to disappoint them. I have some Guardis in most of the big museums. Not too many.' He has been busy during the last few days. The high tide has 'liberated' eighteenth-century paper from a basement around the corner and his flat is festooned with washing lines of drying paper. 'So good to have the real thing.' He prepares his paints exactly as Guardi and Canaletto did, but the paper and canvas is always a problem and now the flood has brought him a rich windfall. As we leave, he presses a small canvas into my hand and gives me his cousin's address. When I go there he is busy making eighteenth-century furniture. His family has, for countless generations, been making furniture in the same manner. He gives me an eighteenth-century picture frame. He's so *proud* and so he should be; this isn't reproduction, this is top of the mark deception. Our time here is becoming more and more splendidly unreal.

At night we have to wait in an improvised bar until the night staff come on because the night electrician at the Danieli is the best tenor. We learn Venetian songs and I improvise an alto line. We sing until dawn. High tide is a horrible thing, but the Venetians are behaving like blitzed Londoners and we have the time of our lives.

I think we love travelling because it stops us from thinking about ourselves. Ourselves – oh, so difficult. Armed insurrections, hunger, thirst, danger – oh, so easy. To move ahead. To move. Interesting. Binding. We never failed to have a good time while engaged on the many journeys we made together. Neither of us was a passive tourist, and life, while we moved about together, was arduous and exhausting and exhilarating. Some of our journeys, marooned in provincial railway stations or stranded in unpromising, unpicturesque spots would have bored and frustrated many, but we always found something interesting to keep ourselves amused. Most of our journeys were, however, more exotic; some were dangerous. Tedious, uncomfortable, glamorous, perilous; it didn't really matter what the conditions were, I think we both travelled for the sake of travelling and consequently we travelled well – almost always.

My trip to Cambodia in 1963 was unexpectedly brief. I arrived in a daring skirt made by a new designer called Mary Quant. It was demurely box-pleated, but it rested an inch and a half above my knee (a bit like my school uniform, which I detested). I had square-toed, stubby-heeled shoes and a modishly straight haircut. O'Toole was appalled. We had a vehement, all the more intense for being whispered, exchange when he suggested I went home on the next flight. 'What have you come as?' he asked in horror. Fortunately, I was able to reassure him that my luggage contained below-the-knee skirts and ordinary shoes, and on the spot I was able to shake my hair into a less fashionable shape. I hated him for greeting me in such a way, but understood by now the tensions of re-unions and – I hated to admit it – he was quite right about the clothes. Skirts were getting shorter and shorter; the one I wore to Cambodia was a restrained version of the London fashion. I had to agree with him when he asked rhetorically, 'What is a tall, thirty-year-old, mother-of-two doing dressed in clothes that would look well on a twelve-year-old?'

We may have been good at travelling, but we were bad at reunions and, rather embarrassed by our own behaviour, we made for the hotel and a soothing bath. A spider, larger than any I had ever seen, fell out of the beautifully folded towel. 'They wear hob-nailed boots here,' said O'Toole, glumly. 'Clump, clump, all over the place.' At the night shoot the film lights sizzled with large, dead, fried night bugs. This place was all snakes and bugs. The loo was a wicker contraption on stilts, the prop-man – prop-men are always my favourite people on a film set – said, delicately, 'Siân – now, not to worry, but we had a really nasty snake in the ladies' tonight and they always go in pairs, so be really care-ful when you – you know.' There was a snake called the Two-Step. You got bitten and then two steps later you fell down dead. O'Toole sent me on a trip round Angkor Wat. 'Wear boots because of the snakes.' I set off into this amazing place and spent the day there. There were soldiers hiding in the bushes, guarding the bits of art that might get chopped off and taken home. Good for them. I wondered if O'Toole had been thinking of 'liberating' a little art.

That same week, news came that the political situation was rapidly worsening and American and British nationals were advised to leave at once. The film unit was disbanded and dispersed quite fast. O'Toole ignored the official evacuation and preferred to trust to his own wits, and I had no doubt my best bet was to follow him. 'Let's go to the airport,' he said. There were no planes. I was installed in the ladies' lava-tory. No luggage (the contentious skirt was now in the possession of the attacking army). How do I know what I'm going to hear next? 'Here, read this and *wait* here, darling.' I had a guidebook to Angkor Wat and nothing else except my passport, which seemed strangely useless in what appeared to be an armed insurrection. I sat on the floor in a cubicle in the ladies' lavatory and read about what I'd seen during the day. It kept me busy for over an hour until a familiar hand appeared under the door. I touched it. 'Open up,' breathed a voice, and I opened the door and O'Toole crept in. 'We've got a plane.' (There were few left in the airport.)

'Oh, good.'

'But not for five hours.'

'Oh hell.'

We sat on the floor of that horrible lavatory, alternately whispering and reading and actually having quite a nice time (I learned a lot about Angkor), until the appointed hour when we straightened up and cautiously moved out and on to the runway. O'Toole thought he recognised our small plane. 'OK, run!' he whispered and we belted out across the airfield and up the staircase. It was the right plane. Money changed hands and we were off. Where to? 'Don't ask.' We landed in Hong Kong where O'Toole had been filming before arriving in Cambodia. O'Toole hadn't trusted the film company to get us out of a war zone, but once in Hong Kong he summoned the might of the company to get us a hotel. They may not know about politics, but film companies sure know hotels. We were directed to the newly built Mandarin and rolled up – dirty and hungry, no baggage – to inaugurate the Presidential Suite. There was a lot to play with; lying on the vast bed I opened curtains, raised televisions, altered the temperature – I'm not sure I didn't run a bath while lying down. O'Toole proved surprisingly adept at acquiring toothbrushes and paste and combs and shampoo and also summoned tailors to the room to measure us for clothes. I ordered a modest frock (skirt on the knee) and a jacket and coat, and O'Toole ordered a few pairs of slacks and shirts and a jacket or two.

He showed me around the Hong Kong he had become familiar with and into the bar frequented by 'Hot Pants Molly Malone' (a bit of a disappointment), whose card he'd retained. Who wouldn't? Then he ventured into more interesting territory. 'There's this square mile owned by a feudal war lord.' 'Ah yes.' 'But no one goes there. The police don't dare. Let's go and have a look.' 'Sure.' I was in my new Chinese 'Chanel' coat and dress, still clutching the Hermès handbag (the only thing I'd brought out from Cambodia). Our taxi driver said, 'No! No! Please!' as he set us down. 'Just wait here,' said O'Toole sweetly. 'No, sir! You cannot go there. Not the lady.'

'Be all right, old son,' murmured O'Toole as we ducked into a dark alleyway, the entrance to the forbidden city. So this was the place where criminals went, knowing the law could not pursue them. 'Now, are you sure . . .?' 'Come *on*!' After a few twists and turns I felt horribly conspicuous. There wasn't a lot to look at, either. My Hermès bag seemed to be sending out signals. 'O'Toole—' 'Yes?' 'This is very interesting but do you notice how the women are taking the children indoors?' 'Yes.' 'D'you think this is a bad sign?' No reply. The dark, narrow, foetid alleyway ahead was now deserted, save for a few moody-looking young men.

'Mmm, don't look frightened. Just turn around casually, make a left and *stroll* back – no, *STROLL* dammit.' As we turned around we saw that the street behind us had emptied as well. Was this prior to some act of violence? Or did they think *we* were dangerous? We strolled, God, how hard we strolled. I have no sense of direction and couldn't think how to get back to law-abiding, everyday Hong Kong. O'Toole sauntered confidently, his casual amble at odds with the vice-like grip in which he held my hand. Light ahead. Daylight. Not quickening our step, we made for what turned out to be a version of Oxford Street, and our taxi – thank God O'Toole had a great sense of direction. The driver practically wept when he saw us. I suppose it would have been very awkward for him if he'd reported back to Columbia Pictures without its star.

'Yeah, well – you can't think about all that,' said O'Toole, recovering his high spirits as we made for the Mandarin. 'You go back to the hotel. I've got a chance to buy a little bit of Korean something or other. Bit dodgy. Tell you what – have a read and just *wait for me*.'

I waited for a long time in that huge suite before he returned with a lovely bulky piece of bas-relief – horsemen rushing into battle.

'Excuse me, but I'm awfully itchy.'

'Well, so am I.'

'How strange.'

Strange indeed that the first guests in the Presidential Suite should be lousy from their spell in the public lavatory at Phnom Penh Airport. They fumigated the rooms – and us – and O'Toole said, 'Let's go to Japan.'

Chapter Twenty-four

As we walk down a Tokyo street, nasty as the Edgware Road and twice as noisy, I glance into a small sandwich bar and see an empty piece of Formica countertop and on it, in a jar, a single branch of flowering cherry. Behind the deep-fryer is an open door leading to a postage-stamp of garden – cool and quiet. It's a tiny, powerful piece of calm and beauty holding its own against the tumult. Pressing forward into the unbearable over-congestion of the street, I feel excitedly that once again I am in a truly foreign place – already I've encountered ten things I do not comprehend. I decide not to try to understand anything and begin to review the contradictions of the day. Mrs Kawakita is our contact as head of Toho Films. She is tiny, dressed in traditional costume, perpetually smiling and polite. I'm told that grown men have been known to cry after bruising business encounters with her. When things get really tough, voices remain low, but terrified underlings in the outer office fancy they see Western blood seeping under the door before Mrs Kawakita emerges, head nodding, smiling and eyes lowered, a favourable contract completed.

I tower over her in my Hong Kong pretend-Chanel and feel, as I try to gauge my bows to correspond with and not exceed hers – otherwise we'll be here all day – that she looks quaint and a bit odd in that get-up. It takes only a week for me to begin to marvel at the beauty of her hair and make-up, the complexity of her dress, the delicacy of her movements and the subtlety of her expression, while feeling more and more like a clod-hopping land-girl; too big, too loud, too vulgar of face. Even my perfume – that year Mitsouko by Guerlain – seems too obvious by half. I feel ugly.

We have elected to stay in a Japanese hotel. Walking up the white-lined corridor to the suite, we notice tears here and there in the paper walls. 'Looks as though someone bad with props, like Johnny G, has been here,' remarks O'Toole. He is great with props. I am not, as I demonstrate within minutes of entering the huge, empty, beautiful set of rooms. Exploring what might be a bedroom, I withdraw the wooden bolt in the wall in order to open a window and find that I have the entire wall in my hands and am precariously balanced, leaning outwards over a lovely moss garden one floor below. I dare not move. I breathe, 'Pete – Pete! Help! Help!' It seems an age before O'Toole, thinking he hears something, drifts into the room and, anchoring me around the waist with one arm, takes possession of the wall with the other and, shaking his head resignedly, much as he does when I mess up a bit of business on stage, replaces the wall and leaves me to unpack while he goes in search of a bar.

I tiptoe around the dividing screens. So much in the rooms is so light and breakable, but at the same time the deep, narrow bath, the bedroll which is laid out at night only, the headrest, the dark wooden floor, are so confidently heavy and in their correct, immovable place that I am constantly wrong-footed as I move around, at one moment behaving rather patronisingly like a grown-up in a doll's house and the next submitting to an alien but mightily convincing arrangement of objects.

O'Toole returns, having discovered not only a bar (the Japanese are crazy about whisky, it seems) but a massage parlour below where a little lady *walked* up his spine. I settle for a shampoo and set, but even so my little lady shampooer does something unprecedented to my skull. We're two Brobdingnags in paradise. 'I'll bet they laugh at us,' says O'Toole. 'Apparently we smell awful and they call us "the Big Noses".' He's probably right. My nose – rather unremarkable I always thought – seems to be growing.

Sleep. Such sleep. My first night on a Japanese bed-on-the-floor. No book, no radio, no television, big darkness, the polished floor near my right hand and sleep that I can almost taste.

In the morning, film representatives come to call. They're discouraging about the possibility of buying art. 'You'd swear they don't *want* to sell anything,' says one. 'I've been rooting around for ten years – nothing.' O'Toole nods gravely and we promise to ring the office if we need anything in the way of restaurant reservations, cars and so on. This must be a horrible job, looking after movie stars and their whims. We have a couple of numbers we've found for ourselves. Eureka! Kurosawa rings back; he's filming *The Red Doctor* and we're invited to watch him. Our cups run over completely when the most famous of all Japanese actors, Toshiro Mifune, calls. It's going to be very hard to behave like rational beings around these two men. They're like mythical beasts to me. I owe my knowledge of them to O'Toole and am overwhelmed now by the magnitude of my debt to him. I don't actually want to meet these men at all. But I do want to *watch* them; however, meeting is a part of all that.

The set of *The Red Doctor* is wonderful. If this were movie making then I would want to do little else but make Kurosawa movies. He is a master, Kurosawa – and he's tall! He's a good-looking cowboy of a Japanese. His mother is tiny and she cooks and runs the kitchen on the film set. It's like filming in his parlour, except one is aware that he is one of the most illustrious directors in the world, but oh, the difference from anything I've seen . . . He doesn't act great. His mother doesn't treat him as great. The unit mills about like family retainers, the actors behave with modest dignity; no one is treated exceptionally well. But there it is – hanging over the ramshackle location – the impact of great quality.

Watching movies being made is low on the list of spectator sports, but I could have sat on my orange box for months – and I didn't understand a word of text. It seems the financiers are exasperated by the length of the shoot; Kurosawa is being hounded and harried. His great talent and reputation don't save him from being treated badly. I make a mental note once again *never* to feel bad when I'm badly treated. Much better talents than mine are treated shamefully by people who are actually only trying to hang on to their jobs, trying to save a bit of money.

Toshiro Mifune appears! This is a star! He, also, is tall, another Japanese cowboy, and when he walks he displaces a lot of air . . . It's a pleasure to see him and he and O'Toole fall on each other. O'Toole has adored 'Tosher' since he was a boy in Leeds; it must be wonderful to stand on Japanese soil and embrace one of the best Japanese actors, and to find that they like each other on sight! I hang back slightly and watch the meeting. They arrange to see each other later.

Where do we meet? I'm getting used to the unexpected and don't blink when we enter a huge, ghastly, dark, pleasure-drome where they serve – of course – many kinds of whisky. Toshiro loves whisky. O'Toole loves whisky only too much and becomes a mad person when he drinks it, so he's forsworn it and I'm impressed when he refuses one now. Whisky is a big treat. Toshiro is buying. O'Toole is choosing – who knows what? – it's not whisky and I'm silently overcome with admiration. He wants to make a good impression on Mifune, but not at the expense of turning into a mad person. They talk through an interpreter and I sit, enjoying this meeting, hating the venue and only vaguely understanding what is being discussed. The noise is *tremendous*! This is worse than Annabel's.

We now have a longer list of phone numbers. I'm getting to understand that in this country, without a personal recommendation, it is very difficult to reach anyone significant. Kurosawa and Mifune between them pass us on to the best kimono maker in the country, the best antique dealer and the best lacquer man, and we make calls and wait. Then we embark on a series of visits that feel a bit like auditions.

And in the interim the film company arranges visits to the theatre. They are touchingly eager to please a big Star and I think that they must be keenly grateful for an easy few weeks now that the Star has the Wife in tow. Nothing is required except visits to special monuments and trips to the theatre and they must wonder what we do with our time. 'This play goes on all day, you don't have to stay,' we're told as we go backstage at the theatre. Backstage is huge. Actors sit in front of cheval mirrors, hands on knees, legs apart. Silently they look at themselves as they are transformed into the character they will inhabit for the rest of the day. Old men become young girls. Young men become elderly. I believe it all. Here, in the ordinary light of day, the atmosphere is church-like. Out front, I settle into an uncomfortable seat next to an old lady who is sitting on her feet. On the floor in front of her is a primus stove and food and tea. The play opens with the most compelling entrance I've ever seen an actor make: slow, slow, lateral walk to the acting area, but the acting, the diction, are at first grotesque and after a mere ten minutes, totally believable and natural. The audience gasps and cries as one; red ribbons are as real as the blood in a Peckinpah movie, blue cloth is a believable, impassable river. The movie representative appears in the aisle to 'rescue' us. No way am I leaving. My old lady busies herself with a bit of cooking and I wish she'd offer me a bite, as we settle down for another couple of hours of drama. Eventually, shaken and exhausted and exhilarated, I emerge into the Tokyo afternoon. We have an evening appointment, otherwise I *could* have stayed there all day. Why? I find it quite difficult to sit through a long play in London. I've read about people sitting through a day of theatre in Ancient Greece and wondered how they could do that. Maybe there has to be this degree of mutually accepted tradition and commitment before the experience becomes possible? Come to think of it, I'm rarely convinced

– this carried away – in a theatre at home. Back in my empty Japanese room I sit and wonder at the day.

Our phone calls lead us to people who are distinguished artists and not about to start making a sale to just anyone; not even at the say-so of their important and successful friends. Sometimes it's O'Toole's reputation and charisma that gets us by, but sometimes it's my patience and sincere admiration that wins the day. We sit day after day in what looks like a council flat in North London (except our feet are dangling over a fire-pit under the dining table) and gradually the Lacquer Man brings out small objects for our consideration. Kurosawa has explained to me that this man marks a tree he will use in ten years' time and he waits and waits for it to mature and his output is wonderful and prized but tiny, and he will never be rich, but he is the greatest lacquer artist in Japan, and, sitting in his dowdy living room and knowing nothing, even I can tell that he is great. My ideas are getting such a shake-up. Actually, I'm learning to forget what I've been absorbing over the last ten years. What was that? Style, I suppose. I'm unprepared for the person who lives in an unappealing house like this, wears undistinguished clothes like this, eats dull food such as this, but thinking back, I recall that Johns the Postman in Cwmllynfell, in my home in Wales, drank too much, looked like a cleaned-up tramp, lived in a little house with a Mabel Lucie Attwell calendar on the wall and antimacassars on the uncut moquette chairs, and wrote Welsh poetry, the complexity of which would bear comparison with the best Greek poetry. And now, I'm sitting in a little living room with nasty wallpaper and awful little ornaments and the man of the house is showing us great art, wrapped up in tea towels. O'Toole can see that I'm making an impression and he leaves the negotiating to me. Well – I don't talk about *money* – I ask about being *allowed* to *acquire*.

Eventually, we leave with eight superb bowls. I've had such an intense few nights with this man, but I don't say, 'We'll be in touch.' What would have been the point? He hasn't any idea of who we are, but we have connected quite strongly. Maybe he can see that I will remember these few days for ever. I hope he can. I will.

The Kimono Man is a bit more of a showbiz character, more accustomed to visiting stars. We order kimonos that bear no relation to the ordinary kimonos sold in the shops here or in England. (When they wore out I tried to have them copied and no one could master the intricacy of their making.)

Art is so much more difficult to find. The film people – Westerners who live in Tokyo – are almost right when they say that the barrier between 'us and them' is as good as impenetrable. We sit, night after night, drinking tea in suburban houses. Occasionally, our host says 'Let's go and visit X' and off we trundle to another little sitting room and drink more tea. Still no art appears. A week goes by before a bundle is produced and, unwrapped, proves to be an actor's mask from the eighteenth century – holly wood, painted for the Old Man's character. The owner gestures to me to put it on and I do and I am very moved by the gesture and, taking it off, I sniff a bit, and pass it to O'Toole. He puts it on and the company roars with laughter to see the beautiful star face transformed to decrepit old age. He lays it reverently back on its cloth and we drink tea for hours. As we leave, the mask is bundled up and pressed into O'Toole's hands. Our interpreter must have agreed to pay; these negotiations are always rather lordly.

The Mask Man hands us on to another dealer and after many nights in back rooms we buy almost my favourite object of all, a terracotta head, so simple it is scarcely formed at all.

When I say 'we', that is of course completely misleading. O'Toole chose to spend a major part of his earnings on art and I was an enthusiastic helper, but he was spending *his* money, not mine. I spent a large portion of *my* earnings on antique furniture, but I never felt a great sense of ownership except in a few, emotional, instances. I rarely bought art. Here, in Japan, I'm becoming acquisitive. I buy an eighteenth-century scroll – I want to live in a low, Japanese house. I want a garden of mosses. I'd like to be smaller, quieter, less scrutable.

Chapter Twenty-five

Back in Heath Street in Hampstead, fitting our acquisitions into this lovely fortress of a house, our life in it continues to be workable, as well as intermittently ecstatic or unbelievably dreadful. We've acquired a family of cats who live downstairs and a bulldog called Scobie who lives in the basement and in the Green Room and who absorbs a great deal of household energy. O'Toole bought him as a protector for the houseful of girls he has to leave behind when he goes filming. Fierce to look at, Scobie became a well-known feature of street-life in Hampstead, plodding out twice daily on what looked like a glum walk, occasionally slipping his lead on the Heath and once, during such a moment of freedom when the fair was paying its Easter visit to Hampstead, charging up the steps of a fairground caravan – he wasn't named after a jockey for nothing – and, unable to stop, smashing his way into a china cabinet. 'Very good china,' said the vengeful and formidable old fairground woman when she visited us and her eyes alighted on O'Toole's name here and there in the Green Room, and then, taking in a poster on the wall, 'Royal Doulton mostly – and some *Limoges* as well, and then there's the *crystal!*' 'Yes, yes,' I said soothingly as I pressed bundles of notes into her hand.

Scobie had already been in a spot of bother with the law and I didn't feel he was well placed to survive more trouble. Although every time one of the many burglar alarms in the house went off at night, he greeted the police, tail wagging, dribbling affectionately on their trousers; he'd taken against being loaded into a Black Maria when he, along with his young walkers, had been arrested on an apple-scrumping expedition and hauled off to Rosslyn Hill police station. The schoolboys obediently trooped into the sinister van, but Scobie exerted all of his not inconsiderable strength, summoned up the indomitable spirit of his breed, and would not budge; policemen overbalanced and sat down suddenly on the pavement, helmets rolled down the road, and as passers-by clutched each other, crying with laughter, Scobie glowered at everyone and phone calls were made to the house to 'Get this damned ferocious beast out of here. NOW!' It was my mother who hurried down the hill and murmured reproachfully, 'Oh, Scobie!' and he trotted over and sat at her heels. She apologised to the recovering officers, glared at the boys cowering in the van, and in the voice that could still make me jump with fright said, 'And as for you. Just you wait . . .'

At home, when he inadvertently knocked someone to the ground, he stood there mournfully, breathing hard, bestowing the odd wet lick on the prone figure until, to his evident relief, it righted itself. He arrived 'toilet-trained', but he'd got the message wrong and would stand for hours on the Heath, longing to pee, legs crossed, practically hopping with anxiety. Then, once back in the house, he would lean against the closed door in the hall in a 'Thank God' position and the floodgates would open. He had to be sent back to school to relearn the lesson, but he was never entirely sure that he'd got it right. Nor had he when he appeared in the film, *Great Catherine*, as the dog belonging to the British Ambassador, played by Jack Hawkins. He rode to Shepperton in the Rolls, sitting motionless up front and dribbling steadily on the upholstery to Lionel's frustrated fury. 'I'd like to *murder* him,' he muttered. He lived for thirteen years and was the longest lasting of O'Toole's Petruchio's servants – adorable and totally useless in the job for which he'd been engaged.

Scobie personified our home life – sweet and slightly cockeyed.

In spite of my earnest efforts, there were times when I found it almost impossible to contain my frustration over work. Time and again I failed to embrace my hero Sydney Smith's dictum, 'If my lot be to crawl, I will crawl contentedly; if to fly, I will fly with alacrity; but, as long as I can possibly avoid it, I will never be unhappy.'

Desperate to be 'flying', in a place where it counted in those days (and London seemed to be the only place that really signified), I jumped at the chance to play Cleopatra at the Vic. O'Toole wanted to know all the details of the production (none of which I knew), saying that a 'true professional' would not embark on such a job without making sure that all the conditions were perfect, down to the smallest piece of casting and costume. (He added that the play rarely worked.) Very differently situated from him, I was not in a position to make demands and exhaustive enquiries. Nor was I convinced that a guarantee of perfection was any guarantee of a successful outcome, but as the arguments raged at home and they became more concerned with my character and less about the job, I withdrew from it and domestic harmony was instantly restored, but I was sick at heart as I resumed a modest crawl.

I lost *The Cherry Orchard* in much the same way. When I began to quiz my old friend, director Frank Hauser, about the casting, he was outraged that I should be interfering in his production plans. That was the reaction I expected and I wasn't surprised when he withdrew his offer and didn't work with me again for a good ten years. I was disheartened to see how little courage and confidence I was able to muster at home. Defiance was out of the question.

Almost at once, in 1966, I came near to losing *Man and Superman* as well. This time, the order from O'Toole was not to play it without acquiring a major star for Jack Tanner (a role that O'Toole had played brilliantly at the Bristol Old Vic). Philip Wiseman, the director, and Richard Shulman, the producer, were bemused, but obligingly, as requested, offered the part to a few movie stars who they knew were never going to accept the job (and who took months before they bothered to reply). Finally, reality overtook everyone and a list was compiled of major theatre actors who might reasonably want the huge part as well as being able to perform it. As we looked down the impressive list, the crumpled, exhausted production team, *longing* to get on with the job, paused at one name and we read no further. Everyone wanted one of the most exciting actors in the country, only too infrequently seen in the great parts he was born to play. It was just as well that Philip and Richard and I were equally enthusiastic, because it became clear that Alan Badel was as reluctant as any Hollywood tyro to respond to letters or to return phone calls. Weeks and months went by and in despair I called Alan's wife, Vonnie. (Their house was more of a fortress than ours.) Vonnie lifted the phone and there was a very guarded, 'Yes?' 'Vonnie, it's Siân and I'm desperate. Do you think Alan will do the play?' 'Well, I think he should.' 'But *will* he?' 'Leave it with me.' I did and within days we had a message of acceptance. O'Toole approved. Well, how could he not?

When Alan turned up to read the play with a good but hastily assembled cast, Philip and I were only slightly put out when we slowly realised, chatting with Alan over coffee, that he had turned up to rehearse *Arms and the Man*. A copy of *Man and Superman* was hastily but casually slipped on to the table where Alan would sit. I watched him touch it, his face revealing nothing, as he made a mental readjustment and prepared to sightread Tanner. It was the beginning of a long, incident-packed journey, which culminated in one of the longest commercial runs of any Shaw play. The highs were glorious and the lows difficult to look back on without shuddering.

The opening night at the Arts was, on the whole, a low. Alan, busily teasing Philip because he belonged to that hated breed – directors – neglected to thoroughly learn his part. Philip was exhausted from directing the play while keeping out of Alan's sightlines. I was dazed with fatigue from keeping the peace between the two of them and was far from having figured out how to play Anne. Also, I couldn't help noticing that Alan – my friend – having summoned up all his formidable resources in order to get through the long opening duologue with me, was playing it brilliantly but also was playing it pressed up against the backcloth while I (his friend and protector against the wrath of the management) sat, pinned in my chair, down stage. To the uninitiated this is called 'upstaging' someone. I loved acting with him and forgave him completely. O'Toole, in England for a while before leaving for Warsaw to film *Night of the Generals*, arrived at the theatre in a state of mixed emotions and passed out drunk in the corridor backstage, so we made our entrances stepping over his curled-up figure in the corridor. What little stock of embarrassment that remained to me evaporated for ever that night. Alan went on a few weeks later to be superb, and although the long run threw up its share of weekly crises, it was for me one of the most exciting, if erratic, of jobs. During the year Alan and I worked on *Antony and Cleopatra* in our spare time and hoped to mount a production of the play, and when that collapsed I thought I really wasn't *meant* to play the part, except in my head.

My mother in the play was played by Marie Löhr, who, despite the disparity in our ages, became one of my closest friends. Marie, well into her seventies when I met her, was stately, on the stout side, and beautifully dressed in the grand clothes of an earlier time. In spite of a streak of sheer naughtiness, which she retained from a youth studded with some startling romances and adventures, she had the air of a *grande dame* and it wasn't difficult to see her as the actor-manager she had been in her heyday. Living alone now in a small flat, she had developed a few idiosyncratic habits, but her awareness of the absurdity of a great deal of daily life – her own included – quite exempted her from being perceived as eccentric. Lest she should miss something interesting, she kept both radio and television running softly as she dealt with her correspondence, and in order to keep her beloved canary near her when she released him from his cage, she sprinkled birdseed on to the crown of her head so he was never away for long, returning to peck away among her shiny, white curls. This seemed very sensible to me and I would forget about the seeds and it was Marie who would lift her hand halfway to her head, as we sat down in a restaurant, raise an index finger, mouth pursed in comic disapproval, and sail majestically into the Ladies to remove her hat and shake out of her hair the forgotten remnants of Joey's breakfast, before returning to further enslave an adoring bunch of waiters who would never have seen her act, but who knew she was Somebody, all right. Her exquisite manners were camp in a ladylike way and fragments of advice she passed on to me were all too few and so lightly produced as to be in danger of passing unnoticed. She never talked about herself or of the past except when, knowing her better and better, I would press her to look back.

There were great gaps in the story always, but I pieced together enough to make me wish that she'd kept a journal. She'd been an actress since she was sixteen or seventeen, and described the scene up and down Shaftesbury Avenue or the Charing Cross Road as dozens of young actresses ran from theatre to theatre to be seen or to audition for jobs. There is a wide walkway along the side of the Garrick Theatre where we were playing at the time and she remembered it being full of girls – young ladies – all in hats and gloves and carrying little bags with their spirit heaters and curling tongs for smartening up the hair before they went on stage. She became Sir Herbert Beerbohm Tree's leading lady in *Faust* when she was eighteen. He was an actor-manager who was a law unto himself, and when Marie lost her voice he suspended rehearsals and sent her and her mother to Brighton for a week with his own recipe for throat medicine and instructions that she was not to speak until she returned to London. She did as she was told and the play opened triumphantly when he felt that it and she were good and ready.

Marie's mother (I never heard her speak of a father) was an actress called Kate Bishop and Marie was utterly devoted to her. They were living together when Miss Bishop died, and when Marie described her last illness her jauntiness deserted her and the sense of loss was fresh in her voice. Her mother loved and had a way with birds, and as she lay dying, small songbirds sat on the bedhead and on the piled-up pillows and even on her hand where it rested on the coverlet. 'She smiled and smiled at the end,' said Marie.

She herself made a glittering career, becoming an actor-manager, and ran a fine house, somewhere on the river. When she took one of her own productions from her theatre in Shaftesbury Avenue to New York, she recast the play and an actress called Margaret Bannerman was given her star part. The play did not do well in America and she was obliged to come home, where she found that her husband had taken up with her replacement. She lost everything – jewels, furs, grand house – and even saw Miss Bannerman wearing her jewellery. An excruciatingly painful divorce followed and, in court, the judge – an admirer of Marie's – asked plaintively, 'Who *is* Margaret Bannerman?' 'I could have kissed him,' said Marie, her eyes glistening with malice.

When she toured she – an expert player – travelled with her own custom-made, collapsible billiard cues, along with a great deal of luggage. She loved the company of men and she acted with most of the matinée idols of her day; occasionally, when certain very renowned names came up, she would look a little absent and the conversation would halt and I guessed at a *tendresse*, to say the least, but knew better than to ask her to reveal more than she had already volunteered. She was a lady.

Her beloved mother had been a contemporary and a colleague of Ellen Terry, and as small children, Kate Bishop and Ellen Terry had both been engaged as fairies at Bristol, where Mrs Kendal (Madge Robertson) was actor-manager of a stock company. It was awesome to me to realise that some of the voice exercises passed on to me by Marie had been taught to her mother in the middle of the nineteenth century.

After playing my mother for about nine months in *Man and Superman*, things went well for a while; she played in a film and on television with O'Toole and was made much of by visiting Americans, who were inclined to whisk her off to the Connaught, which she loved. Then she had a few falls at home and decided that it was dangerous for her to live alone. Lacking family to live with, a good friend, with the very best intentions, moved her from London to a nursing home in a quiet, prosperous part of Brighton. Lionel moved her in our Rolls and the trip was, he said, hilarious. She was completely disorganised and he did most of the packing before they set off, hours late. They had lunch on the way and he installed her in her nice room in the large, soundless house. Then, I think, the laughter ended for Marie. She sat in her room, with some of her own good furniture around, and whispered,

'I don't see anyone here. They're all *old*, I think.' She became slim again, and then thin and all her lovely clothes had to be given away. She went on dwindling and very soon she was gone, and I miss her still.

Philip, Richard and I worked together for a third time. We missed acquiring the rights to *A Streetcar Named Desire* by a matter of hours only, but Tennessee sent us a rewritten version of *Summer and Smoke*. He called it *The Eccentricities of a Nightingale* and we tried it out at the Yvonne Arnaud Theatre in Guildford. Our doubts about the reaction of the stockbroker belt to Tennessee were dispelled in the first few days. Our reception and favourable press led us to believe that we would have no problem in finding a home in the West End after one month in Surrey. London was, however, packed with plays and we grew anxious as the days went by and every play in town seemed set to run and run for ever. Then, like a miracle, we were offered one of my favourite theatres, the Vaudeville. It was a rush job; closing in Guildford on Saturday, we had to open in the Strand on Tuesday. The revolve at Guildford on and around which Nicholas Georgiardis had devised a beautiful, elaborate set, was as wide, if not wider, than the proscenium arch at the Vaudeville. Catastrophe. We needed to borrow five thousand pounds in order to move the set and rejig it to fit the new theatre. I turned to our company – Keep Films – and, to my surprise, I was told that 'they' ('they' included me, surely?) needed to inspect the management's fiscal health and to 'think' about the transaction. Clement Scott-Gilbert and Richard Shulman, the producers, went to the office armed with their bank statements and balance sheets, confident that all would be well. The following day we were all mortified to be told that in Jules's opinion, Tennessee Williams was too 'chancy' a playwright to merit such a loan. To general stupefaction, we closed the play and sent the set to be broken up. Of all the blows Keep Films dealt me over the years, that one was the most difficult to overcome.

During this time I made infrequent forays into the London that was called the 'Swinging' London of the Sixties. From time to time I read with bewilderment that we were part of the set that embodied it. Nothing could have been less plausible. When I wasn't working I was usually at home with the children and O'Toole was far too busy working or doing the crossword to meet most of the film stars who came to London and called on Keep Films. As a director of Keep Films, I was occasionally deputed to pick them up from the Dorchester or the Grosvenor House and get them in to Tramp's or Annabel's, the first places they wanted to visit. I would have done one, sometimes two, shows before I picked them up. Once installed inside, we would make conversation for a moment or two. 'And what do *you* do?' 'Oh, I work in the theatre here in London, but I have small children – do you mind if I leave you now?' For me to spend an evening in Annabel's was torture; the ceiling was too low, the music too loud. Twice I went there with Jules and Joyce, sat on the banquette, ordered a drink and fainted clean away.

One night after the show, my dresser gave me a message to go to Tiberio – a lovely restaurant off Curzon Street – where the acoustics were so bizarre that from certain tables you could hear every word spoken at some of the other tables (since deals were made at each table at lunchtime, it really paid to know exactly which were the vulnerable spots). I couldn't get a taxi from the Garrick Theatre and sprinted over to Mayfair, where I joined a large table nearing the end of dinner. They were all beautifully dressed in the fashion of the day: soft silk shirts for the men, stiff, beaded frocks for the women, hairpieces, false eyelashes, false nails. I sat down recognising all the famous people – nods and kisses. Peter Sellers! How nice – yes; hello, yes – all round the table. There was one little woman I didn't know – not an actress – speak to her later. Later was a bit too late. The one person I failed to recognise was Princess Margaret. It was only when she switched suddenly into HRH mode and tremors ran around the gathering that I realised my mistake. I rather admired her in her wrath. Lord knows what had inspired it on that night.

Chapter Twenty-six

London – the end of the decade. Another film offer, to be directed by Peter Yates, who had recently made *Bullitt*. I was to play a doctor, working opposite Warren Beatty. 'I absolutely can't. So sorry. But thanks.'

At home, O'Toole said, 'Are you *sure* you don't want to do this film?'

'Oh, absolutely. South America! With the girls coming up to their entrance exams. Not a chance.'

'But South America,' he kept on insisting, 'a wonderful place. Oh, you should go. The girls could visit after their exams.'

Eventually I said, 'Well, maybe. And Warren Beatty is a nice man, they say. And South America does have wonderful vegetation . . . oh well, all right. *Murphy's War* it is.'

After I accepted, O'Toole stopped talking about the film. I went off to the medical centre and was jabbed in dozens of places. I went off to the Quaker Centre in the Euston Road to learn about their attitude to foreign ministries (I was to play a Quaker). I concentrated on life at home, especially on Kate's entrance exam to a school I had chosen above all others – the North London Collegiate. Visiting, I had embarrassingly dropped a little curtsey to the headmistress, Madeleine McLauchlin. My mother was also besotted by the school. We *had* to get both girls in, somehow. (We entered them for Camden and Francis Holland as well, just in case.) My mother was appalled by the results of the new methods of teaching: classroom walls being torn down; grammar despised; mathematical tables not to be learned, nor poetry memorised; the children measuring the walls of their classroom and shaking powder from cocoa tin to cocoa tin and doing unbelievable things with empty egg boxes. Not only had Harold Lever advised Harold Wilson to close down every legal tax avoidance scheme so that high earners like O'Toole now paid nineteen shillings and sixpence in the pound in income tax ('Go abroad at once and stay there,' was the advice. O'Toole refused and elected to stay), but the Labour Government that we fought for was now – it seemed to me – also destroying the education system to which I owed my present life. The National Health Service was still intact. But for how long? At the moment it was the education system that worried my mother and me. She went to a few PTA meetings and I watched in awe as she rose to speak against the new system. The hostility and derision were palpable. After one meeting, a man sought us out; ignoring the headmistress, he talked to my mother. 'I just want to thank you – I didn't have the nerve to get up, but thank you – I'm a Maths lecturer at London University and I'm appalled at the ignorance of incoming students and the rot begins right here at primary level.'

'I *know* that,' said my mother, grimly. Unsmiling, they looked at each other and parted, too upset to say goodbye.

'I'm taking them out,' said my mother. 'How d'you mean?' 'They have to know how to read and write and add up and subtract and multiply and divide or they'll never get into a decent school.' I envisaged scandal and endless newspaper attention. 'Just say they're not well. Get a note from Gerry. I'll teach them at home.' 'For how long?' 'Give me four months.' Feebly, I begged sick notes from Gerry and wrote letters describing fictitious family dramas. My mother held classes in the dining room and I took grammar and literature in the Green Room then, feeling like a deserter, I left for South America and my mother was left with the task of getting the two little girls into a *decent* school – the sort of school that, thanks to Rab Butler (a Tory), had been mine by right. The world turns.

'So I'm going to do this job?' (To John Miller, my agent.)

'Yes, dear. Oh, by the way, Warren Beatty isn't doing it.'

'Really?'

'No, he wanted too much money. The producers are being a bit careful; even your part now incorporates three others – a man and two women.'

'I see.'

This is a week before I leave for South America and I say, 'So who *will* be playing Murphy?'

John looks amazed and embarrassed. 'Oh, don't you know? Er – well – O'Toole is the star of the picture. It seems he's mad about South America.'

I return to Hampstead, hatchet-faced. *Ride a Cock Horse* had been a never-to-be-forgotten, horrible experience. How would we get through a four-month movie together?

'Aw, come on – it'll be *great*,' he smiles. The study desk is piled high with books about Simon Bolivar, Eldorado, pre-Columbian art, Spanish primers, dictionaries. I look at him, quivering with excitement, all his attention directed at the desk.

My mother appears, beaming. She's been won over. So much to *learn*, how lovely.

'Don't worry about anything. Sort everything out when we get there. This is going to be a *great adventure* – just you wait.'

Caracas, Venezuela. The Caracas Hilton, isolated in what is a large, hot version of the new Spaghetti Junction in Birmingham and no possibility of going out for a walk. There's a grand welcoming party to wish the film well. The big garish reception room is full of the most beautiful women I've ever seen congregated in one place; their skins range from black to brown to café-au-lait to olive and the effect is devastating. I remember that Miss Venezuela is usually a starry presence in the Miss World line-up and am astonished to realise that the dazzling good looks that are so extraordinary in London are the norm here in this part of South America. And there's something else, as well, the rich pungent smell of expensive perfume and leather and cigars adding up to – what? Later, unwrapping the beautiful piece of jewellery nestling in my bouquet, the gift of a stranger (no address, thank goodness, or I'd have to return it), I realise that the smell is the smell of extreme wealth. Caracas may have been beautiful once. No longer. The slums, a huge shanty town a stone's throw from our smart hotel, are large and appalling. I'm glad to get away to start filming. Our base will be Puerto Ordaz and we're to live on a Greek boat and travel by hovercraft to our locations in the huge delta of the Orinoco. 'No!' shriek our new acquaintances. '*Nobody* goes to the Green Hell.' I've brought all the wrong clothes, as usual, and leave almost everything in Caracas. The delta will be sulphurously, stiflingly hot.

It was. We tried to settle in on board the rather run-down Greek cruise ship. It wasn't a success. The cabins were cramped and, making a stab at running a happy ship, a nameless person put out cheery messages over the ship's loudspeaker. There was a lot of 'Wakey, Wakey! Savoy Grill now open' at breakfast time. Within a week we were all desperately trying to get away from each other – and there was no means of escape. I tried to learn some Amerindian, laboriously compiling a phonetic dictionary of useful phrases I might use in the film in my role as doctor. We got on with wardrobe fittings and make-up tests and grew more and more restless – no filming in sight. On our first outing in the huge hovercraft we encountered very rough water (no one had realised that the Pacific meets the Caribbean hereabouts and the waters are always rough). All the windows smashed in and we took on a great deal of water. My hairdresser, who was calm about most things, shrieked that this was it. No more hovercraft! There was rumbled, sea-sick assent from the unit and we limped home to the accompaniment of audible prayers. So, no way of getting to work and, on board ship, a mutiny. We were taken off and housed in the Rasil Hotel in Puerto Ordaz and helicopters and trucks were ordered to get us into the rainforest and deeper into the delta. All this was desperate for the company and for Peter Yates, the director, who couldn't begin filming. It was decided that it was by now cheaper to continue than to abandon the film. Not having any responsibility beyond knowing my lines and staying upright in the killing climate, I was loving the beginning of the adventure. O'Toole was still up to his eyes in books about Simon Bolivar, the liberator of Venezuela, and the difficulties – the near impossibilities – brought out the best in him. Our companion was Philippe Noiret who, until fairly recently, had been a senior member of the Théâtre Nationale Populaire, the TNP, in France. We ordered ourselves brightly coloured cotton pyjamas and bought identical straw hats and called ourselves the Theatre Nationale Orinoco, the TNO – The tay en oh. We divided our leisure time between the only two restaurants and our sitting room, where Philippe unveiled his cache of champagne and I contributed a large Cheddar cheese and Branston pickle, sent from Jermyn Street by Joyce. Philippe had packed À la recherche du temps perdu in French and we looked at each other in amazement as I opened my trunk and revealed my complete Proust – in English. Working conditions were appalling, but we had a high old time. Peter Yates was kindness and forbearance itself and somehow, slowly and painstakingly, the film got made. It wasn't a 'smart' film, but it was a really good adventure story and how else could we ever have lived in such an outlandish place, for so long?

On my last day I'd been filming alone, and was one of only a few people waiting to be lifted off by helicopter. The chief of police, an unpleasant man who'd been a heavy presence during the last few weeks, treating the movie as a holiday, was fooling around in one of our dug-out canoes on the Orinoco. A few of his men stood on the bank and as we waited there, barely paying attention, tired after a long day, one of the policemen on the bank took out his gun and shot his disliked superior. As my mouth opened, the unit member standing alongside me clamped his hand on my arm and hissed, 'Shut up. Turn your back and look inland.' I obeyed and we stood there for what seemed a very long time, ignoring the cries (of joy? protest? who could tell?) behind us. The helicopter approached, my friend pushed me into it and we lifted off from the delta for the last time. The scene below was quite calm. I'd learned a great deal in four months and knew enough not to talk about what we'd witnessed. I didn't discuss it with anyone when I returned to the hotel. I was scared and fascinated in equal measure by the absence of anything resembling law and order as I'd been raised to perceive it. It was a lesson we'd had to learn quickly: that the so-called absolutes, the codes of behaviour we'd learned to live by, meant nothing here in the remote corners of this continent.

Chapter Twenty-seven

'Everything that can go wrong, will go wrong and at the worst possible time.' So says Murphy's Law and the months of filming on the Orinoco convinced everyone that the Law contained an incontrovertible truth. Even after we moved to the comparative comfort of the Puerto Ordaz hotel, the Rasil, the company still faced the problem of transporting the large unit to work each day. Tracks were cut through the rainforest, tracks which within a week would become impassable under the rampantly returning vegetation. We were soon made to understand why 'nobody goes to the Green Hell'; almost invisible, clouds of small insects bit or stung every scrap of exposed flesh, and the steady drip, drip, of sweat drove the sound operator mad. One night the river rose fifteen feet and our set disappeared, and once, at three in the morning, I was awakened by an Irish crew member who'd been sent to fetch the all-important barge which figured hugely in the film (as Philippe Noiret's home and O'Toole's torpedo carrier) in order to sail it to a new location. Maybe no one else answered the phone or maybe he was too nervous to confide in anyone more important. 'Siân?' he whispered urgently. 'Siân – THE BARGE IS SUNK.' He'd encountered treacherous waters in the sea to the east of the delta and, alive and not too shaken, was making his long way back to base in the casual manner peculiar to those men who like working in inhospitable places. It was left to me to pass on the dreadful message, which galvanised the set department into heroic, round-the-clock work as they reproduced the eccentric vessel. I worked alone for a week with 'my' Indians who played my patients in the film, all of us running for our lives day after day, while enemy planes bombed us and shot at us and the village burned all around. I returned to base thinking that the climate was beginning to get me down and that, moreover, I'd pulled a muscle in my upper back and was having trouble breathing and maybe I should let the doctor have a look at it. 'Got a few days off?' he enquired. I nodded.

'Good,' he said. 'Stay in bed. You're just recovering from pleurisy.' He understood completely that the symptoms of pleurisy could seem like part of the rather poorly feeling that afflicted us all as we struggled to get through the day. Life on the ground was difficult, but the movie was largely about aeronautics and the Frank Tallman team of American aviators had been engaged to do all the Second World War stunts. They purveyed the glamour of danger and they were such stars! Their wives – blonde and glamorous – were never seen, except at night, dining with their dashing husbands. Of course, not everyone realised that Gilbert Chomat, with the camera strapped to his helicopter, had to do everything the Tallman team did. We became fast friends with Gilbert (he *wasn't* starry) and the three of us made trips over the rainforest every weekend. One day he told me, 'You know, this job is too dangerous for a family man – all my helicopter pilot friends are dead. I have four small boys and a beautiful wife in Brittany. I will do only one more movie after this – *The Blue Max* in Ireland.'

Gradually, it occurred to me that O'Toole had a purpose behind all the flying around over the massive delta of the Orinoco. We had been collecting pre-Columbian art for some time and had been assured by a Venezuelan government official in London that there was none to be found in Venezuela. This seemed improbable, if not impossible, so he began to scout about for likely settlement areas. Sheltered spots on rivers seemed favourable and indeed when we were able to touch down and walk to the waterside, we occasionally saw signs of past occupation. One day we arrived at an unusually pleasant curve in a river tributary. We stood there breathing in the calm of the place, when O'Toole whooped – a ghastly Irish sound – and darted to the mud bank. He extracted a beautiful parrot-head handle, which must, once, have been attached to a big bowl. The pre-Columbian art was surrendering to us, falling out of the soft earth. Gilbert and I tentatively joined in the 'dig' and loaded the helicopter with twenty-five beautiful 'bits'.

After that we made frequent weekend forays, not always fruitful, but I can't remember spending more pleasurable times. We found a great many objects – almost two hundred in all, including one entire pot, very precious. I thought that the existence of art was denied through ignorance, but our visit to Angel Falls opened my eyes to a darker purpose and frightened me.

O'Toole: 'Angel Falls! We've got to go there.'

'It's hopeless. They're invisible most of the time.'

'We've got to *try*, though.'

Gilbert said, '*I'd* like to try.'

Bob Willoughby added, '*I'm* in!'

Bob Willoughby, the famous prize-winning photographer, had worked on foreign locations with O'Toole before. He contributed to all the major picture magazines and now, frustrated by the physical difficulty of travelling to our locations, he made it his mission to get us to Angel Falls and then to attempt to travel to the remote reaches of the Orinoco, where it flows through the Amazonas territory, not far from the border of Venezuela and Brazil. He was preparing a book of portraits of women and was desperate to photograph the Waika tribe. He went to work to obtain permission from the government for an expedition.

'But *when*? *How*?' I asked, disbelievingly.

'Oh, later,' said O'Toole, cagily. 'Maybe not at all. Forget it.'

I knew better than to try to question him further, so I *did* forget all about these wild plans until, with a free weekend ahead, I was told to pack a few toothbrushes and a change of knickers and socks and be ready to leave the Rasil Hotel at dawn. I knew we were going to try to land on top of Angel Falls. I also knew that the film company would knock us out and lock us up rather than let the four of us do anything so foolhardy. I spent a sleepless night, guilty and pleasurably excited in equal measure. We were on the little airstrip at daybreak and found Gilbert waiting at his helicopter. He explained to me that we didn't have enough fuel for such a long trip, but that I wasn't to worry because O'Toole and Bob had learned from someone called 'Jungle Rudi' that there was aviation fuel stored nearby his place in Guiana. It had been there for years and the metal drums were all rusted, but *no doubt* it would get us to Angel Falls and then home again. No doubt. Oh, yes. But this was no time for doubts. We were off.

The Guiana Highlands lie in a corner of Eastern Venezuela, Bolivar State. This is El Dorado, the Terra Incognita between the Orinoco and the Amazon. Sir Walter Raleigh was here; one hundred men and five rowing boats and no luck at the end of the journey. Of course, there *has* been gold here. Until the discovery of the Rand goldfields of 1886, Venezuela was the largest gold-producing country in the world. We're after water not gold. Angel Falls, named after the great aviator, Jimmy Angel, whose plane got stuck on the summit.

'Going down,' shouts Gilbert over the noise of the helicopter and we land in a landscape unlike anything I've ever seen. The river and the trees where we stand are dwarfed by the *tepuis* all around; massive, squat, sheer-sided, table-top mountains that seem to belong in a work of fantastic fiction. An unkempt figure appears. Somehow, Gilbert, after flying for hours with no sign of a human being, has located Jungle Rudi, who greets us. They confer and Gilbert says we'll be back later.

'Now hold this.' I'm given a small piece of helicopter and see that Gilbert seems to be taking his machine apart and the men are neatly piling up everything that can be safely detached, and soon there's nothing left but the frame and the seats – no doors, no sides, nothing to hang on to except the frame of the seat in front. 'Okay,' he says cheerily. 'Let's go.' He and O'Toole are in great high spirits. The summit of Angel Falls is more often than not out of sight, blanketed in thick cloud, so it had been far from sure that we would be able to land there, but now, it seems, Gilbert thinks we have a good chance. Bob and I scramble into the back seats and hang on as we whoosh up and away and the ground, only too visible beneath our dangling feet, recedes and at the same moment the rain begins. We're drenched in minutes and that, coupled with the unaccustomed, terrifying feeling of naked vulnerability in a foreign element so disorients me that it is moments before I realise that the shrieking noise I can hear is coming from me. We fly into cloud and that is calming, but as we emerge from it I realise that we're going to put down on a piece of flat ground that to my fevered, disturbed senses doesn't seem to be much bigger than a grand piano. I clutch Bob's arm and scream, 'I can't look! I can't look!' 'Nor can I,' he shouts, 'and I'm taking the pictures!' As we make a perfect landing I open my eyes. 'Get out carefully on the *left side only*,' says Gilbert. 'We have no more than five minutes, then we must lift off before the cloud descends again.'

The summit of the *tepui* is spongy (no wonder Jimmy Angel's plane got stuck there) and it's covered in mosses and ferns which, so I've read, grow nowhere else. I've got gloves and pruning scissors and plastic bags in my pocket and I begin collecting. I believe Gilbert when he says that there's nothing but emptiness on the right-hand side of the helicopter and I stay on the left as I'm told, too frightened to look anywhere except at what lies directly under my feet so, standing where No Foot Has Trod is somewhat wasted on me; I'm seeing very little. The sound of water is deafening, but I can hear O'Toole laughing at my RHS gloves, or my cowardice, or both.

'That's it,' calls Gilbert. 'We have to go.' We obediently jump in and rise sideways and then, dropping slightly and moving in close to the side of the *tepui*, we come face to face with the falls as they emerge from rock and I realise that Gilbert is going to descend *with* the sheet of water thundering down the side of the mountain. I've heard of down draughts (or is it up draughts?) and the dangers of what we are doing, but after the trials of the morning I have no fear left and I am able to admire both the beauty of the sight before me and Gilbert's skill as we gently drop 3,212 feet to the ground below. Purged and quiet, we disembark weak at the knees, floppy like rabbits and smile our gratitude at Gilbert, who is looking very pleased, as well he might. We return to the fuel dump and refuel, Bob filtering the precious stuff through a nylon stocking while Gilbert spoons it off.

The adventures were not over and the day ended on a sombre note. After reassembling the helicopter, we flew a short distance, O'Toole and Gilbert conferring and searching around – for what? Suddenly they spotted a lone figure standing on a piece of level scrub near a small shack. It was Jungle Rudi's home. We put down, switched off the engine, and I followed the group making for the little house, where we sat drinking brandy and Jungle Rudi told us a fantastic tale of plots, of genocide, of danger. As he talked on and on, directing his attention to O'Toole only, speaking in an urgent, low monotone, I tried to separate the real, the probable, the believable from the improbably fantastic. I was tired and the brandy, taken on an empty stomach, was distorting my reason while at the same time in a way enhancing my acceptance of this strange scene. Rudi, his shotgun close to his right hand, talked of the destruction of huge tracts of land, flooded in the service of hydro-electric power. 'You think it is physically possible that they have warned Indian tribes impossible to locate even by expert anthropologists?' he asked rhetorically. I remembered that the student revolt I'd seen begin in the capital when we first arrived had been quelled in record time and when I'd asked how it had been stopped our Caracas friend, Mr Perez-Canto, had airily replied, 'Oh well, they shot quite a few.' I looked down at my precious bag of plants on the ground between my feet. This was a terrifying, beautiful, unruly place. I tried to rearrange my ideas of fair play and justice and my notion of the way things should be done. The intolerable was only too possible. But why was he telling this to O'Toole? 'They'll get me soon,' he said. 'They.' I began to withdraw. He could be just a lonely man, deranged by isolation. 'If you have art made by these so-called inartistic, ignorant, valueless people be very, very careful.' We had been digging and collecting for months, and yes, everyone *had* said that the Venezuelan Indians produced no art worth speaking of. That was the official line. I began to feel depressed, too tired and too inadequate to evaluate what was going on. Rudi and O'Toole walked together as we returned to the helicopter. I looked with relief at Gilbert's healthy Breton face and Bob's slightly sceptical, confident American sideways glance.

We were too tired to shout above the noise of the helicopter and sat silently as we flew over the seemingly endless rainforest. The last quarter of an hour of the journey found us sitting up, very alert and tight-lipped, while the red light on the chopper's panel glowed red for empty as we headed for the makeshift airfield. O'Toole kissed the ground when we landed safely and we headed off to the café to toast Gilbert and his dazzling skill. Back at the hotel, we sauntered through the coffee shop as though we'd been on a short taxi ride. I felt shaky, but I swung my plastic bags of plants as though they contained a little shopping. O'Toole sat down and ordered a coffee. No one was to know what we'd been up to, but Bob couldn't suppress his elation as he took off at speed to develop his pictures in his makeshift dark room. 'Nice day off?' asked someone. My eyes felt as big as saucers and I was sure I didn't look normal after the wonders of the day, all too much to absorb and digest, and I could do no more than nod and smile as I headed to bed and oblivion.

The Spanish Conquistadors had left behind forts which, unlike any subsequent buildings, caught the breeze and made the days bearable. The hospital scenes in the movie took place in such a building and while we were shooting these sequences the girls and my mother came to join us in Puerto Ordaz and made the long journey through the rainforest to watch the filming in the fort. Watching people filming is not a spectator sport and they were relieved to be let off to explore the pleasures of the American oil company compound, which had, glory of glories, a swimming pool and a Coca-Cola machine. Even the Caracas Hilton was more fun for the ten- and seven-year-old girls. So good to see the three of them; my mother had done a terrific job in my absence and under her coaching Kate had passed the entrance examination to three good schools and was all set to go to our first choice: the North London Collegiate School for Girls. My mother had a determined gleam in her eye as she talked about Pat's future. Pat, blonde, immaculate – a stranger to bad-hair days – shrugged and smiled non-committally. My mother permitted herself a half-smile and I could see that Pat had a date with my mother's classroom-for-one in the big kitchen in Guyon House.

When they left, we embarked on the last phase of the movie. Fate was kind to our director, Peter Yates, who had struggled so hard against awful odds, and filming was almost uneventful. When it was over, there was a concerted, mad rush for the exit. Our cases remained unpacked, however, and I assumed that we were to make a leisurely departure, returning via Caracas, the capital, where we had friends to visit. The telegram from our lawyer, Denise Sée, puzzled me. 'Poor Kate and Pat,' it read, 'to think of them as orphans . . .' Orphans? 'What does she mean?' I asked O'Toole. He looked at the telegram and tossed it into the wastepaper basket with a laugh. 'Good old Denise. Nice try,' he said. 'Try? What?' I persisted. 'Oh, everyone is behaving hysterically,' he said, soothingly. 'Pay no attention. We're going to make that little trip I was talking about and Dr Inga Goetz is coming down from Caracas to help us on our way.' Dr Goetz was an anthropologist and I'd read her book about the Yanomama Indians. I'd also read about the difficulty of reaching the headwaters of the Orinoco and I'd thrilled to the accounts of head-hunters and abandoned missions and missing travellers. It had made exciting reading, all right, and I was rather inclined to leave it at that, but already Bob was organising water-purifying tablets and was all set for the trip. O'Toole's contribution to the packing was a couple of bottles of brandy and a few gifts of tin kettles and machetes and sheets of Yanomama words he'd been given by Dr Goetz. 'You could learn these,' he said encouragingly. I didn't waste time arguing. It was very clear that O'Toole was going up the Orinoco and if he was going then I was going. I visited the only store in town, and found three plastic ponchos, folded small. I couldn't find anything else to buy. And it was difficult deciding what to wear, so far from the Army & Navy Stores or Tropicadilly in London. In the end I wore a cotton Yves St Laurent safari jacket and a Herbert Johnson cotton bush hat (they qualified as suitable because of the words 'safari' and 'bush'). My trousers were stuffed into a pair of Charles Jourdan 'riding' boots. I remembered buying an anti-bug burning device from Harrods. It lay unopened in my trunk along with the complete set of *À la recherche du temps perdu*, which I'd intended to read and hadn't. I slipped it into my little rucksack along with the brandy and a toothbrush. It didn't seem enough somehow, so I added some chocolate bars.

Even so, we seemed to be woefully unprepared, but I could see O'Toole's reasoning. We only had two or three weeks at our disposal. If we loitered, trying to make adequate preparations, we simply wouldn't make the trip at all. 'Remember,' he said, 'Englishmen once went up Everest in tennis shoes with a packet of sandwiches.' I supposed he was exaggerating, but I rather agreed with the notion that anything was possible until it turned out to be impossible. 'Okay,' I said and bought more chocolate.

Dr Goetz arrived; German, tall, middle-aged and very sprightly. We were in business. The four of us flew in an alarmingly small plane to the small settlement called Ayacucho (I could have done without being told that this meant 'corner of death'). There, she helped us find a suitable small boat (the soap-dish, O'Toole christened it) and a pair of guides. They were incredibly uncharming and shook their heads gloomily whenever Dr Goetz addressed them. We only had room for one man, but they were adamant that they wouldn't accompany us alone and conveyed to Dr Goetz that they would only go 'so far'. It seemed that most of the missions along the river had been abandoned and only two remained. Dr Goetz would accompany us to the first one and persuade them to let us stay overnight. As we began our journey the following morning, sun shone and the river was alarmingly wide, as it had been where we'd been filming hundreds of miles to the east. The noise of the outboard was deafening and we were silent as we stared at the 'green wall' which was the vast rainforest on both sides. At least the river had a shine on its mud-coloured surface. O'Toole had decided that he wouldn't bother with water purifiers, so we were to start drinking river water as soon as possible 'to get our systems going'. Bob looked incredulous. He was weighed down with the latest thing in camera equipment and water purifiers.

It took us a day to reach the mission; a day spent looking at not very much. It seems absurd but remote jungles and rainforests viewed from the river do present dull, almost blank, high 'walls' of green. I began the journey sitting up straight on the bit of bench that was to be mine during the entire journey, eagerly looking about. After about four hours I sat slumped, wishing I could at least identify the trees which made up 'the wall'. It looked impenetrable and I wondered uneasily how we'd manage when we pulled in.

The landing place looked very small when it appeared, protruding into the immense river. We tied up and Dr Goetz, who was familiar with the place, led us through the trees on to a serviceable pathway which led in turn to the clearing and the somewhat ramshackle mission building. The nuns were welcoming and indicated that they would be very happy for us to eat with them and to stay overnight. We were ravenous and fell on the food, which was laid on a trestle table in a dilapidated room, bare of furniture save for a few benches. The meat was wild pig and was delicious. We were shown to small cells containing narrow wooden-framed beds with straw mattresses. I scarcely remembered undressing and the sun was high in the sky when I woke and scrambled to get ready to leave. Dr Goetz sat with us and gave us a last briefing before she returned to Ayacucho and then to Caracas. The bad news was that one of our guides refused to come any further. It seems he was now voluble with horror stories of the dangers ahead, but I couldn't understand a word he said. Dr Goetz said that we should of course be careful, but that in all probability we wouldn't find any native Indians. She had made thirteen properly organised expeditions and not all of them had been successful in this regard. She wished us luck and reminded us to use our Yanomama words, especially *Shori noji* (good friends) and to be as cheerful and as amusing as possible, should we be fortunate enough to find ourselves surrounded by the Yanomama.

Rested and fed, we were in high good spirits as we set off on our own and the rain began to fall. It didn't just fall, it leapt on us and jumped up and down. I fished out the plastic ponchos and we each retreated into a little brightly coloured tent. We were wet by the time we arranged them over our little places (Bob draped his over his cameras) and then the rain penetrated the neck fastening and ran up our arms as we tried to smoke. We couldn't even look up, the rain was blinding and the noise was deafening as it landed on the metal soap-dish and bounced off our ponchos. There was now a wall of rain between us and the wall of the jungle. There was nothing to do except stare silently at the floor and occasionally glance sideways. The remaining guide was malevolently fed up, as well he might be. I'd given him my chocolate bar, which he accepted with palpable disdain. I wished I could speak to him; we might have enjoyed a bit of a moan together. We seemed to have been travelling for a week already and I thought I sensed him wondering where we would sleep and would there be anything to eat except chocolate. Bob and O'Toole were full of high resolve and in no mood to be bothered with trivial details.

Out of the corner of my left eye I see something – the first *different* something I've seen all day. On a smooth outcrop of rock shining in the rain, backed by the dark green jungle wall, stands a person – a small, stocky figure, legs braced, arms raised, holding a huge bow, taller than himself, the arrow poised for flight. Snuggled under my pixie hood I figure the bow is six feet high, so the man is only four feet something. The arrow is trained on the soap-dish. I nudge O'Toole with my foot. He's sitting opposite me, staring at the ground. He looks at me through the rain. As subtly as I know how, I indicate the bank to my left. He looks and sees the naked figure. As he stiffens, Willoughby, behind me, follows his gaze and automatically his hands tighten on his camera. 'No,' breathes O'Toole. 'Leave it.' Our guide is oblivious, thank God, and we pass up river – oh, so slowly – and the arrow slowly swings around to follow us until we pass out of sight into the rain-soaked dusk. We can't discuss what happened, conversation is impossible, and we plough on. In a way, that little incident has made me less afraid. We've gone over Niagara in a barrel and there's no going back and that makes everything simpler. I no longer have any hope of knowing what time of day it is, or indeed what day it is, but suddenly the rain stops and we see a lawn – I swear – a lawn. It's like a vision, too Pre-Raphaelite bright to be real, and there, standing on the edge of the lawn is a figure in black robes with a huge white Old Testament mane of hair and long, spade beard. It says something for my state of mind and the amount of brandy I'd ingested that I have no recollection in what language we communicated with this priest. But we dined with him in a ramshackle shed and he showed us his work. He was making a dictionary. Yanomama to – what? I'd never make a decent explorer. I don't remember. I fancy it was Armenian. He looked Greek. There was no one left in his mission. And there were no missions left up river. He told us there had been trouble with the Yanomama – there was danger and we should turn back, now.

We ate bits of meat picked from small ribcages (what *were* we eating, I wondered). Now that we were at rest and the rain had stopped, we could hear noises again: birds shrieked and later frogs croaked and crickets filled the air with their sound. We slept in hammocks. I wasn't worried about what lay in store. Only later did I realise that I was living entirely in the present.

Onward up river. Against advice, we are not carrying guns (just as well, I think – my aim is probably as bad as my sense of direction). The rain is intermittent now and the boys have thrown away their red cloaks. Mine is stuffed under my seat, just in case. It's so incredibly boring, this trip up the exotic river. I'm now thinking of the jungle wall as green concrete. Where are we? How far have we come? What will the source of the river – miles away – look like, if we get there? Is it worth it? Plod on. Drink brandy and river water. Smile at guide a lot. He doesn't smile back once. I'm half asleep most of the time. There's a hallucinatory quality about my waking moments.

A small girl appears in a tiny clearing in the forest wall. O'Toole shouts at the guide to pull into the bank. The water is high, but he manages to moor near a small spit of land and we disembark. Reality intrudes as the small child grabs O'Toole's hand and begins pulling him into the forest. Bob and I fluster out of the boat and set off at a run after them. The guide doesn't budge. Waist-high branches and creepers slash across our bodies as we try to keep up with the pair ahead. The little girl is so small that she can run under the impediments. How is O'Toole coping? We're slowing down to a trot and, breathless and scratched, we reach a clearing. Ahead is what looks like a huge, blond ski-slope and I realise it's a massive thatched roof made of palm leaves yellowed with age – it must reach from forty feet down to a little wall-opening just four feet high. The small girl drags O'Toole through the opening. Keen not to be left behind, we half crawl, half stumble after them. We are in a big *shabono*. I've never seen one from the air, but I'm told that from above they look like doughnuts. From ground level they are much more elegant, the roof rising to an open circle, and below as many as forty families occupy a segment each of the circle; hammocks swing in two or three layers over fires which can be reached by hand from the lowest hammock. Behind the hammocks against the wall are makeshift shelves, holding little more than baskets, it seems, and on ground level, pet birds and parrots play. Babies are at all times attached to their mothers. Dusk is falling, it's raining again. The noise of the rain on leaves mingles with the shrill noise of female voices. *That's* what's so odd. There are no men here. And Willoughby and O'Toole have disappeared. I remember what Dr Goetz had told me, 'Say "*Shori noji*" – often! Smile! Lift your eyebrows as often as possible. And allow them to explore your body. They need to know what you are.'

There must be fifty small, small women pressing around me, not one reaching my diaphragm. Tiny hands pull at my St Laurent shirt. The buttons give way (well done, back at the workroom). My black silk trousers give way at the waist and rip down the length of the zipper. My hat is torn off and my hair detached from its rubber band. They scream with laughter – these small, big-breasted women – I'm revealed as an androgynous, flat-chested, wide-shouldered, slim-hipped, flat-stomached – what? So much exercise, so much disciplined dieting to a perfect catwalk size 8 to 10, has resulted in hilarious entertainment for the ladies of the upper reaches of the Orinoco. I tie my clothes back on – I'm not enjoying this much but am trying to keep smiling – and hope that my genuine goodwill is going to get me through the ensuing night. O'Toole and Willoughby appear from the side of the *shabono*. It seems that most of the men are away on a hunt. I'm so dazed I don't ask how they *know* this. 'This is quite lucky for us.'

'We're to be taken to sleep now.'

A little group of women walk us back into the forest until we come to another clearing and there we see a group of nuns. Now, I do feel I'm hallucinating. I'd read that some of the Yanomama, while not accepting Christianity, quite like to live near a mission in order to trade goods. This must be the second of the last remaining missions. These sweet-faced women lead us to a trestle table and yet again we eat unidentifiable bits of meat attached to small ribcages. After much nodding and miming of gratitude we retreat to snug hammocks under a broken-down barn roof. I remember my Harrods anti-bug coils. I light the coils and place them under our hammocks and I lie there listening to the forest noises, looking up at the broken roof, wishing I hadn't read so much about vampire bats.

All night the air was filled with music. The women, alone in the *shabono*, ululated and sang for the success of the hunt. I made that up. They sang all night but I don't know what they were singing about. The men were away hunting. They may have been wishing them success or just enjoying a hen night.

In the morning we thank the nuns and make our way back to the *shabono*. The women are having a kind of lie-in after the musical efforts of the previous night or maybe this is how they spend their days. They lie in their hammocks playing with their babies, decorating them with paint and feathers. The older children play on the floor with the family pets. One woman is working; she is weaving a basket, lying down in her hammock, using her two hands and one foot. The vine is held away from her by her huge big toe. I notice that they all have large big toes that stand away from the other toes. A few men appear and try to engage O'Toole and Bob in some kind of game. We can't work out what they want, but we do a lot of eyebrow work and smile obligingly.

The women roll out of their hammocks and we follow them as they all trot a little way away from the *shabono* (they never seem to move at walking pace; everything is done at a run). Ah – it's to be a contest of strength. They're producing the huge bows and arrows we saw the young man holding on the river bank. O'Toole is almost twice as tall as these men, the contest seems unfair. Everyone is in huge good humour. Some of the men are laughing so much they can barely stay standing. They're calling O'Toole something and I write it down so that Dr Goetz can translate it later. The men give O'Toole a bow and arrow and stand alongside him. He's not a bad archer and now he good-humouredly prepares to shoot with them. Their arrows fly into the air and O'Toole is left struggling. He cannot release the arrow no matter how he tries. They now lie on the floor, they're laughing so much. These tiny men have shoulders and arms like heavyweight boxers at the peak of fitness. We are now loved. O'Toole is patted on his bottom and is obviously being told what a great fellow he is. We trot out our bits of Yanomama and throw in lots of '*Shori noji*'s; greater harmony could not be imagined. The women have got used to me and stroke my clothes and my flat chest, fondly amused this morning. We can't stay, fearful that they might feel they have to feed us – and they don't seem to have anything in the way of food. Almost all of them accompany us (at a run) through the rainforest and down to our boat. The 'guide' and boatman looks appalled and stands apart, hatchet-faced, as we indulge in a prolonged leave-taking and O'Toole produces gifts from our little store of machetes and beads and tin cans. I've never had such a social success anywhere.

As soon as we set off up river it begins to rain again. I can tell that the river is very high. Today, we're seeing things. They were there before, so have we only now learned to notice them? I can't believe that, but we are now seeing birds as they sweep across the water: macaws, I recognise; dark green kingfishers also – although they don't look much like the kingfishers of Carmarthenshire. As I look at the jungle wall, I see an ibis, high up, miss its footing and fall gracelessly down four or five 'floors' of tree. It finds a landing place and, effortlessly elegant again, sits there, pretending nothing embarrassing happened. I catch O'Toole's eye and see that he has been observing the same comical scene.

The rain stops and we are able to look around again. I don't know what time it is – my watch became waterlogged days ago – and it is very hard to be sure how many days we have been travelling. There is a smooth rock and a piece of beaten earth alongside it that could be a landing place. We are very tired and very hungry and quite disoriented (probably a bit drunk as well). Pulling in, we set off into the rainforest. There *is* a path of sorts. The vines and branches lash cruelly across our waists and chests. We're too tall for this vegetation. On we go, each sunk in our thoughts, and suddenly there is another *shabono*, but the drama is *outside* this time – we gradually realise we have walked straight into a hallucinogenic ceremony. There are no women in sight. The men are naked, save for the belt which holds the foreskin tucked up in its correct 'public' place. We freeze on the spot and no one acknowledges our presence. Squatting down, one man, clad only in a loincloth, is about to blow the hallucinogenic dust into the nostrils of another man. I've read about this often, so I know what to expect, but nothing prepares one for the explosion of mucus; the eyes, the nose, the mouth – everything runs violently. As I'd read, this pain seems to go on for half an hour; then, for the next half-hour, the shaman (the wise man) receives auditory instructions and advice for the tribe, then he goes to the river and washes and takes another half-hour to recover. So we watch the full one-and-a-half-hour experience.

Instinctively, we felt that we shouldn't linger in this place. There was none of the friendly curiosity we had experienced earlier. We laid our gifts on the floor, machetes and tin kettles, and while they were unsmilingly picked up and examined we nodded and smiled, said, '*Shori noji!*' and tried to melt into the forest, backing away as casually as we were able. I had found the ceremony alarming. Bob, of course, had snatched some photographs and O'Toole, who prided himself – with reason – on his nose for trouble, murmured, 'Don't hang about, my dears. Back to the soap-dish.' Once we were out of sight of the *shabono* we turned and ran back to the river and continued towards the source. We didn't make it, but we stopped after travelling a very respectable distance. The BBC was in Venezuela making a documentary that year. They were making a proper expedition in a hovercraft with guards carrying submachine guns and it seems that we managed to get four hundred miles further up river than they did. And this gave us a good deal of childish satisfaction at the time.

The return to Ayacucho dragged. We had none of the excitement of the beginning of the adventure and time was running out and we ought to be thinking of returning to England where, in a few weeks, filming would be resumed in the studio. O'Toole was in a 'Let's push on' mood and we took only brief rests on the long journey. The guide was handsomely rewarded for his pains. For an unguarded moment he looked surprised as he swiftly counted the notes O'Toole thrust at him. He hadn't realised that he'd been working for one of the great over-payers of the Western world. We hired a Cessna in Ayacucho and flew to Caracas. Coffee and beds and baths and a spot of scrambled egg were just beginning to feature in my thoughts when we flew into a violent storm. I was too tired to be frightened and looked at the men in disbelief as the little plane was thrown about and the pilot began to shout incoherent bits of advice to us over his shoulder. It was obvious that we had to escape from the storm so down we went – all the way down, in fact. The pilot managed to land and we stood in the middle of nowhere with our bits of luggage – mainly Bob's equipment – until the pilot succeeded in raising a local taxi, who was startled but game when we asked him to drive to Caracas, five or six hours away. Bob and O'Toole pressed a great deal of money into the pilot's hand and off we lurched – it was a *very* old car; all of it rattled, but we slept like infants and it got us to the Hilton, pulling up with a noisy flourish alongside the Bentleys and the Rolls-Royces.

Bob's wife, Dorothy, was waiting for him. 'We're going to Machu Picchu,' they said. 'Not without us,' said O'Toole, and I went upstairs to pack and change the air tickets and telegraph London to say that we were safe and *almost* on the way home. I called Dr Goetz before we left Venezuela. She told us that the name O'Toole had been given was 'High Mountain'.

We rendezvoused with the Willoughbys in Cuzco and obediently followed all the rules for acclimatising to this altitude; no alcohol and a four-hour sleep, then very slow movement for a while. In the 'best' hotel our sheets were grubby and I took them off and we fell asleep under the rough blankets. (Why should we assume that the blankets were cleaner than the sheets, I thought lazily, and at the same moment thought, 'What does it matter?')

Awakening, we strolled – slowly – around Cuzco, marvelling along with all the other visitors at the wonderful stonework. O'Toole and I have a special interest in stone. Connemara in Ireland is a land of granite, the drystone walls of Ireland are beautiful and varied. Looking at the massive drystone walls of Cuzco, we decided that we would try to build a drystone house in Connemara. Like all the visitors, we wanted to go to Machu Picchu. In 1970 it was still an uncomfortable trip and along with a cartload of other tourists we felt slightly adventurous.

There was no place to stay, it was a bit like going to Petra ten years previously, and we were well able to rest curled up under a rock. Nothing can prepare one for Machu Picchu and nothing one can say can add to the descriptions or convey the wonder of it.

We moved on to Lima where O'Toole had a contact in the art world. Bob and his wife left us after the one conventional meal we were to enjoy and they also gave us money; we had run out but there was something called a credit card and it gave you money, no matter where you were. O'Toole and I were mystified and impressed and grateful. Lima was the noisiest city I had ever been in – or was I now unused to urban din? O'Toole went off to 'meet a man – don't ask' and I 'Wait here'. To pass the time, I pressed my dried plants (my mother would be fascinated to see them) and repacked our luggage and sat looking at the dark street. This city scared me somewhat, though I didn't know why. At four in the morning O'Toole returned, exhausted, bearing a few plastic shopping bags. 'Pack these – don't look. God, I'm tired.' Fully clothed, he stretched out on the bed and slept. This man slept better and longer than anyone I knew. Dutifully, I didn't 'look' and I packed the objects in the luggage. When O'Toole woke, we left for the airport and home. In Bogotá we landed unexpectedly and the plane was kept on the ground for hours. 'Sorry, love,' he said. 'I think the game's up. Don't forget you really *don't* know what's in those bags.' I tried to read and not contemplate the punishment for the unlawful liberating of works of art. Suddenly we were off! I couldn't look at him. It was the luck of the Irish, dammit. I felt sick.

In the Green Room of Guyon House, my mother and Kate and Pat and Liz and Manolita unpack and drink tea. 'Oh, thank God for a decent cup of tea,' groans the Irishman. 'Where's the jewellery?' 'What jewellery?' 'You *know* – the jewellery from Lima.' 'Was there any? You said not to look.' 'Oh Jaysus – I'm surrounded by eejits.' 'Wait, wait,' soothes my mother and goes to search through the rubbish. 'Is this what you were looking for?' she says, holding up a ratty plastic shopping bag. 'Could be,' and he drops the most beautiful old necklaces over my head. The pre-Columbian masks are put aside to be sent to our British Museum friend, who will 'blow' the flattened gold back into shape and then they will be sent to Claude de Muzak in Paris to be mounted. We all look at the beautiful, battered, soft gold faces. The girls stroke them and I can't feel too guilty about any of this.

* * *

We leave for Ireland almost at once. Arriving at the cottage in Connemara, I unpack my plants from Angel Falls and see the *Irish Times* on the table. 'Air Tragedy', I read, and before I pick up the paper I know it will tell me of Gilbert's death on *The Blue Max*. A small piece of something or other fell from above and cut Gilbert's rotor blade. It only takes a little something to destroy a helicopter and in this case five lives in Brittany. We look out over the fuchsia hedges, down to the Atlantic; the never far-away melancholy of this piece of Ireland rises up to chime with the desolation we're feeling.

Chapter Twenty-eight

Since my schooldays I had never had anything much to do with people of my sex and age. I spent the most interesting times working with adults where I was 'the girl'. Then as I grew up and played leading parts, I worked largely with men. The other women I worked with were usually considerably older than I was. In private life I was a wife – a wife obliged to keep her private life very private and defined to a large extent by the identity of a husband. As a young mother I felt redefined by my children. Was it my imagination, or were young women years ago constantly in some kind of competition with each other? Certainly there were, as always, too few jobs for too many of us actresses, so that competition was understandable. Those women whose ambition was to marry well seemed also to pursue a solitary path to their goal. As the wife of a rich, talented, glamorous man I was from time to time painfully aware of the unabashed, predatory behaviour of the women we met. From time to time I was astonished to observe that even women whom I regarded as friends were not above making a barely veiled attempt at seducing my husband.

Safe within my small circle of women whom I liked and admired, women whom it was not possible to define especially by their gender – well behaved, hardworking, amusing, clever, good-looking – I looked out somewhat nervously at the liberated woman of the late Sixties and early Seventies.

So when I was asked to play Mrs Pankhurst, the leader of the Suffragettes, in *Shoulder to Shoulder*, a six-part series that Ken Taylor had written about the movement and the women involved in it, even as I unhesitatingly accepted the producer Verity Lambert's offer, at the same moment I thought, 'Oh, this is going to be hell on wheels – six months, virtually living with fifty women.' Half the plays were to be directed by Moira Armstrong, the other three by Waris Hussein – how would he cope with us all? – and even one of the camera operators was female. I

449

could imagine the rows, the tears, the gossiping, the cliques, the jealousies that lay ahead.

The range and diversity of the personalities cooped up together in close quarters for long hours each day as we worked six, sometimes seven, days a week gave rise to amusement and absorbing interest rather than irritation. I realised that I'd turned some kind of corner when I found myself polishing Patricia Quinn's skin-tight leather dress – which she was wearing at the time. It had been bought in a shop in the King's Road in which I wouldn't have been seen dead, but I could appreciate that it looked terrific on Pat. I played Mrs Pankhurst, the leader of the Suffragette Movement, Patricia was my daughter, Christabel, and Angela Down played Sylvia. Angela was as reserved as Pat was extrovert, I hovered somewhere in between and we became the little family which was the nucleus of the drama. Georgia Brown developed the idea for the series along with Midge McKenzie, and Georgia played a leading part as well. Ken Taylor was the writer and as we all became experts on the politics of the turn of the century he grew to dread our pleas for extra scenes – especially 'good' bits of the story that we didn't want left out. If he'd listened to us the series would have been fifty hours long. Verity Lambert, the producer, presided effortlessly over the huge undertaking, helped by the best of buccaneering company managers (shortly to become a producer himself) Graham Benson, who, on our first early morning filming call in the damp, grey countryside outside Halifax (which was playing Manchester, 1890), appeared in the makeshift make-up room bearing trays of champagne and orange juice 'to cheer things up a bit'.

We stayed cheered up for the next seven months, all of us running more or less complicated private lives, and no one pleaded tiredness or illness or heartbreak or buckled under the worries of organising homes and husbands and parents and children by remote control. There wasn't one woman who gave less than her best and I was buoyed up like a cork on the ocean. The men in our lives were a trifle bemused, as well they might be. Many of them found themselves at home while we worked late. This was a different kind of life we were leading and it made us all a little different. Waris Hussein, who shared the directing with Moira Armstrong, accompanied us when we let off steam occasionally and went out on the town, dancing for hours, and Graham Benson made sure we were all packed off home in good order. This was all quite unlike working in a more usual mixed-sex show where the men went out on the spree and the women rushed home to catch up with the housekeeping. I'd never had such a good time and my confidence began to grow. Observing how other women struggled to reconcile the many demands made on them with varying degrees of success and often with utter failure, I began to realise that it was impossible to do everything properly; that feeling slightly inadequate and very guilty all the time was a state common to us all. The current wisdom was that it was easy to Have it All, to Do it All. I had been photographed many times in my 'perfect' room in my 'fashionable' clothes with my clean, 'adorable'- looking children, 'successfully combining my busy working life with my beautiful domestic existence', as the caption would read. What a lie! I thought, with relief. I knew now that I wasn't alone in finding the effort of running three or four lives almost impossibly difficult. It was comforting to feel part of a huge, struggling, largely silent sisterhood. Men weren't expected to help at all; if women wanted to work they had, somehow, to manage everything so as to inconvenience no one and many of us learned for the first time to admit failure and to ask for and give help.

More than a few of us had health worries as well. 'Pains peculiar to ladies', as I'd seen them quaintly described, were ignored, as were minor illnesses and even major illnesses were overcome with a minimum of drama. Both Verity and I were hospitalised with suspected breast cancer. When we went to visit our producer after her exploratory operation, she was holding an IV fluid bottle in one hand, a telephone in the other and gesturing at the champagne with her foot.

The moment that there was an indication that I might have breast cancer, Dr Slattery whisked me back from Bristol where I was spending the weekend with O'Toole, who was doing a season of plays at the Old Vic. I was booked into the London Clinic at once, pausing only to tell Verity that I'd be back at work as soon as possible. She was reassuringly matter-of-fact; with fifty women on board for six months, these crises were depressingly frequent. The watchword was 'Don't get excited; just deal with the situation minute by minute.' O'Toole was more fearful than I was, but he went on rehearsing.

It was winter and before I drove down to Harley Street for surgery, I went to one of my favourite Hampstead places, the High Hill Bookshop, to order the Christmas books for the girls and for my friend, Ricci Burns, and his mother, Lilian. Standing there, suddenly I wasn't able to maintain my chirpy attitude and I wondered morbidly if I would *be* there in Guyon House at Christmas time. I trailed back up the hill, feeling sorry for myself. There was no one at home in whom to confide. My mother most certainly wasn't to know; not many years past she'd survived a double mastectomy and I didn't want her to have to confront another, frightening cancer episode. It would be silly to worry the girls and I had waved them off to school as casually as I was able. As usual, my only confidant was Ricci Burns. I called him and he didn't let me down. 'Oh, my God, I can see it all! You're sitting in that house and you've convinced yourself you're going to die! Stop it! Don't be a drama queen!' I took his advice and stopped organising my funeral service.

O'Toole came to London from Bristol to receive an award and called in to the hospital on the eve of my operation. I think that hospitals and illness distress him beyond measure and am glad when he hurries off. As I'm on the brink of feeling alone and sorry for myself, the nurse comes in bearing a massive, magnificent bunch of red roses; it looks incongruous in this expensive but spartan room. When I look at the note I re-join the land of 'normal', functioning people. It reads, 'Wear these in your hair tonight, love Ricci'. Ricci – thank God for him. I feel like Frida Kahlo in a Buñuel film as I snuggle down to sleep, broadly smiling, surrounded by red blossoms.

After the operation the next day, when I came round, they give me my 'Permission to perform a mastectomy' form to tear up because the papilloma, which had bled so alarmingly, had proved to be benign. My first thought is to call the BBC to say I'll be back at work the following day. I call home. Lionel isn't available to bring me home; he's picking up actors and bringing them to Guyon House before they all set off for another week's rehearsal at Bristol. A little groggy, I thank my nurse and go out into Harley Street to look for a taxi. I feel lucky, standing there, listing slightly to starboard, under the weight of my roses. At home, the Green Room is alight with laughter and storytelling – there are some expert raconteurs in there, sitting and then jumping up to take advantage of the small stage. It's lovely but it's not for me today. O'Toole and I have a short, relieved moment together, but I can tell that I'm expected to have moved on. That moment when I was at the centre of the domestic stage is over. Downstairs, Lionel looks mightily relieved when I flash him a grin. (He would have wanted to pick me up and bring me home, I know.) My mother, knowing nothing, looks a bit disgruntled that I've been away for a night for no good reason. Climbing the stairs from the basement kitchen I meet the troupe setting off for Bristol. I have another brief moment with O'Toole, then they're gone.

As the big Georgian door closes, a profound silence descends on the house. Thanks to Manolita, everything looks beautiful. The big hall with its black-and-white tiled floor glows with the dull brass of the Persian chest, opened to reveal a tumult of oriental silks. The Bró paintings with their violent, vivid mop-headed trees are startling against the grey walls. The stairwell is hung with a large stone bas-relief from China and rubbings from Angkor and deceptively quiet Picasso etchings. Turning into the bedroom with its big bow window shuttered against the winter light and, beyond the garden, the Men's Surgical ward of New End Hospital, I know that three floors below me, Scobie, the bulldog, is plodding to and fro under the fig tree, mute and mutinous; willing someone to let him in. Not I. Not today. My mother and Manolita will be clearing away the cups and glasses and ashtrays in the Green Room. Liz is in the nursery, the children are at school and the bedroom is extra silent. I drop my bag and sit on the bed facing my treasured Louis XIV bureau plat. The walls of cupboards are shut and behind them, I know, there is perfect order; hanging cupboards filled with clean, pressed clothes, blouses filed in order of colour, trousers, all black and white. Shoes, polished and lined up on brass rods – all fitted with their shoe-trees – everything rising unseen to the high ceiling. Gloves are neatly arranged – leather, cotton, suede, string. There are monogrammed handkerchiefs and underwear in scented bags. I know exactly what lies, invisible, behind the blank walls, the multitude of potentially chaotic garments which could fill the calm room, unfurling themselves, filling it with colour and confusion. Manolita's devotion and my anxiety keeps everything at bay, subdued and in its place. There is nothing in this beautiful room to indicate that I live here. Turning back the dark tapestry spread on the bed, I switch on my bedside lamp. Lying down, I think gratefully that when I am alone, there are no surprises in this room, Manolita has seen to that, and I am comforted by our unspoken stand against the misrule and chaos that threaten to engulf me and this house. Yea, though I walk through the valley of the shadow of death, my folded clothes, my shiny shoes, my gloves and my clean handkerchiefs shall comfort me.

Lying there, I know no one will disturb me until the girls get back from school. Few people know this ex ex-directory line and anyway, who would call me in this fortress? I realise that I *had* said goodbye to all this, thinking of my own mortality in a way I had not done since I was a little girl, much preoccupied with death.

The next day I was back at work, feeling terrific.

I was on the whole blessed with rude good health, but illness dogged much of our lives together. When I first met O'Toole he was living with Ken and Doriah Griffith in Belgravia and Doriah confided in me, half admiring, half scandalised, 'He sits there drinking alternate gulps of white ulcer medicine and Scotch. *And* he's smoking Gauloises!' During the Stratford season his ulcers got worse and he was urged to go into hospital. More or less organising his own treatment, O'Toole ordered gallons of white 'stomach medicine' and the kitchen was piled high with Complan. Naturally, he continued to stay up late and drink and smoke prodigiously. When he returned to London after the season, he was completely well again. His extraordinary restorative power, aided by a huge capacity for sleep and a healthy appetite, continued to stand him in good stead. My mother and I worried quietly and were mightily relieved when he underwent a cure before each job. And of course he emerged at the end of a job tired but healthy, after a prolonged bout of discipline. It was the in-between times that were difficult.

Chapter Twenty-nine

In the early Seventies, inexplicable episodes of bad health began to occur. A few years earlier we had acquired the small cottage with a piece of land in 'O'Toole country' on the West Coast of Ireland. Our plan was to acquire yet more of the adjoining land and to build ourselves a family home. As we planned the new house we all squashed into the one-storey croft with two bedrooms and a living room, lean-to bathroom and kitchen, an attic bedroom for the girls under the roof, one turf fire for heat and a Calor gas cooker. Even when I was working and couldn't accompany them, the girls and Liz and my mother spent all the school holidays in Connemara. The girls were given a life that almost duplicated my childhood, disappearing after breakfast and returning at night to a house where there was no television or radio; just talk and books by night and freedom and security by day for girls who had at one time been on the receiving end of kidnap threats in London. In her seventies, my mother was returned to her youth. Her country skills were recollected and became useful again. Isolated and a bit out of our depth, we were dependent on her store of knowledge, and that, I suppose, is what ought to happen in a family, but modern life is rarely conducive to this happy state.

The cottage boasted a garden which had been neglected for years. Brambles and sycamore seedlings, twenty-foot-high thickets of old hydrangea bushes, flowering green-white in the shade, stands of bamboo thickening over the kitchen garden. The soil was superb; friable and dark, chocolate brown (obviously this garden had once been beautifully looked after) and everywhere in the small front garden and in the copse at the side of the house, fresh, green-leaved plants in among the montbretia, all increasing healthily inside the overgrown boundary hedges of fuchsia. I admired the plants and looked them up in my gardening dictionary. My mother and I looked at each other in dismay; 'Bishop's Gout-Weed, Devil's gut,' we read, 'otherwise known as *ground elder* – the most virulent of weeds. Almost impossible to eradicate.' What to do? It was everywhere. We couldn't poison the whole garden – we wanted to start replanting.

Depressed, my mother flew back to London with the children and O'Toole and I, with some time off, stayed behind, for a few days as we thought, and I fretted over the monstrous weeds – the smallest piece of root left in the earth would grow into another plant and it would even go on growing out of earth thrown on the rubbish tip. It was like something from another planet and I began to regard it as a personal enemy and was sitting on the doorstep, wondering moodily what to do about it, when I realised that O'Toole, sitting behind me in the house, was distinctly unwell. Unwell enough to go to bed without argument. Unwell enough not to object when, the following day, frightened, I called the local doctor. He was also worried. O'Toole had dreadful stomach pain and there didn't appear to be an explanation for it. He was too ill to be moved and so began a month of misery. Our patient seemed barely conscious at times and lay there – just enduring pain. The local doctor came and stood, worried, at the foot of the bed. He spoke to Gerry Slattery in London. There was nothing to do but try to keep him as comfortable as possible. Eventually the pain diminished somewhat, and, exhausted, he lay there, drifting in and out of sleep, too weak to move. Twice a day I hand-washed sheets wet with perspiration and laid them out on the brambles to dry. I left the bedroom window open and a few feet away from the bed inside, and sick at heart with worry, I began to work on the ground elder, gently uprooting it by hand. All my misery and fear went into that weeding. Every few minutes I glanced at the bed through the window and for three weeks I worked my way slowly through those innocent-looking, monstrous plants.

When O'Toole was able to stand and walk, I felt that, together, we'd conquered something mysterious and dangerous. The garden also had been tamed, the ground elder banished, the beautiful soil sieved and checked over again and again for a fragment of evil, white, fleshy root. Powerlessness in the sick room had given me the tenacity of an animal, working out there on my hands and knees by day, while at night I listened for his breathing until I fell asleep, exhausted.

Back in London, we were none the wiser. What had it been, pondered Gerry and a few of his friends from the Royal Free Hospital. Well, no sign of anything now. O'Toole went back to work on *Rosebud*, a movie that would take him to seven or eight countries. 'All over for good, let's hope,' said Gerry. But it wasn't over. In Paris, O'Toole became very ill indeed and his make-up man, Bill Lodge, called a halt to the unequal struggle to go to work every day. Otto Preminger, the director, stopped the film without a murmur, got O'Toole into the American Hospital and sent for me. I did little except loiter, worried, in the hospital and spent the rest of the summer days of 1974 alone in the hotel, never straying far from the phone.

There is always a professional need, shared by all actors high and low, to keep illnesses a secret from the press and the public. In my case, this created an additional divide between me and the girls and the outside world as well. O'Toole's parents and his sister were not to be told anything but good news – Jules and Joyce and my mother (up to a point) and I were isolated in our falsehoods. The girls were asked not to talk about their father. And I wasn't told what was wrong.

Otto Preminger was capable of being a difficult director, but he was what Joyce Buck called a 'six o'clock pussy cat', turning into the nicest person imaginable once the day's work was done, and certainly, to us during our troubled month, he was kind and considerate over and above the call of duty. I did see the other side of him once during the filming of *Rosebud* as for no good reason he demanded take after take from Richard Attenborough. There were actors of every nationality in the movie and I was very proud to be, if only by similar training, on Richard Attenborough's 'team'. Throughout the trying day he remained polite and calm and solid as a rock, never allowing Otto to affect his work adversely.

Script writer, Roy Clarke, had been co-opted and flown to Paris to improve O'Toole's dialogue (in a script written by someone else). I met him at the hospital and he gave me the few bright moments I enjoyed during that sad, worrying summer. We shared a coffee after one of our visits to the American Hospital and were sitting silently outside the Café de la Paix, watching the crowds go by. It was 14 July. Roy, in his North Country voice, broke the silence. 'D'you know what day it is today?' 'No.' 'Ah, well, at home tonight they'll all be asking "What did *you* do for Bastille Day then?"'

When O'Toole recovered from his mystery illness and we'd spent some time quietly in the hotel suite while he convalesced, he packed me off home. I was loath to leave him; he looked frail to me, but as usual he hated to be seen to be looked after and I knew Bill Lodge, his make-up man, would watch over him. Before I left I visited the set as they shot a street scene. The only actor I met that day was Peter Lawford, who looked appallingly ravaged. We sat together in a café and I had to make my excuses and leave; there was something unbearably distressing and depressing in his manner and conversation.

I flew home, low in spirits, and the film dragged on in an undistinguished fashion all over Europe. I had finished work on *Shoulder to Shoulder* and then played Mrs Patrick Campbell for the first time in a TV series about Jenny Churchill. Richard Shulman and Philip Wiseman and I tried to reunite to do Tennessee Williams's *Camino Real*, but our plans failed. Sara Randall, the most creative of agents, had commissioned a treatment of the story of Frieda, D.H. Lawrence's wife, and was beginning to negotiate with the BBC, who were interested in producing six hour-long plays, each dealing with Frieda's relationship with a significant man in her life, beginning with her brother, Baron von Richthofen, the First World War flying ace. I began to read all the material available and my enthusiasm grew in spite of an encounter with Sir John Gielgud in Sloane Street. We were on opposite sides of the road, both dressed identically (except he was in brown and I in black) in long, Yves St Laurent trench coats with Herbert Johnson fedoras. John, who seemed to know *everything*, even in the planning stage, called across to the underground side of the road, 'Shawn, Shawn' (he never mastered 'Siân'), 'why d'you want to play that boring German cow?' Taking all my books and Tennessee Williams's new short plays, which his agent, Audrey Wood, had sent me, I left for Connemara and some serious gardening and building. The children were at school and my mother and Liz were left in charge.

Moving swiftly through customs, I located the driver and began the long journey up the West Coast into Connemara. I had a house to build!

'You throw your hat into the air and where it lands, there you build your house.' Leo Mansfield, the architect, told us this and we had stood solemnly on a hill above the vanished village of Eyrephort, which was where we'd bought the land and the small cottage we'd been staying in, and up went O'Toole's hat and we scrambled to the spot where it landed before it disappeared, borne away on the wind over the Atlantic. 'Is it always as – er – as – breezy as this up here?' I enquired. 'Pretty much,' was the reply. All the other houses in Eyrephort, past and present, were built down below in the southern shelter of the hill. Even the castle near Clifden was sheltered (but nevertheless, all its trees had been destroyed in a famous, vicious storm). The cottage nestled down below the inhospitable spot where we were – barely – standing. But what a place on which to perch! We seemed suspended in air; Atlantic to the south and west, an estuary to the north, and to the east Clifden, out of sight, and the Twelve Bens beyond. It was a difficult site from every point of view. It was high and obvious above the coastline and I racked my brain to think of a way of building an unobtrusive house. It was not going to be easy to get planning permission. I asked Leo to draw an elevation of the house. Soon discarded were all my ideas of a long Japanese house ('Yes,' said Leo, 'those low, overhanging Japanese roofs are very nice-looking. First bit of a storm and your house would be up in the air on its way to New York'), or a Roman house built around an atrium ('Have you ever looked inward week after week at an atrium under driving rain?').

Leo was an expert on the Irish vernacular and he persuaded us to build a low house of stone that snaked down the hillside, like a Welsh long-house, its stone walls merging into the granite boulders everywhere. Granite. Ever present in the west. Not far away to the south in the Gaeltacht there were fields as small as dining tables surrounded by lumps of stone taller than a man and beautiful drystone walls; works of art everywhere. The first thing to be done was to level a piece of ground and that meant calling into town for a few experts in the art of handling gelignite. The explosions were dramatic and swift and accurate. In the grey, bitterly cold, wet afternoon, I looked at the flattened site – looking much the same as it had a few hours earlier but without the big outcrops of living rock. There was no water, no electricity, no refuge from the violent wind. Would we ever be allowed to build where the hat had landed?

Winning permission took a long time and I became versed in the arts of patience and very un-English diplomacy. In Wales, I remembered, petitioners came to Uncle Davy's door at all hours, but there was a faint effort to abide by a set of rules formulated in Westminster. Here in Ireland, I couldn't make out what the rules were that I was trying to bend. I wrote letters, submitted plans, tried to convey my good intentions, went to meetings, submitted to interviews and waited and waited and waited. And then, one day over a year later, it was over. Permission was granted to begin work on 'The O'Toole House'. Aware of the great favour extended to enable us to build this high above the spectacular coast, I redoubled my efforts to make a tactful house. Leo

Mansfield was the perfect architect for this project and he not only designed the house but he taught me about stone and weather; the effect they had on the life of the inhabitants of the west and how they determined the style of the houses. I came to see that there was nothing random about the little crofts; every feature was there for a purpose and it became an absorbing game to build a house with six bedrooms, almost as many bathrooms, central heating and plumbing, while incorporating as many aspects as possible of the traditional Irish house. There was the huge hearth in the main 'room' where the turf fire was never allowed to go out and over which hung an iron pot where we could cook all our meals, should the need arise. Near the fire was a recess and a day-bed where the oldest (or sickest) person could sleep near the fire, the floors were made of slabs of stone cut from the cliffs of Moher, each one bearing the imprints of fossil remains of worms. Indoors we used them convex side up and outside, on the wide walkway surrounding the house, we turned them and showed the concave side. The roof was made of the Bangor blue slates of my childhood home, shipped over from North Wales. The doors and stairs and roofs were of pine, the door furniture was a cheat – I bought all the 'traditional' black iron from Beardmore's in London – but the outer walls were the real thing and gave me a thrill of pleasure every time I looked at them. It wasn't easy, finding someone who could drystone an entire house, but I had seen writer Richard Murphy's barn in Cleggan, which he'd had built by John Cosgrove, a local mason who spent a large part of the year odd-jobbing for the Council.

The Harbour Bar at Cleggan had become a centre of my activities as I searched for local craftsmen to work in the house. Eileen O'Malley was my ally in this. She had inherited the bar from her father, Matcher O'Malley, whom I had met on my first visit to the West as a girl when O'Toole and I had spent the entire day sheltering from the driving rain and mist, huddled next to the turf fire in the empty bar while Matcher leaned on the half-door looking out. Two cars passed through the village that day. When night fell and we decided we had to make a move, a lone customer, soaked to the skin, joined us in the bar and uttered a greeting. 'Ah,' said Matcher. 'A wet day and nothin' but cars goin' wesht wesht wesht all day.'

In this same bar I sat and tried to beguile the local building talent (O'Toole called me the Mata Hari of Galway County). Their expertise was hidden under a veneer of jovial insouciance and the menial work they did for the local Council mending roads, flinging up breeze-block bus shelters. Eileen O'Malley arranged a meeting for me with John Cosgrove. It was inconclusive and another was arranged. After a day's gardening I would clean up, shake out my black St Laurent skirt and sweater, and set off for Cleggan, praying that this time I could persuade Mr Cosgrove to build me a house. 'No. No. No,' he demurred again and again after we'd skirted around the subject for an hour or so. 'I've only ever made barns – a few auld walls.' 'But a house is a few old walls,' I pleaded. After weeks of to-ing and fro-ing to Cleggan, he agreed to 'have a go' and began to order stone from a quarry nearby. He brought his son of nineteen with him and I spent hours watching as he selected the granite blocks he needed for each course and asked his son to fetch them and make more 'shtwff' with which to bind the narrow gaps (shtwff – stuff, was a mixture of straw and mud). Miraculously the walls rose.

To ease John's mind, I'd promised that the builders would build a cavity wall inside the stone wall so that, as winter approached, we would have an independent shell to the house, but, as it turned out, John and his son ascended at the same speed as the builders with their breeze-blocks. It was beautiful. I remembered the morning in Cuzco when we had looked at the dramatic pre-Columbian drystone courses at the base of the Spanish buildings and determined to try to make a smaller, Celtic version of this Inca marvel. After the house was completed, someone complimented John and said he must be very proud to see his work. 'Ah, Jaysus no,' he said. 'Every time I pass by I'm afraid to look at the yoke in case it's fallen down.' Nothing could ever overcome the modesty of this man whose skill was of such a high order.

Our first, small cottage, which we now called Mamgu's cottage, drew water from an old, small well on a nearby meadow. It was known as a well that had never been known to go dry, not even in the worst droughts. Now, we needed a much bigger well, high up on the hill. Matter-of-factly, Leo said that he'd order along a dowser. This was a magical development in the building process and on the appointed day, O'Toole and myself, Mamgu, Liz and the girls were out on the meadow waiting – for what, we weren't sure. The ordinary-looking man in flannels and a sports jacket and a mac walked about with his home-made dowsing rod and we watched, entranced, as it occasionally kicked upwards between his hands. 'Just about *here*,' he said finally, as the hazel twig almost flew out of his hands. 'Have a go,' he offered. 'Have a go?'

We looked at each other, wide-eyed. The man had just made our house possible (a house without water is no house at all). On his say-so, we were about to spend a great deal of time and money. Were we, also, capable of this extraordinary feat? Well, I wasn't, nor was Mamgu, nor Pat. Liz said she thought she felt something, but O'Toole and Kate walked about, their hazel twigs twirling like things possessed. It was still a mystery, but it was all systems go for building.

The artesian well was sunk and quite soon we accessed a huge supply of water – we drank it in wine glasses standing in the rain. Halfway through the building the well ran dry after a quarry across the estuary indulged in some over-enthusiastic blasting; we suffered panic-stricken days until the dowser returned and found us another source. Searchlights were put up in the meadow overlooking the estuary and I stood alone in the shell of the house, watching the men drill day and night in the driving rain. The meadow looked like a Texas oilfield. 'If they strike oil I'll commit suicide,' I muttered to Mamgu as I crept off to bed in her cottage. Down and down they drilled into the rock and 176 feet below ground they found water again. I've never been so relieved in my life.

I travelled between the building centres in London and Dublin and Connemara. I bought the *Reader's Digest* do-it-yourself-building book. and learned as I went along about plumbing and damp courses and electrics and generators and septic tanks. Working towards moving the family in was like working towards a big opening night. The children, my mother and Liz had been living it up in an hotel in Clifden as we hiccupped our way towards completion. At last, we were ready. Everything worked. The family arrived. 'Fill every bath,' I cried. 'We have limitless water.' The men waved goodbye and drove their trucks and cars across the lower meadow to the road and off they went for good. 'How's the water?' 'It's grand but it doesn't go away.' The men had laid the pipes too near the surface and had flattened the whole system as they drove away. We now had a houseful of water and no means of getting rid of it. There was nothing in Liz, the nanny's, past to prepare her for this (her name was not Elizabeth de la Court Bogue for nothing – she was rather grand), but sending for more joints and bits of pipe, with the *Reader's Digest* book open at our side, we, together, rebuilt the drainage system and went to bed in a house with perfect plumbing. They say that building a house makes you a philosopher. I don't know about that, but it teaches you many things. The chief of which, in my case, was patience.

There was a time for the girls when, I suspected, they would have preferred to spend their holidays pounding the pavements of the King's Road rather than clambering up and down the West Coast. Temporarily, they had an uneasy time of it, but I was sure it would soon pass. O'Toole and I went to Connemara, together or separately, whenever we were free of work, and between 1970 and 1974 I spent every moment I could there, working on the new house, and often this entailed making the long journey for one afternoon on the site. I was as happy as a clam; rising at daybreak and spending the whole day out of doors, a piece of cheese in my pocket, and the kettle and coffee situated nearby in an open window so that, filthy and often wet, I need not enter the house until it was time to come in and scrub myself clean and begin preparing dinner. Pat rode a bit and went visiting. Kate, on strike from country pursuits, read indoors whatever the weather. Occasionally I bribed them to help me carry water or push wheelbarrows of weeds to the bonfire, but this was not really how they wished to be spending their vacation. They were pathetically pleased when we drove into the town and were able to watch a bit of television before dinner.

Guiltily, I occasionally gave up a day's gardening and organised an outing. My excursions were cursed with bad luck (or bad judgement) and inevitably we found ourselves hopelessly lost, miles from anywhere, or trying to cross a huge bog in the pouring rain, or arriving at our destination to find that the castle was shut or the people we were visiting had gone away. The girls were remarkably patient and there was nothing in the way of outright rebellion, but I did discover from Liz that they raised their eyes to heaven, shaking their heads gloomily when they knew that one of what they bitterly called 'Mummy's little expeditions' was being planned.

Our neighbours, Ann and Eddie Pryce, who farmed on adjoining land, called round regularly and we all sat drinking tea and chatting – 'wasting' time. Old Mr Feste Pryce, Eddie's father, lived with them and my mother always brought him a gift of black-brown, solidly compacted 'plug' tobacco, wrapped in silver foil. The gift was received with a gracious nod and a smile and little else. In fact, I never heard Feste speak until one day, as Liz was driving me back from a shopping expedition to Clifden, we saw Feste and his friend, Tommy, not doing anything as obvious as thumbing a lift but definitely looking hopefully in the direction of home some fifteen miles away. We stopped and they nodded and climbed into the back seat. As we drove along the coastal Sky Road, high above the Atlantic sparkling in the spring sunshine and studded with the tiny islands of the West Coast, I heard Feste say to Tommy, 'You know, one life is too short to enjoy all this beauty.' He had lived in the same house, looking at this same view, for over seventy years.

The road that ran past our land, and in some places through our land, simply circled the peninsula and returned to Clifden, so visitors were few and far between. When the big house was completed, high on its hill, we could see cars approaching from a great distance and one night as my mother and I prepared dinner and O'Toole read near the big fire, the girls who had been hanging out of the gable window watched a car approach and then they saw it stop at our gate and, wonder of wonders, the occupants began the steep, stony ascent to the house. Callers! 'Mummy! Mummy!' they cried as they hurtled downstairs. 'There's an old tinker woman coming up the drive!' When I answered the knock at the kitchen door and peered into the dusk it took me a moment or two to make out behind the shawl wrapped around the raincoat and the scarf tied over the hat, the wonderful features of Kate Hepburn and, behind her, looking considerably more respectable, her companion, Miss Phyllis, and film director, Tony Harvey (who had directed *Lion in Winter*). Abashed to have made such a huge mistake, the girls remained mute for the rest of the evening, sitting at a respectful distance, gawping at the most unusual film star they had ever met. I felt a bit like Moley showing off his house in *The Wind in the Willows*, as I recounted the story of the building of the house and Kate was every bit as obligingly admiring as Ratty as she inspected and approved the arrangements. I think she really did like the plain, solid rooms. She had been to visit Brian Friel to talk about a script and she now wanted to talk to O'Toole, but first she concentrated on my problems with the drains and the septic tank – still so fresh in mind. 'D'you know,' she said, 'if I had a daughter, d'you know what I'd have her train to be?' We leaned forward. 'A *plumber*!' she pronounced forcefully. The girls, pop-eyed, looked nervous.

Not everyone liked my efforts. Robert Shaw, with whom I had a mildly competitive friendship, began building his family home at much the same time as I did. Robert had spent years being dissatisfied with his progress as an actor. Too long a period carrying spears and playing small parts had left him feeling disgruntled and unappreciated, and the on–off success led to his losing patience with the profession and he determined to be a writer instead. His first novel, *The Sun Doctor*, was a success and he was well reviewed. As is the way of things, he immediately became a star actor, the most notable of his movies being *The Sting* with Robert Redford and Paul Newman, and *Jaws*. Rich and successful, he was rebuilding and converting a bishop's country residence in a much gentler part of Western Ireland. He bounded up the half-finished steps into the living room. I waited proudly for him to comment on the enormous flags I'd had cut for the floor and the great wooden 'upturned boat' ceiling and the walls, four feet thick against the constant winds. There was a long pause and he said, 'What are you doing? Where are the carpets? Where is the comfort? You can't live like this from choice. You're *mad*.' We agreed to differ and turned our attention to the safer topic of gardening. He quite admired my plans and said, 'I'll bet I get mine up and running before you do.' I was delighted by the challenge and fancied my chances for once. I was desolate when, soon after, Robert died suddenly, and I always paused on the spot where we had stood outside the house, and thought of him looking down towards the sea and seeing a garden which had not begun to exist.

My life in Connemara was becoming dangerous. It was by far the best part of my existence and I became more and more obsessed with the huge garden I had in my mind. There was a massive amount to learn; for one thing it was difficult for me to learn to think Big. O'Toole generously called me Capability Phillips as I wrestled with walkways and woodlands and planned vistas and hired JCBs. One day, I thought to myself, I might just stay here when it is time to return to London. Then what would happen? Would I be able to change my life completely? Could I really live there in isolation except for the family visits? These faint, uneasy thoughts remained in the back of my mind, but they were sad days when I was driven away to Clifden and then to Shannon Airport. Not since I was a small child in Wales had I felt such an attachment to a place. I looked out of the back window of the car, printing the scene on my mind, as though I might never see it again.

Chapter Thirty

The four years spent building the house in Connemara had demanded such an investment of time and emotion and hard work that now, on its completion in 1974, I felt it to be the centre of my life. There wasn't a scrap of it from the damp course and the insulation to the material of the blinds and the drawer holding the teaspoons that I hadn't scrutinised. O'Toole had let me have my head and when he'd been in the country he had taken a keen interest, not in the furniture and door handles, but very much in the structure of the house; the thick walls, the roof and, above all, the huge fireplace and main chimney. We shared the intense excitement as the walls rose and we walked around the shoreline, learning to identify the spots where one could first glimpse the house. We stood, leaning on the west wall where our bedroom would be, and looked at the sunsets. I don't recall that we ever exchanged a cross word while we were in Ireland. But we didn't spend all our time in Ireland and life in London was very different.

It's hard to describe how fragmented life became when O'Toole was not working. Although he was protected by Jules and the staff at the offices of Keep Films, he was nevertheless besieged on all sides by people who wanted his help, his advice, his money, his company. The hordes of journalists who wanted to talk to him were often fascinating people in their own right and they had the time of their lives with O'Toole, who was a newspaper junkie. Once they'd penetrated the defences, O'Toole found it impossible not to throw himself whole-heartedly into whatever project they had in mind. When he was drinking, sober-sided writers would be whisked off on a pub crawl they were not to forget in a hurry or, stone-cold sober, he would spend hours a day with foreign newspapermen, pouring his enthusiasm and energy into giving them a guided tour of Hampstead or Soho. It seemed mean to begrudge the fine time they were having, but I *was* mean and resentful when O'Toole returned home too exhausted to do anything but rest. It didn't help that I was able to see that my problems were largely of my own making. O'Toole was what he was and avowedly had never intended to make any changes in his behaviour. 'If you don't like me, leave me alone,' he would say, wearily, taxed for the umpteenth time in his life with not behaving like a 'normal' husband or father.

More threatening and only half in jest was the question 'Who owns this house?' It went without saying that the owner of the house made the rules. He and I had both grown up at a time when male-dominated households were normal, so part of me enthusiastically embraced the task of being a 'good' wife; supportive, undemanding, avoiding censure, basking in approval (also, alas, atoning for my past). Few men would willingly give up such a delightfully agreeable domestic arrangement where clothes could be dropped on the floor and reappear washed and pressed, rooms tidied by unseen hands, children raised and fed. Men in those days were not ashamed to say they had 'better' things to think about, the implication being that women did *not* have anything better to think about. Astonishingly, this attitude held even when women were occupied in the same profession as their husbands. Some brave spirits protested against all this and altered the structure of their lives. They were regarded as strident, tiresome, unattractive. I was not a brave spirit. Had I been partnered with any of the other men I'd ever associated with I wouldn't have thought twice about moving with the times and staking my claim for equality. Indeed, outside the house I found it only too easy to assert myself, had no qualms about appearing strident, tiresome, unattractive, but I was linked with the most powerful man I'd ever met, whose chauvinism was equalled only by his attractiveness. 'If you don't like me, leave me alone', indeed. He patronised me; called me 'a silly girl' and there were times when I didn't like him at all. Did I want to leave him alone? No, I did not.

But I wasn't a masochist. I *was* loved – hugely. How did I know? Simple; if you *feel* loved, you *are* loved. There were times when I was thanked for my help. There were times when he asked for my forgiveness and pleaded for my forbearance. There were times when we just had fun. And we were bound by shared prejudices and shared likes in books (a shared fondness for P.G. Wodehouse, which we would read aloud to each other, is not a bad reason for staying with someone).

When, as a girl, I first left Wales and home and safety, Saunders Lewis wrote to me saying, 'You must learn to live your life on the knife-edge of insecurity.' I had learned to do just that, for a time, but now I was unable. I was standing in the 'small place' my mother had predicted for me all those years ago in Stratford-on-Avon, and not only was it small, it occasionally shook beneath my feet. The measure of balance we had achieved was flawed; it was too dependent on my conduct. Were I to be 'difficult' or argumentative, the whole structure of our life would collapse. Then what, for example, would happen to my mother who had come to live with us? She ran the house, made up the accounts, painted the odd ceiling, did all the washing, but if I were dismissed there would be no house for her to take care of. And the children? I would think twice before depriving them of the kind of life they enjoyed in Guyon House. All the money I made was spent on the house, on clothes for the girls and my mother and myself. I saved nothing. Keep Films took care of our medical insurance and Jules said there were now trust funds set up for the girls in Ireland and that they would be entitled to a cottage each on our land. But all that would be in the future – they were eleven and fourteen years of age in 1974. Could I start from scratch and provide for them in the manner to which they were accustomed? I didn't have any idea – I doubted it. On the surface all was well and everyone in the house took the future for granted, and, much as I tried to stifle it, my resentment grew. 'She is my rock,' I would read in the newspaper, or 'She is his still centre.' 'Without her to lean on . . .' What sort of woman was this solid, immovable object? She earned her keep but what kept woman didn't?

Unable to bear the pain when love and approval were withheld, I began gradually to reduce my dependence, to loosen the ties that bound us so tightly, so lethally. Less ecstasy, less despair, would make my life more bearable and I couldn't think beyond this.

In early 1975 it was as if all the small and inexplicable episodes of illness that O'Toole had suffered over the previous five years gathered themselves into one life-threatening attack, so large and frightening that it obliterated all other considerations for many months.

Coming home from a prolonged reunion with his friend, the writer H.A.L. Craig who had just returned to London after a long absence, O'Toole couldn't conceal the fact that he was once again in dreadful pain. Harry looked sheepish and left and I put O'Toole to bed. As usual, he didn't want to see a doctor, but I was so worried by his state that I went against his wishes and called Gerry Slattery (also a friend of Harry Craig). As we had done so many times in the past, Gerry and I sat, one on each side of the big bed in the dimly lit bedroom, and Gerry chatted calmly, trying to piece together the events of the last twenty-four hours. It was pitiful to see O'Toole attempt to talk, even to joke as he answered Gerry's questions. Almost apologetically, Gerry said suddenly that he thought O'Toole should go to hospital. Normally, this would have produced voluble objections ending in stubborn refusal. I was alarmed when O'Toole now remained silent, overcome with pain which was evidently greater than any he had endured and denied. Gerry indicated that I should follow him as he made his way down to the study. Always in the past we had stood in his room while he reassured me that there was nothing to worry about. Even after wild drunken episodes ending in collapse, he had told me that all would be well in the morning.

Now, almost apologetically, he said that O'Toole should immediately be hospitalised. Within minutes, it seemed, O'Toole was taken out into the gathering dusk and I was left to collect together a few things he might need, then follow them by taxi. What was I thinking of? I packed *The Times* crossword, the book on the night table, a toothbrush and an extra night shirt. I couldn't get a taxi so I ran to the Royal Free in Pond Street. There was nothing for me to do at the hospital. Everyone – Gerry included – had disappeared into the business end of the place, where no 'civilian' may follow. I walked down Pond Street towards South End Green and the Heath and sat on a bench, but I couldn't sit still and I walked back up the hill, past the hospital to the taxi rank on the main road, standing there where there were strangers for company. Eventually, I returned and sat alone in the hospital.

Finally, Gerry appeared, looking drawn and grey. I could tell that he was miserably unhappy not to be the bringer of good news and I asked him what I should do. He told me to go home and go to sleep. 'But I want to *be* here when he comes round.' 'Siân, it's not quite like that. It'll be some time before he can see you.' I didn't know much but I could see that things were as bad as they could be short of – no, that was unthinkable. I asked the Sister if she would telephone me if there was any change and climbed the hill to Guyon House, standing dark and empty. The girls and my mother and Liz were all in Ireland for the holidays. Manolita would come in at nine in the morning but no one else would come. The phones were silent. Only Scobie, the bulldog, rumbled and snorted, grumbling to himself in the garden. I went down and unlocked the garden door and he shot into the house and up the stairs to the ground floor, pounding into the Green Room where he liked to spend his evenings. I put the lights on for him and went to sit alone in the study. I couldn't go to our bed upstairs and it was dawn when I went up and, entering, saw the bed and the sheets thrown back where he'd been lifted out, and I sat in the chair near the door and wept. If he was allowed to get better, never, I swore, would I ever entertain a disloyal thought, never would I feel resentment, never would I complain. I would do *anything*, so long as he didn't die. Dammit, I thought, I shall *will him* not to die.

I don't know how long I sat there before I stopped crying, got up and made the bed. Going downstairs I fed Scobie and went up to my bathroom and took a bath and put on more make-up than usual. Then I called Jules, who I knew would be awake in order to make his calls to California, and told him what had happened. Jules, the fixer, the doer, was frustrated when he realised that there was nothing he or I could usefully do, but he had to do something so he drove from Belgravia to Hampstead to see me. When I opened the door he was surprised to see me dressed and painted and assuring him that O'Toole *would* be all right. He nodded obligingly but not very convincingly and said that he'd been talking to Gerry and wanted to go to the hospital to see for himself how things were. I wondered what Gerry had told him.

At the hospital we were allowed to enter the room where O'Toole lay motionless and connected to a battery of instruments. Nothing happened and we were ushered out again. Jules went to the office; he had somehow to withdraw O'Toole from public view without actually admitting that he was seriously ill. There are people in every courtroom, theatre and hospital who ring the papers with 'stories' (and are rewarded very poorly for their pains) and indeed by the time I was home, the phones were ringing. 'Was it true that Peter was at the Royal Free? Was it true that he was terminally ill? Did he have alcoholic poisoning?' . . . and so on, endlessly. I explained to Manolita what had happened and left the house to walk around Hampstead until it was time to go to the hospital again.

At first, I found the papers relatively easy to deal with; I had had long practice in being evasive without being too infuriating, but as the days became weeks and my will to stay optimistic crumbled, it became harder and harder to put on a brave face – or in this case, a brave voice. One night after I'd been sitting in O'Toole's room for most of the day, I went home and sat despondently on my side of the bed. Picking up the phone, I heard the voice of a journalist I knew quite well. 'Look, Siân, it's Peter here. I know it's late but you're a sensible girl, you know what I'm up against and I want to do a good job – could you give me a hand updating the obit?' I couldn't think of anything to say to him but 'No' as I put the phone down before bursting into tears.

As time passed in that side ward I learned to operate the system of tubes and gradually lost my terror of the paraphernalia which had so intimidated me at first. Sister was unhappy and Gerry was so worried that he could scarcely bear to speak to me, unable as he was to give me reassurance and hope.

And then one day it was like sailing into a calm dawn at sea after a stormy night. O'Toole opened his eyes and they were *his* eyes. He couldn't lift his head, but he gave me a lopsided grin and my heart filled with relief and love. We held hands and didn't say a word. One by one the nursing staff popped their heads round the door and smiled and nodded. There was very little talking. 'Very good. Very good,' said Gerry, nodding vigorously, his eyes almost shut, his head tilted back. 'He'll outlive us all, kid,' said Jules brusquely and shook his head as if to wipe out the horror that was past. I felt like a different person. O'Toole was different. We went home thankfully and quietly, so quietly. He went to bed to convalesce. My mother and the girls returned. We had him to ourselves! We had him. I had him. His girls revelled in him. When I looked at him I saw many people, people he did not know who were him, the people who, high up in the Royal Free Hospital, had hated me, reviled me, pleaded with me, adored me, all while he slept. And now he was back. Let us rest.

'I need to go somewhere nice to recuperate. Not too much sun. Quiet. Nice.'

Oh, no.

I had been so reluctant to take him abroad, but the month in Positano was to be transforming. He'd been right again. Now we came home and began to consider the next step in our new life – a life that seemed like a gift.

Chapter Thirty-one

'*Please* let me come with you.'

For the first time, I was pleading to be allowed to accompany O'Toole on location. The response was a firm, dismissive 'No'. He looked surprised that I should even raise the possibility of such a change in our routine and saw no reason that he should break the habit of a lifetime. I understood that it was important to him to be alone and independent while he worked, but I was far too worried about his health not to try to persuade him that he needed to be looked after. He had escaped death by such a narrow margin. Did he fully appreciate this? Or was he deliberately erasing it from his mind? Whatever the reason he refused any discussion. I couldn't bear to see him, frail but straight-backed, determined to be as he was before, rejecting sympathy and help. In a way, I thought his behaviour brave and admirable, but of course I didn't want him to reject *my* sympathy, *my* help. My part in the grim struggle we had endured had made me feel that I was indispensable to him, that our partnership had advanced to another level, and it was a crushing blow to discover that I also was expected to dismiss from my mind the terrors, the pain, the discovery of a new well-spring of love, the perfect happiness that had followed the despair. I tried to show how profound was my disappointment, but the habit of not being a nuisance was too strong and I gave way to his decision with reasonably good grace. I couldn't conceal my sadness, but it went unnoticed amid the usual flurry of preparation for departure. Someone asked me what was the name of the film that he was going to shoot and who was the director, and I realised that for the first time in our life together I had no idea and didn't really care.

How to explain my feelings to myself? I could hardly believe the alienation that had occurred. Never, not at the lowest point of our relationship, had I thought of leaving O'Toole; I had hated him, resented him, wanted to smite him and never entertained the possibility that I wouldn't spend the whole of my life with him. And now for the first time since we met, I felt totally separate from him. It was almost as though my O'Toole *had* died at the Royal Free down the road. How *could* he behave now as though nothing had happened? Near-death had happened, a new beginning had dawned and now another sort of death was happening.

I made plans to return to work myself. I had foolishly assumed that I would be away in Mexico – New Mexico? I wasn't sure which. Now Sara advised me to do a play in the West End, partly because it would be rehearsed in London and would preview there as well, so, at least, I could be at home while I worked. The play, which was one of the scripts I'd read without great enthusiasm in Positano, was *The Gay Lord Quex* by Pinero. John Gielgud was almost alone in loving the play, but he *did* admire it enormously and had now persuaded Eddie Kulukundis to produce it. The Edwardian settings and costumes were hugely expensive and it was to be a lavish production. For the most part my scenes would be with Dan Massey (who played the eponymous hero) and Judi Dench, whom I'd never before worked with but admired enormously and wanted to act with, not least because I was told it was the greatest fun imaginable. I could do with a bit of fun, I thought.

O'Toole was to be gone shooting *Foxtrot* in New Mexico for three months at least. His movies often took a good deal longer than this and Jules was vague even now about the actual date of ending. It was strange to be leading a normal everyday life while grappling with such inner turmoil. And no one noticed; life went on as usual for the girls and my mother and Liz. The house ran on oiled wheels, Manolita and I scarcely needed to consult each other as we began to pack the big trunk and the suitcases; assembling everything that might conceivably be needed during O'Toole's time away, pasting the list of contents inside each lid. And as the hours and days went by, I felt my presence becoming more and more indistinct. It wouldn't have surprised me if one of the family were to have walked right through me where I stood in the hall, an invisible person, as doors opened and shut, telephones were answered, children ran up the stairs, everyone absorbed and full of purpose. Everyone except me. I knew with certainty that I couldn't return to the old life with its long separations and lack of shared experience. When the day came to say goodbye to O'Toole, I felt I was saying goodbye to him for ever. I had been incapable of making him understand what I felt, how urgently I needed to be with him now. He had a hard task ahead of him and I could read the determination in his face and in the set of his shoulders. He would not yield to weakness. He would survive whatever the cost. I admired him for that, but I was admiring him as I would a stranger and that left me desolate.

It was May – a wet May. I went to work as he went to the airport. What did he feel? I had no idea. It was hard to be bright and cheerful as I met the *Quex* company for the first time. Dan Massey was an old friend and he made me laugh as we were photographed in the rain in the churchyard outside our rehearsal room in Piccadilly. 'Great start,' he said, looking at my wet, ruined hair-do. That night I sat alone in the study. Were it not for the presence of the girls, the house would have seemed very gloomy. As it was, when they climbed the stairs to their apartment, all the rooms on the ground and first floors were very quiet indeed and save for my desk lamp in the study, unaccustomedly dark. I went over the events of the morning and our farewells to each other. O'Toole had no idea how I felt, I was sure of that now. His farewells had been as they would usually be before a long absence and he would expect everything to be as usual when he returned in late summer. And of course I would be here – why would I not be? The future had yet to be resolved and I had no idea what it would hold. How quietly it had come about, this revolution in my life.

When I had asked O'Toole if I should come to visit him should the play not enjoy a long run, he'd responded, 'No, no, you'd hate it. Cabo San Lucas is the arsehole of the world.' Now I rose and took down the atlas and looked it up. Baja California didn't seem to be horrible at all. I had always visited him, however awful the locations, and I was puzzled by his determination to keep Cabo San Lucas out of bounds to me. What did I know of O'Toole's life in Mexico?

Before he became ill, he returned from filming *Man Friday* in Mexico and dumped the usual pile of unanswered mail on my desk, and there was one letter written in a neat, childish hand that especially caught my eye and for some reason I put it aside instead of throwing it away with all the other mail, much of it too fatuous to need answering. A girl called Anna wrote sadly that she had obviously misunderstood all that had passed and – God, save her – I thought, apologised for her presumption. There was a greeting-card type of poem as well, a pathetic little adieu. I remembered that a Mexican girl called Anna had been given a job on a co-production of a film we had made without O'Toole. *Was it the same girl?* I wondered, but only for a moment.

It had not occurred to me that he might have another reason for wishing to be alone when away on location. I had always been too occupied trying to burnish my tarnished reputation in his eyes, trying (in vain, I sometimes thought) to convince him that I was trustworthy, faithful beyond reproach. He was quick to criticise looseness in other women also and loud in his condemnation of what he called 'fouling your own doorstep', and I had assumed that he applied the same stringent standards to his own behaviour as he did to mine, and certainly, with the small exception of the sad note from Anna, I had never been confronted with a whisper of infidelity on his part. Nor had I ever read anything of the sort in the mass of newspaper articles about him. Nor had I ever felt that his affections might be engaged elsewhere. When he first became famous, O'Toole had been as taken aback as I by the deluge of attention from women and I was left to deal with the intemperate behaviour and the surprising outpourings of respectable young women who ought to have known better. He was pursued by every manner of woman and I was astonished that he was able to deal with the avalanche of flattery with such grace and restraint. His close friend, Kenneth Griffith, said to me, barely controlling his laughter, 'D'you know – he looked me straight in the eye and said, "I have never been unfaithful to her."' I wasn't sure how he expected me to react and he, sensing my confusion, changed the subject. Now, as I thought of it, I wasn't at all sure that I regarded it as any of my business what O'Toole got up to during those long absences, provided it did not affect our life together. It wasn't anything we'd ever talked about and now it didn't matter in the least. All the same, I was mildly curious about Mexican Anna – if she still existed in his life or whether she had ever been significant in it.

During the remaining weeks of May I spent my evenings at home and went to work by day, scarcely registering the considerable storms brewing in the rehearsal room. Like most sad times, this was laced through with comedy, verging on farce. Dan Massey, the same dear Dan – who wrote such elegant, witty letters, who was such a tower of strength when I put my back out while we were rehearsing *Alpha Beta* together in 1972, who made a game out of our violent fistfight in Act One and laughed me out of my terrors that I was disabled for life – that same Dan was now despondent, black browed, scarcely speaking to anyone. He and John Gielgud did not get on. Worse, they scarcely spoke the same language. Dan, who had just played an acclaimed Lytton Strachey, his first 'character' part, wanted to apply the same principles of research and heavy appearance-changing make-up to Lord Quex. Unfortunately, *The Gay Lord Quex* was a jolly, young man-about-town, handsome as all get-out and a devil with the ladies. Nothing much else to think about.

There was a huge cast, four sets, four changes of costumes – and at the end of it all not a great deal in the way of a story. Judi Dench was playing the little manicurist and John admired her as much as he disliked Dan. When I laid aside my personal unhappiness and began to look around, I became fascinated by John, who came to work each day with a completely new set of ideas. He and the designer devised sets, each of which had a round object in the middle (make-up display counter, table, fountain) and occasionally he would cry, in pain, 'Oh for God's sake stop going *round* and *round and round*! You look as tho' you're dancing round a maypole.' We were – there was nowhere else to go. Occasionally, he would get up and demonstrate how an Edwardian lady would enter, speak and sit, and that was magic. Descended from the great Terry family, he'd kept his eyes open around all those Terry aunties when he was a youth and it was a privilege to be given a glimpse into the manners of another age. But the rest of the time we limped from bad to worse. 'No. No. No! Why are you doing that?' 'Because you told me to.' 'When?' 'Yesterday.' 'But that was another *life*.' He and Dan stopped talking to each other completely. John could not understand why Dan couldn't just bounce on and be a charming roué. Dan retreated further and further behind elaborate make-up drawings.

Judi Dench was the cleverest actress I'd ever watched working. While she wasn't 'getting' the part, she remained calm and cheerful and good-humoured, and then, after about three weeks, she came in and declared that *finally*, after puzzling and puzzling, she'd got hold of the end of a string and, with any luck, if she pulled on it – that would be the solution. And it was! More than anyone I'd known she had a formidable, a huge, actor's intelligence and the solid good sense to get her through the vicissitudes of production week. When she came on at the dress parade in her specially designed dressing gown, Gielgud shrieked, 'Oh God, you look like Richard III.' Many leading ladies would have been put out (Peggy Ashcroft would certainly have locked herself in the dressing room, weeping); Judi – secure in her performance – probably consoled the unfortunate designer who had to make another costume in a hurry.

Almost four weeks into rehearsal, Judi and I decided that maybe we'd better work out our own moves on our own (John's were getting more and more wild). It seemed almost sacrilegious to doubt him, but we *did* have to open and soon. That night we went to see John in his play, *No Man's Land* by Harold Pinter, which he was playing with Ralph Richardson. He was so sublime that, of course, we decided we *were* being sacrilegiously insubordinate and henceforth we would slavishly obey his every whim. 'Did you really like it?' he smiled when we went round afterwards. 'D'you think it's a good play?' (So patrician.) 'I'm frightfully lucky to be playing it, you know.' (Lucky? He?) 'It's only because poor Larry's dead – dying – I mean so much better, thank God.' He beamed at his own success in avoiding a *faux pas*. An awed hush settled over the dressing room. It isn't often you see a legend strut his stuff.

John thought I looked like Mrs Patrick Campbell and he taught me some lovely bits of what he called 'plastique', but when I came on in my ballgown – plumes in my hair – he wailed, 'Sit down, *Shawn*.' 'But John . . .' (common sense overcoming my reverence), 'I've only got to say five lines and get off. It'll take hours if I sit centre stage.' 'I know, but I want you to *sit* in the middle.' 'John, it doesn't make *sense*. I'll be trailing this costume around for minutes with nothing happening.' 'I know, I know, but you must *sit down*. You look so *tall* when you're standing up.' I think this gave Dan the only smile in a dire dress rehearsal.

John was so sweetly apologetic when we opened badly. He gave Judi and myself the most beautiful presents. Neither Judi nor Dan could face doing the obligatory radio interviews. We had all said from time to time – John – 'Wonderful, sublime actor but cannot direct *traffic*.' My old friends at the BBC said *someone* had to do this interview, so I went to Broadcasting House and was vague about the virtues of the play and confined myself to remarks where I could be truthfully praising of John. He sent me flowers and then a card, thanking me for being 'more generous' than he deserved. I turned it over and the picture was of a policeman directing traffic. My blood ran cold. It was a privilege to be in a flop directed by this complex, brilliant man.

The weeks went by. No word from Mexico. I didn't have a number where I could reach O'Toole and anyhow, he didn't like the telephone. And in a way, he had a point; the wires don't support emotion or need over great distances.

During rehearsals I had seen Judi – so much more observant and more caring than I – restrain one of the young men in the play when he made as if to strike John after a particularly tactless piece of direction.

I hadn't been paying any attention at all, but I felt sorry for the pretty youth who sat, mutinously pouting, Judi's restraining hand on his arm. At the same time I thought how callow to react to John in such a way. It was another few weeks before I could take the time to look around at other people and their problems. The young man should have been all right in his part of a glamorous officer, but John had completely incapacitated him. 'Come on and *take the stage*!' he would cry. After four weeks of John's direction, he could scarcely walk straight, let alone dominate a scene. Not my problem, I had no scenes with him. Didn't even know his name.

Weeks went by and predictably the 'notice' to end was put up. Only a fortnight more to play. I had been to the BBC to talk to producer Martin Lisemore about playing Beth Morgan in *How Green Was My Valley*. Still faintly tanned from Positano, I wore a beautiful pale, pastel Missoni dress. When I went to talk to him, Ronnie Wilson, the director, joined us and said, 'This is the part of a *mother*, you know.' 'Yes,' I said, thinking maybe my new Maud Frizon shoes were a mistake. 'Look,' I said. 'I am Welsh and I *am* working class. I may be thin, but I *am* a mother. Thin, tall mothers do exist, you know.' They smiled and dismissed me. I've never 'gone for' jobs and now I think maybe one should *dress* for them? No. If they can't see I can act this part, a change of frock isn't going to help. Ah well. The play was ending and I didn't think I'd got the television part, so what to do with myself? I would go to Connemara and garden, and perhaps as I wrestled with that inhospitable, rocky terrain I would begin to see what I should do next.

Chapter Thirty-two

The girls and my mother and Liz were already on holiday as usual in Connemara. July 1975 was the hottest in years. The theatre was as hot as Hades and I was grateful to get out of my sodden costume and hurry into the alley alongside the Albery Theatre. I stood there, looking for Lionel and wondering where he'd put the car.

'Would you like to go for a drink? I've got a friend in and we're both going for a jar.'

It's the young man who was at odds with John. I'm *so* flattered. No one asks Mrs O'Toole out. Not ever. 'Well, there's the chauffeur . . . and I have an appointment early in the morning. I don't think so.' 'Only a drink.' 'Well, all right. We could pop over to Macready's' (a really depressing actors' club in Covent Garden. Damp). I was a member so that left me more or less in control of the evening. Lionel drove the three of us to Macready's and it was shut. I was at a loss. Whenever O'Toole was away I never went out unless escorted by Jules and Joyce and I only knew really expensive places. 'Look – both of you come back to Hampstead.' We piled, rather uneasily, into the Rolls and, arranging to meet him early in the morning, I said goodnight to Lionel, and took the young men into the house, to the ground-floor Green Room, unlocking the door to the basement floor and the wine cellars reaching under Heath Street.

The drinks tray held only spirits, so we all went down to the cellars for wine. The night was still unbearably hot and I opened up the door to the garden, as well. It was so strange to be alone and using the house in this way. It made me feel rather grand and powerful to be entertaining alone in it. It was partly *mine*, after all, this place I lived in. Drinks. Music. (I *never* played records at night.) We sat and chatted until I thought it was time to end the evening. One young man (what *was* his name?) left and the other helped me lock up the cellars and garden, and before we'd made for the front door his hand was on mine and the key was thrown aside. I couldn't believe what was happening. I had felt myself to be in an aunt-like position to these men and had no wish to complicate my life. I was well aware that the solution to my problems did not lie in displacement activity, and, hopeless with names, I didn't even know who this person was. Knew nothing about him. And I welcomed this happening. Even as I thought to myself that I was making a dreadful mistake, I could feel a smile forming on my face. A smile of approval to some submerged self. Accustomed all my life to untroubled, wonderful sex, the worries and heartbreak of the last six months made this coupling something more extraordinary than usual. I was asleep when he left in the morning. Descending to start the day I looked at my handbag, where I'd left it in the study the night before. My wallet had disappeared. 'Serves you right, you fool,' I thought without rancour. 'He callously turned you over and you deserved it – and it was, in a way, worth it.' I laughed and was abashed later when I saw my wallet, intact, on the Green Room table. I knew so little of this man that I thought he might be a thief.

I went through the motions of running my house, distracted by my extraordinary behaviour of the night before and surprised by my lack of guilt. I felt – almost exhilarated. No, maybe not quite that, but certainly elevated above the rut in which I'd been living. Going to work at the theatre was another matter. I was deeply embarrassed when I made my first entrance that night, feeling as though the audience was pointing at me and whispering, 'Well, there's a fast woman.' I didn't see Robin – I'd checked his name in the programme and discovered that he was the son of one of my favourite British film actresses, Eleanor Summerfield. His father was also famous, but I didn't know him, Leonard Sachs, best known as the chairman of *The Good Old Days*, the Leeds City Varieties Music Hall. I also figured out that Robin must be sixteen years my junior. Well! That was something new. But the play would end soon and that would be the end of the matter. Just a few weeks of awkwardness to get through. The fact that it *wasn't* the end of the matter was every bit as much my fault as Robin's and I felt that 'fault' *did* enter into it, even as I took pleasure in the fault.

Robin and I spent a weekend together in the empty house, camping out in the nursery, and it was domestic in a way that was quite new to me. Robin could cook rather better than I could. He prepared meals and we cleaned up together, and it was highly unusual – wrong, but intriguing. He was a bit forward, I thought. Cheeky, in fact, and disrespectful in a cautious sort of way. No one had ever been bold with me. Monstrous, maybe, diabolical even, but cheeky? No. I rather liked it. My pedestal was niftily kicked into touch and I assumed my place as a grubby, voracious creature, sweating in the August sunshine and praised, and flattered – I had never been so eloquently, endlessly flattered – just for being myself. Or rather, less than myself. When the play ended, we parted, he to Greece with his brother and I to wind up business in London before joining the girls and Liz and my mother in Ireland.

The unbearable heat of 1975 turned my head and before leaving for Ireland I spent a wonderful week with an actor whom I had known and admired for the last twenty years. I knew he liked me, but we had both behaved so well until now when we didn't. What was happening to me? I felt that I'd burned my boats as far as O'Toole was concerned. There was no way in which I could pretend to be the person he'd left in May. I didn't even want to be. Behaving badly was making me happy. Of course, Robin would have been outraged by my behaviour after his departure and I didn't give a damn about that either (though I didn't tell him so). As I boarded the plane for Ireland, I felt terrific.

My brief time with Robin had stopped me shrouding my body in Celtic decency or shame and I gardened in my bikini, covering up only if I saw someone approach – I was a guest in holy, Catholic Ireland and had no wish to give offence.

Martin Lisemore actually managed to get through to Mamgu's cottage telephone, assisted by Miss Heffernan at the Post Office. Yes, they'd like me to star in *How Green Was My Valley* with Stanley Baker and could I get back to London quite soon for pre-production? I told my mother the news. She lifted her gaze from our gardening notes only to say, 'Well, let's hope it's better than that last try.' She was referring to the Hollywood movie based on the novel in which the parts were all played by American-based Irish actors because the Welsh cast was unable to cross the Atlantic in wartime. We continued planning the next stage of the garden. Did she notice I was different, I wondered? *Was* I different?

Back to London, alone. Robin was back from Greece and it was entirely due to me that we met again. Well, maybe he would have braved the castle keep, but I rang him and arranged a meeting in Kensington Gardens. I still felt that there was something odd about us, but there was also a growing sweetness. He was so incredibly encouraging. No man in my emotional life had ever been encouraging or helpful or paid one so much attention. I could tell Robin all my fears and difficulties and he didn't sneer at me or belittle my feelings. I was warily impressed. Part of me now identified with the previously traditional male figures in my life and I sometimes thought, 'This man must be mad. He's so nice, there must be something wrong with him.' Then, 'No, wait a minute, this is really agreeable, this care and attention.' Occasionally, I worried about his attitude to work. During September as I prepared for six months at the BBC he was recalled for an important series. He didn't get the part and said, sincerely, 'The man who's got it is *wonderful* – and I'm happy I've got *you*.' Well, such generosity of spirit was alien to me and what did he mean, he 'had' me? This was proceeding too fast and yet – he was getting something very right and maybe I *was* his already.

Something strange had happened in August. I received the only letter O'Toole wrote to me from Baja California. On what was the night I had first slept with Robin, O'Toole had had a strange experience. I had 'appeared' to him. In the letter he pledged his troth to me anew, implying that he regretted what had drawn him to Mexico, but he did not elaborate on that. He wrote things I would have been so happy to read even four months previously. I couldn't respond. But my silence seemed to go unremarked.

In late August O'Toole returned and quickly settled down to London life. He resolved to take more of an interest in the running of Keep Films, so every day he would leave with Lionel and spend most of the day in Belgravia. His energy was prodigious because he was no longer drinking. The doctors had been uncompromising on this – he must never drink again. Another bout of illness could be fatal. Gone were the days of sleeping until lunchtime, of feeling slightly under par until the drinking began again. I could scarcely imagine how he managed this revolution in his life. As he interfered in everyone's business, read, made notes, wrote poetry, looked at his mail for the first time, tried to understand balance sheets and filled every moment of the day with activity, a friend said, 'Only Peter would try turning not drinking into an art form.' As for us, his assumption seemed to be that everything had settled down as he wished it to. We chatted a great deal less though and he seemed as unaware as before that there was a change in me. I was in pre-production for *How Green Was My Valley*, seeing Robin occasionally for a brief walk, usually in Kensington Gardens. I was astonished that no one ever asked me where I was or what I did. It was amazingly easy to be deceitful.

I left for location in Wales and O'Toole came down with me and dressed as a collier and for a lark appeared as an extra. Stanley Baker played my husband. I'd been wary of him, a tough guy among tough guys. He turned out to be professional in the extreme, courteous, well-prepared, so tactful when, drawing on a wealth of experience, he suggested an alternative, maybe a better way of shooting a scene. He held the cast and unit together in the most unobtrusive way imaginable. When he got to know and like me, he would share his lunch with me on production weekends. 'There you go,' proudly handing me a perfectly nice but unremarkable cheese sandwich. 'Ellen made these.' Ellen, his wife, was perfect in his eyes. We worked well together and people would suggest that maybe we'd become very close. 'You know that look, in that scene – come on. Tell.' Nothing could have been more absurd to either of us. My admiration for him grew and grew.

For six months we lived in each other's pockets, Ronnie Wilson directing this bunch of volatile Welshmen, Martin Lisemore, the producer, keeping a close eye on us all. I travelled from Hampstead to the BBC rehearsal rooms in Acton each day, ran the house, spent a good deal of spare time at the North London Collegiate School, saw the children at night and also Marie Kean, who was staying with us, and went through the motions of being Mrs O'Toole, a role which no longer had any credibility for me. Once Marie said suspiciously, 'What are you up to? Why are you more cheerful than usual?' But no one else noticed my altered state. Very occasionally Robin and I would manage an early dinner together and I discovered a whole raft of cheap restaurants that no one I knew would ever dream of visiting. My liking for being adored was gaining ground. I'd never in my life met a man who was so unafraid to show his feelings, who didn't seem to want to protect himself or take control of the situation.

How Green Was My Valley drew to an end. My actor friends from Wales, who'd been commuting to London for six months, declared that they now had to get jobs to pay for this job, during which they'd spent their salaries in the bar of the Paddington to Cardiff train. There had been a great deal of drinking. On the day of the arrival of Beaujolais Nouveau, Stanley had arrived with the first shipment in his car and the entire company, floating on a sea of red wine, had been sent home early with a severe reprimand.

We held the 'wrap' party in the basement flat of one of the designers. I took part in the cabaret playing Stanley, dressed in his flannel shirt, corduroys and boots. The room was lit by candles placed against the walls. I'd treated myself to a new St Laurent suit in shiny black ciré fabric and as I perched on a side table, talking to Mike Gwilym, who had played one of my sons, he said, 'Siân, don't move,' as he placed his arms around me and hugged me tight. My jacket, too close to a candle, was on fire and melting horribly. The room was packed and mercifully no one saw him put the fire out. Later, as we were searching for my new black raincoat and realised someone had taken it by mistake, Mike, thinking back to the cabaret, said, 'Oh, poor Siân, what a night you've had; you've lost your raincoat, burned your new suit *and* you made a fool of yourself.'

Before I went to the party, when I was still in my dressing room wearing my worn Beth Morgan dress and cracked boots and white wig, Martin Lisemore came in bearing a large pile of scripts. 'Here, have a look at these and tell me if you want to play the part I've marked.'

As I took off my ageing wig and make-up for the last time, I flicked through one of the scripts – 'nearly bald, ancient, she looks up at Caligula' – oh no, not *another* geriatric part. Turning back, I read a scene which made me laugh. Flicking forward, I realised that this was a very camp script, very well written by Jack Pullman. I got Martin on the extension. 'That was quick.' 'Yes, well, I'm obviously doomed to play old bags for ever and this does make me laugh – and we've had a *nice* time over the last six months – haven't we?' 'Is that a "yes", then?' 'Why not.' By the time I left the building I'd agreed to play Livia in *I, Claudius*.

The incessant activity meant that I had very little time in which to review my private life, which was, frankly, absurd. It was also becoming nicer and nicer, and that was absurd *and* bad. I had a husband with whom I was living what a cynic would call a 'normal' married life – not much in the way of communication and totally satisfactory sex. My lover would have been horrified, I realised, had he been aware of this. Young and romantic, he took it for granted that I would have broken off 'relations' with my husband. I didn't care to disabuse him.

For the first time in my life I had a life of my own which was nothing to do with either of these men and I had no intention of sharing it with either of them. I took good care of all our properties (we had now acquired a flat in the West End as well), went on working on the Irish garden, maintained the Irish house and two other Irish cottages and the house in Hampstead ('maintenance' was a major part of my life). And, my main, big jobs aside, I made broadcasts, wrote book reviews, appeared on television shows, went regularly to the girls' school, organised their weekends, went to the cinema with them and supervised lives which, more and more, ran like clockwork. Everyone was having a perfectly fine, busy time. Although I was a part of many people's lives, it seemed to me that I was still shadowy and superfluous. Except to Robin. To him I was becoming more real – more a possible, valid part of his life. To me, this seemed still ridiculous. There was no way in which our relationship could become 'real'; it seemed to me that it could exist only in its present clandestine form. And what would be the outcome? I supposed that it would simply fizzle out. Then what would I do? I would be sad, I was sure of that. O'Toole, leading a completely sober life, was understandably preoccupied with his own problems. The drinks table across the room from his favourite chair was laden, as usual, with bottles. Drink was *pressed* on all our guests. Dr Slattery prescribed large quantities of vitamins and they were conscientiously taken; also Valium, something new, beneficial and harmless, it was said.

Pat became more and more locked into her life at school and with Mamgu and Liz, and Kate began to rebel fairly seriously and demanded to be allowed to leave school after taking her O-Levels, going instead to an A-Level tutorial college in town. She also demanded to be allowed to go on holiday with a mixed-sex group. All this was tricky but pretty standard, I thought. Kate had always been somewhat beyond my control. I admired her independence of spirit and was amused by her escapades, and there was very little I could do to alter whatever course she'd decided upon. Until I realised this, we'd lived at loggerheads. Now, I told her what I thought and left her to make her own decisions. O'Toole said he would have a talk with her but that she should be allowed her freedom. I didn't really feel I was in any position to *tell* her how to behave. I'd done everything my parents wished of me: stayed at school, gone to university, married – well, maybe I'd gone slightly wrong at that point – but eventually I'd settled down in a spectacular way. And where had all that got me, I wondered? My life was unravelling and I was endlessly postponing the day of resolution.

But at Christmas I decided that I had to end the affair with Robin. He was devastated and the scenes were prolonged and painful; I also was distraught and very unnerved to realise how attached I had become to him. However, my problems were twofold and separate, and it was impossible to deal with the difficulties of the marriage while conducting an affair. The parting lasted all of three weeks. We were reunited, feeling relieved but more confused and muddled than ever. We saw each other little, we walked in the park in the cold. We were happy and not happy.

In 1976 O'Toole went to Rome to film *Caligula* with John Gielgud, Malcolm McDowell and Helen Mirren. He rented a house on the Appian Way and began to study Spanish; Mexico still held a potent attraction for him and he determined to learn the language properly. I discovered, by chance, that he had acquired land there and was thinking of building a house. '*Another* house!' I thought indignantly – as though I didn't have enough to look after. Then, realising that I wasn't meant to know about it, I also realised with some relief that I wasn't going to have to look after it, either. So, what did this signify? The language lessons, the Mexican real estate? I remembered Anna and his strange letter describing my appearance in his dream, almost hallucinatory in character. Was it possible that he, also, was looking for a way to terminate or alter this seemingly unbreakable relationship? That would be too easy by half, I thought ruefully. There was a horrendous time ahead and no way of avoiding it.

Cowardly, I put it out of my mind and concentrated on *I, Claudius*. Robin was a constant on the periphery, but I was beginning to realise that, to my sorrow, the affair was going to have to end again. I was simply too busy and too involved in other business to move it 'centre stage' and it was scarcely fair to Robin to keep him on the sidelines. I postponed the moment. There is something so strange in living a life which is totally chaotic in one aspect and so completely happy and coherent in the other. *I, Claudius* was, after a bumpy start, one of the most pleasurable, carefree jobs I'd ever had.

I'd worked with Herbie Wise, the director, before at Granada when he was part of just about the best drama department in television. He and Jack Pullman and Martin Lisemore and the designer Tim Harvey, and head of costume, Barbara Kroenig, and head of the BBC's superb make-up department, Pam Meagher, had been working on the series for a very long time before that first read-through at Acton. I'd worked with or known many of the actors involved: George Baker (not for the first time I was playing the mother of someone who was my senior), Brian Blessed, John Hurt (an old friend), Pat Quinn (my daughter in the Suffragette series), John Castle (whom O'Toole had 'discovered' for *Lion in Winter*), Patsy Byrne (whom I'd been with at Stratford). Herbie laid down the ground rules early on. I had all sorts of ideas about the subtlety of my character, Livia. Derek Jacobi, in one of his first big television parts, was still doubtful about how he was going to play Claudius; we all had our little private problems. After the read-through – pretty dull – Herbie said, 'Okay, let's get up and try a bit.' We played a few scenes. He looked appalled. 'Look,' he said (in effect), 'we don't have much time and we are certainly not playing some kind of English costume drama. *This* is how we're going to do this show – BIG, up-front, poster paint. It's *my* decision. No negotiation.' Consternation and tears (men, as well). Reluctant performances at rehearsals, wails (very British) of 'But this is so *obvious*.' Remorseless, he whipped us on towards the first episode. It was a nightmare. One of my big scenes came right at the end of the last twelve-hour day. 'Sorry, Siân. We have ten minutes to get this. Get a move on.' Somehow, we got it done – on the run. And it was over. Episode One was finished and we were committed to this somewhat un-English style of acting. Would it be good or awful, we wondered? Herbie was confident. Martin was thinking hard.

Chapter Thirty-three

During the rehearsals for Episode Two we all calmed down. Derek was still saying that he might give up the part, Brian was a bit mutinous, but then Brian always is gloriously mutinous. I sat there, rehearsing a scene with George and Brian on the main set (what we called 'the family parlour'). It was a family squabble scene and I noticed, at the end, that Jack and Herbie were smiling, pleased. 'Tell me,' I said. 'Is this a Jewish comedy?' There was a pause before they beamed and said that they hadn't wanted to say anything so crass, but, yes, that was more or less what it was. After that I did as little 'acting' as possible. And the less I did the more approving Herbie was. After the first few weeks everything became terribly easy and hugely enjoyable.

Even so, we had no idea that we were making a classic. As new cast members joined the show, they were sent to a viewing room to see what we'd shot so far. Time after time they came back to the rehearsal room looking doubtful. Close friends said, 'Oh dear, this looks really *strange* – I don't think it's going to do well.' It was so lovely to be in that we stopped caring about the outcome, successful or otherwise. In the summer my character, Livia, 'died'. Martin and Herbie took me to lunch and said we might be on to something. Already, I had begun to worry about my 'life' again and didn't pay much attention. The girls flew back from Ireland and together we went on to Rome to visit their father.

The villa on the Appian Way – pretty enough – had become a 'Petruchio' house, staffed by typical O'Toole Petruchio servants. There was a pool, but it needed cleaning; the sitting room was festooned with wires and recording equipment (Spanish lessons were in full swing). Meals were provided by a small Italian who was prone to fits of hysteria and who was running a busy sideline in stolen jewellery. Where did O'Toole *find* these people? What did the gardener do? Why did the cook confine himself to frying aubergines?

Our visits to the set were even more bizarre. John Gielgud stood there looking grand and pretending not to notice that the girls flanking him were bare-breasted and carrying dildos. In the trailer, Helen Mirren and Malcolm McDowell were beyond caring and very funny about their experiences. O'Toole was playing Tiberius and, as I watched, he nearly drowned, swimming in a huge red robe, surrounded by up-to-no-good under-age boys (Tiberius's 'minnows'). It was so strange to leave the set of *I, Claudius* (which can't have cost much), which had been researched, old BBC-style, for a year before shooting began, and to walk on to this huge set with all that *Penthouse* money behind it and where the actors were paid vastly more than any of us at home, and to see it all going horribly wrong. The costumes and make-up and sets were a mess and as for the script . . . I said nothing.

Kate's boyfriend from Ireland pitched up and came to stay. Michael from Clifden was one of the nicest young men I'd ever met and I was sorry that they were meeting at sixteen, when neither of them had spread their wings. They seemed so perfectly suited (certainly *I* was perfectly poised to be *his* perfect mother-in-law), but they were very young. When they disappeared to her room I felt that maybe we should exert some kind of control over them and asked O'Toole to sort out their living and sleeping arrangements. Telling me that I was a little out of touch, he promised to deal with the situation and I was glad to leave it to him. As for us, we had very little to say to each other; my head was still full of *Claudius* (which I had to return to for a 'ghost' scene) and my infidelity; he, for his part, was preoccupied with his Spanish, and only in bed did we come together easily, mindlessly, pleasurably.

Jerry Bauer, a photographer who always took our family pictures and who now lived in Rome, came out to take photographs and he released a strange, sad picture of us to the press. It was captioned 'The Last of the Summer Wine'. It looked just that – the end of something.

The girls and I returned to London, leaving O'Toole in Rome, and I began rehearsing a play about Janet Achurch, the actress who created Candida for Bernard Shaw and who ended her days, a great nuisance to him, in a fog of drugs and drink. It was a BBC/TV production, written and directed by Don Taylor. *Frieda*, Sara said, was progressing well. Although she had set up the series through Keep Films, James Cellan Jones, the head of drama at the BBC, would ultimately be in charge. I admired him enormously and knew I'd be in safe hands. It was a very big project, six hours of television, and I looked forward to working on it for the whole of the following year, with any luck. O'Toole returned and began to film for the BBC as well. Jack Gold, an old friend, directed him in an adaptation of a book by Geoffrey Household, *Rogue Male*.

It was I suppose a measure of the gulf that had opened between us that my duplicity, my unhappiness, my withdrawal of myself, seemed to go unremarked for so long. Not having any clear idea what I wanted to do, I did nothing and dreaded the storm which would surely break over my head one day. In the back of my mind I calculated that when everything was known, I wouldn't have to make the decision which seemed so beyond me, I would merely have to react to events – whatever they might be. That was more or less how things happened, but they seemed to happen in slow motion and time spread and lengthened as it does in dreams. Finally, when O'Toole noticed that something was seriously amiss – and why did he, I wonder? – he sprang into attack mode and began interrogating me, something to which I was only too accustomed, and I reacted like a frightened rabbit, much as I had all those years ago when we were first married. I couldn't tell him about Robin at first, not wishing to unleash the eloquent and derisive reaction which I could hear before it was spoken.

Secondary to this selfish desire was a wish to protect Robin; the contest between him and O'Toole seemed painfully unequal. Even worse, the passion I had felt for Robin was diminishing; his violent reactions to our partings had made me realise that he in his youth couldn't fully deal with the situation we had created. My recurring concern was the effect of all this on the girls' lives. Robin couldn't be expected to understand this. He wasn't a parent and had never met my children. All he wanted was me. And I worried about my mother, who was oblivious, it seemed, to all that was going on around her. Closed doors and raised voices were things to be complicitly ignored in a house in which alcohol figures so largely. The habit of not acknowledging unpleasantness continued now that sobriety reigned in Guyon House. I went as far as to make it clear that I was unhappy and that I would like us to part, and eventually I confessed Robin's name. Useless to say that he was a symptom, not a cause, useless to say that all I *really* wanted to do was to live apart, on my own.

Somehow, for months we managed to work, plan future work, live our lives without confiding our problems to anyone. We slept little, argued a great deal, advanced not at all. O'Toole still spent a great deal of time as a more active partner of Keep Films, putting in hours in the office when he wasn't working. He and Jules worked on *Frieda*, among other things, and one day as I sat waiting for a taxi in the car park at TV Centre, James Cellan Jones called out to me and told me that after, all the work, the BBC was abandoning *Frieda*. The BBC felt that the demands made by Keep Films were simply too expensive and our company wanted to retain too much control. 'The next time you want to do something,' said Jim, 'do your own negotiating.' It was the end of two years' work. Sara was aghast. I was disbelieving; no one at Keep Films called me to explain what had happened. O'Toole said nothing.

Janet Achurch's photographs featured heavily in Shaw's letters and the BBC went to a great deal of trouble to produce a good photograph of me as her. The play had turned out very well and the photograph was so good that it was decided to make it the cover of the *Radio Times*. Then *Rogue Male* entered the lists and they called me from the BBC to say I'd lost out to my husband. I wasn't surprised, or annoyed. By now I was old in the faith and nothing if not a realist.

Events accelerated. Robin turned up one day to meet me for a snatched coffee and said he'd told his parents about us. I wasn't pleased but said nothing. In the same week, O'Toole summoned Robin to meet him in his palatial office in Belgravia. Robin had called him and asked for an interview. He was glad to have things come to a head, but I felt sorry for him and I feared for him. He seemed strangely unafraid and unaffected, and as far as I could make out, he more or less asked for my hand. I don't know how O'Toole responded. The situation was careering out of control. I wanted my hand to myself. O'Toole told me to end the affair once and for all, and I felt that ending the affair *was* inevitably the right thing to do, but not so I could stay within the marriage. The cheap jokes and the scorn strengthened my wish to leave. To leave and live alone.

But once again I ended the affair and again I was surprised to be overcome with sadness, more affected than I had anticipated I would be. I gave Robin my most treasured small possession and said goodbye and went home to bed where I stayed, crying into my pillow like a foolish girl – as I never *had* done as a foolish girl. I couldn't believe that I was behaving in this way. No one seemed to notice that I wasn't up and about. Life at home became a torment. Autumn dragged into winter and I began to see Robin again. There didn't seem to be any reason not to and I did miss him frightfully. I missed having someone to put me first. It was as potent as any drug.

By Christmas of 1976, which was spent in London, O'Toole and I had both reached exhaustion point. Sidney Gottlieb, O'Toole's friend and a hypnotherapist, came to visit and said that something had to be done; we were living a life of unbearable tension. O'Toole refused to discuss a plan, wouldn't release me in a coherent way, and I couldn't just jump ship. But, feeling desperate, I did once again terminate my affair with Robin – this time for good, I thought.

I'd become immensely fond of the ugly BBC Television rehearsal rooms in North Acton where I spent so much of my time. There were sometimes thirteen shows in rehearsal, so the crowded canteen at the top of the building was like an actors' club. I began to rehearse *Heartbreak House*. Sir John – by far the most illustrious member of our profession in the building – seemed unaware of his status. He adored gossip and scandal and each day he began pointedly looking at his watch a good five or ten minutes before the lunchbreak began. Once in the canteen he would stand there holding his tray, transfixed by the 'famous' faces all around. 'Look, look!' he hissed one day, and I followed his gaze to a table at which sat a very young actress/model/singer/ dancer, mainly famous for going to other people's opening nights. 'So?' I said, 'what's so special about her?' 'Oh, *always* photographed going through airports,' breathed John, admiringly. So different from Rex Harrison. When we were embarking on a long rehearsal period for his first ever television play (*Platonov* by Chekhov), he entered the canteen on the first day, a glamorous vision in oatmeal tweed with a cream silk shirt. Startled, he joined the queue as indicated, helped himself to a little food, then looked disbelievingly at his tray and at the plain, noisy room and, setting down the tray, turned and walked swiftly out of the building in search of his chauffeur and the Bentley, and disappeared to fetch a little light lunch from his house in Belgravia. He could be seen each day after that, moodily picking at a little cold salmon in the back seat of the car.

When I finished *Heartbreak House*, the bitch – reality – began to nip at my heels again. Life at home was grim for me, living as I was in a kind of limbo; not allowed to leave, obliged to stay – for how long? I didn't know. I felt like a fly in a web, only half alive, wrapped in barely discernible threads. I was lonely. It was unthinkable that I should confide in anyone and I missed Robin's company. Everything around us was beginning to disintegrate; Lionel left to take up another job. For me, this was like losing a brother; although we never ever discussed family problems, in his privileged position he saw and heard everything and was the only person who knew exactly how I was placed. Much as he might wish to, he never ventured to defend me, but he was, I knew, deeply upset when I was treated badly. I knew that I could not see him again until I regulated my life. A regulated life seemed beyond our grasp. At one stage it was suggested that we might separate, divorce and continue to live in the same house – we were thrashing around like animals in a net. O'Toole began to fall out with Jules – Jules, who had run our lives, arranged our finances, organised O'Toole's life in the movies, dealt with every manner of trouble imaginable. In my view, for me to confide in Jules would have been disloyal to O'Toole and worrying and embarrassing for Jules, so I kept my distance and, deprived of the company of Jules and Joyce – my 'family' for as long as I'd been married – I was completely isolated.

O'Toole announced that he was going to Mexico alone to recuperate from his illness. It says a great deal about my half-paralysed state that it never entered my head to quiz him about his life in that country or his possible attachment to someone there. I asked O'Toole if I might go and spend some time alone in Connemara. He pointed out that the Irish house was not mine and that my presence there was unacceptable. I realised that I had indeed seen the Sky Road and the house on the hill for the last time. Ordinarily, I would have been heartbroken, but now it just seemed to be one more blow, much like any other.

The weeks of February dragged. Looking at my diary I see that I went to school to talk about Kate's future. I went to listen to a recording I had made of *Antony and Cleopatra* with Robert Stephens and Ronald Pickup, under the direction of Martin Jenkins at the BBC. I tidied my papers, filed everything to within an inch of its life, rearranged books, answered O'Toole's mail, avoided our friends. Why didn't I take some action of my own? My mind darted from one problem to the next. What would happen to the family if I left? Where would I live? I had never saved money – all my earnings went into the houses, furniture and furnishings, and my clothes. What would I live on? O'Toole warned me that the scandal, when made known, might mean I would find work difficult to come by. And what would happen to my mother? Would I be able to take care of her? There were too many questions to which I had no answer. I was immobilised with no one to talk to in my secret life. And worst of all, I didn't feel I had the *right* to do anything.

My capacity for altering my life seemed spent and I waited to hear what O'Toole thought I should do.

He was away in Mexico for six weeks and I kicked my heels in Hampstead. We were not in touch. When he returned it was only for a day or two before he left on private business in Bristol. He had arrived at a solution during his stay in Mexico – it was just as well that one of us had done so. It was clear to him that I should leave Guyon House. I had no reason to disagree with this decision, but I didn't know where to go and when he returned from Bristol a few days later I had made no plans at all. It was 21 February and I agreed with him it was right that I should leave home the following day at four o'clock. Still I did nothing, made no provision. I couldn't argue with his disdain at my paralysis; I rather agreed with him that such feebleness was despicable. Had he not helped devise a means of departure, I might have continued for months to sit, half dead, in that lovely house.

On 22 February he assembled the household; my mother, Kate, Pat and Liz, meeting in the Green Room; the girls and Liz sitting on the big couch, my mother in an armchair and O'Toole in the high Prides leather wing chair I had bought him when he had hurt his back. I sat in the most disadvantageous chair in the room, a Charles Eames chair I had given O'Toole after a particularly well-paid TV job. It was low and luxurious and in its embrace I appeared indolent and relaxed. Unbelievably, I lounged there and told the people to whom I was closest that I was 'exhausted' and needed to leave home for a 'rest'. The family looked at me, silent and uncomprehending. I'd finished what O'Toole called my 'Father Xmas version' of the events of the last two years. No one spoke. Finally O'Toole rose and said, 'Well, that's that then.' He was brisk and benevolent as he moved to the study. It was clear that I was dismissed.

I went to the bedroom, while the family dispersed over the other four floors of the house. I felt numb beyond tiredness as I began to pack, barely acknowledging to myself that the scene I had rehearsed and played had been deeply humiliating. I knew that I would never see O'Toole again; he prided himself on his resolutely unforgiving nature and I had no wish to expose myself ever again to being patronised in this lordly way.

Swiftly, I reviewed the situation. My mother would stay and run Guyon House – she did not know and was not to be told that I would not return. The girls' lives would continue uninterrupted. They went to school at Edgware, so it was important that they remained where they were. Liz was, by now, part of the family and I knew they would be looked after properly and enjoy all the benefits to which they were accustomed. On that day in February I had nothing to offer them. It would not have occurred to me or to anyone in our circle to question O'Toole's decisions. I had sometimes observed people formulate an unspoken question in response to some draconian pronouncement on O'Toole's part, but I never saw anyone defy him or question him. Not once.

I began to fill two suitcases – black things only, something to wear to BAFTA, which was coming up, one pair of black shoes, one black bag, a few toilet things. Where could I go? O'Toole had told me that I wasn't to tell anyone that we were parting. He said there would be unwelcome publicity if anyone found out that I wasn't living at home. I accepted this and it worried me, but in a way, in spite of my efforts to free myself, I was still identifying with him, even against myself. I was looking at the situation from his point of view, not mine; I realised that I wasn't going to be able to handle this change in my life on my own, but I couldn't ask any of 'our' people for help – it would place them in an intolerable position. Everyone was nervous of 'The Guvnor'. The only person I could think of who would not be made nervous by help- ing me was Ricci – Ricci Burns. I called him at his hairdressing salon in George Street. 'I'm leaving home and I have to be out of here in forty-five minutes.' He asked no questions. 'Take a cab and go straight to my flat in Portman Towers. Leave the bags there and then come back here to the salon to see me.' I called a taxi on the bedroom phone and looked around for what I knew would be the last time ever. The room had altered a little and was not quite as perfect as it had been when Joyce and I first designed it. The bed now had its back to the bow window since the night O'Toole had set fire to it when it was placed against the wall, but the room was still beautiful; my 'things' lay behind closed drawers and cupboards.

The months of turmoil were over.

I lifted both bags and walked downstairs and out into the street to wait for the taxi. I met no one on the way out; the house was sweetly scented, shining and quiet and, like water, the air closed behind me as though I had never been there.

Chapter Thirty-four

Ricci was wonderfully, reassuringly flippant, and dispelled the effect of the endless gloomy drama that had prevailed for so long at home. 'Silly cow, get over this nonsense. Say you're sorry and *go home*, for God's sake.' Lilian, his mother, said, 'Have my room. I'll go away for a week – but *listen* to Ricci, please.' She was fond of O'Toole and he of her and we had spent many happy hours together, the four of us, but, like many people, she liked the *idea* of us, the O'Tooles, and knew little of our private life. 'So,' said Ricci when he came home from work, 'you *look* all right. Who have you left him for?' When I told him that there *had* been someone and that it was all over and I was planning to live on my own, he simply didn't believe me. 'I love you but you're lying. I know you.' Ricci and I were so different and so close. He understood me very well and his advice on most matters, even complicated professional matters to which he responded in a purely instinctive manner, was always good and I listened to him even before Sara with her experience, or O'Toole with his huge knowledge of the Business. Now, he was wrong, and we bickered and argued as we cooked supper, and we went on arguing for weeks to come.

He found me a small service flat in Curzon Street and I moved in and began to heal physically. I couldn't remember when I had last slept so well. I was still smoking as heavily as ever, but I didn't drink at all and I lived a hidden life in the flat, seeing no one except Ricci and Lilian and my mother, Liz and Pat. In the evenings, I hung out of my window, watching people entering the Mirabelle restaurant below. My life had changed utterly overnight. (The Mirabelle was probably a thing of the past, I thought.) Our joint bank account was closed and naturally my small allowance ceased; my medical insurance was cancelled; however, I was strangely untroubled as I felt myself becoming rested, stronger and more contented. I had enough money in my own account to live on for the present and I went on working.

I hadn't seen Robin since before I left Guyon House and thought never to see him again. The madness that had possessed me was over. Now living at home with his parents, he found out where I was and asked if he could come to see me. I realised that it no longer mattered to me whether I saw him or not. When he arrived I explained that I had to go out and left him in the flat to wait – or not – till I returned. He was still there at midnight and we spent the night together and it was hugely agreeable, but I told him that I didn't even wish us to meet again. He accepted this, remarking that it seemed such a shame that someone who liked sex so much should consign herself to a celibate life. For a moment, I couldn't follow his thinking. Then I remembered that he had no way of knowing that I had maintained a sexual relationship with my husband. Feeling only momentarily guilty, I assured him that celibacy was probably going to be just fine and we parted. For ever. I realised that I was mightily relieved to have simplified my life.

A few people had to be told where I was. They were sworn to secrecy. Sara (to whom I'd been introduced by Ricci), was wonderful to me. I'd stuck by her early on in our relationship when she'd been hospitalised with a mystery ailment – and now she repaid the debt of loyalty with interest. As a sideline she read scripts for Keep Films and developed projects for O'Toole. Now he told her to choose between Keep and me. Unhesitatingly she chose me. Not only that, but she called me every morning to check that I was all right before she opened the office. My accountant, John Libson, the son of the Keep Films accountant, the great Nyman Libson, also showed that he was not going to abandon me, and between us all we tried to find a financial path forward. It was realised that since I didn't know what O'Toole might suddenly do with regard to my mother or the girls, I had better try to buy a house that would shelter all of them – a four-bedroom house, in fact. How to do this? Out of the blue I received two large cheques – repeat fees for lengthy serials – and John reminded me that, on his advice some years previously, I'd left some film money outside the UK and now it could be retrieved, legally and tax free. I could buy a house! I could hardly believe it. Ricci and I found a house for me in an early Victorian part of Islington.

Miraculously, we kept the story of my separation from O'Toole out of the papers, but I now told my mother the truth. She knew better than to suggest we might patch things up. Marie, who was staying at Guyon House while filming, spent her evenings with me and she also knew better than to suggest that the rift between O'Toole and myself could ever be healed.

Islington in 1977 had not become fashionable; the Georgian bits were fairly desirable but the Victorian section I was to buy into – built on a square mile of old market garden – boasted not too expensive, solid, well-built, airy houses with decent gardens. I found the house through Peter Brooke in the King's Road, a firm I remembered from my undergraduate days and renowned for its blunt descriptions ('Horrible flat in a bad neighbourhood, in need of repair, looks for a loving, mad buyer', etc.). John D. Wood and Chestertons were snooty and depressingly pessimistic. It was raining. At Peter Brooke they took me in, gave me some tea, told me to sit down and get dry, and reassured me that I'd have no trouble buying a house with the money at my disposal. And I didn't. Sara knew that I now needed to make regular money and between us we saw to it that I didn't spend an idle day. Ricci found me a larger flat in Chelsea and it was easy to move my few belongings to this new, secret address. Only Sara, Marie, my mother, Ricci and John Libson had the phone number.

I was preparing to play Boadicea for a Thames Television series called *Boudicca* and was spending a large part of every week in Kingston-on-Thames in an indoor riding school, learning to ride bareback on the nastiest horse I'd ever met – Jasper – who knew that I was vulnerable and took advantage. At weekends, bleeding and barely able to walk, I saw Pat and my mother and Kate, who, I fancied, was rather glad to have got rid of the Wicked Witch of the West, and, looking at it from her standpoint, I didn't entirely blame her. She was at a rebellious age and, no doubt, behaved better when I wasn't there. My mother didn't think much of my flat, after the splendours of 'home'. The girls rather enjoyed pottering around it – it was smaller than their nursery apartment. It seemed that they had deduced correctly that the marriage was over and no one reacted with regret or sorrow or surprise. Pat said consolingly that she only had one friend with two parents living together. There was no possibility that they could move from Hampstead while they were at school, even had they wished to, but I assured them that very soon I would have a house large enough for all of us, should the need arise.

Organising the house purchase was eventful to say the least. *Boudicca* was shot on location all over southern England. I would repair, painted white – or blue – as the script demanded, to the nearest telephone kiosk to plead with my charming young lawyer at Harbottle & Lewis to speed things up. 'How can I *force* her to complete?' 'Oh, it's very easy.' 'Really?' 'Yes, you take hostages and every day when she doesn't do it, you shoot one.' I stopped nagging him. My life was complicated by the fact that, following O'Toole's instructions, I was pretending to everyone (except those in my small, close circle) that I lived in Hampstead in the family home. In order to be picked up at 5.30 a.m. by the Thames TV car, I had to rise at 3.30 a.m. in my Chelsea flat and then get myself up to Heath Street and wait in the street until the car arrived to pick me up, and at night, after I was dropped off in NW3, I had to make my own way back down to Chelsea again. Tired and furtive, I felt like a member of MI5 on a dangerous mission.

Towards the end of March I went to the British Academy dinner and award ceremony. The organisers wanted to arrange a suitable escort for me when they learned I wouldn't be attending with my husband. I resisted this vigorously; I was really enjoying life on my own and didn't feel the need for an escort. (I had a small dalliance with a really charming writer but decided I couldn't cope with a relationship and firmly told him so with a new-found honesty that I, at least, found refreshing!) I had been nominated as Best Actress for Livia and Beth Morgan, but hadn't really had time to think about the possibility of winning. Ricci pulled me together and organised my appearance – my dress and my hair – and off I went alone in a taxi. I sat halfway up the auditorium next to a well-known comedian, who told me that my position in the auditorium meant that I was *not* going to be a winner. I rather agreed with him and we were both surprised when my name was called.

After the ceremony I found a taxi and went straight home to Chelsea, preoccupied as usual with the problems of the morning pick-up in Hampstead. As I paid off the cab and fished out my front-door key, a figure appeared from the shadows. It was Robin. He'd watched the ceremony on television and had come round to congratulate me. How was it that he always managed to find out where I was and be there to do something really nice for me? I had not been planning to mark the occasion at all, but now we sat up and had a celebratory drink together. He still lived at home with his parents in their house in Bayswater. 'Mind if I stay over?' he asked, trying to sound casual. He *was* forward. And sweet. I would have preferred him to go home, but it seemed a bit mean, considering the fact that he was the only person who'd bothered to say 'well done'. 'Okay, but just for tonight,' I replied. He agreed and went home the following day and I got on with my life.

The post arrived bringing a typed confession for me to sign. I called Sara, asleep in bed, to ask what I should do. 'Sign nothing,' she cried and gave me the name of a lawyer to consult. Now, I was not only trying to buy a house by remote control, I also had a divorce lawyer to see every week. Trevor Williams – the most gentlemanly of lawyers – became a fixture in my life and I met him regularly for the next three years. Having completed *Boudicca*, I was on my way to try on crinolines at Bermans for a BBC serial called *Off to Philadelphia in the Morning*, when O'Toole demanded a meeting where I was to hand over the signed 'confession'. We met on the pavement and I told him that my lawyer would not countenance my signing such a thing. When he learned I had engaged a lawyer he was enraged. Engaging a lawyer, it seemed, was as bad a deed as having an affair had been in the first place. 'Goodbye,' he snapped, turning towards his chauffeur waiting at the kerb. 'Goodbye,' I replied faintly but resolutely and turned into the costumier's fitting room. It was still only 10 a.m. and I *shook*. They laced me into my Victorian corset and slipped on my opera singer's dress – pale blue taffeta – I heard a buzzing in my ears and the faces around me approached and receded and the voices grew loud and then indistinct and I felt myself beginning to fall, and mercifully for a while I was released from the dreadful day.

I came to, laid out on an elegant couch in the big fitting room, worried, sympathetic figures hovering around me. I wondered how on earth I was going to survive this battle with O'Toole. Obviously the first step was to get on with the fitting so I could do the next job. I apologised and began to get up. My dress felt strange and oh, *merde*! I couldn't believe it – as though things weren't bad enough, for the first time in my life I had wet myself (and ruined yards and yards of expensive silk). 'Oh Lord,' I began, confused and embarrassed, 'I don't know how to apologise.' 'Hah!' barked an elegant young man and deftly tore the soiled length of silk from its moorings at my waist and consigned it to oblivion. 'Think nothing of it,' he said firmly, and calling out 'More silk!' went on with the fitting, and on I went, one step at a time, with very little idea where I was heading or what I would do when I got there.

After about a month Robin telephoned me – we hadn't been in touch at all since the British Academy Award night – and asked if he might come round to visit at the weekend. I was still in hiding and welcomed the company. He stayed the night. The same thing happened the following weekend and a few weeks later he left some of his things in the flat and before long he began spending the greater part of every week there. I was out at work during the day so it made sense that we should stay indoors in the evening. But weekends were difficult. I was nervous of being seen in the street near the flat and it wasn't easy being cooped up indoors, especially when the weather began to improve. On the whole we got on reasonably well, but already I could see that there were difficulties ahead. At weekends I cleaned and laundered and shopped and cooked. Robin loved sunbathing above everything and while the sun shone he lay beneath it, methodically 'working' on his tan. As I hoovered and struggled to come to grips with domestic arts I'd never before had to try to master except briefly at Stratford – which was a long while ago – I looked malevolently at the oiled, brown body on the balcony. O'Toole's words to me after he'd met Robin crossed my mind. 'Watch out for those small, brown eyes,' he'd said, 'and remember, you can't afford him.'

As I worried about the girls and my mother, saving as much money as I could and working all the hours I could, I thought to myself, 'This is very pleasant in many ways but it is going to have to stop,' and finally I plucked up courage to say to Robin that he could not possibly move with me to my house in Islington, when my life would cease to be a clandestine, hole-in-the-corner affair and become 'real' again. 'I cannot see you in the road with my Pickford's removal van,' I told him, trying to make light of it. 'Oh I don't see why not,' he replied breezily. 'I can take care of the whole thing for you.' And he more or less did. When the mood took him he could get a lot done. I was fully occupied with work and my visits to the lawyers' office; mountains of paperwork arrived regularly from O'Toole's lawyers and I had to sit for hours every week, answering all the points and trying to distance myself emotionally, but I came away from each meeting distressed and shaken. It was comforting to have someone take care of me. Robin organised deliveries, took messages and actually moved into the house while I was away at work, and saw to it that we had a table at which to eat, somewhere to sit, somewhere to sleep, a cooker and fridge. With a sudden rush of energy he even built me a broom cupboard, bought groceries, prepared meals and was charm itself to the girls and my mother, who was impressed by the broom cupboard. I had now accompanied Kate on her first day to Davies College where she would do her A-Levels, and my mother was still at

Guyon House to see Pat through her O-Levels (Liz would be in Hampstead as well). Pat couldn't possibly travel from my house in Islington to school in Edgware each day. It wasn't perfect but it was workable and now I *did* have a house in place, in case of emergencies.

This house was the first I'd ever lived in where I took care of everything myself. I cleaned it, did the laundry, struggled with the ironing and, book in hand, I began cooking in earnest. Meals for ten or twelve people became the norm. Robin's family and our friends and the girls sat around the big dining table and, ironing excepted, I began to enjoy the intense domesticity. There were still moments when I wanted to murder Robin as, if the mood took him, he rested while I wrestled with a new job *and* put in long hours in the kitchen, but on the whole it had a great deal of charm, this new life. Robin acted very little, but this didn't seem to bother him. (For how long? I wondered.) My mother gave us a small, cheap car and for my part I began to familiarise myself with public transport. My life could not have changed more completely, and although my vision of myself had been of someone living alone, unencumbered by the demands and irritations of a permanent relationship, there was something rather wonderfully absorbing about living with someone with whom I got on very well indeed, although we had little in common. It was shaking me up in an interesting way and I did, for a while, adopt alternative ways of looking at people and events. And it was exhilarating to feel that I was in charge of our lives. I said what I pleased, did what I pleased, within reason, and nothing in my life made me nervous or afraid. If anything annoyed me I could walk away from it. A horrible thought gave me pause; I was behaving rather as middle-aged men behave when they abandon their wives and take up with a younger, good-looking bimbo with whom they appear to have nothing in common. If that was the case it didn't reflect well on me or on Robin – and there *was* genuine affection between us. Nevertheless, I read something which gave me food for thought. It seems there are two periods in a woman's life when she throws her bonnet over the windmill; one is when she is about twenty-four and the other when she is about forty. At more or less those ages I'd first flown against all advice and married O'Toole and, much later, taken a young lover. It was humbling to feel like a textbook case. But, best of all, I wasn't living in, and being reminded that I was living in, a house that belonged to someone else. The house was constantly filled with people, and I could invite whoever I pleased.

Gradually, the house, which had begun as a pretty but empty shell, took shape. Each time I completed a job I 'did' another room or carpeted the stairs or bought curtains or china. Like many only children, I had been over-attached to my 'things'; pencils, pens, books. I liked to arrange my room exactly as I wished, not really wanting to share my time or my possessions, and very often preferring to be an observer rather than a participator. I had carried much of this behaviour into adulthood, but now I changed my ways. I had lost this attachment to my possessions. I would never again see 'my' garden in Ireland, and if ownership is 'that with which man has mingled his labour' then it surely *was* mine. The Irish house and all my books and notes and furniture were gone, but I realised now that it was the work of building that I most enjoyed, not sitting around luxuriating in the result of that work. As for the beauty of the place, it didn't belong to anyone and it was imprinted on my retina. Every so often I would wish to be standing there. I would feel blowing into my heart 'the air that kills', see in my mind's eye 'the land of lost content'. But those moments were few and I grew to love my bright, cheerful house in the busy, dusty streets of N1, off the unlovely Essex Road.

Robin began taking an interest in horticulture and together we improved the garden at the back of the house – he, learning to lay York stone and build steps. He had no way of knowing that nothing a man could do would impress me more. Everything that we had, we shared with friends, and he helped me turn my private life outwards for the first time.

Chapter Thirty-five

Denise Sée was our Keep Films company lawyer – poached by us from United Artists – small, like a pouter pigeon in a grey barathea business suit and shiny black shoes and briefcase, iron-grey haircut short, in private life a cordon bleu cook, devoted to her husband and her dachshunds. She was content to let her appearance lull her opponents into underestimating her formidable mind and killer instincts, and she took me in hand when I was a young wife under considerable pressure from the paparazzi. 'Whatever the provocation, don't answer back. Never complain. Never explain and above all do not engage in litigation.' I thought of her words each week as I climbed the stairs to Trevor Williams's office in Holborn. It seemed now I couldn't avoid litigation. O'Toole had teams of expensive divorce lawyers who flew wherever he was filming and lengthy affidavits would then come winging to me in London and there was nothing for it but to continue to sit with Trevor and slowly refute them, point by point. O'Toole still had the power to make me laugh and Trevor was occasionally scandalised by my inappropriate reaction to a particularly ridiculous statement. At one stage, O'Toole's lawyers were changed for reasons I could only guess at, and we all went back to square one. There seemed no reason why this divorce business should ever come to an end.

Denise pointed out that she had years ago secured half ownership for me of one of our properties, the house in London. That was all I could legally claim from the marriage, but I requested the rest of my clothes, my grandmother's furniture, my mother's silver and a guarantee that the girls would be assured money for their higher education. O'Toole quite rightly supposed that nothing would induce me to embarrass the children by opposing him in open court publicly raking over my difficulties within the marriage. Also, I didn't feel like presenting such a simple and consequently incomplete picture to the world. In many, so many, regards our life together had been thrilling and happy and exactly what

I wanted. And my high regard for O'Toole's many virtues remained intact. Of course, as Trevor pointed out, this would be construed by the opposing side as weakness; and it soon became clear that his lawyers *did* think that I was stupid, which I wasn't, and my lawyer incompetent, which he was not. Trevor suited me because he was not a thug and not combative, but even he said that he was bound to point out that it was absurd that I should walk away with so little after twenty years. He added that he understood my reasons for leaving quietly and even sympathised with my stance. There was a moment when it seemed as though I would have to fight to keep the house I had just bought with my own money, but the claim was abandoned. Even so, it took almost two years to reach an agreement by which I willingly gave up everything I might reasonably have laid claim to. It was a sad and sorry affair and I was to see all my jewellery – the accumulated birthday, Christmas and anniversary gifts – for sale at Sotheby's. I tried never to think about the divorce the moment I closed the door to Trevor's office and he found the case so depressing that he said he was disinclined to accept another divorce suit. By the time I was divorced, Keep Films had ceased to involve Jules. Naturally, Joyce and I resigned as directors and the Bucks began to think of returning to America.

Trevor took me for a farewell lunch near Chancery Lane. 'There you are,' he said. 'Free – free to make the same mistakes all over again.' I laughed uneasily. It was the winter of 1979 and I'd been working flat out since I'd left Hampstead in 1977. I was driven by the need to achieve some financial security but, or maybe because of that, the work had been variable in quality. The West End play I did, called *Spine Chiller*, was so bad that it acquired a cult following. Friends crept in to see it week after week – to laugh. In January 1978 we received a notice that pronounced confidently, 'This is the worst play of 1978.' It is difficult, going 'on' night after night in a terrible flop. My friend Fenella Fielding called and asked me to get her tickets for the mid-week matinée. I pleaded with her not to come, but she insisted. When the day came I forgot that she was out front and trudged back to the dressing room after the matinée to put my feet up before the next performance. There was a knock on the door and I heard the unmistakable Fielding tones. Opening the door, I moaned, 'Oh God, Fen, I'd forgotten you were in. Please don't say anything. I *know* what it's like.' 'No, no,' she reproved, 'persevering out there in a turkey like this is useful. It *builds muscle*.' And it does, but one wouldn't want to do it too often. My dear friends

Edward Hibbert and Edward Duke – both unknown to me at the time – sneaked in regularly for the curtain to the last act where, dressed in Balenciaga, I sank down, centre stage, cradling the dying, very black murderer in my arms, and he looked up and whispered 'Mother' as the curtain slowly fell on my astonished face. Not as astonished as the audience, believe me. George Baxt, the author, a witty, clever novelist, became a firm friend and ever after we wondered how we had sleep-walked our way into such a disaster.

On top of everything I went down with violent food poisoning the night before we opened that play on the road and I saw the truly sweet side of Robin's nature. He was keeping me company on tour (and that also was a first for me and very agreeable) and now he sat up all night, holding my head, wringing out towels, cleaning me up. I'd never been taken care of in this way – not by anyone – and of course I liked it. But not enough to entertain the prospect of marriage, and that was being proposed more insistently and with greater frequency.

The mere thought filled me with fright. And there was the question of the age difference. Once again, I brought up all the arguments against such a lopsided union. What about children? It seemed unfair that he should be denied a family, and while it was physically *possible* for me to have children, I didn't want a second family and couldn't see how I could fit a child into my already overcrowded life. He assured me that he had no interest in being a father and that he had thought through all the problems. All he wanted was that we should be married and he wasn't going to rest until we were. I persisted in saying that – like him and me in the street with the Pickfords van – I couldn't *see* it. He pointed out that we were having a perfectly nice time, living together, so why *not* get married? The argument went on and on. Well, it wasn't exactly an argument; he remained good-tempered and rational – and adamant – and I shook my head and feebly waved my hands about. Of course, it was *hugely* flattering as well as worrying – and wrong.

The day my divorce became final he came home with a special licence. I was aghast. He'd arranged a party after the wedding ceremony and we'd tell our friends then. We would get married first thing in the morning on Christmas Eve to avoid the press. 'For the last time,' he said, 'give me one reason why *not*.' It seems feeble to say that I'd been ground down, but I'd run out of arguments and yes, we *did* get on better and better. Something was working, that much was obvious.

There wasn't time to do much in the way of preparation for the wedding. I prepared a buffet supper for about fifty people. My main preoccupation was to avoid publicity, but I bought a new grey skirt from Browns and fished a nice old St Laurent coat from the back of the wardrobe. Robin's family attended.

The girls were on holiday and my mother didn't choose to attend. I wasn't surprised or upset. Ricci and Sara came to the Rosebery Avenue registry office, neither of them approving or hopeful of a happy outcome. At the party at home as the news slowly circulated, not a few people asked, '*What* do you think you're doing?' I said, 'Look, I'm not doing. It's done. Don't ask.'

I entered the Eighties, nervous, dreading the newspaper attention, but determined to keep a straight back, and maybe Robin had been right – life at home was now more relaxed than ever. Ricci determined to try to be pleased for me. Sara said, 'Keep your own bank account.' Almost everyone was unexpectedly kind and understanding. Inevitably, in time the press became involved and the papers made a huge business of the age difference. I tried to keep my comments on marriage to a minimum, pointing out that it was people who'd been married only once who were in a position to be knowledgeable and wise about the institution. What did I know?

Reading the tabloids one day I noticed with amusement that O'Toole had moved a Mexican girl called Anna into the house. (He renamed her Malinche after Simon Bolivar's mistress, but she could have been the Anna of the sad note and poem.) So I had after all been right to feel curious, had I? 'How did he manage never to relinquish the high moral ground?' I wondered, unable to keep from smiling at his nerve. My mother completely astonished me. She was still running the Hampstead house and over Sunday lunch at my house she said, 'You know that Malinche has moved in. She had a *beautiful* pair of expensive, new boots yesterday. I said to Peter last week, "I will look after Malinche as though she were my own daughter".' Well! I was lost for words. I was glad that she was taking what could have been an awkward situation in her stride, but did she have to be *quite* so enthusiastically generous towards my successor?

Robin and I were apart a good deal now. He went off on a provincial tour and I got ready to go away to film a TV series about Sean O'Casey in Ireland. Before I left I tried to find a new stage play. After the débâcle of George's *Spine Chiller* I redeemed myself slightly with *You Never Can*

Tell at the Lyric Hammersmith, the play that opened the new theatre there. Our first week was gruelling as the construction workers moved out and earnest efforts were made to clear away the drunks from their usual pitch outside the stage door before we embarked on four days of openings – for dignitaries, the press, fund raisers and, finally, Her Majesty the Queen (the drunks were back for that, I noticed). Smoke alarms went off, the sprinkler system was activated and there were police dogs everywhere sniffing at one's make-up. I love Shaw, but Mrs Clandon is one of those heavy-duty parts that are all hard work and no jam. Paul Rogers was superb as the Waiter and it was a uniformly good cast, but even so, I wasn't sorry when we closed. The plays sitting on my desk weren't spectacular. The best script by far was not a play, it was a musical. But I'd never done a musical. I could read music after a fashion, but I'd never sung alone in public, so I laid it aside and went on reading the plays. But I kept coming back to the musical. No harm in talking to the director, Robert Walker ('What on earth made him think that I could do this show?' I wondered). He was breezy and confident on the phone. I explained why casting me was a terrible idea. 'Nah, nah,' he responded. 'Give it a go. It'll be great.' I was beginning to think he was deranged. 'What's he like?' I asked around. The answers were uniformly favourable: 'talented, bit of a maverick, deeply attractive, law unto himself'. Mmm. I knew the score of the show because I'd been playing the LP at home for at least ten years. 'I'd better come and meet the musical director,' I suggested. If he says 'no' I shan't do it. 'Yeah, okay,' Robert agreed equably and so I found myself in a house in Islington nervously (and presumably very badly) singing through Vera's numbers from *Pal Joey*.

'Yah, great,' said Robert casually. He didn't seem to be paying a great deal of attention. 'What d'you think?' I asked John Fiske, sitting at the piano. 'You'll be all right,' he said, 'if you start taking singing lessons right away and keep at it. Call Ian Adam, he'll get you on.' I walked home through Canonbury hardly believing that I had just agreed to star in an American musical. Of course, it was only for a run of six weeks and the theatre was in the Mile End Road. No one I knew would be there to see me fall on my face. I bought a tuning fork and hoped that Robert Walker knew what he was doing.

Before I had time to begin getting nervous about my new job, I read a TV script that made me laugh so much I almost fell out of bed. It was one episode of a very long and successful Tyne Tees serial called *Barriers*. Unbelievably (in view of the nature of my role) it was targeted at older children. Overriding the dampening comments in the production office ('She'll *never* do it.' 'It's only *one* episode.' 'It goes out late *after-noons*/early evening'), Malcolm Drury, the casting director, said, 'Nothing ventured . . .' and mailed me a script. Even as I finished it, I reached for the phone and accepted the job. I was to play a slightly dazed, glamorous middle-European, retired opera singer, a widow who'd been married to a very small, rich man called Mr Dalgleish who left her lots of money, a castle in Scotland and two Rolls-Royces, and she employed two chauffeurs – very young and beautiful, in pasted-on trousers – 'Two – in case one gets tired, you know.' As it turned out, my contribution apart, the series was very moving. Who had dreamt up this extraordinary character? I turned back the pages and read 'William Corlett'. I looked him up. Former actor, theatre playwright, award-winning novelist, TV writer, award-winning TV writer – for some reason I had never come across him. Paul Rogers was the star of the series and Benedict Taylor was the juvenile lead. It would be lovely to work again with Paul, one of the best actors in the country, and I could just fit this in before *Pal Joey* and *Sean O'Casey*. What could William C. be like? Would I get to meet him?

I called Robin to let him know that I was off, picked up a dress from St Laurent, negotiated the hire of a sable coat for myself, and, with no time to fit a wig, packed a Graham Smith turban. I did *love* dashing around as and when I chose, answerable to no one. It occurred to me that maybe I was enjoying my freedom too much. Undeniably there was an element in it not only of making up for lost time, but of getting my own back on everyone who'd ever cramped my style. Robin might have more trouble to deal with than he could have anticipated.

In Newcastle, Maggie Bottomley, the producer, gave a lavish dinner for Paul, Patti Lawrence (who was playing his secretary), William Corlett and myself. It was a riotous evening and we ate and drank too much and I was in no mood to stop, but Paul coughed gently and indi-cated the lift and bed. I couldn't wait for morning when we would drive to Bamburgh Castle and begin shooting. Mr Corlett – Bill already – had made me laugh more than anyone I'd met for a very, very long time. We had a wonderful time, freezing all over Northumbria (thank God for the sables). Maggie provided real champagne for the picnic scenes and every night Bill and I thawed out, listening to *Pal Joey*, and then, already replete with location catering food and sips of champagne, laid into huge dinners. By the time we took the train back to London we were fast friends and planning to do more work together. We were also a good deal fatter. I felt I'd acquired a brother and I blessed casting director, Malcolm Drury, for sending me the script and Sara for encouraging him to do so.

It was March and *Pal Joey* was not due to start rehearsing until June. I knew all the lyrics and I took the tapes with me to Dublin, where I would stay in Baggot Street with Marie Kean while I played Countess Markievicz in the Sean O'Casey series. Because there was a TV strike on, I had a great deal of time off and Marie and I spent far too much time going to restaurants and staying up late at the Arts Club where she was a member. This was another aspect of my new life in which I was revelling – and far too enthusiastically; for the first time drink was a huge pleasure, with no worries attached. I could drink as and when I pleased because there was no fear that I would be setting a bad example or laying the ground for trouble ahead. If anyone became drunk and objectionable, I could walk away if I pleased. I no longer had to be the good caretaker and it was terrific – for a while.

Waking one morning with a terrible hangover, I looked at Marie and said, 'This, alas, has got to stop.' On the spot I renounced my brief career as a barfly and began to *run* to Marie's masseur's clinic every morning for a treatment before running on to work at the TV studio in Donnybrook. Life in Dublin was just as much fun on tea and orange juice as it had been on wine and I began to get fit. I might not be any *good* in *Pal Joey*, but I was determined to be 'able' for it. I loved working at RTE, and especially enjoyed working with the wonderful Irish actor, John Lynch, who played Sean O'Casey, and only disliked having to learn to handle a rifle. I don't think I managed to make it look more menacing than a handbag.

When I finished in Ireland I joined Robin on tour in Scotland and we spent a lovely week in Edinburgh before returning to London together. He was a skilful driver and I always felt safe with him. Driving down what Ralph Richardson used to call 'the backbone of England' was an unexpected pleasure. I was astonished to see that so much of this small island was still green, unpopulated and unspoiled.

London. *Pal Joey*. My life closed down to contain nothing but the show. I met my vocal coach for the first time and from now on I would see Ian Adam four times a week and every day I would practise his exercises at home. Without Robin I could never have done *Pal Joey*. Well, I *would* have done it, but with great difficulty. Ian, my music teacher, lived in Knightsbridge, I lived in Islington, *Pal Joey* rehearsals took place in the East End and there were wig fittings with Brian Peters in WI and costume fittings in Soho. Without Robin's willingness to drive me all over London every day, to wait for me, to pick me up, to deliver me back to work and to have something prepared for dinner at night, I don't see how I would have managed. I was being paid sixty pounds a week with no prospect of earning more. It would have been ruinous for me to take taxis all over London and public transport would never have got me to my appointments on time.

I was on a strict diet again (I'd given up dieting when I met Robin). The script demanded that the clothes for Vera in *Pal Joey* had to be simply wonderful. The Half-Moon Theatre budget was £200 for six outfits. Impossible. Among my new circle of friends were two of the top British designers, John Bates and Bill Gibb. Lunching at John's apartment one Sunday, I tentatively asked if he might consider designing me just one outfit in which I could sing 'Bewitched, Bothered and Bewildered'. 'I'll do the lot,' he said, casually. 'If I don't have time, Billy there will do them,' indicating Bill Gibb. I was speechless. 'Mind you,' said John, 'no bra – no underpinning and you need to be *thin*'. 'Thinner?' I asked, standing up straight and breathing in. ''Fraid so, dear.' John set about making a breathtaking wardrobe and also took care of the hats, gloves, furs, shoes and bags. He made no charge. Whatever came after, I was going to make a stunning first entrance, looking confident and RICH. No trouble or expense was spared. John's best cutter was on holiday and he looked at the white silk jersey dress that his *second*-best cutter had made and, in a fury, tore it off and flung it to the floor, lifting the phone and summoning the 'genius-with-the-scissors' back to London immediately. Naturally I had to do my bit as well and, weight dropping steadily, I stood for hours in the fitting room, one eye on my watch, with hours of work ahead, worrying desperately if I was up to any of this.

Stuart Hopps had the daunting task of teaching me to dance. Denis Lawson, who played Joey, was a very good dancer and an experienced singer. They were both endlessly patient, going over my routines in corridors and unoccupied corners of the shabby little rehearsal building – rat poison everywhere – overrun with confident, noisy youngsters who seemed to know exactly what *they* were doing. It was, for me, a time of total confusion. Every so often Robert would look at this revered script ('book by John O'Hara') and he'd say, 'Oh, I don't know about this' and set about turning it upside down, enthusiastically tearing out pages and rewriting. The only things that got rehearsed were production numbers; we scarcely looked at the scenes or my songs and I grew more and more despondent and more and more certain that I would never get to grips with the show. A week before we began previews, I sang 'Bewitched' for Robert. Stuart Hopps who was waiting to 'set' the song said, 'Why are you singing it so high?' I told him that that was how it was written in the script. 'Put it in a key that suits *you*,' he insisted. 'Can I do that?' I asked John Fiske, the musical director. 'Yes,' he replied and began to rearrange the orchestrations. My teacher, Ian, optimistic and encouraging, was sure I could sing soprano. Maybe I could have managed it, but it would have been a dreadful worry each time I opened my mouth. All my keys were changed down.

We moved in to the 'theatre', the new premises of the Half-Moon in the Mile End Road, the conversion from Methodist Chapel barely accomplished. There was a block of seats 'raked' in the auditorium, but they were wet with paint. The stage was just the flat bit at the end of the hall, the dressing room was a communal prefabricated building behind the chapel and there were Portaloos outside and duckboard walkways led to the Mile End Road. I realised that I would have to change for my first entrance at the front of the building under the stairs to what used to be the chapel gallery. They'd probably hang a cloth there later, I hoped. We were really short of funds. The production telephone was a red British Telecom kiosk on the pavement, and locals grew impatient as we received and made endless calls, and for a while our production company 'borrowed' electricity from the telegraph pole next to the telephone. Robert beamed, presiding over this mayhem like a prizefighter, hitching up his cotton slacks and executing a little shuffle from time to time, rubbing his hands with pleasure. I didn't doubt that he knew what he was doing, but I had no idea what *I* was doing and he left me to get on with it.

It was hot July weather. Our first preview arrived. The paintwork in the auditorium was still wet. 'Send them away,' said Robert as a rather smart West End audience milled around in the Mile End Road. How *grand* he is, I thought. We still hadn't done a 'dress' run-through a few days later when we decided we *had* to open. (We simply couldn't keep sending people home.) As it was, we had to turn people away for lack of room. I'd tried to ignore the press interest in my involvement. I was playing a middle-aged socialite who'd taken up with a younger man. I was singing and dancing for the first time *and* I was past the great age of forty. The opportunities for column inches were limitless. By now, I *knew*, absolutely knew, that I was on a hiding to nothing. Only dour, dogged professionalism kept me chained to my post. I sat, wrapped in a shawl, eating sticks of celery and wishing I were dead. Outwardly, I smiled. My mother refused to attend the first performance. Sensing my mood (which no one else did) she said, 'I've no wish to be there to see her making a fool of herself.'

My mother . . . What I had feared had happened. My mother called and said she had to move out of Guyon House. She was shattered and could not speak of the circumstances. I told her to come and live with me right away. So, during the rehearsals of *Pal Joey* I had been making a flat for her on the garden floor of the house, buying furniture and making sure that the kitchen and the bathroom were in good working order. The big front bedroom was a half-basement, the large living room and kitchen at the back were light and airy, giving on to the garden. After work and at weekends, I obsessed over the floor, my worries about Pat and my mother and my part in the show projecting themselves on to this huge expanse of dingy tiles, which were meant to be white. With a pail, soft wire wool and a sponge, I slowly scrubbed every inch of floor until it was blindingly clean.

My mother arrived at eight in the morning before we started previews at the theatre. She hated the flat. I looked at it through her eyes and indeed it was a far cry from the luxury of Heath Street. This normally rational, practical woman refused to unpack and I had to leave her sitting, disconsolate, surrounded by luggage. She was almost eighty. It took her a couple of weeks to adapt to her new life; nothing to run and organise, no accounts, no cooking to speak of. She'd lost her role and she, like me, had lost her life in Connemara. Kate was twenty and had flown the nest and for the first time my mother was separated from Pat, her 'baby', who was now seventeen. She'd lived in Guyon House for seventeen years and, curiously, the change was harder for her than it had been for me. She began to smoke. Gradually, we made her comfortable, but I wasn't sure that she would ever be entirely reconciled with her new life.

And that was the background to the opening of *Pal Joey* – a smash hit, which transferred in September to the Albery Theatre in the West

End and played there for over a year. There was enormous excitement, as is usual when one has a success, but I remember very little about the opening except the strange feeling of not being able to go on with the show and not knowing why (I had no idea what 'stopping the show' meant). Indelibly printed on my mind are the opening moments when, having dressed, hidden behind a blanket as the audience, inches away, filed into the theatre, I emerged into the empty foyer in brilliant sunshine and stood just inside the double doors, open to the street. As I turned to make my first entrance, unseen down the side of the steeply raked bank of seats, I was joined by an extremely drunk local who wandered in through the unattended front door. Smiling broadly, he attached himself to me. We scuffled noiselessly, unseen by the spectators above and to the side of us, who were all looking straight ahead at the stage. My cue was approaching and I was desperate. Hitching up my skirt I jabbed him in the shin with my stiletto and hissed, 'Fuck off! I'm IN this.' He went reeling back into the lobby and, adjusting my furs, I sauntered on down the aisle and into the acting area with an assurance I was far from feeling.

I cannot recall one time of success that has not been counterpointed by some kind of sadness or worry. Now, as I settled into a long run, I realised that with the arrival of my mother my time of kicking up my heels and living just as I pleased was once again at an end. Nevertheless, I felt pretty pleased with myself and with the way things were turning out.

Chapter Thirty-six

There is something about being in a long run that stabilises one's life no end. My producer on *Pal Joey* was Ian Albery, son of Donald Albery who gave me my first West End job. We were playing at the Albery Theatre, which had been run by Ian's father and before that by his grandfather, Sir Bronson Albery, and his great grandparents, Charles Wyndham and Mary Moore, who also ran the Criterion Theatre, which dug deep into the bowels of Piccadilly Circus. Mary Moore was, to say the least, careful with money and a stingy employer. One day when workmen were seen digging up the pavement outside the Criterion and someone asked what they were doing, a disgruntled actor passing by replied bitterly, 'Disaster! Mary Moore's lost sixpence.'

When we were all young things in the fifties, Ian, who was training in all branches of theatre management, came out on the road for the first time as company manager when O'Toole and I were in *The Holiday*. He was anxious and zealous and O'Toole's antics exasperated him beyond endurance. The company report book was full of remarks along the lines of 'P. O'Toole *laughed* on stage and made S. Phillips laugh, as well. *Spoke* to them.' There was a lot of *speaking* to. All these years later, he's a very grown-up producer and I'm a very responsible leading lady and we get along just fine. The favourite performance of the week for me is Saturday matinée when a small boy occupies the stage-right box and sings along with the whole show. He knows every word. Stage-struck as ever, I find it very moving to be playing to a small Bronson Albery in the theatre that until recently was named after his great-great-grandfather.

One always imagines that, once a show is up and running, there will be more leisure time in the week. The reality is that as the weeks go by, time shrinks as the need to stay fresh in order to keep the show fresh becomes paramount. Oddly enough, doing another job during the day can help to keep one fresh, but it goes without saying that there isn't a great deal of time left over for home life. However, domesticity – active, hands-on domesticity – was so novel to me that I shopped and cooked like a thing possessed. I was learning more and more about food, and each Sunday I recklessly invited ten or twelve people to join us for brunch – lunch – dinner. Most of my recipes I learned from Bill Corlett, an expert in the kitchen. Every Sunday morning the telephone wires between Islington and the village of Great Bardfield rang with cries of '. . . but *how* do you get the bone out of the leg? Oh, okay – I've got it on the floor and – yes, it's out! – but it looks like a traffic accident.' 'How do I keep the stuffing from falling out? But my sewing's *terrible*. Oh Bill, it looks *awful*. Does it matter? Oh, yes what a good idea. I'll cover it with lots of parsley.' He more or less 'talked me down' from ambitious near-disasters for about two years.

It was one of the blessings of the early Eighties that Bill and I became fond of each other's partners. Grave, wickedly funny Bryn Ellis became as much my friend as Bill was, and Robin was a treasured leavening and rising agent, egging us on to mild follies that we all loved even as we protested against them. We all went to Venice together and Robin very quickly cottoned on to the beneficial nature of an 'eye-opener' in the morning in cold weather. 'Spot of grappa to get us going, I think.' 'What? At nine in the morning? What are you thinking of? Oh, why not.' 'Another round of desserts?' 'Are you mad? But they *are* very nice. Oh, why not.' He was a mild lord of misrule and I loved being with him when we were with Bill and Bryn. I loved it more, I realised, than I did when I was alone with him. We didn't have a great deal in common, now that the urgency of setting up home, getting divorced, and getting married had subsided. There was marvellous sex, of course, but I had never known anything less.

We did share some things; entertaining was a joint effort at this stage and it was enjoyable. Robin, having caught my passion for gardening, very quickly progressed from under-gardener to very capable, equal partner. Above all we shared a love of animals. He gave me my first Burmese cat, Spencer, a large, strong, blue tom-cat with a loud, depressed voice. He was a present for me for the opening of *Pal Joey*, but he bonded with Robin on their journey home from the breeder and he loved him evermore with ferocity. He was like the jealous cat in the story by Colette and I think that there were moments when he would have liked to murder me so he could have Robin all to himself. This didn't make me love him less and he, for his part, allowed me to feed him and love him, and he grew to like me well enough, but passion he reserved for Robin. He came to think it was his right to sleep between us, so we decided to buy another Burmese so that he might spread his affections somewhat. And small, brown Barnaby came into our lives. Spencer 'mothered' him immediately. When Barnaby disappeared, we were frantic, but our distress was nothing compared with Spencer's. He searched and searched for him, returning home dirty and dispirited, moaning loudly. Every day he led me around the house, pawing at closed doors, howling until I opened them so that he might check the interiors. He displayed all the symptoms of deep depression.

Barnaby had to be replaced in the hope of assuaging Spencer's grief. We found a breeder who could let us have a Burmese right away. So Rupert entered the house and took over, boxing Spencer's ears and appropriating the position of Top Cat in every sense. He sat high up on the tops of doors and bookshelves. He tormented us and Spencer. He was a force and he was wonderful, but he didn't replace Barnaby, and Spencer became gloomier. For three weeks Robin and I spent all our spare time searching our neighbourhood and posting 'LOST' notes on trees and in shops, and then I received a call from N19 (we lived in N1) from The Cat Protection League, saying that they had a very troublesome, noisy Burmese on their hands and it might be mine. A 'troublesome' cat, so far away, seemed an unlikely candidate for my small, quiet Barnaby, but off I shot with my cat box. There in the cat refuge, solitary in a cage, alone in a corridor, was a horrible-looking, screeching creature, his face all mouth, with a cut head and a misshapen leg. 'Oh no,' I began and then I saw a small defect on the right foot that told me that this unrecognisable creature had to be – 'Barnaby?' I said. The screeching stopped. The ferocity disappeared and the small cat quietly waited for me to open the cage, lift him out and take him home. He'd been screaming for help from home for three weeks and his screaming had worked or so he must think. As I thanked the staff of the N19 CPL and wrote the biggest cheque I could afford and carried him into the sunny street to look for a taxi, I thought how chancy were one's own hopes of a good result, of happiness, of getting what one wanted. It might seem as though we worked for things, won things, achieved things, but actually one's luck turned on being in when the phone rang.

Barnaby never spoke again. When I opened the front door, Spencer was waiting in the hall. I dropped to my knees, thinking I was going to witness a fantastic reunion. I opened the cat box and lifted Barnaby out.

Spencer looked at the smelly, dirty, bloody animal, backed away and walked through the house into the garden. He never 'mothered' Barnaby again and became the slightly deranged outsider in the trio of cats dominated by Rupert. And they dominated us, as well. From this time on, our lives revolved around that of the cats; we rarely went away at the same time. My mother, a dog woman, with her own dog in her flat, learned to become a cat person and took over Spencer's position in Barnaby's life. He demanded her undivided attention and gradually he won her over. At home, in Wales, cats were workers and lived outside. When Bill, on a visit to the farm, asked my small cousin, Mair, what the cat was called, she looked at him in astonishment and replied 'Cat'. My cousins were disgusted that the cats sat around in the kitchen, watching the cooking, stealing what they could (not Barnaby). Robin and I were slaves to these beautiful creatures – blue, brown and 'red' blonde – and we were completely at one in our care for them. Sometimes, animals keep a relationship flourishing more efficiently than children.

When *Pal Joey* ended I went to Ireland to film for television a play based on Jennifer Johnston's book *How Many Miles to Babylon?* Ms Johnston, who came to visit us in Wicklow, was the epitome of my ideal Irish woman; independent, slightly racy, too stylish to be a victim of fashion or dietary whim. Meeting authors you admire is one of the big bonuses of being an actor *and* I was working in Wicklow *and* I was working for Moira Armstrong again (for the first time since *Shoulder to Shoulder*) *and* I acquired a new 'son'. Now that I'd begun playing mothers in earnest, my children were becoming a distinguished, beautiful bunch. Here was one of the most fascinating; Daniel Day-Lewis, whom I knew as Jill Balcon's son (Jill Balcon, so respectable and rather intimidating, who only a few months before had, along with me, got the giggles so badly during recording of a Greek tragedy that we were both asked to leave the studio and not return until we could control ourselves). I hoped her son was as good, and as jokey, as she was. He was playing his first decent part and within minutes it was evident that he was not only good, but very special (though *not* as jokey). Alec McNaughton was my husband (very jokey). It didn't make me sad, being in Wicklow and Dublin. It was Connemara that had held me in thrall; I couldn't go west.

Afterwards, back in London, I went on working, slowly consolidating my financial position and continuing to improve the house. I bought myself a grand piano and made a second sitting room at the top of the house, next to the guest-room; from there a staircase led to a roof garden that extended over the whole area of the house: white floor, white walls, it was like a Mediterranean garden. I was playing house. There was still something adolescent about my life during these years, in spite of the fact that I was taking care of my mother and seeing more of Pat and her friends than I had when we were living together in Hampstead. Kate I rarely saw these days. She was living with her current boyfriend in Islington, had decided against taking up a place at university and dropped out completely, but finally I tracked her down in Soho where she was working at Ronnie Scott's jazz club. I had made friends with Lynda La Plante while I was playing *Pal Joey* and I now persuaded her and her husband and Robin to come there with me on Kate's birthday so that I could deliver her a present. If there is such a thing as a star waitress, she was certainly it, and I was sincere in my admiration as she whizzed around, placing well-heeled customers as far away from the bar as possible, thereby obliging them to tip her heavily as she made the long journey, carrying heavy trays to them. I was amazed and intrigued; she was good at her job, and while I didn't think she should spend a lifetime being a waitress, it would never have occurred to me to try to divert her at this point. She was quick and smart and observant and sassy – all qualities I would dearly like to possess and never would. Now that I was no longer trying to influence her I found her totally enchanting; I didn't totally understand her, but I really admired her. Nor did I have fears for her. Looking at her, only slightly put out by my presence, I realised that, bringing the whole of my personality to bear on her, I had made little impression on her. And that cheered me up enormously as I sat there in the dark, noisy club, wanting to leave for the relative quiet of the street. We made no plans to meet, but I was sure that she would be in touch when the time was right. She got on well with Robin, but I had a feeling that she found my relationship with him slightly comical; not embarrassing, not irritating, just faintly amusing.

Pat, on the other hand, may have been only too susceptible to the advice lavishly handed down by my mother and, to a lesser extent, myself. She was still the Good Girl that she had been all her life; school-teachers, tutors, chaperons, nannies, all hated to see her go away from them. Her school reports were glowing, but she also decided against taking up her university place – and this hurt my mother, I know – and chose instead to go into the backstage side of the entertainment business. I wasn't displeased. She went on the road with her father as an

ASM, and played a small part in *Pygmalion*. In very little time she was stage-managing a West End show and I was amazed by her expertise in a field I knew nothing about. I was still uncertain in all things practical, and one Sunday when I was making heavy weather of serving a three-course lunch for twelve people and standing in the kitchen, dithering, Pat, sensing trouble, rose from the table and joined me. Taking in the situation and speaking a theatre language she felt I might understand, she said forcefully in stage management speak, 'Okay! Go Roast Lamb!' Lunch was on the table in a trice.

I had believed O'Toole when he told me that when our parting became public knowledge I would find work difficult to come by, but that hadn't happened and, looking back, I couldn't believe that I had been so credulous and so nervous. Weekends, as often as possible, were spent in Bill and Bryn's country cottage in Great Bardfield. There were more friends in my life than ever before and there was fun now along with all the hard work. The dancer and choreographer, Anton Dolin, whom I'd known slightly for years, became a staunch friend and he tried to teach me a little grandeur, which would be good for me – and then gave up and allowed me to be his *un*glamorous chum. John Bates and his partner, John Siggins, became firm friends and saw to it that, though I couldn't always afford it, I was decently turned out – spectacularly turned out, when the occasion demanded.

Lynda La Plante made me laugh more than anyone I'd met since Maggie Smith. She said to me while we were rehearsing something or other, 'I'm giving up acting.' (She was a wonderful comedienne.) 'I'm going to be a writer.' 'Oh, yes,' I replied, hardly listening from this point on. 'Oh yes, I've got this idea and I've written the story *here* – do you have one of these? You must. It's a Chisholm's – from the stationers in Kingsway. Can't live without it.' 'It' was a smallish, leather-bound address book, notebook, account book, diary – combined. 'You organise your life with this.' I made a mental note to go and buy a 'Chisholm's'; it did look lovely. 'Here, you want to see? This is called *Widows* and I'm going to put it on television.' I glanced at the notebook; huge writing with lots of spelling mistakes sprawled over the pages. I looked at her pretty features fired with excitement and felt a pang of sympathy for her. What disappointments lay ahead. How many actors at this moment were saying, 'I've written a film script – a TV series – a novel.' Poor Lynda. Why not stick to what she was good at? Then she told me the story and I thought, 'Heavens, that's good.' Even so, I was astonished when, within a year, *Widows* appeared on TV and Lynda became a star.

She and her husband, Richard, and Robin and I spent much of our leisure time together now. The men began to focus their attention on the gymnasium; on weightlifting, or karate. Neither Lynda nor I could summon much enthusiasm for this preoccupation, or for the spectacular, muscled results. She and I worked like beavers while the men perfected their physiques. We never discussed it, but I think we were both relieved that they had something with which to occupy themselves. Lynda worked hard because she loved writing and I worked so hard partly because I, too, loved my job and partly because I felt I had to prove myself – not least as a breadwinner – and I thought I had to make up for lost time. Sara was a friend as well as my agent, and she knew and understood my need to be constantly employed and colluded with me on this. Wiser heads maybe said, 'Don't panic. Wait for the better jobs.' I couldn't and I did miss a lot of prestigious work because of my infernal drive to work all the time. I was so busy I didn't always pay attention. Maureen Duffy and I met for lunch at old Bianchi's (with Elena presiding) and she and I discussed the possibility of doing a show about Karen Blixen. I had loved *Out of Africa* for some time and thought the show to be a good idea, but I wasn't really listening properly and the script wasn't going to be ready for a while and I wanted to get on. Fool that I was. I should have listened to Maureen and played that part.

Instead, I found a play which would come 'in' quite quickly. The director was Frith Banbury, a great name from the heyday of the West End in its glory days of Binkie and John and Ralph and Peggy and Edith. It was a play about Bernard Shaw and Mrs Patrick Campbell and it was *Dear Liar* by Jerome Kilty. A 'letters' play. Not too much acting, I thought, and nice to play Mrs Pat again; I had played her in a TV series about Jenny Churchill in the early Seventies. Robert Hardy would play Shaw, Bob Ringwood would design the set and John Bates would make me three outfits (one of which ought to get a round of applause for itself). We rehearsed in Knightsbridge and I turned up just before ten to be greeted by an immaculate Frith ('beautifully shod', as Coral Browne, the personification of elegance, would have remarked) who checked his watch, sat straight-backed and said 'Begin' on the stroke of ten. It was like joining a boot camp. Elegant, charming, polite Frith, associated with elegant, charming, polite theatre, was a bloody-minded slave-driver. No director that I ever met before or since expected so much hard work. The hours between 10 a.m. and 1 p.m. and 2 p.m. and 6 p.m. held nothing but work; no chats, no anecdotes, no breathers. He spotted my weaknesses very early on and was unremitting in his efforts to eradicate them. It was a wonderful experience, working for Frith. ('Frothy' Frith I had heard some acquaintance from the early Forties call him – Frothy? Hah!) He did a wonderful job on the play, as did Bob Ringwood and John Bates (whose dress *did* get a round). Robert Hardy and I were pretty good too, by the time Frith had finished with us, but not all the elements for a success were in place. We came 'in' into the new Mermaid. Our producer became mortally ill, the theatre did not have permission to advertise its existence outside the building, there was no way of crossing the road near the theatre (Griff James, the famed company manager, used to go out into the busy highway to escort people across in safety). Frith had to go away on family business after the opening. We subsided quietly and Frith returned to a very sad scene. Good notices and a good show are not enough to ensure success in the West End. Without a well-managed advertising campaign and a good 'shop' one might as well not bother opening. But Ingrid Bergman came to see us one night with Ann Todd! And on the same night April Ashley blew in from – where? She was a vision. Sometimes the dressing-room scenes should have been on stage. We came off.

Almost at once I was given a chance to work again with Peter Gill, now a great figure at the National, but I hadn't worked with him since we were at Nottingham Rep in the late Fifties. My room under the stage was next to Peter's stage manager's room, with the poisonous coke boiler (renowned in repertory circles), between us.

'Next week we will give *'Amlet*. I myself will play the moody Dane and me wife will play Ophalia.'

'Your wife's an old whore.'

'Nevertheless, she will play Ophalia.'

Each night we would chant these ancient theatrical jokes through the cotton sheet that divided us in our gloomy, noxious, underground booths.

Now – how smart – I would play Lady Britomart for Peter in his production of *Major Barbara*. And Penelope Wilton would play Barbara, and best of all, Brewster Mason (my Petruchio from the early Sixties) would play my husband again. It all seemed too good to be true. Penelope was one of O'Toole's favourite actresses. I had seen her, wonderful in his *Vanya* and alongside him when he played a brilliant Darcy Tuck in *Plunder* in his season at the Bristol Old Vic, which Sara had helped put together. Penelope was now married to my old friend, Dan Massey. I had longed to play at the National, but none of the possibilities had ever worked out. I was delighted.

Rehearsals with Peter were so entertaining that I never wanted them to stop (they did go on for months). They didn't take place at the National because Peter didn't much like working there, so we rehearsed in Hammersmith at the Riverside Studio. I would have liked to have been at the National, but Peter was a law unto himself and I was his willing slave. He must be one of the few 'teaching' directors of his generation. There was a time when almost all directors were able to teach actors how to play their parts. Then, as they relinquished lighting to lighting designers and sound to sound designers, many of them relinquished teaching as well, relying on casting directors to find actors who were 'right' for the parts. I watched Peter coax a great performance out of an actor that had neither the technique nor the natural aptitude for it. As for us girls, well, you can always spot a Peter Gill woman. He somehow reminds one of one's femininity and that confidence is retained long after the engagement is over.

We shifted over to the National a week before we opened and I found it very hard to 'learn' the building and never did become entirely confident that I could find my way to the right auditorium at the right time. I wished I had been able to rehearse there. (Subsequently, I fell in love with the confusing building and felt it to be the best place in the world in which to work.) Stage terror strikes at strange times. *Major Barbara* opens with a long duologue between Lady Brit and her son. David Yelland and I – both petrified – met each night before the show and ran the fiendish opening. We *never* felt confident enough to just come in and get on and do it.

Penelope Wilton was a wonderful colleague. Later, when the National went on tour, we both looked after Brewster who, by this time, was unwell and not good at looking after himself. She called herself Nurse Wilton. She and I went on a health kick and ran in the snow each morning before breakfast. And it was in Aberdeen, returning from our run along the riverside, that I learned that my friend, Marie-Lise Grès – John Hurt's partner – had died in a riding accident. We were friends and had been close neighbours in Hampstead. I had no idea how John was or where he was, and I sat there, looking out at the bright, cold Scottish morning, snow on the ground, with no one to share my shock, and I remember Lise and that view as if it were yesterday.

As we were about to open *Major Barbara* at the National, Sara had rung up, very excited, to say that a producer would like to see me about being in a major movie. As usual, at that time, I was stupidly under-whelmed by the prospect of the movies. Although I had been bitterly disappointed many years previously by the collapse of a plan to make *The Lonely Passion of Judith Hearne* and also very cast down when the director of *Ashes and Diamonds*, who had seen me in a play, failed to get finance for his film with me, I had never found it to be a problem turning down movies that didn't excite me. (Robert Atkins' command 'Don't go into the fillums' still sounded in my ears.) I asked the National for permission to go and see the producer. 'Not a chance,' was the reply. We were in the throes of technical rehearsals. 'Sorry,' I told Sara, 'can't go. We have to turn it down.' To my embarrassment, the producer and the director came over the river to see *me*. I slunk into the foyer with a white scarf over my wig and met – of all people – my friend, Silvana Mangano's daughter, Raffaella De Laurentiis. She was the big film producer! (I hadn't seen her since she was a typical naughty teenager in her mother's house in the South of France.) And with her was David Lynch, the director ('*Eraserhead*,' I realised). 'Oh God,' I thought. 'This is the most embarrassing thing that has ever happened to me. I've dragged them all the way down here to sit on a window ledge and have a drink of water.' I apologised and apologised – I couldn't bear to think they'd had to trek over Waterloo Bridge. We parted, I still apologising. 'Have you got the part?' said Sara. 'Heavens, I've no idea,' I replied. '*I feel so bad* they had to come all this way.' 'Oh, be quiet,' she snapped and hung up.

We went on tech-ing. Days later, I remembered the incident in the foyer. 'Hey, have I got the part?' 'Yes, yes, yes,' said Sara, fed up with the whole thing.

'The part' in *Dune* took me to Mexico for almost a year off and on. Mexico. When Jack Hawkins was first diagnosed with throat cancer, after his surgery he and his wife Doreen and O'Toole and I had taken a cruise to Mexico and had fallen in love with the country. Later, we had co-produced films at Churubusco Studio in Mexico City. O'Toole had made it his refuge when we were estranged. This was my chance to come to terms with another piece of my past. A thought: was coming to terms with and overcoming my past taking up too much of my time?

While I was playing *Major Barbara* I had time enough in which to review my personal situation and there was something not quite convincing about it. When one says 'Now I can be *me*,' what, exactly, is meant? In my case it meant being a person enjoying an absence of strain. Yes, that certainly. And freedom from the fear of disapproval. The subsequent increase in confidence, of course, but then ease and confidence tipping over maybe into complacency, self-indulgence, misplaced confidence – *over*-confidence? Relaxation – verging on sloppiness, maybe? Simply getting rid of problems was not the answer to this great step forward that I had had in mind. And furthermore, who was this 'me' that I was now free to be? So many years spent trying to adapt to difficult circumstances not of my choosing had left me strangely diffident about realising 'my' personality. I was having no trouble at all adjusting to the massive change in lifestyle. I travelled by public transport and loved it. Robin adored driving and I bought him cars that reflected my gradually improving financial position, culminating in a BMW, which gave him inordinate pleasure that I did not share. With a sinking heart, I realised that in a much more easy-going, pleasure-driven way, I was again adapting; this time to Robin's congenial idea of what our life together should be. And it wasn't his fault, not in any way. I had divined the scenario and, as well as I was able and without being asked to, I was living it out. There is more, however, to being yourself than changing your circumstances. If one is not careful a change of circumstance can be like a change of scenery; nothing much. ('*A groeso fôr Ni newid onid air.*' Crossing the ocean only gives you a change of air.)

Even work was slightly unreal. I now had to find a few friends who would help me with performances. Wilfrid Lawson used to say that one of the secrets to being a good performer was to 'find a friend'. Alas, not easy. People are very reluctant to be brutally frank and however self-critical you are, you can't see all the things that you're doing wrong, and the director is often too close to his part of the job to be able to help. I had been accustomed to long, fascinating debriefings at home with O'Toole and it was a two-way road, one of the few areas where I was free to speak my mind. No matter how well a show had gone, O'Toole and I spent hours the following day gently pulling the performance to pieces in order to reassemble it better. It was a totally absorbing, interesting process – occasionally painful but overridingly enjoyable. I learned more about acting from O'Toole than I had done from any of my teachers. Once, when I was playing mad Queen Juana of Spain in a play by Montherlant and was struck down by flu, he actually 'fed' me the performance on my sick bed, phrase by phrase, inflection by inflection, and I got up and went to perform the play, virtually with no rehearsal and it worked a treat. I trusted him implicitly. Knowing I would never speak to him again (and neither he nor I would wish to attempt a meeting), I treasured the few words of advice I had had the sense to commit to paper; they proved to be the most useful pieces of acting advice I ever received.

The first time I saw Robin in a play I obligingly read the play carefully beforehand and made notes throughout. He was pleased that I'd liked the performance, but looked aghast when I offered to go through the play the following day for improvements. I could see that the sight of my sheets of notes offended him, so I crumpled them up and hastily threw them away and we never discussed acting ever after. It was odd not to be able to share such a huge part of my life.

Now I was to spend the best part of a year in Mexico. Robin would not accompany me; he needed to find work in England. I knew I would be homesick for my house and my cats and our easy life and our friends, but I also wanted to get away. In the small hours of the morning I could not escape the fear that our relationship, Robin's and mine, was close to ending its course. Born in a series of random chances against a background of confusion and need, the attraction had been real enough, but after seven years the differences between us were becoming more marked. I think it irritated Robin to find all the radios in the house retuned from Radio One to Radio Four as much as it irritated me to walk into a room to find, nine times out of ten, a quiz show playing on television. But these were small things, I told myself, and marriage was a big thing. I couldn't bear to be seen to fail again.

Chapter Thirty-seven

Robin and I have a Venetian holiday with Bill and Bryn before I leave for South America. Bill and I have tried to acquire the rights to the E.F. Benson books featuring Mapp and Lucia and George and mad Irene. No success. London Weekend Television has the rights and is just sitting on them. It's maddening. I don't necessarily want to *play* in the show, but I would love to be a part of getting it done properly – properly, as I see it, that is. Ah well. Our other attempts at producing are also unsuccessful. We both love a book by Russell Hoban called *Turtle Diary*, but we miss the rights by a day. Our other obsession is J.R. Ackerley and we buy the rights to *My Sister and Myself*, but it's regarded as too 'depressing'. It is, in fact, hilariously despondent. We spend a fair bit of money on this before we give up and go on holiday. It's good to share my insider's view of Venice. All the Venetian friends and acquaintances come through magnificently and we have a wonderful time. Then Bill starts a novel and I go to Mexico.

For a month I sat in my bedroom on the twenty-first floor of the Century Hotel in Mexico City waiting vainly to be called to work. The budget was so enormous that they could afford to call actors and pay them to sit in the hotel doing nothing for weeks on end. It was a bizarre experience living at the Century; the lift was out of order, so it took a long time to reach the street by the staircase. The building, like most of the fashionable Zona Rosa, was constructed of artificial fabric; nylon, vinyl, plastic, concrete – all totally unsuited to the climate. I walked to the Zocalo, the big square at the centre of the city, and wandered enviously through the Majestic Hotel, made, Spanish-style, of wood and stone and marble, the deep-set windows catching every breeze. For the whole of that month I stalked through the city, visiting every art gallery and museum, speaking to no one. No one from the production office telephoned me and one day I felt so isolated and unnerved that twice I fell over from a standing position. Robin, in the interest of economy, had ordained that we shouldn't speak on the phone except in the case of emergencies. (It was *very* expensive calling England.) What constituted an emergency, I wondered? The fear that one was losing the power of speech? Driven in on myself, I kept my eyes open and watched everything around me. On Grasshopper Hill, below Maximillian's Palace, I saw a family, out for a Sunday picnic, with a bald turkey on a leash. He seemed very content. One very small obscure exhibition pricked my imagination into seeing Mexico City in a new light. It was an exhibit of drawings and watercolours from the nineteenth century, all executed by the wives and daughters of diplomats from Europe. I had no idea that Mexico City had remained luxurious beyond Parisian standards well into the nineteenth century, when it was still a city built on water – as it had been to a greater extent when the Conquistadors crossed the causeway to be greeted as gods by the inhabitants of the beautiful island. When I was there, Mexico City contained seventeen million inhabitants and the pollution was unbearable. At night I leaned out of my window and watched the smart streets gently invaded by beautiful Indian families who slept in the doorways of the expensive shops. One became sick merely by breathing the foul air, but the romance of the location had gripped me, thanks to those watercolours and drawings, and I never lost my 'inner' view of the city and grew to love living in it.

I was, however, lonely for a few months; we worked very long hours and returned to the city too tired to go out. I spent long hours at night learning new songs, listening to Peggy Lee and Mabel Mercer hour after hour. 'Why?' I wondered. Just for fun? Maybe. Work was slow and the script was difficult to follow, but director David Lynch and the actors were wonderful to work with and I learned something about being a lone lady traveller; I learned not to travel light. I had observed Kate Hepburn arriving in Provence for the filming of *Lion in Winter* with her books and her food and her companion and her record player and her easel and her canvases and paints and special china. At the time I'd thought she was being a trifle eccentric. Now, I saw the good sense of carrying one's world on one's back, like a snail. I acquired books and drawing paper and tapes and a recording machine and vowed never to be caught short far from home again.

During the year I was able to return to London a few times and Robin flew out for a holiday once. We had different ideas about how to spend a holiday, so it was only partially successful; he wanted to lie on a beach and I wanted to explore. I found it hard to spend days on the beach and Robin didn't relish the long, hot journeys in rickety buses into the interior. We compromised. Towards the end of that year Robin got his first really good job in a TV series with Terence Stamp, whom he came to admire enormously. It gave his morale a huge boost and I hoped it would be a turning point in his fortunes.

By now both my daughters had gone into the theatre. I, alone, was surprised by this, which indicates that, far too much, I accepted things at face value; they displayed no interest in drama while they were growing up, so I assumed they *weren't* interested. Now, belatedly, I realised that it must have been hard for them to declare themselves in that intensely theatrical household. Pat had got herself into a drama school in London (informing me of this after the event). When Kate came to the unhappy end of a love affair, her father took her to New York and she began a new life in America, first running somewhat wild in Manhattan and then, effecting a major change, entering Yale where she studied to be a dramaturge and was side-tracked into acting, leaving Yale to study in San Francisco and then in New York, where she began acting professionally at the Irish Arts Centre. She now came home to stay with me for the first time in years and I was mightily impressed by her appearance; drop-dead chic and, typically quirky, combining an elegant wardrobe with a startling punk haircut, and rolling her own cigarettes with flair and skill (one hand). I had watched Pat develop into the radiantly pretty girl she was and wasn't surprised by her control and her enviable insight and good sense, but now I *was* surprised to be getting along so well with this elegant creature whom I had spent so many years trying to alter. Thank goodness I'd had no success at all, I thought again, and counted myself lucky in my grown-up children. It did occur to me, not for the first time, that maybe I wasn't at my best trying to communicate with *small* children.

I was in a musical which was not a success, but which was running in spite of its cool reception by the critics. It often happens that a poor show can lead to something wonderful. In this instance *Peg* led to two important friendships, one with musical director Kevin Amos, with whom I began an enduring musical collaboration, and the other with an actor who became my very close friend and with whom I later shared my house – Edward Duke. At the moment when I met him he had been gathering praise and awards – and lots of money – for his portrayal of P.G. Wodehouse's Jeeves in a play he'd written himself, *Jeeves Takes Charge*.

A nice, eccentric man called Louis Busch Hager was obsessed with a show, which we always referred to as 'Peg-the-Musical'. (It was *Peg*, a musical version of the Laurette Taylor vehicle 'Peg o'My Heart'.) Lou was the scion of not one but two wealthy American families. Someone explained to me that innumerable people drink the Bush beer, Budweiser, and that every home has Hager's hinges on its doors and windows, so there was money raining down from all directions. His wife was sane and lovely, but his mother gave one pause. She was called 'Poomey' (or 'Pumi' or 'Poomi'). We presented the show when it wasn't ready to be seen, because Poomey had flown over on her birthday with a Concorde-ful of friends. In the event, she passed on the opening, but when she did decide to come she sat there, squat and bejewelled, occasionally, when pleased, letting out a loud whoop and exclaiming, 'That's mah boy!', compounding the confusion in the stalls of the Phoenix Theatre.

David Heneker was the composer and musically the show was first rate. Edward became, like Bill and Bryn and Ricci, one of my adopted brothers. We met on a nasty February morning in Pimlico. We'd already been rehearsing for a week and Edward had been detained in America. I'd obligingly written down his moves and what little dialogue we possessed from a threadbare book, which was to be whisked away and rewritten. He was hugely tall, jet-lagged and barely coordinated, long legs and arms and narrow patrician feet and hands shooting off in all directions. During the morning we rehearsed a scene and I told him I'd 'filled in' a script for him. He looked at it as though he'd never seen a script before. (Well, it wasn't *much* of a script at this point and already he'd realised that this was going to be a *sauve qui peut* job.) 'Don't think I want that, love pot. How about a spot of lunch?' Scarcely pausing to shake his head reprovingly at the nourishing grains and fruit generously provided by Lou, he took me by the hand and ran me from the gastronomic wasteland in which we were rehearsing in the direction of the only good restaurant for miles. 'If I don't have a decent lunch I get – unhappy,' he remarked, as we tucked into a large meal at Pomegranate. From that moment on we were inseparable, eating and drinking *far* too much each day, spending most of our salary at the Caprice at night. Never in my entire life had I eaten 'proper' food so regularly. Never in my life had I laughed so much.

When we moved into town the company manager, whom we cordially disliked, had appropriated what should have been his dressing room on the ground floor, so we shared my number one suite and our blossoming friendship made the whole trying experience bearable. Lou gave me orchids instead of the rewritten script and amazingly didn't take offence when, exasperated, I threw them down the corridor. Sir Ronald Millar, who for some reason was engaged to write a new version of a perfectly good book by Robin Miller, delivered bits of text after we'd actually opened on tour. Infuriated by one – as I thought – useless contribution written on the back of an envelope, I was panicked into yelling, furious and exhausted, 'This just won't DO!' He rounded on me. 'How many authors do *you* know,' he demanded, 'who drive a *Rolls-Royce*?' As I struggled to shape a reply I could hear the strangled noise of a hysterical Edward Duke going back to a darkened dressing room for a lie-down.

It was an unusual experience in all respects, but it had another happy outcome. By the terms of my divorce, the girls were to be supported until they'd finished their higher education. Kate's allowance had stopped when she left Yale and she was now living on a shoestring and also needed to pay off her student loan. I was happy to be able to turn over to her my earnings from a show I hadn't been proud of. Of course, if I hadn't spent so much time and money in the best West End restaurants with Ed, I would have had money left over for me as well. As it was, after my grand gesture to Kate and her current boyfriend who was also short of funds, I had to go back to work – fast.

Sara found a play for me that might be suitable for Robin as well and for that reason I agreed to try it. I was to play an older, professional woman who dumps her long-term middle-aged lover (wonderful Moray Watson) for a delivery boy on roller skates (Robin). I noted gloomily that it was *French* and what kind of luck did I ever have with French plays? None. Charles Savage was to direct – very bright and very handy with rewrites so we might stand a chance. Edward, before he left the country, read it and said bluntly, 'Absolutely no, sweetie.' But when did I ever listen to reason? Too late now, anyway.

The play goes its long, predictable way. We try. We really do. Charles is valiant. In the end, after months of struggling, we fail.

The only nice things that happened during the latter part of 1984 were, firstly, that I was to meet Irene Handl and she came to the house for lunch – big hat and all. It so thrilled me, to see her sitting there, eating *my* food at *my* table, that I was struck dumb. I love her acting and her two novels and her love for Elvis Presley. The other was that I was able to do the best thing imaginable for my mother. The University of Wales made me a Doctor of Literature and I took my mother to the ceremony in North Wales and was able to invite her sister, Meriel, as well. The two old women had the time of their lives, seeing people they hadn't met for fifty years. No one paid much attention to me and I stood back and watched Sally and Meriel queening their way demurely around Bangor.

I was moved by the ceremony, but as we were waiting to process into the hall and organs were playing and trumpets were beginning to sound, Sheikh Yamani reached under his Doctor of Law gown and, producing what looked like a medicine bottle, said, 'This is very special perfume – only for my family – made for *me* only, in *my* factory.' I was standing there with five or six distinguished academic gentlemen and we nodded and stood frozen by surprise as he liberally splashed the scent all over our robes, so that, when the doors opened, we marched into the great hall on a tidal wave of what smelled suspiciously like Jungle Juice.

A few weeks later I had reason to feel that my debt of gratitude for that weekend in North Wales could never be repaid. My mother was diagnosed with lung cancer and her doctor told me that she would not live more than six months. Meriel, her sister, was magnificent and navigated her way from Carmarthenshire all over the outer margins of north-east London to be with her sister as they waited for the results of tests and queued endlessly to be seen by a succession of doctors. The first hospital my mother went to was Dickensian and I came upon her, stripped and wrapped in a blanket, sitting up, cold and scared and confused after one of those painful, lung-draining injections. She was confirmed in her fear and dislike of hospitals and I noticed that whenever we drove past a hospice in north-east London – remarkable for its cheerful exterior – she pointedly turned her head away until we were well past it. I took the hint. Hospices were out. I began to plan her last six months. My sitting room was slightly raised above street level and caught whatever sun there was. Her bed could sit in the window. My National Health Service doctor put me in touch with the Islington Social Services and I had good reason to regret joining in the criticisms of the 'Looney Left' which abounded at the time. They asked me if I needed cleaning help – I didn't, or Meals on Wheels – no, or help with bathing and lifting – it might come to that later. Should someone help with shopping? No, but I outlined my plan to bring my mother's bed into the sitting room where she would feel part of our lives and have a good view of the street. The social worker's eyes lifted from her note-pad. She looked surprised. 'Have you consulted your family about this?' 'No,' I answered, thinking what is there to consult about? She nodded and said that I was over-confident to think that I could keep my mother at home until her end but that she would monitor our progress and provide me with extra help, when it was needed.

After she'd gone, I thought again of her question about the reaction of 'the family' to my decision and realised that I was going to keep my mother at home for as long as possible, no matter what Robin's reaction might be. I could see that my decision would cause trouble in our rela-tionship and I was prepared for that. My mother regarded him with a cool eye and he, for his part, seemed divided between fearing and patronising her. He was also anxious that we should move upward in the property market and our choices were limited by my insistence that any house we bought should contain an apartment for my mother and space for at least one daughter. For the moment she was able to live independently in her flat.

Christmas came, uneasy this year, and for me everything was coloured by the awareness that it was Sally's last winter. I discussed my domestic plans with no one. There seemed no sense in precipitating a row with my mother, who wouldn't wish to be dependent, and with Robin, who would not welcome the inconvenience.

February was a month of birthdays in the family. The women took turns in preparing the birthday dinners. It was my mother-in-law Eleanor's turn to prepare Robin's party at their family home in Bayswater. I privately commemorated my father's birthday and filmed some musical sequences for a *Life of Siân* that was being prepared by an independent TV company. But glittering and being gay did not come easily.

On 10 February, the day of Robin's birthday party, I got ready to leave for Eleanor's house. It was so cold. Robin went to the car and I ran down the side path to the garden entrance and knocked at my mother's apartment door. When she opened it I saw that she was look-ing very chic in a Jean Muir outfit; hard to believe that she had ever been chronically overweight. She was shivering, 'I don't think I should come. I'm *so* cold.' 'Oh, come *on*,' I said, bossily. 'Let me get you a warm wrap. You're coming, so there.' We got into the car. She was in the front and she took a long look at the house as we drove off, turning her head to keep it in her vision. Sometimes my mother's sense of drama really annoyed me. I thought to myself, 'I'll bet she's counting the times she'll drive away down Oakley Road never to see it again. *Damn* the drama!'

The Sachs's house in Kildare Terrace was brightly lit on every floor. I noticed my mother straighten her back as we climbed the steps. Glitter and be gay. We were nine for dinner and Eleanor – a wonderful cook – was busy in the basement kitchen. I went to offer help, but she didn't need it. She was looking as pretty and as unruffled as if she'd just popped in for a cocktail. As usual I marvelled at her powers of organisation and her sense of perfect presentation. In the first-floor drawing room, Leonard was dispensing champagne cocktails and my mother, glass in hand, was deep in conversation with her favourite of Robin's relations, his Aunt Toffee – not in showbusiness; bad legs, a slave to her cats, indomitably coping with her long, lonely widowhood. My daughter, Pat, arrived. Because she was taking drama classes in Bayswater she had taken to popping in regularly to Eleanor and Leonard's house. I sat next to Toffee and Sally in the first-floor drawing room. 'D'you know,' said my mother to me in Welsh, 'I don't feel so wonderful.' 'Would you like to lie down?' 'Maybe, for a minute.' There was a day-bed in the closed off 'L' of the drawing room and she lay down while I fetched a glass of water. Pat – devoted to her grandmother – began to say, 'Let's get a doctor.' 'Oh, don't be silly, Pat,' I said. 'Just make her comfortable.'

Pat and I sat on either side of the narrow day-bed and I began to think that something unusual was occurring. Robin and then Eleanor looked around the door and went away. Pat and my mother and I were alone in the room. Sally began to breathe more urgently, deep, rasping breaths. Pat became agitated and I told her to be calm and hold her grandmother's hand. Again she said, 'We should call a doctor.' I was sure that we shouldn't. Then my mother spoke for the first time. Her voice was strong and magisterial. 'Take off these clothes,' she said. I had a moment of not knowing what to do. 'Undress me,' she said in the same strong voice, the voice that, as a child, I had obeyed without question. I looked at Pat and we both rose and began to take off the Jean Muir coat and blouse and skirt. Then the petticoat. Then the spotless white corset with its myriad hooks – how had she ever done them up I wondered. I had never seen my mother's bare flesh and I hesitated now before dealing with the straining hooks and eyes. Pat took the initiative and loosened the suspenders and rolled down the stockings. 'Go on,' said the voice – it seemed there was nothing of my mother except her voice – and I began to push and tug at the hooks and eyes. We discarded the bits of metal and rubber and steel and nylon and elastic and silk and wool. They lay on the floor and Pat and I stood one each side of the smooth, smooth white body. 'We're here. We're with you,' I repeated inadequately. I had a feeling that it no longer mattered to my mother whether or not we were here with her in this back room in Bayswater. Her breathing changed. I had never heard a death rattle, but I recognised it now. I clutched my mother's hand and lowered my head. And after a while, knowing she was gone, I looked up and saw Pat staring, staring at her dead grandmother.

I looked at my watch. Barely fifteen minutes had passed. My mother's dying seemed to have taken longer, a great deal longer.

I did everything badly for the remainder of the night. It was as though I'd lost any sense of how to behave properly. Pat was now the person who needed attention and I didn't give it to her. Eleanor gave me a loose robe and I dressed my mother in it. I was all daughter, nothing of a mother. Unbelievably, after calling the undertaker, I said we should go ahead with dinner. Who knows what everyone wanted to do? I, in my distraction, imposed a form of behaviour on them all. Conversation was impersonal and polite. The men arrived to take my mother away. Sitting across from the dining room door, I saw the bound body as they carried it down and out of the front door. After dinner we went home. I find it hard to believe that we took Pat home to her flat and left her there instead of bringing her home with us. But we did. I find it painful to imagine how she got through the night. When I got home I began to weep for the first time. Robin patted me sympathetically. Later he reminded me that we were now free to move house. I felt a small canker of disdain for him, which never went away.

In my mind I relived that February night in Bayswater, and over and over again I picked and worried at that fifteen minutes. Something had happened that I hadn't noticed, something momentous had occurred when I wasn't paying attention and I'd missed it.

After the funeral in London, a tear-drenched, crowded affair, conducted partly in Welsh and attended not only by our small family, but by Kate's former boyfriend all the way from Clifden in Ireland (my favourite but never-to-be son-in-law) and undergraduates of Kate's and Pat's generation and staff from the North London Collegiate School, I was swamped with letters and, this being a Welsh occasion, poems written for the occasion. Meriel's bore a card saying in Welsh 'One small step behind'. Kate was back in America and unable to return, but as Pat and I stood to say goodbye to the people who had attended the funeral I was surprised to find myself face to face with O'Toole. I hadn't spoken to him since we parted on the pavement outside the costumier Nathan and Bermans, and now we shook hands and he left. We hadn't exchanged a word since we'd parted.

Pat and I went back to work the following morning. Robin had made all the arrangements, dealt with the technicalities of death in a city. There were times when I couldn't imagine how I would manage without him. Now he set me house-hunting. It was something to do when the acting stopped.

Chapter Thirty-eight

Ricci got married! Consternation fought with rejoicing among his many friends, mostly women, to whom he was indispensable and to whom he was always available. Who could not wish him happiness? Nevertheless, it was going to be something of an exercise in timing and limiting one's phone calls and one's demands on his time and attention. House-hunting alone, I found a house on the day of his wedding and rushed on foot from Ripplevale Grove in Islington to the Register Office in W1. Oh, I *was* unreservedly happy for him. His bride, Rachelle, was ravishing and as eccentric as he. Her small child was a dark beauty. After the brief service we lunched rather grandly and privately, and I was proud to be part of the small and select wedding party. Looking at the two of them, I had a feeling that they were going to achieve an unusual and successful union. Almost in passing, I noted that *my* third attempt at marriage seemed to be faltering. I put the thought out of my head and raised my glass to Ricci and Rachelle and J.J., their small boy.

And so in 1985 I began the process of buying another house, a house which was at once a dream and a nightmare. Ripplevale Grove was one of those pretty roads, nestling in a conservation area, immaculately tended, always 'desirable' in the estate agents' lexicon. The houses were late Georgian, two storeys high, double fronted, like doll's houses, with front paths leading to neat front doors, fanlights intact. In fact, the houses were surprisingly intact inside as well as out. There were modern extensions leading into the large gardens overhung with tall, mature trees. It wasn't until I talked to Jack Pullman, the writer of *I, Claudius*, that I realised why the house retained its windows and shutters and was very little affected by ugly 'improvements'. When Jack and his wife, Barbara Young, arrived for dinner in the new house Jack said, 'I have to sit down with a stiff drink. I haven't been back here since I was a boy.' I gave him a drink and he said, 'I swore I'd never come back. I was so glad

537

to get out. This was the roughest area in Islington. Boy Scouts needed police protection to get to the club house.' I couldn't credit what he was saying and, seeing my astonished face, he said, 'When we left our house in Hemingford Road to go out and play, the last thing my mother would shout was "DON'T GO UP RIP!"' (which was what they called Ripplevale Grove). No one had been able to *afford* to improve the houses until they were slowly bought up by sympathetic people from the class of chatterers – of which I was one. I could only just afford to buy the freehold of Number 15 and I suspect that I was able to buy it – heftily mortgaged – only because it needed a new roof, new plumbing, new wiring, new floors, new walls in some rooms and there was dry-rot and rising damp as well. It was a gem, but it was to keep me poor for the next five years as I worked incessantly and poured all I earned into fixing the house and garden. The constant work and the strain of living in a building site was also to put an intolerable burden on my marriage.

The house bought and the builders engaged, I went to Northern California to make a film about Ewoks. The producer was George Lucas. On the plane I developed acute sciatica. Surrounded by beauty and hospitality, courtesy of Edward Duke's incomparable address book, I was in such pain that I slept standing up for a month and suffered appallingly as we worked the long hours six days a week. Kate joined me for a brief holiday, and on the day she nearly missed her plane back to New York I found that although I couldn't lie down or sit or walk, I could run. Thereafter I cranked myself up each day and ran around the quiet neighbourhood in Marin County where people didn't walk *or* run.

Painfully, I flew home and moved house. Having a 'bad back' didn't quite convey the pain of sciatica and I couldn't explain to Robin why suddenly I didn't want to carry heavy objects. My back had been giving out a few days before opening night for almost ten years and I had survived a couple of weeks of bearable pain and then snapped back to normal. Now, it took almost two months of truly severe pain before I recovered. I was worried. I had managed to get through a month's filming, but I could never have opened a play in this acute distress. I saw doctor after doctor, got myself X-rayed, talked to chiropractors and surgeons and, having been told that I was stuck with this condition for life – '. . . look at the X-rays. Wear and tear I'm afraid, my dear' – I still couldn't accept it.

I baulked at surgery, bided my time. We moved, with an army of builders, to the new house and I began rehearsing *Gigi* in Chiswick. It was to move to the Lyric in Shaftesbury Avenue. I was not getting on with my director, John Dexter, but, mercifully, I was on the best of terms with my 'sister', Beryl Reid, and Jean-Pierre Aumont and Geoffrey Burridge and Amanda Waring, who was *Gigi* (and Dorothy Tutin's daughter). Although my sciatica had run its course I knew that, come opening night, I might fall ill again. I was desperate. Robin had been annoying me – playing at helping the builders when it suited him; slowing them up, entertaining them to breakfast. I stood drinking a coffee in what would, one day, be the kitchen while the men sat on the only chairs in the dining-room and talked about 'manly' things before starting work. I could have done with a lift part of the way, but our car sat in the street outside and there was murder in my heart as I left the house and ran past it on my way to the tube to Chiswick and to difficult John Dexter. Within a few weeks Robin and his brother were given a gift of money by their parents and decided to spend all of it going on a wonderful holiday. Robin left a list of things I was to make sure the builders finished before he returned and off he swept to Maui. His behaviour so embarrassed me that I couldn't think of anything to say to him. He didn't notice that I was less than chatty.

After he left, rehearsals became more and more unpleasant. John Dexter antagonised each member of the company in turn – I wondered when it would be mine. Every night I cleaned up after the builders, left a list of things I'd like them to do on the morrow (I had actually built a house so I could see what they were or were not doing), and tried to keep myself reasonably clean and tidy despite the dust and dirt that enveloped me and my clothes. When Robin returned after two weeks, tanned and fit and deeply critical of the lack of progress, I looked at him and wished him buried under the rubble that was the house, with John Dexter for company, but I didn't know how to confront him and could only back further and further away, hiding behind a veneer of good behaviour, implacably determined to keep my distance from him. Unfairly, I blamed him for not seeing that I was angry with him. Unreasonably, I blamed him for not being telepathic. Stupidly, I blamed him for qualities which had drawn me to him in the first place, a kind of sweet laziness.

By Christmas, *Gigi* was almost ready to open in the West End. My turn to be worked over had come, so had Jean-Pierre Aumont's – I'll never forget the look on his face when he realised that he was being insulted. A polite, impenetrable shutter descended, shutting out John Dexter for ever. I think John had an idea that breaking people down was in some way good for them and he was also patronising about the show, looking down his nose at its middle-of-the-road appeal. I met the writer of the show, Alan J. Lerner, in the wings as I was bracing myself to begin a dress rehearsal. 'You leaving?' 'Oh, yes, for good.' 'What do you mean?' 'Look.' He raised his hands; the nails had bitten into the palms of his hands and left a red, bleeding line. 'I have to clench my fists or I'll knock him out – and he's got diabetes, so I can't.' Dexter had just slung the great lyricist out of the theatre where his own show was to play and he was going, deeply, deeply hurt.

I was assured that John Dexter had once been a wonderful director. Right now I could only rejoice at the story that the opera star Julia Migenes had chased him out of the Met in New York when he was running the theatre – she got rid of him for showing disrespect! I hoped I would meet the glorious creature one day. Jean-Pierre and Beryl both wanted to leave, but we all calmed down and I fell completely under Beryl's spell and had more fun on stage than I'd had for a long time. She improvised, flirted with the audience, doubled the playing time of our scenes if they were going well, cut out bits if they were going badly, but never ever took her eyes off me to see if I was coping. I'd been a comic's 'feed' for six months when I was a young girl, so I was accustomed to a comic's lust for the audience's love and approval and laughter. I rather shared that feeling and felt privileged to be part of this great comedienne's nightly love affair with the house. Every weekend she bought presents of game and fish for me from Berwick Street, and I bought fruit and veg for her, and we couldn't have had a better time. And John Dexter never came near us after opening night.

Christmas arrived and the whole family came to visit me in the only-just-completed house. I had Christmas day off and would have liked to have gone to bed for the holiday. The Burmese cats, Spencer, Barnaby and Rupert, sat high up on the tops of cupboards, fascinated by my seasonal efforts down below. As I was trying to stow away the dishes from the turkey part of the meal and tearfully retrieving my mother's Christmas pudding (injected with potheen – illicit, clear, raw Irish spirit) made the previous year, from its long, cloth-bound boil, Spencer decided to descend for a better view and somehow landed in the white rum sauce, at which I dropped the hot pudding. The three cats and I stared at the wreckage on the floor.

'Anything wrong?' cried someone from the dining room. 'No. No. No,' I responded, on my hands and knees, trying to rescue pudding and sauce and leave out the slivers of glass.

As I presented the dish to an unsuspecting table, I hoped I'd got all the glass out. I hoped. But I didn't really care, I was too tired and sadly I never exchanged a straightforward word with Robin after that year, 1985. The year of my mother, Sally's, death.

Chapter Thirty-nine

How do people end relationships 'amicably'? I wish there were a manual. After all these years and all these liaisons, I'm at sea, rudderless. The awful thing is I suspect Robin feels as badly as I do, but when I try to broach the subject he backs off and won't discuss it.

There is a practical problem. No matter how grand or carefree one might try to be, money can be a terrible source of discontent. Robin has always said that he doesn't mind that I am the breadwinner – and at first I was grateful for that. Now, after some twelve years, I'm less grateful. Occasionally, he says that if things don't pick up he's going to have to 'get a job' (meaning a non-acting job); this is offered as the most awful move imaginable, but I think that getting an honest job, *any* sort of job, might help us both feel better. And he does feel awful, I can tell. He and Richard La Plante build their bodies to perfection. He learns karate and does well, and then stops at the point of gaining his black belt. Why? I feel sorry for him as he comes home from the gym and retreats to the garden room to lie on the couch and watch game shows. There is nothing I can do for him – or for myself. He's begun to gamble regularly; he really enjoys it, so I have little objection. I think I understand this desire to have a smart car and be seen in smart clothes at the gaming tables. I may be harassed and overworked, but I am doing a job I love and spend my days with people that are the best possible company. The life of a chronically out-of-work actor is truly awful. The spectre of unemployment terrifies me so much – a legacy of my childhood in Wales – and I can't discuss the problem but pick up the bills and cover the debts. Also, I did take the wedding promises seriously; this is worse rather than better and poorer rather than richer and there is sickness at the heart of our life, but this is what it is. The future seems hopeless.

A few things helped me along the way. Fenella Fielding, when I told her about my despair of ever curing my treacherous back, had suggested that I should consult a friend of hers from Israel, Lily Cohen, who had been a dancer and now taught Tai Chi and the Feldenkrais exercise system and did a lot of voluntary work with old, disabled people. Feeling older than God's mother and twice as disabled, and having exhausted all other avenues, I now embarked on a three-year course of treatment with Lily. We worked in her apartment in Bayswater three times a week and gradually my back grew stronger and I just knew that one day I was going to be completely 'normal' again. The regular exercise also improved my mood and, as an added protection against depression, I joined a drawing class so when I wasn't rehearsing or playing, I nipped into the Mary Ward Centre in Holborn and did a spot of bad but absorbing sketching – anything rather than sit at home. When I had a play to learn, I made that an excuse for going out of town; once I went to stay, alone, in a hotel near Lincoln Cathedral and another time Sara allowed me to use her country house in Norfolk where I learned lines and painted and became cheerful until my return home. I also got it into my head that the whole family should learn to meditate and that was an astounding success. Kate, who was back from America and now working in England, really loved the discipline, but Pat was not so sure; Robin persevered and I added it to my cocktail of activities designed to keep me on an even keel. The garden thrived, the house improved gradually as I acquired well-paid television jobs. I was by no means out of the wood financially because our future seemed so precarious and the house continued to be a heavy drain, but when I got an unexpectedly large cheque, I was able to go back to St Laurent after a considerable absence and kit myself out grandly for the first time in years.

I was working really hard on the TV series, *The Snow Spider*, in Wales when I was asked to go and see Milos Forman and was delighted to have the chance to meet a man I admired so much. Trailing a lot of luggage and destined for Paddington, I made a detour past Blake's Hotel where he was staying. Would I read, asked the Czech fascinator; 'Well sure,' I purred, having rolled over on my back, charmed. And having read, I pushed off to mid-Wales. Sara was furious. 'You didn't have to *read*. You've *never* had to read.'

A few weeks later I was asked back. Again, on my way to work in Wales, I dragged my suitcases down to Blake's and had another enchanting meeting with Mr Forman. Would I read a scene *with* someone? 'Oh, of course,' I crooned, rolling over again. Sara was fit to be tied. 'What are you *doing*?' 'Well, it was fun.' I forgot all about it.

A few weeks later Milos wondered if I could assemble a kind of costume and learn a *scene* and do it with a few people and he would film it. This time I didn't dare tell Sara what I was up to. It was another Monday meeting and again I toiled down with my luggage and a token costume. This time Milos *directed* a scene and it was massive fun. I pushed off to Builth Wells again. Ages later I was told that I was the first person Milos had cast for the movie, *Valmont*. Never can a part have been obtained more light-heartedly or more pleasantly (or more secretly).

So, it was to be Paris for six months. I hadn't been in Paris since I was a rich person, living at the Meurice or in our apartment at the George V, dining out every night at the best restaurants, the newest night clubs. This was a very different life. I no longer knew anyone there and I lived quietly, but I was ravished anew as, this time, I walked and walked around the city and we worked in the most beautiful locations. And I met Annette Bening (playing Mme de Merteuil). She was not only beautiful and talented but good and wise and lots of fun, and I learned a great deal from watching her. She was patient and friendly to everyone in that enviably open American way. When bad things happened she dealt with them by going for a long run along the banks of the Seine. She possessed formidable discipline and a huge sense of the ridiculous. We both loved and admired Milos Forman, who, when he was working, was the most tactless person imaginable. He was so intent on the work in hand that his thoughts sprang from his mouth uncensored and uttered in endearing Mittel European. One day as we were working on an endless tracking shot in the Musée Camondo (which was 'my' house in the film), we repeated our scene over and over and over and over again. The unit grew apprehensive as it looked as though we girls were going to cop it any minute. Sure enough, an anguished scream from Milos: '*Why* are you behaving like ziss? *Why* are you talking in such a peculiar way? *Why* do you *walk* like zat? *Why* can you not be like *peeple*? *Why* not be *natural*? *Tell* me *why* you do it?'

Disconsolate, we turned to go back to our first marks and begin again, and Annette under her breath said to me, 'We do it like *ziss*, Milos, because we want you to hate us. And we do it like *ziss* because we want never to work again.'

I stored her in my mind as an example of good behaviour and there she stayed.

At Christmas, Annette's then husband, Steve Black, came to visit her from America and Robin joined me. It was an uneasy time. Robin was veering between low spirits and the sort of extra high spirits which none of us could match. The long separation was tearing apart the already threadbare fabric of our life together. When I returned to London, Kate came to stay and that helped somewhat. Robin was very well mannered and more good-humoured when she was around. Even so, the atmosphere became more and more strained. I had very little idea now what made up Robin's daily routine. Where did he go in his BMW? What did he do when he wasn't at the gym or the casino? Once, in a family crisis, I needed to find him and I called the place where he'd said he was spending the day – he'd not been there since early morning. When he returned at night I asked if his day had gone well. 'Oh yes,' he replied and I found I had neither the will nor the inclination to question him further. Perversely, I felt guilty about the episode, as though *I* was the one leading a secret life. As I went through the motions of being a 'good' wife I wished that something or someone would happen along radically to alter everything. Since I lacked the courage to force a discussion, there was nothing for it but to hope feebly for a theatrical, *ex-machina* solution. Something along the lines of 'with one bound she was free'.

Robin was marooned in a comfortable world, but dependent on me, where the phones rang for me, a world in which, at almost forty years of age, he was still referred to by journalists as a 'toy-boy', where strangers called him 'Mr Phillips'. He no longer kept my accounts as he used to. It was as though by distancing himself from the practicalities of life he distanced himself from all responsibility for the mortgage payments, the taxes, the insurance and the day-to-day task of maintaining a life.

Gradually, the house grew glossier and the cats thrived; when they weren't fighting each other, they lay on the most comfortable chairs, a beautiful heap of shining brown, grey and red-blonde fur, but I looked at them and myself and felt that they, the house and I had all lost our lustre in Robin's eyes.

There was very little time for moping. I was always busy and the girls were both acting as well, and when I went to see them I found, to my surprise, that watching them brought nothing but pleasure, with none of the fear and torment I used to feel when watching their father (or when I was a child, my father) on stage. Out of the blue I had been commissioned to write a book about needlepoint. Coral Browne had taught me the basic stitches in the Sixties and I had made some large pieces; now I struggled to complete the book (sewing to a deadline was much worse than writing) and continued to film the TV *Life of Siân* that had begun so many months ago. It was meant to be a story told without narrative or interviewer's questions; just pictures and songs, shots of me opening a play, rehearsing, performing songs. This was a difficult concept, made doubly difficult by my unwillingness to reveal anything about my crumbling private life, and it seemed to drag on interminably. Edward Duke came to stay and developed a new hobby – cooking. It was a measure of my fondness for him that I didn't turn a hair as my immaculate kitchen became an impenetrable no-go area, piled high with blackened pots and dirty dishes and spilled sugar, flour and gravy. (The food, though, was spectacular.)

I piled on more and more work – besides writing and sewing and filming musical segments for *The Life*, I began to rehearse a play by Loleh Bellon, *Thursday's Ladies* ('Another French play,' I thought with misgiving). The other Ladies were to be played by Eileen Atkins and Dorothy Tutin, the one handsome young man by Jeremy Brudenell. I was delighted to be directed again by Frank Hauser. It was too much to resist. We played ourselves as toddlers, children, teenagers, young women, switching from one age to another with no warning or preparation. Frank didn't want to help the changes by making lighting adjustments, so we did our level best to age or rejuvenate in an instant, switching from one age to another with startling suddenness, concentrating like mad. The three of us worked hard – and happily – but the play, which was so much fun to do, wasn't, we gathered, nearly as much fun to watch. One of my faithful fans said to me at the stage door, 'Oh, Miss Phillips, some of these foreign plays you're in – I do *dread* them.'

It was a short run, but one night I met a great friend of Eileen's, an actor whom I hadn't met since the Fifties, Ken Parry, a rotund, Dickensian figure, with shiny, round eyes that missed nothing and rosy, pursed lips that conveyed disapproval or disbelief in hefty quantities. We realised that we were neighbours and began to visit each other and became friends. From Wigan, but born in Wales of Welsh extraction, Ken's English was eloquent, sonorous and magisterial, and I began to collect his more ornate tirades against the sheer bloodiness of life. Some of his pronouncements were startling. 'Albert Finney was on a bicycle as I came down the street with me teeth in, and there were six nuns passing.' 'I first met Charlie Kay with a parrot in the Edgware Road.'

'Gloria Swanson told me all those lies. For instance: she told me Rudolph Valentino wasn't gay.'

I moved straight from the play to a musical at the Donmar. Bill Bryden and Sebastian Graham Jones were going to write the show, called simply *Brel*, as we rehearsed the sixteen or so Jacques Brel songs that would make up the evening, and Bob Crowley would design the sets and costumes, and the company was to consist of two 'mature' voices to sing the songs of experience and a young man and woman to sing the love songs. In the event they failed to cast an older man, so I sang all the 'mature' songs, including one for which I was totally unsuited though I struggled (manfully) with it, and Alex Hansen and Kelly Hunter sang the songs of youth. Dressed by Bob in leather, I walked on to his ravishing set (three full-grown trees set on an empty stage and the walls of the Donmar painted *Gauloise* blue right up to the roof) and opened the show singing 'Amsterdam', a tough song about tough, louche sailors. 'Go on. You can do it! Don't fuss!' they cried, and in the end I didn't fuss, although I wasn't convinced I could do it (I think the meditating was taking effect). I loved doing the show and, during the run, something inside me changed. Then, just before Christmas, I experienced one of my rare, strong, Technicolor™ dreams.

Bob's set for the second half of the show was dominated by a vast dining table covered in a white tablecloth, with huge gilded dining chairs set around it. There was a picture of Brel propped on the chair at the head of the table, which was set with large crystal goblets. (One of the songs in Part Two was called '*Le dernier repas*'.) One Saturday night Robin picked me up after the second show and we set off to spend the weekend with Bill and Bryn, now living in Herefordshire. I strapped myself into the back and fell asleep instantly. Over an hour later I woke and saw that we were travelling very fast and that Robin was drinking from a hip flask. He was a responsible driver and this was very unlike him, and for a moment I was speechless before finding far too loud a voice and demanding to know what the hell he thought he was doing. The 'Don't Drink and Drive' campaign was still in its infancy, but, given my early experiences of being terrified in the car of a drunken driver, it was understandable that I should greet the campaign with enthusiasm. Absurdly, I demanded to be put out on the deserted roadside and Robin, refusing, insisted that he was perfectly capable of driving. The flask was, however, put away and we pitched up at the house silent and angry but unharmed at about two in the morning. Sizing up the situation, Bill and Bryn nervously suggested a quick bowl of soup and bed. I awoke from my dream at five in the morning. In it I had been singing and dancing Brel's 'Funeral Tango', which Alex Hansen and I used to do as a duet while Kelly Hunter looked on, and at one point, dancing down the length of the dining table, as I looked down to check where I put my feet, I saw in the dream that all ten goblets were filled with salt instead of wine. The salt was as white as the tablecloth, and the chairs, upholstered in red brocade, which was meant to echo the red of the wine, stood out shockingly as the only splash of colour in the 'room'. I lay there thinking that the goblets held the bitter taste of a souring marriage. I had no glimpse of resolution, but at least I had been brought sharply to a state of awareness. My temporary solution was pretty useless: work harder.

Simon Stokes asked me to play Amanda in Tennessee Williams's *Glass Menagerie* – another of those parts, along with Hermione in *Heartbreak House*, that I was always being told I was 'born' to play. I'd had my fingers burned with some of the 'born to play' parts, but the combination of Simon and Tennessee convinced me to accept the job at the Arts Theatre in Cambridge and after that on tour. Once again, I came to the conclusion that I appeared to do better in roles that seemed unsuitable for me. I never convinced myself as Amanda and also committed the ultimate sin of taking against my character. All my sympathy was with the boy, Tom, who escaped his family; Laura, the lame daughter, got on my nerves, and I would have liked to shake Amanda until her teeth rattled. I just couldn't make a 'case' for her and that is a recipe for failure. I wasn't helped by the fact that I smashed my foot on a concrete block while I was running to have lunch with Colin Firth's mother in Winchester. By the evening my foot had swollen to double its size and we had to cut away half of my stage shoe (off-stage I wore a man's sock on my right foot). We were playing on a vertiginous raked stage – so fashionable in the Eighties – and I could scarcely hobble across it. What the audience made of the play in which the daughter's limp is one of the main features, when her mother's limp – never referred to – was much worse than hers, I can't imagine. The huge foot was extremely painful and showed no signs of subsiding.

The play ended in June and I had a few weeks only in which to pray that I got better soon because I'd agreed to do a play in London for Christopher Renshaw, with whom I'd been working on the score of a musical by Jerry Herman called *Dear World*, which we hoped to do together. Meanwhile, the play we were engaged on was a French comedy, set on the Avenue Foch, which meant clothes from Paris and *very* high-heeled shoes. In the nick of time, the swelling went down and I managed to squeeze my foot into a smart shoe. Another French play, *Paris Match*. Will I never learn? Stephen Murray, Leslie Ash and I bore the brunt of the action and we did everything to that play short of blowing it up and jumping up and down on the bits. The great Ray Galton came in to help and gave me some wonderful, sure-fire laughs, which helped me, but nothing could help the play and a month after we'd opened in town I gratefully hung up my stilettos for the last time. But I couldn't take a break, unable to face the prospect of spending time at home.

Chris and I doggedly went on working on the musical (which never did happen) and at the same time I went into another play, *Vanilla*, this time an American play by Jane Stanton Hitchcock, which was to be directed by Harold Pinter. It was extremely incorrect politically and very funny, and that, coupled with Harold's name and the prospect of working with a wonderful cast under the management of Michael Redington, lured me on board against the advice of friends who now (rightly) sensed an element of panic in my choices. We came into the Lyric on Shaftesbury Avenue and as though doing the play was not enough, after the performances on Saturday night a car would pick me up and take me on the long journey to mid-Wales, where I would work each Sunday and Monday morning on a television series, *Emlyn's Moon*, returning in time for the show at the Lyric on Monday night. During the weekdays I busied myself with broadcasts and recordings. The fact that I loved what I was doing couldn't disguise the fact that it was largely displacement activity. Taking on more and more responsibility at work was the only way I could hide from myself the truth that my life was out of control. The play did not succeed, but I made enduring friendships with the author Jane Stanton Hitchcock and one of my favourite Irish actors, Niall Buggy, with whom I shared a dressing room. We co-existed – I, pin neat, and he, unbelievably untidy – without flying at each other's throats, and continued to keep company harmoniously ever after.

After a long illness, Robin's father died and left him a substantial sum of money. He genuinely forgot to tell me that he was proposing to go to Los Angeles for the period in the spring of the year, known in the television world as the 'pilot season'. For two or three months there is huge activity as innumerable new shows are cast and tried out. Most fall by the wayside, but it is a time to see people and be seen and, of course, some people are lucky and get very lucrative work. Robin was comically mortified when he realised that he had discussed his plans with everyone except me. (I *was* out most of the time.) I considered this to be a good move on his part and helped him all I could, compiling a book of useful addresses and contacts. Ricci, when I told him the news, said, 'Well, that's the last we'll see of *him*.' I was so exasperated; such a glib, superficial, over-dramatic reaction, I thought. On 6 January 1991 I went to Heathrow and waved Robin off. After he'd passed through the barrier I stood unseen, watching his figure grow smaller as he descended a long ramp before disappearing from view. He looked vulnerable and very alone and I prayed that things would go well for him.

The atmosphere at home had been more friendly than it had been for a very long time and the parting had been easy because I was due to visit New York, Los Angeles and Washington within a matter of days, as a guest of Mobil Oil, who presented much of our TV output in America. We were to celebrate the birthday of Masterpiece Theatre on Channel 13. We were flown to New York and went on to L.A. where Robin and I were reunited. He came to stay with me at my smart hotel for a few days. Waking early near Venice Beach, I stood on the balcony and wondered why no one had mentioned that the city was framed by beautiful pale purple mountains. Robin was unexpectedly sweet and affectionate, shedding a tear as we parted after a few days, he to resume settling into his life of flat- and job-hunting and I to attend a dinner in Washington. He was due home in three months.

Our caravan moved on to Washington, where we arrived on the eve of the Gulf War to be entertained by Mobil Oil in the beautiful reception rooms at the top of the State Department Building. There must have been some local doubt about the wisdom of this event, but it was decided to go ahead and some thirteen of us British actors went up in the modern lift through the modern building and stepped out into the eighteenth century – it was *such* a *coup de théâtre* and we were suitably stunned into open-mouthed, silent admiration. The veteran broadcaster Alistair Cooke gave us a tour of the rooms and we sat down to eat, two actors to each table of eight Americans. The tables were charmingly decorated with appropriate 'props' from plays in which we'd appeared. Jeremy Brett was at my table and he shamelessly switched place cards so that he could sit next to me and, as he explained, 'that halves the talking I have to do'. He ate nothing, I remember, and when I urged him to taste something he muttered, 'No, no, no, this is much too impressive and I want to concentrate on it.' We were given a tour of the city late that night and there was a light at every window in every government building. It was overwhelming, being in a place that would see no rest, where the lights would not be extinguished throughout the night. In the morning the United States went to war and we flew home, subdued.

Chapter Forty

I remained subdued until Edward Duke came to stay with me while we worked together at the BBC on a series of Noël Coward playlets, hardly distinguishing ourselves, alas, but having a lovely time at home cooking and watching incomprehensible Indian musical movies late at night, playing with the three cats, enjoying a spot of domesticity. We were juvenile, if not childish – and we were happy. Edward had become ill and I was aware that with the close of the pilot season my problems would reappear as urgent and as fresh as ever, so we ignored the future and took care to keep each other amused. When we finished the long job at the BBC we went our separate ways and for some time to come the laughter ended for both of us.

Before I embarked on another stage play I went to visit Robin in L.A. As I made my travel arrangements I found myself wondering why I was going on the visit; he was due home in a few weeks' time. He wasn't there to meet me when I arrived. I waited, feeling anew that this trip was a stupid mistake. My fellow passengers had all left when he appeared, eating. He explained that – waiting for me – he'd felt hungry and nipped out for some Mexican food. No apology. My uneasiness grew and stayed with me for the whole week. We were in an odd situation, partly estranged and partly over-familiar. I was genuinely pleased for him that he'd done an episode of a TV series and pleased also that he seemed so at home. He'd rented what I thought was a rather nice house, which he shared with another English actor, but he didn't like the neighbourhood, not smart enough, I gathered, and hadn't done anything much to brighten up his part of the house. He seemed to be abstracted, waiting for something else to happen. We made a trip to San Diego, but he was anxious to return to L.A. We saw friends for lunches and dinners, but I felt he was eager to resume his 'normal' life – whatever that might be. I couldn't work out what he did all day. I was uneasy.

It was a long week. My spirits rose slightly as he drove me to the airport. 'See you in a month's time,' we chorused too brightly. The plane was delayed. I suspected that neither of us could endure to be locked together in the intimacy of waiting for a plane and I asked if he'd mind if I went through so I could do a little work on the play (an adaptation of *The Manchurian Candidate*). Robin made a small show of reluctance and we parted. Miserable as I had been, now I fairly skipped through passport control and I imagined that he, too, must be happy to be driving alone through his beloved city. It really was dear to him. A few days previously, as we'd driven down a hideous road – gas stations, low, shoddily built shops, fast-food restaurants stretching for miles, disaffected youth lounging on the pavements – and I was wondering how this endless, messy sprawl had come about, Robin broke the silence saying, 'Isn't it *wonderful*?' I smiled, not speaking. It was charming and disarming, his genuine love of the place. As I pottered about in the airport, feeling better than I'd felt all week, I wondered again what form our future life could possibly take. Was he dreading a return to the poor weather and lack of excitement of London N1? Did London seem dull? Was the British actor's life of lower rewards, lower expectations, dreary in his eyes? When I tried to talk to him about the future, he'd protested that London was 'his' town, his home. But I was sure that he'd fallen in love with Los Angeles. When he'd run out of money, would he want us – me – to maintain a home there? Should I embark on such a costly enterprise? How could I live in L.A. when I didn't drive? I had a score of questions and no answers, so I settled down to work on the play until my flight was called.

The stewardess tapped me on my shoulder as I sat in my economy seat and asked me to come through to the first-class section of the plane. I was nonplussed until I saw Suzanne Bertish. I didn't know her but of course I recognised her. She was returning to London after doing a stage play in L.A. Forceful and authoritative, she'd just *told* someone to move me forward. I was impressed and grateful. I would never have thought of asking. As we talked, I mentioned that I didn't drive, and instead of sympathising as everyone else did with my horrible experiences culminating in car-phobia, she reared up and said that it was *ridiculous* not to be able to drive and that doubtless my fears had nothing to do with cars or traffic and that I ought to *address* the problem and why hadn't I already *done* so? Losing interest in that, she moved on to other areas where I might smarten up a bit – chiefly, as well she might be, astonished that I'd never read anything by Robertson Davies. We talked and talked all the way across the Atlantic and it was one of the most lively and agreeable of long flights. But driving? Despite Suzanne, I couldn't see myself behind the wheel of a car.

The play to which I returned was a version of the novel *The Manchurian Candidate* by Richard Condon (father of my friend, Debbie). John Lahr had cleverly adapted and updated the book. I would play the hateful mother and Gerard Murphy, an actor I much admired, would play my son. We were to tour the play before bringing it to London for a season at the Lyric Hammersmith. Apart from anything else, I thought that this would give me a chance, once and for all, to perfect a good Southern American accent, and I began to work with Joan Washington, my favourite accent and dialogue coach.

Neither the play nor the accent was easy and I had no time in which to worry about myself until, a month later, it was time for Robin's mother and me to collect him at Heathrow. It was morning when we met him and Eleanor drove us back to Islington where I served a very quick lunch of pasta and salad. Robin exclaimed how wonderfully 'Californian' it was. It was evident that anything that might even remotely be considered Californian would be wonderful in his eyes. I felt a little defensive and was glad that it was a lovely spring day and that the garden, while not Californian, was looking very beautiful in its damp English way. Within days I left to open the play in the South of England, rushing home on the last train on Saturday night in order to spend the weekend there before travelling on to the next 'date' in Manchester. I was glad that Kate was staying at the house so that Robin – somewhat disoriented – wasn't all alone. I suspected that he hadn't wanted to leave California. He'd been gone five months, two months longer than he'd intended to be away. As I lunched at a friend's house while I was on tour in Manchester, Kate telephoned, very excited, to say that Robin had auditioned over the phone for a part in the mini-series of *Dynasty*. The actor playing one of the sons had dropped out for some reason and he'd got the part and was needed immediately in L.A. He'd gone while I played a matinée! It was like a fairy tale. Kate and I were beside ourselves with excitement. It was so *American*; the unexpectedness, the speed of it all. Although it wasn't long in duration, this job somehow justified all the time and money he'd spent in L.A. since January.

Later, I sat on my bed back at the little hotel where the company was staying and found myself writing a description of the room with its cheap bamboo furniture, cunning use of small space – the pretty bedside lamp just that bit too small and too low to make reading in bed comfortable, the little ornaments from Spain – noting the dull weather and the view from the window over the suburban backyards and knowing that this was the watershed of our life together. Nothing would henceforth be the same. I looked at the page and thought that maybe I was over-reacting. Robin's last message had been to wish me well and to say that he would be back for the opening of the play in London. I was unreservedly happy for him and if this job went well then it might follow that our lives might begin to make some kind of sense. It wasn't a job I would much want to do, but it *was* a job and it might, with luck, help him on the way to a viable career.

As he dashed to the airport, returning to the balmy weather and the smart hotel, with his car waiting for him, I walked through the drizzle and caught a bus to the Opera House. My life was the usual combination of job satisfaction and anxiety and discomfort. It was not a life that Robin had ever truly embraced. And now he had a job in the beautiful climate that made him happy.

Chapter Forty-one

Our set for *The Manchurian Candidate* – a huge piece of scaffolding –
was difficult to work on and rather dangerous. Actors with vertigo
had a particularly terrible time as they clung on to their moorings
near the top of the proscenium arch. Clive Carter saved Gerard
Murphy from plunging twenty feet to his death or horrible injury by
grabbing at his waistband and praying that the wardrobe department
had done a good job on the seams. We ran out of money in Cardiff.
Our director had to leave to do another job. John Lahr was valiant
(and generous with cash), and his friend Karel Reisz kindly stepped in
to direct us. It was business as usual – part of the rough and tumble of
putting on a play – but it was wearing and I was tired when we
returned to London. The mini-series was soon over and Robin was
expected back any day, so I hastily organised a celebratory garden
party for him. Then he called to say that although the show was over
he was detained in L.A. I cancelled the party. His mother, however,
was not pleased with him. After my opening night she and I went out
for a small dinner with friends and I made excuses for him. In all fairness, I didn't totally disbelieve him. He might be evasive, protective of
his privacy – I sympathised with that – but he had always laid great
store by truthfulness and honesty.

Not only did he not return for the opening, he didn't return for the
whole run of the play at the Lyric. There were 'people to see', hopes of
'another job' – it was all very understandable, I thought, and moved on
to another job, a television series called *The Chestnut Soldier*. One day I
astonished myself as I lifted the telephone receiver and dialled a driving
school that was offering a week's intensive, residential driving course,
culminating in a test at the end of it. I arranged a place for myself the
day after I finished the television series. I replaced the handset and
wondered why it had taken so long for Suzanne's words to goad me into
action.

Now as I nervously got ready for my driving course, I called Robin for reassurance and couldn't locate him. At last he called me and I was relieved to talk to him because he was a brilliant driver and I especially needed his encouragement and advice. I wasn't nervous – I was petrified; and what was propelling me forward? Was it Suzanne or a wish to make it possible for me to live in L.A.? I had no idea. Robin seemed bemused as well and wasn't quite as impressed and helpful as I'd hoped he would be. He seemed distracted. When I hung up, the phone rang and a woman from the driving school said that there had been a clerical error and my place was not available after all. I stood in the dining room in Ripplevale Grove, unable to move or think. If I couldn't begin this feared, dreaded venture and begin it at precisely the moment I'd planned, I didn't think that I would ever be able to begin it. It was established, like a challenging rock-face, in my mind and I couldn't imagine not climbing it.

Barely coherent, I called my daughter Pat and she, sensing that I'd lost my grip, told me to hang up and do nothing until she called me back. In less than half an hour she'd found me an alternative (non-residential) course, an instructor with whom I'd work all day and every day for a week, and she had booked me into a small, quiet boarding house in Chester. She'd found the times of trains and I was to leave London in a few hours. I don't know that I thanked her properly, but I did exactly what she'd told me to do. Before I left, I ran round to the shops at the Angel and my wallet was stolen. Back at the house, cancelling credit cards, I felt defeated before beginning; what if I sat in the car and burst into tears? What if I ran it into a wall? What if I killed someone? What if I simply couldn't move at all? What if in twenty minutes I couldn't leave the house? I called Morag Hood and told her how bad I felt. She had a brainwave. 'Shall I consult the I-Ching?' she asked. This seemed to have a wonderfully calming effect on me and later she told me that she realised at that moment that I was fairly demented. When, before hanging up, I thanked her for her help and remarked that I had been quite sure she would be able to offer 'practical, down-to-earth' help, she had stood there with the I-Ching in her hand half laughing and half seriously concerned for the innocent people of Chester.

I don't recall what the I-Ching said, but it should have told me that I was going to meet an angel in the guise of a driving instructor. He told me on the first day that there was no possibility that I could sit and pass the driving test at the end of a week; such boasts on the part of the driving schools were stupid. Occasionally a young man of around nine-teen might pull it off, but the rest of us didn't stand a chance. 'But you'll be driving in a couple of days,' he said matter-of-factly. It was a mile-stone week in my life. I was so anxious to live up to this lovely man's expectation that I became calm and methodical once I was behind the wheel. My feelings of unease were very near the surface the rest of the time. One day in the break between a daylight and a night driving lesson I went into a church and sat listening to an organist practising for a concert later in the day and found myself overcome with sadness and apprehension. Something was terribly wrong and I felt that if I sat there for another moment I would see clearly what is was that was stalking me. Drying my tears, I hurried into the narrow, busy street. I wasn't ready to confront the beast. Not yet.

I returned to London, having driven with my instructor to Warrington and back – at night! I felt that I *had* climbed the North Face of the Eiger. Bill Corlett, as he did many times, urged me to enjoy my accomplishment for a day or two, but, as usual, I could only think how much more I had to learn and went to the BSM to arrange a course of lessons in London starting at once. I would never again find an instruc-tor like my saviour in Chester, but I no longer needed an angel – I was almost normal.

Robin was not in the flat I'd found for him (Gwen Humble's apart-ment – a smart address, more to his liking) and I had to wait to tell him the incredible news that I was actually up and driving. I had given him the address of an Anglophile with a lovely ranch in Santa Barbara, who had been married to a rich man and, parted from him, had fallen into a lucrative career doing voice-overs. Her ranch – the Red Rooster – was a haven for depressed foreigners, especially Englishmen. I had been urging Robin to call her and finally, after a lot of nagging, he did and was invited to spend a weekend there. He'd gone back to the Red Rooster for a last visit before coming home for good. He was still there when his niece was taken ill and I had to reach him a few days later. Morag Hood, who'd lived in Santa Barbara for many years, said that it was understandable he should linger there as it was one of the most beautiful, seductive places in the world. I urged him to make the drive up to San Francisco as well before returning.

It was October and Bill, Bryn and I made a trip to mid-Wales to visit a wonderful house where I'd spent some time filming in the summer. We always had a good time together, but this visit was cold and dark and wet and we were in unusually low spirits. Robin was due back in two weeks' time and there were preparations to make for his return. Excepting a week at home in May, he'd been gone for ten months during 1991.

I'd convinced myself that life in London would be dull for Robin, so I'd accepted some smart invitations I might otherwise have declined. On his return, as soon as he'd caught up on some sleep, we had a perfectly hideous night out at a smart charity ball, then we were taken to the Ivy by the producer of *Valmont*. I went on with my driving lessons and a dull week went by, during which I went to an award ceremony in Manchester. Understandably, Robin felt he needed some time at home to reactivate his London life, so he didn't accompany me. I was nominated for an award for *The Manchurian Candidate* and Sara and I made the trip together. After a few hours of hilarity at the lunch, I realised how little light-heartedness there had been at home during the past week. Before I set off for London, I called Robin from the station in Manchester and he sounded surprised to hear my voice. I told him that I hadn't won and he seemed confused and confessed that he hadn't realised that I'd even gone to an awards ceremony. 'He must be very jet-lagged,' Sara said. It didn't occur to me that he might meet my train and he didn't. 'Are you all right?' I had asked him from time to time – too often to judge from his impatient reaction. I resolved to stop asking.

On the first day of the second week we arranged to meet a friend near Regent's Park and took a walk beforehand. He was abstracted and hating the weather. The day was just about as raw and as unpleasant as it ever gets in November in London. Everything compared unfavourably with California. I had run out of excuses, but I felt protective towards the dozy waitress, the tepid coffee slopped into the saucer, the miserable geese in Regent's Park, the low, grey sky, the litter drifting about the pavement. I wanted to stand between him and them so he couldn't look down on and despise them. We met his friend, Clive. 'Are you looking after this lovely woman?' Clive asked, as he often did in his kind-hearted, unthinking way. Robin didn't respond at all. Usually, he made a joke in reply. I began to collect myself and grew quieter. Quite suddenly, I felt very uneasy indeed. The beast was coming close.

At home I made a simple supper, which we ate on trays in the garden room, while watching a video of *The Bonfire of the Vanities*. 'You look very sad,' said Robin rather accusingly, and there, in that moment, I felt the thing which had been lurking about the edges of my life detach itself from the shadows, visible only from the corner of my eye, and emerge into the bright light. I looked at it and heard a voice – my own. 'Is there someone else?' Even as I spoke the little cliché, I began to feel the beginning of a surge of energy. The reply hardly mattered, but it would come, after a move into the dining room and a great deal of displacement activity and huffing and puffing and bluster. 'Yes,' he said in the end and his relief was palpable. How long, I wondered, would he have gone on saying everything was fine and he was glad to be home?

As he grew almost elated after his admission, I grew despondent and my resolve to clean up this mess as fast as possible wavered. I felt weak and unconfident and it was common sense alone that got me through the next hour. Life, I reminded myself, had been unsatisfactory and unhappy for years. Since we moved house five years ago, after my mother's death, and since Robin had caught a glimpse of the promised land in America, our life had disintegrated beyond repair. He'd found a new 'family' in Santa Barbara, complete with stepson, dogs, cats, garden pond. We had been wretchedly unhappy. There was nothing to salvage, no loss to regret, nothing worth keeping. Better to end quickly. '*Llosga fe mas. Paid llusgo fe mas*' – 'Burn it out, don't drag it out', was the Welsh saying that came to my mind.

He was so excited now that he showed me snapshots of the ranch – very nice; himself and a very nice-looking woman in fine-weather clothes doing fine-weather things – very nice. I felt that he would like me to enthuse more. 'Very nice,' I said and told him that he should go back there at once. He looked alarmed. As a matter of fact, I told him, I had to be out of the house early in the morning and it would be a good move on his part to move to his mother's apartment before I got home in the evening. He began to protest that we should consider what we were doing and not do anything hasty. I told him I had no intention of taking the scenic route towards the divorce which loomed ahead and that was as nasty as I got that night. In the morning I had promised to be at a press conference for the launch of the TV series I had made for HTV, so I had to take my hopeless, fine hair to the hairdresser very early. There scarcely seemed any point in going to bed, but I had a bath and changed and we sat up in the bedroom talking, and now that all the ties had been loosened and we weren't *supposed* to be getting along with each other, I felt quite well disposed towards him. He was no soulmate, not even a real friend, but I didn't dislike him at all that night.

In the morning I called Bill and Bryn and Sara and she said that Bryn Newton, her partner, would meet me and take me to the press conference for *The Chestnut Soldier*. I pasted a smile on my face, which stayed in place until I saw Bryn and we went for a chilly coffee in Covent Garden. He was so wholeheartedly on my side, so unashamedly supportive, that it shook my composure. At the press conference there were many of the usual questions concerning the difficulty of maintaining a marriage and a career. Bryn's handsome face was grim, but he knew that I wouldn't falter in public. He and Peter Murphy, the producer, and I drank a great deal of coffee and I went for a driving lesson, surprising my instructor as I charged between the buses at the Angel with unaccustomed brio and resolution.

The day was far from over and I went home to change before joining Ricci and Rachelle for a dinner party we'd arranged for Robin in the Caprice in Mayfair. Robin was in the house; he'd almost finished moving out and he said he'd drive me into the West End. As we left, I asked him for the house keys and he seemed startled, but gave them to me without comment. And what would happen to his BMW? It had been an expensive purchase and he said he'd sell it as best he could and return me the money. Arriving at Ricci's house, he came in and asked if he could still come to the Caprice for dinner. He was navigating without a map and his responses were bizarre. Ricci explained to him that it would be quite inappropriate for us all to spend the evening together. He added that Robin would be much better off in California and that we should never have married in the first place and what a blessing it was all over. Robin looked more and more glum and finally left us and drove off. I was exhausted I realised, but there was no doubt in my mind that I was experiencing a lucky escape. And there *had* after all been a *deus* – or *dea* – *ex machina*. I hadn't had to do anything except indicate the exit.

I had arranged a series of dinners at home for Robin and now I decided not to cancel them. I had better start getting used to entertaining alone – officially alone, that is. Robin came to finish his packing as I rushed around preparing dinner. I hitched up my skirt and realised that my waistband was hanging around my hips. I had unbounded energy and I'd lost a huge amount of weight in twenty-four hours. I was shocked when Robin made to embrace me and I flinched away from him, offended. I couldn't even muster a smile and realised that today I was disliking him rather. Was nothing going to remain the same for more than a few hours? He told me to 'go easy' on myself and not push the driving or force myself to go to all the Christmas parties we went to every year – and maybe cancel some dinner parties. He probably meant well, but I was seized with rage and resolved to redouble my efforts to become a driver and that the stove at home should scarcely be allowed to cool between meals and that I'd get Ricci to find me a new wardrobe for gadding about. I kept my fury well under wraps as I wished him well and told him that he'd be free as soon as I could arrange it and that he shouldn't worry unduly about me. 'Anything you want to ask me?' he asked. I couldn't think of anything at all.

I never saw him after that. He went to America and six weeks after his departure – exactly a year after he first went to California – we were divorced. Ricci had been right, in principle, when he'd said in that January of 1991 that that was the last we'd see of him. Now he said, 'You'll never hear from him again.' I tried on my new wardrobe; I was almost two sizes slimmer than I'd been six weeks previously. Large mercies.

Chapter Forty-two

After a roller-coaster life of much happiness and many troubles, a woman of a certain age makes a break for freedom. She makes a critical error of judgement and against all expectations enjoys some years of uncomplicated happiness, but thereafter finds it very difficult to pay for this pleasure when the bill arrives, as it surely does. She is released from her impossible life with the minimum of blame, the maximum of sympathy, some hurt pride and public humiliation, and a greatly improved financial situation, and she recovers her health, not to mention her figure, and knows in every part of her being that what happened is for the best. She proceeds with life. She is content.

For a moment or two it seemed that that was the story, but almost immediately in that winter of 1992, something went terribly wrong. My shiny new clothes hung in my dressing room where I had expanded into all the capacious cupboards. Now that I had only myself to think of, my hair and nails were expensively groomed and tended. The house had the air of 'my house', the phone rang constantly, I was surrounded by new friends as well as the group of friends that I called my 'family'. My real family was solidly there for me. Everyone was relieved for me. Everyone took care of me. The welcome-home dinners for Robin went on, although he was probably back in California. Sara must have called the girls and they both turned up unexpectedly during a dinner party, Kate all the way from Ireland where she now lived, blowing in, dishevelled. I was dangerously overwhelmed with gratitude for my daughters and I looked around the table at them and my friends and thought myself fortunate.

One of my chief tasks in those early days was to console someone who had become a close friend during Robin's absence in America. Kevin Moore's dismay was almost comical. He was the person who had provided me with the Santa Barbara address which I had given to Robin, with much urging to use it. Now he blamed himself for what had happened at the Red Rooster. I tried to convince him that what had happened wasn't his fault at all and that in any case it really was for the best. He had been helping me learn to drive and now he continued to do so. Tart of tongue, maliciously funny, he was also a man of principle and distressed to find someone he had thought to be a friend had behaved shoddily, as he thought. Missing little, he probably sensed that I was not quite as serenely over the upheaval as I thought myself to be. Bill and Bryn monitored my days by telephone.

Sara called me every morning before she opened the office and Bryn (Newton) called later in the day with a carefully prepared, hilarious piece of gossip. Kate stayed with me and was wonderfully, unfairly partisan. Pat was close at hand – all strength and health and sanity. Ken Parry summoned me to his flat and lectured me on how to live my life with the minimum of pain; evidently, and rightly, he wasn't one of the friends who anticipated a problem-free time ahead. I listened to his warning of trials to come without really understanding it.

Ricci and his mother Lilian were pleased at the turn of events and Ricci expected me to snap back to normal at once. For the first time in our friendship he made a misjudgement and it caused our only estrangement. It was temporary, but it came at a bad time for me. He so wanted to see me happily established and looked after that he began to cast around for a new partner ('not necessarily to *marry*') for me. We didn't see each other until he promised to stop introducing me to strange men whom he considered 'suitable'. His childlike hope would have been to see me reconciled to O'Toole and it was very difficult to explain to him that such a thing was unfeasible and undesirable. In any case, we were unlikely ever to be in touch again. The divorce wasn't through when suddenly I began to feel bad. Very bad. For the first time in my life I couldn't sleep more than a few hours a night and would wake at four o'clock in the morning – three cats on the counterpane – and lie there shaking with fright. What was I afraid of? I didn't know. Weeping silently, I would ask myself what I was crying for? I didn't know. Kate would say, 'Why didn't you wake me?' But what would I wake her for? I had no idea what – fear aside – I was feeling. It was clear to me that something bad was overtaking me and I had no idea how to deal with it. By day, I was all right for a great deal of the time, then suddenly I would be overcome with sadness and fright. The hours between four and seven a.m. were hideous. Edward Duke called from San Francisco. He'd just finished a performance and his dressing room seemed jammed

with *I, Claudius* fans. A stranger to economy at the best of times, he put
them all on the phone to me in this worst of times. He had his own
problems, but he spent hours on the phone every week and knowing,
somehow, that I wasn't doing very well, he drew me a road map for
getting through miserable days. On his advice I bought a small notebook and when I felt I couldn't continue some ordinary activity, like
walking across the concourse of Waterloo Station, I would stop, duck
into an empty doorway and write down exactly how I felt; after a few
pages I'd find I could, as he'd promised, resume everyday life again. The
only truly 'safe' time for me was late at night, when I returned home
after an evening out or after work. 'Home to an empty house', words
of misery and foreboding for many, was, and always had been, for me,
a happy phrase of promise. Now, the moment of knowing myself to be
completely alone for a few hours was one of the truly happy times in
what had become an unhappy life.

I didn't know what to do, but I began to realise what I must *not* do.
I dimly understood that the perception of me by many was that I was
good wife material. Wrong though that was, I could see how my industry, good manners, sense of responsibility, cheerful temperament and
general deceitfulness would have brought about such a belief. Once
again, as had happened when O'Toole and I parted, I began to receive
proposals of marriage – mostly from people I had known years previously (and many of those were, I felt, polite gestures), but some, comically, were from total strangers. (One man enclosed a statement of his
assets with letters from his bank manager.) It became obvious to me that
people thought I *ought* to be married and looked after, partly, I suppose,
because for over thirty years I had *been* married. I myself knew that no
one needed less looking after in that married way than I, and I saw
clearly that the one thing I must not do now was to fudge whatever was
happening to me with the distraction of a close relationship. For the
first time in my life I was going to stand alone.

Things took an unexpected and hateful turn and I struggled between
genuine misery and true annoyance. What happened seemed
monstrously unfair and I didn't like it one bit. Every bad thing I had
ever done came back to haunt me. Every mean thought and malicious
deed reared up as though it had happened only yesterday. At first I sat
up in bed in the ugly, small hours and wrote notes about my sins of
omission, my careless cruelties. After a few months of that, I couldn't
bear it any longer and just lay there, appalled at myself. But it seemed

so unfair, to be visited in this way. *Why* was this happening to me, I wondered, resentfully? I confided this to no one. Someone would be sure to say that actually I was quite a nice person and I wanted to be the one to decide that, sometime, maybe never. Conversely, during the days, memories of great *happiness* intruded, no matter where I found myself. I had lived in London for a very long time and had been happy and sad in almost every part of it. Every miserable moment forgotten, I was assailed by recollections of intensely happy times with the children when they were small, with friends, lovers, husbands – even with Robin. I was cursed with the remembrance of the happy years when we first met and the contrast with my present state was torture.

Everything went wrong at home; the vacuum cleaner broke, the washing machine 'died', the downstairs loo jammed, and one rainy day a plumber came and dug up the yard and £400 later was about to begin taking up the utility-room tiles, when a kindly builder across the road took pity on me, came in and fished out a small deodorant container which had lodged in the 'S' bend. I shed tears of self-pity and gratitude. I felt so *clueless*, and kept cutting myself accidentally, and then, worst of all, Spencer, the oldest of the three Burmese cats, became very ill. It rained and rained and Kate and I went to and fro on foot to the vet. Finally, I took him to live in my bedroom, coaxing him to eat from my hand. He was the cat that adored Robin and now I fancied he must sense that Robin was never coming back and for the first time I was filled with real anger. Spencer spent the last week of his life in the vet's surgery, on a drip. He died on the night of 13 December. I asked for his body, not his ashes, and went to Upper Street to fetch him. It was raining when I carried the heavy burden back to be buried in the garden. The ground was hard and Kate and I had to use my mother's favourite gardening tool, a small pickaxe, to dig the grave. We were so cold and wet that we had to keep suspending work to come indoors for cups of hot tea. We cut ridiculous figures – dirty, laughing and crying and shivering and hacking out a grave. We buried Spencer wrapped in the cover of his favourite velvet cushion, broke his feeding bowl and put in the bits, and added a few olives, to which he was very partial. He was twelve years old. Rupert and Barnaby slept, warm and dry, throughout the miserable afternoon.

I planted a rose on Spencer's grave. 'Isfahan' sounded good and it was only after I installed it that I learned that its alternative name was 'Pom Pom des Princes' – just about as unsuitable a name as could be imagined for big, grave, humourless Spencer. The thought of Robin with his new family of cats, taking his ease in the sunshine while we buried Spencer in the rain, so infuriated me that I broke a lot of china that he'd been fond of and felt better immediately. I realised that I was teetering on the brink of very foolish behaviour.

Before Christmas I began rehearsing *Painting Churches* by Tina Howe, a play I had agreed to do before Robin's return. It didn't go well in any sense and Tina, whom I admired and liked enormously, didn't even stay in London for the opening, leaving for Paris in order to avoid what she was sure would be a disastrous production. We were underfunded and came very close to being forbidden by Equity to perform, which would have been a shaming experience. In spite of the difficulties at work, riding home from the Playhouse on the Embankment to Barnsbury and my 'empty house', I realised that I was content to be working, doing what I was meant to do. That was no small thing, I told myself.

Kevin and Kate and I went to the country to Bill and Bryn's for Christmas. People say that however bad things are, they seem worse at Christmas, but I didn't feel that at all and we all had a lovely time. But even I smiled as I unpacked and laid my bedside reading on my night table and wondered how many people would have included *Living with Grief* along with the Christmas presents. Bill was one of the few people (Edward was another) with whom I could be totally honest, and he bore the brunt as I talked and talked. He and Kenny and Kevin all let me ramble on and on during those months when I needed to be allowed to ramble and I could only hope that they had a mechanism which filtered some of the nonsense I must have been speaking. I had never before confided in anyone, had always had a horror of boring people or embarrassing them or being a nuisance, and now that I'd begun to talk, the floodgates opened and washed over my closest friends. John Ehrman, the director, sent me books and advice from America. I clutched at everything indiscriminately and gratefully.

After months of this I wondered desperately whether I would ever again be free of fear. All the while I meditated night and morning and never missed doing the Feldenkrais back exercises I'd been taught by Lily Cohen, though I found I was at my most vulnerable and sad during the solitary twenty minutes of exercise. I longed to escape from the house but, ironically, work now kept me chained to London. Kate went home and before Edward returned, I schooled myself to live quietly with my unhappiness and to accept and come to terms with my own deficiencies, turning over and over in my mind the harm I'd inflicted on other people, the absence of kindness I'd shown only too often. My mother had never asked me for anything, but I knew what she would have liked to have and what mean-spirited arrogance it was that made me deny her a fur coat for her old age. I knew what she had in mind when she talked of fur; a musquash, no shape, grey, smooth and warm, as worn by the senior mistress at my grammar school. The coat of a woman who, though she could not afford a motor, went to Bruges for her holiday and once to Oberammergau for the passion play and who, if she chose, could go to see an Ivor Novello show in London. It was the coat of the woman my mother could have been. 'Fur? No, no liberal-minded, caring person wears FUR nowadays!' My mother, transported from the Welsh countryside to the expensive shops of Hampstead, struggled politely with this glimpse of fashionable caring and nodded her thanks for the gift of a lovely and costly woollen cape. What mean impulse made me deny her the thing that would have made her harmlessly proud? It wasn't a small thing and it was one of a host of misdeeds that crowded into my mind, clamouring for attention. I was being brought very low.

My strongest resource, my reasonableness, was useful now, if only to preserve the framework of 'normal' life, enabling me to work and even to play a little. What I thought of as 'real' (hidden and secret) life was all tumult and confusion and I moved through the unfamiliar territories guided only by instinct; I neither questioned nor challenged the rhythms of this interior existence. As I sat alone with myself, I grew less appalled by myself and less interested in myself, but I knew that this miserable period was not over by a long chalk. Less and less I wished that I knew where I was going or what I hoped to achieve, and I stopped worrying about my lack of purpose. The natural world exerted the same power over me as it always had and I didn't worry at my inconsistency in finding myself in a sad mood, then suddenly engulfed for a moment or two in happiness; a change in the weather, a trick of the light in the garden was still enough to surprise me into delight. The cats made me laugh. I laughed a great deal the day a blackbird walked portentously into the kitchen and looked at me and two inscrutable Burmese faces hanging over cupboard tops, before turning tail and walking out again.

The days began to lengthen and I vigorously reclaimed the garden for myself, uprooting without a qualm all the plants that Robin had chosen and which I rather disliked. It was deeply satisfying to be re-arranging and replanting and learning the workings of the lawnmower (previously considered too 'difficult' for me). As I wrestled with the pond and its pump (also too difficult), I realised as well that I would never achieve Robin's way with animals. The fish ignored me; they used to feed from his hand. But it was deeply satisfying to see the garden looking just as *I* wanted it. I turned my attention to the house, which for a while had become an object of hatred, and gradually I came to like it again as I rearranged it and altered it. On impulse, one day I heaved the matrimonial bed into the front garden and bought a lovely new one from Heal's. Recalling Bob Crowley's set for Brel, I had the front hall and the staircase and the landing painted the colour of a *Gauloise* ciga-rette packet. Every morning I felt a surge of energy as I stepped into the wonderful blast of blue.

I still felt fear and pain, but I had lost the wish to chatter and the need to validate everything I saw or did by sharing it. I was content to look and then stop looking, and it didn't hurt me when what I did went unseen and unremarked upon, except in exceptional circumstances; when I passed my driving test I came home and telephoned everyone I knew, demanding astonishment and praise.

Chapter Forty-three

Sara thinks it a good idea for me to accept a job in America. I think she's probably right, but I'm scared. I've only visited New York briefly in the Sixties and Seventies as a celebrity wife, living in the grandest hotels, travelling by limo, insulated from the frightening city outside. I remember the terrifying wave of traffic surging down Fifth Avenue. Will I get around safely? Will I learn to live with the noise? The film is *The Age of Innocence*, which Martin Scorsese will direct. Daniel Day-Lewis and Michelle Pfeiffer will play the lovers and I suspect they need a fair number of actors who will look comfortable in period clothes and appear and sound like well-heeled, turn-of-the-century Americans, as they munch their way through lengthy and complicated meals which feature so heavily in books of that period.

Early spring in Troy in upstate New York. Location catering is wonderful and I've eaten rather more than my period stays will allow. The leaves on the trees will soon be in bud and Alec McCowen and I are making our way back to our trailers. I can't help myself and I blurt out, 'Oh, isn't this all *wonderful*?' Alec, mildly surprised and mildly pitying, shakes his head and says, 'Oh Siân, you're *very* easily pleased.' I suppose I am – thank God. I'm so pleased that nothing awful is happening, that I'm actively *not* suffering what Edward Duke has christened 'NDs' – nameless dreads.

There's a rail strike so I'm put in a taxi to travel to New York where most of the filming will take place. My driver is appalled that he has to go to New York, which is full of 'bad people', he says. He's so frightened that I become quite brave and when he gets lost somewhere in the Bronx, I take over the map and begin navigating and have no trouble in getting up safely to the Wyndham Hotel. I'm impressed by myself. He's too scared to say thanks or stop for a coffee, and heads off to Troy, never to return if he can help it, he assures me.

The Wyndham is a smallish hotel, home from home for English actors. I walk around my 'neighbourhood' and very soon it begins to feel like home. Where is that intimidating city which used to scare me so much? Debbie Condon's friend from schooldays, Louise Emmett, calls me and takes me on a smart outing and teaches me a bit about the bus system. I feel as though I'm mastering demotic Aramaic as I board my first bus and then *change* buses.

The early rising and the long hours of work are familiar and soothing. When I'm not working I take huge walks and realise that I'm writing very little in my notebooks these days. It's also soothing to be with people who know nothing about me. This is most unexpected but New York is being just that – soothing. I begin to make friends. Meeting Louise was a piece of luck. She and Debbie attended a ladies' seminary here in the city. They wore white gloves and learned lovely manners, which have endured. I had not expected just yet that anyone would make me laugh uncontrollably, then I met Alexis Smith. We had to be separated because of bad behaviour during the party scene in the film. The first assistant was cross and I avoided Daniel's eye; I don't suppose he'd believe me if I told him that the last person to be evicted with me from a studio for laughing was his mother, Jill.

I loved watching Martin Scorsese at work. He wore crisp, rather military-looking cotton shirts and belted slacks and bounced through the day on the balls of his feet. Never did we see him looking doubtful or uncertain or even dissatisfied. From the first moment of the day's work, for twelve or fourteen hours, he knew exactly what would happen next and all precautions were taken to make sure that everything was exactly as he wished it to be. His sets had a cloister-like quiet – even his carpenters seemed to be able to hammer noiselessly. Occasionally, if there was an unauthorised snatch of conversation in the distance, he would stop what he was doing and, smiling, say, 'Did I hear something? Sh! Listen! No. Nothing. My imagination.' Those smiling moments were blood chilling, but I liked and admired him.

Jane Stanton Hitchcock, the author of *Vanilla*, invited me to stay with her on the Upper East Side. We were both wary of the venture. Jane was a full-time novelist and filming hours make actors unsatisfactory guests. Also, I wasn't at all sure that I wanted to *be* a guest; hotel life was undemanding and I'd become used to living in the Fifties. When I arrived at Jane's duplex on the East River, I realised that she lived in breathtaking style. I had my own entrance to the prettiest guest suite imaginable. I adjusted my ideas. 'Jane, I had no idea. Are you wonderfully rich!' Simple, sweet thing, she merely smiled. I stayed with Jane for the rest of my time in New York. She didn't want a guest and I didn't want to be one, so we got on famously. Occasionally, Jane would stop writing and we'd chat. I told her about heaving the king-size mattress into the street. When she stopped laughing she asked, 'Have you ever been in therapy?' I saw what she meant. It *was* rather extreme behaviour. (I was blissfully Freudianly unaware of myself.) '*Don't* go into open-ended therapy,' she counselled. 'Do a sixteen-hour course of *cognitive* therapy when you get home. It's called *CAT* and it will polish you up nicely!' I admired Jane for her chic, her industry, her expensive allure, her brains and her furniture. It would never have occurred to me not to promise to do as she told me.

Sara arranged for me to go and stay with June Havoc in Connecticut. Ageless at over eighty years, beautiful and gallant, she lived with her friend and assistant, Tana, in a wonderful farmhouse – the outhouses and fields full of the halt, the maimed and the blind of the animal world – and in the barn stood her sister, Gypsy Rose Lee's, piano. It was all a bit too much for me and I lay on the grass and slept for a whole afternoon. June let me do some gardening for her and then took advantage of Tana's absence for a day, visiting her family nearby, to move a great deal of huge, heavy furniture from one room to another. Exhausted – I more than she – we had an early supper and went to bed. I woke very early, not knowing where I was for a moment, and lay there looking at the New England sky, aware that something was different. I sat up abruptly and grinned broadly as I realised that for the first time in ages I wasn't scared, I was just awake. It wasn't a wonderful, exciting moment; it was lovely that something bad was absent. I went downstairs and sat with June and Tana and wished I could tell them what had happened, but I couldn't because they didn't know my story and nothing *had* happened. Something had stopped, that was all. Tana took us to visit her enormous Italian/American family and for a moment I felt a pang of envy as I watched them cooking and playing and interfering in each other's lives, but, standing alone on the veranda overlooking the sea, I reminded myself that my life was programmed to be very different and that we cannot have everything or do everything. Having It All had been too exhausting and time-consuming and finally it had defeated me. It was a relief to stop trying.

Back in the city, I begin to think about going back to London. I shan't be there for more than a few days because I've arranged to do a job in Austria. I've started packing. Walking along 71st Street towards the park, I find I'm suddenly running from high spirits, as I can't remember running since I was a girl at home, but I don't have anywhere to run to and although I have a house in London, I no longer know where 'home' is. Since Central Park is ahead of me, I run there and go on running until, winded, I flop down on a bench. Bending over, catching my breath, I'm glad to have a moment where my face is hidden because I can't stop smiling and feel I look foolish. Finally, I sit up, exhausted. Two young men passing by smile at me sitting there, smiling. As they pass on I realise that at this moment I am not merely *not unhappy*, I am perfectly *happy* and secure, surrounded by strangers, my suitcases half packed at Jane's and a sheaf of travel arrangements in my bag. I haven't any idea what will happen to me. Will I ever get another, 'proper', exciting job? Will I go on working? How will I live? What country shall I live in? Shall I live alone? Why do I feel terrific?

Rising and, still moving fast, going east towards the river and up towards Gracie Square, I realise that I don't really care to look for answers to these questions; I no longer have an impulse to look into the future, but there is a swing in my step that I had not thought to feel again as I continue my way through the smart neighbourhood; 75th, 79th, 81st. Streets that are a world away from the places where I grew up but they feel as familiar and safe under my feet as the tracks across the low, Welsh mountains of my first home. The skies, the houses, the trees – green overnight in the swift astonishing New York spring – are improbably bright today with the Pre-Raphaelite clarity of a world seen with the eyes of youth – or of love.

When I was a girl, a moment ago, Saunders Lewis told me to 'Learn to live on the knife-edge of insecurity.' It seemed to me an uncomfortable place to want to be, but maybe that is where I have arrived and it begins to seem that maybe he was right; to live perilously is to live safely. Maybe. This is so undramatic, this afternoon in New York. So undramatic, so wonderful. No event has taken place. Nothing of significance has been said, but my life has changed. There is no solution, no resolution, no conclusion; but I am happy and I am at home and unafraid of what the future will bring.

List of films, theatre and TV (1959–2001)

1959 *Siwan* (Theatre and TV), *Land of Song* (TV series), *The Garden of Loneliness* (TV), *Granite* (TV), *Treason* (TV and Radio), *The Tortoise and the Hare* (TV), *Game for Eskimos* (TV)

1960 *The Taming of the Shrew* (Theatre), *The Duchess of Malfi* (Theatre), *Strangers in the Room* (TV)

1961 *The Duchess of Malfi* (Theatre cont.), *Ondine* (Theatre), *The Lizard on the Rock* (Theatre)

1962 *Don Juan in Hell* (TV), *The Maids* (Radio), *The Afternoon of M. Andesmas* (Radio)

1963 *Gentle Jack* (Theatre), *This is Not King's Cross* (TV), *Becket* (Film), *The Other Man* (TV Film), *Espionage* (Film)

1964 *Gentle Jack* (Theatre cont.), *Maxibules* (Theatre), *The Sex Game* (TV)

1965 *The Night of the Iguana* (Theatre), *Ride a Cock Horse* (Theatre)

1966 *Ride a Cock Horse* (Theatre cont.), *Man and Superman* (Theatre), *Man of Destiny* (Theatre), *Eh Joe* (TV)

1967 *Man and Superman* (Theatre cont.), *The Burglar* (Theatre)

1968 *The Beast in the Jungle* (TV Film)

1969 *Goodbye Mr Chips* (Film), *The Cardinal of Spain* (Theatre), *City 69* (TV), *Vessel of Wrath* (TV), *The Eccentricities of a Nightingale* (Theatre)

1970 *Murphy's War* (Film)

1971 *Under Milk Wood* (Film), *Platonov* (TV)

1972 *Lady Windermere's Fan* (TV), *Epitaph for George Dillon* (Theatre), *Alpha Beta* (Theatre)

1973 *Gloriana* (Theatre), *A Nightingale in Bloomsbury Square* (Theatre), *Shoulder to Shoulder* (TV series)

1974 *Shoulder to Shoulder* (TV series cont.)

1975 *Pilgrim Fathers* (TV Film), *How Green Was My Valley* (TV series), *The Gay Lord Quex* (Theatre)

1976 *How Green Was My Valley* (TV series cont.), *The Achurch Letters* (TV), *I, Claudius* (TV series)

1977 *Heartbreak House* (TV), *Off to Philadelphia in the Morning* (TV mini-series), *Boudicca* (TV series)

1978 *Spine Chiller* (Theatre), *Clash of the Titans* (Film), *Oresteia* (TV)

1979 *Crime and Punishment* (TV), *The Doctor and the Devils* (Film), *A Woman of No Importance* (Theatre), *Tinker Tailor Soldier Spy* (TV), *The Inconstant Couple* (Theatre)

1980 *You Never Can Tell* (Theatre), *Sean* (TV series), *Pal Joey* (Theatre), *Barriers* (TV series), *Churchill: The Wilderness Years* (TV series)

1981 *Pal Joey* (Theatre cont.), *How Many Miles to Babylon* (Film), *Barriers* (TV series)

1982 *Dear Liar* (Theatre), *Major Barbara* (Theatre), *Smiley's People* (TV)

1983 *Dune* (Film)

1984 *Peg* (Theatre), *Love Affair* (Theatre)

1985 *Gigi* (Theatre), *Return to Endor* (Film), *'Life of Siân'* (TV documentary)

1986 *Gigi* (Theatre cont.), *The Two Mrs Grenvilles* (TV), *A Painful Case* (TV Film), *Lost In Time* (TV), *The Snow Spider* (TV series)

1987 *Thursday's Ladies* (Theatre), *Brel* (Theatre), *Vanity Fair* (TV series), *George Borrow* (TV), *A Killing on the Exchange* (TV series)

1988 *Brel* (Theatre cont.), *Mother Knows Best* (TV), *Shadow of the Noose* (TV), *Emlyn's Moon* (TV series)

1989 *Valmont* (Film), *The Glass Menagerie* (Theatre), *Dark River* (Film), *Paris Match* (Theatre)

1990 *Perfect Scoundrels* (TV), *Freddie and Max* (TV), *Red Empire* (TV), *Vanilla* (Theatre), *Landscape and Legend* (TV)

1991 *The Manchurian Candidate* (Theatre), *Emlyn's Moon* (TV series), *Tonight at 8.30* (TV), *The Chestnut Soldier* (TV series)

1992 *Painting Churches* (Theatre), *The Age of Innocence* (Film), *The Borrowers* (TV series), *Heidi* (Disney Film)

1993 Novello Concert, *Ghosts* (Theatre), *Covington Cross* (TV)

1994 *The Lion in Winter* (Theatre), *Marlene* (Theatre), *The Borrowers* (TV), *A Mind to Kill* (TV series), *Nearest and Dearest* (Theatre)

1995 *An Inspector Calls* (Theatre US), *A Little Night Music* (Theatre)

1996 *A Little Night Music* (Theatre US), *House of America* (Film), *Marlene* (Theatre)

1997 *Marlene* (Theatre US), *The Scold's Bridle* (TV), *Nikita* (TV)

1998 *Marlene* (Theatre cont.), *Alice Through the Looking Glass* (Film), *Aristocrats* (TV series), *Falling in Love Again* – Cabaret (Theatre Israel), *The Magician's House* (TV series)

1999 *Marlene* (Theatre cont.), *Falling in Love Again* – Cabaret (Theatre), *The Magician's House* (TV series)

2000 *Falling in Love Again* (Theatre cont.), *Coming and Going* (Film), *Ballykissangel* (TV)

2001 *Lettice and Lovage* (Theatre), *Falling in Love Again* (Theatre cont.), *The Leopard in Autumn* (Radio series), *Almost Like Being in Love* – Cabaret (Theatre), *Divas at the Donmar* – Cabaret (Theatre)